W9-BQW-304

Managing Your
Personal Finances

6e

Joan S. Ryan

M.B.A., Ph.D., C.M.A.

Business Department Chair
Clackamas Community College
Oregon City College, Oregon

SOUTH-WESTERN
CENGAGE Learning™

Australia • Brazil • Japan • Korea • Mexico • Singapore • Spain • United Kingdom • United States

SOUTH-WESTERN
CENGAGE Learning™

**Managing Your Personal Finances,
6th edition**
Joan S. Ryan

Vice President of Editorial, Business: Jack W. Calhoun

Vice President/Editor-in-Chief: Karen Schmohe

Executive Editor: Eve Lewis

Senior Developmental Editor: Penny Shank

Marketing Manager: Michael Cloran

Associate Content Project Manager: Jana Lewis

Senior Media Editor: Michael Jackson

Website Project Manager: Ed Stubenrauch

Senior Manufacturing Coordinator: Kevin Kluck

Consulting Editor: Peggy Shelton, LEAP Publishing Services

Production Service: Macmillan Publishing Solutions

Art Director: Tippy McIntosh

Internal Designer: Lou Ann Thesing

Cover Designer: Lou Ann Thesing

Cover Image: ©Veer Incorporated

Permissions Account Manager, Images: Don Schlotman

Photo Researcher: Peggy Shelton

For product information and technology assistance, contact us at
Cengage Learning Customer & Sales Support, 1-800-354-9706
For permission to use material from this text or product,
submit all requests online at **www.cengage.com/permissions**
Further permissions questions can be emailed to
permissionrequest@cengage.com

**These 16 Career Cluster icons are being used with permission of the:

States' Career Clusters Initiative, 2009, www.careerclusters.org

ISBN-13: 978-0-538-44937-3

ISBN-10: 0-538-44937-3

South-Western Cengage Learning
5191 Natorp Boulevard
Mason, OH 45040
USA

Cengage Learning products are represented in Canada by Nelson Education, Ltd.

For your course and learning solutions, visit **www.cengage.com/school**

Printed in the United States of America
1 2 3 4 5 6 7   13 12 11 10 09

Secure Students'
Financial Futures

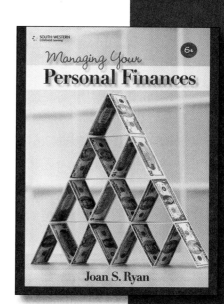

While focusing on the student's role as citizen, student, family member, consumer, and active participant in the business world, *Managing Your Personal Finances 6e* informs readers of their various financial responsibilities. It provides opportunities for self-awareness, expression, and satisfaction in a highly technical and competitive society. Students will discover new ways to maximize their earning potential, develop strategies for managing resources, explore skills for the wise use of credit, and gain insight into the different ways of investing money. Special sections in each chapter focus on current trends and issues that consumers face in the marketplace and help students learn to secure their financial future!

- Ensuring that basic personal financial management skills are attained, this content is aligned with the Jump$tart Coalition's national standards for personal financial literacy.

- To prepare students to become knowledgeable and ethical consumers, this content meets the standards for personal financial literacy established by the National Business Education Association (NBEA).

Turn the page to learn more about how to secure students' financial futures with *Managing Your Personal Finances 6e!*

Presenting the Most Comprehensive

Lessons make the text easy to use in all classroom environments.

Goals are clearly stated learning objectives representing sections of the lesson.

Engaging features within each **Lesson Assessment** give students a chance to check their understanding of the terms and content before advancing to the next lesson.

• Key Terms Review
• Check Your Understanding
• Apply Your Knowledge

Chapter Assessments give students the opportunity to tie their learning together. The **Summary** is a bulleted list of chapter concepts for quick review. **Apply What You Know, Make Academic Connections, Solve Problems and Explore Issues,** and **Extend Your Learning** challenge students to dig deeper into the issues.

10.1

Growing Money: Why, Where, and How

GOALS
- Describe the purpose of saving.
- Explain how money grows through compounding.
- List and describe financial institutions where you can save.

TERMS
- short-term needs, p. 219
- long-term needs, p. 220
- scholarships, p. 220
- student loans, p. 220
- loan consolidation, p. 221
- grants, p. 221
- work-study, p. 221
- principal, p. 222
- interest, p. 222
- annual percentage yield (APY), p. 222

WHY YOU SHOULD SAVE

The best reason to save money is to provide for future needs, both expected and unexpected. If you set nothing aside for these inevitable needs, you will constantly live on the edge of financial disaster. Saving regularly will help you meet your short-term and long-term needs.

SHORT-TERM NEEDS

Often you will have short-term needs, which are expenses beyond your regular monthly items. Unless you have extra cash income during the month, you will have to pay for these things out of savings. Some short-term needs are predictable. Others you can't foresee. Examples of short-term needs include the following:

- Emergencies—such as unemployment, sickness, accident, or a death in the family.
- Vacations—short weekend trips or longer excursions.
- Social events—weddings, family gatherings, or other potentially costly special occasions.
- Repairs—cars, appliances, plumbing, and other items. Occasionally, major unplanned repairs become immediately necessary.
- Major purchases—a car, major appliances, furniture, remodeling, or other items. Things eventually have to be replaced.

What are some short-term needs that could require you to save?

Chapter 10 Saving for the Future 219

10.1

Assessment

KEY TERMS REVIEW
Match the terms with the definitions.

_____ 1. Money borrowed to pay for education

_____ 2. A program where students work on campus to earn money

_____ 3. Combining many loans into one large loan with one monthly payment

_____ 4. The amount of money deposited

_____ 5. Expenses beyond your regular monthly items

_____ 6. Earnings on principal

_____ 7. Forms of educational funding that do not have to be repaid

_____ 8. Cash allowances awarded to students to pay education costs

_____ 9. The actual interest rate an account earns stated on a yearly basis

_____ 10. Expenses that are costly and require years of planning and saving

a. annual percentage yield (APY)
b. grants
c. interest
d. loan consolidation
e. long-term needs
f. principal
g. scholarships
h. short-term needs
i. student loans
j. work-study

CHECK YOUR UNDERSTANDING

11. Why is it important to start saving early to meet your short-term and long-term needs?

12. Explain the concept of compounding and how your money grows.

13. List the financial institutions where you can have a savings account.

APPLY YOUR KNOWLEDGE

14. Describe the advantages and disadvantages of spending now rather than saving for a future goal. Give three examples of how saving money can improve your financial well being.

THINK CRITICALLY

15. There are many places where you can save money. Some are insured and others are not. The safer your money (less risk), the lower your rate of return (APY). Are you willing to take more risk in order to earn more interest on your savings? Explain your answer.

16. Getting advanced training, such as a college degree, requires planning. Do you plan to get some type of post-secondary education? How will you pay for it?

Chapter 10 Saving for the Future 227

SOLVE PROBLEMS AND EXPLORE ISSUES

10. Your friend is considering two career opportunities—one in which she would be an independent contractor and have no benefits provided, and one in which she would work as an employee of a company and have full health insurance as well as other benefits. Explain to her how their differ...

APPLY WHAT YOU KNOW

1. Interview a person who has recently had surgery or been in the hospital for several days or longer. Ask this person about the type of services provided and the approximate cost per day of those services. Ask him or her how much of the cost was paid by insurance and how much (percentage or dollar amount) he or she will have to pay. Write a report on ...

...chure describing the benefits of a group health insurance ...on't know someone who belongs to this type of plan, your ...and the Internet will have information about group plans. ...summarizing your findings regarding the types of coverage ...their provisions for deductibles, copayments, exclusions,

...net for information on Medicare. A good place to start is ...nt site for Medicare at www.medicare.gov. Find out what ...al/hospital/surgical and major medical coverage it provides ...f these costs the patients must pay. Then look into ...nce. Based on your findings, do you feel that medigap ...ood value for a person on Medicare?

...American Association of Retired Persons) web site and ...oducts and services it offers to its members, including ...alth insurance. Do you see value to these services for ...50 or older but not yet age 65 and retired?

...are working full time, are married, and have one ...analysis of your disability needs. Select a career that you ...n, and use a realistic income figure for someone with ...of experience.

...life insurance needs shown in Figure 27.1. Can you add ...? Would you delete anything? Prepare a list of life ...ed on your personal situation as you imagine it will

...CONNECTIONS

...out-of-pocket expenses in the following situation. ...nce will pay 80 percent of the cost of a procedure. ...wable limit for the procedure at $1,000. Tom's ...for $1,300. How much will Tom have to pay?

...e a paper about the uninsured and underinsured ...Internet research to get current statistics. What ...the problem? How can we control medical costs ...affordable to all citizens?

...rmanent life insurance policy that meets your ...amount of coverage you want. Then, visit an ...ne to find out more about the policy and its ...t summarizing why you selected the policy and ...it from the insurer.

...nce/mypf

...th Insurance 623

27

Chapter Assessment

SUMMARY

27.1
- Group health insurance policies provide broad coverage at lower rates than do individual policies.
- COBRA allows people who leave their jobs to keep their employer-provided health insurance for a limited time.
- HIPAA limits exclusions for pre-existing conditions and makes it illegal to deny coverage based on health status.
- A Flex 125 Plan allows employees to set aside money, pretax, to help pay deductibles, copayments, and other health expenses not covered by insurance.
- People without a group plan can buy individual health insurance, but they may have to pass a physical exam.
- Typical health insurance includes basic medical and major medical coverage. Some offer dental and vision coverage for a higher premium.
- Unmanaged care plans allow employees to select their own providers and be reimbursed a percentage of expenses after a deductible. An HSA may be used in association with a high-deductible medical plan.
- Managed care plans contract with a network of health care providers. With an HMO, patients must choose providers from within the network. A PPO is more flexible and allows patients to choose doctors outside the plan. A POS combines features from HMOs and PPOs.

27.2
- Disability insurance replaces your income if you are injured or ill and cannot work. Social Security and workers' compensation insurance provide some disability insurance benefits.
- Life insurance provides funds to beneficiaries when the insured dies.
- Insurers set life insurance premiums based on life expectancy and death rates compiled in mortality tables.
- Temporary life insurance remains in effect for a specified time. If the insured survives beyond that time, coverage ceases with no remaining value. Term life insurance is the most common type of temporary life insurance.
- Permanent life insurance remains in effect for the insured's lifetime and has a savings component (cash value) as well as a death benefit. Common types of permanent life policies are whole life, limited-pay life, universal life, and variable life.

Chapter 27 Health and Life Insurance 621

Personal Finance Program Available!

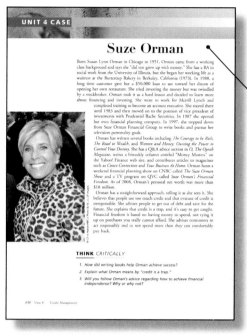

Unit Cases profile real people and describe how they applied the skills presented in this text to their own lives.

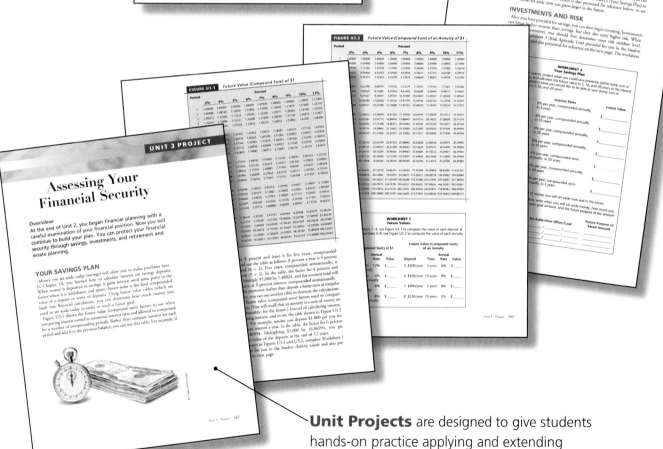

Unit Projects are designed to give students hands-on practice applying and extending what they have learned in the book.

Personal and Professional Success

ISSUES IN YOUR WORLD

UNINSURED AND UNDERINSURED IN AMERICA

All people need adequate health care to maintain a high quality of life. To have access to the quality of health care available in this country, health insurance is essential to help pay the high and rising costs. Yet Census Bureau statistics and the National Coalition on Health Care show that between 45 and 47 million Americans were uninsured in 2007. Eight in ten uninsured Americans come from working families, nearly 20 percent (8.4 million) are children, and young adults (age 18 to 24 years) are the least likely of any age group to have insurance. Every 30 seconds, an American files for bankruptcy after having a health problem. Many of these people have health insurance, but it isn't enough.

According to the Public Broadcasting Service, more than 25 million Americans were underinsured in 2007. Underinsured people spent more than 10 percent of their total income on out-of-pocket medical expenses. This rate has jumped 60 percent in the last four years. Over 6.8 million Americans spend more than a third of their total income on health care.

The United States spends nearly $100 billion per year to provide uninsured residents with health services, often for preventable diseases that physicians could have treated more efficiently with earlier diagnosis.

The United States spends a greater portion of gross domestic product on health care than any other industrialized country, yet it is the only industrialized country that does not have a national health care plan.

Lack of insurance results in poor health and shorter lives for many Americans. There are costs to society as well, such as:

- *Developmental deficiencies from insufficient health care during infancy*
- *Expenses for chronic health conditions not treated until they become emergencies*
- *Lost income due to reduced job productivity and employment*
- *Diminished overall health in the country due to low immunization and lack of access to preventive health care*
- *Health care expenses paid by taxpayers for uninsured patients*
- *Higher program costs (such as Social Security, criminal justice, and Medicare)*
- *Social inequality (with lower-income Americans being at a definite health disadvantage)*

Some say a single-payer, government-sponsored health plan is the answer. This is the type of system that exists in many other nations, such as Canada and most western European countries. Others say we can reform the system we have so that health insurance becomes portable—that is, you can take it with you from job to job. Whatever the answer, we as a country must find a way to provide access to affordable health care for all Americans.

THINK *CRITICALLY*

1. *Suppose you had no health insurance. How would this fact affect the decisions you make about your health care?*
2. *Conduct some Internet research about the problem of uninsured Americans. Is the problem getting better or worse? Explain.*

Chapter 27   Health and Life Insurance

Issues in Your World is a full-page feature that enriches students' knowledge by acquainting them with real-world issues.

Planning a Career in... **Estate Planning**

Estate planners and financial advisers help people get ready for retirement. Their advice includes both analysis and guidance in making investment choices to meet their clients' long-term objectives and to suit their income and lifestyles. Many planners are accountants who specialize in estate tax laws.

Estate planners use their knowledge of investments, tax laws, and insurance to recommend options for individuals. They help clients with retirement choices as well as provide tax advice and sell life insurance. They develop a comprehensive plan that identifies problem areas, makes recommendations for improvement, and selects investments compatible with the client's goals.

Yearly updates keep clients and accounts protected from economic conditions and market changes. Most advisers also sell financial products, such as securities and insurance. They make fees based on the sales.

Employment Outlook
- A much faster than average rate of employment growth is expected.

Job Titles
- Estate planner
- Financial adviser
- Wealth manager
- Personal financial analyst

Needed Skills
- A bachelor's or master's degree is required, with emphasis in finance, business, or accounting.

- A license is typically required by the FINRA for those selling securities to investors.
- A CFP (certified financial planner) certification is needed for estate planners.
- Excellent math, analytical, and problem solving skills are required.

What's it like to work in...
Estate Planning

Ruth has a group of 15 clients that she works with to maintain retirement portfolios. Most of her clients are already retired. Some of them are middle aged, and a few are in their mid-30s. She provides financial planning advice for her clients, based on their age, life stage, and financial goals.

Ruth works independently and is an insurance broker. She has a CFP and a stock broker's license, enabling her to sell securities to investors.

Today she is meeting with new clients who were referred to her by a retired couple. She accepts new clients by referral only. Her days consist of reviewing client accounts, watching financial and market conditions, and making recommendations for changes.

What About You?

Would you like working with people to help them achieve their lifelong goals? Do you enjoy working with financial analysis and numbers? Would you like to be an estate planner?

330 Unit 3   Financial Security

Planning a Career in... offers robust career information related to the chapter's topic, and it incorporates the 16 Career Clusters.

Exceptional Features Enhance Learning!

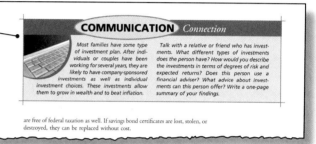

Global View features show international connections relevant to personal finance.

Communication Connection offers speaking and writing activities related to the chapter content.

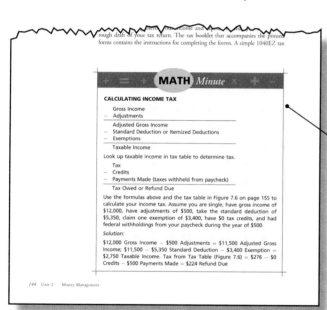

Math Minute offers a review and practice in basic math skills linked to the chapter topics.

Viewpoints provide opportunities for students to think critically about issues that have no clear-cut answers.

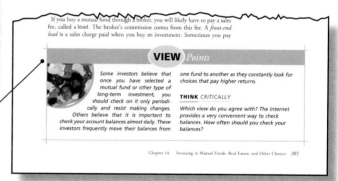

NET Bookmark is a short feature that provides chapter-related activities for students to complete using information found on the Internet.

Comprehensive Teaching and Learning Tools

Annotated Instructor's Edition [978-0-538-44938-0]
Find everything you need to create a dynamic learning environment with minimal preparation. Student pages are surrounded by margin notes that provide comprehensive teaching notes and tips.

Text/eBook Bundle [978-0-324-81862-8]

Student Activity Guide [978-0-538-44939-7]

Printed Tests [978-0-538-44940-3]

ExamView® CD [978-0-538-44941-0]

Instructor's Resource CD [978-0-538-44942-7]
- Lesson Plans
- Lesson Outlines
- Instructor's Resource Manual
- Teaching Tools
- PowerPoint Presentations
- Spanish Glossary
- Instructor's Edition of Printed Tests
- Instructor's Edition of Student Activity Guide

Web site — www.cengage.com/school/pfinance/mypf

Above and Beyond

iMPACT
Interactive Text *is now available!*

Text/iMPACT Interactive Text CD Bundle [978-0-324-81861-1]

Bring students into the front row of the classroom with a new iMPACT Interactive Text, which is a fully functioning textbook delivered via CD-ROM. Appealing to all types of learning styles, the interactive text offers key learning elements such as hypertext linking to subsections of the text, key terms definitions, forms for completing assessment activities, and animations of key concepts.

Get the benefit of having a regular printed textbook along with the added benefit of interactivity. You and your students will be more motivated and engaged in the learning process. **Try it out today!**

Order the demo iMPACT CD: 978-0-538-44997-7.

Contents

Managing Your Personal Finances, 6E

PHOTO: ©Getty Images

PHOTO: ©istockphoto

PHOTO: ©istockphoto

PHOTO: ©istockphoto

PHOTO: ©Getty Images

Reviewers

Nancy A. Backus
Personal Finance Teacher,
Business Department
Winneconne High School
Winneconne, Wisconsin

Theresa L. Badgett
Teacher
Ladue Horton Watkins
High School
Ladue, Missouri

Tatyana Berkovich
President and Founder
Ivy Academia
K-12th Grade Entrepreneurial
Charter School
Woodland Hills, California

Robert B. Blair
Director, Center for Economic
Education
Middle Tennessee State University
Murfreesboro, Tennessee

Karen N. Ceh
Teacher, Business and
Information Technology
Parkland School District
Allentown, Pennsylvania

Scott Christy
Business and Information
Technology Instructor
Green Bay East High School
Green Bay, Wisconsin

Nancy M. Everson
Business Education Chair
Sun Prairie High School
Sun Prairie, Wisconsin

Lance Garvin
Business Teacher
Pike High School
Indianapolis, Indiana

Paige Graves
Business Teacher
William Mason High School
Mason, Ohio

Madge Gregg
Finance Academy Director
Hoover High School
Hoover, Alabama

Renetta L. Meddick
Teacher, Business/Technology
Delsea Regional High School
Franklinville, New Jersey

Diana L. Penning
Teacher, Career and Technology
Education
Columbia High School
Columbia, South Carolina

Karen Phipps
Business Teacher
Ansonia High School
Ansonia, Connecticut

Patricia Pritz
Instructor, Family and Consumer
Science
Great Oaks Institute of
Technology and Career
Development
Cincinnati, Ohio

Annika Russell
Teacher, Business Department
Mitchell School District
Mitchell, South Dakota

Judith P. Sams
Program Specialist, Business and
Information Technology
Virginia Department of
Education
Richmond, Virginia

Nancy K. Talmo
Teacher, Business Department
William Penn High School
New Castle, Delaware

Madeline Tucker
Career Technical Education
Curriculum Coordinator
Onslow County Schools
Jacksonville, North Carolina

Stephanie Williams
Teacher, Marketing/Business
Department
Cameron High School
Cameron, Missouri

Jasper L. Wilson
Business Education Supervisor
Prince George's County Public
Schools
Upper Marlboro, Maryland

Unit 1

Career Decisions

Unit 1 prepares you to make career plans and to develop the tools you'll need to get and keep temporary, part-time, or full-time employment, now and in the future. Wise career decisions are a key part of financial success.

The chapters in this unit explore career options and ways to cope with market changes that will affect your job choices. You will learn why people work, how to begin career planning, and where to find up-to-date information. You also will find out how to compete successfully in the job application and interviewing processes. Finally, you will learn how to adapt to a changing work environment, reinvent yourself as necessary, and stay employable—important life skills that will help you meet your future goals.

1

Choosing Your Career

1.1 | Jobs and Careers

1.2 | Coping with Change and Reinventing Yourself

Consider **THIS**

"To be truly happy in what you do for a living, there are three basic requirements: You must be good at what you do, it must come easily for you, and you must enjoy it. And for those going into a caring profession, a fourth requirement: You must care!"

—*Unknown*

Rafael was a junior in high school who worked every afternoon sorting and delivering packages. He didn't like going to work and was always complaining about his job. His friends told him it was because he wasn't paid enough money. But Rafael knew that there was more to it. He was bored with the work itself, and he found himself dreading going to work. To keep himself motivated, he would remind himself that the job was just part time, after school, to earn spending money—it wasn't permanent.

"When I choose my career, I'll be sure to pick something that I enjoy doing so I can look forward to going to work," he told himself. Now Rafael must begin the process of planning his future career.

Jobs and Careers

GOALS

- Discuss career and job trends, and describe sources of job information.
- Complete a job analysis, listing positive and negative features of potential career choices.

TERMS

- job analysis, *p. 9*
- salary, *p. 10*
- benefits, *p. 10*
- promotion, *p. 10*
- employee expenses, *p. 11*
- work characteristics, *p. 11*
- entrepreneur, *p. 11*

CAREERS OF THE FUTURE

Work enables you to earn a living. It provides money to buy food, clothing, shelter, and other important things, such as education and medical care. Your career path will likely look much different from that of your parents. New products and services, together with an expanding global economy and rapidly changing technology, have created new and challenging pathways for career development. Career-oriented people will need to retrain, upgrade, and reinvent themselves many times during their working lives. Today's technology opens up many options. More and more people are finding it possible to work from home while interacting with colleagues in other countries. Many choose the exciting path of self-employment.

Technology creates better and faster ways of getting things done. In today's global economy, businesses seek ways to improve quality, increase output, and lower costs. To stay in business, companies must offer products that meet diverse and changing needs of customers near and far. The Internet has opened worldwide markets, and it has also created global competition for businesses of all sizes. Employers today look different from the past as they explore diverse ways to meet changing demand. For example, many companies exist only in cyberspace and have no brick-and-mortar building. Others specialize in efficiently providing to companies the services that were traditionally done by inside employees. No matter what career path you choose, technology and the world economy will affect the way you work. They will also affect your job choices and how you must prepare for your future.

© Photodisc/Getty Images

Why is it likely that you will retrain, upgrade, and reinvent yourself many times during your working life?

■ MAJOR OCCUPATIONAL GROUPS

Many of today's growing occupations focus on the collection, use, and distribution of information. Computers and the Internet are key tools for gathering, transmitting, and storing data. The skills required to succeed in today's jobs change rapidly.

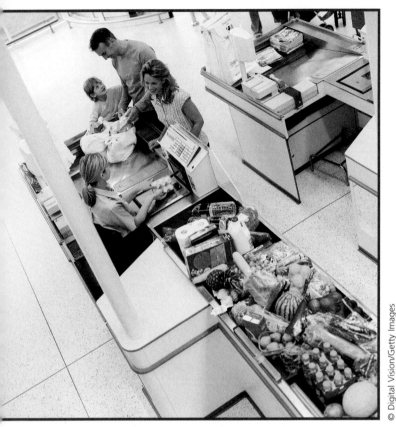

Why are service jobs increasing while manufacturing jobs are disappearing?

One of the highest paying career groups is called *professional*, where being knowledgeable is a key job skill. For professionals (such as lawyers, economists, and teachers), much of the job involves creating, processing, storing, retrieving, and transmitting information. As technology continues to evolve, new professional careers will emerge. Consider how medical records have changed from the hardcopy file system to an electronic distribution of data. Today, your medical information can travel around the world with the click of a mouse. A technician in India can read the CT-scan just taken at a clinic in your hometown.

Service jobs are a large and increasing sector of the market. They also are dominated by technology and information needs that determine what will be produced and how it will be made available. Service employees use highly sophisticated information storage and retrieval devices, from point-of-sale computers to optical scanners for inventory management and customer databases.

This extraordinary transformation of occupations has been variously labeled the "electronic era," "global village," "technological revolution," and "information age." All of these terms refer to technology and the rapid increase of knowledge that affect virtually all career choices today.

■ JOB TITLES AND DESCRIPTIONS

Careful research into descriptions of potential careers will help you make good career choices. Several U.S. government publications, available online and in most libraries, provide detailed job descriptions:

- *Dictionary of Occupational Titles (DOT)*, available online as *O*NET* (http://online.onetcenter.org)
- *Occupational Outlook Handbook (OOH)* (http://www.bls.gov/oco)
- *Monthly Labor Review* (http://stats.bls.gov/opub/mlr/mlrhome.htm)

O*NET is the *DOT* in the form of an online searchable database. At the *O*NET* site, you can search the database in several ways. You can look for occupations by entering keywords or selecting from a list of job families. Or, you can enter your skills into a checklist to search for occupations that match the skills you have. Figure 1.1 shows a portion of the "Tasks" in an *O*NET* job summary. As you can see, *O*NET* also provides links to knowledge, skills, and other information about this job.

FIGURE 1.1 O*NET *Job Description*

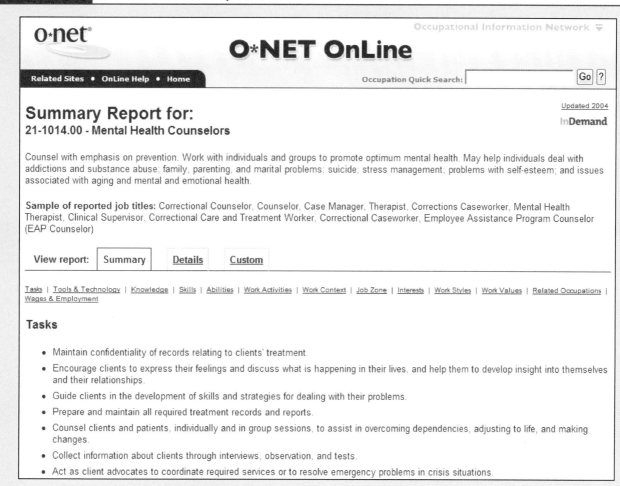

Source: Excerpted from O*NET Online, U.S. Department of Labor, Dictionary of Occupational Titles, 5th Edition, http://online.onetcenter.org/link/summary/21-1014.00, accessed June 3, 2008.

The *Occupational Outlook Handbook* provides in-depth job descriptions and information about job opportunities nationwide. It gives job descriptions in eleven categories (2008-09), as follows:

- Management
- Professional
- Service
- Sales
- Administrative
- Farming

- Construction
- Installation
- Production
- Transportation
- Armed Forces

Additional statistics and graphic information are available in the *Monthly Labor Review*. Articles in this publication provide current information about specific occupation clusters (groups of similar occupations) across the nation.

You can continue your research with the subject headings in your library's catalog, as well as magazine indexes such as the *Business Periodicals Index* and the *Readers' Guide to Periodical Literature*. Libraries typically provide Internet access and online research assistance. Online career sites, such as *Monster* (www.monster.com), provide career advice and information about different jobs.

Figure 1.2 illustrates the kinds of information you will find in the *OOH*. The *OOH* is very helpful in conducting industry- or career-specific research.

FIGURE 1.2 — *Portions of a 2008–09* Occupational Outlook Handbook *Job Description*

Counselors

Significant Points
- A master's degree is required to become a licensed counselor.
- Job opportunities should be very good because job openings are expected to exceed the number of graduates from counseling programs.
- The health care and social assistance fields employ about 47 percent of counselors; state and local governments employ about 11 percent.

Nature of the Work
Counselors assist people with personal, family, educational, mental health, and career problems. Their duties vary greatly depending on their occupational specialty. For example, educational or school counselors provide career and academic advising. Marriage and family therapists help families prevent family crises through enhancing communication and understanding among family members.

Work Environment
Work environment can vary widely depending on occupational specialty. School counselors work in schools where they usually have an office. Other counselors may work in a private practice, community health organization, or hospital. Many work in an office where they see clients throughout the day.

Employment
Counselors held about 635,000 jobs in 2006. About 260,000 were school counselors, 141,000 were rehabilitation counselors, and 100,000 were mental health counselors.

Licensure and Other Requirements
Some states require licensure; school counselors usually must have a state school counseling certification. Requirements for licensure often include a master's degree and 3,000 or more hours of supervised clinical experience. People interested in counseling should have a strong desire to help others and the ability to inspire respect, trust, and confidence. They should work well independently or on a team.

Job Outlook
Overall employment in counseling is expected to increase by 21% between 2006 and 2016, which is much faster than the average for all occupations. Employment for school counselors is expected to grow at 13%, which is about as fast as all occupations. Employment for substance abuse and mental health counselors is expected to grow by 34%, which is much faster than all occupations. Other types of counselors can expect growth from 23–30% in areas of mental health, rehabilitation, and marriage and family therapists.

Earnings
Median annual earnings of full-time school counselors were about $47,530. Median annual earnings in the other areas of counseling for 2006 were as follows:

Substance abuse counselors	$34,040
Mental health counselors	34,380
Rehabilitation counselors	29,200
Marriage and family therapists	43,210
Self-employed therapists and counselors	Highest

OOH ONET Codes
21–1011.00, 21–1012.00, 21–1013.00, 21–1014.00, 21–1015.00, 21–1019.99

Source: Abridged from the U.S. Department of Labor, *Occupational Outlook Handbook, 2008–09 Edition,* Counselors, on the Internet at http://www.bls.gov/oco/ocos067.htm (visited April 10, 2008).

JOB ANALYSIS

A **job analysis** is an evaluation of the positive and negative attributes of a given type of work. An example of a job analysis form is shown in Figure 1.3. A job analysis can help you identify types of work that would be a good fit for you. Gaining the skills you need for a career costs money. You may have to attend college or a training program. By taking the time now to identify a career that is right for you, you won't have to spend additional money later to change direction.

Preparing for your chosen career is worth the cost. The salary you will earn depends on your skills, experience, and education. These factors are under your control. You must be willing to obtain the training and needed skills to be successful on the job. Your salary also depends on the supply and demand for workers in your chosen field. Supply and demand are not constant, but change with the economy. While you cannot control these factors, you can look for

---

FIGURE 1.3   *Job Analysis Form*

JOB ANALYSIS

Job title: _____ Beginning salary: _____

Skills required: _____

Education required: _____

Experience required: _____

Positive Features:

Benefits:

_____

_____

_____

_____

Promotion opportunities:

_____

_____

_____

_____

Other considerations*:

_____

_____

_____

_____

Negative Features:

Employee expenses:

_____

_____

_____

_____

Work requirements:

_____

_____

_____

_____

Other considerations*:

_____

_____

_____

_____

*Such as travel, expense accounts, bonuses, working hours, training programs, etc.

VIEW *Points*

To cut costs, many businesses are seeking outside help. Insourcing, near-sourcing, and outsourcing are three ways of getting the work done outside the company that used to be done by employees. Internal cost centers are the most likely to be eliminated. Cost centers are departments within companies that do not generate profits, but merely provide support services. With insourcing, businesses pay for work to be done by another U.S. company that provides a specialized service, such as PayChex or ADP (U.S. companies that provide payroll services). Insourcing can also be done internally within an organization by a stand-alone entity, such as a subcontractor, that specializes in the service being provided. With near-sourcing, companies pay for work done in countries close by, such as Canada or Mexico. With outsourcing, companies pay for work to be done in countries far away, such as India or China. In many cases, American companies are hiring firms outside of the United States to handle work that inside employees used to do, from managing customer service call centers to manufacturing the products to be sold. Companies argue that they must control costs and provide shareholder value in the form of higher profits. Workers argue that good jobs are being lost to foreign workers and Americans are unable to find jobs to pay the high cost of living in America.

THINK *CRITICALLY*

Do you agree with the claims of each side? What point could you make to support each side? How do you think this trend will affect your job prospects in the future?

---

career paths in which demand for workers is expected to grow. You can find out what skills are needed for entry-level work. You also need to plan for upgrading your skills while you are working. How well you are able and willing to do this will affect your income and your job security well into the future.

▌ POSITIVE FEATURES OF EMPLOYMENT

Your chosen career will provide you with many positive features. The most important is usually the **salary**, which is the amount of monthly or annual pay that you will earn for your labor. You should also consider whether there are scheduled salary increases after a month, six months, or a year. Some companies offer frequent evaluations, merit raises, bonuses, and pay schedules that allow you to advance. Benefits are also important. **Benefits** are company-provided supplements to salary, such as sick pay, vacation time, profit-sharing plans, and health insurance, as will be discussed in Chapter 6.

Another important feature is the opportunity for **promotion**—the ability to advance to positions of greater responsibility and higher pay. Promotions give you recognition for your achievements, provide more challenging work, and often come with greater authority and prestige. For example, a retail clerk will want to work for a company in which advancement to store manager is possible.

You may also want to consider commuting distance and parking, company stability in the community, work hours and flexibility, and personnel policies. It's important to examine all features of a field of work and specific jobs, so you will have some idea where the career path may lead you. You should evaluate both rewards and additional investments you may need to make. These investments can include retraining and upgrading, moving to a new location, and advanced education or specialized skill development, such as learning how to use new computer programs, new electronic equipment, and other industry-specific technology.

NEGATIVE FEATURES OF EMPLOYMENT

Every job also has negative features. Try to see these negatives as challenges that go along with the positive aspects of employment.

Employee expenses include any costs of working paid by the employee that are not reimbursed by the employer. Examples include the costs of parking and transportation, such as gasoline or bus fare. Other costs include uniforms and the expense of cleaning, maintaining, and replacing them. Although such expenses may be tax deductible, they can be very costly and can make the job less attractive. It is important to carefully balance employee expenses against benefits for a prospective job.

Work characteristics are the daily activities of the job and the environment in which they must be performed. They might include working indoors versus outdoors, working alone versus working on a team, and having a high or low degree of stress. Time between breaks, supervisory relationships, time spent at a computer terminal, and company rules and policies are all work characteristics to consider. Because you will do this work for eight or more hours a day in a full-time job, it is important to match work characteristics to your own preferences.

ENTREPRENEURSHIP

An **entrepreneur** is someone who organizes, manages, and assumes the ownership risks of a new business. For many people, owning their own business would be a dream come true. There are many opportunities for business ownership. You could continue a family business, purchase an existing business or franchise, or start a new business from scratch. While long hours of work and dedication usually accompany such an undertaking, the rewards can be great. You would get to make the decisions and be your own boss, instead of working for someone else. You would feel in control of your own future. And, you would get to keep the profits.

But owning your own business requires a large amount of planning and consulting, as well as a large investment of money. It's risky too, since statistics show that most new small businesses do not succeed. The two most common reasons for failure are a lack of financing (not enough money to get a good start) and a lack of skills to know how to effectively run a small business.

You can learn more about how to start and run a successful small business by taking entrepreneurial and business management classes in high school or community college. You can get information and assistance from local business organizations, such as Junior Achievement. Local nonprofit organizations, such as Small Business Development Centers, can also provide assistance. For example, they can connect you with government-run incubator projects that provide reduced-cost space to help you get your business up and running. These centers are funded through the Small Business Administration (SBA), an agency of the federal government. The SBA web site is a valuable resource for new and small businesses. Visit the SBA online at www.sba.gov.

ransportation,
Distribution
& Logistics

Every time you board an airplane, you are putting your life into the hands of many professional workers, such as air traffic controllers.

The air traffic control system is a complex network of people and machines. The monitoring of air traffic is critical to ensure that airplanes stay a safe distance apart, whether they are on the ground, in the air, landing, or taking off.

Air traffic controllers direct each plane. A flight plan tells the controller when to expect the plane; radar allows tracking of planes. When the path is clear, the controller directs the pilot to a runway. Controllers are watching the planes, monitoring runways, delaying departures that might interfere with take offs or landings, and directing planes to assigned gates.

Employment Outlook
- As fast as average rate of employment is expected.

Job Titles
- Airport tower controller
- Terminal controller
- Radar controller
- Flight service specialist

Needed Skills
- Must complete FAA-approved program.

- Must pass pre-employment test, physical exam, drug screening.
- Must have security clearance.

What's it like to work in... *Transportation*

Mark finished jogging at 6 a.m. and reported for work by 6:30 a.m. He understands the need to have a clear mind to be able to work rapidly and efficiently and to work under extreme mental stress.

He works the busiest day shift, early morning, when most flights originate. He is able to concentrate and keep track of multiple instructions at the same time. Being responsible for the safety of numerous aircraft and their passengers is challenging.

Today the temperature is lower than average and Mark needs to do additional monitoring to be sure that deicing is being used when needed. Although he works a 40-hour week, he often is asked to work more hours when other controllers take time off for various reasons.

What About You?

Are you willing to stay in top physical and mental condition so you can concentrate and perform critical tasks? Are you willing to be responsible for the lives of other people? Would you like to become an air traffic controller?

Assessment

KEY TERMS REVIEW

Match the terms with the definitions. Some terms may not be used.

_____ 1. Daily activities of the job and the environment in which they must be performed

_____ 2. An evaluation of the positive and negative attributes of a given career choice

_____ 3. Any costs of working paid by the employee and not reimbursed by the employer

_____ 4. Advancement to a position of greater responsibility and higher pay

a. benefits

b. employee expenses

c. entrepreneur

d. job analysis

e. promotion

f. salary

g. work characteristics

_____ 5. The amount of monthly or annual pay that you will earn for your labor

_____ 6. Someone who assumes the ownership risks of a new business

CHECK YOUR UNDERSTANDING

7. How is today's job market different from what it was 10 or 20 years ago? How can you prepare for the new and rapidly changing environment?

8. What are some U.S. government publications to help you research careers?

9. What are some positive features of employment? What are some negative features?

APPLY YOUR KNOWLEDGE

10. Describe a new technology or invention that has been introduced in the last few years. How has it changed your life? Then describe a technological advance that was considered groundbreaking a few years ago, but that is obsolete today. As you think of your future career choice, how might changes such as these affect you?

THINK CRITICALLY

11. How can you start preparing today for your future career? Assess how your career plans will be different from the career plans of your parents.

12. Does the idea of owning your own small business appeal to you? Why or why not?

Coping with Change and Reinventing Yourself

GOALS

- Explain techniques for coping with change and reinventing yourself.
- Discuss the need for job networking for long-term career success.

TERMS

- lifelong learner, *p. 14*
- upgrading, *p. 15*
- retraining, *p. 15*
- advanced degrees, *p. 15*
- self-assessment inventory, *p. 16*
- placement centers, *p. 16*
- networks, *p. 18*

COPING WITH CHANGE

With rapidly advancing technologies, change is certain. You have three options when it comes to change: you can accept it, reject it, or ignore it. If you accept change, you can help shape it. If you reject change, you will be run over by it, because progress cannot be stopped. If you ignore change, you will be left behind. By rejecting or ignoring change, you will end up frustrated, unemployed, or both. By staying informed, becoming a lifelong learner, and taking classes, you can be aware of changes. By completing a self-assessment, you can make an action plan that will enable you to cope and reduce the stress of uncertainty.

STAY INFORMED

A variety of resources follow national and international trends, from general technology to specific industries. Computer magazines or online technology news sources, such as *CNET* and *WIRED* magazine, can keep you informed of technological advances. You can read newspapers and magazines in order to keep up with what is going on in the United States and around the world. You can watch the news and pay attention to what's happening with the economy, with job fields, and with businesses. You can also go to shows, expos, and other events that discuss emerging trends and cutting-edge technology. Participate and be active in the changes.

BE A LIFELONG LEARNER

The knowledge and skills required in the workplace change over time. Being a lifelong learner means actively seeking new knowledge, skills, and experiences that will add to your professional and personal growth throughout your life. You can join professional associations and service organizations that will keep you informed of what's new in specific job areas. You can attend workshops and seminars to learn about current trends. Attending these events will help make you a more knowledgeable and interesting person, as well as increase your opportunities to interact with others in your profession. Lifelong learning is essential to your successful career development.

TAKE CLASSES

Sometimes technology brings change that requires new skills—skills you cannot learn by yourself. When this happens, it's time to actively seek new knowledge by taking classes.

Upgrading means advancing to a higher level of skill to increase your usefulness to an employer. Many jobs, especially those affected by technological improvements, will require regular upgrading by employees.

Retraining involves learning new and different skills so that an employee can retain the same level of employability. Community college and vocational training is geared as much to retraining displaced employees as to preparing employees for entry-level positions. There are numerous sources of retraining:

The Princeton Review Career Quiz helps you match your interests and personality with a career that is right for you. Access school.cengage.com/pfinance/mypf and click on the link for Chapter 1. Read the overview of the quiz and identify the four behavioral dimensions measured by the test. Then click the link *Take the Princeton Review Career Quiz* to take the short quiz. What were your results? What careers were recommended? Do the results seem accurate? Why or why not?

www.cengage.com/school/pfinance/mypf

- Many companies offer technical courses to retrain their own employees. Those who volunteer and are eager to learn will position themselves for advancement.
- Training is available through technical schools, vocational centers, job placement services, business colleges, and community colleges. Many employers reimburse employees for the cost of classes related to their jobs.
- Training over the Internet (online learning) is becoming increasingly common. Employer-sponsored training is often free for employees.

For many careers, applicants will need a college or technical degree and skills before they will be considered for employment.

Many young people are staying in college longer before entering the workforce. **Advanced degrees** are specialized, intensive programs (taken after obtaining the first college degree) that prepare students for higher-level work responsibilities with more challenges and higher pay. An advanced degree may include any of the following:

- Master's degree
- Doctorate in a specialized field
- Professional degree in medicine, law, engineering, and so on

A master's degree often requires one year beyond the first college degree. A Ph.D. may require an additional three years after a master's degree. It is also possible to earn a Ph.D. without first obtaining a master's degree. This path usually takes longer (up to five years).

COMPLETE A SELF-ASSESSMENT

As you go through life, your needs and values will change. It is important to look inward to define what is important to you and then use this knowledge to plan your future. You should think about what you like doing, what you do well, and what skills and knowledge you want to enhance.

A **self-assessment inventory** lists your strong and weak points along with plans for improvement as you prepare for a career. As you improve your weak points, they become strengths in your inventory.

Figure 1.4 is a self-assessment inventory that lists a typical high school student's strengths and weaknesses, along with a plan of action. Completing a similar inventory based on your personal characteristics as compared to the requirements of your desired career area can help you determine areas that need work.

You might also ask another person to objectively assess your strengths and weaknesses. A different point of view can sometimes help clarify your self-assessment.

You can find many self-assessment questionnaires at online career sites or by searching with the keyword "self-assessment."

Many high schools, colleges, and technical training institutes have **placement centers** that offer services related to careers and employment. In addition to assisting with self-assessment inventories, they provide the following services:

- Advice and counseling to help you determine a career direction.
- Vocational, interest, and personal testing. You can compare your interests with those of successful people in various professions. A values clarification test will help you determine what is important to you both personally and professionally.
- Notification of job openings and assistance with applying and interviewing.

Private career counselors are listed in *The Yellow Pages*. They offer their services for an hourly or fixed fee. A less expensive approach is to do your own research, using the sources listed in this chapter as well as in *The American Almanac of Jobs and Salaries*. This book evaluates job opportunities in many career fields and

FIGURE 1.4   *Self-Assessment Inventory*

Strengths	Weaknesses	Plan of Action
Education: High school diploma, including business courses	*Education:* Weak in basic math skills; need to learn more software packages such as Excel	Take extra classes in algebra; learn Excel and other software
Experience: Internship in office—part-time summer job as administrative assistant; volunteer at church	*Experience:* Need experience using database programs	Look for part-time job that involves using database applications; take an online course in Access
Aptitudes and Abilities: Good hand-eye coordination; work well with people	*Aptitudes and Abilities:* Poor public speaker	Practice speaking in small groups; lead a class at church; attend more social functions
Appearance: Neat and clean	*Appearance:* Wardrobe needs more professional work clothes	Start buying clothes that are appropriate for work

gives a full range of salaries for positions and levels. You can do industry research and look into major job categories (service, professional, and so on).

Specific company research will help you determine which companies can offer you the best career opportunities.

- Check your library for sources such as Standard & Poor's *Register of Corporations, Directors, and Executives—United States and Canada* or *The 100 Best Companies to Work for in America*. In these publications, you can read about major American companies and why they are successful.
- Visit company web sites and read each company's description of itself. Check out the company's online job postings and read the requirements of positions that interest you.
- Do field research. Talk to people working in careers that interest you. These informal discussions may reveal positive and negative features of a career that you might not have anticipated.
- Talk to friends and relatives who have or are working in positions that interest you.

All this information is crucial in determining your needs and matching them to an appropriate career.

© Digital Vision/Getty Images

How could a self-assessment inventory help you prepare for change in your career and work life?

CHANGING CAREER OPPORTUNITIES

Career planning is a process that never ends. Your first career may not be permanent, even if you want it to be. All occupations, all types of businesses, and all career fields are subject to rapid and often unpredictable change. To understand how the job market will be affected, let's examine some of the major trends sweeping the country and the world.

LONG-TERM SUSTAINABILITY

Businesses must continually reinvent themselves to meet changing market needs. Individuals also must develop long-term plans to protect themselves from the effects of rapidly changing technology. You must embrace change and adapt to it. Your career plans should span several decades and be broad, diversified, and open to future opportunities and challenges. When you plan for changes and reinvent yourself, you will continue to be of value in the changing workplace.

■ A WORLD ECONOMY

We are part of a worldwide, interdependent economy. The Internet has opened the world market to companies of all sizes. To survive, American companies must find ways to compete successfully with businesses around the world. Competition will likely intensify for new markets in developing countries. *Developing countries* are nations that currently have little industry and a low standard of living. These places represent opportunities for international businesses to invest.

The 20 fastest-growing economies of the 21st century are all in developing nations, including the oil-exporting countries, South Korea, India, Singapore, the Dominican Republic, Taiwan, Mexico, and Brazil.

NAFTA (the North American Free Trade Agreement) has opened doors for American businesses to move their production facilities to Mexico and Canada and to hire their workers. This has caused the loss of thousands of U.S. jobs. But it isn't all bad news. Economists expect that in the future, because citizens in these countries have increased purchasing power, they will be able to buy our products, broadening the market for American goods.

Our nation is part of a worldwide, interdependent economy. How does this affect the U.S. job market? How will it affect your future job?

© Photodisc/Getty Images

Should we try to recapture our role as leader of a modern Industrial Revolution? Many experts say no. Instead, we should adapt and move forward in the area in which we are the leader—information—as we develop new technologies, jobs, and products for the future.

■ NETWORKING

Networking is an effective way to obtain useful information. **Networks** are informal groups of people with common interests who interact for mutual assistance. Networking includes making phone calls, sharing lunch, and creating opportunities to share ideas with your group of acquaintances. To get into and advance in a career, you will need to establish a network of contacts—people you know who have information you need. Through networking, you can get inside information without being an "insider."

You can begin now to create your network by making a master list of people you know through your parents, school and business acquaintances, and personal friends and associates. By communicating within your network, you will learn how to prepare for a job, where job openings exist, and how to pursue them.

ISSUES IN YOUR WORLD

BEING A LIFELONG LEARNER

Graduating from high school or its equivalent is a major milestone. It is the first step toward securing your financial future. You may choose additional or specialized training, an apprenticeship program, an associate's degree, a bachelor's degree, or beyond. Regardless of the highest level of formal education you attain, your opportunities for learning will continue throughout your life.

Lifelong learning is a commitment to professional and personal growth. It involves gaining new knowledge, skills, and experiences. Upgrading your skills will do the following:

- *Keep you marketable, both in your current job and in future jobs.*
- *Enhance your resume, showing you are interested and actively pursuing new skills, talents, or enrichment.*
- *Empower you to change direction when you feel it is time to move on, try new things, or pursue a different path.*
- *Open new opportunities for growth and fulfillment.*

Your choices are virtually unlimited! You can learn a new hobby, improve and maintain your health, polish your leadership skills, discover new opportunities you would never have considered, meet new people who will become your friends, or get involved in community service. Lifelong learning will provide you with a versatility that will allow you to explore new directions, discover hidden talents and interests, and enrich your life.

Lifelong learning will keep you active—mentally as well as physically—as you find new paths to explore and add to your base of knowledge. When times change, you'll be ready!

THINK *CRITICALLY*

1. *Is there something you'd like to explore that is not your major career objective, such as playing an instrument, learning a new sport, making something, or learning a new skill?*
2. *How has lifelong learning been a significant part of the life of someone you know?*
3. *Why would a prospective employer be impressed with an applicant who was involved in community activities?*

Assessment

KEY TERMS REVIEW

Match the terms with the definitions. Some terms may not be used.

_____ 1. Informal groups of people with common interests who interact for mutual assistance

_____ 2. A list of your strong and weak points along with plans for improvement

_____ 3. Organizations that offer services related to careers and employment

_____ 4. Specialized, intensive programs that prepare students for higher-level work responsibilities

_____ 5. Advancing to a higher level of skill to increase your usefulness

_____ 6. Learning new and different skills to retain the same level of employability

a. advanced degrees

b. lifelong learner

c. networks

d. placement centers

e. retraining

f. self-assessment inventory

g. upgrading

CHECK YOUR UNDERSTANDING

7. What steps can you take today, and as you go through life, to deal with change and reduce uncertainty in your career?

8. What is meant by a world economy that is based on interdependence? How can we benefit if our country loses jobs to developing countries with cheaper labor?

APPLY YOUR KNOWLEDGE

9. Describe a business that you have observed making changes over the years to meet the changing needs and wants of consumers. (Hint: Look at how McDonald's has changed.) How might you reinvent yourself to meet changing demands in the workplace?

THINK CRITICALLY

10. Explain the concept of a one-world economy. How has it affected you and your family?

11. Do you have friends, business associates, employers and coworkers, and others who act as your information network? What have you done, and what can you do in the future, to expand your network?

Chapter Assessment

SUMMARY

1.1

- *Careers of the future will be based on technology and information management and will change rapidly in regards to requirements and skills.*

- *Service jobs will grow, while manufacturing and cost center jobs will be insourced, near-sourced, and outsourced.*

- *Sources of job information include the DOT, O*NET, OOH, and Monthly Labor Review.*

- *A job analysis can help you identify types of work that would be a good fit for you.*

- *When making job and career choices, evaluate the positive features, such as salary, benefits, and opportunities for promotion.*

- *When making job and career choices, also consider the negative features, such as employee expenses and work characteristics that do not match your preferences.*

- *You may aspire to be an entrepreneur because of the many advantages of being your own boss, but running your own small business is also very risky.*

1.2

- *You can stay informed of current trends by reading widely, watching the news, and attending shows, expos, and other events.*

- *You can be a lifelong learner by joining professional associations and service organizations that will keep you informed of what's new in specific job areas and provide learning opportunities.*

- *Lifelong learning involves taking classes as a means of upgrading, retraining, and obtaining advanced degrees.*

- *Completing a self-assessment inventory can help you to pinpoint your strengths and weaknesses and to plan a long-term strategy.*

- *Placement centers, online career sites, and private career counselors can provide tools to help you determine a career direction.*

- *You should recognize the dynamics of a worldwide, interdependent economy and take steps to stay competitive and reinvent yourself on an ongoing basis.*

- *To help achieve your career goals, you should develop a network of contacts with which you share interests and interact for mutual assistance.*

APPLY WHAT YOU KNOW

1. What is the focus of most jobs and careers in the United States today, from professionals to service employees?

2. What are some of the highest-paying career groups today? How do you prepare for these types of jobs?

3. List three publications of the U.S. government that will assist you with career choices. Access one of them online and print out a job description that interests you.

4. Describe the types of information listed in a job analysis. Prepare a job analysis based on a part-time job that you are considering.

5. List some negative features you have observed in the jobs of your parents and others. Then list some positive features of the same jobs, not including the paycheck.

6. What can a person do about change? List three ways you can cope with and be successful in preparing for career moves based on change.

7. Based on three potential career choices that interest you, how much education and specialized training will you need to achieve?

8. Do online research to discover the current employment picture in the United States, along with rates of insourcing, near-sourcing, and outsourcing. Explain how the results of your research will affect your current and future job choices and your career planning.

MAKE ACADEMIC CONNECTIONS

9. **Research** Look up three career choices in the Dictionary of Occupational Titles. Summarize your findings in one paragraph about each choice. Look up the same three occupations in the Occupational Outlook Handbook and add a second paragraph about each. If you have Internet access, use the online versions of these publications.

10. **Economics** Write a one-page essay on interdependence, comparative advantage, and absolute advantage. Explain why, in terms of scarce and diminishing world resources, nations should focus on producing those things they can do most efficiently. Connect your research to our study of jobs being near-sourced and outsourced to other countries.

11. **Communication** Review recent newspaper and business magazine articles about the U.S. economy and what's happening in the job market. Are businesses hiring, holding steady, or laying off workers? What are the reasons given? What career fields are growing? Shrinking? Explain how this type of information will affect your job and career choices and your career planning, now and in the future.

12. **International Studies** Identify three countries that are receiving large amounts of near-sourced or outsourced work from the United States. In a one-page report, explain the impact on their economies (jobs for their workers) and standards of living. Use Internet sources and be sure to properly cite them.

SOLVE *PROBLEMS* AND

EXPLORE *ISSUES*

13. *Visit the* Monthly Labor Review Online *at the following web address: http://www.bls.gov/opub/mlr/welcome.htm. Click on the* Index *link to find published articles since 1981. Choose the most recent year, and look up an article or report that discusses earnings and wages, economic growth, or job earnings based on education level. Write a one-page report on your findings.*

14. *Complete a job analysis, using Figure 1.3 as a guide, for three different occupations. To get this information, consult resources listed in this chapter or interview persons who work in these fields. List your source(s) of information on the job analysis form.*

15. *In writing, explain to a friend why it is necessary to be aware of what is happening technologically in the world. Give suggestions as to what she or he can do to keep up with changes.*

16. *Choose a large company for which you believe you would like to work in the future. Do some research to learn more about the company. (Suggestions: Check Standard & Poor's* The 100 Best Companies to Work for in America. *Also, access the company's web site and read the company's description of itself.) Summarize your findings in one or two paragraphs.*

17. *Develop a networking plan—a list of all your possible communication sources—and add to it each time you make a new contact. List contacts you plan to set up, people you would like to meet, and places you would like to visit.*

18. *Choose three career choices that might interest you, each from a different career field. Use print or online resources to find typical salaries for each career. Write a paragraph explaining possible reasons salaries differ among these career choices.*

EXTEND YOUR LEARNING

19. **Ethics** *Networking involves making contacts and forming a group of people who mutually benefit and help each other. When you make contacts with people for the sole purpose of getting something but giving nothing in return, are you taking advantage of them? Networks provide valuable support and assistance, but when a person becomes labeled as a "user" (person who takes but never gives), the network contacts may refuse to lend a hand. Explain why it is important to be a contributing member of your network and not simply a user, or a person who benefits but does not contribute.*

For related activities and links, go to **www.cengage.com/school/pfinance/mypf**

2

Planning Your Career

| 2.1 | **Finding the Right Career Fit** |
| 2.2 | **Finding Career Opportunities** |

Consider **THIS**

"To be happy in your work life, you must be able to work as if you don't have to."

—*Dr. Alfred Mukakis*

Larissa was energetic and outgoing. She enjoyed being around other people and helping them. She often volunteered in the community center, and it made her happy to support others in doing things they couldn't do by themselves. Larissa was strong and physically fit but not especially interested in athletics. She hoped to find a career that would allow her to use her natural talents and help others at the same time.

"I think I'd like to be a physical therapist," she told her high school counselor. "What steps should I take now, while I'm still in high school, to help me decide if this career is really right for me? If the career is a good fit for me, then what can I do to get there as quickly as possible?"

Finding the Right Career Fit

WHY PEOPLE WORK

People work to meet their needs, wants, and goals. The main reason people work is so they can buy things they need, such as houses, cars, and furniture, as well as fun things they enjoy, like TVs and video games. Working also provides a sense of purpose—such as helping others, contributing to society, and making a difference in the world. You can gain this sense of purpose at the same time you earn a living and provide for life's necessities.

People also work to gain a sense of **identity**—of who they are and how they fit in. In the United States, work is typically the central activity of a person's life, and thus becomes strongly linked to a person's sense of identity.

Right now, your identity is that of a student. One of the first questions you are asked is "How old are you?" or "What grade are you in?" Some students also work part time. When you finish school, your work identity will be based on the career you've chosen and what you do with your time. No one will ask you about your age or grade level. Instead they will be asking, "What do you do?" Your answer will be what you do at work.

People who are happy with their work lives are more likely to be happy in other areas of their lives. This is partly because most workers have difficulty leaving work at the office door; they take it home with them at the end of the day. They continue to think about work issues and talk about work with friends and family members.

© Digital Vision/Getty Images

What are some reasons why people work?

Remember, what you do for a living will affect your home and family life as well.

FACTORS AFFECTING CAREER CHOICE

Because your career will affect nearly every part of your life, your choice of career is very important. Many factors will affect your decision. Among them are your values and lifestyle, aptitudes and interests, and personal qualities.

▌ VALUES AND LIFESTYLE

Values are the ideals in life that are important to you. Values are based on life experiences as well as perceptions and beliefs. Each person chooses what he or she believes to be true, meaningful, and important. Your values are shaped by your family, social and cultural groups, and religion. They are also influenced by the media and society as a whole. Ultimately, you must establish your own value system. A common value is the desire to help others. Values can also include spending time with family and loved ones, taking annual vacations, leaving the world a better place, and raising a family.

Lifestyle is the way people choose to live their lives, based on the values they have chosen. Your lifestyle is evident from the clothes you wear and the things you buy, use, do, say, and enjoy. Most people desire to have a lifestyle that is either the same or better than what they experienced growing up. A career is an important part of most people's lifestyle. Your career establishes not only the way you spend a large part of your time but also your level of income. For example, if you seek a lavish lifestyle, you will need a high-income job to achieve that lifestyle. Many people want a higher-level lifestyle but aren't willing to put the time or money into an education that will allow for the lifestyle. It's important for you to understand the connection between your lifestyle choices and the commitments required of you to achieve those goals. Another choice, of course, is to decide to live a simpler lifestyle that requires less time and commitment for education and career goals.

▌ APTITUDES AND INTERESTS

An **aptitude** is a natural physical or mental ability that allows you to do certain tasks well. For example, you may have an aptitude for working with

GLOBAL *View*

A recent study revealed that nearly one-fourth of all U.S. workers receive no paid vacation or holidays. Nearly half of all private sector workers receive no paid sick leave. In contrast, full-time workers in most European countries, such as Finland, receive six to eight weeks of vacation and holiday time annually. The United States is the only wealthy country that does not mandate paid vacation and sick leave.

THINK CRITICALLY

Do you think the U.S. government should pass laws about paid time off? How could you convince an employer that offering more paid time off would be beneficial to it?

numbers. If so, a career that requires calculations, such as engineering, might be a good fit for you. Aptitude tests can help you identify your natural abilities so that you can focus your career search on jobs that use those aptitudes.

Your career search should also consider your **interests**—the things you like to do. By examining the types of activities you enjoy, you can choose a career that involves tasks you find interesting and satisfying. For example, if you enjoy interacting with people, you will likely prefer a job working with others, such as in sales or a helping profession, to one that involves working alone. Use Figure 2.1 to help identify your interests.

The Internet offers a number of questionnaires to help job seekers identify their interests. Use keywords such as "interest test" to search for these questionnaires. They are fun to fill out. Plus, they may reveal something about you that will help you find a good career fit.

PERSONAL QUALITIES

Your **personality** is made up of the many individual qualities that make you unique. Personal qualities include such things as your intelligence, creativity, sense of humor, and general attitude. Most jobs require a particular set of personal qualities. For example, a person who represents a company to potential customers needs an outgoing, friendly personality. A job that involves working alone at a computer needs someone with a more introverted personality. You will be happiest in a job that fits your personality. Which qualities listed in Figure 2.2 on the next page describe you?

CAREER PLANNING

Planning for your future career is an important task. Consider the total time spent working: 8 hours a day, 5 days a week, 50 weeks a year totals 2,000 hours each year, not including any overtime. If you work the average career span of 43 years (from age 22 to age 65), you will spend 86,000 hours or more on the job! Because your work will likely take so much of your time, you will need to plan your career carefully.

FIGURE 2.1	*Types of Work Activities*

Which of these work activities appeal to you?	
analyzing and recording	*physically inactive work*
creating and designing	*presenting or speaking*
following directions	*repetitive tasks*
helping others	*self-motivated work*
indoor work	*thinking and problem solving*
managing people and resources	*variety of tasks*
manual work	*working alone*
outdoor work	*working on a computer*
physically active work	*working with machines*

FIGURE 2.2   *Personal Qualities*

1. I am ambitious and willing to work hard to reach my goals.
2. I prefer a low-stress work environment.
3. I am happiest working alone.
4. I enjoy working with a group to achieve goals.
5. I am friendly and outgoing.
6. I am shy, and meeting new people is difficult for me.
7. I like to lead group activities.
8. I am more of a follower than a leader.
9. I am a high-energy person who must be constantly on the move.
10. I enjoy sitting quietly and reading for long periods of time.
11. I like my activities to vary a lot.
12. I am most comfortable when I follow a regular routine.
13. I like to be in a setting where I can help others.
14. I like working in a setting where I can meet personal goals.

■ STEPS IN CAREER PLANNING

Effective career planning involves careful investigation and analysis—a process that you should start now and revisit throughout your work life. The steps in career planning involve self-analysis, research, a plan of action, and periodic re-evaluation.

Self-Analysis

Using resources available from schools, employment offices, testing services, and online, explore personal factors that relate to your career choice.

1. Determine your wants and needs.
2. Determine your values and desired lifestyle.
3. Assess your aptitudes and interests and determine how they match job tasks.
4. Analyze your personal qualities and the kinds of job tasks that best suit your personality.

Research

Based on a good self-analysis, determine the careers that best suit your interests and aptitudes and will help you meet your lifestyle goals.

1. Seek information in books, magazines, and web sites; use resources available from libraries, counseling centers, and employment offices.

NETBookmark

The U.S. Office of Education has grouped careers into 16 different "clusters" based on similar job characteristics. The occupations within each cluster may seem quite different, but many of the people who work in them have similar interests, skills, and personalities. Access www.cengage.com/school/pfinance/mypf and click on the link for Chapter 2. Identify the 16 different career clusters. Select a cluster that interests you, read its online brochure, and describe the employment outlook for the occupations in that cluster.

www.cengage.com/school/pfinance/mypf

2. Compare your interests, aptitudes, and personal qualities to job descriptions and requirements. Most jobs can fit into one of the categories shown in Figure 2.3, which contains various occupations described in the *Occupational Outlook Handbook (OOH)*. In which category does the job of your choice fit? What training do you need to qualify for this job?

3. Talk to people in the fields of work you find interesting.

4. Observe occupations, spend time learning about jobs and companies, and seek part-time work to get direct experience. Sometimes following someone throughout his or her workday will give you real insight into the daily activities and requirements of a career.

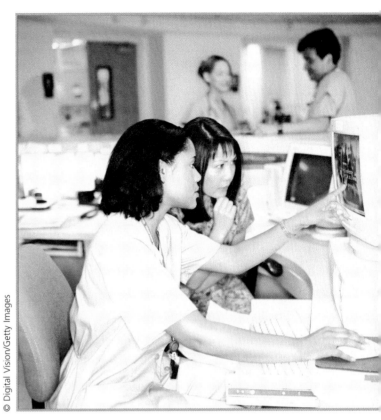

© Digital Vision/Getty Images

What steps are involved in career planning?

Plan of Action

After you have done some job research, develop a plan of action that will eventually bring you to your career goals.

1. Use good job search techniques. Get organized, make a plan, follow through, and don't give up.

2. Develop necessary skills by taking courses (traditional or online) and gaining exposure to the field in which you want to pursue a career.

3. Seek a part-time or volunteer job to gain experience in your area of choice.

4. Evaluate your choices over time. People change and so do jobs. If you discover you are following the wrong career path, change your direction before you stay on it too long.

Re-evaluation

Because the world changes rapidly, we all need to prepare ourselves to meet the challenges ahead. You may wish to prepare for career changes in order to take advantage of new opportunities. About every five years, think about what you will be doing and where you would like to be in the next five years.

THE IMPORTANCE OF GOALS

A **goal** is a desired end toward which efforts are directed. Goals provide a sense of direction and purpose in life. There are three types of goals: short-term, intermediate, and long-term.

- A *short-term goal* is one you expect to reach in a few days or weeks. A short-term goal could be to achieve at least a B on next week's math test. You know you must plan time to study soon to meet your goal.

FIGURE 2.3   OOH Occupation Categories

Occupations	Job Examples	Description of Environment*	Training/Education*	Working Hours*	Beginning Salary/Wages*
Management	**Sales manager,** marketing manager, systems administrator	Work in offices close to top managers; under pressure to meet goals	Bachelor's degree; MBA or specialized master's degree preferred	40-hour work week plus travel and extended hours as needed	Median salary plus bonus: $34,000 to $40,000
Professional	**Engineer,** teacher, architect, economist, lawyer	Work in offices, laboratories, and specialized work sites	Bachelor's degree; advanced work or master's degree often required	40-hour work week plus extended hours as needed	Highest paid bachelor's degree: $50,000 to $75,000
Service	**Police detective,** pharmacy aide, chef, flight attendant	Work in and out of office; complete field work investigations	High school plus law enforcement training; associates or bachelor's degree preferred	Shift schedule varies; often nights and weekends	$48,000 to $56,000, depending on rank and years of service
Sales	**Retail sales clerk,** cashier, real estate sales agent	Assist customers in store or on location of goods being sold	High school; must have associate's or bachelor's degree for advancement	Varied; often evening, weekend, and holiday	$8 to $13 per hour; advancements with years of service
Office and Administrative	**File clerk,** order clerk, teller, dispatcher, postal worker	Work in offices entering/retrieving data	High school/GED; additional training or education preferred	40-hour work week	$7 to $13 per hour; advancements with years of service
Farming	**Agricultural workers,** fishers, forest and conservation workers	Work outdoors raising crops and animals	Skills learned on the job and with experience; little formal training	When needed (feeding, planting, harvesting) and seasonal peaks	Piece rate based on output (crops produced)
Construction	**Carpenter,** laborer, electrician, roofer, painter	Work at site where construction occurs, much of it outdoors	Apprenticeship and special on-the-job training	40-hour work week plus overtime as needed to meet deadlines	$11 to $30 per hour; more with experience and skill
Installation/ Repair	**Auto mechanic,** home appliance repair person, equipment installer	Work in shops using specialized equipment and following precise procedures	High school vocational training program preferred plus specialized or on-the-job training	40-hour work week	$12 to $28 per hour; more with experience and skill
Production	**Assembler,** textile operator, machinist, welder, jeweler	Work in factories using tools and machines focusing on quality	High school/GED plus specialized or on-the-job training	40-hour work week	$9 to $22 per hour
Transportation	**Air traffic controller,** bus driver, pilot, flight engineer	Work in tight spaces under stressful conditions focusing on safety	FAA or other approved program and pre-employment test	Shift schedule varies; often nights and weekends	$40,000 to $50,000

*Based on first example in bold.

- *Intermediate goals* are those you wish to accomplish in the next few months or years. Some examples are graduation from high school, a vacation trip, or plans for summer employment. These goals take longer to achieve and also require more planning.
- *Long-term goals* are those you wish to achieve in five to ten years or longer. They might include a college degree, career, marriage, or family. Many people find it helpful to write down goals and then revisit them every year to evaluate their progress.

If goals are to be meaningful, they should be well defined and realistic. They should also be written down to become a part of your life. If you are like most people, your goals will change every few years, either because you have accomplished them or because your values have changed. You may decide to take a different path. Many people find a checklist to be a handy way to help them reach their goals. Figure 2.4 shows a typical goals checklist. Use it as a guide to create your own checklist.

THE ROLE OF EXPERIENCE

Experience is the knowledge and skills acquired from working in a career field. As you gain experience in a field, you become more valuable to an employer. Most employers give wage increases that reflect the increased value of an employee's experience. When you change career fields, however, you no longer have the advantage of experience. You may need to accept a lower wage as you work to gain experience in your new career field.

| FIGURE 2.4 | *Goals Checklist* |

GOALS CHECKLIST

Week of _____

	Accomplished
Short-term goals (today/this week):	
1. Buy birthday gift for mom	_____
2. Get haircut (Saturday)	_____
3. See counselor about chemistry class	_____
Intermediate goals (next month/year)	
1. Get a C or better in Chemistry	_____
2. Prepare for SAT (test in May)	_____
3. Finish term report (due December 14)	_____
Long-term goals (future)	
1. Graduate from college	_____
2. Buy a car	_____
3. Get a full-time job	_____

ISSUES IN YOUR WORLD

HELP WANTED

The following is a typical ad from a newspaper's Help Wanted section. It poses a dilemma for many young people today. How can you have education and *experience? If no one will hire you, how can you ever get that "experience"?*

There are a number of ways you can meet this employer's requirements of both education and experience. As you complete your formal education, you can prepare for your future career in the following ways:

> WANTED: Web site manager. Must have course work in HTML programming, graphic design, and platform management. Degree preferred. Two years of sales experience required. Starting salary $36,000 plus benefits.

1. Cooperative Work Experience. *A job after class, part time, evenings, and weekends while you are in school will add valuable experience. It will give you insight into the work environment and the tasks, skills, and activities that are performed day to day.*

2. Summer Work. *During the summers, you could work at a job that sounds exciting or interesting to you. To do this, try:*

   a. Temporary Work. *A company that places temporary help may be able to find you a job filling in for a regular employee. While the position is only temporary, it gives you valuable insight and work experience.*

   b. Volunteer Work. *As a volunteer worker, you may be giving up pay, but you will gain important skills and be able to observe working conditions.*

   c. Community Service. *Get involved in the community by serving on committees, working on clean-up projects, or serving food in a homeless shelter. These activities give you general work experience and tell a prospective employer about your character.*

3. Internship. *An internship is an on-the-job training experience that usually pays only your cost of getting to work and any extra expenses you incur. You receive training and exposure to the job requirements.*

These suggestions will help you find ways to avoid the "education but no experience" dilemma. Plan ahead and be ready for that opening!

THINK *CRITICALLY*

1. *Does the career you want require experience for an entry-level position?*
2. *What are some specific ways you can gather experience for the career of your choice while completing your formal education?*

Assessment

KEY TERMS REVIEW

Match the terms with the definitions. Some terms may not be used.

_____ 1. The sum of the many individual qualities that make you unique

_____ 2. Ideals in life that are important to you

_____ 3. A natural physical or mental ability

_____ 4. A desired end toward which efforts are directed

_____ 5. A sense of who you are as a person and how you fit in with the world

_____ 6. The way people choose to live their lives, based on their values

_____ 7. The things you like to do

a. aptitude
b. experience
c. goal
d. identity
e. interests
f. lifestyle
g. personality
h. values

CHECK YOUR UNDERSTANDING

8. If your job does not help you achieve your personal goals, what will likely happen?

9. Describe your interests—what do you like to do with your free time?

10. Why is it important for you to have a career plan of action?

APPLY YOUR KNOWLEDGE

11. Using Figure 2.1 as an example, list activities that appeal to you. Identify several occupations related to these activities. Are you willing to get the education and experience needed for these occupations? Would your choice of occupations support your chosen lifestyle? Based on your answers, do you think your choice of occupations is the right one? Why or why not?

THINK CRITICALLY

12. Job-related contacts can help you get the inside track on finding job openings. How many contacts do you currently have? How can you add more names to the list?

13. Do you set goals for yourself, both personal goals and work-related goals? Create a written list of your short-term, intermediate, and long-term goals. Explain why goals that are written down are more often achieved than those that are not written down.

Finding Career Opportunities

SOURCES OF JOB OPPORTUNITY INFORMATION

You can find out about job opportunities in a number of ways: word of mouth from personal contacts; school counseling and placement services; periodicals, books, and other publications; public and private employment agencies; newspaper, business telephone directory, and private job listings; and the Internet through online career and employment sites and company web sites.

CONTACTS

Many job openings are never advertised. They are filled from within the company or with people from outside who were privately informed of the opening by a contact within the company. A **contact** is a member of your network, such as a relative, friend, member of a group to which you belong, or a former work associate. Contacts can provide you with inside information on job openings. Therefore, the larger your network, the better your chances of hearing about a desired job opening.

If you are seeking a job in a field in which you have no contacts, try to get to know people who can tell you about openings. Start by letting it be known to the current members of your network that you are looking for a particular type of job. If, for example, you want to work at a bank, ask the people you know whether they have any contacts in the banking industry. You might also participate in student and professional organizations and community activities that could provide links to banking professionals. You can also meet and talk with bank personnel through school-sponsored visits, job shadowing, and job fairs. **Job shadowing** is spending a morning or afternoon with a worker in the type of job that interests you. You can see how activities are performed in a typical day firsthand. Job shadowing can give you an inside track on finding out about future job openings.

SCHOOL COUNSELING AND PLACEMENT SERVICES

Many schools have programs to assist students in preparing for careers, making career choices, and securing part- or full-time work. One such program is called **cooperative education**, where students attend classes part of the day and then go to a job that provides supervised field experience. Students receive credits for on-the-job experience that directly relates to classroom studies in a chosen career field. Students placed in work situations are given grades on their work and are paid minimum wage for their efforts. Employers often receive tax credits for the wages they pay the students during training.

School counselors and teachers are also good sources of job opportunity information. They are often asked by employers to recommend students for specific job openings. If you are interested in an office job, you should talk to counselors and business teachers as you complete business courses.

Placement centers help students find jobs. Their services are usually offered free of charge. Placement centers post job openings at the school and provide information to qualified students so they can apply. They also keep a placement folder on each student that contains school records, including attendance, academic, and disciplinary records. When employers ask for information about a student, they receive copies of information from the student's placement folder. If your school has a placement center, examine your folder and have teachers and other adults write recommendations to put in it. You should also confirm that all school records are in the folder. Be sure to check at your school to see what other types of assistance are available.

© Digital Vision/Getty Images

How could you find out about job openings that aren't advertised?

PUBLIC AND PRIVATE EMPLOYMENT AGENCIES

All major cities have public and private employment agencies. **Employment agencies** help job seekers find a job for which they are qualified. They also help employers locate the best applicants for job openings. Private employment agencies may or may not charge a fee for their services. Such fees vary from agency to agency, so you should compare prices before you sign with one. Some of these agencies charge a fee to the employer. Others charge the prospective employee when a job is found, and still others divide the fee between the employer and the hired employee.

A **headhunter** is a type of employment agency that seeks out highly qualified people to fill important positions for an employer. For example, a company may need a new manager or vice president. Rather than post a job

Think of a job you would like to have or a company for which you would like to work in the future. Assume you are going to contact the Human Resources Director for that company and set up an informational interview. An informational interview *is one in which you are not applying for a specific job, but learning more about the job, the industry, or the company itself. It is a good way to explore careers and can help you achieve career goals. To prepare for your informational interview, compile a list of questions you might ask.*

opening and go through an open interview process, the company may hire a headhunter to recruit an executive with the skills and experience needed. Often those being recruited are already gainfully employed and not actively seeking a new job. The headhunter contacts them, explains to them the open position, and asks them if they would be interested. These job offers often entice highly paid workers to switch jobs for better pay and/or better working conditions. Headhunter fees are paid by the companies seeking employees.

The state employment office does not charge a fee because it is a government agency. There you can also obtain information about government job-training assistance programs, YES (Youth Employment Services), Youth Corps, Civil Service (state and federal), and apprenticeship boards, as well as other government employment programs that exist from time to time. You may qualify for one or more of these types of work programs.

If you initially have trouble finding a permanent position in your desired field, you may want to start out working for a temp agency. A **temporary agency**, commonly referred to as a "temp agency," provides part- or full-time temporary job placement. Working in a temporary job for a company gives you a chance to make an impression and expand your network. When the company sees that you are a good fit, it may try to buy out your contract with the temp agency. Or, it may contact you at a later time when a full-time position is available.

■ NEWSPAPER, YELLOW PAGES, AND PRIVATE JOB LISTINGS

The help wanted ads in the classified section of your local newspaper list job openings in your area. The ads will give a brief description of the job, the requirements of job candidates, and often the salary range. Watch these ads closely and respond quickly when a new job enters the market. Both employers and employment agencies advertise job openings to attract qualified applicants.

The Yellow Pages is an alphabetically arranged subject listing of businesses advertising their services. If you are looking for a job in a certain field, you can search *The Yellow Pages* to find a listing of local businesses in that given field. You can then send an unsolicited letter of application to those businesses that interest you or stop by to see if they have openings.

Many companies, government offices, and schools place job opening announcements on bulletin boards, circulate them within their organization, and post them on their web sites. Checking in these places may give you the current information you need to apply for a position when it opens.

ONLINE JOB INFORMATION

Searching the Internet using keywords related to your chosen career field will provide many new sources of job information. Some web sites are specifically designed to help people find jobs. These online career and employment sites offer *online job postings* and provide assistance in matching job openings with applicants. Many of these sites allow you to post your resume for employers to see. Some allow you to apply for a job online.

Examples of general online career and employment sites that provide information on a variety of industries include CoolJobs.com, Yahoo! HotJobs, Monster, CareerBuilder.com, craigslist, and ResumeBlaster.com. Others, such as Guru.com and TechCareers.com, are more specialized. Many local newspapers also list web sites with searchable job listings.

Companies often list their job openings on their own web sites. Go to the web site of a company for which you would like to work. Read the information the company supplies about itself. Then follow the links to its list of open positions. The site will tell you how to apply.

Professional associations often allow job seekers to post resumes and browse their database of job openings. For example, if you have trained for a career as a paralegal, you can post your resume and search for job openings at the National Paralegal Association web site. Professional associations usually include job openings in their print publications as well.

JOB SEARCH TECHNIQUES

Finding and getting the right job takes hard work, careful planning, and often a great deal of time. Nevertheless, a careful search can land you a job you will enjoy for many years. Dissatisfaction leads to frequent job changing, which may damage your employment chances in the future.

Your **work history** is a record of the jobs you have held and how long you stayed with each employer. Employers will evaluate your work history when you apply for a job. If it shows that you have changed jobs frequently without a logical career progression, potential employers might think hiring you is risky. They do not want to invest in training you for a

© Digital Vision/Getty Images

How could your work history affect your chances of getting a job?

position only to have you leave. You do not want to invest your time and effort in the wrong job either. So, take time to do what is necessary to find the job that is the right fit for you. To find the right job, you will need to get organized, make a plan, follow up, and don't give up on your search.

▌ GET ORGANIZED

After you decide what kind of job you want, the first step toward getting that job is to get organized. Prepare a checklist of things to do and check them off as you complete them. The checklist may contain the following items:

- Assemble all the information you will need about the type of work you want to do.
- List prospective companies for which you would like to work.
- Gather your sources of information and research job descriptions, skills and aptitudes needed, and other job requirements.
- Make lists of personal contacts, places to go, and people to see.
- Prepare a current resume and a letter of application (to be discussed in Chapter 3).
- Ask previous employers, teachers, coaches, counselors, or others to write letters of recommendation for you. Also, ask them if you may give their names and contact information as references for employment purposes.
- Update your placement folder at school.

▌ MAKE A PLAN

A plan is important to the success of your job search because it keeps you organized, shows what you have done, and indicates what you need to do in the immediate future. A good plan lists all your goals and shows a timeframe for achieving them. As you accomplish each step or goal, check it off. Your plan might look similar to Figure 2.5.

FIGURE 2.5   *Plan to Get a Job*

Job Leads:

State employment office

Help wanted ads (newspaper)

School placement office

Marketing teacher

Online search

Contacts:

Aunt Jessica (knows manager)

Time Line—*Week 1*

Day 1:

Prepare resume and letter of application.

Check help wanted ads in newspaper.

Make a list of local stores from The Yellow Pages.

Check store web sites for job openings.

Day 2:

Send two application letters.

Get two personal references.

Call Aunt Jessica to set up lunch date to talk.

Check for online job postings.

Often after an interview, you may wonder why you weren't hired. There may be many reasons why you didn't get the job. Don't feel bad about it or let it hurt your self-worth. Competition is fierce in the job market. Here is a partial list of what may have happened:

- They were looking for applicants to hold on file for future openings.
- There were more qualified applicants.
- The position was taken by someone with an inside track.
- Your skills didn't match up with their immediate needs.
- They liked you, but someone else interviewed slightly better than you did.
- You didn't "click" with the interviewer.

There can be many reasons why you are not the first choice for a job opening. Don't assume the worst! It is acceptable for you to ask for feedback. Contact the interviewer and ask what you could have done better. The information will help you prepare better for future interviews.

THINK *CRITICALLY*

If you were the person hiring a new employee, how would you decide between two or more applicants that appear to be equally qualified? What are some questions you might ask the seemingly equal applicants to help you determine which one would be best for the job?

FOLLOW UP

After you have contacted a potential employer by letter or by filling out an application for a job opening, check back from time to time to let the employer know you are still interested in working for the company. At this time, you may ask when the company expects to make its hiring decision.

If you had a formal interview with the Human Resources Director or a manager, follow up with a thank-you letter. Express your appreciation for the opportunity to interview. Convey your continued interest in the position. Remind the interviewer of your skills and point out how they match the needs of the company. The follow-up letter is common business etiquette and will serve to keep your name in the forefront of the decision-maker's mind. Employers will be impressed with those individuals who follow up promptly with a thank-you letter.

DON'T GIVE UP

You can expect to apply, and be turned down, for several jobs before you are hired. Continue to remain courteous and upbeat, and keep checking back for openings. Try all your job leads. Be prepared, so that if you are called for an interview on short notice—even on the same day—you can go. Continually check the want ads for new openings. Check with your contacts frequently. Although a good job search may take several weeks or months, the effort will pay off.

Whenever anything is built, from a building to a highway to a factory, there are construction workers who make it happen. They give us shelter, comfort, and convenience. Their work is vitally important to the economy.

Construction workers do physically demanding work. They lift and carry heavy objects; they stoop, kneel, and crawl in awkward positions. Some work at great heights or in extremely small and uncomfortable spaces.

When Hoover Dam was completed in 1935, it was the world's largest concrete structure. Located on the border between Arizona and Nevada, it impounds the Colorado River and creates Lake Mead. There were 7,000 construction workers, of which 112 died due to the hazards of their job. Today, Hoover Dam is a landmark, a recreation site, and a major power facility attracting more than seven million visitors annually.

Employment Outlook

- Employment is expected to grow by 11 percent between 2008 and 2016.
- The industry is expected to grow more slowly than in recent years, since it is very sensitive to cyclical changes in the economy. Automation also eliminates many jobs each year.

Job Titles

- Construction worker
- Drywall installer
- Carpenter
- Roofer
- Painter

Needed Skills

- No specific degrees are required, but apprenticeship and specialized skills are desirable.
- Trade-related training is available at vocational schools and community colleges.

What's it like to work in... *Construction*

Jim started his day at the work site by unloading, identifying, and distributing building materials. He took roofing materials to one house and drywall to another. He also checked the machinery to be sure it was operational.

He put on his helmet, safety goggles, and protective clothing before entering the demolition site of an older building that contained hazardous building materials. It was his responsibility to load the asbestos materials into the receptacle so that they could be removed from the site.

Jim went to another job site to meet with a stonemason who would be laying brick for the house. Jim loved watching the houses go up and becoming the dream homes of satisfied customers and their families.

What About You?

Why is the construction industry important to our economy? What work characteristics of this industry do you like and dislike?

Assessment

KEY TERMS REVIEW

Match the terms with the definitions. Some terms may not be used.

_____ 1. *A type of employment agency that seeks out highly qualified people to fill important positions for an employer*

_____ 2. *A member of your network*

_____ 3. *A record of the jobs you have held and how long you stayed with each employer*

_____ 4. *Organization that helps job seekers find a job for which they are qualified*

_____ 5. *An agency that offers part-time and temporary full-time work*

_____ 6. *Spending a morning or afternoon with a worker in the type of job that interests you*

a. contact

b. cooperative education

c. employment agency

d. headhunter

e. job shadowing

f. temporary agency

g. work history

CHECK YOUR UNDERSTANDING

7. *How do companies fill jobs without advertising?*

8. *How can cooperative education help you get a job?*

9. *How can the Internet help your job search?*

APPLY YOUR KNOWLEDGE

10. *Using your phone directory and online research, list five employment agencies in your area. With your instructor's permission, call one of the agencies and ask about its fee structure. What would be charged for placement of a job that paid $2,000 per month? Would fees be paid by the employer, employee, or both?*

THINK CRITICALLY

11. *Networking can help you get the inside track on job openings. What can you do if you are seeking a job in a field in which you have no contacts?*

12. *Posting your resume online can be risky. It is easy for predators to post bogus job openings in order to get people to apply and give them personal information found on a resume. How can you protect yourself when applying for jobs on the Internet?*

Chapter Assessment

SUMMARY

2.1

- *People work to buy the things they need and to gain a sense of purpose and identity.*

- *Factors affecting career choices include values and lifestyle, aptitudes and interests, and personality.*

- *Steps in career planning include performing self-analysis, completing research, developing a plan of action, and periodically re-evaluating your career path.*

- *Goals provide a sense of direction as you develop your career plan.*

- *Create a checklist of your short-term, intermediate, and long-term goals, and check them off as you accomplish them.*

- *As you gain experience in your chosen field, you become more valuable to employers. When you switch career fields, you lose the advantage of experience.*

2.2

- *Many job opportunities are never advertised, but you can learn about them through your contacts (networking). You can expand your network and learn about careers through job shadowing and informational interviews.*

- *You can find jobs through placement services, employment agencies, newspaper ads, The Yellow Pages, private job listings, and online job postings.*

- *If you initially have trouble finding a permanent position in your desired field, you may want to start out working for a temp agency.*

- *Once you are established in your career, a headhunter may seek you out to fill an important position for an employer.*

- *Employers will evaluate your work history when you apply for a job.*

- *For a successful job search, get organized, make a plan, follow up, and don't give up.*

APPLY WHAT YOU KNOW

1. *Explain why people work. Why are people's jobs so important to them?*

2. *What is an aptitude? Why is it important to know what your aptitudes are?*

3. *What are personal qualities? List three of yours.*

4. *Look at the want ads in the classified section of your local newspaper. Find an ad that appeals to you. Does it fit well with your aptitudes and personal qualities? Explain your answer.*

5. *List the four major steps in career planning. What are you doing to prepare your career plans?*

6. *Describe your desired lifestyle in ten years. Develop a plan of action to get a job that will support your desired lifestyle.*

7. *Using Figure 2.4 as an example, prepare a checklist of your short-term, intermediate, and long-term goals. At the end of one week, check to see what you have accomplished.*

8. *Find the web site of a major national company that has job openings listed. Briefly describe the available jobs. Then find the company's description of its business. Make a list of key information about the company. How could you use this information in an interview with the company?*

9. *Write a paragraph describing your work history. It can be current or what you would like it to be in ten years.*

10. *Using Figure 2.5 as an example, prepare a plan for getting a job using a one-week timetable. List your job leads, your contacts (or potential contacts), and a list of several items you would like to accomplish each day.*

MAKE ACADEMIC CONNECTIONS

11. **Research** *Use the Internet to locate four different sources of current job opportunities. Develop a table that compares the sites in terms of their effectiveness in providing information about the job, the company, and the procedure applicants should follow in applying for a job.*

12. **International Studies** *Do Internet research on three countries, two of which are wealthy (first-world) nations and one of which is a third-world (developing) nation. Compare jobs and working conditions, along with annual wage and salaries earned by citizens of those countries. Also find out what you can about benefits such as sick pay and holiday pay. Compare their average work week with that of U.S. workers.*

13. **Math** *You are considering the services of three different employment agencies, all of which can get you a job that starts at $2,000 a month. Agency A charges 50 percent of the first month's gross salary. Agency B charges 10 percent of your monthly salary for the first six months. Agency C charges a $100 up-front fee and a flat fee of $500 when you are placed. Compare the three choices. Which of these offers the least expensive overall fee?*

SOLVE PROBLEMS AND

EXPLORE ISSUES

14. Tracy Alegro has decided that her long-term goal in life is to become a mechanical engineer. She is now a sophomore in high school and hasn't done any planning. Tracy's grades are average. She is active, outgoing, and bright. What can Tracy do now, in the next few years, and beyond to prepare herself for a career as an engineer?

15. Research the jobs listed below to determine the working environment, skills and education required, working hours, and beginning pay. Compile the information in a chart. Next to each occupation, indicate whether or not you would be interested in this type of career

    a. webmaster

    b. court reporter

    c. sheet-metal worker

    d. technical writer

    e. building custodian

    f. civil engineer

    g. physical therapist

    h. cosmetologist

    i. radio announcer

    j. tailor

    k. infantry officer

    l. administrative assistant

16. Dunghoon Lee would like to work as a merchandising manager for a large department store. He has the education and needed skills. His experience to this point has been with a medium-sized retailer. He currently doesn't have any contacts inside a large store. Most openings seem to be filled before he even knows they exist. What can Dunghoon do to find out about job openings in a large department store?

17. Julie Lopez has worked part time after school for the past two years. She worked for two weeks as a cook, but she rarely got to work on time and was fired. She worked for two months as a waitress but quit because she didn't get enough tips. Julie also worked for three weeks as a hotel maid but was laid off. Finally, she worked for four months as an administrative assistant but quit because working on the computer hurt her wrist. Would you hire Julie? What does her work history say to potential employers?

EXTEND YOUR LEARNING

18. **Legal Issues** When you go to work for a temp agency, you will sign a contract. The contract is a legally binding agreement where you agree to work for a set period of time for a set rate of pay. Your employer is the temp agency and will provide paychecks and other benefits. After they have started their job assignments, some workers will try to get out of the contract with the temp agency prior to the stated time period in order to work directly for the employer. Doing this denies the temp agency of its lawful fees (source of income). Explain why it is important for those entering into agreements to fulfill their legal responsibilities.

For related activities and links, go to **www.cengage.com/school/pfinance/mypf**

Chapter 3

Getting the Job

3.1 *Getting an Interview*

3.2 *Applying, Interviewing, and Following Up*

Consider **THIS**

Brandi wanted to work a part-time job while she finished high school in order to save money toward college expenses. She decided to apply for three openings she found posted on craigslist. The postings had asked for applicants to e-mail their resumes. For each open position, she wanted to write an e-mail message that would serve as an appealing application letter to which she would attach her resume.

Brandi wanted to be prepared for any upcoming interviews. "Getting a job can be a job in itself," Brandi told her mother. "I need to have all my materials in order. I'm really glad I have two reference letters ready to go. I don't have much experience, but I think I have a good chance at one of these openings. This isn't easy. In fact, it's pretty hard. Now I know what my teacher meant when she talked about 'marketing yourself.' It just isn't comfortable. I feel like I'm bragging, but I need to speak highly of myself in the letter and at the interview so that I stand out from the other applicants."

Getting an Interview

GOALS

- Prepare an application letter.
- Prepare a resume based on guidelines.
- Explain the importance of references and reference letters.

TERMS

- application letter, *p. 46*
- return address, *p. 48*
- letter address, *p. 48*
- salutation, *p. 49*
- body, *p. 50*
- complimentary close, *p. 50*
- resume, *p. 51*
- references, *p. 54*
- reference letter, *p. 55*

THE APPLICATION LETTER

Getting a job begins with the job application process. The **application letter**, or *cover letter*, serves to introduce you to a potential employer. It should accompany your resume. The application letter gives you a chance to briefly "sell" your qualifications and create interest in the enclosed resume. It really is a sales letter. It is often your first contact with an employer and your first opportunity to make a good impression.

CONTENTS OF AN APPLICATION LETTER

The application letter should be specific, interesting, and direct.

- The first paragraph should identify the purpose of the letter—why you are writing. Be specific. Tell the employer what job you want. If you know of an opening, tell the employer how you learned about it.
- The middle paragraph or paragraphs should give reasons why you are a good choice for the job. Explain your key qualifications—those that best fit the job. Express interest in the company as well. Briefly describe experiences, classes, or skills that relate to the job. Your tone should be enthusiastic, and your writing style friendly, upbeat, and conversational.
- The closing paragraph should wrap up the letter in a friendly yet assertive manner. Be direct. Ask for an interview. Give the employer your phone number and indicate a good time to call. Make it clear that you want an opportunity to discuss the open position.

PREPARING AN APPLICATION LETTER

Generally, when you send an application letter by mail, use white, standard-size (8½ × 11-inch) paper of good quality. Choose a mailing envelope of the same color and quality. Your printer should make clear, crisp copies.

Figure 3.1 shows a typical application letter. A standard 12-point font, such as Arial or Times Roman, is recommended for ease of reading. You may use a different font and size if you want, but don't get overly fancy. Your letter should look business professional.

With your letter of application, always enclose a copy of your resume. Also include a copy of any other items requested in the job posting, such as your transcripts (school grade records) or reference letters. Be sure to refer to all enclosed items in the body of your letter. Then list them at the end of the letter in a separate notation.

PARTS OF AN APPLICATION LETTER

An application letter should contain the five basic parts of a formal business letter. As you can see from Figure 3.2, the parts of a business letter are the return address, letter address, salutation, body, and complimentary close.

FIGURE 3.1   *Application Letter*

1274 Grant Avenue
Portland, OR 97224
becarter@internet.com
June 15, 20--

Mr. Jackson Phillips, Manager
Star Gaze Museum
4484 Grand Avenue
Portland, OR 97201

Dear Mr. Phillips

In response to the opening posted on your web site, please consider me an applicant for the summer tour guide position at your downtown location.

As you can see from my resume, I have volunteered as a host or guide for several special events in the past. I enjoy learning new information, making presentations, interacting with people, and helping others learn new facts and ideas. Your posting indicates that you need someone to work on weekends and to be on call for extra duties. I am available and eager to work on weekends and have a flexible weekday schedule that will allow me to fit in extra duties as needs may arise.

I am available now and would love to begin work as soon as possible. You can reach me at (971) 555-3344 every day after 2 p.m. I look forward to hearing from you about an interview and discussing the tour guide position with you.

Sincerely

Brandon Carter

Brandon Carter

Enclosure: Resume

Return Address

The **return address** is the first thing to appear at the top of the letter. It contains your complete mailing address and the date. If you have an e-mail address, add it below your city, state, and ZIP Code. You may add blank lines above the return address to center the letter on the paper.

Letter Address

The **letter address**, also called the inside address, contains the name and address of the person or company to whom you are writing. Use a specific

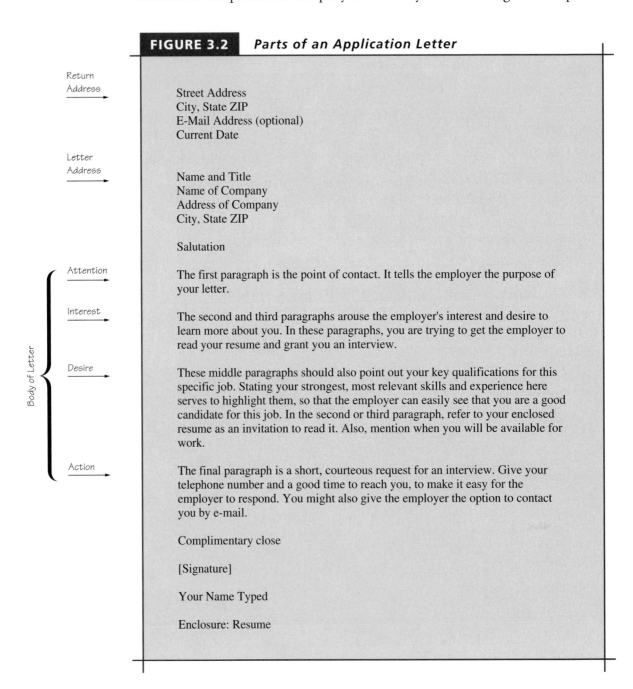

FIGURE 3.2   *Parts of an Application Letter*

Return Address →

Street Address
City, State ZIP
E-Mail Address (optional)
Current Date

Letter Address →

Name and Title
Name of Company
Address of Company
City, State ZIP

Salutation

Attention →

The first paragraph is the point of contact. It tells the employer the purpose of your letter.

Interest →

The second and third paragraphs arouse the employer's interest and desire to learn more about you. In these paragraphs, you are trying to get the employer to read your resume and grant you an interview.

Desire →

These middle paragraphs should also point out your key qualifications for this specific job. Stating your strongest, most relevant skills and experience here serves to highlight them, so that the employer can easily see that you are a good candidate for this job. In the second or third paragraph, refer to your enclosed resume as an invitation to read it. Also, mention when you will be available for work.

Action →

The final paragraph is a short, courteous request for an interview. Give your telephone number and a good time to reach you, to make it easy for the employer to respond. You might also give the employer the option to contact you by e-mail.

Complimentary close

[Signature]

Your Name Typed

Enclosure: Resume

Body of Letter

person's name and title if you can. If you can't find out the person's name or you don't know whether the person is male or female, use the simplified letter format shown in Figure 3.3.

Salutation

The **salutation** is the greeting that begins your letter. Use the person's name or other form of address (such as "Department Manager"). Avoid addressing application letters "To Whom It May Concern." The simplified format has no salutation. Instead, it has a subject line. This makes the letter less personal but

---

FIGURE 3.3 *Simplified Letter Format*

1274 Grant Avenue
Portland, OR 97224
becarter@internet.com
June 15, 20--

General Manager
Star Gaze Museum
4484 Grand Avenue
Portland, OR 97201

JOB OPENING FOR TOUR GUIDE

In response to the opening posted on your web site, please consider me an applicant for the summer tour guide position at your downtown location.

As you can see from my resume, I have volunteered as a host or guide for several special events in the past. I enjoy learning new information, making presentations, interacting with people, and helping others learn new facts and ideas. Your posting indicates that you need someone to work on weekends and to be on call for extra duties. I am available and eager to work on weekends and have a flexible weekday schedule that will allow me to fit in extra duties as needs may arise.

I am available now and would love to begin work as soon as possible. You can reach me at (971) 555-3344 every day after 2 p.m. I look forward to hearing from you for an interview and discussing the tour guide position with you.

Brandon Carter

Brandon Carter

Enclosure: Resume

---

avoids choosing a title, such as Mr., Ms., Mrs., Miss, or Dr., when you don't know which is appropriate.

Body

The **body** is the message section of the letter. As you can see in Figure 3.2, the body should be three or four paragraphs long. These paragraphs should attract the employer's *attention*, inspire the employer's *interest* in learning more about you, create the employer's *desire* to read your resume, and request that the employer take *action* in the form of an interview. These parts of the body are often referred to as AIDA—attention, interest, desire, and action.

Complimentary Close

The **complimentary close** is a courteous phrase used to end a letter. Phrases commonly used in business are "Sincerely" and "Cordially." Your typed name should appear four lines below the complimentary close to allow space for your signature. The simplified format does not include the complimentary close but goes directly to your name. Below your typed name are notations for enclosures that accompany the letter.

▌ PREPARING AN E-MAIL APPLICATION LETTER

With e-mail, what you see on your screen is not necessarily what the receiver will see on his or her screen. The receiver's software may not accept special formatting. Therefore, set your e-mail to plain text, as shown in Figure 3.4. Place everything at the left margin. Use no special formatting or tabs.

- Prepare your application letter in your e-mail message window. Your message will be dated automatically, so you need not type the date. Put the title of the job you are seeking in the subject line. If possible, include a qualification to catch the employer's attention. For example, the applicant in Figure 3.4 included years of experience in the subject line. Keep it short, however!

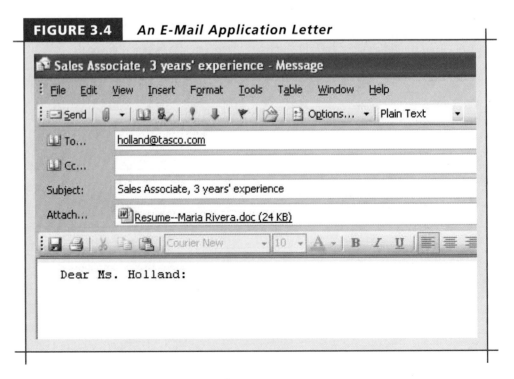

FIGURE 3.4   *An E-Mail Application Letter*

- Start your message with the salutation. Omit the inside address and move your return address to the bottom of the message, below your name.
- The body of your message should contain the same content as any other application letter. End the message with a complimentary close and your typed name, along with your mailing address, e-mail address, and phone number. Send your resume as an e-mail attachment. You need not include an enclosure notation since the attachment will show automatically.

THE RESUME

The **resume** is often called a personal data sheet, biographical summary, professional profile, or vita. It describes your work experience, education, abilities, interests, and other information that may be of interest to an employer. The resume tells the employer neatly and concisely who you are, what you can do, and what your special interests are. Always have an up-to-date resume ready for potential employers. Figure 3.5 shows a commonly used resume style. For more examples, go to an online career and employment site, such as Monster, and look for resume samples.

GENERAL GUIDELINES FOR A RESUME

There are no set rules for preparing a resume. You should choose the style that best presents you to an employer. However, here are some helpful guidelines:

- Early in your career, keep your resume to one page by carefully arranging the information you choose to include. Employers are busy people. They want a quick overview of you—not a lot of words to read. If you don't have enough information to fill a page, center what you have vertically on the page to make it attractive. After you have more education and work experience to summarize, your resume may extend to a second page. Resumes for professional applicants with extensive work experience may run several pages.
- Include all information pertinent to the job for which you are applying. An employer wants to know that you are interested in the specific job opening. Rather than prepare a "generic" resume to fit all possible openings, use key words from a job posting or ad to show that your skills match that particular job.

COMMUNICATION *Connection*

It is a good idea to keep a folder containing records for all the jobs you have ever had, including dates, places, wage rates, and contact information for supervisors. Also keep copies of evaluations, job descriptions, and special projects. This information can help you prepare a master resume that lists everything possible. You can then tailor the master resume for specific job openings.

Compile a list of what you can include on a master resume at this time. Evaluate your list to determine what is missing that could make your resume more exciting and relevant for your desired career. Based on what you think is missing, write a one-page report explaining how you can acquire the skills or experience needed to make your resume more complete.

- Carefully choose fonts, bold, italic, spacing, and other tools to arrange your information in a way that is attractive yet professional looking and easy to read. Place the most important items in the upper third of the page.
- Proofread thoroughly. Remember, your word processor's spell-check catches only misspelled words. For example, it will not catch occurrences of "then" that were intended to be "than." Your resume must have zero errors.
- For hard copies, use a high-resolution printer and good quality 8½ × 11-inch paper. Avoid bright colors, odd sizes, and stained or discolored paper.

FIGURE 3.5   *Resume*

Anisa Newkirk
162 NW Marshall Street
Portland, OR 97209-4323
(971) 555-4021
anisan@internet.com

CAREER OBJECTIVE

To assist with animal training for service dog programs in the local area; desire to work with dogs on emergency and trauma response teams.

EDUCATION

Hoover High School, Portland, Oregon (graduate 2009)
   GPA 3.3, Dean's List two years

Relevant Course Work:	**Relevant Skills:**
Biology	Work well with animals
Environmental Science	American Sign Language (ASL)
Public Speaking and Forensics	Excel (spreadsheets)
	Word (word processing)

Extracurricular Activities:
Volunteer: Red Cross Emergency Response
Debate Team (two years)
Member: National Honor Society (two years)
Athletics: Tennis and volleyball

EXPERIENCE

Volunteer, Noah Animal Hospital, Portland, Oregon (one year)
   Worked with injured animals, gave them food and medication; worked at the all-night emergency room, took data from animal owners; assisted veterinary staff with medical procedures.

Caregiver, County Animal Shelter (two summers)
   Cared for animals; made calls to help find them new homes.

Pet Sitter/Dog Walker (two years)
   Provided care for dogs, cats, rabbits, birds, and snakes while owners were away on vacation; provided daily dog walking services.

REFERENCES

Provided gladly on request.

PARTS OF THE RESUME

A simple resume should include personal contact information, a career objective (optional), education, experience, additional qualifications or special items of interest (if applicable), and references. You may arrange your resume according to personal preference. However, generally you should show your most favorable section first. For example, if your work experience relates to the open position more closely than your education does, list experience first.

Personal Information

This information appears first on the resume and includes your name, address, telephone number, and e-mail address. You may also wish to include a cell phone or pager number. Include your area code. Omit information such as age, gender, marital status, number of dependents, and ethnic background.

Career Objective

The career objective is optional. As your resume gets fuller, you may wish to omit it. If used, keep it short, indicating your career goal. For example, your goal might be to rise to a particular position. Make the statement forward looking, interesting, and specific. This statement helps the employer see how your plans fit with the company. Avoid weak statements such as "any type of work."

Education

List all high school and post-high school institutions you have attended, starting with the most recent. You may include areas of study, grade point average, activities, honors, specific courses that apply to the job opening, or other facts that you think will create a favorable impression. For example, extracurricular activities tell an employer that you are a well-rounded person; offices held in school organizations show that you have leadership skills.

Experience

List jobs, paid and unpaid, that you have held, including assisting at school functions, working as a teacher's aide, and any part- or full-time summer or vacation jobs (such as camp counselor). You may write this section in paragraph or outline form. Include information such as name and address of employer, job title, work duties, employment dates or length of time employed, and specific achievements while with this employer. Emphasize tasks you performed that relate to the open position.

Additional Qualifications

You may have additional skills to bring to an employer's attention. For example, you may list special equipment you have learned to operate, software you can use, or foreign languages you know. You can also list awards you have received. All of these things give an employer a fuller picture of you.

© Digital Vision/Getty Images

Why is work experience an important part of the resume?

Should you give out personal information, such as your Social Security number, before you get a job? Employers want complete information. In some cases, they need your Social Security number to do a credit check or a background report. If information is incomplete, an applicant may not be considered. Job applicants must be careful to whom they give very private and confidential information. With your name, address, phone, and Social Security number, you can be subject to identity theft. If employers are careless with how they handle this private information, you can suffer as a result.

So what should you do? Some applicants mark personal information requests with "will provide information at the job interview," or "will provide information when hired." They feel that this response protects them, especially when they are making online applications with employers they do not know.

THINK *CRITICALLY*

Do you agree with the claims of each side (employer and job applicant)? What point could you make to support each side? How will you handle this tricky issue in the future?

■ SCANNABLE RESUMES

Some employers use scanners and special software to search for key words and phrases that match the skills required in their job descriptions. They can scan hard copy as well as electronic resumes. The scan determines which resumes will be considered further and which will not.

A *scannable resume* has been designed for easy reading by a scanner and contains key words from the applicant's career field. To make the scanner's cut, describe your qualifications using key words from your field. For example, a publisher looking for an editor might scan for key words such as English or journalism degree, writing, and editing. To make your resume easy for the scanner, use the following formatting:

- A simple, standard font, such as Times Roman or Arial
- Type size of 11 or 12 point for the body of the resume
- Headings no larger than 14 point bold or caps

Avoid the following:

- Fancy fonts, italic, underlines, condensed type, shading, shadows, and white type on a black background
- Multiple columns
- Horizontal or vertical lines, boxes, and graphics

REFERENCES

References are people who have known you for at least a year and can provide information about your skills, character, and achievements. References should be over age 18 and not related to you. The best types of references include teachers, advisors, current and former employers, counselors, coaches, and adults in business. Be sure to ask permission before listing people on your resume. If you choose not to list references on your resume, state "references available on request." Then have a list of names, addresses, and phone numbers available for employers who ask for them.

A **reference letter** is a statement attesting to your character, abilities, and experience, written by someone who can be relied upon to give a sincere report. It is helpful to give those writing a reference letter a copy of your current resume or a short summary of your accomplishments and background. The letter should be on company letterhead. A sample reference letter is shown in Figure 3.6. Note that "To Whom It May Concern" is an acceptable salutation in this case, since copies may be provided to multiple prospective employers.

When you get a reference letter, make copies to give to potential employers along with your resume and application letter. Keep the original for your files, because you may need to make additional copies for other job applications.

FIGURE 3.6   *Reference Letter*

FARWEST TRUCK CENTER
402 First Street, NW
Eugene, OR 97402-2143

June 4, 20--

Re: Maribel Boswell

To Whom It May Concern

I have known Maribel for the past three years. She was an employee in our customer service division. Maribel began work here as an intern. She was an excellent employee, so at the end of her internship we hired her on a temporary basis. That temporary job lasted three years until Maribel moved away.

Maribel proved to be energetic and competent. She learned quickly and was a valuable member of our team. She took great pride in her work. She was able to work well independently and as a team member.

Without reservation, I can recommend Maribel to you as a potential employee. I would gladly hire her again if she were to move back to our area.

If you have any further questions, please do not hesitate to call me.

Sincerely

Harry Chen

Harry Chen
Manager

ISSUES IN YOUR WORLD

BEFORE YOU QUIT YOUR CURRENT JOB

Whether you want to leave your job to look for better pay, growth opportunities, more satisfying work, or for some other reason, you should keep several important things in mind:

- *Find a new job before quitting your old job. Then you can conduct your job search carefully, not hastily.*

- *Before leaving your current job, establish good relations with both coworkers and managers who will be helpful references for you. Employers usually check the backgrounds of people they consider hiring.*

- *Don't talk negatively about your old job, boss, or company in job interviews. Be positive and talk about the future. Don't emphasize how important money is to you. Talk about such things as your desire to find a challenging position that would inspire you and the importance of making a contribution in your field. To give the impression that you are looking for a new job only to increase your salary would be a mistake.*

- *In your current job, you may have many opportunities to learn about openings in other companies, especially with clients, vendors, and competitors in the same industry. Proceed with caution as you discuss with these potential employers possible jobs, your current job, or other factors affecting your decision. It is important to maintain confidentiality and good relations in your current position both before and after you leave.*

- *Don't burn your bridges. You never know; in the future, you may want to go back to a previous employer to work or to ask for a positive reference. Also, people at your previous company know people in other companies. If you leave on bad terms, word of your bad reputation may travel to other potential employers.*

Changing jobs to move your career forward is an accepted practice. But take care to set a good track record as you change jobs.

THINK *CRITICALLY*

1. *Suppose you are on your own and supporting yourself. One day your boss makes you angry, so you quit your job without having another job lined up. How would you feel as you interview for new jobs? What mistakes might you make under these circumstances?*

2. *Talk to someone who has changed jobs within the same field. Why did that person change jobs? Did the change accomplish his or her goal?*

Assessment

KEY TERMS REVIEW

Match the terms with the definitions. Some terms may not be used.

_____ 1. The first thing to appear at the top of a letter

_____ 2. The message section of a letter

_____ 3. People who have known you for at least a year and can provide information about your skills, character, and achievements

_____ 4. The greeting that begins your letter

_____ 5. A statement attesting to your character, abilities, and experience

_____ 6. A courteous phrase used to end a letter

a. application letter
b. body
c. complimentary close
d. letter address
e. reference letter
f. references
g. resume
h. return address
i. salutation

_____ 7. A document that describes your work experience, education, abilities, interests, and other information of interest to an employer

CHECK YOUR UNDERSTANDING

8. List the parts of an application letter.

9. What information is contained in a resume? List its parts.

10. List three people who would be good references to list on your resume or who would write a letter of reference for you. Explain your choices.

APPLY YOUR KNOWLEDGE

11. Following the guidelines discussed in the chapter, prepare an application letter and a resume for a job opening you find posted on a company web site. Ask at least three people to critique your work before drafting final versions.

THINK CRITICALLY

12. Applying for jobs online can be very convenient. You can find out about job openings, download applications, and submit resumes with the click of a mouse. Are there any disadvantages to the online application process? Discuss.

13. You will need references when you apply for jobs. How can you be sure that your references will say good things about you? Why should you keep reference letters directed to employers of past jobs?

Applying, Interviewing, and Following Up

GOALS

- List steps for properly completing an employment application form.
- Explain how to prepare for and make a good impression on a job interview.
- Prepare a thank-you letter as follow-up to a job interview.

TERMS

- employment application, p. 58
- job interview, p. 58
- open-ended questions, p. 60
- transcripts, p. 60
- follow-up, p. 61
- thank-you letter, p. 61

THE APPLICATION FORM

When you apply for a job opening, you will have to complete an employment application, like the one shown in Figure 3.7. An **employment application**, or *job application*, is a form that asks questions of people who apply for a job. When possible, take the form home to fill it out carefully at your leisure. Many companies today expect you to fill out the application form at their web site. You may be able to download the form, fill it out on your computer, and submit it electronically. When completing an employment application, follow these steps:

- Write neatly using a black or dark blue pen that does not skip or blot. Stay within the space provided.
- Fill in all the blanks. When you cannot answer a question, write "N/A" (for "not applicable") or use a line (——) to show that you have not skipped the question.
- Be truthful. Give complete answers. Do not abbreviate if there is any chance the abbreviation could be misread.
- Have with you all information that might be requested on the application form, such as telephone numbers, dates, and addresses.
- Proofread carefully; check every word.

THE JOB INTERVIEW

A **job interview** is a face-to-face meeting with a potential employer to discuss a job opening. During the interview, the employer will have your completed application, resume, application letter, and reference letter(s). The interviewer may ask you about information on any of these documents or about any other job-related matters. Thus, you should spend at least as much time preparing for the interview as you did getting the interview.

FIGURE 3.7 *Employment Application*

EMPLOYMENT APPLICATION

Date: _7/15/20 --_ Job you are applying for: _Clerk/Office Assistant_ ☐ Full Time ☒ Part Time

Social Security Number: _Provided at employment_

First Name: _Terrell_ Middle Initial: _B._ Last Name: _Adams_

Mailing Address: _234 Maple Street_ City: _Eugene_ State: _OR_ ZIP: _97401_

Home Phone: _(503) 555-2000_ Work Phone: (   ) _--_

Have you worked for this company before? ☐ **Yes** ☒ **No** **From:** ___ **To:** ___ **What location?**

Your name at that time: _--_ Position when you left: _--_

If you are under 18, give your birthdate: _-- / -- / --_ and work permit number (if applicable): _--_

Date available for work: _7/15/20--_

Please indicate the hours that you are available to work on each of these days.

(Hours)	SUNDAY	MONDAY	TUESDAY	WEDNESDAY	THURSDAY	FRIDAY	SATURDAY
From	8	1	1	1	1	1	8
To	8	8	8	8	8	8	8

START WITH CURRENT OR LAST EMPLOYER—INCLUDE MONTH AND YEAR IN DATES

FROM	COMPANY		POSITION HELD	
Mo. 9 Yr. 07	Video Image Plus		Accounting Clerk	BEGINNING PAY _Min. Wage_
TO	STREET and NUMBER	CITY and STATE		ENDING
Mo. 2 Yr. 08	1121 West 18th, Springfield, OR 97477			PAY _Min. Wage_
SUPERVISOR'S NAME	TITLE	REASON FOR LEAVING		
Jewel Clark	CWE Coordinator	end of program		

FROM	COMPANY		POSITION HELD	
Mo. 9 Yr. 06	Madison High School		Office Assistant	BEGINNING PAY _Volunteer_
TO	STREET and NUMBER	CITY and STATE		ENDING
Mo. 6 Yr. 07	Eugene, OR 97401			PAY _Volunteer_
SUPERVISOR'S NAME	TITLE	REASON FOR LEAVING		
Andy Williamson	Office Manager	end of year		

FROM	COMPANY		POSITION HELD	
Mo. 6 Yr. 02	Register-Guard		Newspaper Carrier	BEGINNING PAY _Commission_
TO	STREET and NUMBER	CITY and STATE		ENDING
Mo. 9 Yr. 04	Eugene, OR 97401			PAY _Commission_
SUPERVISOR'S NAME	TITLE	REASON FOR LEAVING		
Mary Adamson	Supervisor	to go to school		

MAY WE CONTACT YOUR PRESENT EMPLOYER? ☒ Yes ☐ No

SCHOOL NAME	ADDRESS	FROM	TO	DEGREE/DIPLOMA
HIGH SCHOOL				DIPLOMA ☒ Yes ☐ No
Madison High School	Eugene, OR 97401	2004	2008	TYPE:
BUSINESS/VOCATION SCHOOL				DIPLOMA ☐ Yes ☐ No
				TYPE:
COMMUNITY COLLEGE/UNIVERSITY				DIPLOMA ☐ Yes ☐ No
				TYPE:
UNDERGRADUATE COURSEWORK EMPHASIS				CUM GPA
GRADUATE COURSEWORK EMPHASIS				CUM GPA

I understand that any offer of employment is conditioned upon the satisfactory completion of this verification process and that the complany will hire only those individuals who are legally authorized to work in the United States and who present acceptable proof of their lawful employment status and identity.

Terrell B. Adams   _7 / 15 / 20 --_
SIGN HERE   **DATE**

Why should you spend time preparing for a job interview?

■ PREPARING FOR THE INTERVIEW

Review your resume so that all your qualifications will be fresh in your mind. Be prepared to answer **open-ended questions**, which require you to respond in paragraphs (rather than "yes" or "no") and talk about yourself. These questions may include, "Tell me about yourself," "Why do you want to work for us?" or "What would you like to be doing in five years?" Your responses show how well you organize your thoughts, speak, and think under pressure. Emphasize your skills, achievements, and career plans. Avoid speaking negatively of others. Prepare a list of likely questions and rehearse how you will answer them.

It is also important to learn something about your potential employer prior to the interview. Think of questions you might ask the interviewer about the company and the open position. You want to be able to speak intelligently about the company. Do some *company research* ahead of time, where you find out what the company makes or sells, its history, and what its prospects are for the future. This kind of information can be obtained from sources such as these:

- *The Yellow Pages* may list the company's products or services.
- The company's web site tells about its products, history, financial performance, and other data.
- A contact from your network who works for the company can provide first-hand knowledge.
- Annual reports (often available on the company web site) describe the company and its financial resources.
- Articles in current magazines and newspapers, including online publications, may discuss the company's economic health or plans for expansion.

■ MAKING A GOOD FIRST IMPRESSION

Since it may affect your whole future, the interview is an important moment in your life. Prepare for it carefully. Make a good impression.

- *Arrive on Time.* Better yet, arrive ten minutes early so you can check your appearance and compose yourself. Never be late.
- *Dress Appropriately.* Be neat and clean. Be conservative in dress, hairstyle, jewelry, perfume, cologne, makeup, and appearance. It is best to err on the side of being overly dressy than overly casual.
- *Go Alone.* Don't bring along a friend or relative.
- *Be Prepared.* Bring copies of your resume, reference letters, and transcripts. **Transcripts** are school records that include a listing of courses you have taken along with the credits and grades you've received for them. Bring a pad of paper, a pen, and any information you may need. Use a briefcase or some type of folder to keep your papers organized.
- *Appear Self-Confident.* It's normal to be nervous, but don't let your emotions control you. Give the appearance of being relaxed and

comfortable by maintaining good eye contact and giving an occasional smile. Don't chew gum or display nervous habits. Allow the interviewer to lead the discussion.

- *Be Courteous.* Even if you are asked to wait, respond with courtesy and understanding. Be composed and relaxed. Use "please" and "thank you."

- *Think Before You Speak.* Take a moment to organize your thoughts before speaking. Don't be afraid of the silent pause; the interviewer will not be put off. Be polite, accurate, and honest. Use proper grammar. Avoid slang and informal speech. Say "yes" rather than "yeah." Speak slowly and clearly.

NET Bookmark

Many state and federal laws prohibit employers from asking certain types of questions during job interviews. Access www.cengage.com/school/pfinance/mypf and click on the link for Chapter 3. Read the article about inappropriate questions. List three types of questions employers cannot ask and the relevant laws barring them. Then suppose you are a job candidate who is asked, "Do you plan to start a family soon?" during a job interview. How would you respond to this question?

www.cengage.com/school/pfinance/mypf

- *Emphasize Your Strong Points.* Talk about your favorite school subjects, grades, attendance, skills, experience, activities, and goals in a positive manner. Avoid negative comments.

- *Be Enthusiastic.* Act interested in the company and the job. Show that you are energetic and ready to work. Let the interviewer know that you are excited about the company, the job, and your future.

- *Look for Cues.* Nonverbal cues from the interviewer will tell you when to say less or more. Watch and listen carefully, then respond appropriately.

When the interview is over, thank the interviewer for his or her time. Say you will check back later. Then do so. Exit with a smile and a positive comment, such as "I look forward to hearing from you."

THE FOLLOW-UP

After the interview, the employer will have various candidates to consider. Your follow-up may help you stand out from the crowd. **Follow-up** is contact with the employer after the interview but before hiring occurs. It reminds the employer of who you are and could improve your chance of getting the job.

THANK-YOU LETTER

A thank-you letter is one form of follow-up. The **thank-you letter** shows appreciation to the employer for taking time to speak with you. It also brings you to the forefront of the interviewer's mind, providing a reminder of your qualifications and interest in the company.

When writing a thank-you letter, follow the same guidelines that you used in preparing your application letter. You may want to enclose an additional reference or other information that may help convince the interviewer to hire you. Address the interviewer by name. If more than one person interviewed you during your visit, write a brief letter to each person.

Keep your letter short and to the point, and make sure it is error free. This final opportunity to represent yourself to the potential employer may make the difference that will get you the job. Figure 3.8 is a sample follow-up thank-you letter. The important components of the letter are as follows:

- The first paragraph thanks the interviewer.
- The second paragraph reminds the interviewer of your desire to work for the company.
- The final paragraph closes with a positive note.

■ OTHER FORMS OF FOLLOW-UP

In addition to a letter, you may wish to call or stop by and check with the place of business about the status of your application. Such contacts should be courteous and friendly.

FIGURE 3.8	*Thank-You Letter*

1274 Grant Avenue
Portland, OR 97224
becarter@internet.com
July 10, 20--

Mr. Jackson Phillips, Manager
Star Gaze Museum
4484 Grand Avenue
Portland, OR 97201

Dear Mr. Phillips

Thank you for the time you spent with me during our interview yesterday. I enjoyed meeting you and members of your staff.

I am very excited about the prospect of working for your company. The tour guide position is exactly what I was hoping for. As you recall, I have experience and background that make it possible for me to "hit the ground running." I am enclosing another reference who can attest to my ability to learn quickly and fit in well.

If there is any other information I could provide, please feel free to contact me at (971) 555-3344. I look forward to hearing from you.

Sincerely

Brandon Carter

Brandon Carter

Enclosure: Reference

Planning a Career in... Agriculture

Agriculture, Food & Natural Resources

Do you enjoy fresh pineapple or freshly squeezed orange juice from citrus grown in California or Florida? When you shop your local food store, are you able to buy fresh (not frozen) turkey, chicken, or other meat? Are you into organic foods that have no pesticides, preservatives, or additives? Perhaps you have your own garden or enjoy the fresh produce from your local farmer's market.

Food you buy is planted, grown, and harvested by workers across the country. Some of it may be grown locally, but to have year-around, farm-fresh vegetables, fruit, meat, eggs, and milk, many workers must harvest, process, and take the steps necessary to ensure its fresh arrival to your local supermarket.

Employment Outlook

- Employment opportunities will have little or no change. For agricultural equipment operators, employment will decline moderately.
- Prospects for growth of jobs are slower than average, and few new jobs are expected.
- Work is often seasonal in nature.

Job Titles

- Crop worker
- Nursery and greenhouse worker
- Farm and animal worker
- Agricultural equipment operator
- Dairy operator
- Animal breeder
- Animal inspector

Needed Skills

- Skills are learned on the job; many do not require a high school diploma.
- Experience is helpful, specialized work like breeding requires training.

What's it like to work in... *Agriculture*

Raoul works two jobs. In the spring and summer, he plants, cares for, and helps harvest crops. In the late fall and winter, he takes care of greenhouse plants and buildings.

During the summer months, work is strenuous and outdoors, often during very hot and humid days. He has learned to wear sun protection and pack bottles of water to stay hydrated. Planting and harvesting requires much bending, stooping, and lifting.

For Raoul, it is tough but rewarding work. He starts very early in the morning and often works until dark. He enjoys watching the plants grow from seeds. Raoul has to work two jobs in order to have income all year, and the jobs are not secure. Storms, droughts, floods, and other natural events could wipe out the crops, leaving him with no work to do. But he couldn't imagine himself doing anything else. He really loves the land.

What About You?

Would you like to work outdoors with plants, animals, and farm equipment and provide others with fresh food?

Assessment

KEY TERMS REVIEW

Match the terms with the definitions.

_____ 1. Types of questions that require you to talk about yourself in paragraphs

_____ 2. A form that asks questions of people who apply for a job

_____ 3. A letter that shows appreciation to the employer for taking time to speak with you

_____ 4. School records that include a listing of courses you have taken along with credits and grades received for them

_____ 5. A face-to-face meeting with a potential employer to discuss a job opening

_____ 6. Contact with the employer after the interview but before hiring occurs

a. employment application

b. follow-up

c. job interview

d. open-ended questions

e. thank-you letter

f. transcripts

CHECK YOUR UNDERSTANDING

7. What are some important things to remember when filling out an employment application?

8. What are some ways to make a good first impression at a job interview?

9. Discuss the purpose(s) of the thank-you letter.

APPLY YOUR KNOWLEDGE

10. Visit the Career Consulting Corner web site or a similar career and employment web site that offers resume advice. Write a paragraph about the resume tips you find. Which tips do you plan to use when you prepare your own resume?

THINK CRITICALLY

11. Why is it important to show extracurricular and volunteer activities on your resume?

12. You may have heard that "everybody exaggerates on their resume." Do you think this is true? Do you plan to exaggerate? Why or why not?

Chapter Assessment

SUMMARY

3.1

- *The purpose of an application letter is to interest the employer in reading your resume and granting you an interview.*

- *The paragraphs of the application letter should (1) identify the purpose (why you are writing), (2) give reasons why you are a good choice for the job, and (3) ask for an interview.*

- *An application letter sent by mail should include a return address, letter address, salutation, body, and complimentary close.*

- *When an e-mail serves as the application letter, use plain text, avoid special formatting and tabs, put the job title on the subject line, omit the letter address, and move the return address to the bottom. The salutation, body, and close will be the same.*

- *A resume is a concise summary of your work experience, education, abilities, and interests.*

- *Guidelines for resume preparation include (1) keep it short, (2) use key words from the job posting, (3) place the most important items in the upper third of the page, (4) keep formatting simple and professional looking, (5) proofread thoroughly, and (6) print using high-resolution printer and quality standard-size paper.*

- *To make your resume easy for a scanner to read, avoid fancy fonts and formatting.*

- *Reference letters from past employers, coworkers, teachers, and adults confirm your skills, character, and experience for prospective employers.*

3.2

- *Fill out employment application forms neatly, completely, accurately, and honestly. Then proofread carefully.*

- *Prepare for a job interview by reviewing your materials, performing company research, and rehearsing answers to open-ended questions you might be asked.*

- *Tips for making a good impression on a job interview include (1) arrive on time, (2) dress appropriately, (3) be prepared with copies of documents such as school transcripts, (4) show self-confidence, (5) be courteous, (6) think before you speak, (7) emphasize your strong points, (8) be enthusiastic, and (9) look for cues from the interviewer.*

- *After an interview, follow up with a short thank-you letter that reminds the interviewer of your qualifications and interest in the job.*

APPLY WHAT YOU KNOW

1. List and describe the parts of an application letter. Write a sample letter that contains the needed content.

2. Prepare a master resume as described in the Communication Connection feature on page 51. It should list a career objective and all of your experience, education, skills, achievements, and references. Keep this resume as a source that can be used when compiling future resumes for specific job openings.

3. Prepare a scannable resume and e-mail it to a friend with a different operating system. How does it look? Is there extra formatting that doesn't open properly?

4. Why is follow-up important after a job interview? What types of follow-up will you use?

5. Write a letter to each of the people you would like to use as a reference. Ask permission to use their names on your resume and employment applications. Ask one person to write a reference letter for you.

6. Obtain and complete an employment application form from a local business or company web site.

7. Write a thank-you letter for a job interview. Assume you were interviewed by the person to whom you addressed your application letter in Number 1 above.

MAKE ACADEMIC CONNECTIONS

8. **Communication** Write three letters of application—one for an unsolicited job at a company for which you'd like to work (but for which there is no opening), one for a job opening you found on the Internet with an unknown company, and the third for a job you learned about from a friend. How will these letters be different? Focus on content as well as writing style.

9. **History** The workforce has changed considerably over the years. Compare the job market today with what it was like in the 1950s and the 1850s. How has it changed for all types of job applicants? How has it changed for women in particular? If possible, talk to someone who was in the work force 50 or more years ago.

10. **International Studies** Do online research about the job application process in other countries. Choose a country in Europe and one in South America. How are they different from what you would expect in the United States? Would you like to work in a foreign country? Would you be qualified?

11. **Research** Perform library or Internet research to discover what, if any, relationship exists between level of education and wage or salary levels for workers. Explain how education affects a person's resume (qualifications) and expectations of salary.

SOLVE PROBLEMS AND

EXPLORE ISSUES

12. Jaclyn Ross wants to work as a forest ranger when she graduates from college. She knows that the local Bureau of Land Management occasionally hires students during summers to help with forest management of public lands. Jaclyn takes science courses and does well. She is available to work all summer and would even be willing to work without pay if her living expenses were covered. Help Jaclyn write an application letter. Make up a return address, letter address, salutation, body, and complimentary close. Use the application letters in the chapter as guides.

13. Linda Lee must provide a resume to answer an advertisement in the local paper. Write in outline form a summary of the basic rules of writing a resume. Then, sketch a resume and label its parts. Briefly describe the kind of information Linda will need to provide in each part.

14. Sarah Hooper tells you she has a job interview tomorrow. She has never had one before, and she is very nervous. Sarah asks you to point out what she should and should not do. Make a list of five things Sarah should do and five things she should not do.

15. Yi-Ling Chou just completed a job interview. Competition is tough, but he believes he stands a good chance because he has taken three marketing courses, has high grades, and can begin work right away. Would you advise him to write a follow-up letter? What should he say in the letter?

16. When Mark Ramirez completed his job interview, he knew he was lacking in many of the requirements the employer was seeking. He didn't have enough experience. He knew of several other candidates who possessed the desired qualifications. Thus, Mark concluded he needed to do more than just send a simple thank-you letter to follow-up. He needed to do something that would remind the interviewer of his enthusiasm and how much he wanted the job. So, he wrapped up an old tennis shoe and sent it to the interviewer with his thank-you letter that read, "I just want to get my foot in the door." He got the job. Why did he get the job?

EXTEND YOUR LEARNING

17. **Ethics** Many people embellish or exaggerate facts on their resumes, leading employers to believe they have skills, experience, or education that they don't really have. The same is true of employment applications. Both of these documents make representations that are often relied on by employers. Many people who embellish and exaggerate use the excuse that "everybody does it." Does this make it right? Why should you be honest on your resume and employment application?

For related activities and links, go to **www.cengage.com/school/pfinance/mypf**

Adapting to Work

| 4.1 | **Communicating in the Workplace** |

| 4.2 | **Thriving in the Workplace** |

Consider **THIS**

Stage fright is a common fear experienced by people who perform before audiences. It refers to the anxiety felt by a person who is confronted with doing something he or she is not comfortable doing.

Hugh had to give a presentation to his marketing class. He remembered the important things he learned in a previous speech class—to relax, look directly at the audience, speak slowly, and take deep breaths—but still he didn't feel comfortable. According to Hugh, "My dad says I have to get used to this sort of thing. He says I'll have to communicate at work every day. Sometimes it will be one-on-one, but at times I'll have to speak in front of a group. He says this class presentation will be good for me. Fine, but I'm still nervous. The good thing is that I get a little less nervous every time I do this."

Communicating in the Workplace

EFFECTIVE COMMUNICATION AT WORK

Success on the job depends on good communication skills. Of all the job activities you perform in a day, 80 percent involve communication in one form or another. More than half of all job communication involves listening and speaking. Many job ads list good communication skills as a must. Figure 4.1 on the next page illustrates the relative importance of each form of communication (listening, speaking, writing, and reading) during the average workday.

LISTENING

Hearing is the process of perceiving sound. It requires little thinking and very little effort. **Listening** is an active hearing process that requires concentration and effort. To be a good listener, look at the speaker and maintain eye contact. Ask questions and get involved in the conversation. Simple head nods can also show the speaker that you are listening. Avoid interrupting or changing the subject. Control your emotions. Listen to what the speaker says, and then evaluate it with an open mind.

Sympathetic listening, often called *empathetic listening*, is the ability to perceive another person's point of view and to sense what the person is feeling. To listen with empathy, keep your attention on the speaker. Do not interrupt. Ask questions that lead the speaker to make further analysis. Ask clarifying questions to make sure you fully understand the speaker. Try to find out why the speaker thinks or feels a certain way. Avoid giving approval or disapproval. With sympathetic listening, you do not give your own opinion unless it is requested.

© Digital Vision/Getty Images

What is the difference between hearing and listening?

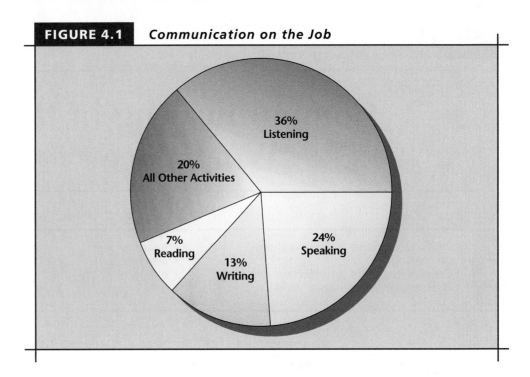

FIGURE 4.1 *Communication on the Job*

36%
Listening

20%
All Other Activities

7%
Reading

13%
Writing

24%
Speaking

Critical listening is the ability to differentiate facts from opinion. When analyzing information about a product or service you are considering purchasing, use critical listening. For example, claims that a product is "the best buy" or "top quality" are useless. They are opinions, not facts. But when you hear factual information, such as "100 percent cotton" or "one-year guarantee," this is useful information.

Creative listening means listening with an open mind to new ideas. Group problem-solving techniques, such as brainstorming, require creative listening. In brainstorming, all ideas are received without judgment. Then, after all ideas are presented, the group votes on the best ideas and incorporates them into a plan of action.

▌ SPEAKING

At most workplaces, about a quarter of the average employee's time is spent in oral communication. Most oral communication is informal. It can involve talking with a supervisor or coworker or talking with clients on the phone or in person. Informal speech can be used in the following circumstances:

- Making contact with others
- Exchanging information
- Influencing others
- Solving problems

At some time in your work life, you may need to give a formal speech. Formal speeches are prepared in advance and designed for a particular purpose. Common purposes for formal speeches include the following:

- *To Inform.* In this type of presentation, your goal is to convey information to your audience in an understandable manner. You can give facts and then reach your conclusions (inductive reasoning), or give conclusions first followed by supporting facts (deductive reasoning).

- *To Entertain.* The purpose of this type of speech is to get your audience to relax and enjoy themselves. Entertainment speech is difficult because it depends on the audience's reaction. For example, if the audience doesn't respond favorably, you may find it difficult to keep going.
- *To Persuade or Sell.* This type of speech is designed to convince your audience to take some action or to believe something. To be convincing, you must use solid facts and statistics. You must appear to be honest and to believe in what you are saying. If you are not sincere, your audience will sense it.

To give your formal speech added style, use visual aids. For example, consider using video, computerized slide shows, audio recordings, display boards, flip charts, objects, models, or handouts. The setting, which includes lighting, room layout, seating, speaker's stand, and microphone, can also contribute to the positive acceptance of your speech.

Stage fright (nervousness) is a natural and common reaction. Many experienced speakers are tense before speaking. To control stage fright, use the following tips:

- *Build Your Confidence.* Prepare in relatively nonthreatening speaking situations. Talk before small groups, including friends and family. Take speech classes and observe other speakers.
- *Be Well Prepared.* First, outline what you want to say. Then time yourself giving the speech on several occasions. Prepare an additional "comfort zone" of several minutes' worth of material in case your speech goes faster than you think it will. Most people talk faster when they are nervous, so make allowances for this possibility.
- *Practice Public Speaking.* Begin with short speeches and build to longer ones. Practice speaking slowly when expressing your thoughts. Keep your voice low-pitched, clear, and reasonably paced. Volunteer to speak to classes and other groups. Record your voice and evaluate its effectiveness.

COMMUNICATION FLOW IN THE WORKPLACE

Workplace communication flows in several directions: horizontally, downward, and upward. *Horizontal communication* occurs among coworkers of equal rank. Most horizontal communication takes place informally in small groups, one-on-one, and by e-mail. Coworkers share information and solve problems together to complete their tasks. Horizontal communication also serves as the company "grapevine," transmitting rumors and office gossip.

Downward communication flows from higher to lower levels of the organization. Managers give employees job-related instructions, performance feedback, and company news. Employees also communicate with managers about work problems, policies, and suggestions for improving company practices. This communication flow from lower to higher levels of the organization is *upward communication.* The effectiveness of both downward and upward communication depends on building open, trusting relationships between managers and employees. Employees often don't tell their employers everything they are thinking or feeling because they are afraid of losing their jobs or creating an unfavorable impression.

Downsizing has been defined as the elimination of part of the workforce, especially in business and government, in order to achieve a more efficient and cost-effective organization. Economic downturns and the resulting downsizing can create a tense workplace. Management insists that in order to remain competitive, jobs must be cut. Employees, particularly those with many years of service, believe their work and their loyalty are not important to management anymore.

THINK *CRITICALLY*

Do you agree with the claims of each side? What point could you make to support each side? How does the state of the economy play a role in this issue?

■ E-MAIL COMMUNICATION

E-mail is the most common form of communication in business today. Messages between employees and managers are generally worded more formally than messages between employees of the same rank. However, the rules of good writing still apply. When you write an e-mail message, use good grammar and proofread before sending. Keep your messages concise. Always read through your entire e-mail before sending it to be sure you are communicating the intended message.

E-mail has several advantages as a communication tool. It is fast. Messages go from one computer to another almost instantly. It is inexpensive. Messages can be sent all over the world without having to pay postage or long-distance charges. Messages can also be sent to many people at the same time. Finally, e-mail is easy to learn and use.

One disadvantage of e-mail arises from an advantage. E-mail is so easy that people tend to use it too much. Business people often complain of information overload caused by e-mail boxes full of unnecessary messages. To be a good e-mail communicator at work, resist the temptation to send unnecessary messages, including jokes or office gossip. Another disadvantage of e-mail is that, unlike face-to-face or telephone conversations, you won't have cues from a person's reactions to know if the recipient fully understands the message.

Remember that e-mail is not private. Employers can monitor employees' e-mails. Even if you delete messages from your computer at work, they remain on servers. You may be fired for using e-mail or the Internet at work for nonbusiness purposes.

HUMAN RELATIONS AT WORK

Human relations is the art of getting along with others. To be truly competent in human relations, you need to have a good understanding of yourself and of others and a genuine concern for their needs and feelings. Here are some ways you can improve your relationships:

- *Accept Differences.* Everyone is different. Accept others as they are, tolerate differences of opinion, and recognize that other ways of doing things may also be effective. Learn to disagree without being disagreeable. Think of disagreements as differences in personal preference rather than as right or wrong. There are often several ways to do things; people simply choose the method that works best for them.

- *Treat Others as Individuals.* Take time to discover the individuality in others. Learn people's names and use them. Take an interest in what others are doing. Try to remember what people say and follow up later. If someone tells you it's his birthday next month, remember to wish him a happy birthday. It feels nice when others remember things about you. Every person deserves respect as a human being.

- *Empathize with Others.* Empathy is the ability to see others' points of view and understand their feelings. It does not mean you agree with them but rather that you understand what they are saying, feeling, or experiencing.

- *Praise Others.* Be consistent in praising the achievements of others. Seek good things that are true and complimentary, and praise them freely. Avoid untrue or exaggerated claims that appear insincere. The more you praise others for their accomplishments, the more they will praise you for yours.

- *Focus on Problems, Not People.* When problems with someone occur, you will get cooperation by focusing on the problem rather than verbally attacking him or her personally. For example, say, "The auditors would like a cost breakdown in your report," rather than, "You did a poor job on that report." Assume it was a simple mistake rather than a lack of competence. Nobody likes to be accused of making mistakes on purpose.

- *Accept Responsibility.* Take responsibility for your actions. Don't blame others for your mistakes. Your coworkers and boss will respect your willingness to accept responsibility and say, "I messed up."

- *Avoid Dogmatic Statements.* A dogmatic statement asserts an opinion as if it were a fact. Present your opinions as possibilities rather than absolute truths. Let people know where you heard the information or why you think a certain way, and be prepared to listen to another opinion.

- *Treat Others as Equals.* Respect each person's contributions. Don't talk down to people by telling them what they should know or do. Allow others to make their own decisions without criticism.

- *Trust Others.* People will live up to, or down to, your expectations. Think the best of others and expect the best. When they know you trust them, most people will prove to be trustworthy.

- *Control Your Emotions.* Withhold judgments, comments, and decisions until you gather enough information to evaluate the situation thoughtfully. You may later regret reacting emotionally.

© Digital Vision/Getty Images

Why are human relations at work important to job success?

Arts, A/V Technology & Communications

Whenever you hear or read the news, it began because reporters did their job. They investigated leads and news tips, took notes, observed events, researched documents, and maybe even recorded video images. Back at the office, they organized and determined their focus, wrote the story, edited it and its accompanying video, and prepared the information for publication.

The news reporters are often not the people behind the camera that read the story to the television audience. But they did the work nevertheless. They wrote the story and submitted it, sometimes from remote locations and most often electronically. Occasionally, their work is even dangerous as they report stories in volatile environments such as war zones.

Employment Outlook

- Little or no change in overall employment through 2016 is expected.
- Competition will continue to be keen in large metro areas and for television stations and networks.

Job Titles

- News reporters and writers
- Photojournalists
- Announcers and interpreters
- Correspondents
- Editors

Needed Skills

- A bachelor's degree is preferred.
- Excellent communication skills and attention to detail and accuracy are needed.

What's it like to work in... *Communications*

Kaitlin works in the newsroom for a local television station. She is currently a news reporter assigned to the courthouse. She checks the case dockets daily and reads the police reports. When there is a breaking story, such as a robbery in progress, she is at the scene reporting what happened. Many of her video clips are used on the evening news. She hopes someday to be that person sitting behind the desk and on camera.

Today has been pretty eventful. It is an election year, and a candidate for governor is in town. She will be there and have questions ready to ask the candidate. She reviews her notes, grabs her identity badge, and heads toward the town square where the candidate will be within the hour. She loves her job because it keeps her involved in what is going on in the world.

What About You?

What are some positive and negative aspects of the field of news reporting? Do the positive aspects of this career appeal to you?

Assessment

KEY TERMS REVIEW

Match the terms with the definitions.

_____ 1. The process of perceiving sound

_____ 2. Listening to differentiate facts from opinion

_____ 3. The art of getting along with others

_____ 4. Listening with an open mind to new ideas

_____ 5. Listening to perceive another person's point of view and to sense what the person is feeling

a. creative listening

b. critical listening

c. hearing

d. human relations

e. listening

f. sympathetic listening

_____ 6. An active hearing process that requires concentration and effort

CHECK YOUR UNDERSTANDING

7. Describe the difference between hearing and listening. How can you tell if someone is listening?

8. List situations in which you do sympathetic, critical, and creative listening.

APPLY YOUR KNOWLEDGE

9. Think about a time when you were not listening to someone, such as a parent, teacher, or friend. What happened as a result of not listening? What can you do to improve listening skills?

THINK CRITICALLY

10. Recall the last speech or presentation you gave. Was it informational, entertaining, or persuasive? Describe it. Critique your performance; what could you have done better?

11. Stage fright is often very obvious and hard to overcome. Describe a situation you observed where stage fright was apparent. Describe ways to overcome it. What will you do in the future to make better speeches or presentations and avoid stage fright?

12. Good human relations are critical to successful work environments. Describe a situation you've observed or experienced where two or more people on a project or team did not get along well. What was the result? How could each party have better handled the situation?

Thriving in the Workplace

GOALS
- Describe employer expectations related to work rules, work attitudes, and work attendance.
- Discuss two theories of motivation and the results of job satisfaction.

TERMS
- work rules, *p. 76*
- absenteeism, *p. 78*
- self-esteem, *p. 81*
- self-actualization, *p. 81*
- hygiene factors, *p. 81*
- motivators, *p. 81*
- productivity, *p. 82*

EMPLOYER EXPECTATIONS

Employers expect employees to behave in ways that will help meet the goals of the business. To inform employees of expected behavior, employers create work rules and policies. Employees who thrive in the workplace exceed these expectations.

WORK RULES

Most businesses have written and unwritten work rules. **Work rules** are the do's and don'ts of fitting in successfully and having a positive work experience. *Unwritten work rules* often are commonly understood without being documented or verbally communicated. An informal dress code is one example. A new employee observes how other employees dress and then dresses in a similar manner. An employer expects employees to know from common sense some of the work rules that apply to their jobs. Courtesy and teamwork are expected. Loyalty, a positive attitude, safety, punctuality, and good grooming are rules that are often unwritten and unspoken.

Written work rules are usually posted in employee work areas or included in an employee manual. These rules are generally written for the benefit and protection of all employees. Companies that deal with hazardous chemicals or potentially dangerous machinery enforce strict written safety rules. When everyone shares in the

© Digital Vision/Getty Images

What are some common-sense rules that apply to the workplace?

FIGURE 4.2 *Work Rules*

COMPANY WORK RULES
Sanders Department Store

1. Work begins promptly at 8 a.m. or 2 p.m. and ends promptly at 5 p.m. or 10 p.m. An employee must be present at all times during our hours of operation.

2. Food and drink are permitted only in the break room areas.

3. No smoking is permitted in the building. Outside smoking areas are provided at the south and north entrances. Please do not smoke within 15 feet of the doorway.

4. All employees must be clean and properly groomed at all times. Facial hair is permitted if it is well groomed. Use good judgment in what you wear.

5. When a worker is ill, he or she must call in by 7 a.m. for the day shift or by 4 p.m. for the night shift.

6. Vacations are taken according to seniority; no more than three employees may take vacations during the same week. All vacations must be arranged two weeks in advance.

responsibilities and adheres to the rules, the work flows smoothly and safely. Figure 4.2 is an example of work rules that might be posted in an employee break room.

Because the rules shown in Figure 4.2 are basic, employees who break them are subject to immediate discipline. If one employee is permitted to break the rules, others will notice and feel justified in doing the same thing. While infractions are not acceptable for established employees, they are tolerated even less for new employees. New employees should arrive early, leave on time, and never take extra time on a break. They should pay attention to policies regarding having food in the work area or making personal phone calls.

WORK ATTITUDES

Employees' work attitudes are important to employers because they affect morale, output (production), and public relations. Every employee in a company represents that company to the public. A good attitude makes a favorable impression. Good public relations are important to a company's future growth and profitability. The list below offers tips on how to leave a favorable impression.

- Remember customers' names and preferences.
- Make an extra effort to be helpful.
- Demonstrate knowledge, enthusiasm, and interest in customers.
- Display genuine concern for the quality of products and services.
- Care about people and meeting their needs.
- Listen sympathetically to customer complaints.
- Take pride in yourself and your work.

Employers appreciate employees who "go the extra mile." This means doing more than required and doing it with a positive attitude.

▌ ABSENTEEISM

Absenteeism is the record and pattern of absence rates for workers. It can be a special kind of problem. How to deal with it depends on the reasons for the absences. One expert observed that of all absences, the following apply:

- 60 percent are due to serious or chronic illnesses, injuries, or family emergencies.
- 20 percent are due to acute, short-term illnesses (such as the flu), work-related accidents, or personal problems.
- 10 percent are due to minor illnesses, such as a cold. Whether or not employees decide to report to work with a minor illness depends on their attitudes about their jobs.
- 10 percent are due to pretend illnesses so that employees can enjoy a day off.

The absentees making up the last 20 percent are of greatest concern to businesses. Industrial psychologists call this "voluntary absence syndrome" and warn that these patterns can lead to serious emotional imbalance and disturbance in the absentees' lives.

Frequent absentees face consequences ranging from pay deductions and warnings to temporary layoffs, poor recommendations, lack of respect (from employers and fellow employees), and eventually to termination of employment. When employers do not take action, they are in effect giving their approval to the absences, thereby encouraging other employees to be absent often. Working employees often resent having to continually cover missing employees' duties while the employer takes no corrective action.

High rates of absenteeism cost companies thousands of dollars annually. The U.S. Department of Labor uses the formulas shown in the Math Minute feature to compute the rate of absenteeism and the costs of absenteeism to a business. Most labor experts agree that an absentee rate of 2.0 is low, while a rate of 5.0 is high.

In the Math Minute example, Bascom's Health Foods Market has an absentee rate of 2.08 percent. The company can conclude that its absenteeism is reasonable. However, Goldstein's has a rate of 4.69 percent. From this number, Goldstein's can see that it has a problem with absent employees and should search for causes and solutions.

NETBookmark

Employers are concerned about the impact of unscheduled absenteeism on their businesses. Nearly one in three report that absenteeism is a "serious problem." The average cost of absenteeism in the United States is almost $700 per person per year, as measured by direct payroll costs for paid, unproductive time. Absenteeism hurts organizations even more when other costs—such as lost productivity, morale, and temporary labor costs—are considered. Access www.cengage.com/school/pfinance/mypf and click on the link for Chapter 4. Read the article about how employers can deal with employee absenteeism and summarize the methods presented.

www.cengage.com/school/pfinance/mypf

COST OF ABSENTEEISM

If your career path leads to business ownership, it is likely that you'll have to hire employees and deal with the costs of absenteeism.

Harry Bascom owns Bascom's Health Foods Market, which operates 24 hours a day, 365 days a year. Employees work three 8-hour shifts. In an average month, a total of 12 employees work 30 days. On average, a total of 180 hours are missed from work per month, which is the equivalent of 7.5 days (180 hours ÷ 8-hour shift ÷ 3 shifts). The *rate of absenteeism* is determined as follows:

$$\text{Rate of Absenteeism} = \frac{\text{Absent Days per Month}}{\text{Work Days per Month} \times \text{Number of Employees}}$$

Using this formula, Bascom's absenteeism rate is 2.08%, or 7.5 ÷ (30 × 12).

The following formula determines the *cost of absenteeism*:

$$\text{Cost of Absenteeism} = \text{Annual Lost Time} \times \text{Average Wage Rate} \times 2$$

The formula multiplies the cost of wages by 2 to include the costs of benefits paid to absent employees and the costs of paying temporary workers to replace the absent workers.

Bascom's average wage rate is $7.50 per hour. Using the formula, the cost of absenteeism is determined as follows:

$$\text{Annual Lost Time} = 180 \text{ Hours per Month} \times 12 \text{ Months per Year}$$
$$= 2,160 \text{ Hours}$$

$$\text{Cost} = 2,160 \text{ hours} \times \$7.50 = \$16,200 \text{ Wages Paid to Absent Employees}$$

$$\$16,200 \times 2 = \$32,400 \text{ Annual Cost of Absenteeism}$$

Based on the preceding example, compute the absenteeism rate and its annual cost for another business based on the following information:

Goldstein's operates two 8-hour shifts a day. A total of eight employees work 24 days per month. On average, a total of 144 hours are missed from work per month, which is the equivalent of 9 days (144 hours ÷ 8-hour shift ÷ 2 shifts). The average wage rate is $12 per hour.

Solution:

$$9 \div (24 \times 8) = 4.69\% \text{ Rate of Absenteeism}$$
$$144 \times 12 = 1,728 \text{ Hours Lost Annually}$$
$$1,728 \times \$12 = \$20,736 \text{ Wages Paid to Absent Employees}$$
$$\$20,736 \times 2 = \$41,472 \text{ Annual Cost of Absenteeism}$$

MOTIVATION AND NEEDS

All human beings have some needs that are basic to survival and other needs that go beyond mere physical existence. Unfulfilled needs motivate people to work toward satisfying those needs. For example, hunger motivates a person to look for food.

■ MASLOW'S HIERARCHY OF NEEDS

Abraham Maslow, a psychologist, developed a human behavior model called the *hierarchy of needs*, as shown in Figure 4.3. Employment can help satisfy all five levels of needs. Levels 1 and 2 are things that are essential to physical survival: employees need pay that is adequate to provide food, clothing, and housing and sufficient job security to feel safe and comfortable. Until the job meets these basic needs, the employee will not be motivated to greater achievement. According to Maslow, in general, lower-level needs must be satisfied first. Once a need is met, the next higher one in the hierarchy begins to motivate the person's behavior. However, the progression is not so clear cut. Several needs may influence a person's behavior at the same time.

Every person needs fulfillment beyond physical requirements. Most businesses consider it the responsibility of management to provide opportunities for employees to meet their needs. In striving to satisfy higher-order needs, employees will likely achieve greater productivity, which will benefit the business.

FIGURE 4.3 *Maslow's Hierarchy of Needs*

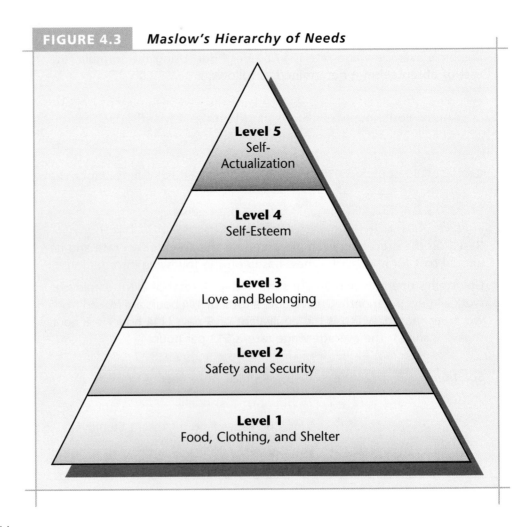

Level 5
Self-Actualization

Level 4
Self-Esteem

Level 3
Love and Belonging

Level 2
Safety and Security

Level 1
Food, Clothing, and Shelter

Maslow's Level 3 is the need for "love" (acceptance) and the need to belong to a group: to have friends and to be valued as a member of the team. In the workplace, employees can meet this need through caring work relationships and through working and socializing with groups of coworkers.

Level 4 is the need for **self-esteem**, or self-respect and recognition from others. When work is challenging and rewarding, employees feel good about their jobs and about themselves, and they want to do more. Workers trying to meet their need for self-esteem will be motivated by praise and recognition.

Level 5 is the need for **self-actualization**, which is the need to reach one's full potential, to grow, and to be creative. Workers can fulfill this need if they are able to do the work they choose, as they choose, and receive appropriate rewards for a job well done. To aid employees in achieving their full potential, many managers challenge employees by providing greater decision-making responsibility and more complex work gradually as the employees become capable of handling it.

HERZBERG'S TWO-FACTOR THEORY

Frederick Herzberg studied employees to find out what satisfied and dissatisfied them about their jobs. From his research, he formulated his two-factor theory. Herzberg found that elements of a job that lead to job satisfaction or dissatisfaction fall into two groups: hygiene factors and motivators.

Hygiene factors are job elements that dissatisfy when absent but do not add to satisfaction when present. For example, pay, fringe benefits, and the workplace environment are hygiene factors. A clean, roomy workspace will help maintain a level of satisfaction but will not increase motivation to work hard or increase satisfaction. However, a dirty, cramped workspace would decrease job satisfaction.

Motivators are job elements that increase job satisfaction. For example, challenging work, responsibility, recognition, achievement, and opportunities for personal growth motivate workers to greater productivity and add to satisfaction in the job. Therefore, to motivate employees to achieve and to promote greater job satisfaction, employers must offer hygiene factors to avoid dissatisfaction plus provide motivators. For example, jobs need to be designed

GLOBAL *View*

In Australia, "career break schemes" enable an employee to negotiate a fixed period of up to several years away from work for educational study or for family commitments, while maintaining a guaranteed job. Career break schemes frequently involve full-time work for short periods and part-time work for phase-out and phase-in stages. During these stages, pay and benefits are usually available. Career break schemes act as a motivating factor and can reduce the loss of experienced staff. Employers help employees who are on a career break maintain their skills and knowledge by providing training courses or by ensuring access to current work-related information. These activities make it easier for employees to return to work.

THINK *CRITICALLY*

How might offering career break schemes lead to greater work satisfaction? Can you relate this to Maslow's hierarchy of needs?

to meet employees' need for challenging, rewarding work. In order for employees to do their best and continue their career with an employer, they need adequate pay and benefits along with opportunities for advancement and praise for a job well done.

RESULTS OF JOB SATISFACTION

When employees can meet their needs in their jobs, several positive outcomes benefit both the employees and the employer.

Increased Productivity

When employees are motivated, they are more productive. **Productivity** is the relationship between the cost of paying for workers and the output that is received from their work. Businesses rely on high worker productivity to make profits. Productive workers use time wisely and produce more and higher-quality work in less time. Increased productivity leads to higher profits for the employer and subsequent rewards for the employees—both tangible (raises, bonuses, or promotions) and intangible (praise and self-esteem).

Self-Esteem and Self-Actualization

To put forth your best effort, to win the praise of your employer and coworkers, to strive for new challenges—all are valid bases for career development and satisfaction. As you achieve these goals, you gain personal pride and enjoyment that are satisfying beyond the paycheck. Because you will probably work most of your adult life, why not strive to achieve to the best of your ability?

Rewards and Opportunities

Employers often seek to motivate employees by using praise and rewards as reinforcements for desirable results. Your rewards will vary: oral or written commendations; admiration and respect of others; pay raises (often called merit pay); increased opportunities for challenging work; and opportunities for advancement to positions of higher pay and responsibility. You could become recognized as "one of the best in the field." This not only makes you valuable to your own employer, but it also makes you more employable in the future should you desire to move to another job. Achieving excellence in your work increases your opportunities and should be a part of your long-term career plans.

© Digital Vision/Getty Images

How can job satisfaction benefit employees?

ISSUES IN YOUR WORLD

WORK ETHICS

Work ethics or codes of conduct exist both formally and informally throughout corporate America. Companies are finding that employees, customers, and government agencies are looking at their values, integrity, and sense of fairness in the workplace.

A corporate study concluded that "outstanding employees will only want to work for companies whose leadership they trust and values they respect." Many American companies, both large and small, are participating in integrity web sites—places for customers and other stakeholders to go and examine values policies, from employee and customer privacy statements to workplace ethics enforcement. To attract and retain customers, stockholders, and financial partners, companies are becoming increasingly aware of the need for values, trust, and commitment.

Many employers are using a work ethics test for pre-employment screening. Why? To select the best workers, defined as people who adhere to high ethical principles. Work ethics for employees include giving the employer consistently high-quality work—a full day's work for a full day's pay.

When faced with an ethical dilemma at work, ask yourself these questions before taking action:

- *Is it legal?*
- *Is it morally right?*
- *Who is affected?*
- *Would it cause harm?*
- *Would I feel pride or shame if my action becomes public knowledge?*
- *What does it say about me?*

Many ethical issues have no clear-cut right or wrong solutions. How you choose to act depends on your values and moral standards. Each person must decide for himself/herself where to draw the line.

THINK CRITICALLY

1. *Describe a situation in which you believe a company acted unethically. How would these actions affect your decision to work for the company?*
2. *Describe a situation in which you faced an ethical dilemma. Are you comfortable with the choice you made? If an action is legal, does that make it ethical? Explain.*

Assessment

KEY TERMS REVIEW

Match the terms with the definitions.

_____ 1. The need to reach one's full potential, to grow, and to be creative

_____ 2. Job elements that dissatisfy when absent but do not add to satisfaction when present

_____ 3. The relationship between the cost of paying for workers and the output that is received from their work

_____ 4. Self-respect and recognition from others

_____ 5. The do's and don'ts of fitting in successfully and having a positive work experience

_____ 6. The record and pattern of absence rates for workers

_____ 7. Job elements that increase job satisfaction

a. absenteeism

b. hygiene factors

c. motivators

d. productivity

e. self-actualization

f. self-esteem

g. work rules

CHECK YOUR UNDERSTANDING

8. Why are work rules, both written and unwritten, important to employers and employees?

9. What are some things you can do to create a favorable impression with an employer?

10. How are motivators different from hygiene factors, according to Herzberg?

APPLY YOUR KNOWLEDGE

11. Think about a job you have held or work you have done as part of a school or community group. What kinds of things motivated you to do your tasks well? Did these same things make the job more satisfying for you? What kinds of things made you less satisfied with the work?

THINK CRITICALLY

12. Have you ever worked at a job at which there were certain rules to follow? If you were writing work rules, what items would you include?

13. Have you ever been treated rudely at a business? Explain what happened? Describe how the employee should have acted.

14. Explain how hygiene factors apply to your life. Provide a specific example.

Chapter Assessment

SUMMARY

4.1

- *Listening involves more than hearing; effective communication requires sympathetic, critical, and creative listening.*

- *People speak informally to make contact, exchange information, influence others, and solve problems.*

- *A formal speech may be designed to inform, entertain, or persuade.*

- *To control stage fright: build your confidence, be well prepared, and practice public speaking.*

- *Workplace communication flows horizontally, upward, and downward.*

- *E-mail is fast, inexpensive, efficient, and easy to use, which leads people to overuse it, creating information overload.*

- *To improve human relationships: accept differences; treat others as individuals; empathize; praise others; focus on problems, not people; accept responsibility; avoid dogmatic statements; treat others as equals; trust others; and control your emotions.*

4.2

- *Most businesses have both written and unwritten work rules.*

- *A good work attitude creates a favorable impression on customers and your employer.*

- *Frequent absenteeism results in high costs to both the absent employee and the employer.*

- *Maslow's theory holds that people behave in ways that will meet their needs from lower to higher levels on a hierarchy.*

- *Herzberg's theory suggests that to motivate greater achievement, employers must offer both hygiene factors and motivators.*

- *Job satisfaction results in increased productivity for businesses and greater self-esteem and opportunities for employees.*

APPLY WHAT YOU KNOW

1. Success on the job depends on good communication skills. Your success as a student also depends on good communication skills. Explain why.

2. List four ways informal speaking is used on the job. Explain how you have used these styles at a job or other occasion.

3. What type of speech or presentation did you hear recently (informational, entertaining, or persuasive)? Describe it.

4. Distinguish among horizontal, upward, and downward communication. Explain ways you have used each one.

5. Discuss advantages and disadvantages of e-mail as a business communication tool. Do you re-read your e-mail messages before you hit the Send button? Describe a situation where you or someone else sent a message that was misinterpreted.

6. Why are human relations important in any career or workplace? Explain scenarios where you have seen (a) good human relations practiced and (b) poor human relations practiced.

7. Explain how your job or a family member's or friend's job helps to meet each level of needs on Maslow's hierarchy. Are you or the other person happy and motivated on the job?

8. Explain why productivity is important to businesses. Why is it important to workers as well?

MAKE ACADEMIC CONNECTIONS

9. **International Studies** Use the Internet to research employee absenteeism worldwide. Compare absenteeism in the United States with that of other countries. Write a report describing what you learn.

10. **Economics** Explain productivity from an economic perspective. What does it mean to a state, region, or nation? The Monthly Labor Review often reports productivity statistics. Prepare a chart listing how productivity has changed in the United States over the last ten years.

11. **Communication** Prepare a formal five-minute speech to inform, entertain, or persuade your classmates. Pick a topic that interests you and plan ways to overcome stage fright. Before giving your speech in class, practice it so that it flows smoothly and adheres to the five-minute limit.

12. **Language Arts** Compose a fictional story about a person whose career helps him or her satisfy the needs identified on Maslow's hierarchy of needs. Provide examples for each of the five levels. The story should also illustrate the correct order of need satisfaction.

SOLVE *PROBLEMS* AND
EXPLORE *ISSUES*

13. *Search the Internet using the keyword "emoticon." Write a brief explanation of what an emoticon is. Then print out or copy several emoticons to share with the class. Together with your classmates, discuss how emoticons can aid e-mail communication.*

14. *Use the questions below to interview employees about the need to get along with others at work. Then ask an employer the same questions.*

    - *Do you feel that human relations are an important part of each job where you work?*
    - *Does the employer (supervisor) feel that human relations are important?*
    - *What types of company policies or unwritten rules are in place to ensure good human relations?*

    Based on your research, write a two-page report that explains your findings. What can you conclude from your research?

15. *Selena works for a small delivery service and believes that she is underpaid. She tells her friends, "When I'm making deliveries, sometimes I stop for a pizza. Sometimes I even visit my boyfriend. Why should I knock myself out on what I earn?" What advice would you give Selena?*

16. *Use the formula given in the Math Minute to compute the rate of absenteeism and annual cost of absenteeism based on these facts:*

    - *Number of employees: 45*
    - *Number of 8-hour shifts: 3*
    - *Number of workdays in an average month: 22*
    - *Work hours lost during an average month: 624*
    - *Average hourly wage: $8*

EXTEND YOUR LEARNING

17. **Ethics** *Some workers believe that time allowed for sick leave and personal leave belongs to them to use as they wish. Thus, if they are allowed ten days a year for sick time, they take off ten days, even if they are not sick. Is it ethical to take time off when you are not sick? Do you feel this takes advantage of employers? In a two-page report, describe the ethical considerations for both employers and employees regarding sick leave and personal leave. What is the impact of absenteeism on employees, employers, coworkers, and customers?*

For related activities and links, go to **www.cengage.com/school/pfinance/mypf**

Chapter 5

Work Laws and Responsibilities

5.1 *Work-Related Forms and Laws*

5.2 *Responsibilities on the Job*

Consider **THIS**

Alexander worked part time after school during high school and full time during the summers. He decided to stay with his job while attending college because the manager was willing to give him flexible hours. This enabled him to study and earn money to pay for college at the same time.

"I like my job because my employer deals with me fairly," Alexander told a friend. "I'm paid adequately, working conditions are good, and I like my supervisor. As a part-timer, I don't get many benefits, but I'm able to attend classes to get my degree. That flexibility makes me feel good about my job, and I'm motivated to give my best. It's a win-win situation. My employer wins because I'm loyal and serve the customers well. I win because I'm able to pursue my career goals and have a job that helps me pay for college expenses too."

Work-Related Forms and Laws

GOALS
- Discuss the purpose of various work-related forms.
- Explain the provisions of major employment laws.

TERMS
- Form W-4, *p. 89*
- allowances, *p. 89*
- exempt status, *p. 89*
- Form W-2, *p. 91*
- unemployment insurance, *p. 93*
- minimum wage, *p. 93*
- workers' compensation, *p. 94*

REQUIRED WORK FORMS

When you get a job, the government will require a number of forms containing information about you. You will fill out some. Others, your employer will complete. If you are under age 16, you may also need a work permit. Some forms, such as Forms W-2 and W-4, are part of the income tax process.

FORM W-4

When you report to work, you will be asked to fill out a Form W-4. **Form W-4** asks for your name, address, Social Security number, marital status, and the number of exemptions you are claiming for income tax purposes. The information determines the amount your employer will withhold from your paycheck for income taxes. The employer sends this money to the government as partial payment of your income taxes.

The form includes a simple worksheet to help you calculate your allowances. **Allowances** are reductions in the amount of tax withheld from your paycheck. The more allowances you claim, the less tax you will have withheld. However, claiming more allowances does not decrease your tax liability. It only decreases the tax payments your employer makes for you from your paycheck during the year. If you have too little withheld, you will have to pay the difference when you file your tax return.

If you qualify, you may claim exempt status. **Exempt status** is available only to people who will not earn enough in the year to owe any federal income tax. Line 7 of the form in Figure 5.1 shows the requirements to claim exempt status. If you qualify, simply write the word *exempt* on Form W-4. Then no money will be withheld from your paycheck for federal income taxes. The

© Photodisc/Getty Images

Why would student workers want to claim exempt status on Form W-4?

FIGURE 5.1 *Form W-4*

Form **W-4**	**Employee's Withholding Allowance Certificate**	OMB No. 1545-0074
Department of the Treasury Internal Revenue Service	▶ Whether you are entitled to claim a certain number of allowances or exemption from withholding is subject to review by the IRS. Your employer may be required to send a copy of this form to the IRS.	20—

1 Type or print your first name and middle initial.	Last name	2 Your social security number
Marisa M.	Clark	999 00 5896

Home address (number and street or rural route)	3 ☑ Single ☐ Married ☐ Married, but withhold at higher Single rate.
685 West Circle Avenue	Note. If married, but legally separated, or spouse is a nonresident alien, check the "Single" box.
City or town, state, and ZIP code	4 If your last name differs from that shown on your social security card, check here. You must call 1-800-772-1213 for a replacement card. ▶ ☐
Cincinnati, OH 45227-6287	

5	Total number of allowances you are claiming (from line **H** above **or** from the applicable worksheet on page 2)	5	
6	Additional amount, if any, you want withheld from each paycheck	6	$
7	I claim exemption from withholding for 20—, and I certify that I meet **both** of the following conditions for exemption.		

• Last year I had a right to a refund of **all** federal income tax withheld because I had **no** tax liability **and**
• This year I expect a refund of **all** federal income tax withheld because I expect to have **no** tax liability.

If you meet both conditions, write "Exempt" here . . . . ▶	7		Exempt

Under penalties of perjury, I declare that I have examined this certificate and to the best of my knowledge and belief, it is true, correct, and complete.

Employee's signature
(Form is not valid unless you sign it.) ▶ *Marisa M. Clark*   Date ▶ **January 3, 20—**

8 Employer's name and address (Employer: Complete lines 8 and 10 only if sending to the IRS.)	9 Office code (optional)	10 Employer identification number (EIN)

For Privacy Act and Paperwork Reduction Act Notice, see page 2.	Cat. No. 10220Q	Form **W-4** (20—)

maximum amount of earnings allowable to qualify for exempt status changes annually.

▮ SOCIAL SECURITY FORMS

Because workers in the United States must pay a Social Security tax from wages earned, all must have a Social Security number. Your *Social Security number* is your permanent work identification number. Employers withhold Social Security taxes from your pay and contribute matching amounts. The amounts you earn and the amounts contributed for Social Security throughout your work life are credited to your Social Security account number. When you become eligible, usually at retirement, benefits are paid to you monthly, based upon how much you have paid into your account.

If you don't already have a Social Security number and card, or if you have misplaced your card and need a replacement, you can get one free of charge. The application and instructions for completing it are on the Social Security Administration web site (www.ssa.gov). You can complete and submit the application form online, or you can print it, fill it out, and mail it to the Social Security Administration.

You should check with the Social Security Administration to see that your earnings have been properly credited to your account. The Social Security Administration provides a form for you to complete for this purpose (see Figure 5.2). To request a statement online, go to the Social Security Administration site. Then follow the links to request a statement. Within 30 days, you should receive a report that shows your income according to the Social Security Administration's records. There is no charge for this service. If you notice any errors in your record, report them immediately. Once you have requested the statement, you will automatically receive an updated statement on a yearly basis.

FIGURE 5.2 *Request for Social Security Statement of Earnings*

Form Approved
OMB No. 0960-0446 [   ] SP

Request for *Social Security Statement*

[ ] Please check this box if you want to get your *Statement* in Spanish instead of English.

Please print or type your answers. When you have completed the form, fold it and mail it to us. If you prefer to send your request using the Internet, contact us at *www.socialsecurity.gov.*

1. Name shown on your Social Security card:

   Marisa _____ M. ____
   First Name   Middle Initial

   Clark _____
   Last Name Only

2. Your Social Security number as shown on your card:

   [9][9][9] - [0][0] - [5][8][9][6]

3. Your date of birth (Mo.-Day-Yr.)

   [0][8] - [2][1] - [1][9][8][8]

4. Other Social Security numbers you have used:

   [ ][ ][ ] - [ ][ ] - [ ][ ][ ][ ]
   [ ][ ][ ] - [ ][ ] - [ ][ ][ ][ ]

5. Your Sex: [ ] Male   [X] Female

For items 6 and 8 show only earnings covered by Social Security. Do NOT include wages from state, local or federal government employment that are NOT covered by Social Security or that are covered ONLY by Medicare.

6. Show your actual earnings (wages and/or net self-employment income) for last year and your estimated earnings for this year.

   A. Last year's actual earnings: *(Dollars Only)*

   $[ ][ ][2],[0][8][4].[0][0]

   B. This year's estimated earnings: *(Dollars Only)*

   $[ ][ ][4],[0][0][0].[0][0]

7. Show the age at which you plan to stop working:

   [6][5] *(Show only one age)*

8. Below, show the average yearly amount (not your total future lifetime earnings) that you think you will earn between now and when you plan to stop working. Include performance or scheduled pay increases or bonuses, but not cost-of-living increases.

   If you expect to earn significantly more or less in the future due to promotions, job changes, part-time work, or an absence from the work force, enter the amount that most closely reflects your future average yearly earnings.

   If you don't expect any significant changes, show the same amount you are earning now (the amount in 6B).

   Future average yearly earnings: *(Dollars Only)*

   $[ ][ ][4],[0][0][0].[0][0]

9. Do you want us to send the *Statement:*
   • To you? Enter your name and mailing address.
   • To someone else (your accountant, pension plan, etc.)? Enter your name with "c/o" and the name and address of that person or organization.

   Marisa M. Clark
   "C/O" or Street Address (Include Apt. No., P.O. Box, Rural Route)
   685 West Circle Avenue
   Street Address

   _____
   Street Address (If Foreign Address, enter City, Province, Postal Code)
   Cincinnati, OH 45227-6287
   U.S. City, State, ZIP code (If Foreign Address, enter Name of Country only)

   NOTICE:
   I am asking for information about my own Social Security record or the record of a person I am authorized to represent. I declare under penalty of perjury that I have examined all the information on this form, and on any accompanying statements or forms, and it is true and correct to the best of my knowledge. I authorize you to use a contractor to send the *Social Security Statement* to the person and address in item 9.

   ► *Marisa M. Clark*
   Please sign your name (Do Not Print)

   1/9/—   (513)555-8684
   Date   (Area Code) Daytime Telephone No.

Form **SSA-7004-SM** (10-2006) EF (10-2006)   ✲ Printed on recycled paper

WORK PERMIT APPLICATION

Many states require *minors*—people under the age of legal adulthood—to obtain a work permit before they are allowed to work. You can obtain an application for a work permit from your state Department of Labor, a school counseling center, or work experience coordinator. There is usually no charge. You will have to provide your Social Security number and proof of age and have your parent or legal guardian's permission. Apply early to allow time for processing.

FORM W-2

Each company for which you worked during the year will give you a Form W-2, like the one shown in Figure 5.3. **Form W-2** is a summary of the income you earned during the year and all amounts the employer withheld for taxes. These amounts include federal, state, and local income taxes and Social Security tax. Compare your W-2 to your paycheck stubs to be sure that the reported amounts are accurate. Your employer will also send a copy of your Form W-2 to the government.

The employer must provide you with a Form W-2 for the previous tax year no later than January 31 of the current year. This is true even if you worked only part of the year and were not working as of December 31. If you do not receive a Form W-2 from each employer for which you worked during the year, contact the delinquent employer. You must file your W-2 forms with your tax return.

FIGURE 5.3   *Form W-2*

22222	**a** Employee's social security number 999-00-5896	OMB No. 1545-0008	

b Employer identification number (EIN) 93-81256791	**1** Wages, tips, other compensation $2,084.00	**2** Federal income tax withheld
c Employer's name, address, and ZIP code	**3** Social security wages $2,084.00	**4** Social security tax withheld $129.21
Hanson Motors 85 Briar Street Cincinnati, OH 45230-5162	**5** Medicare wages and tips $2,084.00	**6** Medicare tax withheld $30.22
	7 Social security tips	**8** Allocated tips
d Control number	**9** Advance EIC payment	**10** Dependent care benefits
e Employee's first name and initial Last name Suff. Marisa M. Clark 685 West Circle Avenue Cincinnati, OH 45227-6287	**11** Nonqualified plans	**12a**
	13 Statutory employee [X] Retirement plan [ ] Third-party sick pay [ ]	**12b**
	14 Other	**12c**
f Employee's address and ZIP code		**12d**

15 State Employer's state ID number	**16** State wages, tips, etc. $2,084.00	**17** State income tax $14.04	**18** Local wages, tips, etc. $2,084.00	**19** Local income tax $41.60	**20** Locality name Cincinnati

Form **W-2** Wage and Tax Statement   20—   Department of the Treasury—Internal Revenue Service

FORM I-9

Before you start working, you and your employer must complete an Employment Eligibility Verification form, or *Form I-9*. The purpose of this form is to verify the employee's identity and eligibility to work in the United States. Along with the form, you will be required to present forms of identification, which could include a driver's license, passport, Social Security card, or birth certificate.

EMPLOYMENT LAWS

The federal government has enacted many laws to protect workers. The Department of Labor is responsible for enforcing labor laws that:

- Provide unemployment, disability, and retirement insurance benefits
- Establish a minimum wage and regular working hours
- Establish rules regarding overtime pay
- Help workers injured on the job
- Provide equal employment opportunities and prohibit discrimination
- Establish safe working conditions

Laws covering minors require more safety precautions than for adult workers. Laws also specify a maximum number of hours minors can work during the school year. A work permit for those under age 16 is required in some states.

Employees who believe they have not received the protections required by law may turn to the government (Department of Labor) for *recourse*, or remedy.

SOCIAL SECURITY ACT

The Social Security Act, passed in 1935, established a national social insurance program that provides federal aid for the elderly and for disabled workers. In 1965, the Medicare provision was added. It provides hospital and medical insurance for those 65 and older. Originally known as OASDHI, Social Security provides these benefits:

- Old age retirement income (OA)
- Survivorship income (S)
- Disability income (D)
- Health insurance (HI)

Benefits received depend on the amount of contributions made. Contributions are mandatory for all workers. Employers deduct Social Security and Medicare taxes (FICA) from employees' pay and send it to the U.S. Treasury for proper crediting to employees' Social Security accounts. Self-employed workers pay their Social Security contributions when they pay their income tax.

UNEMPLOYMENT COMPENSATION

The Social Security Act requires every state to have an unemployment insurance program. **Unemployment insurance** provides benefits to workers who lose their jobs through no fault of their own. After a waiting period, laid-off or terminated workers may collect a portion of their regular pay for a certain length of time. Premiums for unemployment insurance are usually paid by employers.

Each state has its own regulations for waiting periods, maximum benefits, and deadlines for filing claims. Usually, benefits are paid for a maximum of 26 weeks through the local state employment office. In most states, an unemployed worker must wait for at least one week before receiving benefits. To receive benefits, a worker must have been employed for a minimum period of time (6 months to one year, depending on the state) and for a minimum amount of earnings ($400 or more per month in most states). Workers fired for a valid reason, such as poor performance, are usually not entitled to receive benefits.

© Digital Vision/Getty Images

What is the purpose of unemployment compensation?

FAIR LABOR STANDARDS ACT

The Fair Labor Standards Act, which is also known as the Wage and Hour Act, establishes a minimum wage. It also requires hourly workers to be paid "overtime wages" of 1½ times their hourly rate for hours worked beyond 40 per week. A **minimum wage** is the lowest wage that an employer may pay an employee as established by law. Tips are not considered wages, so they are not included in calculating the minimum wage. In 2008, the federal minimum wage was $6.55 an hour (and is set to rise to $7.25 in July of 2009). Some states require employers to pay higher minimum wages than the federal government requires. To compare the minimum wages of different states, visit the U.S. Department of Labor site at www.dol.gov and follow links to minimum wage information. You can find more information about your state's labor laws at your state's Department of Labor web site.

▌ WORKERS' COMPENSATION

Workers' compensation is an insurance program that pays benefits to workers and/or their families for injury, illness, or death that occurs as a result of the job. The employer is responsible for employee injuries and illnesses that are the result of employment, regardless of fault. Today, all 50 states have workers' compensation laws. Employers pay the insurance premiums in most states. Benefits include payments to doctors and hospitals, to the employee for temporary or permanent disability, and to survivors in the event of death.

▌ THE FAMILY AND MEDICAL LEAVE ACT

The Family and Medical Leave Act (FMLA) of 1993 allows employees to take up to 12 weeks of unpaid leave in a 12-month period for certain medical and family situations. Some employers may choose to pay employees during some types of leave, such as sick leave, but they are not required by law to do so. Valid circumstances for unpaid leave under the FMLA include the following:

- Birth and care of a newborn child, including adoption of a child
- Care of an immediate family member (spouse, child, or parent) with a serious health condition
- Medical leave when the employee is unable to work because of a serious health condition

To find out more about FMLA, go to the Employment Standards Administration web site at www.dol.gov/esa/welcome.html and follow the links to FMLA.

▌ LAWS AGAINST DISCRIMINATION IN EMPLOYMENT

A number of laws protect workers from unfair treatment in the workplace. Here is a brief description of the most important of these laws.

- *Equal Pay Act:* Prohibits unequal pay for men and women doing substantially similar work
- *Civil Rights Act of 1964:* Prohibits discrimination in hiring, training, and promotion on the basis of race, color, gender, religion, or national origin
- *Age Discrimination in Employment Act:* Prohibits discrimination in employment decisions against people age 40 and over
- *Americans with Disabilities Act:* Prohibits discrimination on the basis of physical or mental disabilities

These laws are enforced by the Equal Employment Opportunity Commission (EEOC).

NET Bookmark

Sadly, discrimination in the workplace still happens today. The Equal Employment Opportunity Commission (EEOC) enforces the laws that protect workers from unfair treatment by employers. Access www.cengage.com/school/pfinance/mypf and click on the link for Chapter 5. Find the number of discrimination charges handled by the EEOC in the most recent year. (*Hint:* Under the heading "Statistics," first click the *Enforcement Statistics* link, and then click *Charge Statistics*.) What three categories accounted for the largest percentage of claims?

www.cengage.com/school/pfinance/mypf

Planning a Career in... Engineering

Science, Technology, Engineering & Mathematics

Engineers apply the principles of science and math to develop solutions to technical problems. They develop new products and assure that they will be precise and safe for human use.

In addition to design and development, many engineers work in testing, production, or maintenance. Engineers use computers extensively to produce and analyze designs, to simulate and test, to generate specifications, and to monitor product quality.

Most engineers specialize in an area of interest. Civil engineering includes structural and transportation design work. Aerospace engineers design, develop, and test aircraft, spacecraft, and missiles. There are also biomedical, chemical, electrical, environmental, industrial, marine, mechanical, and nuclear engineers. Engineers are creative, inquisitive, analytical, and detail-oriented. They work on teams and must communicate very well because they interact with other engineers and coworkers.

Employment Outlook

- As fast as average rate of employment is expected.

Job Titles

- Civil engineer
- Mechanical engineer
- Electrical engineer
- Agricultural engineer

Needed Skills

- Bachelor's degree in engineering is required.
- Licensure is required by all 50 states when the engineer works with the public.
- Strong math and science skills are needed.

What's it like to work in... *Engineering*

Morgan is working with a team of engineers at the engineering firm where she is a general partner. She specializes in civil engineering and has designed a number of prominent buildings and park sites in the state.

Her current project involves the design of a new theater, hotel, and shopping complex at the airport. She is meeting with a team of environmental engineers to make sure the design of the structure does not pose any risks to the surrounding environment. The structure must be visually pleasing, strong enough to sustain an 8.0 earthquake, and easily accessible by airline customers.

Today Morgan will present her overall design and will explain the scale model she built. She is excited to get the project underway and start the construction phase.

What About You?

Are you creative? Do you like to design and build things? Are you curious about how things work and how to make them work better? Would you like to become an engineer?

Assessment

KEY TERMS REVIEW

Match the terms with the definitions. Some terms may not be used.

_____ 1. A program that provides benefits to workers who lose their jobs through no fault of their own

_____ 2. The lowest wage an employer may pay an employee as established by law

_____ 3. Reductions in the amount of tax withheld from your paycheck

_____ 4. A summary of the income you earned and taxes withheld during the year

_____ 5. An insurance program that pays benefits to workers and/or their families for injury, illness, or death that occurs as a result of the job

_____ 6. Claimed by people who will not earn enough during the year to owe federal income tax

a. allowances

b. exempt status

c. Form W-2

d. Form W-4

e. minimum wage

f. unemployment insurance

g. workers' compensation

CHECK YOUR UNDERSTANDING

7. If you do not fill out your Form W-4 properly, what is likely to happen?

8. What should you do if you lose your Social Security card?

9. What law protects you if you or your spouse wants time off to have a baby?

APPLY YOUR KNOWLEDGE

10. Minimum wage began at 25 cents an hour in 1938. Today there is a federal minimum wage and some states have set a minimum that is higher than the federal rate. What is the minimum wage in your state? How does it compare to federal and other state rates?

THINK CRITICALLY

11. When you are hired, you and your employer must fill out Form I-9 to verify you are working legally in the United States. You must also show forms of identification. Why is this type of documentation necessary? Do you agree with it? Explain.

12. Using the Internet, research one of the numerous laws against discrimination in the workplace. Why was the law passed? Who does it protect? Is it still a relevant law for today? Why or why not?

Responsibilities on the Job

EMPLOYEE RESPONSIBILITIES

To be successful as a new employee, you will have to meet a number of responsibilities. These include personal responsibilities to your employer, to other employees, and to customers.

RESPONSIBILITIES TO EMPLOYERS

Your employer hires you and pays you at stated intervals. In return for this pay and other benefits, the employer expects certain things from you.

Competent Work

You should do your best to produce the highest-quality finished product for your employer. The work needs to be **marketable**—that is, of such quality that the employer can sell it or use it to favorably represent the company. If, for example, you send an e-mail message to a client that has so many mistakes in it that it would make the company look incompetent or uncaring to the client, the message is not a marketable product. Also, when using an employer's property, you should be as thrifty as possible. You should conserve supplies and care for equipment.

Punctuality

Arrive at work on time, do not exceed the allotted time for breaks, and don't leave before quitting time. **Punctuality** means being ready to start work at the appointed time. For example, rather than arriving at the building at 8 a.m. (starting time), you should be at your workstation at 8 a.m.

Pleasant Attitude

On any job, it is important to be pleasant and easy to get along with. You should be willing to follow orders and accept feedback. Your employer also has the right to expect you to be courteous to customers, because you represent the company to others.

Loyalty and Respect

While working for a company, you should never spread rumors or gossip about your employer or job. As long as you are on the company "team," you are expected to be loyal. **Loyalty** is a work habit based on respect. It means that you show respect for your employer and the company for which you work, both on and off the job.

Dependability

When you say you will do something, follow through. **Dependability** is a character trait that means you can be counted on to do what you say you will do. The employer should be able to depend on you to do what you were hired to do. A person who is dependable has a good reputation and will be considered for increased responsibilities and promotions.

Initiative

You should not have to be told everything to do. Employees who stand idle after completing a task are of little value to employers. You should show initiative. **Initiative** is taking the lead, recognizing what needs to be done, and doing it without having to be told.

Interest

It is important for you to show an interest in your job and your company. You should project an attitude of wanting to learn all you can and of giving all tasks your best effort. Being enthusiastic about your job shows an employer your sincere interest in being a cooperative and productive worker.

Self-Evaluation

The ability to take criticism and to assess your own progress is important to you and your employer. You cannot improve your weak points unless you are willing to admit they exist and to work on them. Employers must evaluate employees' work to determine raises and promotions. Employees should be able to recognize their own strong points and limitations and do a realistic self-evaluation of their job performance.

Why is it important for employees to take initiative?

© Photodisc/Getty Images

RESPONSIBILITIES TO OTHER EMPLOYEES

In addition to your responsibilities to your employer, you also have obligations to your coworkers such as those described below.

Teamwork

You are part of a team when you work with others in a company, and you need to do your share of the work. **Teamwork** means working cooperatively in order to achieve a group goal. Workers are expected to produce a high-quality final product. When friction and personality conflicts occur, the productivity of the whole company decreases.

Thoughtfulness

Be considerate of coworkers to promote a good work atmosphere for everyone, including customers. Having a pleasant attitude will result in a more enjoyable time for yourself and others. Avoid bringing personal problems and conflicts to work. Save cell phone calls and checking personal messages until you are on your break or lunch hour.

Loyalty

In addition to being loyal to your employer, you should be loyal to coworkers. This includes not spreading rumors about them. Gossiping leads to a breakdown of teamwork.

RESPONSIBILITIES TO CUSTOMERS

As an employee, you represent the company. To the customer who walks in the front door, you *are* the company. Your attitude toward a customer often will be the deciding factor in whether the customer continues to do business with your company. On behalf of your employer, you have the responsibility to greet the customer with an attitude of helpfulness and courtesy.

Helpfulness

It is your responsibility to help customers find what they want or to do what is needed to make a sale. When customers contact you with a problem, you are responsible for solving the problem or finding another employee who can. An attitude of helpfulness reflects well on the company and is an important part of any job.

Courtesy and Respect

Whether or not you like a customer, the customer actually pays your wages by keeping your employer in business. Without customers, the business could not exist. Therefore, your attitude toward customers should always be respectful and courteous, never hostile or unfriendly. Friendly, helpful employees build customer loyalty to the business.

EMPLOYER RESPONSIBILITIES

Employers also have responsibilities to employees. Some require compliance with employment laws, as previously discussed. Others are simply sensible practices for keeping employees happy and on the job. Failure to meet these responsibilities can result in a high employee turnover (with resulting high costs for finding and training new workers), increased premiums for unemployment insurance, and employer fines for unfair labor practices.

ADEQUATE SUPERVISION

Employees need proper supervision to do a good job. Supervision is providing new and current employees with the information and training they need to do their jobs well. It includes the following:

- Providing appropriate instruction in the safe use of equipment
- Providing adequate training for new employees

- Helping employees solve problems on the job
- Distributing information downward from management and upward to management to ensure an effective communication flow

▋ FAIR HUMAN RESOURCE POLICIES

Policies on hiring, firing, raises, promotions, and dispute resolution need to be fair and well defined. Employees need to fully understand the following:

- What is considered acceptable and unacceptable performance
- What the standards are for advancements and raises
- What constitutes grounds for suspension or discharge

▋ SAFE WORKING CONDITIONS

All employees must be provided with safe equipment, a safe working environment, and adequate training for working under dangerous conditions. Special protective equipment and clothing and warning signs must be provided to employees working in hazardous situations. Laws governing working conditions for minors are often stricter than those for adults.

▋ OPEN CHANNELS OF COMMUNICATION

Employers need to communicate clearly with employees. Open channels of communication mean that all employees have the opportunity to express concerns, ask questions, and make suggestions.

Lack of open channels of communication can result in poor worker morale and low worker output. Employees need to know they are an important part of the company and that their opinions are valuable.

▋ RECOGNITION OF ACHIEVEMENT

Employers need to provide some form of reward for above-average performance. An employee **evaluation** is a report that discusses the employee's strengths and weaknesses in performing the job and how well the employee helped to meet company goals. As a result of evaluations, employees are given merit pay raises, bonuses, and advancement opportunities.

Employees also respond well to nonmonetary rewards, such as providing extra time off or simply complimenting exceptional work in front of other employees. Recognizing achievement will motivate workers.

COMMUNICATION *Connection*

Customer service employees play a big role in the success of a business. Describe your latest shopping experience as a customer in the last 30 days. How did employees of that business treat you? What were the positive aspects of your shopping trip? What were the negative aspects?

Based on your experience, develop a list of customer relations policies for the business you visited. Be sure to consider the employees' responsibilities to the customer. Assume you will share your list with store management. Use a word processing program to prepare it professionally.

ISSUES IN YOUR WORLD

SEXUAL HARASSMENT

A safe working environment also means one that is comfortable and free of unwanted conduct that interferes with work performance. Sexual harassment is any unwelcome advance, request for sexual favors, and other verbal or physical conduct that is offensive.

Workers are protected by the Equal Employment Opportunity Commission (EEOC) from these types of behaviors. Sexual harassment violates the Civil Rights Act of 1964, and employers have the responsibility to prevent it in the workplace. EEOC guidelines state that an employer is responsible for the actions of employees as well as non-employees on work premises.

Unfortunately, sexual harassment is widespread. Studies show that at least 50 percent of working women and 15 percent of working men have experienced sexual harassment on the job. Fortunately, steps are being taken to reduce this problem.

Until a little over decade ago, a victim's only recourse was to sue the offending person. Today, the EEOC investigates complaints. When it finds sexual harassment, the victim may receive a remedy such as back pay, a promotion, or reinstatement if he or she had been fired. When the victim's rights are not protected, the EEOC will sue the employer.

Many companies have policies to prevent sexual harassment. All employees are entitled to respect, courtesy, and tactful behavior. Abusing the dignity of anyone through ethnic, sexist, or racial slurs or other objectionable conduct is cause for disciplinary action. Objectionable conduct includes suggestive remarks, physical contact, and intimidation.

All employees should be aware of what sexual harassment is and how to avoid it. For example, employees who tell inappropriate jokes or engage in suggestive behavior, such as flirting, may find themselves in embarrassing situations. It is important to dress and act professionally at all times, so that you can truly say you did nothing to contribute to the situation.

THINK CRITICALLY

1. *What would you do if you were the target of inappropriate physical or verbal conduct on the job?*
2. *What are some things you can do to reduce your risk of sexual harassment?*

Assessment

KEY TERMS REVIEW

Match the terms with the definitions.

_____ 1. A character trait that means you can be counted on to do what you say you will do

_____ 2. A report that discusses the employee's strengths and weaknesses in performing the job and how well the employee helped to meet company goals

_____ 3. Being ready to start work at the appointed time

_____ 4. Work that is of a quality that may be sold or used to favorably represent the company

_____ 5. Working cooperatively in order to achieve a group goal

_____ 6. A work habit based on respect

_____ 7. Providing the information and training needed for employees to do their jobs well

_____ 8. Taking the lead, recognizing what needs to be done, and doing it without having to be told

a. dependability

b. evaluation

c. initiative

d. loyalty

e. marketable

f. punctuality

g. supervision

h. teamwork

CHECK YOUR UNDERSTANDING

9. What responsibilities do you have to your employer? What responsibilities do you have to your coworkers?

10. What kinds of things do you expect from an employer in exchange for your time and hard work?

APPLY YOUR KNOWLEDGE

11. If you are unhappy with your job, you may be inclined to complain to others. Complaining about your current employer or job shows disrespect (lack of loyalty). Explain ways you can talk about your job without being disrespectful.

THINK CRITICALLY

12. Why should you avoid using your cell phone or hand-held computer while on the job? Give three reasons.

13. Employers should provide fair human resource policies for employees. What policies would you like to see in the areas of annual evaluation, raises, and grounds for discipline?

Chapter Assessment

SUMMARY

5.1

- *The information you provide on Form W-4 regarding your number of allowances or exempt status determines the amount your employer will withhold from your paycheck for taxes.*

- *Your contributions to Social Security throughout your work life determine the payments you will receive during retirement.*

- *If you are under age 16, you may need a work permit to hold a job.*

- *The employer must provide a Form W-2 to employees by January 31 of the following tax year. It summarizes wages and amounts withheld for taxes during the year.*

- *The Social Security Act established a national social insurance program. Provisions have been added for Medicare and unemployment insurance.*

- *The Fair Labor Standards Act sets a minimum wage and overtime pay.*

- *Workers' compensation is an insurance program that pays benefits to workers and/or their families for injury, illness, or death that occurs as a result of the job.*

- *The Family and Medical Leave Act allows employees to take unpaid leave for family and medical reasons.*

- *The Equal Pay Act, Civil Rights Act of 1964, Age Discrimination in Employment Act, and Americans with Disabilities Act protect employees from discrimination in the workplace. These laws are enforced by the EEOC.*

5.2

- *Your responsibilities to your employer include competent work, punctuality, a pleasant attitude, loyalty, dependability, initiative, interest, and self-evaluation.*

- *Your responsibilities to your coworkers include teamwork, thoughtfulness, and loyalty.*

- *Your responsibilities to customers include helpfulness, courtesy, and respect.*

- *Your employer's responsibilities include compliance with employment laws, adequate supervision, fair human resource policies, safe working conditions, open channels of communication, and recognition of achievement.*

APPLY WHAT YOU KNOW

1. *What is the purpose of Form W-4? Obtain a Form W-4 from the nearest office of the Internal Revenue Service or download one from the IRS web site (go to www.irs.gov and follow the links to forms and publications). Complete the W-4 form properly, claiming exempt status if you are entitled to do so.*

2. *Why should you request a Social Security earnings statement? Complete a Request for a Social Security Statement online by going to the Social Security Administration's web site (go to www.ssa.gov and follow the links to the statement request form). When you receive your statement in the mail, check it for accuracy.*

3. *Use the Internet to research the Social Security Act. (Hint: Visit the Social Security Administration online at www.ssa.gov.). Obtain the following information: (a) Who was the president at the time of this Act? (b) Why did the president consider Social Security necessary? (c) Describe the history of benefits, deductions from paychecks, and purpose of Social Security.*

4. *Obtain from your state Department of Labor the provisions of state laws regarding employment of minors. Find out: (a) the maximum hours per week that can be worked, (b) latest hour in the evening that a minor can work, (c) whether a work permit is required for workers under age 16, and (d) any other provisions to protect a minor working part or full time.*

5. *List five responsibilities that employees have to their employers in the order you think most important. Then ask a working parent or other working person to list five employee responsibilities in their order of importance. Compare the two lists. How are they similar? How are they different?*

MAKE ACADEMIC CONNECTIONS

6. **Government** *Go to the Department of Labor's web site at www.dol.gov and review the information provided there. List the categories of information that are available to you. The Department of Labor is a federal agency. There should be a similar state agency in your state. Go to your state's web site and do similar research. (Many states have stricter labor laws than the federal government.)*

7. **Communication** *Assume the role of employer. Think of a job and create a list of job responsibilities and a salary or wage for the position. Prepare a written evaluation for a person who has performed according to your work standards. Recommend an appropriate raise. Write a one-page paper that outlines what the employee is doing well relative to his or her job title and responsibilities and why he or she deserves a raise.*

8. **History** *Research the history leading up to the Civil Rights Act of 1964. Write a two-page paper describing the controversy surrounding this law and how it eventually won passage.*

SOLVE PROBLEMS AND

EXPLORE ISSUES

9. Your friend Eric believes that the amount of wages he received during the year is different from the amount listed on the W-2 he received from his employer. He asks you what to do. How would you reply?

10. Trang did not earn enough money at his part-time job last year to require him to pay any federal taxes. His employer asks him if he would like to claim exempt status on his W-4 this year. Explain to Trang how he can claim exempt status and how it will affect him.

11. Bianca, age 14, has decided that she wants to work part time this summer doing whatever kind of work she can find to earn money to buy clothes. Explain to her what things she should do to prepare for work. Also explain what forms she may have to complete when she begins work.

12. Gena worked for over a year for the same employer but then was laid off because business was slow. She is looking for another job, but she needs income now to make her rent payment. You told Gena that she might be eligible for unemployment insurance payments. Explain how she could qualify and whom she should talk to about unemployment benefits.

13. Aaron, who has a visual disability, applied for a position as an assistant credit manager at a local retail store. The store's human resource manager tested Aaron's eyesight by having him read a chart written in small print. Aaron failed the test and, on that basis alone, was rejected for the position. Have Aaron's employment rights been violated? Explain your answer and discuss any pertinent laws.

14. You work as a sales associate in a retail store. Your manager is always stressing the importance of "total customer satisfaction." What do you think this expression means? Do you believe it is wise for a business to adopt this expression as policy?

EXTEND YOUR LEARNING

15. **Ethics** A sales associate at a home entertainment electronics store works on commission, which means his salary is based on the amount of sales he makes. He is assisting a customer who wants to buy a new plasma TV. After talking with the customer, he knows there are several models with various prices that would satisfy the customer's needs. However, he persuades the customer to buy the higher-priced model. Why do you think the sales associate did this? Was this fair to the customer? What ethical issues are involved when pay is directly tied to sales?

For related activities and links, go to **www.cengage.com/school/pfinance/mypf**

Coretta Scott King

© AP Photo/Ric Feld

Coretta Scott was born on a farm in Alabama in 1927. She showed an early love for music and academics. She was valedictorian of her class at Lincoln High School and earned a scholarship to Antioch College (Ohio) where she completed her bachelor's degree in music. She continued her studies in concert singing and completed an advanced degree in voice and violin at the New England Conservatory of Music. While living in Boston, she met Martin Luther King, Jr., who was completing his doctorate degree in theology. They were married in 1953.

Coretta Scott King raised four children and assisted her husband at the Dexter Avenue Baptist Church in Montgomery, Alabama. As passionate for civil rights as her husband, she conceived and performed a series of critically acclaimed Freedom Concerts, where she combined music, poetry, and narration to tell the story of the civil rights movement.

In the 1960s, Mrs. King was in great demand as a public speaker. She was the first woman to deliver the Class Day address at Harvard and to preach at a statutory service at London's St. Paul's Cathedral. She served as a delegate to the Disarmament Conference in Geneva in 1962. When her husband was assassinated in 1968, Mrs. King carried on his dream. For 27 years, she was at the helm of The King Center, the memorial to her husband and his life's work for non-violent social change, in Atlanta, Georgia.

Throughout her life, Mrs. King remained active for racial and economic justice and inspired many others to dedicate their lives to making the world a better place for those who follow. Coretta Scott King died in 2006 at age 78 and is buried next to her husband at The King Center.

THINK *CRITICALLY*

1. *Coretta Scott King had a fulfilling career that spanned many different areas of interest. What does this tell you about career progression and how it relates to one's values and goals?*

2. *Would you identify Mrs. King as a lifelong learner? Explain your answer.*

3. *Considering their involvement in the civil rights movement, do you think Dr. and Mrs. King had a role in shaping the employment laws of today? Explain your answer.*

Career Development: Planning and Leading a Meeting

Overview

This project is designed to develop leadership skills. If you've ever attended a meeting that failed—people were bored, there was no clear direction, or nothing was decided—you know why it is important to run effective meetings. Your group, whether formal or informal, work- or school-related, will benefit from following standard procedures that allow for binding decisions and good planning.

PLANNING A SUCCESSFUL MEETING

If you are merely announcing information, an e-mail will do. The time to have a meeting is when you need input or opinions, when you want the group to make a decision that affects all of them, when you need a creative solution to a problem, or when you want everyone to hear important information at the same time. Here are some guidelines for planning a successful meeting.

- *Time Limit.* Whenever possible, plan meetings to last no more than an hour. If the meeting must exceed an hour, provide drinks and a break. If it must last more than two hours, you should also provide food.

© Digital Vision/Getty Images

- *Adequate Space.* Make sure the meeting space is sufficient for participants to be comfortable. It must be large enough, have enough chairs, provide the right atmosphere, and include needed accessories, such as a flipchart, white board, or audiovisual equipment.
- *Adequate Notice.* Give at least a week's notice, or preferably two, so people can plan their schedules to attend. Figure U1.1 is a typical meeting notice.
- *Convenient Time.* Avoid calling a meeting late in the afternoon, unless you also have arranged a time of relaxation and entertainment. Friday afternoons are rarely a good time to schedule meetings.
- *Send Agenda.* Provide in advance an agenda of topics to be discussed, so that people can prepare their contributions and bring related information with them. Figure U1.2 is a typical agenda.
- *Stick to Agenda.* Plan topics that can be completed in the scheduled time. Attention wanes when a meeting runs longer than participants expect. Be consistent from meeting to meeting.

FIGURE U1.1   *Meeting Notice*

Meeting Notice

The Teen Consumers Group will have its monthly meeting and will hear a presentation by Eva Diaz of the Better Business Bureau. Ms. Diaz will discuss Internet shopping.

Date: Thursday, February 15, 20—
Time: 3:00 p.m. to 4:30 p.m.
Place: Western High School Library

If you can't attend, please call LaMont Russell at 555-7825 or e-mail him at 1russell@omega.net

---

FIGURE U1.2   *Agenda*

Agenda

Teen Consumers Group
February 15, 20—
3:00 p.m.

Facilitator: LaMont Russell
Notetaker: Sun-Yi Wong

1. Opening comments (LaMont Russell)

2. Report on next month's fundraising car wash (Midori Tanaka)

3. Report on consumer web sites of interest (Barry Coogan)

4. Presentation on Internet shopping (Eva Diaz, Better Business Bureau)

5. Closing comments (LaMont Russell)

SETTING UP THE MEETING

A round table or circle is often a good way to encourage participation at a meeting. Prepare and copy handouts before the meeting and have them waiting for people to arrive. Have extra paper and pencils available.

Set up and test your audiovisual tools ahead of time, such as computer presentation or video equipment, flipcharts, white boards, and markers. Make sure everything is ready to go when the meeting starts. Each participant should be able to see without obstruction. If you expect participants to write, make sure the table offers ample space.

Video participants should be able to hear and see everything going on in the room. Those attending the meeting should be able to see and hear the video participants. Today's technology allows this type of accommodation for people who can't travel to the meeting in person.

Room ambiance is also important. If the room is too cold or dark, group members will be unable to concentrate. If the room is too hot or bright, group members will be in a hurry to leave rather than to participate.

Make prearrangements to avoid meeting interruptions. For example, if refreshments will be served, arrange to have them delivered at a set time. You should stay at the meeting at all times rather than attend to details that you could have taken care of in advance.

CONDUCTING A SUCCESSFUL MEETING

As the meeting leader, you are responsible for keeping the meeting moving along and staying on track. Stick to the agenda. If a new item should be added, put it at the end of the agenda or on the next meeting's agenda. Here are some suggestions for keeping the meeting productive.

- *Give a Preview.* Before you start the meeting, tell the participants what will happen, what will be expected from them, and what outcomes are desired.
- *Make Introductions.* Unless everyone in the room already knows each other, have group members introduce themselves, or give a short introduction of each person yourself, briefly describing each person's role in the group.
- *Take Meeting Notes.* Assign someone to take notes and prepare the meeting summary (also called *minutes*). Figure U1.3 shows a sample meeting summary.
- *Stay on Task.* Keep the group focused on the purpose of the meeting. Some rambling is normal, but avoid getting sidetracked.
- *Brainstorm.* If the purpose of the meeting is to generate ideas or come up with a creative solution to a problem, try brainstorming. With this technique, you present the topic or problem and ask participants to say their ideas out loud as they come to mind, no matter how wild the ideas. Do not judge the responses at this point. Just record them where participants can see them. The purpose of brainstorming is to allow a free flow of ideas. One person's wild idea may trigger a more workable idea from someone else. To encourage everyone to make suggestions, you could try going around the table, asking each person, in turn, for an idea, but allowing people to pass if they don't have one. Then keep going around the table until the group seems to have run out of ideas. Once all ideas are recorded, lead the group in discussing the ideas and selecting the best one to implement.

Meeting Summary

Teen Consumers Group
February 15, 20—
3:00 p.m.

Attendees: Barry Coogan; Joel D'Aurizio; Cate Ewing; Deondra Holcomb; Danny Martinez; LaMont Russell; Midori Tanaka; Nancy Williams; Sun-Yi Wong; Mishelle Zambito

1. LaMont reminded the group that our picture for the school yearbook will be taken on Friday, February 23, in the lobby. Everyone should meet there at noon.

2. Midori handed out instructions for March's fundraising car wash which takes place in the school parking lot. If you have questions, see her.

3. Barry provided a list of new web sites that we should look at before our next meeting. Each group member will review one site and prepare a one-paragraph description. E-mail your information to Barry at bcoogan@omega.net by March 10.

4. Eva Diaz presented a helpful and informative discussion on the pros and cons of Internet shopping. She distributed some brochures from the Better Business Bureau and suggested that we contact the BBB if we experience problems.

5. LaMont closed the meeting with a reminder that the next meeting will take place on Thursday, March 15, at 3:00 p.m. in the library. Last-minute details about the car wash will be discussed, and the reports on the consumer web sites will be reviewed.

- *Involve Everyone.* No matter what your meeting format, keep everyone involved. Some people tend to be more reluctant to speak than others. To encourage their participation, use written feedback or ask directly for every person's opinion, allowing each person the same time to express his or her view. Everyone should feel safe and free to make contributions that will help accomplish the purpose of the meeting.

- *Disarm Disrupters.* To disarm disrupters (those who cause disorder or confusion), place time limits on comments. Acknowledge what they say with a comment such as "We hear you," and then move on to the next item or ask someone else to speak. Ask the group as a whole if they want to stop and address the issue at hand or deal with it at another time. When negativity creeps in, use humor to change the mood back to a positive tone. To deal with disrupters who come prepared to sabotage the meeting, meet them head on by acknowledging their concerns and setting a separate meeting time to deal with their issues specifically.

- *Use Consensus Decision Making When Possible.* With consensus decisions, every person in the group agrees to and "buys into" the final outcome. This means negotiating until all participants feel they have been heard and each person is willing to accept the group's final decision. You will need to ask questions such as "What will it take to make you comfortable with our decision?" until everyone is satisfied that the best possible agreement has been reached.

- *Summarize.* Wrap up the meeting with a summary of what the group decided and the next steps to be taken. People who have agreed to certain actions should be reminded of their commitments. Congratulate everyone for their hard work and contributions.

AFTER THE MEETING

Soon after the meeting, distribute a copy of the meeting summary or minutes to each participant and to group members who could not attend. Include handouts for absent group members and reminders of subsequent actions to be taken and their timeframes. File the meeting summary for future reference. Include the names of all people who attended and the date of the meeting.

FOLLOW-UP ASSIGNMENT

1. Ask someone you know who works in an office to arrange for you to observe a meeting. As an alternative, observe a meeting at school, such as a student council meeting. Take notes on the following issues and write a report for your class:

   a. Was an agenda distributed ahead of the meeting?

   b. Was the meeting room adequate? Was the audiovisual equipment set up and in working order at the start of the meeting? What elements of the physical environment could have been improved?

   c. What was the purpose of the meeting? Did the purpose seem clear to everyone?

   d. How well did the discussion stay focused on the purpose? What sidetracking occurred? How did the leader bring the discussion back to the purpose?

   e. How did the group go about accomplishing the meeting purpose? How did the leader help this process? How could the group process have been improved?

   f. Did everyone participate? How did the leader encourage participation? Were there disrupters? How did the leader handle disruptions? What could have been done to improve participation?

   g. What were the outcomes of the meeting? Did the meeting accomplish its purpose? Did everyone seem to agree with the decisions made and know their responsibilities for further action?

   h. Overall, how productive do you think the meeting was? Explain.

2. Using the issues listed in question 1, critique a meeting that you attend as a participating member. Summarize your findings in a report.

Unit

2

Money Management

CHAPTERS

Unit 2 begins with an examination of your paycheck and benefits, trends in the workplace that affect your career, and opportunities for advancement. Then you will learn about preparing your income tax.

Next you will study financial management, beginning with preparing budgets and other financial records. You will also find out about informal and formal contracts that you enter into daily.

Finally, you will learn how to use a checking account, including writing checks, keeping a checkbook register, and reconciling your account. You will discover how to choose the right bank and services that meet your needs.

6

Pay, Benefits, and Working Conditions

6.1 *Understanding Pay and Benefits*

6.2 *Work Schedules and Unions*

Consider **THIS**

Enrique just got a job. When he was hired, his employer provided a packet containing all kinds of information, from union membership to sick pay. He will receive two weeks of paid vacation every year, after his first year of employment. The company allows ten paid sick days per year and will grant a leave of absence in the case of pregnancy or death of a family member. It also offers a 401(k) plan, which allows employees to make contributions to a savings account to help plan for retirement. Also provided for employees is a full package of group health, dental, vision, and life insurance coverage. In addition, the company has a child-care facility, altered workweeks, and job sharing.

"Wow, I'm going to need to read that entire packet," Enrique thought to himself. "There are a lot of things I need to understand."

Understanding Pay and Benefits

GOALS
- Compute payroll deductions and net pay.
- Identify optional and required employee benefits.

TERMS
- gross pay, *p. 115*
- overtime, *p. 115*
- deductions, *p. 117*
- net pay, *p. 117*
- self-employment tax, *p. 121*
- incentive pay, *p. 121*
- vested, *p. 123*

GROSS PAY, DEDUCTIONS, AND NET PAY

When you take a job, you agree to perform certain tasks in exchange for regular pay. **Gross pay** is the total amount you earn before any deductions are subtracted. If you work for an hourly wage, any overtime pay you earned during the pay period must be added to your regular pay to determine your gross pay.

HOURLY WAGES

Figure 6.1 shows a paycheck for Shari Gregson, who works for $8.00 per hour. Her employer keeps a record of the hours she works. For this pay period, she worked 40 regular hours. To determine Shari's pay for regular hours worked, multiply the pay rate by the number of hours:

$$\text{Rate} \times \text{Hours Worked} = \text{Gross Pay}$$
$$\$8.00 \times \quad 40 \text{ hours} \quad = \$320.00$$

OVERTIME

Shari also worked 4 hours of overtime during this pay period. **Overtime** is time worked beyond the regular hours. A standard workday is 8 continuous hours with scheduled paid breaks plus an unpaid lunch period. A standard workweek is 40 hours in a five-day period of 8 hours each day. According to the Fair Labor Standards Act, employers must pay hourly employees overtime at the rate of 1½ times the regular rate. Shari's overtime rate is $12.00 an hour (8.00 × 1½). Her gross pay is computed as follows:

$$\text{Regular Pay} + \text{Overtime Pay} = \text{Gross Pay}$$

40 hours × $8.00 an hour (regular pay)	$320.00
4 hours × $12.00 an hour (overtime pay)	+ 48.00
Gross pay	$368.00

Shari's gross pay appears under "Gross" at the bottom left of her paycheck stub. The letters "YTD" mean "year-to-date." The amounts on this line are cumulative totals up to this point in the year.

FIGURE 6.1   *Paycheck with Stub*

Marshall Manufacturing Co.

14 Ault Street, Bates, OR 97817-2341

88-0581
1120

PAYROLL CHECK

Co. Code	Department	File No.	Clock No. ID	Social Security No.	TO THE ORDER OF	Pay Date	Check No.
R&T	000108	43329	501 A	999 00 7426	SHARI GREGSON	02 10 —	BELOW

PAY THIS AMOUNT		NET PAY
Two hundred forty-four and 34/100 dollars		$244.34

SHARI GREGSON
1133 ELM STREET,
BATES, OR 97817-1234

DISBURSING AGENT FOR ABOVE EMPLOYER

Jermaine Davis

AUTHORIZED SIGNATURE

BATES BANK
BATES, OREGON

⑀11200581 2⑀   010450   001995⑈

Marshall Manufacturing Co.

14 Ault Street, Bates, OR 97817-2341

Co. Code	Department	File No.	Fed. Status	Name	Pay Period Ending	Pay Date
R&T	000108	43329	501 A	GREGSON, SHARI	02 10 —	02 10 —

Hours Units	Rate	Earnings	Type	Deduction	Type	Deduction	Type
40 00	8 00	320 00	REG	25 00	CR UN		
5 00	12 00	48 00	OT	16 50	H INS		
				3 00	UN DUES		

	Gross	Fed. With. Tax	State With. Tax	Social Security	Medicare	Other Deductions	Net Pay
This Pay	368 00	30 00	21 00	22 82	5 34	44 50	
YTD	2,208 00	180 00	126 00	136 92	32 04	267 00	244 34

SALARY

Perhaps you will work for a salary rather than an hourly wage. Salaried employees usually do not receive additional pay for overtime work. Therefore, your gross pay would be the same as your salary.

Your salary may be stated as an annual (yearly) amount. Your employer will divide the annual salary into equal amounts to be paid each pay period. If you work for $24,000 a year and are paid monthly, your gross pay per paycheck will be $2,000 ($24,000 ÷ 12). If you are paid every two weeks, your gross pay per paycheck will be $923.08, calculated as follows:

52 Weeks in a Year ÷ 2 Weeks per Pay Period = 26 Pay Periods
$24,000 ÷ 26 Pay Periods = $923.08 per Paycheck

If you were paid twice a month rather than every two weeks, you would receive only 24 paychecks (12 months in a year × 2 paychecks per month).

DEDUCTIONS

Amounts subtracted from your gross pay are called **deductions**. Some deductions, such as Social Security tax and federal income tax, are required by law. Other deductions are optional. For example, you can have your employer deduct an amount to deposit into your company-sponsored savings account. In Figure 6.1, Shari has deductions for a credit union payment, health insurance, and union dues.

Employers are required to keep detailed records of wages earned and hours worked for inspection by the Department of Labor. With each paycheck, you will receive a detailed list of all deductions taken from your gross pay. Optional deductions may not be withheld without your written consent except by court order. This does not apply to taxes, Social Security, and other deductions required by law to be withheld from all paychecks.

NET PAY

When all deductions are taken out of your gross pay, the amount left is your **net pay**. It is the amount of your paycheck, which is often referred to as "take-home pay." It is the amount you can actually spend as you wish. Stated mathematically:

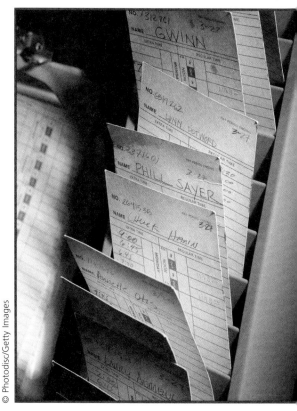
© Photodisc/Getty Images

Why would an employer track the number of hours that an employee works?

Regular Pay (Wages or Salary) + Overtime Pay = Gross Pay
Gross Pay − Deductions = Net Pay

Figure 6.2 shows Shari Gregson's withholding sheet. It lists weekly gross pay, deductions, and net pay. Save your withholding sheets or paycheck stubs that list the amounts withheld from your gross pay. You can use these to check the accuracy of the Form W-2 your employer gives you for your income tax return. Required deductions include federal, state, and local income taxes, as well as Social Security and Medicare taxes. In Figure 6.1, the deductions for Shari appear at the bottom of the paycheck stub.

GLOBAL *View*

Article 7 of Mexico's Federal Labor Law requires employers to employ at least 90 percent Mexican workers in their enterprises. All technical and professional workers must be Mexican, unless there are no Mexican workers qualified in a particular specialty. In that case, the employer may employ foreign workers, but only to the extent of 10 percent of the labor force engaged in the specialty. The employer and the foreign workers are required to train the Mexican workers in the specialty. Article 7 is not applicable to company directors, administrators, and general managers.

THINK *CRITICALLY*

Does Article 7 help or hinder development of the Mexican workforce? What might be its impact on emigration from foreign countries to Mexico?

FIGURE 6.2 *Employee Withholding Sheet*

EMPLOYEE WITHHOLDING SHEET

Employee Name Shari Gregson   Social Security Number 999-00-7426

Pay Period: ☒ weekly   ☐ bimonthly   ☐ monthly

Number of allowances: 1   ☐ married   ☒ single

GROSS PAY

   1. Regular Wages: 40 hours at $ 8.00 /hr. = $ 320.00

or

   2. Regular Salary: =

   3. Overtime: 4 hours at $ 12.00/hr. =   48.00

   GROSS PAY ....$ 368.00

REQUIRED DEDUCTIONS

   4. Federal Income Tax (use tax tables) ....$ 30.00

   5. State Income Tax (use tax tables) 21.00

   6. Social Security Tax (use 6.2% × gross pay, up to $87,900) 22.82

   7. Medicare Tax (use 1.45% × gross pay) 5.34

OTHER DEDUCTIONS

   8. Insurance. 16.50

   9. Union Dues 3.00

   10. Credit Union 25.00

   11. Savings . . . .

   12. Retirement. . . . .

   13. Charity . . . .

   14. Other: _____ . . . . _____

           _____ . . . . _____

     TOTAL DEDUCTIONS (total lines 4 through 14) ....$ 123.66

NET PAY (subtract total deductions from gross pay) ....$ 244.34

The amounts to be withheld are determined from tax withholding tables. Figure 6.3 shows part of the weekly withholding table for the state of Oregon. Figure 6.4 shows part of the weekly federal withholding tax table. If you were paid monthly, you would use tax tables provided for a monthly pay period.

To determine the proper amount to withhold, first identify the appropriate withholding table for your pay period. For example, Shari Gregson in Figure 6.2 is being paid weekly, so you can use the weekly table in Figure 6.3 to find her state withholding. Move your finger down the left side of the table to the range that includes the employee's gross pay. Shari's gross pay of $368.00 falls in the table's range of $360–$380. Then run your finger to the right until you get to

FIGURE 6.3 *State Tax Withholding Table—Weekly Payroll*

Weekly payroll period (Oregon)

Amount of tax to be withheld

Wage		Number of Withholding Allowances																
		Two or Less						Three or More										
At	But Less	Single			Married			Single or Married										
Least	Than	0	1	2	0	1	2	3	4	5	6	7	8	9	10	11	12	13	14
0 –	20	0	0	0	0	0	0	0	0	0	0	0	0	0	0	0	0	0	0
20 –	40	0	0	0	0	0	0	0	0	0	0	0	0	0	0	0	0	0	0
40 –	60	1	0	0	0	0	0	0	0	0	0	0	0	0	0	0	0	0	0
60 –	80	2	0	0	0	0	0	0	0	0	0	0	0	0	0	0	0	0	0
80 –	100	3	0	0	1	0	0	0	0	0	0	0	0	0	0	0	0	0	0
100 –	120	4	1	0	2	0	0	0	0	0	0	0	0	0	0	0	0	0	0
120 –	140	5	2	0	3	0	0	0	0	0	0	0	0	0	0	0	0	0	0
140 –	160	7	4	1	4	1	0	0	0	0	0	0	0	0	0	0	0	0	0
160 –	180	8	5	2	5	2	0	0	0	0	0	0	0	0	0	0	0	0	0
180 –	200	9	7	4	6	3	0	0	0	0	0	0	0	0	0	0	0	0	0
200 –	220	11	8	5	7	4	1	0	0	0	0	0	0	0	0	0	0	0	0
220 –	240	12	10	7	9	6	3	0	0	0	0	0	0	0	0	0	0	0	0
240 –	260	14	12	9	10	7	4	1	0	0	0	0	0	0	0	0	0	0	0
260 –	280	16	13	11	11	9	5	2	0	0	0	0	0	0	0	0	0	0	0
280 –	300	17	15	12	12	10	7	4	0	0	0	0	0	0	0	0	0	0	0
300 –	320	19	16	14	14	11	8	5	2	0	0	0	0	0	0	0	0	0	0
320 –	340	20	18	15	15	12	10	6	3	0	0	0	0	0	0	0	0	0	0
340 –	360	22	19	17	16	14	11	8	5	1	0	0	0	0	0	0	0	0	0
360 –	380	23	21	19	18	15	12	10	6	3	0	0	0	0	0	0	0	0	0
380 –	400	25	23	20	19	17	14	11	8	5	2	0	0	0	0	0	0	0	0
400 –	420	26	24	22	21	18	16	13	10	7	4	1	0	0	0	0	0	0	0

the proper number of allowances and marital status. Shari's form shows that she is single and claims 1 allowance. In Figure 6.3, the number that falls in the column for a single person with 1 allowance, making between $360 and $380, is $21. Notice that $21 shows in the state income tax line on Shari's withholding sheet.

Following the same process, you can find Shari's federal withholding from Figure 6.4. Try it. Did you find the number $30 in the table, as shown on Shari's withholding sheet for federal income tax?

The Social Security deduction is withheld at the standard rate of 6.2 percent of the first $102,000 (for 2008). The Medicare tax deduction is withheld at the rate of 1.45 percent of all pay earned. Employers must contribute matching amounts into each employee's Medicare and Social Security accounts. For example, Figure 6.2 shows Shari's Medicare tax withholding as $5.34 this week. As a result, Shari's employer will also contribute $5.34 into Shari's Medicare account. Congress periodically increases the withholding rate and maximum amount as needed to keep enough tax money coming in to pay Social Security benefits.

In addition to required deductions, the optional deductions an employee has authorized will be subtracted from gross pay to arrive at net pay. The most common of these deductions are insurance payments, union dues, credit union payments, savings deposits, retirement contributions, and charitable contributions.

FIGURE 6.4   *Federal Tax Withholding Table—Weekly Payroll*

SINGLE Persons—WEEKLY Payroll Period
(For Wages Paid in 2008)

| If the wages are— | | And the number of withholding allowances claimed is— | | | | | | | | | | |
At least	But less than	0	1	2	3	4	5	6	7	8	9	10
		The amount of income tax to be withheld is—										
$0	$55	$0	$0	$0	$0	$0	$0	$0	$0	$0	$0	$0
55	60	1	0	0	0	0	0	0	0	0	0	0
60	65	1	0	0	0	0	0	0	0	0	0	0
65	70	2	0	0	0	0	0	0	0	0	0	0
70	75	2	0	0	0	0	0	0	0	0	0	0
75	80	3	0	0	0	0	0	0	0	0	0	0
80	85	3	0	0	0	0	0	0	0	0	0	0
85	90	4	0	0	0	0	0	0	0	0	0	0
90	95	4	0	0	0	0	0	0	0	0	0	0
95	100	5	0	0	0	0	0	0	0	0	0	0
100	105	5	0	0	0	0	0	0	0	0	0	0
105	110	6	0	0	0	0	0	0	0	0	0	0
110	115	6	0	0	0	0	0	0	0	0	0	0
115	120	7	0	0	0	0	0	0	0	0	0	0
120	125	7	0	0	0	0	0	0	0	0	0	0
125	130	8	1	0	0	0	0	0	0	0	0	0
130	135	8	1	0	0	0	0	0	0	0	0	0
135	140	9	2	0	0	0	0	0	0	0	0	0
140	145	9	2	0	0	0	0	0	0	0	0	0
145	150	10	3	0	0	0	0	0	0	0	0	0
150	155	10	3	0	0	0	0	0	0	0	0	0
155	160	11	4	0	0	0	0	0	0	0	0	0
160	165	11	4	0	0	0	0	0	0	0	0	0
165	170	12	5	0	0	0	0	0	0	0	0	0
170	175	12	5	0	0	0	0	0	0	0	0	0
175	180	13	6	0	0	0	0	0	0	0	0	0
180	185	13	6	0	0	0	0	0	0	0	0	0
185	190	14	7	0	0	0	0	0	0	0	0	0
190	195	14	7	1	0	0	0	0	0	0	0	0
195	200	15	8	1	0	0	0	0	0	0	0	0
200	210	16	9	2	0	0	0	0	0	0	0	0
210	220	17	10	3	0	0	0	0	0	0	0	0
220	230	19	11	4	0	0	0	0	0	0	0	0
230	240	20	12	5	0	0	0	0	0	0	0	0
240	250	22	13	6	0	0	0	0	0	0	0	0
250	260	23	14	7	0	0	0	0	0	0	0	0
260	270	25	15	8	1	0	0	0	0	0	0	0
270	280	26	16	9	2	0	0	0	0	0	0	0
280	290	28	18	10	3	0	0	0	0	0	0	0
290	300	29	19	11	4	0	0	0	0	0	0	0
300	310	31	21	12	5	0	0	0	0	0	0	0
310	320	32	22	13	6	0	0	0	0	0	0	0
320	330	34	24	14	7	0	0	0	0	0	0	0
330	340	35	25	15	8	1	0	0	0	0	0	0
340	350	37	27	17	9	2	0	0	0	0	0	0
350	360	38	28	18	10	3	0	0	0	0	0	0
360	370	40	30	20	11	4	0	0	0	0	0	0
370	380	41	31	21	12	5	0	0	0	0	0	0
380	390	43	33	23	13	6	0	0	0	0	0	0
390	400	44	34	24	14	7	1	0	0	0	0	0
400	410	46	36	26	15	8	2	0	0	0	0	0
410	420	47	37	27	17	9	3	0	0	0	0	0

SELF-EMPLOYED REQUIREMENTS

People who are self-employed do not have employee deductions and withholdings. Instead, they must make estimated tax payments quarterly (four times during the year). To do this, self-employed people estimate the total amount they will owe in taxes for the coming year. They divide this number by 4 to determine the amount to pay each quarter. The IRS credits each payment toward their tax obligation for the year.

Like other workers, self-employed people must pay Social Security tax and Medicare tax. However, since self-employed people are both employee and employer, they must pay both the employee and employer-matching contributions to Social Security and Medicare. Thus, for Social Security tax, self-employed people pay 12.4 percent of gross income (6.2% × 2). For Medicare tax, they pay 2.9 percent (1.45% × 2). The total of 15.3 percent is called the **self-employment tax**. It is the total Social Security and Medicare tax, including employer-matching contributions, paid by people who work for themselves.

BENEFITS AND INCENTIVES

Many employers offer *benefits*, which are forms of employee compensation in addition to pay. Common benefits include health insurance, retirement savings plans, pension plans, paid sick leave and vacations, and profit sharing. Some of these benefits are required by law (such as unemployment compensation, workers' compensation, and matching Social Security and Medicare taxes). Others are at the option of the employer. Benefits are often offered to full-time employees only.

PROFIT SHARING

Profit sharing is a plan that allows employees to receive a portion of the company's profits at the end of the corporate year. The more profits the company makes, the more the company has to share with employees. Profit sharing is considered **incentive pay**—money offered to encourage employees to strive for higher levels of performance. Employers offer profit sharing because it links part of employee pay with company profit goals, giving employees an incentive to work harder and reduce inefficiencies.

PAID VACATIONS AND HOLIDAYS

Most businesses provide full-time employees with a set amount of paid vacation time. This means that while you are on vacation, you are paid as usual. It is not uncommon to receive a week's paid vacation after a year of full-time employment, two weeks after two years, three weeks after five years' employment, and so on.

A benefit that you are likely to receive for any full-time job is paid time off for holidays. Paid holidays typically include:

- Christmas
- Thanksgiving
- Fourth of July
- Labor Day
- Memorial Day

Other holidays that many companies consider paid holidays are New Year's Day, Veterans Day, Martin Luther King Day, and Presidents Day. An employee required to work on a holiday is usually paid double or more than double the regular hourly rate of pay.

EMPLOYEE SERVICES

Employee services are the extras that companies offer in order to improve employee morale and working conditions. Many companies offer employee discounts, social and recreational programs, free parking, tuition reimbursement for college courses, wellness programs, and counseling for employee problems.

▮ CHILD CARE

Child care is a major issue for working parents. Many companies provide on-site child-care facilities as well as coverage of child-care expenses as a part of employee benefit packages. In years to come, federal laws are likely to include more child-care incentives for employers of working parents.

▮ SICK PAY

Many businesses also provide an allowance of days each year for illness, with pay as usual. It is customary to receive three to ten days a year as "sick days" without deductions from pay.

▮ LEAVES OF ABSENCE

Some employers allow employees to temporarily leave their jobs (without pay) for certain reasons, such as having children or completing their education, and return to their jobs at a later time. While a leave of absence may be unpaid, it has an important advantage: it gives job security and permits you to take time off for important events in your life. In addition, employers sometimes allow personal days (absences for personal reasons) so that employees can attend to important matters without calling in "sick" when they aren't sick.

▮ INSURANCE

Most large companies provide group insurance plans for all employees. (All kinds of group insurance are covered in more detail in Chapter 27.) A few plans are paid for almost entirely by the employer, as a part of employee compensation. Most plans require that employees pay for part of their own coverage, as well as to cover dependents (spouse and children).

- *Group Health Insurance.* Most employers provide full-time employees with one or more options for group health insurance plans.
- *Group Life Insurance.* Many companies offer group life insurance. However, when you leave your current employment, the group policy may not go with you. The employer may pay an amount each month for standard coverage for each employee. Employees who want additional coverage often can pay for it through payroll deductions.

© Image Source/Getty Images

What types of group insurance plans do employers usually offer?

- *Group Dental Insurance.* Most dental plans provide a maximum benefit per year per family member. Orthodontia (braces) often is not covered.
- *Group Vision Insurance.* Vision insurance covers the cost of prescription lenses and eye examinations once every few years.

BONUSES AND STOCK OPTIONS

Bonuses are incentive pay based on quality of work done, years of service, or company sales or profits. Holiday bonuses are often based on years of service. If a company reaches its sales and profit goals in a year, employees may receive bonuses to reward their efforts in achieving those goals.

Stock options give employees the right to buy a set number of shares of the company's stock at a fixed price. The employees benefit as long as the stock price goes up. Many types of stock option plans exist.

PENSION AND SAVINGS PLANS

Some employers provide pension plans for retirement. Pension plans are funded by the employer. When an employee retires, he or she receives a monthly check. Employees become **vested** (entitled to the full retirement account) after a specified period of time, such as five years.

Employer-sponsored retirement savings plans include the 401(k) for private employers or a 403(b) for government employers. Employers do not bear the full cost of these plans, and as a result, many companies are switching from pensions to these savings plans. Employees put money aside in these accounts; the employer may also (but is not required to) contribute money to the employee's account. Generally, withdrawing funds from savings plans before retirement will result in financial penalties. However, some 401(k) plans allow employees to take out loans without penalty based on certain restrictions.

TRAVEL EXPENSES

Companies that require employees to travel in the course of their work often provide a company car or a mileage allowance if employees use their own car. Generally, car insurance, gasoline, and repair and maintenance expenses for the company automobile are also provided. While out of town, employees may receive a daily allowance to cover their hotel, meals, and other travel expenses. In some cases, expenses may be charged to a company credit card. Other times, employees will have to submit an expense report along with receipts for reimbursement at a later date.

EVALUATING EMPLOYEE BENEFITS

Many of these optional benefits are of great value to employees. Benefits generally are not taxable to employees (except bonuses and other benefits paid in cash), yet they provide valuable coverage and advantages. Generally, large companies provide more extensive optional benefits than do small companies.

In recent years, employee benefits have been expanded to meet the needs of different life situations. *Cafeteria-style employee benefits* are programs that allow workers to select from a range of employer-paid benefits up to a certain total value, based on personal needs. Flexibility in the selection of benefits has become quite common. For example, a married employee with children might opt for increased life and health insurance, while a single parent may choose child-care services.

Business Management & Administration

Payroll clerks may work in human resource departments, or they may work for large corporations that specialize in outsourced payroll services. Wherever they work, they perform vital functions—ensuring that employees get paid on time and that their pay is accurate.

Payroll clerks are found in or for every business or industry. Workers train on the job and have very good computer skills. They process large amounts of data and perform a variety of tasks, from entering data to preparing federal tax forms (for reporting payroll and its deductions).

The work of payroll clerks is more difficult with the advent of new types of work benefits, from 401(k) accounts to HSAs (Health Savings Accounts). They must always be on top of change.

Employment Outlook

- Slower than average employment growth is expected.

Job Titles

- Payroll clerk
- Timekeeping clerk
- Payroll office specialist

Needed Skills

- A high school diploma or GED is required.
- Excellent computer skills and an aptitude for math are needed.
- Good interpersonal and communication skills are helpful.

What's it like to work in... *Payroll*

Carolyn works a typical 40-hour week job. She sometimes works overtime if a new payroll contract is signed. As a payroll specialist for a large corporation that provides outsourced payroll services, Carolyn knows the importance of doing accurate work and meeting deadlines.

Her cubicle looks a lot like that of the other 45 workers on her floor of the office building. It's clean, pleasant, and comfortable. Her computer is state-of-the-art. She knows the best and newest software programs available in the payroll industry.

Carolyn understands the need for privacy and confidentiality. Her work involves very sensitive information about employees for many companies.

In her spare time, Carolyn is preparing to take an exam to become certified. A CPP (certified payroll professional) is a designation that will bring her a raise and possibly a promotion. After three years on the job, she is eager to move into a supervisory role.

What About You?

Do you have an aptitude for math and accounting? Do you like learning to use new computer programs? Would you consider a career in payroll?

Assessment

KEY TERMS REVIEW

Match the terms with the definitions.

_____ 1. Time worked beyond the regular hours

_____ 2. Money offered to encourage employees to strive for higher levels of performance

_____ 3. Amounts subtracted from gross pay

_____ 4. The total amount earned before any deductions are subtracted

_____ 5. The amount left after deductions are taken out of gross pay

a. deductions

b. gross pay

c. incentive pay

d. net pay

e. overtime

f. self-employment tax

g. vested

_____ 6. The point at which employees have full rights to their retirement accounts

_____ 7. The total of 15.3 percent for Social Security and Medicare tax paid by people who work for themselves

CHECK YOUR UNDERSTANDING

8. What is included in gross pay? List optional and required deductions from gross pay.

9. What are some employee benefits and incentives provided at many workplaces?

APPLY YOUR KNOWLEDGE

10. Based on the following information, compute gross pay: Regular hours worked are 40; overtime hours worked are 5. Regular rate of pay is $8.55 per hour.

THINK CRITICALLY

11. Some people work for companies because they want lots of overtime. Other people avoid jobs that require overtime. While overtime hours pay 1½ times the regular rate, they take away personal time. What is your position regarding overtime? Explain your answer.

12. Employee benefits are worth a large sum and, in some cases, are more important to workers than the amount of take-home pay. List benefits that are of value to you, in order of importance. Give a reason for each choice.

Work Schedules and Unions

GOALS

- Describe flexible work arrangements for employees.
- Describe the role of unions and professional organizations.

TERMS

- flextime, *p. 126*
- compressed workweek, *p. 127*
- job rotation, *p. 127*
- job sharing, *p. 127*
- labor union, *p. 128*
- collective bargaining, *p. 128*
- seniority, *p. 128*
- lobbying, *p. 129*

FLEXIBLE WORK ARRANGEMENTS

Many employers are responding to the changing lifestyles and needs of their employees. By designing more flexible jobs, employers can reduce absenteeism, burnout, and turnover.

ALTERED WORKWEEKS

Many firms have experimented with altered workweeks to get away from the standard eight-hours-a-day, five-days-a-week work schedule.

Flextime

Flexible scheduling, or **flextime**, is a type of work schedule that allows employees to choose their working hours within defined limits. Flextime plans generally require all employees to be present during a core time period. Employees can then choose the rest of their work hours around this core period. Employees negotiate their starting times, usually within a three- to four-hour period. They may begin working as early as 6 a.m. or as late as 9 or 10 a.m.

Even though starting times are flexible, most employers require employees to work a set number of hours per day. For example, a person arriving at 6 a.m. would be finished by 3 p.m. (having a one-hour unpaid lunch break), while a person arriving at 10 a.m. would be finished at 7 p.m. The core time period is a crucial time during the day when all employees must be working. This core period may be between 10 a.m. and 3 p.m., the peak hours for business activity.

Flextime is good for business because employees are responsible for working a full day regardless of when they arrive on the job. Employees experience greater job satisfaction because flextime helps them fulfill their personal needs. For example, employees who need to pick up children from school would find it convenient to be off at 3 p.m. Flextime also allows for the scheduling of medical or other appointments, and it reduces stress caused by the pressure of meeting strict work schedules.

Compressed Workweek

A **compressed workweek** is a work schedule that fits the normal 40-hour workweek into less than five days. The typical compressed workweek is ten hours a day for four days, followed by three days off. Some types of work are better suited to a compressed schedule than are others. For example, some kinds of strenuous physical or mental work are probably not suitable for a compressed workweek.

JOB ROTATION

Job rotation is a job design in which employees are trained to do more than one specialized task. Employees "rotate" from one task to another. Job rotation gives employees more variety in their work and allows them to use different skills. It reduces boredom and burnout, leading to greater job satisfaction. A major advantage of job rotation for both employer and employee is that information and ideas are freely exchanged among employees, so that everyone knows how to do each task. If one worker is absent, another can take over and keep the work flowing.

JOB SHARING

Job sharing is a job design in which two people share one full-time position. They split the salary and benefits according to each person's contributions. Job sharing is especially attractive to people who want part-time work. By satisfying employees' needs for more personal time, job sharing reduces absenteeism and tardiness, lowers fatigue, and improves productivity.

PERMANENT PART-TIME

Many employees choose to work only part time (16–25 hours a week). Companies can save on salary and benefits by hiring permanent part-time employees. Part-time work usually provides some benefits to the employee, such as job security, while allowing freedom to spend more time away from work. Parents with small children, older employees, and others may find that permanent part-time work best meets their needs.

Why would a worker want to participate in job sharing?

© Digital Vision/Getty Images

TELECOMMUTING

Advances in technology have made *telecommuting* possible. Telecommuters can work at home or on the road and stay in contact with their manager and coworkers through e-mail, fax, and cell phone. They may participate in meetings through videoconferencing technology, allowing them to see and interact with other meeting participants. Employees who telecommute often do computer-related work, such as data entry, Web design, information processing, or software development. Working at home is convenient and gives the worker flexibility. Telecommuting does not work well in jobs that require frequent face-to-face interaction among employees or that require employees to work together in one place to create a product.

LABOR UNIONS AND PROFESSIONAL ORGANIZATIONS

Many jobs involve union membership or participation in a professional organization as a requirement of employment. Unions are groups of people joined together for a common purpose. A **labor union** is a group of people who work in the same or similar occupations, organized for the benefit of all employees in these occupations.

FUNCTIONS OF UNIONS

Labor unions have four major functions:

- Recruit new members
- Engage in collective bargaining
- Support political candidates who support members' interests
- Provide support services for members

Unions support their members by helping to keep them employed, negotiating wages and working conditions, providing credentials for job-seeking employees, and providing the training members need to obtain and keep jobs.

The main function of unions is **collective bargaining**, which is the process of negotiating a work contract for union members. Terms of the contract set working conditions, wages, overtime rates, hours of work, and benefits. The contract also spells out a grievance procedure. A *grievance* is a formal complaint, by an employee or by the union, that the employer has violated some aspect of the work contract.

Work contracts often provide for *seniority rights.* **Seniority** refers to the length of time on the job and is used to determine transfers, promotions, and vacation time according to most union contracts. Under this policy, the longer you work for an employer, the more job security you have. If layoffs become necessary, the most recent hires will be the first to lose their jobs.

When the union and employer cannot agree on the terms of a new contract, the dispute can be mediated. Through *mediation*, a neutral third party (the *mediator* or *arbitrator*) helps the two parties reach a compromise. If they still cannot agree, the union may decide to *strike*, or refuse to work until an agreement is reached.

TYPES OF UNIONS

Unions are self-governing organizations that can be classified into three types: craft unions, industrial unions, and public-employee unions. Elected union leaders often work full time in

NET Bookmark

Starbucks Coffee Company is the largest coffee chain in the world. The Starbucks Workers Union is an organization of Starbucks employees united to improve their wages and working conditions. Access www.cengage.com/school/pfinance/mypf and click on the link for Chapter 6. Browse the union home page and list some of the union's specific goals. With which larger labor organization is the Starbucks Workers Union affiliated? (*Hint:* Click the *About Us* link at the left of the home page.) Do you think Starbucks workers are justified in wanting to unionize? Explain.

www.cengage.com/school/pfinance/mypf

their positions. Unions often employ their own lawyers, doctors, economists, educators, and public relations officials. Dues collected from members pay for the services of these professionals.

Membership in a *craft union* is limited to those who practice that craft or trade (for example, bricklayers, carpenters, or plasterers). Major craft unions exist in the building, printing, and maritime trades, and for railroad employees.

Members of *industrial unions* are skilled, semi-skilled, or unskilled employees in a particular place, industry, or group of industries. Examples include the AFL-CIO, Teamsters, and United Auto Workers. Most of this country's basic industries (steel, automobiles, rubber, glass, machinery, and mining) are heavily unionized.

Municipal, county, state, or federal employees such as firefighters, teachers, and police officers may organize *public-employee unions*. These unions are organized much like craft and industrial unions except that they generally do not hire outside officers. Members serve as union representatives and officers, sometimes with pay from union dues.

What kinds of workers could be members of a craft union?

PROFESSIONAL ORGANIZATIONS

A *professional organization* consists of people in a particular occupation that requires considerable training and specialized skills. Professional organizations also collect dues from members and provide support services. Notable professional organizations include the following:

- American Bar Association (for lawyers)
- American Medical Association (for doctors)
- National Education Association (for educators)

In some cases, membership in a professional organization is required. For example, the IMA (Institute of Management Accountants) administers a national exam for the CMA (certified management accountant), but individual state Boards of Accountancy rather than the AICPA (American Institute of Certified Public Accountants) administer the CPA (certified public accountant) exam. Both the IMA and the AICPA provide most other functions of a professional organization.

Professional organizations provide the following types of services for members:

- Establish and maintain professional standards
- Administer exams, accreditations, and admission requirements
- Publish professional journals to help keep members up to date
- Provide pension, retirement, and insurance benefits for members
- Participate in political action activities, such as **lobbying**, which is an attempt to influence public officials to pass laws and make decisions that benefit the profession

ISSUES IN YOUR WORLD

STARTING A SUMMER BUSINESS

It's the American dream—owning your own business and working for yourself. As a student in high school, you can also share a part of that dream by starting a summer business. You'll gain valuable experience, know what it's like to work independently, and maybe even pave the way for owning your own company in the future.

If a summer business sounds exciting to you, consider these questions:

- *Do you have a skill that you could offer to others, such as light housekeeping, mowing lawns, or delivering newspapers?*

- *Can you make and/or sell a product that others would be interested in buying— for example, flower planters, gift baskets, or crafts?*

To start a summer business, here are some steps to take.

- Get organized. *Capture your business idea on paper. Write down what you wish to accomplish and how to finance it.*

- Talk with people who can help you get started. *These people may be parents, relatives, friends, or others who can assist you with ideas, financing, and/or finding potential customers.*

- Decide how to advertise your business and find customers. *Will you go door to door? Place an ad in the paper? Sometimes you have to spend money to make money. Can you save some money between now and summer to give you that needed cash?*

- Start small and build a solid customer base. *When someone places trust in you and hires you to provide a product or service, do a great job. Your business will grow from word of mouth.*

- Keep good records. *Keep track of money you spend, money you earn, and who owes you money.*

- Give good value to your customers. *Provide a quality product or service and take pride in your work.*

- Keep a list of what went well and what went wrong. *You can learn from your past experience.*

THINK *CRITICALLY*

1. *Have you ever wanted to own your own small business? If so, what type of business would you like to have?*

2. *Do you know people who own their own business? If so, ask how they got started. If not, go into a small business and ask the owner to answer those questions for you. What advice did you receive?*

Assessment

KEY TERMS REVIEW

Match the terms with the definitions. Some terms may not be used.

_____ 1. A policy where the longer you work for an employer, the more job security and rights you have

_____ 2. A schedule that allows employees to choose their working hours within limits

_____ 3. An attempt to influence public officials to pass laws and make decisions that benefit a particular group

_____ 4. The process of negotiating a work contract for union members

_____ 5. A job design in which employees are trained to do more than one specialized task

_____ 6. A work schedule that fits 40 hours of work into less than five days

_____ 7. A group of people who work in the same or similar occupations, organized for the benefit of all employees in these occupations

a. collective bargaining

b. compressed work-week

c. flextime

d. job rotation

e. job sharing

f. labor union

g. lobbying

h. seniority

CHECK YOUR UNDERSTANDING

8. Explain what is meant by an altered workweek. Give several examples.

9. Name several types of labor unions. What is the purpose of a labor union?

APPLY YOUR KNOWLEDGE

10. Interview a person who is working full time and belongs to a labor union or a professional organization. Ask what benefits members receive and what it costs to participate.

THINK CRITICALLY

11. Today's workers may be offered flexible work arrangements such as flextime, compressed workweek, job rotation, job sharing, permanent part-time status, or telecommuting. Why do you think employers offer these alternatives to their employees?

12. Compare and contrast flextime, a compressed workweek, job rotation, and job sharing. List the advantages and disadvantages of each. At which stage in life would you want to have one or more of these options?

Chapter Assessment

SUMMARY

6.1

- Gross pay includes your regular pay (wages or salary) plus overtime wages earned during the pay period.

- Deductions (both required and voluntary) are subtracted from gross pay to determine net pay—the money you actually take home.

- Self-employed people pay both the employee and employer portions of Social Security and Medicare taxes.

- Benefits in addition to pay may include paid time off, employee services, child care, sick pay, leaves of absence, insurance plans, and retirement plans.

- Employees become vested in pension plans and employer-funded savings plans after they have worked a specified number of years for the company.

- Incentive pay offered to encourage employees to strive for higher levels of performance may include profit sharing, bonuses, and stock options.

- Cafeteria-style plans allow employees to choose the benefits that best meet their needs.

6.2

- Flextime, a compressed workweek, job rotation, job sharing, permanent part-time jobs, and telecommuting offer employees flexibility.

- Labor unions—including craft unions, industrial unions, and public-employee unions—use collective bargaining to negotiate the terms of work contracts with employers on behalf of their members.

- Negotiated work contracts often provide for seniority rights.

- Professional organizations serve people in highly skilled occupations. These organizations maintain standards and keep members current in their fields.

- Through lobbying, professional organizations try to influence public officials to take political action that benefits the profession.

APPLY WHAT YOU KNOW

1. How much must an employer pay an hourly employee for hours worked beyond a regular workweek, assuming a regular rate of pay of $12 per hour and 16 overtime hours?

2. Using the payroll tax withholding tables in Figures 6.3 and 6.4, find the state and federal withholding amounts for each of the following cases:

   - For a single person, one allowance, who made $109 last week
   - For a single person, no allowances, who made $222 last week
   - For a single person, three allowances, who made $291 last week

3. Compute the self-employment taxes for a self-employed person who made $40,000 this year. Separate the Social Security and Medicare components.

4. Visit the Social Security Administration online at www.ssa.gov and look up the current-year Social Security changes. List the maximum taxable earnings for Social Security and for Medicare, and the current tax rate on earnings.

5. Visit the American Medical Association online at www.ama-assn.org, click on the About AMA link, and view its mission and what it hopes to accomplish. Who is encouraged to join the association? How do members benefit? What are the AMA's primary goals?

6. Visit the American Bar Association online at www.abanet.org and list or print out the goals of the association.

MAKE ACADEMIC CONNECTIONS

7. **Research** Visit the National Education Association (NEA) online at www.nea.org. Click on an article at the home page and read about a current concern or direction that is the focus of the NEA. Write a report that explains the purpose of its web site, the mission of the NEA, and what services are available to members.

8. **International Studies** Perform Internet research on unions and professional organizations in other countries, including one country in Europe and one country in another continent. Find out how working conditions compare in countries that do and do not have organized labor.

9. **Math** Prepare an employee withholding sheet similar to the one shown in Figure 6.2, using the following information: Mike Anderson, whose Social Security number is 999-00-9962, is paid weekly. He is single and has one withholding allowance. He works in Oregon (use Figures 6.3 and 6.4 to determine his income tax withholdings). He worked 40 hours at his regular rate of $7.70 an hour, and 6 overtime hours last week. In addition to required deductions, he had $22 for insurance, $12 for union dues, and $10 for charitable contributions withheld from his paycheck.

SOLVE PROBLEMS AND

EXPLORE ISSUES

10. Tatum Gibb works for a weekly paycheck. She is single and claims no allowances. Last week she worked five days for a total of 44 hours. Her regular rate of pay is $8.40 an hour. In addition to withholding for federal income tax, state income tax (use Figures 6.3 and 6.4), Medicare, and Social Security, Tatum also has insurance premiums of $16 a week withheld and puts 6 percent of her gross pay into a retirement account. Compute her gross pay, deductions, and net pay.

11. Bret Countryman receives a weekly paycheck. He is single and claims one allowance. Last week, he worked five days for a total of 48 hours. His regular rate of pay is $7.80 an hour. In addition to required deductions, he has $10 a week deducted for his credit union account and gives $2 a week to a charity fund. Compute his gross pay, deductions, and net pay.

12. Alina Delgado works for herself. She estimates that her gross income this year will be $44,000, and she will owe about $12,000 in federal taxes. How much should she pay when she files each quarterly tax return? How much Social Security tax and Medicare tax will she owe for the year? What is the total amount of Alina's self-employment tax?

13. Tone Chin works for an annual salary and is paid every two weeks. His annual salary is $20,700. How much is his gross pay for each paycheck?

14. Andrea Ghani makes an annual salary of $31,200. However, she is paid monthly. How much is her gross pay for each paycheck?

15. Many businesses do not wish to have labor unions at their companies. While legally they cannot forbid them, they offer wage rates that are equal to or higher than union wages, thus giving workers little reason to want a union. The workers enjoy the same benefits as their unionized colleagues without having to pay union dues. Employees in such companies are called "freeloaders," because they benefit from unions but do not help pay for them. Would you want to join a union if you could avoid it (thus having more take-home pay)? Why or why not?

EXTEND YOUR LEARNING

16. **Ethics** Lobbying is often thought to be a legalized form of bribing public officials. Some groups, such as the American Medical Association and the National Education Association, do extensive lobbying of legislators, at both the state and federal levels. Some citizens feel this is an unfair use of political power. As individuals, they cannot afford to hire a lobbyist to represent them to gain influence. They argue that big unions and professional organizations shouldn't be able to do so either. Do you agree or disagree? What ethical issues are involved?

For related activities and links, go to **www.cengage.com/school/pfinance/mypf**

Federal Income Tax

7.1   *Our Tax System*

7.2   *Filing Tax Returns*

Consider **THIS**

When Jacob started his after-school part-time job last year, he filled out a Form W-4 declaring zero exemptions. At the end of the year, his employer sent him a Form W-2 listing the amounts that were withheld for taxes. Jacob must now prepare his first tax return, so he downloads a copy of Form 1040EZ and its instructions from the IRS web site.

"This is great," says Jacob, as he completes the rough draft of his tax return. "I'm looking at a refund. I had a lot more withheld than I'll owe in taxes. Next year, I think I'll plan a little better. It's nice to have a refund, but it would be better to have the right amount withheld so I have full use of my money throughout the year. I could have earned interest on that money if I had put it in a savings account."

Our Tax System

GOALS

- Explain the purpose of taxes and describe the different types of taxes.
- Describe the U.S. tax system and explain how it works.

TERMS

- revenue, *p. 136*
- progressive taxes, *p. 136*
- regressive taxes, *p. 136*
- proportional taxes, *p. 136*
- tax brackets, *p. 137*
- voluntary compliance, *p. 138*
- tax evasion, *p. 138*
- audit, *p. 138*

TYPES OF TAXES

In a free enterprise system such as ours, the government collects money from citizens and businesses in the form of taxes. These incoming funds to the government are called **revenue**. The government spends the revenues received according to priorities set by Congress. The largest source of government revenue is income taxes. Other taxes providing government revenue include Social Security taxes, unemployment insurance taxes, inheritance and estate taxes, excise taxes, import duties, and property taxes.

A commonly accepted principle of tax fairness is that individuals with high incomes should pay more taxes than people with low incomes. This theory is called the *ability-to-pay principle*.

Progressive taxes take a larger share of income as the amount of income grows. Federal income taxes are progressive. For example, someone with low income may pay 15 percent of income as taxes, while someone with higher income may pay 28 percent.

Regressive taxes take a smaller share of income as the amount of income grows. Sales taxes are regressive, because people with lower incomes pay a larger percentage of their income for sales taxes than do people with higher incomes. For example, your state may charge a 5 percent sales tax. If you buy an item worth $10, your tax would be 50 cents ($10 × 0.05 = $0.50), and you would pay $10.50 for the item. For someone who earns $50 a week, this 50 cents represents 1 percent of income ($0.50/$50 = .01 = 1%). For someone who earns $100 a week, this 50 cents represents only half a percent of income ($0.50/$100 = .005 = .5%). Because the price of a product is the same regardless of income, the sales tax paid is also the same and is a bigger burden on the lower-income person.

Almost all consumption taxes (taxes on goods and services) are regressive. Another type of tax on consumption is an excise tax. *Excise taxes* are sales taxes imposed on specific goods and services, such as gasoline, cigarettes, alcoholic beverages, air travel, and telephone service.

Proportional taxes, or *flat taxes*, are taxes for which the rate stays the same, regardless of income. Property taxes are proportional. For example, all people owning property in the same community pay the same tax rate, whether their property is worth $50,000 or $500,000. Everyone owning a house that has the same assessed value would pay the same tax, regardless of income. However, since lower-income people are likely to own property with a lower value, they will pay proportionally less in property taxes than higher-income people.

On a local level, taxes provide services such as education, parks, roads, and police, fire, and health departments. On a national level, they provide salaries for Congress and funds for national defense, highways, wildlife refuges, welfare, foreign aid, and other services. Most of the services (local, state, and national) are provided for the general welfare of all citizens.

THE TAX SYSTEM

Our tax system is complex. Both businesses and individuals pay income taxes and must file income tax returns each year. The basic components that allow the tax system to operate are the IRS, the country's power to tax income, and each taxpayer's willingness to pay his or her fair share.

THE IRS

The *Internal Revenue Service* is an agency of the Department of the Treasury. It has headquarters in Washington, D.C., and seven regional offices throughout the country. The main functions of the IRS are to collect income taxes and to enforce tax laws.

The IRS also provides services to taxpayers. In local offices, IRS employees assist taxpayers in finding information and forms. The IRS prints pamphlets to aid taxpayers in preparing their returns. It also furnishes tax information and instruction booklets free to schools and colleges. The IRS maintains a web site at www.irs.gov, where citizens can get tax information, download tax forms, and even file their taxes electronically.

THE POWER TO TAX

The power to levy taxes rests with Congress. The Constitution provides that "all bills for raising revenue shall originate in the House of Representatives." Proposals to increase or decrease taxes may come from the President, the Department of the Treasury, or a member of Congress representing the interests of a geographic area. The House Ways and Means Committee studies the proposals and makes recommendations to the full House. Revenue bills must pass a vote in both the House and the Senate and then be signed by the President before they become law.

PAYING YOUR FAIR SHARE

Our income tax system is graduated. This means that tax rates increase as taxable income increases. Tax rates apply to income ranges, or **tax brackets**.

© Digital Vision/Getty Images

Do you think the U.S. tax system is fair? Why or why not?

A significant portion of local public school budgets is typically based upon taxes paid by property owners who live within school districts. Elderly people, who often have fixed and limited incomes, may feel that they should not have to fund schools since they no longer have school-age children.

THINK *CRITICALLY*

How do you feel about this point of view? Should elderly property owners be given a tax break or even be exempt from taxes that fund school districts?

Currently, there are six tax brackets, ranging from 10 percent at the low end to 35 percent at the high end. For example, in a recent year, if you had taxable income of $30,000, you would have been in the 15 percent tax bracket. Congress increases the tax rates when needed to bring in more money to balance its budget. When the government spends more than it receives in revenue, it has a *deficit*, or shortage. It must then borrow money to pay its expenses.

Our income tax system is based on **voluntary compliance**, which means that all citizens are expected to prepare and file tax returns of their own accord without force. Responsibility for filing a tax return and paying taxes due rests with the individual. Failure to do so can result in a penalty: interest charges on the taxes owed plus a possible fine. Willful failure to pay taxes is called **tax evasion**, which is a serious crime punishable by a fine, imprisonment, or both.

AN IRS AUDIT

Every year, the IRS calls millions of taxpayers for an **audit**, which is an examination of their tax returns. Taxpayers being audited have three choices:

- They can represent themselves.
- They can give someone the power to take their place, as long as the designated person is a lawyer, certified public accountant, a member of the immediate family, or an enrolled agent (someone who is licensed to prepare tax returns).
- They can bring someone (tax preparer, attorney, or other representative) for support during the session.

Most audit sessions involve nothing more than confirming supporting documentation. Therefore, most taxpayers can go alone unless the matter is unusually complicated. There are three types of audits:

- In an *office audit*, the taxpayer sits down with the auditor to answer questions and produce records.
- In a *correspondence audit*, the IRS sends a letter, asking the taxpayer to respond to specific questions or produce evidence of deductions or other entries on the tax return.
- A *field audit* is similar to an office audit, except that an IRS agent or local representative visits the taxpayer's home or business to examine records or assets, verify information, and ask specific questions.

ISSUES IN YOUR WORLD

SURVIVING AN AUDIT

Every year, the IRS audits millions of American taxpayers. You may be one of them if you make math errors on your tax form or report income that does not match the income on your Form W-2. To avoid the audit, here are some helpful tips:

- Check your math. *Make sure all your additions and subtractions are correct. Many audits result from simple math errors.*
- Fill out the form neatly. *A neat form is easy to read and provokes fewer questions.*
- Use a tax software program. *Tax software will output a neat form and help prevent math errors. It will also help you take advantage of all the credits and deductions you deserve.*
- Keep good records. *Keep receipts for all deductions and credits you claim on your tax return.*
- File on time. *File your tax return by April 15 to avoid penalties and interest.*

Once you receive the audit notice, remember:

- *You have 30 days in which to respond. Get advice and help if needed, and respond to the notice within the time limit.*
- *You can have a representative with you or in your place, such as a CPA, enrolled agent, or attorney.*
- *Bring all of your receipts, forms, instructions, and other documentation with you to prove your case.*
- *Learn more about audits and how to prepare for them from Publication 556 (available at www.irs.gov) and from other print and online resources.*
- *The IRS can make mistakes too. You have rights as a taxpayer (see Publication 1), and in many cases, the Tax Court rules in favor of the taxpayer.*
- *Don't sign forms that take away your rights. Before you sign anything, be sure to get advice from a tax professional.*
- *Stay calm and collected. Behave responsibly, return calls, ask questions, give reasonable explanations, and listen carefully.*

After the audit is complete, you can appeal the auditor's decision if you feel you have good cause.

THINK CRITICALLY

1. *Do you know someone who has been audited by the IRS? Ask that person to share general information about the process. As an alternative, use the Internet to research the audit process. Share what you learned with the class.*
2. *What can you do to avoid an IRS audit?*

Assessment

KEY TERMS REVIEW

Match the terms with the definitions.

_____ 1. *Flat taxes for which the tax rate remains the same regardless of income*

_____ 2. *Taxes that take a smaller share of income as the amount of income grows*

_____ 3. *Willful failure to pay taxes*

_____ 4. *Incoming funds*

_____ 5. *An examination of your tax return and records by the IRS*

_____ 6. *Income tax ranges from 10 to 35 percent based on income*

_____ 7. *A system in which all citizens are expected to prepare and file income tax returns of their own accord without force*

_____ 8. *Taxes that take a larger share of income as the amount of income grows*

a. audit

b. progressive taxes

c. proportional taxes

d. regressive taxes

e. revenue

f. tax brackets

g. tax evasion

h. voluntary compliance

CHECK YOUR UNDERSTANDING

9. *List three types of taxes levied in the United States. Give examples.*

10. *What is the IRS and what is it empowered (by Congress) to do?*

APPLY YOUR KNOWLEDGE

11. *List the types of taxes you and your family pay in a year's time and provide specific examples. Include items such as income tax, sales tax, gasoline tax, excise tax, etc. Categorize those taxes by their type—are they progressive, proportional, or regressive?*

THINK *CRITICALLY*

12. *Some people believe that there are too many taxes and that tax rates are too high. They refuse to pay income taxes to the federal government because they disagree with how the government spends the money. Do you agree with these arguments? Why or why not?*

13. *The IRS is empowered by the U.S. Congress to collect taxes from individuals and businesses. Some people feel that the IRS is too powerful and is abusive in its practices. Do you agree? Explain your answer. Why do taxpayers often hire a lawyer as a form of protection when dealing with the IRS?*

Filing Tax Returns

GOALS
- Define basic tax terminology.
- Prepare tax forms 1040EZ and 1040A.

TERMS
- filing status, *p. 141*
- exemption, *p. 141*
- dependent, *p. 142*
- gross income, *p. 142*
- adjusted gross income, *p. 143*
- itemized deductions, *p. 143*
- standard deduction, *p. 143*
- taxable income, *p. 143*
- tax credit, *p. 144*

TAX TERMINOLOGY

You should prepare your tax forms with the idea of paying your fair share while taking advantage of the tax breaks legally available to you. Let's look at some basic tax terminology.

FILING STATUS

Filing status describes your tax-filing group, which is based on your marital status as of the last day of the tax year. You must mark one of the following as your filing status on your tax form:

- Single person (not married)
- Married person filing a joint return (even though only one spouse may have earned income)
- Married person filing a separate return
- "Head of household" (you may qualify as a head of household whether you are married or single if you meet certain conditions in providing a home for people dependent on you)
- Qualifying widow(er)

The tax instruction booklet contains a more detailed description of these classifications.

EXEMPTIONS

When figuring taxes, an **exemption** is an amount you may subtract from your income for each person who depends on your income to live. Each exemption reduces your taxable income and thus your total tax. As a taxpayer you are

© Photodisc/Getty Images

Why is marital status important when filing taxes?

automatically allowed one exemption for yourself unless someone else (such as a parent) claims you as a dependent on his or her return. If you are filing a joint return, you can take an exemption for your spouse.

You are also allowed exemptions for your dependents. A **dependent** is a person who lives with you and for whom you pay more than half his or her living expenses. Dependents can include children, a spouse, elderly parents, or disabled relatives living with and depending on the taxpayer.

■ GROSS INCOME

Gross income is all the taxable income you receive. *Earned income* refers to money you earned from working. *Unearned income* refers to money you received from passive activity (other than working). Some forms of income are not taxable and are not reported for tax purposes. The most common types of each form of income are listed below.

Earned Income	Unearned Income	Non-Taxable Income
Wages	Interest	Child support
Salaries	Dividends	Gifts
Tips	Alimony	Inheritances
	Unemployment compensation	Life insurance benefits
	Workers' compensation benefits	Veteran's benefits

Scholarships and grants are a form of unearned income. They may be taxable for amounts used for expenses other than tuition and books. Employer-paid tuition is often taxable.

You are also taxed on other forms of income, including winnings from gambling, bartering income, pensions and annuities, Social Security benefits, income from self-employment, rental income, royalties, estate and trust income, and income on sale of property.

Wages, Salaries, and Tips

This category on your Form W-2 includes all income you receive through employment. If you receive tips on your job, you must report your tips to your employer. These earnings must be reported as income and are included with your wages on Form W-2.

Interest Income

Interest income includes all taxable interest from banks, savings and loan associations, credit unions, series HH savings bonds, and so on. You should receive a Form 1099-INT for each investment that earned interest during the year. This form reports the amount of interest you earned from that investment.

Dividend Income

Dividends are money, stock, or other property that corporations pay to stockholders in return for their investment. You will receive a Form 1099-DIV for each stock investment, listing the dividend income. According to the Jobs and Growth Tax Relief Reconciliation Act of 2003, these dividends may be subject to a maximum 15 percent tax rate.

Unemployment Compensation

If you receive any unemployment compensation during the year, you will receive a Form 1099-G, which shows the total you received. You must enter this amount as income on the tax return.

Social Security Benefits

If you receive Social Security payments during the year, 85 percent of this money is taxable if your total income exceeds $25,000 for single taxpayers and $32,000 for married taxpayers filing jointly. You would receive a Form SSA-1099, listing the total paid for the year.

Alimony and Child Support

Money paid to support a former spouse is called *alimony*. It is taxable for the person receiving it and deductible for the person paying it. Money paid to a former spouse for support of dependent children is called *child support*. This income is not taxable for the person receiving it, nor is it deductible for the person paying it.

ADJUSTED GROSS INCOME

The law allows you to subtract some types of spending from gross income. You can "adjust" your income by subtracting such things as contributions to individual retirement accounts (IRAs), student loan interest, and tuition and fees. These adjustments are subtracted from gross income to determine **adjusted gross income**. These adjustments reduce income that is subject to tax. Note that these adjustments are not available on Form 1040EZ.

TAXABLE INCOME

In Chapter 6, you learned that deductions are amounts subtracted from your gross pay to arrive at your take-home pay. On tax returns, **itemized deductions** are expenses you can subtract from adjusted gross income to determine your taxable income. Since your tax is based on your taxable income, anything that reduces taxable income also reduces your tax.

To itemize deductions, you must use Schedule A and Form 1040. Common expenses you may deduct are medical and dental expenses beyond a specified percentage of your income, state and local income taxes, property taxes, home mortgage interest, gifts to charity, losses from theft or property damage, and moving expenses.

If you do not have many deductions, your tax may be less if you take the **standard deduction**. This is a stated amount that you may subtract from adjusted gross income instead of itemizing your deductions. This amount changes each year.

After subtracting your standard deduction (or itemized deductions), you need to compute exemptions. You may deduct a stated amount for each exemption to arrive at your **taxable income**, which is the income on which you will pay tax. You can then determine your tax by looking up your taxable income in a tax table. The Math Minute feature shows formulas for computing income tax.

▮ TAX CREDITS

After determining the tax you owe from the tax table, you may deduct any tax credits for which you qualify. A **tax credit** is an amount subtracted directly from the tax owed. It is different from a deduction. A deduction is subtracted from adjusted gross income. It reduces your tax by reducing the amount of income on which the tax is figured. A tax credit, on the other hand, reduces the tax itself. For example, if the tax table shows that your total tax is $1,000 and you can claim a tax credit of $100, then your tax drops to $900.

The government allows tax credits for certain education expenses, child-care expenses, and other reasons from time to time. The IRS publishes instructions outlining the requirements to qualify for each type of tax credit.

PREPARING YOUR INCOME TAX RETURN

Once you have gathered your income and expense records, you can make a rough draft of your tax return. The tax booklet that accompanies the printed forms contains the instructions for completing the forms. A simple 1040EZ tax

---

MATH *Minute*

CALCULATING INCOME TAX

Gross Income
− Adjustments
_____
Adjusted Gross Income
− Standard Deduction or Itemized Deductions
− Exemptions
_____
Taxable Income

Look up taxable income in tax table to determine tax.

Tax
− Credits
− Payments Made (taxes withheld from paycheck)
_____
Tax Owed or Refund Due

Use the formulas above and the tax table in Figure 7.6 on page 155 to calculate your income tax. Assume you are single, have gross income of $12,000, have adjustments of $500, take the standard deduction of $5,350, claim one exemption of $3,400, have $0 tax credits, and had federal withholdings from your paycheck during the year of $500.

Solution:

$12,000 Gross Income − $500 Adjustments = $11,500 Adjusted Gross Income; $11,500 − $5,350 Standard Deduction − $3,400 Exemption = $2,750 Taxable Income. Tax from Tax Table (Figure 7.6) = $276 − $0 Credits − $500 Payments Made = $224 Refund Due

---

return may require only 15 minutes to prepare. The long Form 1040 may require most of a day after you have gathered all information. In addition to a federal tax return, you may have to file state and local income tax returns.

WHO MUST FILE?

You must file a tax return if you earned enough income to owe taxes. In a recent year, a single person under the age of 65 whose income exceeded $8,750 likely owed taxes and had to file a return. If you did not earn enough to owe taxes but taxes were withheld from your paychecks, you should file a return to claim a refund. You can check the IRS web site to see if you must file.

WHEN TO FILE?

You must file no later than April 15 of the year after you earned income. If April 15 falls on a weekend or holiday, your tax return is due on the next weekday. If you file late, you will have to pay penalties and interest charges.

WHICH FORM TO USE?

All taxpayers must use one of three basic forms (1040, 1040A, or 1040EZ) when filing their return. There are many other supporting forms that may be required to support line items on the basic form. In all, there are nearly 400 federal tax forms. For your first tax return, you will probably use either Form 1040EZ or Form 1040A. Which form you choose will depend on the type and amount of your income, the number of your deductions, and your tax situation.

In general, if your deductions add up to more than the standard deduction, your total tax will be lower if you use Form 1040 and itemize your deductions. Taxpayers who earn more than $100,000 in taxable income must use Form 1040. Those with taxable income less than $100,000 may use any of the three forms. If you have no deductions or credits, less than $1,500 in interest income, and no dependents, you should use Form 1040EZ, which is the easiest form. However, if you qualify for any credits and deductions listed on Form 1040A, use that form. If you have enough deductions to benefit from itemizing, use Form 1040.

WHERE TO BEGIN?

During the year, save all receipts and proofs of payment for your itemized deductions. You will need these receipts to prove the accuracy of your tax return if you are audited. Save all employee withholding records, such as your paycheck stubs. By January 31 you should receive a Form W-2 from each of your employers. Compare it with your records to check for accuracy. Any discrepancies between the Form W-2 and your records should be reported immediately to the employer and corrected.

Gather all other necessary information, including instruction booklets and last year's tax return as a model for preparing this year's return. Once you have gathered all your information, prepare both the short and the long form to see if you can save money by itemizing deductions.

Even if you hire a professional tax preparer, you are responsible for supplying accurate and complete information. Hiring a tax preparer will not guarantee that you are paying the correct amount. You must check the form before you sign it. If you discover an error after the return has been filed, you may file an amended return (Form 1040X) to make corrections.

Save copies of your tax returns, together with all supporting evidence (receipts) and Forms W-2 and other forms such as Form 1099, for six years.

FILING ELECTRONICALLY

You can choose to file your return electronically through the IRS e-file program. Instructions for electronic filing appear on the IRS web site at www .irs.gov/efile. E-filing is free if your income is under $54,000. The web site also allows you to pay taxes online using a debit or credit card. If the government owes you a refund, you can have the refund transferred to your bank account electronically. If you file online, be sure to print a copy of the tax return for your records.

TAX PREPARATION SOFTWARE

Most professional tax preparers use a tax preparation computer program. You can use tax preparation software to do your own taxes if you like. Good software provides all the necessary forms and leads you through the process of filling out the forms. Most tax software also provides tips and additional information to help you identify all the deductions and credits you are allowed. Search the Internet to find information about different brands of tax software. Software producers usually provide a feature tour at their web site.

FORM 1040EZ

You may use Form 1040EZ if you are single or married filing jointly and claim no dependents. Your taxable income must be less than $100,000. Line-by-line instructions for filling out Form 1040EZ are given on the back of the form. Highlights of the instructions are described in the following paragraphs.

Figure 7.1 shows Form W-2 for Roberto Flores. Figure 7.2 shows his completed Form 1040EZ tax return. Roberto is single and claims one exemption. His wages are found on the W-2. Follow along on Roberto's Form 1040EZ as you read the instructions.

Step 1: Name, Address, and Social Security Number

Fill in your name, address, and Social Security number. If you receive a tax forms booklet in the mail, it will include a self-adhesive label that you can place in this section of the form.

Check the "Yes" box if you want $3 to go to the Presidential Election Campaign Fund. This is a fund established by Congress so that taxpayers can share in the costs of election campaigns. The $3 contribution will not increase your tax or reduce your refund.

Step 2: Report Income

- First, enter your total wages, salaries, and tips, as shown on your W-2 form(s). On Roberto's Form W-2, you can see that he earned $14,720. He entered this amount on line 1.

NET Bookmark

Each year, the number of available tax preparation software programs seems to increase. It can be difficult to decide which program will best meet your income tax preparation needs. To make your decision easier, access www.cengage.com/school/pfinance/mypf and click on the link for Chapter 7. Which tax preparation program received the highest rating? What are five features you should look for when choosing a tax program?

www.cengage.com/school/pfinance/mypf

FIGURE 7.1   W-2 for Roberto Flores

22222

a Employee's social security number
999-00-3894

OMB No. 1545-0008

b Employer identification number (EIN)
93-899348488

c Employer's name, address, and ZIP code
Blanton School District T-31
23855 SW 85th
Portland, OR 97215-4562

d Control number

e Employee's first name and initial   Last name   Suff.
Roberto J. Flores
285 SW 28th Street, #8
Portland, OR 97214-4562

f Employee's address and ZIP code

1 Wages, tips, other compensation
$14,720.00

2 Federal income tax withheld
$1,501.00

3 Social security wages
$14,720.00

4 Social security tax withheld
$912.64

5 Medicare wages and tips
$14,720.00

6 Medicare tax withheld
$213.44

7 Social security tips

8 Allocated tips

9 Advance EIC payment

10 Dependent care benefits

11 Nonqualified plans

12a

13 Statutory employee / Retirement plan / Third-party sick pay

12b

14 Other

12c

12d

15 State	Employer's state ID number	16 State wages, tips, etc.	17 State income tax	18 Local wages, tips, etc.	19 Local income tax	20 Locality name
OR	2384762	$14,720.00	$946.00			

Form **W-2** Wage and Tax Statement

20—

Department of the Treasury—Internal Revenue Service

- Second, enter interest earned on savings accounts and any unemployment compensation you may have received. Roberto Flores recorded the $234 of interest he earned on his savings. Add these income figures to the earnings shown in line 1. The result is your adjusted gross income, line 4.
- Next, check if you are claimed as a dependent on another person's tax return. If not, you can enter the amount shown on line 5. This is both the standard deduction and your exemption added together ($5,350 + $3,400 = $8,750).

Step 3: Compute Tax

On line 7, enter the total federal tax withheld, as shown on the W-2 form(s). This is the amount of tax you have already paid. To figure tax owed, look up your taxable income from line 6 in the tax table that comes with your return. It will look similar to the one in Figure 7.3. In the tax table in Figure 7.3, Roberto found that his taxable income of $6,204 fell within the range of $6,200–$6,250. In that row, he located his total tax liability of $623 in the "Single" column and recorded it on line 10.

Step 4: Refund or Amount Owed

If the amount of federal taxes withheld (the amount you already paid) is larger than your total tax (from the tax table), you will receive a refund. If you owe more tax than was withheld, you must pay the difference. Write your check to the United States Treasury and enclose it with your return.

When Roberto subtracted his total tax of $623 from his taxes withheld of $1,501, the difference was $878, which he recorded on line 11a. He decided to have his refund deposited electronically into his checking account. He entered the routing number (the first 9 numbers printed on the bottom of his checks) and account number (the last 7 numbers on the bottom of his checks) in the Refund section of his tax form and checked the box for account type: Checking.

FIGURE 7.2 *1040EZ Tax Return for Roberto Flores*

Department of the Treasury—Internal Revenue Service

Form
1040EZ

**Income Tax Return for Single and
Joint Filers With No Dependents** **20—**

OMB No. 1545-0074

Label

(See page 8.)

Use the IRS label.
Otherwise, please print or type.

L A B E L	H E R E

Your first name and initial — Roberto J.   Last name — Flores

If a joint return, spouse's first name and initial — --------   Last name

Home address (number and street). If you have a P.O. box, see page 9. — 285 SW 28th Street   Apt. no.

City, town or post office, state, and ZIP code. If you have a foreign address, see page 9. — Portland, OR 97214-4562

Your social security number 999 00 3894

Spouse's social security number

▲ You **must** enter your SSN(s) above. ▲

Checking a box below will not change your tax or refund.

Presidential Election Campaign (page 9) ▶

Check here if you, or your spouse if a joint return, want $3 to go to this fund . . . ▶ ☑ **You**   ☐ **Spouse**

Income

Attach Form(s) W-2 here.

Enclose, but do not attach, any payment.

1	Wages, salaries, and tips. This should be shown in box 1 of your Form(s) W-2. Attach your Form(s) W-2.	1	14,720 00
2	Taxable interest. If the total is over $1,500, you cannot use Form 1040EZ.	2	234 00
3	Unemployment compensation and Alaska Permanent Fund dividends (see page 10).	3	0
4	Add lines 1, 2, and 3. This is your **adjusted gross income.**	4	14,954 00
5	If someone can claim you (or your spouse if a joint return) as a dependent, check the applicable box(es) below and enter the amount from the worksheet on back. ☐ **You** ☐ **Spouse** If no one can claim you (or your spouse if a joint return), enter $8,750 if **single;** $17,500 if **married filing jointly.** See back for explanation.	5	8,750 00
6	Subtract line 5 from line 4. If line 5 is larger than line 4, enter -0-. This is your **taxable income.** ▶	6	6,204 00

Payments and tax

7	Federal income tax withheld from box 2 of your Form(s) W-2.	7	1,501 00
8a	**Earned income credit (EIC).**	8a	0
b	Nontaxable combat pay election. 8b		
9	Add lines 7 and 8a. These are your **total payments.** ▶	9	1,501 00
10	**Tax.** Use the amount on **line 6 above** to find your tax in the tax table on pages 18–26 of the booklet. Then, enter the tax from the table on this line.	10	623 00

Refund

Have it directly deposited! See page 15 and fill in 11b, 11c, and 11d or Form 8888.

11a	If line 9 is larger than line 10, subtract line 10 from line 9. This is your **refund.** If Form 8888 is attached, check here ▶ ☐	11a	878 00

▶ **b** Routing number 0 0 1 0 7 3 2 6 4   ▶ **c** Type: ☑ Checking ☐ Savings

▶ **d** Account number 4 1 1 2 0 3 6

Amount you owe

12	If line 10 is larger than line 9, subtract line 9 from line 10. This is the **amount you owe.** For details on how to pay, see page 16. ▶	12	

Third party designee

Do you want to allow another person to discuss this return with the IRS (see page 16)? ☐ **Yes.** Complete the following. ☐ **No**

Designee's name ▶   Phone no. ▶ (   )   Personal identification number (PIN)

Sign here

Joint return? See page 6.

Keep a copy for your records.

Under penalties of perjury, I declare that I have examined this return, and to the best of my knowledge and belief, it is true, correct, and accurately lists all amounts and sources of income I received during the tax year. Declaration of preparer (other than the taxpayer) is based on all information of which the preparer has any knowledge.

Your signature — *Roberto J. Flores*   Date — 3/15/20—   Your occupation — mechanic   Daytime phone number — (503) 555-0052

Spouse's signature. If a joint return, **both** must sign.   Date   Spouse's occupation

Paid preparer's use only

Preparer's signature ▶   Date   Check if self-employed ☐   Preparer's SSN or PTIN

Firm's name (or yours if self-employed), address, and ZIP code ▶   EIN   Phone no. (   )

For Disclosure, Privacy Act, and Paperwork Reduction Act Notice, see page 32.

Cat. No. 11329W

Form **1040EZ** (20—)

FIGURE 7.3 *Part of 1040EZ Tax Table*

20— Tax Table

Example. Mr. Brown is single. His taxable income on line 6 of Form 1040EZ is $26,250. First, he finds the $26,250-26,300 income line. Next, he finds the "Single" column and reads down the column. The amount shown where the income line and filing status column meet is $3,550. This is the tax amount he should enter on line 10 of Form 1040EZ.

At least	But less than	Single	Married filing jointly
		Your tax is—	
26,200	26,250	3,543	3,151
26,250	26,300	(3,550)	3,159
26,300	26,350	3,558	3,166
26,350	26,400	3,565	3,174

If Form 1040EZ, line 6, is —		And you are –	
At least	But less than	Single	Married filing jointly
		Your tax is –	
0	5	0	0
5	15	1	1
15	25	2	2
25	50	4	4
50	75	6	6
75	100	9	9
100	125	11	11
125	150	14	14
150	175	16	16
175	200	19	19
200	225	21	21
225	250	24	24
250	275	26	26
275	300	29	29
300	325	31	31
325	350	34	34
350	375	36	36
375	400	39	39
400	425	41	41
425	450	44	44
450	475	46	46
475	500	49	49
500	525	51	51
525	550	54	54
550	575	56	56
575	600	59	59
600	625	61	61
625	650	64	64
650	675	66	66
675	700	69	69
700	725	71	71
725	750	74	74
750	775	76	76
775	800	79	79
800	825	81	81
825	850	84	84
850	875	86	86
875	900	89	89
900	925	91	91
925	950	94	94
950	975	96	96
975	1,000	99	99

1,000

At least	But less than	Single	Married filing jointly
1,000	1,025	101	101
1,025	1,050	104	104
1,050	1,075	106	106
1,075	1,100	109	109
1,100	1,125	111	111
1,125	1,150	114	114
1,150	1,175	116	116
1,175	1,200	119	119
1,200	1,225	121	121
1,225	1,250	124	124
1,250	1,275	126	126
1,275	1,300	129	129
1,300	1,325	131	131
1,325	1,350	134	134
1,350	1,375	136	136
1,375	1,400	139	139
1,400	1,425	141	141
1,425	1,450	144	144
1,450	1,475	146	146
1,475	1,500	149	149

If Form 1040EZ, line 6, is —		And you are –	
At least	But less than	Single	Married filing jointly
		Your tax is –	
1,500	1,525	151	151
1,525	1,550	154	154
1,550	1,575	156	156
1,575	1,600	159	159
1,600	1,625	161	161
1,625	1,650	164	164
1,650	1,675	166	166
1,675	1,700	169	169
1,700	1,725	171	171
1,725	1,750	174	174
1,750	1,775	176	176
1,775	1,800	179	179
1,800	1,825	181	181
1,825	1,850	184	184
1,850	1,875	186	186
1,875	1,900	189	189
1,900	1,925	191	191
1,925	1,950	194	194
1,950	1,975	196	196
1,975	2,000	199	199

2,000

At least	But less than	Single	Married filing jointly
2,000	2,025	201	201
2,025	2,050	204	204
2,050	2,075	206	206
2,075	2,100	209	209
2,100	2,125	211	211
2,125	2,150	214	214
2,150	2,175	216	216
2,175	2,200	219	219
2,200	2,225	221	221
2,225	2,250	224	224
2,250	2,275	226	226
2,275	2,300	229	229
2,300	2,325	231	231
2,325	2,350	234	234
2,350	2,375	236	236
2,375	2,400	239	239
2,400	2,425	241	241
2,425	2,450	244	244
2,450	2,475	246	246
2,475	2,500	249	249
2,500	2,525	251	251
2,525	2,550	254	254
2,550	2,575	256	256
2,575	2,600	259	259
2,600	2,625	261	261
2,625	2,650	264	264
2,650	2,675	266	266
2,675	2,700	269	269
2,700	2,725	271	271
2,725	2,750	274	274
2,750	2,775	276	276
2,775	2,800	279	279
2,800	2,825	281	281
2,825	2,850	284	284
2,850	2,875	286	286
2,875	2,900	289	289
2,900	2,925	291	291
2,925	2,950	294	294
2,950	2,975	296	296
2,975	3,000	299	299

If Form 1040EZ, line 6, is —		And you are –	
At least	But less than	Single	Married filing jointly
		Your tax is –	

3,000

At least	But less than	Single	Married filing jointly
3,000	3,050	303	303
3,050	3,100	308	308
3,100	3,150	313	313
3,150	3,200	318	318
3,200	3,250	323	323
3,250	3,300	328	328
3,300	3,350	333	333
3,350	3,400	338	338
3,400	3,450	343	343
3,450	3,500	348	348
3,500	3,550	353	353
3,550	3,600	358	358
3,600	3,650	363	363
3,650	3,700	368	368
3,700	3,750	373	373
3,750	3,800	378	378
3,800	3,850	383	383
3,850	3,900	388	388
3,900	3,950	393	393
3,950	4,000	398	398

4,000

At least	But less than	Single	Married filing jointly
4,000	4,050	403	403
4,050	4,100	408	408
4,100	4,150	413	413
4,150	4,200	418	418
4,200	4,250	423	423
4,250	4,300	428	428
4,300	4,350	433	433
4,350	4,400	438	438
4,400	4,450	443	443
4,450	4,500	448	448
4,500	4,550	453	453
4,550	4,600	458	458
4,600	4,650	463	463
4,650	4,700	468	468
4,700	4,750	473	473
4,750	4,800	478	478
4,800	4,850	483	483
4,850	4,900	488	488
4,900	4,950	493	493
4,950	5,000	498	498

5,000

At least	But less than	Single	Married filing jointly
5,000	5,050	503	503
5,050	5,100	508	508
5,100	5,150	513	513
5,150	5,200	518	518
5,200	5,250	523	523
5,250	5,300	528	528
5,300	5,350	533	533
5,350	5,400	538	538
5,400	5,450	543	543
5,450	5,500	548	548
5,500	5,550	553	553
5,550	5,600	558	558
5,600	5,650	563	563
5,650	5,700	568	568
5,700	5,750	573	573
5,750	5,800	578	578
5,800	5,850	583	583
5,850	5,900	588	588
5,900	5,950	593	593
5,950	6,000	598	598

If Form 1040EZ, line 6, is —		And you are –	
At least	But less than	Single	Married filing jointly
		Your tax is –	

6,000

At least	But less than	Single	Married filing jointly
6,000	6,050	603	603
6,050	6,100	608	608
6,100	6,150	613	613
6,150	6,200	618	618
6,200	6,250	623	623
6,250	6,300	628	628
6,300	6,350	633	633
6,350	6,400	638	638
6,400	6,450	643	643
6,450	6,500	648	648
6,500	6,550	653	653
6,550	6,600	658	658
6,600	6,650	663	663
6,650	6,700	668	668
6,700	6,750	673	673
6,750	6,800	678	678
6,800	6,850	683	683
6,850	6,900	688	688
6,900	6,950	693	693
6,950	7,000	698	698

7,000

At least	But less than	Single	Married filing jointly
7,000	7,050	703	703
7,050	7,100	708	708
7,100	7,150	713	713
7,150	7,200	718	718
7,200	7,250	723	723
7,250	7,300	728	728
7,300	7,350	733	733
7,350	7,400	738	738
7,400	7,450	743	743
7,450	7,500	748	748
7,500	7,550	753	753
7,550	7,600	758	758
7,600	7,650	763	763
7,650	7,700	768	768
7,700	7,750	773	773
7,750	7,800	778	778
7,800	7,850	783	783
7,850	7,900	790	788
7,900	7,950	798	793
7,950	8,000	805	798

8,000

At least	But less than	Single	Married filing jointly
8,000	8,050	813	803
8,050	8,100	820	808
8,100	8,150	828	813
8,150	8,200	835	818
8,200	8,250	843	823
8,250	8,300	850	828
8,300	8,350	858	833
8,350	8,400	865	838
8,400	8,450	873	843
8,450	8,500	880	848
8,500	8,550	888	853
8,550	8,600	895	858
8,600	8,650	903	863
8,650	8,700	910	868
8,700	8,750	918	873
8,750	8,800	925	878
8,800	8,850	933	883
8,850	8,900	940	888
8,900	8,950	948	893
8,950	9,000	955	898

Sign and date your tax return. Make sure your W-2 form(s) and check (if applicable) are included with the completed return, and mail them to the regional IRS office designated for your area.

▌FORM 1040A

Individuals who earn less than $100,000 in taxable income can also use Form 1040A. With Form 1040A, you can take more deductions than with the 1040EZ. It is a two-page form. Figure 7.4 shows Forms W-2 for Melissa B. and Michael J. Anderson. Figure 7.5 on pages 152–153 shows their joint return using Form 1040A. Follow along on the form as you read the instructions that follow.

FIGURE 7.4 *Forms W-2 for Melissa Anderson and Michael Anderson*

22222	**a** Employee's social security number 999-00-3214	OMB No. 1545-0008		
b Employer identification number (EIN) 92-186848			**1** Wages, tips, other compensation $18,072.40	**2** Federal income tax withheld $611.00
c Employer's name, address, and ZIP code A&W Welding Supply 85 West Bensington Blvd. Chicago, IL 60615-2358			**3** Social security wages $18,072.40	**4** Social security tax withheld $1,120.49
			5 Medicare wages and tips $18,072.40	**6** Medicare tax withheld $262.05
			7 Social security tips	**8** Allocated tips
d Control number			**9** Advance EIC payment	**10** Dependent care benefits
e Employee's first name and initial Last name Suff. Melissa B. Anderson 312 East 34th Street Chicago, IL 60604-5214			**11** Nonqualified plans	**12a**
			13 Statutory employee ☐ Retirement plan ☐ Third-party sick pay ☐	**12b**
			14 Other	**12c**
				12d
f Employee's address and ZIP code				

15 State Employer's state ID number IL 33-261	**16** State wages, tips, etc. $18,072.40	**17** State income tax $820.00	**18** Local wages, tips, etc.	**19** Local income tax	**20** Locality name

Form **W-2** Wage and Tax Statement   **20—**   Department of the Treasury—Internal Revenue Service

22222	**a** Employee's social security number 999-00-6128	OMB No. 1545-0008		
b Employer identification number (EIN) 91-4813141			**1** Wages, tips, other compensation $11,028.60	**2** Federal income tax withheld $591.00
c Employer's name, address, and ZIP code A Art Studios 48 East 11th Avenue Des Plaines, IL 60601-3132			**3** Social security wages $11,028.60	**4** Social security tax withheld $683.77
			5 Medicare wages and tips $11,028.60	**6** Medicare tax withheld $159.91
			7 Social security tips	**8** Allocated tips
d Control number			**9** Advance EIC payment	**10** Dependent care benefits
e Employee's first name and initial Last name Suff. Michael J. Anderson 312 East 34th Street Chicago, IL 60604-5214			**11** Nonqualified plans	**12a**
			13 Statutory employee ☐ Retirement plan ☐ Third-party sick pay ☐	**12b**
			14 Other	**12c**
				12d
f Employee's address and ZIP code				

15 State Employer's state ID number IL 226421	**16** State wages, tips, etc. $11,028.60	**17** State income tax $706.00	**18** Local wages, tips, etc.	**19** Local income tax	**20** Locality name

Form **W-2** Wage and Tax Statement   **20—**   Department of the Treasury—Internal Revenue Service

Step 1: Name and Address

Write the name, address, and Social Security number for each person filing the return. If you receive a tax forms booklet in the mail, it will include a self-adhesive label that you can place in this section of the form so long as the information on the label still applies.

Michael and Melissa are filing a joint return. Each person filing can elect to give or not give to the Presidential Election Campaign Fund.

Step 2: Filing Status

In this section, select your tax filing status. If married filing separately, you must fill in your spouse's name and Social Security number. If filing as head of household, insert names of any qualifying children who are not your dependents.

Why would a taxpayer elect to use Form 1040?

Step 3: Exemptions

In the Exemptions section, claim yourself and your spouse if you are filing jointly, and enter the names and Social Security numbers of your dependents. Total your exemptions on line 6d.

Step 4: Income

On line 7, enter wages, salaries, tips, and other income as shown on your Form W-2. The Andersons, filing jointly, entered the total earnings from their two Forms W-2.

On lines 8 and 9, report taxable interest and dividend income. If you received over $1,500 in interest, you must complete Schedule 1. The same is true of dividend income.

If you received any tax-exempt interest, list it on line 8b, even though you would not have to pay tax on it. The rest of the Income section of Form 1040A requires you to report the taxable amount of any money received from IRAs, pensions, unemployment compensation, and Social Security benefits.

After listing income received from all sources, you would add them to determine total income for line 15 of Form 1040A.

Step 5: Adjusted Gross Income

You can deduct educator expenses, contributions to an individual retirement account (IRA), student loan interest, and tuition fees in this section of the form. You would then subtract the total adjustments from gross income (line 20) to determine your adjusted gross income (line 21).

FIGURE 7.5 *Joint Tax Return*

Form

1040A

Department of the Treasury—Internal Revenue Service

U.S. Individual Income Tax Return   **20—**

IRS Use Only—Do not write or staple in this space.

Label
(See page 15.)

Use the IRS label.
Otherwise, please print or type.

L
A
B
E
L

H
E
R
E

Your first name and initial: Melissa B.
Last name: Anderson

If a joint return, spouse's first name and initial: Michael J.
Last name: Anderson

Home address (number and street). If you have a P.O. box, see page 15.
312 East 34th Street

Apt. no.

City, town or post office, state, and ZIP code. If you have a foreign address, see page 15.
Chicago, IL 60604-5214

OMB No. 1545-0074

Your social security number
999 00 3214

Spouse's social security number
999 00 6128

▲ You **must** enter your SSN(s) above. ▲

Presidential Election Campaign ▶ Check here if you, or your spouse if filing jointly, want $3 to go to this fund (see page 15) ▶

Checking a box below will not change your tax or refund.

☐ You   ☐ Spouse

Filing status
Check only one box.

1 ☐ Single
2 ☑ Married filing jointly (even if only one had income)
3 ☐ Married filing separately. Enter spouse's SSN above and full name here. ▶
4 ☐ Head of household (with qualifying person). (See page 16.) If the qualifying person is a child but not your dependent, enter this child's name here. ▶ _____
5 ☐ Qualifying widow(er) with dependent child (see page 17)

Exemptions

If more than six dependents, see page 18.

6a ☑ **Yourself.** If someone can claim you as a dependent, **do not** check box 6a.

b ☑ **Spouse**

c **Dependents:**

(1) First name Last name	(2) Dependent's social security number	(3) Dependent's relationship to you	(4) ✓ if qualifying child for child tax credit (see page 18)
William Anderson	999 00 2915	Son	☐
Diane Anderson	999 00 4814	Daughter	☐
			☐
			☐
			☐
			☐

Boxes checked on 6a and 6b: **2**

No. of children on 6c who:
• lived with you **2**
• did not live with you due to divorce or separation (see page 19) ____

Dependents on 6c not entered above ____

Add numbers on lines above ▶ **4**

d Total number of exemptions claimed.

Income

Attach Form(s) W-2 here. Also attach Form(s) 1099-R if tax was withheld.

If you did not get a W-2, see page 21.

Enclose, but do not attach, any payment.

7 Wages, salaries, tips, etc. Attach Form(s) W-2.   7   29,101 | 00

8a **Taxable** interest. Attach Schedule 1 if required.   8a   284 | 00
 b **Tax-exempt** interest. **Do not** include on line 8a.   8b

9a Ordinary dividends. Attach Schedule 1 if required.   9a   168 | 00
 b Qualified dividends (see page 22).   9b

10 Capital gain distributions (see page 22).   10   ---

11a IRA distributions. 11a | 11b Taxable amount (see page 22). 11b   ---

12a Pensions and annuities. 12a | 12b Taxable amount (see page 23). 12b   ---

13 Unemployment compensation and Alaska Permanent Fund dividends.   13   ---

14a Social security benefits. 14a | 14b Taxable amount (see page 25). 14b   ---

15 Add lines 7 through 14b (far right column). This is your **total income.** ▶   15   29,553 | 00

Adjusted gross income

16 Educator expenses (see page 25).   16

17 IRA deduction (see page 27).   17   500 | 00

18 Student loan interest deduction (see page 29).   18   500 | 00

19 Tuition and fees deduction. Attach Form 8917.   19

20 Add lines 16 through 19. These are your **total adjustments.**   20   1,000 | 00

21 Subtract line 20 from line 15. This is your **adjusted gross income.** ▶   21   28,553 | 00

For Disclosure, Privacy Act, and Paperwork Reduction Act Notice, see page 74.   Cat. No. 11327A   Form **1040A** (20—)

FIGURE 7.5 *Joint Tax Return* (Concluded)

Form 1040A (20—)   Page **2**

	22	Enter the amount from line 21 (adjusted gross income).	22	28,553	00

Tax, credits, and payments

	23a	Check if: ☐ **You** were born before January 2, 1943, ☐ Blind — ☐ **Spouse** was born before January 2, 1943, ☐ Blind. **Total boxes checked ▶** 23a			
	b	If you are married filing separately and your spouse itemizes deductions, see page 30 and check here ▶ 23b ☐			

Standard Deduction for—

- People who checked any box on line 23a or 23b **or** who can be claimed as a dependent, see page 30.
- All others:

Single or Married filing separately, $5,350

Married filing jointly or Qualifying widow(er), $10,700

Head of household, $7,850

	24	Enter your **standard deduction** (see left margin).	24	10,700	00
	25	Subtract line 24 from line 22. If line 24 is more than line 22, enter -0-.	25	17,853	00
	26	If line 22 is $117,300 or less, multiply $3,400 by the total number of exemptions claimed on line 6d. If line 22 is over $117,300, see the worksheet on page 32.	26	13,600	00
	27	Subtract line 26 from line 25. If line 26 is more than line 25, enter -0-. This is your **taxable income.** ▶	27	4,253	00
	28	**Tax,** including any alternative minimum tax (see page 30).	28	428	00
	29	Credit for child and dependent care expenses. Attach Schedule 2.	29		
	30	Credit for the elderly or the disabled. Attach Schedule 3.	30		
	31	Education credits. Attach Form 8863.	31		
	32	Child tax credit (see page 35). Attach Form 8901 if required.	32		
	33	Retirement savings contributions credit. Attach Form 8880.	33		
	34	Add lines 29 through 33. These are your **total credits.**	34	0	
	35	Subtract line 34 from line 28. If line 34 is more than line 28, enter -0-.	35	428	00
	36	Advance earned income credit payments from Form(s) W-2, box 9.	36	0	
	37	Add lines 35 and 36. This is your **total tax.** ▶	37	428	00
	38	Federal income tax withheld from Forms W-2 and 1099. 38	1,202	00	
	39	2007 estimated tax payments and amount applied from 2006 return. 39			

If you have a qualifying child, attach Schedule EIC.

	40a	**Earned income credit (EIC).** 40a			
	b	Nontaxable combat pay election. 40b			
	41	Additional child tax credit. Attach Form 8812. 41			
	42	Add lines 38, 39, 40a, and 41. These are your **total payments.** ▶	42	1,202	00

Refund

Direct deposit? See page 52 and fill in 44b, 44c, and 44d or Form 8888.

	43	If line 42 is more than line 37, subtract line 37 from line 42. This is the amount you **overpaid.**	43	774	00
▶	44a	Amount of line 43 you want **refunded to you.** If Form 8888 is attached, check here ▶ ☐ 44a		774	00
▶ b		Routing number ☐☐☐☐☐☐☐☐☐ ▶ c Type: ☐ Checking ☐ Savings			
▶ d		Account number ☐☐☐☐☐☐☐☐☐☐☐☐☐☐☐☐☐			
	45	Amount of line 43 you want **applied to your 2008 estimated tax.** 45			

Amount you owe

	46	**Amount you owe.** Subtract line 42 from line 37. For details on how to pay, see page 53. ▶	46		
	47	Estimated tax penalty (see page 53). 47			

Third party designee

Do you want to allow another person to discuss this return with the IRS (see page 54)? ☐ **Yes.** Complete the following. ☐ **No**

Designee's name ▶	Phone no. ▶ ( )	Personal identification number (PIN) ▶ ☐☐☐☐☐

Sign here

Joint return? See page 15. Keep a copy for your records.

Under penalties of perjury, I declare that I have examined this return and accompanying schedules and statements, and to the best of my knowledge and belief, they are true, correct, and accurately list all amounts and sources of income I received during the tax year. Declaration of preparer (other than the taxpayer) is based on all information of which the preparer has any knowledge.

Your signature *Melissa B. Anderson*	Date 4/15/20—	Your occupation student/cashier	Daytime phone number (312) 555-2211
Spouse's signature. If a joint return, **both** must sign. *Michael J. Anderson*	Date 4/15/20—	Spouse's occupation student/clerk	

Paid preparer's use only

Preparer's signature ▶	Date	Check if self-employed ☐	Preparer's SSN or PTIN
Firm's name (or yours if self-employed), address, and ZIP code ▶		EIN	
		Phone no. ( )	

Form **1040A** (20—)

Step 6: Taxable Income

Next you would compute your taxable income. First, copy your adjusted gross income from the bottom of the first page to line 22 at the top of the second page. Then enter the standard deduction stated on the form for your filing status. In Figure 7.5, the Andersons entered $10,700 because they are married filing jointly.

Subtract the standard deduction from adjusted gross income, and enter the result on line 25. Then multiply the number of exemptions claimed by the amount allowed for each exemption. Line 26 of the form shows the amount per exemption for this tax year as $3,400 (it changes yearly). On the first page of their form, the Andersons had claimed four exemptions, so they multiplied $3,400 by 4 to arrive at their $13,600 deduction. Subtract the result from adjusted gross income to determine taxable income for line 27.

Step 7: Tax, Credits, and Payments

Find your tax by looking up your taxable income in the tax table in your instruction booklet. Figure 7.6 shows a recent tax table for use with Form 1040A. With a taxable income of $4,253, this amount falls in the $4,250–$4,300 range. Reading across to the "Married filing jointly" column, their tax is $428. This amount is entered on line 28.

You may qualify for other credits; if so, enter the amounts on lines 29–33 as appropriate and record the total on line 34. Subtract total credits from the tax on line 28 and enter the difference on line 35. On line 36 enter the amount of any advance earned income credit payments indicated on Form W-2 and add it to line 35 to obtain the amount of total tax on line 37. The Andersons do not claim any of the credits listed on lines 29–33, so they enter a zero on lines 34 and 36 and enter $428 on lines 35 and 37. This is their total income tax.

Finally, enter the amount of federal income tax withheld, as shown on Form W-2. The Andersons had $1,202 ($611 + $591) withheld during the year and entered this amount on line 42. If they had qualified for the earned income credit (EIC), they would have entered it on line 40a and included it as part of the total payments made on line 42.

Step 8: Refund or Amount Owed

If the total payments on line 42 exceed the total tax shown in line 37, the difference is your refund. If your total tax is greater than payments, you owe taxes. Record the amount you owe on line 46 and enclose a check for that amount. The Andersons show a $774 refund on lines 43 and 44a.

Step 9: Signature

Both spouses must sign and date a joint return, even if only one had income. Anyone who is paid to prepare a tax return must sign and date the return as well.

What determines the number of exemptions you can claim?

FIGURE 7.6   *Part of 1040A Tax Table*

20— Tax Table

Example. Mr. and Mrs. Green are filing a joint return. Their taxable income on Form 1040A, line 27, is $23,300. First, they find the $23,300–23,350 taxable income line. Next, they find the column for married filing jointly and read down the column. The amount shown where the taxable income line and filing status column meet is $2,716. This is the tax amount they should enter on Form 1040A, line 28.

Sample Table

At least	But less than	Single	Married filing jointly *	Married filing separately	Head of a house- hold
			Your tax is—		
23,200	23,250	3,093	2,701	3,093	2,924
23,250	23,300	3,100	2,709	3,100	2,931
23,300	23,350	3,108	(2,716)	3,108	2,939
23,350	23,400	3,115	2,724	3,115	2,946

If line 27 (taxable income) is—		And you are—			
At least	But less than	Single	Married filing jointly *	Married filing separately	Head of a house- hold
			Your tax is—		
0	5	0	0	0	0
5	15	1	1	1	1
15	25	2	2	2	2
25	50	4	4	4	4
50	75	6	6	6	6
75	100	9	9	9	9
100	125	11	11	11	11
125	150	14	14	14	14
150	175	16	16	16	16
175	200	19	19	19	19
200	225	21	21	21	21
225	250	24	24	24	24
250	275	26	26	26	26
275	300	29	29	29	29
300	325	31	31	31	31
325	350	34	34	34	34
350	375	36	36	36	36
375	400	39	39	39	39
400	425	41	41	41	41
425	450	44	44	44	44
450	475	46	46	46	46
475	500	49	49	49	49
500	525	51	51	51	51
525	550	54	54	54	54
550	575	56	56	56	56
575	600	59	59	59	59
600	625	61	61	61	61
625	650	64	64	64	64
650	675	66	66	66	66
675	700	69	69	69	69
700	725	71	71	71	71
725	750	74	74	74	74
750	775	76	76	76	76
775	800	79	79	79	79
800	825	81	81	81	81
825	850	84	84	84	84
850	875	86	86	86	86
875	900	89	89	89	89
900	925	91	91	91	91
925	950	94	94	94	94
950	975	96	96	96	96
975	1,000	99	99	99	99

1,000

At least	But less than	Single	Married filing jointly *	Married filing separately	Head of a house- hold
1,000	1,025	101	101	101	101
1,025	1,050	104	104	104	104
1,050	1,075	106	106	106	106
1,075	1,100	109	109	109	109
1,100	1,125	111	111	111	111
1,125	1,150	114	114	114	114
1,150	1,175	116	116	116	116
1,175	1,200	119	119	119	119
1,200	1,225	121	121	121	121
1,225	1,250	124	124	124	124
1,250	1,275	126	126	126	126
1,275	1,300	129	129	129	129

If line 27 (taxable income) is—		And you are—			
At least	But less than	Single	Married filing jointly *	Married filing separately	Head of a house- hold
			Your tax is—		
1,300	1,325	131	131	131	131
1,325	1,350	134	134	134	134
1,350	1,375	136	136	136	136
1,375	1,400	139	139	139	139
1,400	1,425	141	141	141	141
1,425	1,450	144	144	144	144
1,450	1,475	146	146	146	146
1,475	1,500	149	149	149	149
1,500	1,525	151	151	151	151
1,525	1,550	154	154	154	154
1,550	1,575	156	156	156	156
1,575	1,600	159	159	159	159
1,600	1,625	161	161	161	161
1,625	1,650	164	164	164	164
1,650	1,675	166	166	166	166
1,675	1,700	169	169	169	169
1,700	1,725	171	171	171	171
1,725	1,750	174	174	174	174
1,750	1,775	176	176	176	176
1,775	1,800	179	179	179	179
1,800	1,825	181	181	181	181
1,825	1,850	184	184	184	184
1,850	1,875	186	186	186	186
1,875	1,900	189	189	189	189
1,900	1,925	191	191	191	191
1,925	1,950	194	194	194	194
1,950	1,975	196	196	196	196
1,975	2,000	199	199	199	199

2,000

At least	But less than	Single	Married filing jointly *	Married filing separately	Head of a house- hold
2,000	2,025	201	201	201	201
2,025	2,050	204	204	204	204
2,050	2,075	206	206	206	206
2,075	2,100	209	209	209	209
2,100	2,125	211	211	211	211
2,125	2,150	214	214	214	214
2,150	2,175	216	216	216	216
2,175	2,200	219	219	219	219
2,200	2,225	221	221	221	221
2,225	2,250	224	224	224	224
2,250	2,275	226	226	226	226
2,275	2,300	229	229	229	229
2,300	2,325	231	231	231	231
2,325	2,350	234	234	234	234
2,350	2,375	236	236	236	236
2,375	2,400	239	239	239	239
2,400	2,425	241	241	241	241
2,425	2,450	244	244	244	244
2,450	2,475	246	246	246	246
2,475	2,500	249	249	249	249
2,500	2,525	251	251	251	251
2,525	2,550	254	254	254	254
2,550	2,575	256	256	256	256
2,575	2,600	259	259	259	259
2,600	2,625	261	261	261	261
2,625	2,650	264	264	264	264
2,650	2,675	266	266	266	266
2,675	2,700	269	269	269	269

If line 27 (taxable income) is—		And you are—			
At least	But less than	Single	Married filing jointly *	Married filing separately	Head of a house- hold
			Your tax is—		
2,700	2,725	271	271	271	271
2,725	2,750	274	274	274	274
2,750	2,775	276	276	276	276
2,775	2,800	279	279	279	279
2,800	2,825	281	281	281	281
2,825	2,850	284	284	284	284
2,850	2,875	286	286	286	286
2,875	2,900	289	289	289	289
2,900	2,925	291	291	291	291
2,925	2,950	294	294	294	294
2,950	2,975	296	296	296	296
2,975	3,000	299	299	299	299

3,000

At least	But less than	Single	Married filing jointly *	Married filing separately	Head of a house- hold
3,000	3,050	303	303	303	303
3,050	3,100	308	308	308	308
3,100	3,150	313	313	313	313
3,150	3,200	318	318	318	318
3,200	3,250	323	323	323	323
3,250	3,300	328	328	328	328
3,300	3,350	333	333	333	333
3,350	3,400	338	338	338	338
3,400	3,450	343	343	343	343
3,450	3,500	348	348	348	348
3,500	3,550	353	353	353	353
3,550	3,600	358	358	358	358
3,600	3,650	363	363	363	363
3,650	3,700	368	368	368	368
3,700	3,750	373	373	373	373
3,750	3,800	378	378	378	378
3,800	3,850	383	383	383	383
3,850	3,900	388	388	388	388
3,900	3,950	393	393	393	393
3,950	4,000	398	398	398	398

4,000

At least	But less than	Single	Married filing jointly *	Married filing separately	Head of a house- hold
4,000	4,050	403	403	403	403
4,050	4,100	408	408	408	408
4,100	4,150	413	413	413	413
4,150	4,200	418	418	418	418
4,200	4,250	423	423	423	423
4,250	4,300	428	428	428	428
4,300	4,350	433	433	433	433
4,350	4,400	438	438	438	438
4,400	4,450	443	443	443	443
4,450	4,500	448	448	448	448
4,500	4,550	453	453	453	453
4,550	4,600	458	458	458	458
4,600	4,650	463	463	463	463
4,650	4,700	468	468	468	468
4,700	4,750	473	473	473	473
4,750	4,800	478	478	478	478
4,800	4,850	483	483	483	483
4,850	4,900	488	488	488	488
4,900	4,950	493	493	493	493
4,950	5,000	498	498	498	498

Government & Public Administration

Tax examiners, collectors, and revenue agents work for federal, state, and local governments. They review tax returns to determine the accuracy of the math as well as the credits and deductions claimed. They also identify tax debt and collect taxes owed. Some deal with individual taxpayers, and others work with profit and nonprofit organizations.

Wherever money is collected on behalf of government units, there are revenue agents and officers sending out reports, calling, and communicating findings. For each case, careful records are kept and shared among the federal, state, and local governments.

Sometimes travel is needed, but a significant amount of time is spent in offices doing detailed work. Stress results from working under tight deadlines as well as confronting delinquent and often hostile taxpayers.

Employment Outlook

- Little or no change in employment growth is expected.
- Competition will be higher for positions with the IRS.

Job Titles

- Tax examiner
- Tax collector
- Revenue agent

Needed Skills

- A bachelor's degree is preferred.

- Specialized experience is desirable.
- Excellent analytical and communication skills are needed.

What's it like to work in... *Tax Collection*

Alice enjoys analyzing and verifying information contained in tax returns. She compares tax returns with records from other sources such as employers and banks. When there is a discrepancy, she may tag the files for a full audit; in other cases, she is able to determine accuracy with a phone call or a written letter.

The government building where she works is old and historic, but comfortable. Her office is among many others in the Department of Revenue for the state where she lives.

Today is like most others—it involves detailed work that requires concentration, patience, and organization. Her filing system allows her to retrieve information quickly, compare data, produce communication, and follow-up with action when needed.

Alice had to pass a strict background check because she works with confidential information. She is trustworthy, honest, and dedicated to enforcing the tax code.

What About You?

Do you like analyzing data and adhering to procedures? How do your skills and aptitudes match up with those required in the tax collection field?

Assessment

KEY TERMS REVIEW

Match the terms with the definitions.

____ 1. All taxable income you receive, including wages, salaries, and tips

____ 2. Expenses listed on Schedule A that you can subtract from adjusted gross income to determine taxable income

____ 3. A stated amount you can subtract from adjusted gross income if you do not itemize deductions

____ 4. Your tax-filing group based on your marital status

____ 5. Gross income less adjustments

____ 6. An amount you may subtract from your income for each person who depends on your income to live

____ 7. The amount on which you will pay income tax

____ 8. An amount subtracted directly from the tax owed

____ 9. A person who lives with you and for whom you pay more than half of his or her living expenses

a. adjusted gross income

b. dependent

c. exemption

d. filing status

e. gross income

f. itemized deductions

g. standard deduction

h. tax credit

i. taxable income

CHECK YOUR UNDERSTANDING

10. How is gross income different from taxable income?

11. How are tax deductions different from tax credits?

12. What is the difference between Form 1040EZ and Form 1040A?

APPLY YOUR KNOWLEDGE

13. Explain the differences between Form 1040A and Form 1040. Describe circumstances when each should be used.

THINK CRITICALLY

14. Is it a good idea to prepare your taxes twice—once using Form 1040 and then again using one of the other tax return forms—so that you can compare the results? Explain your answer.

15. Making simple mathematical errors on your tax form could result in your tax return being targeted for an audit. Use of tax preparation software helps prevent this type of error. Do you think hiring a professional tax preparer would reduce the chances of being audited? Why or why not?

Chapter Assessment

SUMMARY

7.1

- *The government collects money, or revenue, from citizens and businesses to spend as specified by Congress.*

- *As income grows, progressive taxes take a larger share of income and regressive taxes take a smaller share.*

- *Proportional or flat taxes take the same percentage regardless of income.*

- *The IRS is the government agency in charge of collecting taxes, enforcing tax laws, and supplying information to help taxpayers prepare their tax returns.*

- *The income tax system is graduated. Different tax rates apply to different income ranges, or tax brackets.*

- *Our income tax system is based on voluntary compliance.*

- *Willful failure to pay taxes is called tax evasion and is a serious crime punishable by a fine, imprisonment, or both.*

- *Every year the IRS calls millions of taxpayers for an audit.*

7.2

- *You may claim an exemption for each of your dependents.*

- *Gross income consists of taxable income received from all sources.*

- *Gross income less certain allowable adjustments is called adjusted gross income.*

- *To determine taxable income, subtract adjustments, deductions, and exemptions from gross income.*

- *Tax deductions reduce taxable income, while tax credits are subtracted directly from taxes owed.*

- *You may take a standard deduction or itemize deductions on Schedule A if they will exceed the standard deduction.*

- *File the short form, 1040EZ, if your income is less than $100,000 and you have no dependents.*

- *File Form 1040A if you do not have enough deductions to itemize and have less than $100,000 of income.*

- *If the amount of taxes withheld from your paychecks exceeds your total tax, you will receive a refund. If the amount withheld is less than your total tax, you must pay the difference when you file your tax return.*

APPLY WHAT YOU KNOW

1. How do new tax laws get passed?

2. Why are regressive taxes considered unfair to lower-income people?

3. How does your filing status affect the amount of taxes you will pay?

4. How does the number of exemptions claimed affect the amount of taxes you will pay?

5. What are deductible expenses?

6. Which would reduce your income tax more—a $300 tax deduction or a $300 tax credit? Explain.

7. Search the Internet for a tax calculator. Some calculators figure the income taxes you would pay if our country had a flat tax. Others calculate taxes based on today's system and rates. If you have a job, enter numbers based on your earnings. Estimate any numbers you don't have. Then enter different income levels to see how the tax changes as income rises. Based on these calculations, summarize what you learned about the tax system in one or two paragraphs.

8. What must you do if you are married and wish to deduct charitable contributions on your tax return?

9. Visit www.irs.gov, follow the link to Forms and Publications, and download this year's Form 1040EZ and instruction booklet. Fill out the form using estimates if you don't know the real amounts for yourself. Use the tax tables in the booklet to find your tax obligation based on your estimates.

MAKE ACADEMIC CONNECTIONS

10. **Research** Visit the IRS web site at www.irs.gov and explore the resources available. Learn how to file taxes electronically using the web site as a tool. Write a one-page report describing what you learned.

11. **International Studies** Use the Internet to research taxes assessed in foreign countries, including one country in Europe and one country on another continent. What benefits do taxpayers receive in exchange for their taxes? Compare and contrast your findings with U.S. taxes and benefits.

12. **History** Do a report on the history of taxes in this country or in another country. Describe the kinds of taxes, including when they were first introduced and for what purpose.

13. **Government** Compare your state's tax system with that of other states. Which states are considered the worst (in terms of high taxes)? Which states are considered the best (in terms of low taxes)? Prepare a report of your findings.

SOLVE PROBLEMS AND

EXPLORE ISSUES

14. Acquire a copy of Form 1040EZ. Prepare a tax return for Tomeka Hunt. Use the tax table in Figure 7.3 and the following information:

   - Tomeka M. Hunt (Social Security number 999-00-9892)
   - 54 Center Street
   - San Francisco, CA 96214-3627

   Tomeka is a part-time engineer. She wants $3 to go to the Presidential Election Campaign Fund. She is single and claims only herself as an exemption. Tomeka's salary is $16,200, plus interest of $155. No one else claims her as a dependent, and she had $1,660 in federal taxes withheld.

15. Using Form 1040A and the tax table in Figure 7.6, calculate the total tax for Mack R. Rueoff, a part-time auto mechanic. Mack's gross income is $13,255. He has a $1,000 IRA deduction, claims the standard deduction, and had $350 in federal taxes withheld. He is single and is entitled to one exemption. Based on this information, how much does Mack owe or how much is his refund?

16. Using Form 1040A and the tax table in Figure 7.6, calculate the total tax for Yi Chang, a part-time teacher. Yi's wages total $12,201. He received $190 of taxable interest income, made an IRA contribution of $500, claims the standard deduction, and had $520 in federal taxes withheld from his wages. He is married filing separately and claims only himself as an exemption. How much does Yi owe in taxes, or how much is his refund?

EXTEND YOUR LEARNING

17. **Legal Issues** Voluntary compliance is an important part of our tax system. When everyone contributes their fair share, the country is able to meet its obligations to its citizens. Willful refusal to file a tax return or pay taxes is a federal crime. However, many people called tax protestors believe that the U.S. Constitution does not require them to pay federal income taxes and that payment of the tax is voluntary. Look up "tax protestors" in Wikipedia online. Write a paper about tax resisters and those who refuse to pay taxes. Is their argument rational? On what is it based? What would happen if all people took the same approach and refused to pay federal and/or state income taxes? Do you believe the claims that more than 40 percent of all Americans pay no federal income tax? What is the attitude of the U.S. government toward these protestors? What is your position on this issue?

For related activities and links, go to **www.cengage.com/school/pfinance/mypf**

Chapter 8

Budgets and Financial Records

8.1   *Budgeting and Planning*

8.2   *Legal Agreements and Record Keeping*

Consider **THIS**

Sarah has a part-time job, attends school six hours a day, and participates in two after-school sports. She no longer receives a monthly allowance from her parents. She pays for all of her own clothes, gas, insurance, and entertainment. Last year, she was able to save over $600.

"How do you do it?" asked her friend Anna. "I work more hours than you do, my parents pay for my clothes and most of my expenses, and I still don't have any money left over for entertainment. I didn't save a dime last year!"

"I have a budget," said Sarah. "Every time I get paid, I put aside money for savings. I know how much I spend on everything I buy. Keeping a good record of income and expenses helps me plan better, so I don't run out of money. That doesn't mean I can buy anything I want, but it does mean that I know how much I can spend, which helps me stretch my money to cover as many things as possible ."

Budgeting and Planning

GOALS

- Explain the purpose of financial planning and prepare a personal budget.
- Explain the need for and create a net worth statement and a personal property inventory.

TERMS

- disposable income, p. 162
- financial plan, p. 162
- budget, p. 163
- fixed expenses, p. 164
- variable expenses, p. 164
- assets, p. 166
- liabilities, p. 166
- net worth, p. 167

FINANCIAL PLANNING BASICS

Do you have unlimited resources to buy all the things you want? Some people do, but if you are like most Americans, to achieve financial success, you will have to plan and work for it. Planning, budgeting and keeping good records provide the road map that leads to financial security.

GETTING STARTED

We all have to start somewhere. Even if you don't have much income, it will help to make a plan. There are two elements to consider—your income and your expenses. Your gross income is important, but it doesn't represent money over which you have control. Your **disposable income** is the money you have left to spend or save after taxes and other required deductions are taken. If you spend all of your income, there won't be money to set aside for the future. In order to use your income to your best advantage, you need a financial plan.

All the money you receive is spent, saved, or invested. You may spend it for things you need or want, save it for future needs, or invest it to earn more money. A **financial plan** is a set of goals for spending, saving, and investing the money you receive. Financial planning helps you do the following:

- Determine and evaluate your choices.
- Prioritize your choices so your money goes as far as possible.
- Avoid careless and wasteful spending.
- Organize your financial resources (sources of income) so you can achieve your financial goals.
- Avoid money worries by planning your saving, spending, and borrowing to live within your income.

The first step in financial planning is understanding your *resources*—the sources and amounts of money you expect to receive—as well as understanding your obligations. Before you can prepare a budget, you may wish to keep track of money coming in and going out for a month or two. This will give you a clearer idea of what you can expect. Many people keep a journal or log where they record everything they spend. They may keep receipts for cash items. This record forms the basis of understanding what's going on in your current financial picture.

VISUALIZING YOUR FUTURE

Once you have a good idea of what comes in and how it goes out, you can then start thinking about ways you'd like to change that. For many people, just keeping track of what you receive and how you spend it makes a difference. When people can actually see how much they spend on something, they may decide there are other things they'd rather do. But taking the next step—actually preparing a budget—will take your financial planning visions to reality.

NETBookmark

Envelope budgeting is the first type of budget system many people use when they move out on their own. Access www.cengage.com/school/pfinance/mypf and click on the link for Chapter 8. Read the article about envelope budgeting and briefly describe how it works. Then name at least one advantage and one possible drawback to this style of budgeting.

www.cengage.com/school/pfinance/mypf

PREPARING A BUDGET

The next step toward achieving your financial goals is to prepare a budget. A **budget** is a spending and saving plan based on your expected income and expenses. In a budget, money coming in (earnings plus borrowing) must equal money going out (spending plus saving). The budget must balance. A budget helps you plan your spending and saving so that you won't have to borrow money or use credit to meet your daily needs.

Steps in Preparing a Budget

The steps in preparing a budget are as follows:

1. Estimate your total expected income for a certain time period. Include all money you expect to receive. Use a weekly, biweekly, or monthly budget—whichever best matches how often you expect to receive money.
2. Estimate your expenses, or money you will need for day-to-day purchases—for example, lunches, fees, personal care items, and clothing.
3. Decide how much of your income you want to save—to set aside for future needs. Most experts advise saving 10 percent of your disposable income each pay period. By saving, you will have money to pay for future needs, both expected and unexpected.
4. Balance your budget. If your expenses plus savings exceed your income, adjust your budget to make them balance. To do this, you may have to delay buying some items you want but don't need. Or, you may decide to save a little less this month. If you can't cut your expenses, then you have to increase your income.

Figure 8.1 on the next page shows a high school student's budget for one month. This student expects to receive a total of $380 and plans to use the money for certain needs and wants and to save part of it as well. Notice that the total income equals the total of expenses plus savings. The budget balances.

A Typical Monthly Budget

Some people create a monthly budget by taking an annual budget and dividing it into 12 months. This can be very helpful for those people who do

FIGURE 8.1 *Simple Budget*

Evan Anderson
Budget for September

Income

Part-time job (15 hours/week)	$320
Allowance for household chores	20
Birthday gift (check from grandparents)	40
Total Income	$380

Expenses

Daily lunches	$ 80
Supplies	20
Clothes	40
Entertainment (movies and golfing)	140
Total expenses	$280

Savings

Credit union account	$100
Total expenses plus savings	$380

not have a regular monthly income. A budget will help them plan and adjust spending to cover expenses during the low-income times.

Figure 8.2 shows a monthly budget for a married couple. Mike and Jennifer both work and have no children. They estimate their income by adding together the net pay from both of their paychecks. They also expect income from savings and investments.

There are two types of expenses. **Fixed expenses** are costs that do not change from month to month. You are obligated to pay them regardless of income changes. For example, people must pay rent or a house payment, utility bills, a car loan, and insurance premiums when they are due. Most financial experts recommend that a family have fixed expenses of no more than 50 to 60 percent of take-home, or net, pay. However, this standard is difficult to achieve for young people just starting life on their own. But with time, pay raises, and careful budgeting, a family can achieve that goal.

Variable expenses are costs that vary in amount and type, depending on the choices you make. For example, your grocery bill can be larger or smaller, depending on what you choose to buy. Other examples of variable expenses are costs for eating out, going to movies, and buying clothes.

Mike and Jennifer aren't sure how much they can save each month. By subtracting estimated expenses from estimated income, they determine that they have a *cash surplus* (income exceeds expenses). They apply the cash surplus to savings, which is approximately 12 percent of their monthly income ($430 ÷ $3,500). This enables them to set aside money for emergencies, short-term savings, and long-term investing.

FIGURE 8.2 *Budget for a Couple*

Mike and Jennifer Harris Budget

	Monthly	Yearly
Income		
Salary (Mike) after taxes	$1,600	$19,200
Salary (Jennifer) after taxes	1,800	21,600
Interest on savings	50	600
Earnings on investments	50	600
Total income	$3,500	$42,000
Expenses		
Fixed expenses:		
Rent	$1,000	$12,000
Utilities	150	1,800
Car payment	300	3,600
Insurance:		
Car	100	1,200
Life and Health	75	900
Total fixed expenses	$1,625	$19,500
Variable expenses:		
Cell phones	$ 60	$ 720
Gasoline	150	1,800
Car repairs and maintenance	60	720
Cable/Internet	90	1,080
Groceries	400	4,800
Clothing	200	2,400
Personal care:		
Dry cleaning, household	50	600
Medicine, cosmetics	50	600
Insurance deductibles and co-pays	50	600
Recreation and entertainment	100	1,200
Gifts, donations, miscellaneous	300	3,600
Total variable expenses	$1,510	$18,120
Total fixed and variable expenses	$3,135	$37,620
Cash surplus (total income minus total expenses)	$ 365	$ 4,380
Savings (allocation of cash surplus)		
Emergency savings fund	$ 35	$ 420
Short-term savings	100	1,200
Long-term investments	230	2,760
Total savings and investments	$ 365	$ 4,380
Total expenses plus savings	$3,500	$42,000

PERSONAL RECORDS

Good personal records makes budgeting and long-range planning easier. Your records also make it easier to prepare income tax returns, credit applications, and other financial forms. You should keep five types of personal records: income and expense records, your net worth statement, a personal property inventory, tax records, and other miscellaneous documents.

■ INCOME AND EXPENSES RECORDS

Your W-2 forms show the money earned and deductions taken from your paycheck during the year. The W-2 forms also state the amount of taxes, including Social Security taxes, withheld. You may need these forms later as proof of earnings and deductions when you want to collect benefits, such as Social Security. Other records of income include statements from banks showing interest earned on savings and statements from investment companies listing dividends earned from stock or other investments.

Expense items include receipts listing charitable contributions, medical bills, or work-related expenses. When you prepare your budgets and tax returns, these receipts and statements serve as documentation (proof) of income and expenses. Store these documents in a safe place for future reference.

■ NET WORTH STATEMENT

A *net worth statement*, such as the one shown in Figure 8.3, shows a person's net worth based on his or her assets and liabilities. **Assets** are items of value that a person owns. Assets accumulate over your lifetime and are called wealth. A wealthy person has many assets of different types, from cash in accounts to real estate owned.

Money or debts you owe to others are called **liabilities**. A responsible person plans to pay off his or her debts in the future. Short-term liabilities will be paid

FIGURE 8.3	*Net Worth Statement*

Net Worth Statement
Anisa Newkirk
January 1, 20—

Assets		Liabilities	
Checking account	$ 500	Loan on car	$1,800
Savings account	800	Loan from parents	100
Car value	3,000		
Personal property:		Total liabilities	$1,900
(inventory attached)	5,000		
		Net Worth	
Total assets	$9,300		
		Assets minus liabilities	$7,400
		Total	$9,300

off soon, usually within a year or less. This might be money you borrowed from a friend. Long-term liabilities are paid off over several years, such as a car loan.

When you subtract your liabilities from your assets, the difference is known as **net worth**. As net worth increases, you are growing in overall wealth. Over time, your assets are increasing while you are paying off debts. When assets are greater than liabilities, a person is said to be *solvent*, or in a favorable financial position. When liabilities are greater than assets (you owe more than you own), a person is said to be *insolvent*, or in a poor financial position. Many people are insolvent at certain times during their lives, such as when they are attending college and until they can get a good job to start paying off their student loans.

You will need your net worth information (lists of assets and liabilities) when you apply for a loan or credit. The bank or other financial institution will want you to be a good risk—a person who will likely pay back the loan. A net worth statement also helps you keep track of how you spend your money and what you have to show for it at the end of the year. If you create a net worth statement yearly throughout your life, you can check to be sure that your financial position is improving over time.

PERSONAL PROPERTY INVENTORY

A *personal property inventory* is a list of the valuable items you own, along with their purchase prices and approximate current values. Personal property includes anything of value inside your home—clothing, furniture, appliances, and so forth. A personal property inventory is useful in the event of fire, theft, or property damage. The inventory will help you list lost items and their value when you make an insurance claim. As a further safeguard, photograph items of value, attach the photographs to the inventory, and keep this information in a safe deposit box or other secure place to use as evidence in the event the property is damaged, lost, or stolen.

A personal property inventory also helps you see what you have to show for the money you have spent. It should include other items you own as well, including investments, savings accounts, and CDs. Reviewing it will help you assess your spending patterns. As you buy new items and dispose of others, you should revise the inventory.

Figure 8.4 is a personal property inventory for a young adult. Keeping track of your assets is a good idea.

© Digital Vision/Getty Images

What items would you include in your personal property inventory?

FIGURE 8.4 *Personal Property Inventory*

Personal Property Inventory
Anisa Newkirk
January 2, 20—

Item	Year Purchased	Purchase Price	Approximate Current Value
Sphinx XTL DVD Player with big-screen TV	2008	$ 3,200	$1,300
Bedroom furniture (bed, dresser, lamp, clock)	2006	2,000	1,200
Clothing, jewelry	------	3,000	500
MBD motor bike	2005	1,800	1,000
CD collection, digital camera, scanner, CD burner	2006	2,000	1,000
		$12,000	$5,000

TAX RECORDS

All taxpayers should keep copies of their tax records for at least three years after they file their tax return. *Tax records* include the tax return itself (a copy of the signed form), W-2 forms, and other receipts verifying income and expenses listed on each return. Keep your tax records in a safe place in case of an audit. The IRS has the legal right to audit your tax returns and supporting records for three years from the date of filing (longer if fraud or intentional wrongdoing on your part can be proved).

OTHER RECORDS

Many consumers also keep lists of credit card numbers and phone numbers to call if those cards are lost or stolen. As a part of your financial plan, it's a good idea to reflect on the number of credit accounts you have along with the balances for each, the interest rates being charged, and the monthly payments required. It's important to use credit wisely. You must have good credit for the times when you will need it (such as buying a house), but you must also be careful not to overuse credit and hurt your ability to plan for your financial future.

You may choose to keep other records as well, including the following:

- Car titles
- Insurance policies
- Birth and marriage certificates
- Passports

These documents are sometimes needed for certain financial transactions. The original documents should be placed in a safe place (such as a safe deposit box), and photocopies should be kept for easy reference.

Issues in Your World

LIVING WITHIN YOUR INCOME

To be financially responsible, you must recognize that you are responsible for your own financial future.

A balanced personal budget is the first step to financial security. Living within your income means that you spend less than you make and that you plan savings for future as well as current needs.

Setting financial goals is the next step to securing your financial future. You can't achieve future financial goals if you aren't paying your current bills on time.

It is easy to believe advertisements that create demand. Emotional appeals are designed to get you to buy things you don't need in order to be more popular or to keep up with your friends. Ask yourself the following questions:

- *Do I need it?*
- *Why am I buying it?*
- *How else could I spend the same money?*
- *How will buying it affect my financial goals?*

Many people have a limit on how much money they will spend without a careful analysis and a family decision to spend the money. Whatever your limit, before spending a large sum or accepting a loan that will take a big bite from your future earnings, think through the decision carefully.

Living within your income is an important part of being happy. Regardless of the amount of your income, careful planning and budgeting can enhance your lifestyle and secure your future.

THINK CRITICALLY

1. *Make a list of things you'd like to have, along with the purchase price of each. Read this list a week from now. Do you still want the same things? If so, what do you plan to do to buy one or more of them?*

2. *Do you know people who live within their income? If so, ask one of them to share how he or she does it. Based on the advice you receive, create a list of budgeting tips.*

3. *Do you know people who live beyond their income? What do you observe about their stress, financial stability, and financial goals?*

Assessment

KEY TERMS REVIEW

Match the terms with the definitions.

_____ 1. Costs that change in amount and type, based on your choices

_____ 2. A spending and savings plan

_____ 3. Money you have left to spend each month

_____ 4. The difference between assets and liabilities

_____ 5. Costs that do not change from month to month

_____ 6. Debts you owe to others

_____ 7. A set of goals for spending, saving, and investing money

_____ 8. Items of value that you own

a. assets

b. budget

c. disposable income

d. financial plan

e. fixed expenses

f. liabilities

g. net worth

h. variable expenses

CHECK YOUR UNDERSTANDING

9. What is the first step in budgeting?

10. How are fixed expenses different from variable expenses?

11. Why would you prepare a net worth statement?

APPLY YOUR KNOWLEDGE

12. Using Figure 8.1 as a model, prepare a simple budget for yourself. If your budget does not balance, make adjustments until it does. How much will you set aside for savings? Assume that you can set aside this same amount each month. Locate a savings planner tool and calculate your total savings after 12 months, at 6 percent interest, starting with $0 savings.

THINK *CRITICALLY*

13. Financial planning should begin early in your life. Many people revise their plans as major life events occur, such as getting married or having children. Explain how a financial plan is based on personal values and choices and why some people choose not to do any planning.

14. Why is it important to save personal records, such as receipts and credit card statements? Provide an example of a time when you did not save something and found that you later needed it.

Legal Agreements and Record Keeping

GOALS

- List the elements of a legally binding agreement.
- Design an effective filing system for your personal records.

TERMS

- contract, *p. 171*
- counteroffer, *p. 173*
- consideration, *p. 173*
- notarized, *p. 174*
- negotiable, *p. 175*
- co-signer, *p. 175*
- warranty, *p. 176*
- spreadsheet, *p. 178*
- database, *p. 178*

LEGALLY BINDING AGREEMENTS

As your finances become more complex, it is likely that you will enter into legally binding agreements. A **contract** is a legally enforceable agreement between two or more people. For example, if you buy a suit and you want it altered, the sales clerk fills out a ticket. The ticket lists the changes requested and the promised date of completion. This ticket is a contract between you and the store. The store agrees to make the alterations by the stated date and for the stated price, and you agree to pay the price.

Other common legal agreements are credit accounts, mortgage loans, and rental agreements. When you sign up for a retail credit card, the store agrees to give you products now in exchange for payment on your account later. When you rent an apartment, the landlord agrees to let you live in the apartment, and you agree to pay the rent by a certain day each month. Each of these cases constitutes an *express contract*. Express contracts can be oral or written. What makes them express is that the parties have stated the terms of their agreement in words.

Figure 8.5 shows a credit application from a retail store. A credit application asks you to agree to certain conditions before opening an account. Attached to the application will be an explanation of finance charges and how they are computed. When you sign the application, you are agreeing to pay finance charges if your balance is not paid in full each month. Be sure you have read everything contained in the agreement before you sign it. If something is not clear, ask for an explanation so you can understand your rights and responsibilities before you enter into the contract.

© Digital Vision/Getty Images

Why do people enter into legal agreements?

In addition to written agreements, you take part in many unwritten agreements. An *implied contract* is not written but is created by the actions or conduct of someone. The "terms" of an implied contract are assumed. For example, suppose you mow your neighbor's lawn and she pays you $25. You continue to mow her lawn, and she continues to pay you. This is an implied contract based on the actions of each person. One person accepts something of value, knowing that the other person expects something of value in return. Although the terms of your agreement were never explicitly stated, it would be unfair or unjust if the neighbor stops paying you for mowing her lawn.

FIGURE 8.5 *Credit Application*

CREDIT CARD APPLICATION
(Please print. Not valid unless signed below.)

Title (optional): Mr. ☒ Mrs. ☐ Ms. ☐ Other _____

First Name __Richard__ MI __J__ Last Name __Washington__

Street Address __45 Cleveland Avenue__ Apt. # _____

City __Portland__ State __OR__ Zip + 4 __97201-1072__

Home Phone __(513)555-0181__ Business Phone __(513)555-9213__ E-Mail _____

Soc. Sec. # __999-00-9384__ Est. Monthly Charges __$100.00__ # Cards Desired __1__

Former Address __-----__
(if less than 1 year at current address)

City _____ State _____ Zip + 4 _____

Mother's Maiden Name __Hawkins__ Years Employed __3__ Position __Payroll specialist__

Present Housing: Own ☐ Rent ☒ Live with Parents ☐

# of Dependents (exc. self) __1__ Student? Full ☒ Part ☐

> **Note:** An applicant, though married, may apply for a separate Account in his or her own name. If your spouse will use this Account, please indicate his or her name, and social security number for credit reporting purposes.

First Name of Spouse __----__ MI ___ Last _____ Soc. Sec. # _____

I HAVE READ AND AGREE TO BE BOUND BY THE TERMS OF THIS APPLICATION (INCLUDING THE ADDITIONAL APPLICATION PROVISIONS AND ACCOMPANYING FEDERAL AND STATE NOTICES AND SUMMARY OF CREDIT TERMS PRINTED TO THE RIGHT AND BACK).

I understand and agree that if I am approved for an Account, (i) the Central Credit Bank, N.A., Retail Installment Credit Agreement (the "Agreement") that I will receive with my credit card, will govern my Account, (ii) the Agreement is incorporated by reference into and made a part of the Application, and (iii) THE AGREEMENT INCLUDES AN ARBITRATION PROVISION THAT MAY SUBSTANTIALLY LIMIT MY RIGHTS IN THE EVENT OF A DISPUTE, INCLUDING MY RIGHT TO LITIGATE IN COURT OR HAVE A JURY TRIAL, DISCOVERY AND APPEAL RIGHTS, AND THE RIGHT TO PARTICIPATE AS A REPRESENTATIVE OR MEMBER OF A CLASS IN A CLASS ACTION. I MAY REQUEST THE COMMERCIAL ARBITRATION RULES OF THE AMERICAN ARBITRATION ASSOCIATION, WHICH SERVES AS ARBITRATION ADMINISTRATOR, BY CALLING 1-800-555-0155. I understand and agree that the Bank will first consider this application with respect to the credit card program described in this application. If for any reason, at the Bank's sole discretion, I do not qualify for this program, I request the Bank consider this application with respect to alternative credit card programs. My signature on this Application represents my signature on the Agreement.

NOTICE TO THE APPLICANT: (1) DO NOT SIGN THIS APPLICATION/AGREEMENT BEFORE YOU READ IT OR IF IT CONTAINS ANY BLANK SPACES. (2) YOU ARE ENTITLED TO A COMPLETELY FILLED IN COPY OF THE RETAIL INSTALLMENT CREDIT AGREEMENT

x *Richard J. Washington* 3/11/--
Signature of Card Applicant Date

CONTRACT ELEMENTS

To accomplish its purpose, a contract must be *binding*. That is, all who enter into the contract are legally bound to abide by its terms. A contract is legally binding when it contains these four elements:

- Agreement
- Consideration
- Contractual capacity
- Legality

Agreement

A contract has legal agreement when a valid offer is made and accepted. Both the *offer* (made by a person called the offeror) and *acceptance* (made by a person called the offeree) must express a voluntary intent to be bound. When one person makes an offer and another person changes it, the second person is making a counteroffer. The **counteroffer** is a new offer because it changes the original offer. It has to be accepted or rejected by the first person.

On the Internet, you may click on an "acceptance" of an offer. This click-on acceptance is considered a voluntary intent to be bound. If you do not intend to enter a binding agreement, or if you accidentally hit the wrong button, notify the online seller immediately of your error (and lack of intent to be bound).

It is important that both parties to an agreement genuinely agree to the contract terms. Genuine agreement does not exist when there is a mistake, fraud (an intentional misrepresentation), duress (threats), or undue influence (having free will overcome by a person who has a special interest, such as a parent or guardian).

Consideration

Consideration is something of value exchanged for something else of value. Consideration may be an item of value, money, a promise, or a performed service. If one person is to receive something but gives nothing in return, the contract may not be enforceable. The idea behind consideration is that each party to the agreement receives something of value. When you buy a pair of shoes, you get the shoes and the store gets your money. The shoes and the money are items of consideration.

© Photodisc/Getty Images

Why is consideration an important element of a contract?

Contractual Capacity

Contractual *capacity* refers to the competence (legal ability) of the parties to enter a contract. Competent parties are people who are legally capable of agreeing to a binding offer. Those who are unable to protect themselves because of mental deficiency or illness, or who are otherwise incapable of understanding the consequences of their actions, cannot be held to contracts. Minors have *limited contractual capacity*, which means that they may legally set aside contractual obligations. This privilege is allowed in order to protect minors from those who would take advantage of them.

Legality

To be legally enforceable, a contract must have a lawful purpose. A court will not require a person to perform an agreed-upon act if it is illegal. Some contracts must have a special form in order to be legally enforceable. For example, a contract for sale of real estate would have to contain a specific legal description of the property. A deed to transfer title to property would have to be notarized. When a document is **notarized**, the signature is verified by a notary public, who then applies a notary seal.

STATUTE OF FRAUDS

Every state has a statute of frauds. The purpose of this law is to prevent harm due to fraudulent conduct. This law requires that some contracts be in writing and signed to be legally binding. Examples include the following:

- Contracts for the sale of real property (homes and land)
- Contracts that cannot be fully performed in less than a year
- Contracts involving the sale of goods for $500 and over
- Contracts in which one person agrees to pay the debts of another
- Contracts in consideration of marriage

These types of agreements must be in writing because they involve special rules. For example, a *prenuptial agreement* is a contract that specifies what will happen if a marriage ends in divorce. Generally, if two parties of unequal wealth enter into a marriage, a prenuptial agreement may be required in which the person without wealth agrees that he or she will receive a set amount as a settlement, rather than half of what the other person owns, if the marriage ends. This type of agreement serves to protect an individual's assets from a spouse who may have entered into the marriage fraudulently for financial gain.

RESPONSIBILITIES IN AGREEMENTS

When people enter into contracts, they have several responsibilities. They should do the following:

- Fill in all blank spaces or indicate N/A for items that are not applicable.
- Write all terms clearly. Vague phrases are often not enforceable.
- Enter dates, amounts, and other numbers correctly and clearly.
- Be sure the seller has supplied all relevant information, including rate of interest, total finance charges, cash payment price, and so on.
- Understand all terms contained in the agreement. Do not sign it until you have read it. Your signature acknowledges that you have read and understood the contract.
- Check that no changes have been made after you have signed it. Your initials at the bottom of each page will prevent substitution of pages.
- Keep a copy of the agreement. Put it in a safe place for future use.

Although as a consumer, you are protected by numerous consumer protection laws, you may need legal services occasionally. Your best protection is to arm yourself in advance by understanding the agreements into which you enter.

NEGOTIABLE INSTRUMENTS

In contracts, the word **negotiable** means legally collectible. A negotiable instrument is an unconditional written promise to pay a specified sum of money upon demand of the holder. The negotiable instruments most people use are checks (discussed in Chapter 9) and, to a lesser extent, promissory notes.

A promissory note, like the one shown in Figure 8.6, is a written promise to pay a certain sum of money to another person or to the holder of the note on a specified date. A promissory note is a legal document, and payment can be enforced by law.

The person who creates and signs the promissory note and agrees to pay it on a certain date is called the *maker*. The person to whom the note is made payable is known as the *payee*. A promissory note is normally used when borrowing a large sum of money from a financial institution.

In some cases, creditors (those extending credit) will require a co-signer with a good credit rating as additional security for repayment of a note. A **co-signer** is a person who promises to pay the debt of another person. The co-signer's signature is also on a note. Young people and people who have not established a credit rating are often asked to provide a co-signer for their first loan. If someone asks you to co-sign a loan, do so only if you are sure the person is financially responsible. If that person fails to repay the debt, you will be legally responsible to repay it.

When one person agrees to pay the debts of another person, that agreement must be in writing (signed by the co-signer) to be enforceable.

FIGURE 8.6	*Promissory Note*

PROMISSORY NOTE

$ 400.00   January 15   , 20 - -

I (we) Marilyn Huykamp   , jointly and severally, do agree and promise to pay to Emerald Furniture Co. the sum of Four hundred and 00/100   dollars with interest at the rate of 9 % from January 15, 20 - - , payable in monthly installments of $ 69.67 beginning February 1   , 20 - - and on a like day each month until paid in full, the last payment due July 1   , 20 - -. Said payment shall include interest. In the event of default, the maker hereof agrees to pay attorneys' fees and court costs in collection of this note.

Marilyn Huykamp
Maker

■ WARRANTIES

A **warranty**, also called a *guarantee*, is a statement assuring quality and performance of a product or service. If the product fails, the warranty usually states what remedies are available, such as return of the product for the purchase price or repair of the product at no extra charge. The warranty may be in writing or assumed to exist by the nature of the product. Still, a warranty is not a safeguard against a consumer's poor buying decision.

All products contain *implied warranties*. For example, all products have the warranty of merchantability. This means that a product will do what it is made to do. For example, a new tennis ball must bounce. If it does not bounce, you can return the defective ball, even if there is no written warranty.

Specific *written warranties* often guarantee that a product will perform to your satisfaction for a certain period of time. Many written warranties state that you may return a product for repair or replacement if it ceases to work because of a defect. However, warranties will not protect against normal wear and tear of the product.

Figure 8.7 illustrates a limited warranty that might accompany a home product. Read it carefully to determine what the manufacturer does and does not guarantee.

FIGURE 8.7	*Limited Warranty*

Limited Warranty   12 Y 845

This product is guaranteed for one year from the date of purchase to be free of mechanical and electrical defects in material and workmanship. The manufacturer's obligations hereunder are limited to repair of such defects during the warranty period, provided such product is returned to the address below within the warranty period.

This guarantee does not cover normal wear of parts or damages resulting from negligent use or misuse of the product. In addition, this guarantee is void if the purchaser breaks the seal and disassembles, repairs, or alters the product in any way.

The warranty period begins on the date of purchase. The card below must be received by the manufacturer within 30 days of purchase or receipt of said merchandise. Fill out the card completely and return it to the address shown.

Owner's Name: _____
Address: _____
City, State, Zip: _____
E-Mail Address: _____
Date of Purchase: _____
Store Where Purchased: _____

Return to: ALCOVE ELECTRICAL, INC.
42 West Cabana
Arlington, VA 23445-2909

To register your warranty online, visit our web site at www.alcoveelectrical.com.

Serial No.   12 Y 845

PERSONAL RECORD KEEPING

As you begin to accumulate financial records and legal documents, you should have a good filing system to help organize, store, and retrieve needed information. Many people use a simple paper filing system. An electronic filing system may be a more convenient way to organize some records.

PAPER FILING SYSTEM

A typical home filing system would include folders and labels and a file cabinet. Most households need folders for each category shown in Figure 8.8. You may have additional categories. Name your folders with a descriptive word or short phrase that tells you immediately what records it contains. File your folders alphabetically.

Keep records and receipts in the appropriate folder. For example, in the "automobile" folder, you might want to keep track of oil changes, tune-ups, repairs, and other car expenses. You may also want to keep copies of car titles, car insurance policies, insurance cards, car payment records, and other related information. This way they will be easy to find when you need them.

ELECTRONIC RECORD KEEPING

Many people invest in home computers and software for personal financial planning and record keeping. The advantages of computerized systems include the following:

- Ease of updating information
- Ease of record storage and retrieval
- Speed of making new computations and comparisons

FIGURE 8.8   *Home Filing System*

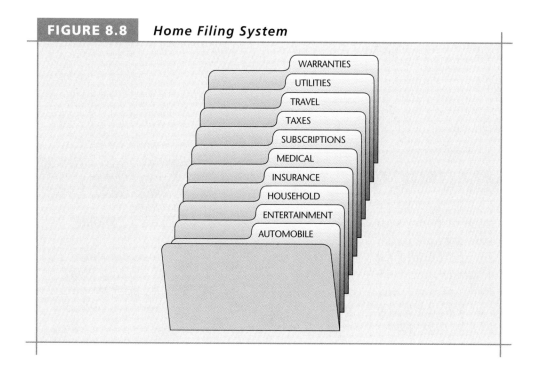

WARRANTIES
UTILITIES
TRAVEL
TAXES
SUBSCRIPTIONS
MEDICAL
INSURANCE
HOUSEHOLD
ENTERTAINMENT
AUTOMOBILE

Many people keep financial records on their computer, usually password-protected, or on a travel or flash drive. As with any important files you keep electronically, always keep a current backup of your financial records.

Many software programs can help you keep better records. A **spreadsheet** is a computer program that organizes data in columns and rows and can perform calculations using the data. You can use a general-purpose spreadsheet program to maintain a list of your income and expenses. You can enter a formula that will perform math calculations, such as addition. When you enter a new expense, the formula will recalculate the new sum automatically. You can even design your own budget worksheet in a spreadsheet program. Spreadsheet programs, such as Excel (Microsoft), are easy to use and help you keep information up to date.

A **database** is a computer program that organizes data for easy search and retrieval. The program can sort the data in many ways. For example, if you entered all of your expenses into a database program, you could ask it to give you a report of all expenses associated with travel.

A general-purpose database program can be rather sophisticated. However, several available software packages are specially designed for financial planning and record keeping. These programs provide spreadsheet and database forms already set up for personal financial management. For example, Microsoft Money and Quicken are popular financial management programs designed to help you keep track of your income and expenses, keep an electronic checkbook, and create budgets.

How can you benefit from having a good filing system?

© Richard Ransier/Corbis

COMMUNICATION *Connection*

Gather a stack of paper slips or index cards. Set up a paper filing system appropriate for you or your family's personal records. On each slip or card, write the name of a folder along with the various records that folder would contain. Then file your "folders" alphabetically.

After setting up the filing system, write a brief summary explaining the benefits of using your filing system to your family. Your paper should persuade them to get their records better organized.

Finance officers and managers are responsible for making sure a business or client has money when it is needed. Almost every firm, government agency, and other type of organization have one or more financial managers. They oversee the preparation of financial reports, manage investments, and implement cash management strategies. By doing so, they keep the company on solid financial footing, allowing for growth and expansion.

Financial managers are creative thinkers and problem solvers. They are computer savvy and are very knowledgeable about all aspects of finance, including global issues. They are also very familiar with tax laws and regulations, ensuring the company is in compliance with them.

Employment Outlook

- An average rate of employment growth is expected.
- Those with a master's degree will have the best opportunities.

Job Titles

- Loan officer
- Finance officer
- Treasurer
- Credit manager

Needed Skills

- A bachelor's degree in finance, accounting, or a related field is required.

- Certifications and advance degrees are preferable.
- Experience and analytical skills are essential.

What's it like to work in... *Finance*

Rajiv works in a comfortable office, right next door to the company president. He reports directly to the president and has frequent informal conversations throughout the day. As chief financial officer (CFO), Rajiv has many responsibilities.

Today he will present his financial analysis to meet the CEO's strategic plan for the next three years. With help from the accounting department, he prepares and revises a forecast of financing options and their costs, along with projected cash management changes. His recommendations include major changes in how the company can operate more efficiently. If his decisions are implemented, many people in the company will have to follow new operating policies to help cut costs and increase profits.

What About You?

Would you like to be involved in helping a company grow by analyzing its finances and increasing its ability to operate more efficiently? Would you consider a career in finance?

Assessment

KEY TERMS REVIEW

Match the terms with the definitions.

_____ 1. A process that verifies the signature of a person who signs a document

_____ 2. A computer program that organizes data in columns and rows

_____ 3. Something of value exchanged for something else of value

_____ 4. A person who agrees to pay the debt of another person

_____ 5. An instrument that is legally collectible

_____ 6. A legally enforceable agreement

_____ 7. A statement assuring quality and performance of a product or service

a. consideration
b. contract
c. co-signer
d. counteroffer
e. database
f. negotiable
g. notarized
h. spreadsheet
i. warranty

_____ 8. A computer program that sorts data for easy search and retrieval

_____ 9. Changing an original offer to make a new offer

CHECK YOUR UNDERSTANDING

10. What are the four elements of a binding contract? How is an express contract different from an implied contract?

11. Explain a paper filing system and an electronic filing system. Why do you need backup copies in both systems?

APPLY YOUR KNOWLEDGE

12. Using Figure 8.6 as a model, write a promissory note from you to John Doe. The note is payable in one year in the amount of $50 with interest of 11 percent and monthly payments of $4.63. Are you the maker or the payee of the note? What is the total amount you will pay on the note?

THINK _CRITICALLY_

13. Once you enter into an agreement, you are obligated to perform as agreed. Why do people who enter into agreements later refuse to do what they agreed to do?

14. Why is it important to keep good financial records? If you fail to keep a backup copy and your house burns down, how will you be able to recreate your records?

Chapter (Assessment)

SUMMARY

8.1

- *Disposable income is the money you have left over to spend or save after paying taxes.*

- *A budget is a spending and saving plan based on expected income and expenses.*

- *To prepare a budget, you should estimate your income and expenses and set a savings goal.*

- *If expenses plus savings exceed income, adjust your spending or saving to balance your budget, or find a new source of income.*

- *Fixed expenses are costs that do not change monthly, while variable expenses change depending on choices made.*

- *Four types of personal records to keep include income and expense records, a net worth statement, a personal property inventory, and tax records.*

- *Net worth is the difference between assets (items of value owned) and liabilities (money owed).*

8.2

- *Contracts are legally binding agreements. They can be express or implied.*

- *An enforceable contract has agreement (offer and acceptance), consideration (an exchange of something of value), contractual capacity (legal ability), and legality (lawful purpose).*

- *Negotiable instruments, such as checks and promissory notes, are promises to pay a specified sum to the holder.*

- *A warranty guarantees a product's quality and performance. It can be written or implied.*

- *Good filing systems can be paper or electronic. Spreadsheet and database programs can facilitate budgeting and record keeping.*

APPLY WHAT YOU KNOW

1. What choices do you have if your budget doesn't balance? If you had to reduce your spending to balance your budget, which would you try to reduce first: fixed or variable expenses? Why?

2. The Statute of Frauds requires that some contracts must be in writing to be enforceable. Give three examples of contracts that must be in writing in order to be enforceable. Why is a written form necessary?

3. Using Figure 8.3 as a model, prepare a net worth statement. List your assets and liabilities. Compute your net worth. How can you use this information?

4. Using Figure 8.4 as a model, prepare a personal property inventory, listing items of personal property in your room at home. Why should you and your family keep a record such as this?

5. After examining the credit application in Figure 8.5 , list the kinds of information requested by a retail store. Why do you think a store wants this type of information?

6. Bring to class an express warranty from a product you or your family recently purchased. What does the warranty specifically promise to do? List any restrictions (exceptions) that the manufacturer has placed in the warranty.

7. Search online for articles or reviews about financial planning software. Write a one-page description of what you could do with the software and what features make one software better than another.

MAKE ACADEMIC CONNECTIONS

8. **Economics** Use the Internet to search for information regarding the budget of the United States, prepared by the President. List the major categories of proposed revenues and expenditures. What are some important provisions of the budget? What is the process for getting the federal budget approved?

9. **Communication** Write a one-page narrative of the goals you would like to include in your life's financial plan. What would you like to achieve (in general terms) and how do you propose to cover the cost of meeting your objectives?

10. **Social Studies** Discuss the role of law in society, such as contract law governing the relationships between people. Explain why laws and rules are important, both in the establishment of and in the enforcement of agreements. What remedies are available to people when the other person in a contract breaches that contract?

11. **Technology** Use a spreadsheet program to create a budget template that could be used for a monthly and yearly budget. Use the categories shown in Figure 8.2. Insert formulas for calculating totals.

Solve Problems and

Explore Issues

12. Based on the following information, prepare a monthly and yearly budget for Brandy and Kenneth Harbour. Use Figure 8.2 as a model.

Average Income

Net paychecks = $1,800 monthly

Interest on savings = $50 monthly

Average Monthly Expenses

Rent payment	$400
Utilities	120
Gasoline	100
Insurance	150
Groceries	200
Clothing	100
Car payment	210
Car maintenance	50
Cell phone	40
Entertainment and recreation	200

Cash Surplus

Savings	To be determined
Investment fund	60
Miscellaneous	120

13. Based on the following information, prepare a monthly and yearly budget for Cathy Kudyrko. Follow the style shown in Figure 8.2.

Average Income

Net monthly pay is $1,400

Average Monthly Expenses

Rent	$410
Insurance	60
Utilities	50
Gasoline	60
Clothing	60
Entertainment	100
Savings	120
Telephone (landline)	15
Car payment	150
Car repairs	20
Groceries	150
Personal care	50
Miscellaneous	155

14. Revise Cathy's budget when she agrees to share her apartment with a friend. Some expenses can be shared equally. Assume the telephone expense increases to $30, utilities to $60, and insurance to $70. These expenses along with rent are shared equally. What will you advise her to do with the added funds?

15. Based on the following information, prepare a net worth statement for Sako Masuta. Follow Figure 8.3. Sako owns a car worth about $3,000 but owes $1,500 on it to the bank. He has $500 in savings and $100 in checking. His personal property totals $3,000, and he also owes $90 to his credit union.

16. Based on the following information, prepare a personal property inventory for Sako Masuta. Follow Figure 8.4.

    Sako has these furnishings in his apartment:

    - JWA entertainment system, Model 252, SN 975923, bought last year for $600, presently worth $500
    - Sofa, presently worth about $800
    - Bright alarm clock, SN 630AM and Blare radio, Model 2602, SN 413T, bought four years ago, total worth about $100.

    Sako also has the following personal items:

    - Miscellaneous clothing and jewelry, presently worth about $800
    - Quantex wristwatch, presently worth about $100
    - Coin collection, valued last year at $600.

    Sako has photographs of these items. (List a hypothetical purchase price for all items except the entertainment system in preparing your property inventory.)

EXTEND YOUR LEARNING

17. **Legal Issues** Fraud is misrepresentation of a material (important) fact with intent to deceive another person or company. People who claim to own assets that they did not purchase and then report them lost or stolen are committing insurance fraud. Or they may claim their vehicle or property was stolen and damaged just to collect insurance. Fraud is a serious crime (felony). Insurance companies investigate claims to be certain that people who file claims legitimately owned those items or that the property was actually stolen and/or damaged. Do you know someone who filed a false insurance claim? How can keeping good records, such as a personal property inventory, protect you from being accused of insurance fraud? What other types of records do you think would be helpful in resolving insurance claims?

For related activities and links, go to **www.cengage.com/school/pfinance/mypf**

Chapter 9

Checking Accounts and Banking Services

9.1	*Checking Accounts*

9.2	*Banking Services and Fees*

Consider **THIS**

Rochelle works part time after school and one weekend a month. She receives a paycheck once a week from her employer.

"I can't cash my paychecks," Rochelle told her boyfriend, "unless my mom goes with me to her bank. They told me that I need my own account. They recommended a checking account along with a savings account. That way I can transfer the money I don't need each month into savings, where I can earn higher interest."

The bank teller told Rochelle that her mother or other adult has to be a joint account holder with her until she reaches age 18. Then she can have her own private account. But for now, a joint account with her mother will allow Rochelle to deposit her checks into her checking account and manage her own money.

Checking Accounts

CHECKING ACCOUNT BASICS

Financial institutions such as banks and credit unions offer a number of services. The first service you will likely want is a checking account. A *checking account* allows you to write checks to make payments. A **check** is a written order to a bank to pay the amount stated to the person or business named on it.

A checking account is also called a **demand deposit**, because the money may be withdrawn at any time—that is, "on demand." Only you, the depositor, also known as the *maker*, can write checks on the account.

Checks follow a process through the banking system. The *payee* cashes your check. The bank that cashed the check returns it to your bank. Your bank withdraws the money from your account and sends it to the other bank. Your bank then stamps the back of your check, indicating that it has *cleared*, which means it has been processed by the bank. A **canceled check** is a check that has cleared your account. It can be used as proof of payment if a dispute arises.

Many banks no longer send paper checks to other banks for processing. To make processing faster and more efficient, they exchange check information electronically by transmitting an image of the check, called a *substitute check*. A substitute check can be used in the same way as an original check.

A checking account offers several advantages.

- It provides a convenient way to pay your bills.
- Writing a check is often safer than using cash, especially when making major purchases, paying bills, or buying through the mail.
- It has a built-in record keeping system that you can use to track expenses and create budgets.
- It gives you access to other bank services, such as loans, online banking, and 24-hour access to your money through automated teller machines (ATMs).

As an account holder, you should write checks carefully and keep accurate records. You should check the accuracy of the bank statement you receive each month. In the past, canceled checks were returned with the statement. Today, most banks either send copies of canceled checks or simply describe your canceled checks on the statement. Merchants can also use *electronic check conversion* to convert a check into a debit transaction instead of processing the check. With this process, the check may either be destroyed or returned to you immediately after the transaction is processed. It is your responsibility to keep track of all of these entries in your checking account.

You must also maintain enough money in your account to cover all the checks you write. A check written for more money than your account contains is called an **overdraft**. A bank that does not honor a check usually stamps the check with the words "not sufficient funds" (NSF) and returns the check to the payee's bank. When this occurs, the check has *bounced*. Your bank will charge you a fee of $25 or more for each NSF check processed.

Many people write checks, hoping to deposit money to cover them before they clear. This is called **floating a check**. Floating a check is very risky because today's electronic systems allow checks to process very quickly. Floating a check is illegal in most states. Intentionally writing bad checks can result in penalties and hurt your credit record.

OPENING A CHECKING ACCOUNT

To open a checking account, you must fill out and sign a signature authorization form, such as the one shown in Figure 9.1. The signature form provides an official signature that the bank can compare to the signature you write on your checks. Most banks also require that you have an initial deposit of $50 or more.

In Figure 9.1, Ardys Johnson completed and signed the form. Signature forms look different at various banks, but they contain the same basic information. Ardys also listed her mother's maiden name for use in identification.

FIGURE 9.1	*Signature Authorization Form*

First Independent Mutual Savings Bank
Checking Signature Verification

Customer Name	Ardys Johnson	Date	4/28/--
Account No.	08 40 856	Individual X Joint	
Address	4250 West 18th Avenue	Home Phone	555-8925
City/State/ZIP	Chicago, IL 60601-2180	Work Phone	555-0100
Social Security No.	999-00-8696	Birthdate	11/20/80
Occupation	Accountant	How long?	2 years
Employer	Cho and Jackson, Inc.	Phone	555-8925
Contact in case of emergency:	Harold Johnson	Phone	555-2322
Relationship	father		
Mother's Maiden Name or other code word	Williams		

SIGNATURE: _Ardys Johnson_   Date _4/28/--_

(Use second page for joint account holders.)

Someone forging Ardys's signature is not likely to know her mother's maiden name when questioned by a teller.

◼ PARTS OF A CHECK

A check consists of the following parts. Look at the lettered elements of the check in Figure 9.2 as you read the following explanations.

Ⓐ *Check Number.* Checks are numbered for easy identification. In Figure 9.2, Check 581 has been prenumbered by the bank.

Ⓑ *ABA Number.* The American Bankers Association (ABA) number appears in fraction form in the upper right corner of each check. The top half of the fraction identifies the location and district of the bank from which the check is drawn. The bottom half helps in routing the check to the specific area and bank on which it is drawn.

Ⓒ *Name and Address of Maker.* The maker, or *drawer*, is the person authorized to write checks on the account. Ardys Johnson is the maker of the check in Figure 9.2. You should have your name, address, and phone number printed on your checks.

Ⓓ *Date.* In this blank, fill in the date you write the check. Do not *postdate* (write a future date on) checks.

Ⓔ *Payee.* The *payee* is the person or company to whom the check is made payable. Food Mart is the payee in Figure 9.2.

Ⓕ *Numeric Amount.* Write the amount neatly and clearly as close as possible to the dollar sign, with the dollars and cents clearly distinguished.

Ⓖ *Written Amount.* The written amount shows the amount of dollars and cents being paid, written in words. The word "dollars" is preprinted at the end of the line. Write the word "and" to separate dollar amounts from cents.

Ⓗ *Signature.* Sign your check on the signature line, the same way you wrote it on your signature card.

Ⓘ *Account and Routing Numbers.* The account number appears in bank coding at the bottom of each check. In Figure 9.2, 08 40 856 is Ardys's checking account number. The number 071000741 is the bank's routing number for the electronic sorting and routing of checks.

Ⓙ *Memo.* The memo line at the bottom left of each check provides a place to write the purpose of the check. Filling in this line is optional.

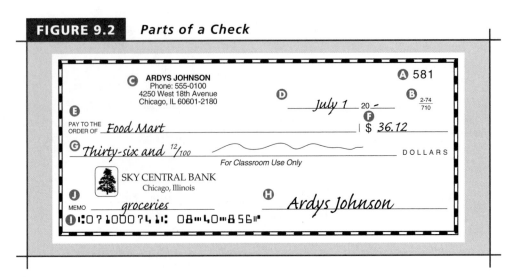

FIGURE 9.2 *Parts of a Check*

Banks sell checks to customers. They often provide checks of basic design free to account holders who maintain minimum balances. You can also choose to buy checks with special designs or colors, either from your bank or from a check-printing company.

USING YOUR CHECKING ACCOUNT

Checking accounts can help you manage your personal finances but only if you use them correctly. Careless or improper use of a checking account can result in financial loss. Here are some tips on using a checking account.

WRITING CHECKS

When writing checks, be sure to do the following:

- Always use a pen, preferably one with dark ink that does not skip or blot.
- Write legibly. Keep numbers and letters clear and distinct, without extra space before, between, or after them.
- Sign your name as it appears preprinted on the check and on the signature card.
- Avoid mistakes. If you make a mistake, write "VOID" across the face of the check to cancel it and then write a new check.
- Be certain you have deposited adequate funds in your account to cover each check you write.

PAYING BILLS ONLINE

Instead of writing checks to pay bills, you can pay bills online. It is safer than sending checks through the mail and faster because money leaves your account right away. It's also convenient and saves both postage and the cost of checks.

To pay bills online, you have two choices. First, you can register at the web site of the business to which you will be making payments. You will give them your routing number and checking account number. Each month you can authorize a payment, or you can allow the business to take automatic payments from your account.

Second, you can pay bills from your own bank. To do this, you must first register at your bank's web site. In that process, you establish your *personal identification number (PIN)* or password to gain entry into your account. Screen prompts will lead you to the bank's online bill payment page, such as the one shown in Figure 9.3.

© Digital Vision/Getty Images

Why do people pay their bills online?

FIGURE 9.3 *Online Bill Payment Page*

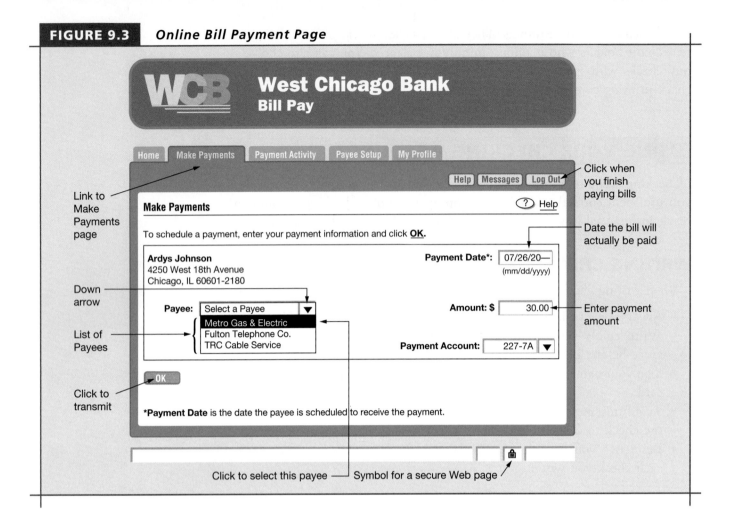

After you set up your list of payees, you can pay bills each month by simply selecting the payee from the list and entering the payment amount. The bank will remove the money from your checking account and send it to the payee's account. Be sure to record these payments in your checkbook register.

Some banks charge a monthly fee for online bill payment privileges. Some limit the number of bills you can pay online each month. Consider the fees and restrictions for online banking when you choose a bank.

■ MAKING DEPOSITS

You should complete a *deposit slip* each time you want to deposit money in your account. Figure 9.4 illustrates a deposit slip. To prepare a deposit slip, follow these guidelines:

1. Insert the date of the transaction.
2. In the "Cash" section, write in the amount of currency (paper money) and coins you are depositing.
3. If you are depositing checks, write the amount of each check, together with the check's ABA number (top part of fraction), in the "Checks" section of the slip.
4. Total the currency, coin, and check amounts. Write this figure on the "Subtotal" line.

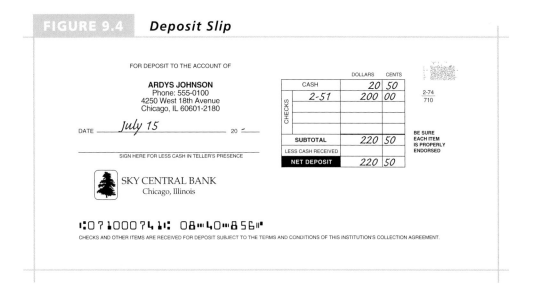

FIGURE 9.4 *Deposit Slip*

5. If you wish to receive some cash at the time of your deposit, fill in the desired amount on the "Less Cash Received" line.

6. If cash is received, subtract it from the subtotal. Write the final amount of the deposit on the "Net Deposit" line.

7. If you will receive cash, write your signature on the line above the words "Sign here for less cash in teller's presence" (this wording will vary).

8. The teller will give you either a copy of this deposit slip or a receipt. Keep the copy or receipt as proof of your deposit.

Checking account deposits can also be made at your bank's ATM machine or in a night deposit. Be sure the deposit slip is filled out accurately.

USING A CHECKBOOK REGISTER

A **checkbook register** is a booklet used to record checking account transactions. Figure 9.5 shows a page from the checkbook register of Ardys Johnson. Ardys lists all checks, online payments, fees, interest, and deposits for her account. Follow along in Figure 9.5 as you read the following guidelines for recording transactions in a checkbook register.

1. Record the current amount in your account at the top of the "Balance" column. (When you go to the next page in your register, copy your account balance from the bottom of the previous page to the top of the new page).

2. As soon as you write a check, make an online payment, or make a deposit, record the transaction in your checkbook register.

3. Write the preprinted check number in the first column. If the transaction is not a check, make up a code to represent the kind of transaction it is, such as DEP for deposit, WD for withdrawal, ON for online transaction, SC for service charge, and INT for interest.

4. Write the month, day, and year of the transaction in the "Date" column.

5. Enter the name of the payee on the first line of the "Description" section. On the second line, write the purpose of the check or any description of the transaction you find useful.

6. If the transaction will reduce your balance, write the amount in the "Payment/Debit" column. If the transaction will add to your balance, record the amount in the "Deposit/Credit" column.

FIGURE 9.5   *Checkbook Register*

CHECK NO. OR TRANSACTION CODE	DATE	DESCRIPTION OF TRANSACTION	PAYMENT/ DEBIT(−)		FEE (−)	✓	DEPOSIT/ CREDIT (+)		BALANCE $800	00
581	7/1/--	Food Mart	$ 36	12	.20		$		36	32
		Groceries							763	68
DEP	7/15/--	Deposit Paycheck					220	50	220	50
									984	18
WD	7/16/--	ATM Withdrawal	20	00					20	00
									964	18
582	7/20/--	Bellvue Apts.	600	00	.20				600	20
		Rent							363	98
ON	7/22/--	Metro Gas & Electric	32	50					32	50
		Online Payment							331	48
SC	7/31/--	Monthly Account Fee			5.00				5	00
		July							326	48

7. Some banks charge a fee for each check written. In this case, record the fee in the "Fee" column next to the check.

8. Add the amount of the check to the check fee, and record the result in the "Balance" column. For a deposit, simply repeat the amount in the "Balance" column.

9. If the amount is a debit transaction, subtract it from the previous balance. If the amount is a deposit or other credit transaction, add it to the previous balance. Write the new balance on the next line of the "Balance" column.

10. The column headed by a check mark is provided so that you can check off each transaction when it appears on your monthly bank statement. The check mark shows that the transaction was cleared by the bank and is no longer outstanding (unprocessed).

Always keep your checkbook register handy so you can write down the necessary information each time you make a transaction. If you don't record it promptly, you could forget a transaction and accidentally overdraw your account.

∎ RECONCILING YOUR CHECKING ACCOUNT

Financial institutions that offer checking accounts provide each customer with a monthly statement. This statement lists checks received and processed by the bank, plus all other withdrawals, deposits, service charges, and interest. Your canceled checks, or copies of them, may also be included with your statement.

The process of matching your checkbook register with the bank statement is known as **bank reconciliation**. The back of the bank statement is usually printed with a form to aid you in reconciling your account. Figure 9.6 represents both sides of a typical bank statement.

The left side of Figure 9.6 is a statement showing the bank's record of activity on Ardys Johnson's checking account. The statement lists all checks that have cleared as well as all withdrawals, online bill payments, and fees that the bank subtracted from the account. It also shows all deposits added to the balance that month. After subtracting all debit transactions and adding all deposits, the bank arrives at the ending, or current, balance for the account.

FIGURE 9.6   *Bank Reconciliation*

Bank Statement
SKY CENTRAL BANK

Ardys Johnson
4250 West 18th Avenue
Chicago, IL 60601-2180

Statement Date: July 31, 20—
Opening Balance: $800.00
Ending Balance: $926.68

Checks

Check No.	Date Paid	Amount
581	7/4/—	36.12

Debits and Withdrawals

Date	Amount	Description
7/16/—	20.00	ATM withdrawal
7/22/—	32.50	Online bill payment
7/31/—	.20	Check fee ($0.20 per check)
7/31/—	5.00	Monthly account fee

Deposits

Date	Amount	Description
7/15/—	220.50	Deposit

Account Reconciliation

1. Ending balance shown on the bank statement: *926.68*

2. Total of all credits and deposits made but not shown on statement: *0*

3. Total lines 1 and 2: *926.68*

4. List all checks, withdrawals, and debits made but not shown on statement:

Check No. or Transaction Code	Amount	
582	600	00
SC		20

5. Total of outstanding debit transactions: *600.20*

6. Subtract line 5 from line 3: (Result should match checkbook balance.) *326.48*

The balance your checkbook register shows will not always match the ending balance shown on the bank statement. A check does not appear on the statement until the payee has cashed it and the check completes its route through the banking system. Since you recorded the check and subtracted the amount from your balance when you wrote it, your balance will be lower than the bank's until the check clears and the bank removes the payment from your account. As you can see by comparing Ardys's checkbook register (Figure 9.5) to her bank statement (Figure 9.6), the ending balances do not match. When this occurs, you can check for errors by reconciling your account. Follow along on the right side of Figure 9.6 as Ardys reconciles her account.

1. Write the ending balance shown on the bank statement.
2. From your checkbook register, total any deposits you made that do not appear on the bank statement.
3. Add the outstanding deposits to the ending bank balance.
4. List all debit transactions from your checkbook register that do not appear on the statement. Debit transactions are any transactions that reduce your balance, including checks, online bill payments, withdrawals, and fees. Ardys listed check #582 and its check fee, since these did not appear on her statement.
5. Total all outstanding debit transactions.
6. Subtract the total debits from the previous total. The result should match the balance shown in your checkbook register.

If the balances do not match, check your addition and subtraction in the reconciliation process. Next, make certain that you have deducted service charges from and added any interest earned to your check register balance. For example, Ardys recorded the $5 monthly account fee in her check register. Check all addition and subtraction for the period covered by the statement. Finally, if you still cannot reconcile your account, ask a bank representative for help in discovering where the error lies. Be sure to take your checkbook, canceled checks, and bank statement with you.

Do the reconciliation immediately upon receipt of the bank statement. This will allow you to report any problems to the bank as soon as possible. Occasionally the bank does make an error, which it will correct when you report the mistake. You can also view your current balance and all transactions with online banking.

▌ ENDORSING CHECKS

A check generally cannot be cashed until it is endorsed. When two or more people are named as payees, all must endorse the check if the names are separated by "and." If the names are separated by "or," only one person must endorse it. To endorse a check, the payee named on the check signs the top part of the back of the check in ink. There are three major types of endorsements.

Blank Endorsement

A **blank endorsement** is the signature of the payee written exactly as his or her name appears on the front of the check.

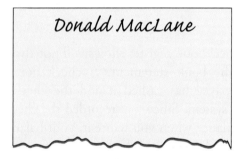

If Donald's name had been written incorrectly on the face of the check, he would correct the mistake by endorsing the check with the misspelled version first and then with the correct version of his name, as shown here.

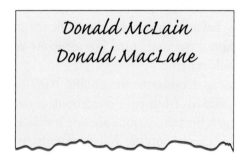

Special Endorsement

A **special endorsement**, or an endorsement in full, is an endorsement that transfers the right to cash the check to someone else. It consists of the words "Pay to the order of [new payee's name]" and the signature of the original payee. In the following illustration, for example, Donald MacLane uses a check written to him to pay a debt owed to Diane Jones. By using a special endorsement, Donald avoids having to cash the check before repaying Diane.

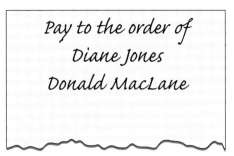

Pay to the order of
Diane Jones
Donald MacLane

Restrictive Endorsement

A **restrictive endorsement** restricts or limits the use of a check. For example, a check endorsed with the words "For Deposit Only" above the payee's signature can be deposited only to the account specified. The restrictive endorsement is safer than the blank endorsement for use in mailing deposits, in night deposit systems, or in other circumstances that may result in loss of a check. If a check with a restrictive endorsement is lost, the finder cannot cash it.

For Deposit Only
United California Bank
Acct. #8-2011-4
Donald MacLane

TYPES OF CHECKING ACCOUNTS

Financial institutions offer many types of checking accounts. You should carefully study your options, because a wise choice can save you money. Most banks still offer *free checking* (no service fees) accounts. These accounts do not pay interest and may come with certain conditions. For example, you may be required to maintain a certain balance or limit your use of teller services. Free checking is also available to senior citizens, nonprofit groups, and to others during special bank promotions.

JOINT ACCOUNTS

Accounts can be either joint or individual. A *joint account* is opened by two or more people. Such an account is also called a *survivorship account* because any person who signs on the account has the right to the entire amount deposited. If one person using the account dies, the other (the survivor) then becomes the sole owner of the funds in the account.

© Photodisc/Getty Images

Why might a person open a joint account?

SPECIAL ACCOUNTS

Most banks offer a *special checking account* to customers who have a small amount of activity in their accounts each month. Service fees are charged at a flat rate per month with an additional fee for each check written (for example, $8 per month plus 15 cents for each check cashed). In some instances, banks may charge service fees only when the number of checks written or deposits made in a month exceeds a set limit (such as more than ten checks or three deposits in a given month). If you write only a few checks each month, this type of account might be right for you.

Another type of special account assesses a small or no monthly fee, but charges for each teller service. If you make a deposit or withdrawal at a teller station, you will be assessed a fee for the personal service. This type of account is good for people who have their paychecks electronically deposited by their employers and who use ATMs for most of their withdrawals and other transactions.

STANDARD ACCOUNTS

A *standard account* usually has a small or no monthly service fee and no per-check fee. To avoid a monthly service fee, you are usually required to maintain an average minimum balance in the account. Many banks offer a package of services for this type of account, such as free traveler's checks, an ATM card, or a free safe deposit box. Some banks offer reduced interest rates on credit card balances to customers who also have checking, savings, and other accounts at their bank.

INTEREST-BEARING ACCOUNTS

Most financial institutions offer checking accounts that earn interest. With these accounts, your account balance usually must not fall below a minimum average set by the bank during any month. The minimum may be $500 or more.

Interest rates rise and fall with economic conditions. When overall interest rates drop, you may receive less than 1 percent. When overall interest rates rise, you might expect 5 percent or more. A *money market account* is an interest-bearing checking account that pays a higher rate of interest, but it usually has more restrictions.

SHARE ACCOUNTS

Most credit unions offer *share accounts*. These are checking accounts with low (or no) average daily balance requirements and, generally, no service fees. If you are eligible for credit union membership, this type of account may be the least expensive and most convenient option.

NETBookmark

Omaha State Bank operates several branches on the west side of Omaha, Nebraska. The bank offers its customers a wide array of checking account choices. Access www.cengage.com/school/pfinance/mypf and click on the link for Chapter 9. Browse the site and review the options for the various plans. (*Hint:* Under "Deposits," click the *Checking* link.) Then answer: Which account requires the smallest minimum balance? What is the monthly maintenance fee for the Prime Time Checking account, and when does it apply? Does the Ultimate Choice plan allow unlimited check writing? If you wanted to open a checking account at Omaha State Bank, which account would you choose? Why?

www.cengage.com/school/pfinance/mypf

Planning a Career in... Accounting

Business Management & Administration

Accountants are analytical and trained to keep good, accurate records. They work in companies, for individual clients, and for government units. Their jobs focus on information—preparing, analyzing, and verifying it. Through audits and verification procedures, accountants ensure that accuracy standards are met. Many people depend on the integrity of the information reported by businesses. Accountants ensure that an organization reports its results of operations and current financial condition in a full and transparent manner.

Employment Outlook

- Strong growth in overall employment through 2016 is expected.
- CPAs will experience the highest demand; growth at 18 percent is faster than average for all occupations.

Job Titles

- Certified public accountant (CPA)
- Government accountant
- Internal auditor
- Management accountant
- Forensic accountant

Needed Skills

- Bachelor's degree in accounting or related field, with CPA designation and four years experience is preferred.
- Excellent communication skills; attention to detail and accuracy.
- Excellent technology skills, including proficiency in accounting, tax, and spreadsheet software.

What's it like to work in... *Accounting*

Bill works many 12-hour days as a junior accountant. He plans to become a junior partner within 5 years and a full partner within 15 years. That means long days learning the intricacies of financial audits, information consulting, and tax laws. Bill took and passed the CPA exam right after college graduation. When he completed two years of work experience with a CPA, he was granted the CPA designation, which now hangs proudly on the wall at the accounting firm.

Bill enjoys meeting with his firm's clients and discussing their needs, both in terms of reporting and assessing their business operations effectively, and in terms of planning the security of their assets and business information. He knows that it is critical for businesses to protect their information system as well as use it effectively to make good economic decisions.

What About You?

Would you consider a career in accounting? Are you analytical and detail-oriented? Do you like working with people? How do ethics affect those working in this field?

Assessment

KEY TERMS REVIEW

Match the terms with the definitions. Some terms may not be used.

_____ 1. A type of bank account from which funds may be withdrawn at any time

_____ 2. A booklet used to record checking account transactions

_____ 3. An endorsement that transfers the right to cash a check to someone else

_____ 4. Writing a check and hoping to cover it with a deposit before it clears

_____ 5. A check that has cleared your account

_____ 6. A written order to a bank to pay the amount stated to the person or business named on it

_____ 7. A check written for more money than your account contains

_____ 8. An endorsement that limits the use of a check

_____ 9. The process of matching your checkbook register with the bank statement

a. bank reconciliation

b. blank endorsement

c. canceled check

d. check

e. checkbook register

f. demand deposit

g. floating a check

h. overdraft

i. restrictive endorsement

j. special endorsement

CHECK YOUR UNDERSTANDING

10. What is an overdraft? Why is it important to avoid it? How can keeping a checkbook register up to date help?

11. Name five types of checking accounts available at many banks.

APPLY YOUR KNOWLEDGE

12. Using a blank piece of paper, prepare three endorsements—blank, special, and restrictive. Label each one and explain when it would be used.

THINK CRITICALLY

13. Explain why it is important to protect your own account number by shredding unused deposit slips and voided checks.

14. A checking account offers you convenience for bill paying. Many people choose to use cash only. Which viewpoint do you agree with? Why?

15. Bank reconciliation allows you to catch errors in your account—your own and the bank's. Many people do not take time to reconcile their accounts. Is this okay? Why or why not?

Banking Services and Fees

GOALS

- Describe banking services available at most financial institutions.
- List and explain fees charged by financial institutions for their services.

TERMS

- certified check, *p. 199*
- cashier's check, *p. 199*
- traveler's checks, *p. 200*
- debit card, *p. 200*
- overdraft protection, *p. 201*
- electronic funds transfer (EFT), *p. 201*
- stop-payment order, *p. 201*
- safe deposit box, *p. 202*

BANKING SERVICES

A *full-service bank* is one that offers every possible kind of service, from savings and checking accounts to credit cards, safe deposit boxes, loans, and ATMs. Other services commonly offered are online banking, telephone banking, certified checks, cashier's checks, money orders, and debit cards. Most banks offer FDIC (Federal Deposit Insurance Corporation) insurance, which protects the deposits of customers against loss up to $250,000 per account.

GUARANTEED-PAYMENT CHECKS

A **certified check** is a personal check that the bank guarantees or certifies to be good. Sometimes a payee might want you to get your personal check certified to reduce the risk of accepting your check for payment. For example, if you buy a used car from someone, the owner might want a certified check before allowing you to take the car.

To get a check certified, write your check in the normal manner. Then take it to your bank. A bank officer will immediately deduct the amount from your checking account, stamp the word "certified" on the check, and initial it. In effect, the bank holds in reserve the check amount from your account for specific payment of that check. Most financial institutions charge the account holder for this service. Typically, the fee ranges from $2.50 to $5.00 per check.

A **cashier's check**, also called a *bank draft*, is a check written by a bank on its own funds. You can pay for a cashier's check through a withdrawal from your savings or checking account, or in cash. After receiving your payment, the teller makes out the cashier's check to your payee, and an officer of the bank signs it.

Cashier's checks are generally used when the payee requires a guaranteed payment but cash is not desirable. A cashier's check also can be used for transactions in which you wish to remain anonymous. The bank is listed as the maker of the check, and your identity need not be revealed. As with certified checks, many banks charge a fee for issuing cashier's checks.

Women's World Banking (WWB) is a nonprofit organization based in New York that is committed to expanding the economic assets, participation, and power of low-income women as entrepreneurs and economic agents. WWB supports a network of financial organizations that provide women with easier access to finance, knowledge, and markets. WWB has more than 23 million end users (women borrowing money) who are low-income borrowers. The network of organizations finances small business loans and health insurance to help increase family incomes, improve nutrition and health, raise education standards, and reduce poverty around the globe.

THINK *CRITICALLY*

How can WWB help reduce poverty by making small business loans?

Many financial institutions also provide traveler's checks for their customers. **Traveler's checks** are check forms in specific denominations that are used instead of cash while traveling. Many businesses that will not accept an out-of-state personal check will accept a traveler's check for payment. When traveler's checks are purchased, money is taken from your bank account to cover them. You sign each traveler's check in one place immediately upon purchase. When cashed, you present identification and sign in another place. Traveler's checks are safer than carrying cash, since they are payable only upon comparison of the purchaser's endorsement against the original signature on the check.

MONEY ORDERS

Banks sell *money orders* to people who do not wish to use cash or do not have a checking account. A money order is like a check, except that it can never bounce. There is a charge for purchasing a money order. It can cost from 50 cents to $5 or more, depending on the amount of the money order. You also can purchase money orders through the post office and local merchants.

DEBIT CARDS

A **debit card** is a plastic card that deducts money from a checking account almost immediately to pay for purchases. The debit card is presented at the time of purchase. When a debit card is used, the amount of the purchase is quickly deducted from the customer's checking account and paid to the merchant. The debit card transaction is similar to writing a check to pay for purchases. The issuing bank may charge an annual fee for the card or a fee for each transaction. A debit card is not the same as a credit card. No credit is extended. Instead, payment occurs instantly because funds are quickly withdrawn from your checking account. Debit cards can also be used for cash withdrawals at ATMs. Be sure to record these transactions in your check register.

BANK CREDIT CARDS

You can apply to a full-service bank for a bank credit card, such as a Visa or MasterCard. If you meet the requirements and are issued a card, you can use it instead of cash at any business that accepts credit cards. Banks offering national credit cards usually charge both an annual fee for use of the card and interest on the unpaid account balance. The topics of credit and credit cards will be discussed in detail in Unit 4.

OVERDRAFT PROTECTION

Overdraft protection allows you to cover checks or withdrawals up to a specified amount, usually between $100 and $1,000, depending on the typical balance in your account. With **overdraft protection**, your checks will be covered even if you have insufficient funds in your checking account. Protection may be offered in the form of an instant "loan" with high interest rates. Other banks may charge a flat fee. With some overdraft-protection agreements, the amount of the overdraft may be pulled from your savings account or charged to your bank credit card. Banks may charge transfer fees for this type of protection.

AUTOMATED TELLER MACHINES

Many banks provide ATMs for their customers. At an ATM, you can make cash withdrawals (using your debit card) from your checking or savings account. Using a Visa or MasterCard, you can receive a cash advance electronically. To use 24-hour ATMs, you must have a card that is electronically coded. You also must know your personal identification number (PIN), which usually is some combination of numbers and letters. For safety, do not carry your PIN in written form. Commit it to memory.

ONLINE AND TELEPHONE BANKING

Most financial institutions offer online and telephone banking services to their customers. These services give you the ability to access your accounts from a computer or telephone, transfer money from one account to another, and pay bills by authorizing the bank to disburse money. You can find out your current balance, what checks have cleared, and which deposits have been entered. Online and telephone banking enable you to access your account anytime, day or night.

Most banks also allow and encourage electronic transfers of money. An **electronic funds transfer (EFT)** uses a computer-based system that enables you to move money from one account to another without writing a check or exchanging cash. This can be done by telephone, by computer, or in person. Money is available immediately (there is no delay as with waiting for a check to clear). Electronic transfers can also be made between banking institutions, and funds are available immediately.

STOP-PAYMENT ORDERS

A **stop-payment order** is a request that the bank not honor a specific check. The usual reason for stopping payment is that the check has been lost or stolen. By issuing a stop-payment order, the check

© Photodisc/Getty Images

Why do people use automated teller machines?

writer can safely write a new check, knowing that the original check cannot be cashed if it is found and presented to the bank. Most banks charge a fee (usually $20 or more) for stopping payment on a check. The stop-payment order is usually good for only six months. After that, the check will no longer be honored because checks over six-months old are not valid for cashing or depositing.

SAFE DEPOSIT BOXES

Financial institutions offer customers a **safe deposit box** to store valuable items or documents. They charge a yearly fee based on the size of the box. Annual rental fees may range from $50–$150 or more. The customer is given two keys for the box. The bank will also have a key. Both the customer's key and bank's key must be used to open the box. Documents commonly kept in a safe deposit box are birth certificates, marriage and death certificates, deeds and mortgages, and stocks and bonds. Jewelry, coin collections, and other small valuables also are commonly stored there. Keeping important documents and other items in a safe deposit box ensures that the items won't be stolen, lost, or destroyed. Documents that can be easily replaced with a duplicate need not be stored there.

When you rent a safe deposit box, you will fill out a signature card. Then each time you enter your safe deposit box, you must sign a form so that your signature can be compared to the one on file. This procedure prevents unlawful entry to your box by an unauthorized person.

LOANS AND TRUSTS

Financial institutions also make loans to finance the purchase of cars, homes, vacations, home improvements, and other items. Banks can also provide advice for estate planning and trusts. (You'll learn more about estates and trusts in Chapter 15.) In addition, banks can act as trustees of estates for minors and others. A *trustee* is a person or an institution that manages property for the benefit of someone else under a special agreement.

NOTARY PUBLIC

A *notary public* verifies a person's identity, witnesses the person's signature on a legal document, and then "notarizes" the signature as valid. Financial institutions typically have a person on their staff who is a notary public. This person provides notary services for account holders, usually without charge. For non-customers, however, there is typically a small fee.

FINANCIAL SERVICES

Many banks offer financial services to their depositors, such as purchasing or selling savings bonds and investment brokerage services. You may buy and sell stocks and bonds through the brokerage service. The purchases and sales are "cleared" through your checking or savings accounts with the bank. Brokerage services will be discussed in Chapter 12. Many banks also purchase a block of bonds (debt obligations) that they allow their members and depositors to purchase. Generally there is no additional fee to buy or sell these securities (the fee is included in the purchase price). However, a minimum purchase such as $1,000 is often required.

BANK FEES

Banks charge fees to their customers to help cover their operating costs. For example, when a bank grants you a loan, it charges you a loan fee. When the bank acts as the trustee of an estate, it charges a fee for this service.

Banks also charge noncustomers for services such as check cashing. If you want to cash a check at a bank where you do not have an account, the bank may charge you a fee or refuse to cash the check. Nondepositors pay for other services that may be free to depositors, such as traveler's checks and notary services.

Under the Truth-in-Savings Act (1993), checking advertised as "free" must carry no hidden charges or conditions. The bank or savings institution cannot charge regular maintenance or per-check fees or require balance minimums to avoid fees. However, it still may charge for a box of checks and for ATM transactions.

Most banks charge these fees to their customers who have checking accounts:

- Monthly service fees, averaging $5 to $15
- Overdraft fees of $25 to $30 per event
- NSF check charges of $25 to $30 per event
- ATM fees of $1 to $5 per transaction
- Safe deposit box fees of $50 to $150 per year

Unless you have a regular checking account, you may also be charged fees for teller services, account balances that fall below the stated minimum, cashier's and certified checks, traveler's checks, notary services, and online bill payment services. In addition, some banks charge a fee to return canceled checks.

The best way to avoid fees is to choose the right kind of account. For example, if you need to write a large number of checks each month, sign up for an account that does not charge a per-check fee. Some accounts charge a fee for using a teller. Only sign up for such an account if you have your paycheck directly deposited by your employer and can do almost all of your transactions online or by ATM. Shop around and find the account that is right for you. Be aware of the rules of your account, so that you don't violate them, resulting in high fees. If your account requires a minimum balance, plan enough cushion so that your balance will not drop below that amount.

One way to avoid service charges is to have more than one account and to link them together. For example, if you have a retirement savings account, it can be "linked" to your checking account. The combined balances of your retirement account and checking account can give you the minimum balance you need to avoid service fees on your checking account.

© Photodisc/Getty Images

Why is it important to know the rules in your bank account agreement?

ISSUES IN YOUR WORLD

SHOPPING FOR THE RIGHT BANK

A checking account is a personal choice. Some people choose the bank closest to their home or work. Others choose the biggest bank or the one with the most ATMs. While all of these are good reasons, there are many other considerations in choosing your bank. Sometimes the best choice is a credit union where you can have the same services and possibly lower fees.

Finding the right bank can take a lot of time. All banks and services are not the same; they vary a great deal. A good way to start is to make a list of the features that are important to you. Rank them 1 to 10. For example, #1 may be a low interest rate on a Visa card; #2 may be a low minimum deposit for a free or interest-bearing account; and #3 may be low or no service fees. Arrange your features into a table, either on paper or in a word processor or spreadsheet. At the top, list the banks that you are considering. Your table might look like this:

	Bank 1	**Bank 2**	**Bank 3**
Free online bill payment	_____	_____	_____
Low/no minimum deposit	_____	_____	_____
Low/no service fee	_____	_____	_____
Online banking available	_____	_____	_____
Low-cost credit card available	_____	_____	_____
Conveniently located ATMs	_____	_____	_____

Fill in your table by inserting information you find out about the different banks. Then compare information to determine which bank overall provides the best services at the lowest costs for you.

THINK *CRITICALLY*

1. *Which is your favorite bank or credit union? Why?*
2. *What features do you think are the most important when choosing a financial institution for your checking account?*
3. *What would cause you to switch from one financial institution to another?*

Assessment

KEY TERMS REVIEW

Match the terms with the definitions.

_____ 1. Check forms in specific denominations that are used instead of cash while traveling

_____ 2. A request that the bank not honor a specific check

_____ 3. A plastic card that deducts money from a checking account almost immediately to pay for purchases

_____ 4. A personal check that the bank guarantees to be good

_____ 5. A computer-based system that moves money from one account to another without writing a check or using cash

a. cashier's check

b. certified check

c. debit card

d. electronic funds transfer

e. overdraft protection

f. safe deposit box

g. stop-payment order

h. traveler's checks

_____ 6. A check written by a bank on its own funds

_____ 7. A place at your bank available to store valuable items or documents

_____ 8. A bank service that covers checks even if you have insufficient funds in your checking account

CHECK YOUR UNDERSTANDING

9. List five banking services that are found at full-service banks.

10. List bank fees charged to customers and to noncustomers for services provided.

APPLY YOUR KNOWLEDGE

11. Checking accounts may have many good features, such as overdraft protection. List banking services that appeal to you and indicate whether each is of high, medium, or low value. Would you be willing to pay a monthly service fee to have the service?

THINK CRITICALLY

12. When customers write too many bad checks, banks may close their accounts. It may be difficult for such a person to get an account at another bank. Do you agree with the banks' actions? Why or why not?

13. Many people feel that bank fees are too high. They believe that banks make money off of account deposits but pay depositors insufficient interest for use of their money. Do you agree? Why or why not?

Chapter Assessment

SUMMARY

9.1

- *A checking account is a demand deposit that provides a safe, convenient way to pay bills.*

- *To open a checking account, fill out a signature authorization form and make a deposit.*

- *To write a check, fill in the current date, name of the payee, and the amount in figures and words. Then sign the form.*

- *As soon as you make a checking transaction, record it in your checkbook register.*

- *A canceled check is one that has been cleared, or processed by your bank and deducted from your account.*

- *If you float a check, you are risking the possibility of an overdraft on your account, since today's electronic systems process checks so quickly.*

- *Reconcile your bank statement with your register each month and correct any errors.*

- *To cash a check, you must endorse it with a blank, special, or restrictive endorsement.*

9.2

- *Certified checks and cashier's checks are guaranteed by the bank to be paid.*

- *Traveler's checks provide a readily acceptable and safe form of payment for people who are traveling.*

- *You can pay for purchases or make ATM transactions using a debit card, which allows immediate deductions from your checking account.*

- *With overdraft protection, your checks will be covered even if you have insufficient funds in your checking account.*

- *Online and telephone banking enable you to make electronic transfers and access your account 24 hours a day.*

- *A stop-payment order is a request that the bank not honor a specific check.*

- *Financial institutions offer safe deposit boxes for customers to store valuable items or documents.*

- *To avoid high bank fees, choose the type of account that best fits your needs and follow the account rules.*

APPLY WHAT YOU KNOW

1. Using Figure 9.2 as an example and following the guidelines on pages 188–189, write these checks:

   ▪ Check No. 12 to Melvin Quigly for $34.44, written today.
   ▪ Check No. 322 to Save-Now Stores for $15.01, written today. The purpose of your check is to buy school supplies.
   ▪ Check No. 484 to M.A. Rosario for $91.10, written today.

   Note: Blank checks are available in the Student Activity Guide.

2. Using Figure 9.4 as an example and following the guidelines on pages 190–191, prepare these deposit slips:

   ▪ Today's date; currency $40.00; coins $1.44; ABA No. 18-81 for $51.00; no cash received back with the deposit transaction.
   ▪ Today's date; ABA No. 40-22 for $300.00 and ABA No. 24-12 for $32.00; $20.00 cash received back with the deposit transaction.

   Note: Blank deposit slips are available in the Student Activity Guide.

3. Using Figure 9.6 as an example, determine your ending reconciled checkbook balance when all of the following six conditions exist:

   ▪ Your ending checkbook balance is $311.40 before the monthly account fee (service charge) is deducted.
   ▪ You made a math error, resulting in $30.00 less showing in your account than should be.
   ▪ The monthly account fee is $6.00.
   ▪ The ending bank balance is $402.00.
   ▪ Outstanding deposits total $100.00.
   ▪ Outstanding checks total $166.60.

MAKE ACADEMIC CONNECTIONS

4. **Communication** Write a one-page paper discussing bank services and fees and how the banking industry depends on charging fees to its customers to make a profit. Also discuss other ways that banks make money and ways depositors may avoid fees.

5. **History** Today's banking system has a long history. Use the Internet to research the roots of U.S. banking. Write a report explaining why banks were created. Describe the first banks and discuss any laws that helped lay the foundation for today's banks.

6. **International Studies** Conduct online research to explore banking systems in foreign countries. How are they similar to and different from the U.S. banking system? Do they depend as much on electronic transfers and ATMs? Do customers pay bills on the Internet? Is there as much Internet fraud, such as identify theft, in foreign countries as there is in the United States?

7. **Technology** Visit a bank web site that offers online bill payment. Write a summary of how the process works. How do you set up your list of payees? Share your summary with the class.

SOLVE PROBLEMS AND

EXPLORE ISSUES

8. Find the errors in the following check.

```
                                                              518
        RICHARD McGUIRE
        Phone: 555-0109
        2802 Saratoga Street                                  97-145
        Ogden, UT 79393-4081       June 1    20 --            1243

PAY TO THE
ORDER OF _____ Best Buys _____ | $ ___ 35 00 ___

_____ Thirty five and °°/100 _____ DOLLARS
                          For Classroom Use Only

        PEAK BANK AND TRUST
        OGDEN, UTAH
                                          Rick McGuire
MEMO _____

⑈1243014452⑈ 0518 024⑈90759⑈
```

9. The deposit slip shown here was written to deposit the check in Number 8 above. Find the errors on the deposit slip.

```
                  DEPOSIT SLIP

        BEST BUYS FOODS              CURRENCY                 24/12-7
        Ogden, Utah                  COIN                       33

                                 C  1243      35 00
                                 H
DATE  June 1              20 ═══ E
                                 C
      SIGN HERE FOR LESS CASH IN K
      TELLER'S PRESENCE           S
                                     TOTAL FROM
                                     OTHER SIDE
                                     TOTAL       35 00    A hold for uncollected funds
        STATE BANK OF                LESS CASH RECEIVED   may be placed on checks or
                                                          similar instruments you de-
        UTAH                         NET DEPOSIT  30 00   posit. Any delay will not ex-
                                                          ceed the period of time per-
        Main Branch   Ogden, Utah                         mitted by law.

⑈123000 123⑈017 0 30123⑈    FOR CLASSROOM USE ONLY
                                                          RM 552 (0584)
```

10. Complete the bank reconciliation form included with the bank statement on the next page. Start by finishing the checkbook register below; enter the service charge and then compute balances. (Don't write in your textbook. Use another piece of paper.)

CHECK NO. OR TRANSACTION CODE	DATE	DESCRIPTION OF TRANSACTION	PAYMENT/ DEBIT(–)		FEE (–)	✓	DEPOSIT/ CREDIT (+)		BALANCE $ 100 00	
101	3/1/--	Grocery Mart	$ 24	75			$		24	75
		Groceries							75	25
ON	3/3/--	Independent Phone Co.	13	00					13	00
		Online Payment								
DEP	3/5/--	ATM Deposit					30	00	30	00
102	3/8/--	Local High School	10	00					10	00
		Band Donation								
103	3/10/--	Alan's Bakery	3	80					3	80
		Bread								
104	3/15/--	Grocery Mart	18	20					18	20
		Groceries								
DEP	3/18/--	Deposit					42	00	42	00
105	3/20/--	Acme Hardware	4	18					4	18
		Hammer								

Bank Statement
HOMETOWN BANK

Statement Date: March 31, 20—
Opening Balance: $100.00
Ending Balance: $77.25

Checks

Check No.	Date Paid	Amount
101	3/4/—	24.75
102	3/11/—	10.00
103	3/11/—	3.80

Debits and Withdrawals

Date	Amount	Description
3/3/—	13.00	Online bill payment
3/31/—	1.20	Service charge

Deposits

Date	Amount	Description
3/5/—	30.00	ATM Deposit

Account Reconciliation

1. Ending balance shown on the bank statement: _____

2. Total of all credits and deposits made but not shown on statement: _____

3. Total lines 1 and 2: _____

4. List all checks, withdrawals, and debits made but not shown on statement:

Check No. or Transaction Code	Amount	

5. Total of outstanding debit transactions: _____

6. Subtract line 5 from line 3: _____
(Result should match checkbook balance.)

EXTEND YOUR LEARNING

11. **Legal Issues** *Many serious crimes involving checks and checking accounts are committed every day. Depending on the state and the amount of the check, writing bad (NSF) checks can be considered a felony crime. Forgery is another crime committed with checks. It involves making or altering a document, such as a check, with the intent to steal money from another person's account. Research the laws in your state related to these criminal activities. What are the penalties? How can financial institutions and other businesses help prevent these crimes? What can you do to avoid becoming a victim of forgery?*

For related activities and links, go to **www.cengage.com/school/pfinance/mypf**

Robert (Ted) Turner

Ted Turner was born in Cincinnati, Ohio, in 1938 and moved to Savanna, Georgia, as a child. He attended Brown University, where he majored in economics and was active in debate. He began sailing when he was nine and went on to compete in the Olympic trials in 1964. In 1977, he defended the America's Cup for the United States as skipper of the Courageous.

Ted started his business career at age 24 when he inherited his father's business. The business was worth approximately $1 million at the time.

© AP Photo/Ric Feld

Today, his empire is worth more than $2 billion. Turner is best known as the founder of CNN, the first 24-hour cable news channel (1980), with which he established the first "all news, all the time" format.

As a businessman, he has also successfully ventured into sports team ownership (the Atlanta Braves), environmental initiatives, billboard advertisement (Turner Outdoor Advertising), and restaurant ownership (Ted's Montana Grill) in Bozeman, Montana, just to mention a few.

Along the way, Mr. Turner has also given back. In 1989, he created the Turner Tomorrow Fellowship, which offers positive solutions to global problems. As a philanthropist, he is best known for his $1 billion pledge to the United Nations (one-third of his $3 billion worth at the time). In 1991, Ted Turner was named *TIME* magazine's Man of the Year.

Throughout his life, Ted Turner has devoted his assets to a blend of environmentalism and capitalism. He owns more land than any other American and owns the largest herd of bison in the world. He has taken many risks and grown his business ventures into well-known enterprises. At the same time, he has cared deeply about the environment and the social issues of the times.

THINK CRITICALLY

1. Comment on Ted Turner's success in money management. How did he grow his net worth from $1 million to $3 billion?

2. What kinds of financial records, filing system, and personal records would you imagine someone like Ted Turner would need? What kind of banking services would a financier such as Ted Turner use?

3. How does philanthropy help our country? Why do wealthy people establish foundations and give large sums of money?

Assessing Your Financial Health

Overview

This project is designed to help you begin the financial planning process. Here you will assess your financial health by carefully examining your present financial condition. By taking inventory of where you are now, you can begin to build a plan for the future.

YOUR JOB

Let's begin with your job. The money you earn affects what you are able to purchase and save now as well as your future prospects for financial stability. You will want to examine your current job in terms of your opportunities for advancement, the company's chances for survival, and job satisfaction. If you feel you are in a dead-end job, working for a weak or financially unstable company or in an obsolete industry, it's time to start looking for a more promising opportunity. On the other hand, if you like your job, and the future looks good for the company and the industry, then examine your opportunities for advancement. In addition, consider your own mental attitude, skills, and aptitudes for higher-level positions. If you aren't currently working or are in a dead-end job, get started by interviewing a person who has the type of job you'd like to have.

Complete Worksheet 1 (Rate Your Job) provided for you in the *Student Activity Guide* and also presented on the next page. Worksheet 1 is designed to help you assess your current job and any potential job you might consider. When you examine your scores, you will have a clearer picture of the direction

© Photodisc/Getty Images

you should pursue. The time to do career research is now, not after you've invested several years of your life in advanced education and training, the wrong job, the wrong employer, or the wrong industry.

A score of 25 points is possible for each section. A score between 20 and 25 for any section indicates stability and good prospects for the future. A score between 15 and 20 indicates that you should examine the characteristics carefully before making long-term commitments. A score between 10 and 15 indicates that you should start looking for a new job, a new employer, or a new type of career soon. A score under 10 indicates that you are in a dead-end job, which should be viewed as only temporary.

WORKSHEET 1
Rate Your Job

Directions: Rate each of the following characteristics on a 1 to 5 point scale. A score of 5 means *always;* a score of 4 means *usually;* a score of 3 means *as often as needed;* a score of 2 means *sometimes;* a score of 1 means *never;* and a score of 0 means *not applicable.* If you do not have a job, complete this worksheet after doing research about your desired future job.

Your Score

1. You enjoy the work you do, and you look forward to going to work each day. _____

2. You are willing to get extra training, education, or extra skills in order to be challenged. _____

3. You seek additional responsibility and can do the job well. _____

4. You like the work environment, and others recognize you as someone who will help and be a team player. _____

5. You receive regular pay raises large enough to keep you ahead of inflation and support your desired lifestyle. _____

Your total _____

Job Score

1. The product or service is in demand and prospects look good for the future. _____

2. The industry is growing as a whole, with opportunities for advancement in other companies similar to yours. _____

3. The product or service is economy-resistant (rising prices or economic downturns don't greatly affect sales). _____

4. Turnover among employees is generally low. _____

5. Pay scale and fringe benefits compare well with other companies in the same field. _____

Job total _____

Employer's Score

1. Your boss calls on you to handle tough assignments and gives you credit for your accomplishments. _____

2. The boss regularly solicits your suggestions and follows them. _____

3. The company promotes from within. _____

4. The company has a large number of customers rather than just a few big ones. _____

5. The company is well established and still growing. _____

Employer's total _____

Total of all points _____

YOUR INCOME AND OUTGO (CASH FLOW)

Having completed the budgeting exercises in Chapter 8, you recognize the importance of keeping track of dollars that regularly flow through your hands. Complete Worksheet 2 (Cash Flow Statement) provided for you in the *Student Activity Guide* and also presented for reference below. Worksheet 2 will help you identify where your money comes from and where it goes. In addition, it allows you to make projections for future income and outgo on a yearly basis. It's important to pinpoint your spending habits, analyze them, and take steps to improve your financial picture.

Examine your cash flow closely, looking for places where your income may be leaking. Plugging the small leaks will help you build larger cash reserves and spend money more wisely. Think about three things you bought last year and later regretted. What is the total amount of money you could have saved? What other things could you have purchased?

WORKSHEET 2
Cash Flow Statement

Directions: Keep a record of income and expenses for a month (you might want to do this for a year to build a budget base for the following year). In the first column, list each item you receive or spend in a month. In the second column, project your annual income or expense for each item. In the third column, check any items that need attention. In the fourth column, indicate how much (increase or decrease) each item should change monthly. Add a plus sign (increase) or minus sign (decrease) to each entry. In the fifth column, indicate how much additional money you would save or spend annually by making the changes in the fourth column. Use a plus sign (save) or minus sign (spend) for each entry. See the example below.

Example:	THIS MONTH	YEARLY TOTAL	NEED CHANGE	MONTHLY CHANGE	YEARLY EFFECT
Entertainment expense	$38.00	$456.00		+$12.00	−$144.00

	1 THIS MONTH	2 YEARLY TOTAL	3 NEED CHANGE	4 MONTHLY CHANGE	5 YEARLY EFFECT
ITEM					
Income:					
Take-home pay	_____	_____	_____	_____	_____
Bonuses/gifts	_____	_____	_____	_____	_____
Interest income	_____	_____	_____	_____	_____
Other_____	_____	_____	_____	_____	_____
Totals	_____	_____	_____	_____	_____
Outgo:					
	_____	_____	_____	_____	_____
	_____	_____	_____	_____	_____
	_____	_____	_____	_____	_____
	_____	_____	_____	_____	_____
	_____	_____	_____	_____	_____
	_____	_____	_____	_____	_____
	_____	_____	_____	_____	_____
	_____	_____	_____	_____	_____
Savings	_____	_____	_____	_____	_____
Totals	_____	_____	_____	_____	_____

Analysis:
List ways you can cut expenses or increase income (such as by substituting activities, buying cheaper products, or working odd jobs in the summer).

YOUR NET WORTH

An assessment of where you stand begins with what you own and owe at the moment. Complete Worksheet 3 (Net Worth Analysis) provided for you in the *Student Activity Guide* and also presented for reference below. Worksheet 3 is used for listing your assets and liabilities and making projections of where you would like to be at some future date (such as a month, a year, or five years). The purpose of the net worth analysis is threefold: (1) to show you your strong and weak areas, (2) to help you plan for specific short-term changes, and (3) to allow you to project goals into the future based on those decisions.

WORKSHEET 3
Net Worth Analysis

Directions: Fill in the blanks below. In column 1, write in the market value of each item you possess or debt you owe. See Chapter 8 for definitions of terms (assets, liabilities, and net worth). In column 2, write in what each item will be worth in one year. In column 3, indicate the value of each item in five years. You can assume an item will increase it if gains in value over time (through interest or inflation) or if you add to or purchase an item from that category.

ITEM	1 TODAY'S BALANCE	2 ONE-YEAR PROJECTION	3 FIVE-YEAR PROJECTION
Assets:			
_____	$_____	$_____	$_____
_____	_____	_____	_____
_____	_____	_____	_____
_____	_____	_____	_____
_____	_____	_____	_____
_____	_____	_____	_____
_____	_____	_____	_____
_____	_____	_____	_____
_____	_____	_____	_____
_____	_____	_____	_____
_____	_____	_____	_____
_____	_____	_____	_____
Total assets	=========	=========	=========
Liabilities:			
_____	_____	_____	_____
_____	_____	_____	_____
_____	_____	_____	_____
_____	_____	_____	_____
_____	_____	_____	_____
_____	_____	_____	_____
Total liabilities	=========	=========	=========
Net worth	=========	=========	=========

Analysis: List major purchases that you wish to make and how you plan to pay for them.

YOUR TAX LIABILITY

Based on the income tax returns you prepared in Chapter 7, use Worksheet 4 (Tax Liability) to analyze your total tax and determine whether or not you can reduce your taxes through careful planning. Worksheet 4 is provided for you in the *Student Activity Guide* and also presented for reference below. Keep copies of your tax returns. Compare total tax by preparing Forms 1040EZ, 1040A, and the long Form 1040. Use the form that gives the greatest tax advantage (that is, the lowest amount of taxes). Then study tax booklets and other information to see where you can benefit from taking more deductions.

WORKSHEET 4
Tax Liability

Directions: To complete this worksheet, first list your gross income, taxable income, tax before credits, and total tax for the last three years you have filed tax returns and paid income taxes. If you have not yet filed a tax return, use the projected gross income that you would receive in the entry-level position of your choice (used for Worksheet 1). Compute taxes owed on that amount (see Chapter 7). Then compute how much you could save in income taxes if you made changes as shown. Finally, list some of the tax deductions and credits available on the Form 1040 in the *Student Activity Guide* that you might use to decrease your tax liability.

YEAR	GROSS INCOME	ADJUSTED GROSS INCOME	TAXABLE INCOME	TAX (BEFORE CREDITS)	TOTAL TAX (AFTER CREDITS)
1. _____	_____	_____	_____	_____	_____
2. _____	_____	_____	_____	_____	_____
3. _____	_____	_____	_____	_____	_____

How would each of the above years' tax liabilities have changed *if* you could have had the following changes:

YEAR	CHANGE	TAX DECREASE
1	IRA deduction of $2,000	$_____
2	Child care credit of $500	$_____
3	One more exemption	$_____

Analysis:
Examine Schedule A of Form 1040 (itemized deductions) in the *Student Activity Guide*. Identify some deductions you might wish to take advantage of to reduce your tax liability.

Examine Form 1040 in the *Student Activity Guide* and list additional types of income, deductions, and credits that are required and/or permitted when this form is used.

3

Financial Security

CHAPTERS

CASE: Ben S. Bernanke

PROJECT: Assessing Your Financial Security

Unit 3 begins with a basic explanation of how to get started with saving and investing. We then explore options for saving and investing, followed by investment alternatives, investment risks, and how to invest wisely. We will examine types of stock and reasons why investors choose them.

We will also examine other investment choices, such as bonds, mutual funds, real estate, precious metals, gems, and collectibles, as well as futures and options.

We wrap up this unit learning about retirement and estate planning, wills, trusts, and estate taxes.

10

Saving for the Future

10.1   *Growing Money: Why, Where, and How*

10.2   *Savings Options, Features, and Plans*

Consider **THIS**

Isaac saves regularly from his allowance and the money he gets from relatives and friends for special occasions. He makes it a point to set aside some of what he receives, rather than spending all of it.

"For every dollar I save, Dad contributes 10 cents to my savings," Isaac told his best friend. "That gives me a 10 percent return, in addition to the interest I earn on my savings account. Dad wants me to save money for the future. I'm going to college some day, and I want to minimize the amount of financial aid I'll need. It may not seem like a lot of money each month, but every year my savings grow. This year, I'll have enough to get a certificate of deposit at the bank. That way, I get a higher interest rate on money deposited. Sure, it's tempting to spend some of my savings on fun stuff, but I have to pay back the 10 percent to my dad on everything I take out. It's kind of like a tax on spending, isn't it?"

Growing Money: Why, Where, and How

GOALS

- Describe the purpose of saving.
- Explain how money grows through compounding.
- List and describe financial institutions where you can save.

TERMS

- short-term needs, p. 219
- long-term needs, p. 220
- scholarships, p. 220
- student loans, p. 220
- loan consolidation, p. 221
- grants, p. 221
- work-study, p. 221
- principal, p. 222
- interest, p. 222
- annual percentage yield (APY), p. 222

WHY YOU SHOULD SAVE

The best reason to save money is to provide for future needs, both expected and unexpected. If you set nothing aside for these inevitable needs, you will constantly live on the edge of financial disaster. Saving regularly will help you meet your short-term and long-term needs.

SHORT-TERM NEEDS

Often you will have **short-term needs**, which are expenses beyond your regular monthly items. Unless you have extra cash income during the month, you will have to pay for these things out of savings. Some short-term needs are predictable. Others you can't foresee. Examples of short-term needs include the following:

- Emergencies—such as unemployment, sickness, accident, or a death in the family.
- Vacations—short weekend trips or longer excursions.
- Social events—weddings, family gatherings, or other potentially costly special occasions.
- Repairs—cars, appliances, plumbing, and other items. Occasionally, major unplanned repairs become immediately necessary.
- Major purchases—a car, major appliances, furniture, remodeling, or other items. Things eventually have to be replaced.

© Photodisc/Getty Images

What are some short-term needs that could require you to save?

▮ LONG-TERM NEEDS

While you need savings to meet emergencies and short-term needs, you must also provide for long-term needs. **Long-term needs** are expenses that are costly and require years of planning and saving. These include predictable costs such as home ownership, education, and retirement. Saving money now will enable you to make larger purchases in the future. It will also allow you to invest and accumulate enough money for a secure retirement.

Home Ownership

Many people want to own their own house. At the time of purchase, you will likely have to pay a large sum of cash, or a *down payment*. This amount is often 10 to 20 percent of the purchase price. The balance will be paid with a mortgage (home loan) for which you will make monthly payments. The larger the down payment you make, the smaller your monthly mortgage payments will be.

Education

Many young people desire to complete some form of post-secondary education or training. Education is a long-term investment that pays off in higher income potential. Many couples begin a savings plan when children are born. When the time comes for college, they have all or some of the money needed for their children's higher education. If there are no savings (or not enough) to pay for a college education, it is usually financed through a variety of other sources, as described below.

Work   Students may choose to work part time, full time, summers, or any combination. Working full time while attending college is a pay-as-you-go system. Its advantage is that when you finish your education, you are debt-free. The disadvantage is that it takes longer to finish your education. Many students choose a combination of work and other forms of financing to pay for their education.

Scholarships   Cash allowances awarded to students to help pay education costs are called **scholarships**. Generally, these monies are paid directly to educational institutions. They are often obtained from donations from private or public sources. For example, professional organizations in a field (such as accounting) may sponsor scholarships for accounting majors. Many scholarships are available based on scholastic achievement, which includes grades earned in high school, high scores on tests, or other qualifying criteria. Scholarships are also awarded for athletic achievement. Other scholarships are based on need, and to qualify, you must show that you do not have other sources to pay for your education (such as parents). The biggest advantage of scholarships is that they do not have to be repaid if you complete your education. But scholarships usually require students to meet certain standards, such as maintaining a certain GPA. Unfortunately, some scholarships become taxable or must be repaid if the student drops out or does not fulfill the requirements.

Student Loans   Money may be borrowed for your education in the form of **student loans**. They are available from the federal government or from other lenders, such as banks. Student loans may be *subsidized,* which means you pay no interest or payments until after you graduate from college, or *unsubsidized,* which means interest accrues as the loan goes along. Generally, government student loans are subsidized because they are guaranteed by the government.

The view of many people is that a college education will get you much further in life than if you don't have one. They say the college degree will get you an interview for a job where you don't need the degree to do the work. Because so many people do have degrees, the competition is much greater. Others believe that college isn't for everyone. It's expensive and time-consuming. Default rates on student loans show that many people can't afford to pay back their student-loan debt. There are many reasons for this, including changes in demand for workers in certain career fields for which students trained.

THINK *CRITICALLY*

How do you feel about the long-term value of a college education? Do you agree that time spent now getting an education will be rewarded later in the form of higher income over your lifetime? Why or why not? Do you feel that student loans should be repaid with interest, even when the graduate can't get a job in the field for which he or she was trained? Why or why not?

In most cases, students who finance their education with student loans will obtain many loans throughout their years of study. Before they start making payments after graduation, they will consolidate those loans. **Loan consolidation** means that all their student loans are combined into one large loan, which results in one monthly payment, rather than many payments.

Grants and Work-Study Programs   Students who are eligible for student loans may also get some money from grants and work-study programs. **Grants** are forms of educational funding that do not have to be repaid and usually do not require students to maintain certain standards. They are often funded by the government. Students may also be able to access federal and state funding in the form of **work-study** programs, whereby students can work at the campus or other college location to earn money. Generally, the amount of work-study earnings will not offset the need for loans and grants.

Retirement

The Social Security system was never designed to provide a comfortable retirement. It is meant to be a supplement to an individual's own savings. To have a financially secure retirement, you must begin to save regularly as early in life as you can.

Investing

After you have saved enough to cover daily expenses and emergencies, you can afford to invest your extra savings. Investing in stocks, bonds, mutual funds, real estate, and other investments can make your money grow faster than it would if left in a regular savings account. Because investments are often risky, you should make them in addition to—not instead of—regular savings. Types of investments will be described in later chapters.

FINANCIAL SECURITY

Probably the best reason to save is the peace of mind that comes from knowing that when needs arise, you will have adequate money to pay for them. The amount of money you save will vary according to several factors, including the following:

- The amount of your discretionary or disposable income—what you have left over to spend or save as you wish
- The importance you attach to savings
- Your anticipated needs and wants
- Your willpower, or ability to give up present spending in order to provide for your future

HOW MONEY GROWS

The amount of money you deposit into a savings account is called the **principal**. It is the base on which your savings will grow. For the use of your money, the financial institution pays you money called interest. **Interest** represents earnings on principal. As principal and interest grow, more interest accumulates. This is known as *compound interest,* or interest paid on the original principal plus accumulated interest.

Figure 10.1 illustrates how interest is compounded annually. Notice how the interest earned increases each year because the saver is earning interest on the previous year's interest as well as on the initial deposit.

The more often interest is compounded, the greater your interest earnings will be (see the Math Minute feature on page 224). Figure 10.2 illustrates what happens when 6 percent interest is compounded quarterly (every three months) and added to the principal before more interest is calculated. If you compare the ending balances in Figure 10.1 and Figure 10.2, you will notice that you earn more interest with quarterly compounding than with annual compounding. Today, many financial institutions offer interest compounded each day savings are on deposit. They use computers to rapidly compute the compounding daily interest.

Earnings on savings can be measured by the rate of return or yield. *Yield* is the percentage of increase in the value of your savings due to earned interest. Because financial institutions compound interest in many ways, comparing yields can be difficult. To solve this problem, the law requires all financial institutions to tell consumers the **annual percentage yield (APY)** on their accounts. This is the actual interest rate an account pays, stated on a yearly basis with the compounding included. Because all financial institutions must calculate APY the same way, you can use APY to easily compare the yields on different accounts.

FIGURE 10.1	*Interest Compounded Annually*		
Year	Beginning Balance	Interest Earned (6%)	Ending Balance
1	$100.00	$6.00	$106.00
2	$106.00	$6.36	$112.36
3	$112.36	$6.74	$119.10

FIGURE 10.2   *Interest Compounded Quarterly*

Year	Beginning Balance	Rate	Quarterly Interest				Ending Balance
			1	2	3	4	
1	$100.00	.015	$1.50	$1.52	$1.55	$1.57	$106.14
2	$106.14	.015	$1.59	$1.62	$1.64	$1.66	$112.65
3	$112.65	.015	$1.69	$1.72	$1.74	$1.77	$119.57

Quarterly Compounding
Annual Interest Rate = 6%

WHERE TO SAVE

Most cities have several commercial banks, savings banks, savings and loan associations, credit unions, and brokerage firms from which you can choose to open an account. Savings accounts are also available through online banks and financial institutions, including credit card companies. Most of these institutions have greatly expanded their services in recent years, so the differences among them are becoming increasingly blurred. Interest rates vary among savings institutions and among the various types of accounts offered. You will have to study your options and determine which type of institution and account is the best deal for you.

COMMERCIAL BANKS

Commercial banks, also known as *full-service banks,* provide the widest variety of banking services of any of the financial institutions. Many people prefer to keep their checking and savings accounts in the same bank for ease in transferring funds and making deposits and withdrawals. Commercial banks offer many kinds of savings and checking accounts. Almost all commercial banks are insured by the Federal Deposit Insurance Corporation (FDIC). This insurance protects depositors from loss due to bank failure, up to $250,000 per account.

SAVINGS BANKS

Savings banks are usually referred to as *mutual savings banks.* These financial institutions are few in number—about 500 of them in roughly a dozen states, mostly throughout New England and the Northeast—but substantial in size. Savings banks are insured by the FDIC. Two primary services offered by these institutions are savings accounts and loans on real property, including mortgages and home-improvement loans.

© Photodisc/Getty Images

Why might people prefer to keep their checking and savings accounts in the same bank?

COMPUTING INTEREST COMPOUNDED QUARTERLY

Compound interest means earning interest on principal, and then allowing the interest to remain on deposit so you will then earn interest on both your principal and your previous interest. To compute interest compounded quarterly, divide the annual interest rate by 4 to get the quarterly rate. For monthly compounding, divide the annual interest rate by 12. For interest compounded every 6 months (a half year), divide the annual rate by 2.

Suppose you deposit $100 in a savings account that will pay you 6 percent per year, compounded quarterly. This means that for each quarter, you will receive ¼ of the yearly interest. Six percent divided by 4 is 1.5 percent (or .015) each quarter. At the end of the first quarter, you earn $1.50 in interest, using the following computation:

$$\$100 \times .015 = \$1.50$$

At the beginning of the second quarter, you now have $101.50 in your account ($100 + $1.50). At the end of the second quarter, you earn interest as follows:

$$\$101.50 \times .015 = \$1.52$$

At the beginning of the third quarter, you have $103.02 ($101.50 + $1.52). At the end of the third quarter, you earn interest as follows:

$$\$103.02 \times .015 = \$1.55$$

At the beginning of the fourth quarter, you have $104.57 ($103.02 + $1.55). At the end of the fourth quarter (the end of the first year), you earn interest as follows:

$$\$104.57 \times .015 = \$1.57$$

Your balance at the end of the first year is $106.14 ($104.57 + $1.57). You earned a total of $6.14 in interest for the year. At the end of Year 3, your balance is $119.57. That's a total interest of $19.57 on your original deposit of $100, as shown in Figure 10.2. Based on the previous example, compute your quarterly interest for three years if you deposit $500 at 8 percent, compounded quarterly.

Year	Beginning Balance	Rate	Quarterly Interest 1	2	3	4	Ending Balance
1	$500.00	____	$____	$____	$____	$____	$_____
2	$_____	____	$____	$____	$____	$____	$_____
3	$_____	____	$____	$____	$____	$____	$_____

Solution:

Year	Beginning Balance	Rate	Quarterly Interest 1	2	3	4	Ending Balance
1	$500.00	.02	$10.00	$10.20	$10.40	$10.61	$541.21
2	$541.21	.02	$10.82	$11.04	$11.26	$11.49	$585.82
3	$585.82	.02	$11.72	$11.95	$12.19	$12.43	$634.11

SAVINGS AND LOAN ASSOCIATIONS

Savings and loan associations (S&Ls) are organized primarily to lend money for home mortgages. S&Ls offer many of the services of commercial banks, including interest-bearing checking accounts and special savings plans. You may find a slightly higher interest rate on savings at an S&L. S&Ls are insured by the FDIC.

CREDIT UNIONS

Credit unions are not-for-profit organizations established by groups of people, such as employees in similar occupations who pool their money. To use a credit union, you must be a member of the group. Credit unions generally offer higher interest rates on savings and lower interest rates on loans. Their membership in the National Credit Union Administration (NCUA) provides insurance for depositors' accounts, up to $250,000.

Credit unions are owned by their members. Savings and checking accounts at a credit union are usually called *share accounts*. The checking accounts have low (or no) average daily balance requirements and, generally, no service fees. If you are eligible for credit union membership, this type of checking account may be the least expensive and most convenient option.

Credit union members save their money in the form of "shares," or part ownership in the credit union. From funds accumulated by these shares, the credit union makes loans to its members. Credit unions also offer IRAs (Individual Retirement Accounts) and other financial services to members, including savings and investing plans that may pay higher rates of return than other banking options.

BROKERAGE FIRMS

Brokerage firms buy and sell different types of securities. *Securities* are stocks and bonds issued by corporations or by the government. Stocks represent equity, or ownership. Bonds represent debt, or a loan. In other words, when you buy stock, you become an owner of the company. When you buy a bond, you are loaning money to the company or to the government. Investors buy and sell securities through a *stockbroker,* who works for the brokerage firm. As you will learn in a later chapter, you can buy stocks, bonds, and mutual funds directly or through brokerage firms. *Discount brokerage firms* offer broker services for reduced fees. They also offer checking and savings account options. Accounts in brokerage firms are usually not insured.

ONLINE ACCOUNTS

Credit card companies and financial services companies offer online savings accounts that often work in tandem with your credit card. These savings accounts generally pay higher, or market, rates of interest. And, as a result of having the online savings account, you can expect to receive a lower rate of interest with your credit card agreement. However, these accounts can be risky. If the account provider is not a financial institution, these accounts are not insured. As a general rule, the higher the amount of interest you can earn, the higher the risk associated with the account.

Business Management & Administration

Managers exist in every type of business. A manager's job is to coordinate resources to match the needs of the business. Some managers are top-level executives. Others are middle managers. First-line supervisors are at the lowest level of management.

A branch manager for a financial institution administers all the functions of a branch office. Branch managers are generally considered middle-level managers. Duties include hiring employees, approving loans and lines of credit, establishing rapport with the community, and assisting customers with account problems. Branch managers must also be familiar with sales and service and understand a growing array of financial services and products.

Employment Outlook

- Overall employment is expected to grow about as fast as average for all jobs.

Job Titles

- Branch manager
- Credit manager
- Loan department manager
- Financial manager

Needed Skills

- Bachelor's degree in finance, accounting, or business administration is needed.
- Master's degree in business area is preferred.
- Experience in banking and financial services is essential.

What's it like to work in... *Bank Management*

Marty is meeting with corporate representatives to discuss the branch's financial goals for the coming year. Her branch is required to perform in accordance with local economic conditions, compared to previous years and compared to other branches of the same size and demographics.

Marty knows and understands banking because she started as a teller several years ago. After completing her bachelor's degree, she entered the bank's management training program. She worked as an assistant manager for two years before she was assigned as manager of her own branch.

Marty oversees her staff of tellers and loan and account specialists. She sets policies and procedures to meet company goals. She must ensure that her branch is operating smoothly and efficiently. She works with customers to help them resolve problems and advises them about the various financial accounts and services available to them. Her performance is rewarded with an annual salary review, along with a bonus and other perks.

What About You?

Would you like a job managing people and resources? Would you enjoy resolving conflicts and setting policies? Would a job as a branch manager appeal to you?

Assessment

KEY TERMS REVIEW

Match the terms with the definitions.

_____ 1. Money borrowed to pay for education

_____ 2. A program where students work on campus to earn money

_____ 3. Combining many loans into one large loan with one monthly payment

_____ 4. The amount of money deposited

_____ 5. Expenses beyond your regular monthly items

_____ 6. Earnings on principal

_____ 7. Forms of educational funding that do not have to be repaid

_____ 8. Cash allowances awarded to students to pay education costs

_____ 9. The actual interest rate an account earns stated on a yearly basis

_____ 10. Expenses that are costly and require years of planning and saving

a. annual percentage yield (APY)

b. grants

c. interest

d. loan consolidation

e. long-term needs

f. principal

g. scholarships

h. short-term needs

i. student loans

j. work-study

CHECK YOUR UNDERSTANDING

11. Why is it important to start saving early to meet your short-term and long-term needs?

12. Explain the concept of compounding and how your money grows.

13. List the financial institutions where you can have a savings account.

APPLY YOUR KNOWLEDGE

14. Describe the advantages and disadvantages of spending now rather than saving for a future goal. Give three examples of how saving money can improve your financial well being.

THINK CRITICALLY

15. There are many places where you can save money. Some are insured and others are not. The safer your money (less risk), the lower your rate of return (APY). Are you willing to take more risk in order to earn more interest on your savings? Explain your answer.

16. Getting advanced training, such as a college degree, requires planning. Do you plan to get some type of post-secondary education? How will you pay for it?

Savings Options, Features, and Plans

GOALS

- Explain the features and purposes of different savings options.
- Discuss factors that influence selection of a savings plan.
- Describe ways to save regularly.

TERMS

- liquidity, *p. 228*
- certificate of deposit (CD), *p. 228*
- maturity date, *p. 229*
- money market account, *p. 229*
- safety of principal, *p. 230*
- direct deposit, *p. 232*
- automatic deductions, *p. 232*
- payroll savings plan, *p. 232*

SAVINGS OPTIONS

Once you have decided to establish a savings program, you need to know about the different savings options available to you. You may want to deposit money in several types of accounts, because each can contribute to your overall plan in different ways.

REGULAR SAVINGS ACCOUNT

A regular savings account has a major advantage—high liquidity. **Liquidity** is a measure of how quickly you can get your cash without loss of value. A regular savings account is said to be very *liquid* because you can withdraw your money at any time without penalty. The tradeoff for high liquidity, however, is a lower interest rate. A regular savings account generally pays the least amount of interest of all savings options.

Once you have opened the account, you are free to make withdrawals and deposits. Some financial institutions charge service fees when you make more than a maximum number of withdrawals in a certain period of time. Other institutions charge a monthly fee if your balance falls below a set minimum. In most cases, you will receive a debit or ATM card that goes with the account so that you can make withdrawals and deposits at ATMs. You can also check your balance and transfer money between your checking and savings accounts online and by telephone.

CERTIFICATE OF DEPOSIT

A **certificate of deposit (CD)**, or time deposit, is a deposit that earns a fixed interest rate for a specified length of time—for example, 5 percent for six months. A CD requires a minimum deposit. The interest rate on a CD is usually higher than on regular savings accounts because CDs are less liquid. You must leave the money in the CD for the full time period. If you take out any part of your money early, you will pay an early withdrawal penalty. This penalty could be 90 days interest. You could even lose part of your principal if you withdraw all of your money early.

A CD has a set **maturity date**, which is the date on which an investment becomes due for payment. Within a stated number of days after the maturity date, your certificate will renew automatically. When a CD *renews,* it is extended for another six months or whatever the original time period was. You may prefer to redeem it for cash or purchase a new certificate for a different time period. Financial institutions offer CDs that allow the interest to accumulate to maturity. Often you can choose to receive a check periodically for the interest earned or have the interest deposited in a separate regular account.

© Photodisc/Getty Images

Why is a regular savings account said to be very liquid?

MONEY MARKET ACCOUNT

A **money market account** is a type of savings account that offers a more competitive interest rate than a regular savings account. Brokerage firms as well as banks and other financial institutions offer money market accounts.

There are two different kinds of money market accounts: money market deposit accounts and money market funds. A *money market deposit account* is similar to a regular savings account, but it offers a higher rate of interest in exchange for larger than normal deposits. In addition, the interest rate may increase as your balance increases. These accounts are insured by the FDIC.

A *money market fund* is a type of mutual fund that invests in low-risk securities. Money market funds are not FDIC insured, but they are generally considered safe because they invest in short-term government securities. Therefore, the chance of losing your principal (amount deposited) is very low. On average, money market funds will pay a higher interest rate than money market deposit accounts. Before investing in a money market fund, you should carefully read all of the fund's available information.

Unlike CDs, there is no penalty for taking money out of money market accounts. As a result, these accounts are quite liquid. However, you usually are limited to a certain number of withdrawals each month. In addition, money market accounts require minimum opening deposits and minimum balances.

SELECTING A SAVINGS PLAN

There are important factors to consider when selecting a savings account and a savings institution. All savings or investment options involve a tradeoff between liquidity or safety and yield. The safer or more liquid an investment, the less earning potential it is likely to have. Use the following criteria in judging which savings options best meet your needs: liquidity, safety, convenience, interest earning potential (yield), and fees and restrictions.

▌ LIQUIDITY

Liquidity is how quickly you can turn savings into cash when you want it. The need for liquidity will vary, based on your age, health, family situation, and overall wealth. For example, if you have little money left over after paying your bills, you may need to keep this money liquid so you can get it quickly, without penalty, if you face some emergency. In this case, a regular savings account or money market account would be best for you. CDs impose a penalty if you withdraw early, so you should choose this option when you don't expect to need the money before the maturity date.

▌ SAFETY

You want your money to be safe from loss. **Safety of principal** means that you are guaranteed not to lose your savings deposit, even if the bank or other financial institution fails and goes out of business. Most financial institutions are insured by a government agency, the Federal Deposit Insurance Corporation (FDIC) or National Credit Union Association (NCUA). Accounts protected by insurance are safe for up to $250,000. You should be sure the financial institution of your choice has federal insurance to protect your deposit. Deposits in banks, no matter what type, are almost always safer than investments in the stock market.

▌ CONVENIENCE

People often choose their financial institution because of convenience of location and the services offered. Interest rates on various savings accounts and certificates of deposit may vary only slightly. Fees charged are often very similar within a community.

Many banks have several branches within a limited geographic area, which makes your banking convenient. If a bank has only one branch located several miles from your home, the inconvenience of driving there might outweigh a slightly higher interest rate at this bank. A very large bank may have branches in other states, giving you banking privileges while out of town.

Many banks offer drive-up windows with expanded hours. Telephone and online banking make most savings plans very accessible. Branches are often located in grocery stores or residential areas. You may want to

© Photodisc/Getty Images

What are some important factors to consider when selecting a type of savings plan and a financial institution?

look for a bank that offers ATMs near your home, job, or shopping area you frequent.

INTEREST-EARNING POTENTIAL (YIELD)

You want to earn as much interest as you can on your deposit, while maintaining the degree of liquidity, safety, and convenience you want. Shop around for the best APY in your area for the type of account you want. Usually, the more liquid your deposit, the less interest it will earn. A regular savings account usually earns a low rate of interest because you can maintain a low minimum balance and withdraw money as needed. CDs tie up your money for some length of time. In exchange for your commitment to leave this money with the bank for this time period, you will usually earn higher interest.

FEES AND RESTRICTIONS

Different accounts and institutions have different rules. Before you open an account, be sure to understand the withdrawal restrictions, minimum balances, service charges, fees, and any other requirements. For example, some accounts charge a fee for using a human teller rather than completing transactions through an ATM. CDs may incur a heavy cost in lost interest for withdrawing money before maturity. Fees for use of an ATM can vary as well. Some banks may charge nothing to use their ATMs but charge a hefty fee for using another bank's ATM.

Why should you make a habit of saving regularly?

SAVING REGULARLY

Saving regularly will help you meet all of your financial goals. You can grow your savings only by spending less than you take in. It is important not just to save but to save regularly. Over time, and with compounding interest, your savings can grow into a substantial sum. Figure 10.3 illustrates the effect of compounding when you make regular deposits and earn interest on interest.

Obviously, no savings plan is effective unless you have the willpower to set aside money. The safe storage of funds for future use is a basic need of every individual. There are ways to make regular saving easier, including direct deposits and payroll deductions.

FIGURE 10.3   *Compounding with Additional Deposits*

Year	Beginning Balance	Deposits	Interest Earned (5%)	Ending Balance
1	$0.00	$100.00	$5.00	$105.00
2	$105.00	$100.00	$10.25	$215.25
3	$215.25	$100.00	$15.76	$331.01
4	$331.01	$100.00	$21.55	$452.56

DIRECT DEPOSIT

Both employers and financial institutions offer direct deposit. With **direct deposit**, your net pay is deposited electronically into your bank account. This service helps you because your money is available in your account faster. You do not have to make a special trip to the bank to deposit your paycheck. Instead, your employer gives you a nonnegotiable copy of your check and stub, notifying you of the amount deposited directly into your account. You can also have your automatic deposit split between accounts, with some going into savings and some going into checking to cover your bills. This way, you are truly paying yourself first. You can earmark the money you set aside for a vacation or some other special purpose.

AUTOMATIC DEDUCTIONS

Automatic deductions represent money you have authorized your bank or other organization to move from one account to another at regular intervals. For example, you can automatically have money moved from your checking account to your savings account.

With a **payroll savings plan**, you authorize your employer to make automatic deductions from your paycheck each pay period. For example, this money may be deposited into a retirement account or used to buy government savings bonds.

COLLECTING COINS AND CASH

Some people find it convenient to set aside their spare change and money left over each day or week. They may put it into a piggy bank, a jar, or other storage area. Once a month or several times a year, they take the cash out and have it counted and deposited to their savings accounts. Setting aside small amounts of change each day will lead to large sums over time. It's surprising how pennies can add up to make dollars!

NETBookmark

Collecting your loose change may be an easy way to save money, but cashing in all those coins may not be as easy. Sorting, counting, and rolling coins can take a long time, and many banks charge a fee to do it for you. Access www.cengage.com/school/pfinance/mypf and click on the link for Chapter 10. After reading the article from Bankrate.com, explain whether you think it is appropriate for banks to charge customers for accepting coins. If you had a jar full of coins, would you use the Coinstar machine described in the article to cash them in? Why or why not?

www.cengage.com/school/pfinance/mypf

ISSUES IN YOUR WORLD

SAVING TO KEEP LIFE SIMPLE

Saving is often defined as deferred spending. In other words, you set money aside today so you can spend it in the future. But saving money can be more than providing for some future need. Saving itself can be a virtue.

Abraham Lincoln said, "Most people are about as happy as they make up their minds to be." But what is happiness? According to many philosophers, it is enjoying what you have, not wishing for more. Consider what some people learn well into their lives—that the accumulation of possessions does not bring happiness! By keeping your life simple, you don't get used to having more and more and keeping up with what everyone else is buying. This means not continually buying "things" that have to be protected and maintained. Instead, you can enjoy life without having to earn large sums of money to achieve some high standard of consumer spending.

In today's competitive marketplace, people frequently lose their jobs and must retrain and even find a new career. If you keep your life simple, you won't have a lot of payments to make. Then, if you lose your job, you will be less likely to lose your house, car, and other possessions. If you stay liquid, you can more easily move and start a new career and have money on hand to carry you through jobless periods.

Most people "buy things they don't need, with money they don't have, to impress people they don't like." Those who love and care about you aren't impressed with how much money you spend or all the possessions you own. Wouldn't it be better to put money aside so that you can retire early, enjoy traveling, or live comfortably without the stress of keeping up with the rat race? Remember, even if you win the rat race, you're still a rat!

THINK CRITICALLY

1. *Do you sometimes buy things that you later wish you hadn't? If you had the money back, what would you do with it instead?*

2. *Do you know someone who is "happy" and at peace with his or her life? If so, describe the person's lifestyle.*

Assessment

KEY TERMS REVIEW

Match the terms with the definitions. Some terms may not be used.

_____ 1. The date on which an investment becomes due for payment

_____ 2. A guarantee that you will not lose your savings deposit

_____ 3. A plan in which you authorize your employer to deduct money from each paycheck for retirement, savings, or investments

_____ 4. A measure of how quickly you can get your cash without loss of value

_____ 5. Money you have authorized your bank or other organization to move from one account to another at regular intervals

a. automatic deduction

b. certificate of deposit (CD)

c. direct deposit

d. liquidity

e. maturity date

f. money market account

g. payroll savings plan

h. safety of principal

_____ 6. A time deposit where a fixed rate of interest is earned for a specified length of time

CHECK YOUR UNDERSTANDING

7. How is a savings account more liquid than a CD? Why is liquidity important?

8. To earn a higher interest rate, what tradeoff will you likely have to make? Why?

9. How is a money market account different from a regular savings account?

APPLY YOUR KNOWLEDGE

10. Why is it important to understand fees and restrictions before choosing a savings option?

THINK _CRITICALLY_

11. If you tie up money in a one-year CD but need to withdraw it for emergency repairs, could you? Would there be consequences? How could you avoid this situation?

12. Saving regularly is important. Do you keep a coin jar where you can stash spare change? What are some other ways you can start putting money aside (money that will stay put aside)?

Chapter *Assessment*

SUMMARY

10.1

- Savings provide money for short-term and long-term needs.

- Examples of short-term needs include emergencies, vacations, social events, repairs, and major purchases (replacement).

- Long-term needs are expenses that are costly and require years of planning and saving, such as home ownership, education, and retirement.

- The best reason to start saving is to provide for your own future financial security.

- Compounding, or interest earned on principal and previous interest, makes money grow faster.

- To compare accounts with different compounding methods, simply compare the stated annual percentage yields (APY).

- Commercial banks, savings banks, savings and loan associations, credit unions, brokerage firms, and online accounts are available for savings.

10.2

- Savings account options include regular savings accounts, certificates of deposit (CDs), and money market accounts.

- The criteria used in judging which savings options best meet your needs include liquidity, safety of principal, convenience, interest earning potential (yield), and fees and restrictions.

- Among the savings options, regular savings accounts usually pay the lowest interest but offer the highest liquidity and safety.

- Certificates of deposit (CDs) have a set maturity date and are less liquid, but they pay a higher rate of return than regular savings accounts.

- Money market accounts pay more interest when economic conditions are good (and growing).

- Most financial institutions offer safety of principal through insurance programs offered by government agencies, such as FDIC or NCUA.

- Saving regularly helps you meet your goals more quickly.

- Direct deposit, automatic deductions, and payroll savings plans are ways to force you to save.

APPLY WHAT YOU KNOW

1. List several short-term needs that you expect to have in the next few months or years. List your long-term needs that will require money in the next five years or more.

2. Write out your savings plans, listing your short-term and long-term goals and how you plan to achieve them. How much money will you have to save to meet them? On the Internet, locate a savings planner tool and calculate how much you would have to save to meet your short-term goals. Assume you will be saving for five years and will earn 7 percent on your savings.

3. Why might people choose to save their money in a commercial bank when another type of financial institution offers a higher interest rate?

4. What things would you consider when choosing a financial institution for your savings?

5. Describe ways you can force yourself to save. What does discretionary income have to do with saving?

6. If two savings accounts offered 5 percent interest but one was compounded quarterly and the other was compounded daily, which account would have the higher APY? Why?

MAKE ACADEMIC CONNECTIONS

7. **Communication** Assume that you and your friend are planning a trip upon graduation in two years. You estimate that you will each need $1,000. Write a savings plan for you and your friend to help you save the money needed. Consider the different savings options and the characteristics of each one, such as safety, liquidity, and compounding.

8. **Research** Use the Internet to research the type of online-only accounts available to consumers. Review web sites of credit card companies, insurance companies, brokerage companies, and any other source you may find that allows consumers to have online savings accounts. Some may be tied to credit cards or other types of accounts. Prepare a written report of your findings, assessing the safety, liquidity, and return that savers can expect to receive.

9. **Economics** The Federal Reserve manages the money supply in the United States. Define "money supply" and explain how the different kinds of savings, such as time deposits, are part of the money supply. (Hint: Search for M1, M2, and M3 money measurements.)

10. **Technology** Search the Internet for a savings calculator. Plug in different numbers and note the results. For example, enter a savings amount compounded annually, then quarterly, then monthly. Note the differences that occur because of the different compounding method. Then try different savings amounts using the same compounding method. How does saving just a little more each month affect your total savings in, say, ten years? Then try different interest rates with the same savings amounts and compounding method. Summarize your conclusions.

Solve Problems and

Explore Issues

11. Collect advertisements offering various financial services. What factors would you consider before using these services and the financial institutions that offer them?

12. Visit a financial institution in your community and describe the following:

    - types of savings accounts
    - services available to depositors
    - fees charged for services
    - requirements, such as minimum deposits
    - other enticements to get your business

13. Call a credit union in your area or find one online. Who can be a member of this credit union? What services does the credit union offer its members?

14. Bianca Araya is considering buying a certificate of deposit with the $500 she has in regular savings. Explain to her what factors she should consider when choosing a certificate of deposit.

15. Investigate the advantages and disadvantages of investing in a long-term CD (such as a two-year CD). What should you consider before doing so? Speak to a local bank manager to help answer these questions.

16. Compute the interest and ending balance for Lindsay Dolan, assuming that she deposits $1,000 in a CD with interest compounded every six months at the rate of 8½ percent. The certificate matures in three years. Use the following format on a separate sheet of paper.

Year	Beginning Balance	First-Half Interest	Second-Half Interest	Total Interest	Ending Balance
1	$1,000	_____	_____	_____	_____
2	_____	_____	_____	_____	_____
3	_____	_____	_____	_____	_____

17. Compute the interest compounded quarterly on a deposit of $500 for three years at 8 percent APY. Use the following format on a separate sheet of paper.

			Interest				
Year	Beginning Balance	First Quarter	Second Quarter	Third Quarter	Fourth Quarter	Total Interest	Ending Balance
1	$500	_____	_____	_____	_____	_____	_____
2	_____	_____	_____	_____	_____	_____	_____
3	_____	_____	_____	_____	_____	_____	_____

18. Jan Aguilar plans to deposit $100 a month into her savings account. Her bank compounds interest monthly. The current rate for a regular savings account is 5½ percent. Compute the ending balance in her account after one year. Use the format shown below on a separate sheet of paper. The first line has been completed as an example.

Month	Beginning Balance	+ Deposit =	Total	+ Interest =	Ending Balance
1	$0.00	$100.00	$100.00	$0.46	$100.46
2					
3					
4					
5					
6					
7					
8					
9					
10					
11					
12					

19. Compute your total savings if you keep $1,000 in a regular savings account at 5¼ percent, compounded quarterly, for two years. Use the following format on a separate sheet of paper.

		Interest					
Year	Beginning Balance	First Quarter	Second Quarter	Third Quarter	Fourth Quarter	Total Interest	Ending Balance
1	$1,000						
2							

EXTEND YOUR LEARNING

20. **Ethics** Financial aid is available to those who need assistance to pay for their college education. When people fail to repay their student loans, taxpayers are left paying the bill and less money is available for others to use. Some people feel that student loans do not have to be repaid. Nationwide, there is a high student default rate. The U.S. Department of Education releases default rates each year. For those schools that have extremely high default rates (for student loans granted through their institution), their access to future federal student aid funds may be limited. Why should people repay their student loans? If loans aren't repaid, what are the negative effects?

For related activities and links, go to **www.cengage.com/school/pfinance/mypf**

Investing for the Future

| 11.1 | Basic Investing Concepts |
| 11.2 | Making Investment Choices |

Consider **THIS**

Pavel has saved some money that he will use for college expenses in a few years. Right now, it's in a regular savings account, earning 3 percent a year.

"My parents say I can do better," Pavel told his best friend. "If I invest the money, I could get 6 to 8 percent, or maybe even better. So I've been checking my options. You know what I've found so far? That investing is filled with risk, and there are many types of risk. If I'm willing to take a lot of risk, then I may be able to earn more money. But I also stand a chance of losing part or all of my money. So I have to decide what my goals are, weigh the tradeoffs, and make the best choice to meet my goals. This is interesting stuff, but it isn't as easy as it sounds."

Basic Investing Concepts

GOALS

- Explain why you should consider investing.
- Discuss the stages of investing.
- Explain the concept of risk.
- Describe investment strategies and options.

TERMS

- investing, *p. 240*
- inflation, *p. 240*
- Rule of 72, *p. 240*
- portfolio, *p. 243*
- investing risk, *p. 243*
- diversification, *p. 243*
- temporary investments, *p. 246*
- permanent investments, *p. 246*

WHY INVEST?

Investing is the use of long-term savings to earn a financial return. Investing is a proven and powerful way to strengthen your financial position over time. It is an essential part of providing for future needs. It provides a source of income in addition to a paycheck, allowing you to make money on money.

INVESTING HELPS BEAT INFLATION

© Image Source

What can you do to help protect yourself from rising prices?

Inflation is a rise in the general level of prices. Inflation reduces purchasing power over time. As prices rise, it takes more money to buy the same goods and services. Thus, investors seek investments that will grow faster than the inflation rate. For example, if the annual inflation rate is 4 percent, you will want your investments to yield a rate of return higher than 4 percent.

Thus, investing will help protect your purchasing power. As prices rise, your investments will keep your net worth rising. Investments allow your net worth to grow at a faster rate than general price levels.

A quick way to evaluate an investment's rate of return is to use the Rule of 72. The **Rule of 72** is a technique for estimating the number of years required to double your money at a given rate of return. Simply divide the percentage rate of return into 72. For example, if an investment is yielding an average of 6 percent, it will take 12 years to double your money ($72 \div 6$). As shown in the Math Minute feature, you can also use the Rule of 72 to estimate the rate of return needed to double your money in a given number of years.

THE RULE OF 72

The Rule of 72 is a rule of thumb or approximation technique. You can use it to estimate either the number of years or rate of return needed to double your money.

If you want to find the number of years, divide 72 by the rate of return.

Example: You are earning 10% on your money. How long will it take to double your money?

Solution: $72 \div 10 = 7.2$ years

If you want to find the rate of return, divide 72 by the number of years in which you want your money to double.

Example: You have $5,000 and want to double it in 6 years. What rate must your investment earn to achieve $10,000 in 6 years?

Solution: $72 \div 6 = 12\%$. At 12% your money will double in 6 years.

INVESTING INCREASES WEALTH

Financial success grows from the assets that you build up over time. Investing helps you accumulate wealth faster than if you simply saved your excess cash in a savings account. When you invest in stocks and bonds, you are participating in helping businesses make and sell new products and services. You will be rewarded with dividends and interest.

INVESTING IS FUN AND CHALLENGING

Investors make choices and hope to pick winners. Once you gain experience, you can have fun choosing investments, buying and selling when the time is right, and using your knowledge to plan for your financial security.

STAGES OF INVESTING

Before you begin investing, you must consider your budget, including your income, expenses, and savings. Typically, as your income grows and exceed your expenses, you can progress through stages from temporary savings into different kinds of investing and greater amounts of risk.

STAGE 1. PUT-AND-TAKE ACCOUNT

When you first begin to earn a paycheck, you will put it into an account and take money out as needed to pay your bills. This money is your emergency fund, or your "put-and-take" account. (See Figure 11.1.) The purpose of this money is to pay for your short-term needs with enough left over to cover unexpected expenses. Thus, you want to put your money in an account that offers security, or safety of principal.

FIGURE 11.1 *Stages of Investing*

BUDGET
- Income
- Expenses
- Savings

	Type of Investment	Strategy	Considerations
❶ Put-and-Take Account	Short-term savings (3–6 months' pay)	Safety	• Security • Liquidity • Short-term needs
(excess)			
❷ Initial Investing	Conservative, low risk securities	Higher rates of return than savings	• Reasonable purchase price
(excess)			
❸ Systematic Investing	Retirement funding	Long-range planning	• Growth • Future financial security
(excess)			
❹ Strategic Investing	Portfolio expansion	Maximization of return in the medium term (5–10 years)	• Diversifying • Planning • Hedging against risk
(excess)			
❺ Speculative Investing	High-risk options	High profits	• Uncertain future income • Short-term profit potential

Many financial advisers recommend that you have three to six months' net pay set aside in this type of fund. Then, should a need arise, you won't dip into permanent, long-term investments to pay for temporary, short-term needs. Your main concerns should be safety and liquidity.

▌ STAGE 2. INITIAL INVESTING

Investing really begins when you have "excess" savings beyond what you need for daily expenses and emergencies. Your *initial investing* should be conservative with low risk. At this stage, you don't have a lot of money to invest, so you don't want to risk losing it. Once you have established a safe cushion of investment, you can afford to make riskier (and potentially more profitable) investments. Typically, young workers in their 20s and early 30s begin investing when their spending is stable and their excess cash is increasing.

STAGE 3. SYSTEMATIC INVESTING

Once you are comfortable with your initial investments, you can then enter a stage called systematic investing. *Systematic investing* is making investments on a regular and planned basis. Money is set aside regularly for investing each month. As income grows, the amount invested also grows. At this stage, your goals are long-range. You are investing for a financially secure future. This ability to contribute regular sums of money usually happens in your 30s and 40s, when earning potential is highest.

STAGE 4. STRATEGIC INVESTING

Strategic investing is the careful management of investment alternatives to maximize growth of your **portfolio** (collection of investments) over the next five to ten years. For example, when the growth prospects for one investment seem to be declining, you would move your money into another investment where the prospects for growth seem greater. You would invest in different types of securities (stocks and bonds) to try to maximize your returns.

STAGE 5. SPECULATIVE INVESTING

When you are investing regularly in a broad collection of investments but you still have money available to take bigger risks, then you can choose to move into the final stage, called speculation. *Speculative investing* happens when you make bold and high-risk investment choices. In this stage, you can make—or lose—a great deal of money in a short period of time. You must be aware of the risks and be prepared to lose. Typically, odds are small that you will make a profit in a speculative investment, but when it does pay off, the profit is enormous. Beginning investors should avoid speculative investments because they cannot afford the loss that is likely to occur. High-risk investing is not for everyone; some people prefer to avoid it altogether.

RISK AND RETURN

Investing risk is the chance that an investment's value will decrease. All types of investing involve some degree of risk. The greater the risk you are willing to take, the greater the potential returns. A safe investment has little risk of loss. Some people are willing to take more risks than others. Those who are willing to accept a reasonable amount of risk will likely make considerably more in the long run than investors who are *risk averse* (afraid to make investments in which they might lose some or all of their investment). However, *risk-takers* (investors who like to take on a great deal of risk) could make a lot or lose a lot. The best plan for most investors is to plot a moderate course, somewhere between no risk and extreme risk, where they feel comfortable.

DIVERSIFICATION

One way to minimize risk is through **diversification**, which is the spreading of risk among many types of investments. Rather than buying only one kind of investment, you should choose several types of investments, such as stocks, bonds, and real estate. Also, you should diversify among types of stocks. For example, you might select some low-risk stocks to balance others with greater risk. Diversification reduces overall risk because not all of your choices will perform poorly at the same time. If one choice does not do well, the others will likely make up some or all of the loss.

TYPES OF RISK

Short-term investments are generally less risky than long-term investments. You can predict much more accurately what will happen in a week, a month, or a year than you can in 10–20 years.

Interest-Rate Risk

Interest-rate risk is the chance that inflation will rise faster than the return on your investments. Inflation makes your fixed-rate investments worth less because they are "locked in" at lower rates. The value of a fixed-rate investment decreases when overall interest rates increase. Their value increases when overall interest rates decrease. For example, if you own a security paying a fixed interest rate (say, 5 percent) and interest rates are increasing (to a level greater than 5 percent), your investment will be worth less over time.

Political Risk

Political risk refers to actions the government might take that would reduce the value of your investment. Increased taxes and certain regulations, such as costly environmental controls that businesses are required to apply, can make some investments less attractive.

Market Risk

Market risk is caused by the business cycle—periods of economic growth or decline. When the economy is doing well, the financial markets usually follow (and vice versa).

Nonmarket Risk

Nonmarket risk is unrelated to market trends. Nonmarket risk is entirely unpredictable and uncontrollable. For example, terrorism threats affect all investments in the short term. Because of the violent and unpredictable nature of such events, people change their behavior and seek ways to protect themselves. This causes markets to suffer as people sell their investments to hold more cash for personal security.

Company and Industry Risk

Company risk is associated with owning one company's stock. If that company fails, you lose your investment. *Industry risk* affects groups of businesses. For example, if you invest in the candy industry, a nationwide trend toward dieting or the avoidance of sugar may adversely affect the value of your investment.

How can you minimize your investing risk?

© Photodisc/Getty Images

The euro is the official currency of the European Union (EU). It is used in 15 member nations, known collectively as the Euro-zone. It is also used in nine other countries around the world that are not members of the EU. All European countries are eligible to join the EU, but not all EU members have chosen to adopt the currency. Sweden turned down the euro in 2003. Three other European states (Vatican City, Monaco, and San Marino) have adopted the euro, though they haven't joined the EU.

THINK *CRITICALLY*

Some nations are members of the European Union but have chosen not to adopt the euro as their currency. What do you think might be reasons for this? Why would nations who are not part of the European Union adopt the euro as their currency?

INVESTMENT STRATEGIES

Many individuals never start an investment program because they think they don't have enough money. But even small sums of money grow over time. To achieve financial security, start investing as soon as you can and continue to invest over your lifetime. The suggestions that follow will help you make wise investment decisions.

CRITERIA FOR CHOOSING AN INVESTMENT

Some investments increase in value at a rate higher than the rate of inflation. Some do not. Some investments provide for increases in value that do not show up as taxable income for many years. Evaluate your investment choices based on these factors:

- Degree of safety (risk of loss)
- Degree of liquidity (ability to get your money quickly)
- Expected dividends or interest
- Expected growth in value, preferably exceeding the inflation rate
- Reasonable purchase price and fees
- Tax benefits (saving or postponing tax liability)

No investment offers a high degree of all of these. Each investment choice represents a tradeoff. For example, in exchange for tax benefits, you would likely have to give up a high return and liquidity. However, you should choose investments that offer, for example, the highest degree of safety you can get for the expected return. A diversified portfolio of investments achieves a balance among these factors. It would include some safe but low-yield investments as well as some riskier, higher-growth choices plus some tax-deferred investments. These factors will be examined in the discussion of specific types of investments in Chapters 12–15.

WISE INVESTMENT PRACTICES

People commonly make investment mistakes. Some mistakes are minor and can be corrected easily. Others cause serious financial damage. To avoid investment mistakes and maximize your investing returns, follow the investment practices described on the next page.

Define Your Financial Goals

Clearly defined financial goals will help you to identify which investments to purchase. To be useful, investment goals must be specific and measurable. Set specific monetary targets. Identify how you plan to use the money and how soon you need to accomplish each goal.

Go Slowly

Before making investments, gather the information you need to make a wise decision. Make temporary investments until you are certain they will meet your needs. **Temporary investments** are investment choices that will be reevaluated within a year or less. If they aren't performing as expected, they will be sold and other choices selected. Avoid get-rich-quick schemes—if they sound too good to be true, they probably are!

Follow Through

A common mistake is keeping temporary investments too long and not reevaluating them regularly to determine how well they are performing. **Permanent investments** are investment choices that will be held for the long run—five or ten years, or longer. These securities will become the "critical mass" of your investment portfolio. They will sustain good solid returns over long periods of time and will grow substantially in principal as well.

Keep Good Records

To keep a clear view of your progress toward future needs and goals, keep good financial records. Pay attention to how your investments are doing. Every year, compare your investments' current balances with their previous years' balances. Keep statements to verify your account balances and make transfers when needed. Unless you know where you have been and where you are now, it is difficult to plan where you are going.

Seek Good Investment Advice

Don't be afraid to ask questions. Seek competent advice from a trained professional as you make investment decisions. To get this advice at low cost and without a commitment, consider attending an investment seminar. Here you can learn about products, costs, and risks. Then you can decide what to do in your own home without pressure.

Keep Investment Knowledge Current

Be aware of what is new in the financial market, what kinds of investments are currently good prospects, when to sell, and when to buy. It is your responsibility to know when to ask questions and to make the final decisions about your investments. Understanding the economy and how it works will help you make better investment choices.

Know Your Limits

Understand your risk tolerance and the amount of money you can afford to risk, so you can maximize returns within your risk comfort zone. If you are uncomfortable taking large risks, then avoid them. The chance of making huge profits is not worth being stressed out by the risk.

Computer Programming

Wherever people are successfully meeting the needs of a large quantity of customers, there is a computer program that keeps the records and processes the accounts. Computer programmers design all types of software, including the financial planning tools that are available to consumers.

Computer programmers write, test, and maintain detailed instructions, called programs, so that computers can operate as needed. Programmers also conceive and design software. Programmers know a variety of programming languages, and they tend to work on databases, mainframe, or Web programs. Most programmers are either applications programmers or systems programmers.

Employment Outlook

- Employment in this field is expected to decline slowly.

Job Titles

- Software engineer
- Systems analyst
- Computer programmer
- Systems programmer
- Applications programmer

Needed Skills

- A bachelor's degree is commonly required, although a two-year degree may be adequate.
- Relevant programming skills and experience are highly valued.

What's it like to work in... *Computer Programming*

Janeece works a typical 40-hour workweek. This week, she and the entire systems engineering department have been hard at work creating a new investment software package for a major client. They must meet the deadline and have the program up and running within two months.

Today, Janeece is writing program code so that the client can perform needed tasks. The company has many requirements for the software package. Janeece must incorporate a calculator that will perform various functions, which the company's financial advisers will use to compute asset growth and payout for their clients. The program must also have the capability to access live data from various stock exchange web sites to obtain current stock prices.

Janeece will be responsible for testing the program upon its completion to ensure it produces the desired result for the client. If problems occur, she will make the appropriate changes to the code and recheck it again until the program is functioning properly. Janeece will continue to offer product support for as long as the program is in use.

What About You?

Do you have an aptitude for writing detailed instructions that are logical and systematic? Do you enjoy working with the computer for most of the day? Is a career in computer programming right for you?

Assessment

KEY TERMS REVIEW

Match the terms with the definitions.

_____ 1. The spreading of risk among many types of investments

_____ 2. Investment choices held for the long run

_____ 3. The use of long-term saving to generate a financial return

_____ 4. The chance that an investment's value will decrease

_____ 5. A technique for estimating the number of years required to double your money at a given rate of return

_____ 6. Investment choices that will be reevaluated in the short term

_____ 7. A rise in the general level of prices

_____ 8. A collection of investments

a. diversification

b. inflation

c. investing

d. investing risk

e. permanent investments

f. portfolio

g. Rule of 72

h. temporary investments

CHECK YOUR UNDERSTANDING

9. Why do you need to establish an emergency fund before you start investing?

10. How does investing help you beat inflation?

11. What is diversification and what is its purpose?

APPLY YOUR KNOWLEDGE

12. Why is it important to start with temporary investments that lead to permanent investments?

THINK CRITICALLY

13. Why is risk an important consideration when investing? Write a paragraph explaining your comfort level with risk and how it will affect your investment decisions.

14. Explain the connection between keeping good records and making good investment choices.

15. Financial advice is only as good as its source. Explain why you should seek several sources of information before making investment decisions. Is it a good idea to use relatives and friends for advice? Why or why not?

Making Investment Choices

- List and describe sources of investment information.
- Describe basic investment choices and rate them by risk.

- annual report, *p. 251*
- bonds, *p. 252*
- discount bond, *p. 252*
- stock, *p. 253*
- mutual fund, *p. 254*
- annuity, *p. 254*
- futures, *p. 255*
- option, *p. 255*
- penny stocks, *p. 255*

SOURCES OF FINANCIAL INFORMATION

To make good investment choices, you must have good information. Investment information can be found in print, online, and through other sources to help you evaluate investment options.

NEWSPAPERS

Found in your local newspaper, *financial pages* list all types of securities, including stocks and bonds, as well as other information related to investing. Reading these pages daily will help you keep track of financial markets and obtain information needed to make wise investment decisions.

The Wall Street Journal is a daily paper that provides detailed coverage of the business and financial world. *Barron's* is a weekly paper that also provides charts of trends, financial news, and technical analysis of financial data. Both of these publications offer online subscriptions as well as free articles and data available at their web sites.

INVESTOR SERVICES AND NEWSLETTERS

Companies called *investor services* provide extensive financial data to clients. Major services include the following:

- Moody's Investors Service
- Standard and Poor's Reports
- Value Line

These publications are found in public libraries and brokerage firms, as well as online. They contain precise current and historical financial data. Many investors subscribe to weekly or monthly investment newsletters, which give them the latest financial data and information.

FINANCIAL MAGAZINES

A number of weekly and monthly magazines specialize in business and financial information. Most of them interpret financial data and give opinions and recommendations. Choices include the following:

- *Business Week*
- *Forbes*
- *Money*
- *Fortune*
- *Kiplinger's Personal Finance*
- *The Economist*

These magazines will keep you current, so you can determine when it is time to buy, hold, or sell securities. All of these publications offer financial news and stock market performance data at their web sites.

▌ BROKERS

Full-service brokers provide clients with analysis and opinions based on their judgments and the opinions of experts at the company they represent. However, you cannot expect a broker to pick winners for you every time. Almost all full-service brokerage firms provide monthly market letters giving advice on the purchase and sale of certain securities. Some well-known full-service brokerage companies include the following:

- Merrill Lynch
- Fidelity Investments
- American Express

Some people are well informed and know what they want to buy and sell. For these investors, a discount broker is adequate. *Discount brokers* buy and sell securities for clients at a reduced commission. A discount broker usually provides little or no investment advice to a client. Examples include the following:

- Charles Schwab
- TD Ameritrade
- E*TRADE

Because of the increasing popularity of inexpensive trading, many full-service brokers also offer discount trading at their web sites. Some banks, credit unions, and other financial institutions also assist their customers with buying and selling securities. Money can be transferred out of your checking or savings account to pay for securities purchased or transferred into your account for securities sold. You will receive statements showing the current value of your securities.

© Photodisc/Getty Images

What are some sources of financial information useful for investing?

With most types of brokerage accounts, you can manage your account online. You can give buy and sell orders, transfer money among investment accounts, and track the progress of your investments, either with your own software or with a platform supplied by the broker or bank.

FINANCIAL ADVISERS

Professional investment planners are called financial advisers or *certified financial planners* (CFPs). They are trained to give investment advice based on your goals, age, lifestyle, and other factors. The adviser will ask you to supply confidential information about your assets, liabilities, net worth, income, and budget, as well as your financial goals. The adviser usually receives a fee for consulting services, although some also receive a commission when they sell you investment products (such as stocks, bonds, or life insurance policies). Generally, you will get better overall advice when the adviser does not stand to make a profit on the investments you choose to buy.

ANNUAL REPORTS

An **annual report** is a summary of a corporation's financial results for the year and its prospects for the future. The Securities and Exchange Commission (SEC) requires all public corporations to prepare this report each year and send it to their stockholders. Investors can use the information contained in the report to evaluate the corporation as an investment prospect.

You can find annual reports online at the SEC web site (www.sec.gov). Corporations often publish their financial performance data in the investor section of their web sites. If you are interested in investing in a corporation, you can receive a copy of the annual report by writing to the company or submitting a request at the company's web site. Also, some large libraries keep copies of annual reports of major corporations.

NETBookmark

The annual reports of many corporations, such as McDonald's, can be found online for investors to examine. Access www.cengage.com/school/pfinance/mypf and click on the link for Chapter 11. At the McDonald's web site, follow the link to the most current annual report posted. Read the letter to shareholders near the beginning of the report and summarize the information in it in your own words. What were the company's revenues for the most recent year? How much did McDonald's pay in dividends to shareholders? What other types of financial information is available in the annual report?

www.cengage.com/school/pfinance/mypf

ONLINE INVESTOR EDUCATION

In addition to the web sites of print publications and brokers, the Internet offers many educational sites for new investors. Teenvestor is a web site dedicated to helping teens learn how to invest and manage their money. The Motley Fool web site offers money management tips in its personal finance section. Its "fool's school" presents investment basics in reader-friendly language. The National Association of Investors Corporation is a nonprofit site dedicated to investor education. This organization also helps investment clubs get started. These are just a few of the many educational sites available to investors online. A web search using a search engine or a directory from a popular home page, such as Yahoo!, will produce many more.

INVESTMENT CHOICES

Once you are ready to make permanent investments, it's time to consider all of your investment choices. Investments can be categorized by their degree of risk and expected return. In Chapters 12 through 15, you will explore each type of investment more thoroughly.

▌LOW RISK/LOW RETURN

For your first investments, you will likely want to consider fairly safe investments, even though their returns will be relatively low. Even as you grow as a sophisticated investor, however, you should continue to include some low-risk investments as part of your diversified portfolio.

Corporate and Municipal Bonds

Bonds are debt obligations of corporations (corporate bonds) or state or local governments (municipal bonds). When a corporation or government body sells a bond, it is borrowing from an investor. When you invest in a corporate bond, the corporation pays you a fixed amount of money (called interest) at a fixed interval (usually every six months). The corporation also must repay the principal (amount borrowed) at maturity. The *maturity date* of a bond is the date on which the borrowed money must be repaid.

When you loan money to a state or local government unit, such as a city, county, community college district, or utility district, you are also paid interest on your investment. Your principal is repaid when the bond matures. Typically, interest earned on municipal bonds is tax-free, giving the investor a tax advantage. Bonds are explained in detail in Chapter 13.

U.S. Government Savings Bonds

When you buy a savings bond, you are lending money to the United States government. U.S. savings bonds are available in two forms as follows:

- *Series EE Savings Bonds.* These bonds are known as discount bonds. A **discount bond** is purchased for less than the maturity value. The purchase price of a Series EE bond is one half of its maturity value. For example, you could buy a $50 bond for $25 and a $100 bond for $50. At maturity, you receive the full value of the bond. If you don't cash the bond at maturity, it continues to earn interest for up to 30 years.
- *Series I Savings Bonds.* These bonds are designed for investors wanting to protect against inflation and earn a guaranteed rate of return. With I bonds, interest is added to the bond monthly and is paid when the bond is cashed. I bonds are sold at face value (you pay $50 for a $50 bond), and they grow with inflation-indexed earnings for up to 30 years. In other words, the I bond pays a fixed rate combined with a semiannual inflation adjustment to help protect purchasing power.

You can buy savings bonds from commercial banks, through payroll deduction plans, or online. Savings bond certificates should be stored in a safe deposit box. If you are seeking safety, savings bonds are a good choice. You can hold them to maturity or cash them in at a bank for their current value after holding them for at least one year. Their interest is not subject to state or local taxes, only federal. Some savings bonds used to finance a college education are free of federal taxation as well. If savings bond certificates are lost, stolen, or destroyed, they can be replaced without cost.

Treasury Securities

For those with cash to invest, there are three types of U.S. Treasury securities. All of these are taxed by the federal government but are exempt from state and local income taxes. You can learn more about these securities at the TreasuryDirect web site (www.treasurydirect.gov).

- *U.S. Treasury Bills.* These bills (called T-bills) are available for a minimum purchase of $100. The maturity date for these bills ranges from a few days to 52 weeks (one year).
- *U.S. Treasury Notes.* These notes (called T-notes) are available for a minimum purchase of $100. Maturities are 2, 5, or 10 years. Interest rates for Treasury notes are slightly higher than for Treasury bills.
- *U.S. Treasury Bonds.* These bonds are issued for a minimum of $100 with a 30-year maturity. Interest rates are generally higher than rates for either T-bills or T-notes because of the longer maturity. Interest is paid every six months.

MEDIUM RISK/MEDIUM RETURN

When you feel secure enough to take more risk and you have additional money to invest, you are ready to step up to the medium-risk range to increase your return. Some of these medium-risk options involve investing with companies that manage the investment.

Stocks

Stock is a unit of ownership in a corporation. The owner of stock is called a *stockholder*. A stockholder receives a stock certificate, which is evidence of the ownership. When you are a stockholder, you will share in a corporation's profits, which are paid to you as dividends. If the company does well, you earn returns in two ways: in dividends and in the increased value of the stock you own.

Stocks generally carry more risk than choices with fixed interest, such as savings bonds, because a stockholder's earnings can go up or down, depending on the company's profits. Stocks in well-established companies are reasonably safe, while stocks in less-stable companies can be quite risky. However, a diversified portfolio of stocks of various risk levels can achieve a medium overall risk. You will learn more about investing in stocks in Chapter 12.

Mutual Funds

Suppose you have $500, which is not enough to buy a diversified portfolio of stocks. You can buy shares in a large, professionally managed group of investments called a mutual fund. A **mutual fund** is the pooling of money from many investors to buy a large selection of securities. Security funds are grouped to meet the fund's stated investment goals. Two major advantages of a mutual fund for investors are professional management and diversification. Since the fund invests in a wide variety of securities, it provides diversification that small investors could not otherwise achieve with their limited resources.

Although some mutual funds fall in the speculative category and others fall in the low-risk category, such as those that specialize in money market securities, most mutual funds fall somewhere in the broad medium range in terms of risk and return. You can further diversify your portfolio by investing in mutual funds with different objectives. For example, some funds buy securities in riskier small companies, hoping to earn a higher return. Others stick to well-established, safe companies to earn a lower but stable return. By investing money in both funds, you are diversifying your investments. If your riskier fund does not do well, your stable fund will limit your losses.

Mutual funds are the fastest-growing segment of the American financial services industry. You will learn more about mutual funds in Chapter 14.

Annuities

An **annuity** is a contract that provides the investor with a series of regular payments, usually after retirement. Generally, you receive income monthly, with payments to continue as long as you live. You usually buy an annuity directly from a life insurance company. The interest on the principal, as well as the interest compounded on that interest, builds up free of current income tax. Taxes are *deferred* until you receive payments from your annuity (these are called tax-deferred annuities). The payments from an annuity are normally used to supplement retirement income. The annuity is often described as the opposite of life insurance. It pays while you are alive; life insurance pays when you die.

Real Estate

Many people like to invest in real estate—houses and land. While this type of investment usually represents a large and often nonliquid investment of cash, it has proven to be protection against inflation in most parts of the United States. In

What are some advantages of investing in real estate?

© Digital Vision/Getty Images

some areas, market values of homes have increased faster than the inflation rate. Real estate investments also have tax benefits. Certain costs associated with home ownership are deductible from gross income, and thus lower taxable income. While investing in your own home carries little risk, investment in other types of real estate can be very risky. Investing in real estate is covered in greater depth in Chapter 14.

HIGH RISK/HIGH RETURN

High-risk/high-return choices involve considerable uncertainty. Returns can be high, but they can also be low or even negative, resulting in a loss of principal (the amount of the original investment). If you are willing to take the risks involved with these choices, you stand to make high returns over time. But you also risk high losses if your investments prove to be poor performers.

Futures

Futures are contracts to buy and sell commodities (products that are mined or grown) or stocks for a specified price on a specified date in the future. The investor is betting that the price of the commodity or stock will be higher on that future date than it is at the time of the contract. Thus, trading in futures is very risky speculation. If prices fall, the investor loses. If prices rise, the investor stands to make a lot of money. This type of investment is not for beginners or for individuals who cannot afford to lose their investment.

Options

An **option** is the right, but not the obligation, to buy or sell a commodity or stock for a specified price within a specified time period. As with futures, the investor is betting that, during the option period, the price of the stock will rise. If it does, the investor can choose to buy it at the lower option price, resulting in an instant profit. Typically, options are short-term investment devices used by speculators to make a quick profit. They are risky and not for inexperienced investors.

Penny Stocks

Penny stocks are low-priced stocks of small companies that have no track record. The stock usually sells for under $5 per share. The small companies often have low revenues and few assets to assure future growth. Dot-com (Internet) companies typically begin this way. Many of them fail, and the stock is worthless. Occasionally, a penny stock will be successful, and the investor will make a large windfall. Generally, penny stocks are highly risky.

Collectibles

Many people like to collect items such as coins, art, memorabilia, ceramics, or other items that are popular from time to time, such as Beanie Babies or baseball cards. If you collect an item that goes up in value rapidly, you can reap large rewards. If, however, you don't sell when your items are a hot commodity, they are likely to lose their value just as quickly, making them a risky investment. Collectors must be aware of the market and realize that their collections are subject to changing public tastes and can be difficult to resell.

ISSUES IN YOUR WORLD

CHOOSING THE RIGHT FINANCIAL ADVISER

Selecting the right financial adviser can be tricky. The most important factor is trust. You must feel comfortable with your adviser, be willing to give him or her a complete picture of your finances and financial goals, and then follow his or her advice.

Many people begin their investing with a trusted family friend who is in the business of giving financial advice at a bank, brokerage firm, or other financial institution. Or, you may know someone who has worked with a particular adviser for many years and can recommend that adviser to you. If so, your choice will be somewhat easier.

Some people consult with financial advisers at credit unions or through employee assistance plans. Others participate in group seminars offered by employers or professional organizations. In many cases, these choices provide good general advice about investment strategies that are effective for people with investment goals similar to yours.

The trick to finding and building a relationship of trust with a financial adviser involves taking the time to ask questions and thoroughly discuss your income, assets, liabilities, risk comfort level, and financial goals. Be sure to ask potential financial advisers about their training, background, and experience. Ask about their philosophy of investing, fees (how they earn money), and investment strategies. You also should know how clients have done in the past with their investment recommendations. Ask for references. Good advisers will tell you about their past successes. You can also check up on the past performance of stockbrokers through the Financial Industry Regulatory Authority. It monitors complaints and takes actions against its members when they are in violation of its rules. Remember: If you don't feel comfortable with a prospective financial adviser, keep looking until you find one who you feel can help you achieve your investment goals.

THINK *CRITICALLY*

1. *If you needed financial advice, whom would you ask? Why?*
2. *What are the characteristics you would look for in a successful financial adviser? What would it take to build your trust?*
3. *Locate the names and addresses of three or more financial advisers in your area.*

Assessment

KEY TERMS REVIEW

Match the terms with the definitions. Some terms may not be used.

_____ 1. A savings bond that is purchased for less than its maturity value

_____ 2. Low-priced stocks of small companies that have no track record

_____ 3. A summary of a corporation's financial results for the year and future prospects

_____ 4. A contract that provides the investor with a series of regular payments

_____ 5. Debt obligations of corporations or state or local governments

_____ 6. Unit of ownership in a corporation

_____ 7. Pooling of money from many investors to buy securities

a. annual report

b. annuity

c. bonds

d. discount bond

e. futures

f. mutual fund

g. option

h. penny stocks

i. stock

CHECK YOUR UNDERSTANDING

8. What are some sources of financial information useful for making investment decisions?

9. Why should beginning investors choose low-risk investments?

10. Why is investing in stock considered more risky than investing in bonds?

APPLY YOUR KNOWLEDGE

11. Visit a library or go online to obtain a copy of a current annual report of a major corporation that does business in your state. Outline the contents of the report and decide whether or not this corporation would be a good investment choice. Explain why or why not.

THINK CRITICALLY

12. What are advantages and disadvantages of investing through a discount broker rather than a full-service broker?

13. Explain why it is not possible for one investment to offer both low risk and a high return. Which is most important to you?

14. Compare U.S. government savings bonds to mutual funds and collectibles in terms of risk and potential return. Explain why these investments are categorized as they are.

Chapter Assessment

SUMMARY

11.1

- *Investing helps you beat inflation when your investments give you a return that is higher than the inflation rate.*

- *As your income grows beyond current needs, you can progress through investment stages involving greater amounts of risk.*

- *All investments involve some risk that your investment will lose value. Diversification helps minimize overall risk.*

- *Types of investment risk include interest-rate risk, political risk, market risk, nonmarket risk, company risk, and industry risk.*

- *Evaluate investment options for their degree of safety, liquidity, dividends or interest, growth, cost, and tax benefits. All investments involve trade-offs among these criteria.*

- *To make wise investments, define your goals, go slowly, keep good records, get good advice, keep your investment knowledge current, and know your limits.*

11.2

- *You can get investment information from newspapers, investor news-letters, financial magazines, annual reports, and brokers and financial advisers as well as from online sources.*

- *Full-service brokers give you advice in buying and selling securities; discount brokers do not give advice, but their cost is lower.*

- *Generally, the more risk you are willing to take, the more you stand to gain or lose from an investment.*

- *Investment choices can be low risk, medium risk, or high risk—depending on the investor's ability and willingness to take risks.*

- *Low-risk/low-return investment options include corporate and municipal bonds, U.S. government savings bonds, and U.S. Treasury securities.*

- *Medium-risk/medium-return investments include stocks, mutual funds, annuities, and real estate.*

- *Futures, options, penny stocks, and collectibles carry a high risk of loss but also offer large gains if they are successful.*

APPLY WHAT YOU KNOW

1. Read the financial section of your local newspaper. Write a few paragraphs summarizing the type of information covered and its usefulness to you as an investor.

2. Visit a discount brokerage firm online to find out how to open an account. Summarize their requirements in a paragraph.

3. Using keywords such as "investment," "stock," or some others you can think of, search the Internet for resources to help you make investing choices. List the names and URLs of three sites that you think would help you most. Briefly describe the types of investment information available at those sites.

4. Consult a financial newspaper or magazine or search the Internet to find the current rate for each of the following securities:

   - Series EE savings bonds

   - one-year Treasury bills

   - two-year Treasury notes

   - thirty-year Treasury bonds

5. Describe the five stages of investing. Which stage do you think is most important? Explain why.

6. Identify criteria you can use to evaluate an investment. Which criteria is most important to you? Why?

MAKE ACADEMIC CONNECTIONS

7. **Math** Using the Rule of 72, compute how long it would take to double your money at 1%, 3%, 5%, 7%, 9%,11%, and 13% annual rates of return. Assuming the inflation rate is 5.5% in a given year, how do these rates of return meet your needs?

8. **Research** Conduct research on a famous person (past or present) who has invested wisely over his or her life, resulting in substantial wealth. Consult their biography (if available) and other sources and explain their investment strategies. Write a report on your findings.

9. **Economics** Explain the concept of a business cycle. If the economy is growing, how would that affect your choices of investment? If the economy is slowing, how would that affect your choices? Consult The Economist magazine and find an article about the business cycle. Where are we at this point in time (recession, recovery, peak, or trough)? Explain what those terms mean in terms of investing.

10. **Careers** Assume you would like to work as a broker some day. Research the qualifications and skills required. What are the educational requirements? Describe the work environment and characteristics of this occupation. What is the average salary? Compile your research into a "career profile" of a broker.

Solve Problems and

Explore Issues

11. Ryan, who is 19 and in college, has just inherited $1,000. He does not need the money for his put-and-take account. What would you tell him to do with it? If Ryan invested the money in a stock that earned, on average, a 10 percent return, how much would his investment be worth in five years? Using the Internet, locate a savings planner tool for help.

12. If Ryan invested his $1,000 at a 5 percent average return, how many years would it take for his investment to be worth $2,000?

13. Allison is considering investing $500. Explain to her what factors she should consider when choosing investment alternatives.

14. Karmyn would like to invest in XYZ Corporation. You've never heard of it. What kinds of information should she have before she invests in this company? Where can she get that information?

15. Diane plans to invest $10,000 that she inherited from her uncle. She would like to have the money for her daughter's college education. Her daughter is now 10 years old and will start college in eight years. She does not want to take a lot of risk because she cannot afford to lose the $10,000. What course of action would you suggest for Diane?

16. Assume that Diane (in number 15) invested her $10,000 in a way that earned, on average, a 6 percent annual return. On the Internet, locate a college planner tool to find out how much more she would have to invest each year to cover her daughter's college costs. Assume that college will cost $10,000 a year for four years.

17. Choose six of the investment alternatives presented in this chapter. Rank the choices from high to low on the factors of safety, risk, and liquidity. Assume that 3 is the highest score and 1 is the lowest score for each factor. Based on the results of your review of possible investments, which three alternatives would you select as permanent investments? Why?

EXTEND YOUR LEARNING

18. **Legal Issues** Insider trading occurs when someone who has inside information about a company makes stock market transactions that create wealth for that individual. Why is insider trading illegal? What are the consequences or penalties? What is the Security and Exchange Commission's (SEC) role in enforcing laws against insider trading?

For related activities and links, go to **www.cengage.com/school/pfinance/mypf**

12

Investing in Stocks

12.1 *Evaluating Stocks*

12.2 *Buying and Selling Stock*

Consider **THIS**

Jon worked during the summer and managed to save $500 to invest. He decided he wanted to buy some stock and see if he could double his money in the next year or two.

"I've been doing research about a medical research company, and I think it's on the verge of something big," he said to a discount broker he met through his father. "I've been reading about this company and I think the stock price is low now because the company isn't paying dividends. Instead, they are using company profits to develop new products. Some of those products are on the cutting edge of research. All the information I've gathered suggests that the company is solid, growing, and will be a leader in its industry. I think this company's stock is worth the risk. Please buy me as many shares as my money will purchase."

Evaluating Stocks

GOALS

- Describe features of stock and types of stocks.
- Explain how to value a stock and decide a fair price to pay for a stock purchase.

TERMS

- stockholders, *p. 262*
- dividends, *p. 262*
- common stock, *p. 262*
- proxy, *p. 263*
- preferred stock, *p. 263*
- income stocks, *p. 263*
- growth stocks, *p. 263*
- blue chip stocks, *p. 264*
- par value, *p. 265*
- market value, *p. 265*

OWNING STOCK

Nearly 50 million people in the United States own stocks. There are more than 34,000 public corporations from which to choose. A *public corporation* is a company whose stock is traded openly on stock markets.

People who own shares of stock are called **stockholders**, or *shareholders*, of the corporation. If the corporation does well, stockholders will profit in two ways. One is through dividends. **Dividends** are money paid to stockholders from the corporation's earnings (profits). The other way stockholders profit is through *capital gains*. This is an increase in the value of the stock over time. For example, if you bought stock for $5 per share and the corporation thrived, its stock price might go up to $10 per share. If it did, you could sell it for a substantial profit. Part of the risk in owning stock, however, is that the price could also go down below the price initially paid for it, resulting in a *capital loss*. Also, a capital gain becomes profit only when you sell the stock. Until then, it is a profit only "on paper."

Stockholders can also lose all of their investment if the company fails or goes out of business. However, one advantage to owning stock is that stockholders can lose no more than their investment in the stock. The owner of a small business, on the other hand, can also lose personal assets if the business fails.

Stocks are traded in round lots or odd lots. A *round lot* is 100 shares or multiples of 100 shares of a particular stock. An *odd lot* is fewer than 100 shares of a particular stock. Brokerage firms usually charge higher per-share fees for trading in odd lots. Odd lots are usually combined into round lots before they are traded.

COMMON STOCK

Common stock represents a type of stock that pays a variable dividend and gives the holder voting rights. The board of directors, which guides the corporation and decides the amount of dividends to pay each year, is elected by the common stockholders. Common stockholders vote on major policy decisions, such as whether to issue additional stock, sell the company, or change the board of directors. Each share of common stock has the same voting power, so the more shares a stockholder owns, the greater the power to influence corporate policy.

Common stockholders may vote in person at the stockholders' meeting or by proxy. A **proxy** is a stockholder's written authorization to transfer his or her voting rights to someone else, usually a company manager. Most common stockholders vote by proxy rather than by attending the annual meetings.

Why is owning stock risky?

PREFERRED STOCK

Preferred stock represents a type of stock that pays a fixed dividend but has no voting rights. Preferred stockholders earn the stated dividend, regardless of how the company is doing. Thus, preferred stock is less risky than common stock. In the event the company fails, the preferred stock-holders would be paid ahead of common stockholders. As with most investments, however, the tradeoff for less risk is lower return. Dividends on preferred stock may be lower than common stockholders would earn, if the company is thriving over time.

TYPES OF STOCK INVESTMENTS

When evaluating stock investments, investors often classify stocks into different categories. Categories of stocks include income, growth, emerging, blue chip, defensive, and cyclical. Some stocks may fall into more than one category. Which category is best for you will depend on how much risk you are willing to assume for a chance to earn larger returns on your investments. Also, most investors buy stocks in several of these categories to diversify their risk.

Income Stocks

Corporations can use their profits in two ways. They can distribute the profits to stockholders as dividends, or they can reinvest the profits in the business to help it grow. Stocks that have a consistent history of paying high dividends are known as **income stocks**. Investors choose income stocks in order to receive current income in the form of dividends. Preferred income stocks pay the most certain and predictable dividends and are often the choice of retired people and others needing regular and dependable sources of income.

Growth Stocks

Growth stocks are stocks in corporations that reinvest their profits into the business so that it can grow. These corporations may pay little or no dividends. Instead of current income, investors buy growth stocks for future capital gains. If the reinvested profits do make the business grow, the stock will be worth substantially more in the future, when the investor is ready to sell it. As a result, growth stocks are long-term investments. They are often selected by younger people who have more time to let investments grow. If the value of the stock increases, stockholders must decide whether to sell it at the higher price now or to continue to hold it, hoping that it will go up even more. When stockholders decide to sell, the difference between their original purchase price and the selling price they receive is their capital gain.

Emerging Stocks

Stocks in young, often small corporations that have higher overall risk than stocks of companies that have been successful for many years are called *emerging stocks*. These young companies may be on their way to becoming highly profitable. Or, they may be among the many small companies that fail every year. Because the future of these companies is so uncertain, their stocks are often inexpensive but risky.

Blue Chip Stocks

Blue chip stocks are stocks of large, well-established corporations with a solid record of profitability. Most people have heard of these companies because their products and services have been around for decades. They are companies like IBM and Coca-Cola. Blue chip stocks are a conservative investment. Investors choose them for relatively safe, stable, but moderate returns.

Defensive Stocks

A *defensive stock*, or *non-cyclical stock*, is one that remains stable and pays dividends during an economic decline. Generally, companies in this category have a history of stable earnings. A defensive stock is not affected as much by the ups and downs of business cycles. Examples include utilities, pharmaceuticals, food, and health care stocks. In other words, the demand for these products remains fairly consistent regardless of economic conditions. Therefore, stocks in these industries protect the investor from sharp losses during bad economic times.

Cyclical Stocks

Cyclical stocks do well when the economy is stable or growing but often do poorly during recessions, when the economy slows down. Examples of cyclical stocks are travel-related companies such as airlines and resorts, manufacturing companies such as auto makers, and housing/construction companies. For example, during a recession, many people lose their jobs or earn less than they would during good economic times. As a result, people have less money for luxuries, such as leisure travel, causing reduced profits for travel-related companies. In response to this poor profit performance, the value of the stocks in these companies will likely decline.

VALUING STOCK

When you buy stock, you expect to hold it for a period of time and then sell it, hopefully for a profit. Whether or not you make a profit depends on how much someone else is willing to pay for it when you are ready to sell.

When you purchase stock, you may receive a stock certificate or have it held electronically. The certificate states the number of shares you own, the name of the company, the type of stock (common or preferred), and the par value. The **par value** is an assigned dollar value given to each share of stock. For common stock, par value is often meaningless. Common stock can be issued without a par value (no-par value stock). However, for preferred stock, par value is used to calculate dividend payments.

Par value has nothing to do with a stock's **market value**, which is the price for which the stock is bought and sold in the marketplace. The market value of a stock reflects the price investors are willing to pay for the stock. How a company currently is performing, its track record, and how well it is expected to perform in the future determine market value.

Some stocks perform very well, yet their market value seems too low—or a "real bargain." These "undervalued" stocks are worth more than the price for which they are selling. Stocks that are undervalued make good bargains for investors, while creating a dangerous situation for businesses by leaving them vulnerable to a takeover by a large investor or company. Takeovers may be unfavorable for employees but can be very favorable for stockholders, because the market value of the stock is likely to rise.

On the other hand, stocks can be "overvalued," which means they are selling at a price that is perceived to be too high. The price of the stock is not justified by its earnings but is based on its superior growth potential in the future. This situation is very risky for the investor, because it is likely that the price of the stock will drop. The wider the price swings, the riskier the stock.

STOCK PRICE

Several factors affect the price you will pay for a share of stock. These factors include the company's financial situation, current interest rates, the market for the company's products or services, and earnings per share.

- *The Company.* When a company is performing well (paying its current debts and earning a profit), the company's stock is attractive. Investors consider the company's earning power (its ability to continue to make a strong profit), as well as its debt (how much the company owes). If the company seems to be in a good financial position, the stock price will continue rising.

- *Interest Rates.* When interest rates are low, people who would normally put money in savings accounts and CDs look for more profitable places to invest their money. As interest rates rise, however, people tend to move their money to the safer investments. Generally, when interest rates fall below the current rate of inflation, people buy more stock, and stock prices rise.

- *The Market.* The marketplace determines a company's ability to sell its product or service now and in the future. If the company is in a popular industry and its products or services are selling well, its stock price will rise. For example, when people are buying computers, software, and related items, companies in the high-tech industry are considered wise investments.

If the demand for a particular product or service declines, the price of the stock will decline.

- *Earnings per Share.* Earnings per share are a corporation's after-tax earnings divided by the number of common stock shares outstanding, that is, shares in the hands of investors. For example, assume that in a given year, XYZ Corporation had after-tax earnings (net profit) of $1,000,000. It had 100,000 shares of common stock outstanding. Therefore, its earnings per share at that time were $10 ($1,000,000/100,000). Stockholders use earnings per share as a measure of a company's profitability.

■ RETURN ON INVESTMENT

Because you can make money on stocks from dividends and from an increase in the price of the stock (capital gain), you should consider both when computing the return on your investment. Figure 12.1 shows the formula for computing a stock's *return on investment (ROI)*. Your profit is the difference between what you paid for the stock and what you sold it for, plus any dividends you earned. To compute the total costs, add any commission you paid to the stockbroker to the purchase price of the stock.

■ STOCK INDEXES

A *stock index* is a benchmark that investors use to judge the performance of their investments. One widely followed stock index is the Dow Jones Industrial Average. Often called simply *the Dow*, it is an average of the price movements of 30 major stocks listed on the New York Stock Exchange. This average provides a general overview of how stock prices are doing in the stock market as a whole. Investors compare the price fluctuations of their stocks against this average to judge how well their stocks are performing compared to the overall stock market. Indexes for judging the performance of all kinds of stocks are available online and in print publications. Other commonly used indexes are the Standard & Poor's 500 and the NASDAQ Composite Index.

FIGURE 12.1	*Computing Return on Investment*

Computing a Stock's One-Year ROI

$$\frac{\text{Current Profit on Stock}}{\text{Purchase Price} + \text{Commission}} = \text{Return on Investment (ROI)}$$

Example: Selling price (or current stock price): $40/share
Dividends received during the year: $1/share
Purchase price: $38/share
Discount brokerage fee: $19
Number of shares owned: 100

Computations:
Current profit: $40/share − $38/share = $2/share × 100 = $200 + $100 dividends = total profits of $300

$$\frac{\$300}{(100 \times \$38) + \$19} = \frac{\$300}{\$3,819} = 7.86\%$$

Probably the number one career for inspiring others is teaching. As a teacher, one has the opportunity to touch, influence, and change more lives during his or her career than any other type of job.

Education careers occur at many levels, including pre-school, elementary, secondary (middle and high school), and post-secondary (community college, junior college, and four-year university).

Private industry also has educators. They do corporate training and help workers learn new skills and prepare them for higher positions within the company. Corporate educators have similar skills to those working at colleges and universities; they impart knowledge and help students reach their full potential.

Employment Outlook

- An average rate of employment growth is expected.

Job Titles

- Teacher
- Professor
- Corporate trainer

Needed Skills

- Bachelor's degree in subject matter; master's degree in education (teaching).
- Licensure in all 50 states for public education careers.
- Specialized knowledge and skills for private industry educators and trainers.

What's it like to work in... *Education*

Mike uses his teaching skills to help prepare workers at a large investment portfolio corporation. With his degree in education, he understands adult learning strategies. He also has worked for several years in the industry, so he has a good understanding of clients' needs.

Mike's company is incorporating a new investment planning strategy to help clients reach their investment objectives. He has planned a two-hour training session for the company's financial advisers. He will use a combination of print materials and visual aids during his presentation to accommodate all learning styles. Mike has also prepared several learning tools, including a chart that lists a variety of investment objectives and the correlating new stock options available to clients. These tools are designed to help advisers implement the new strategy more quickly and efficiently.

After the training session, Mike will conduct follow-up sessions with advisers to answer questions and address problems. He will conduct the training program for a new group of workers every six months.

What About You?

Do you enjoy training others to help them improve their performance? Would you like a job as a corporate trainer?

Assessment

KEY TERMS REVIEW

Match the terms with definitions. Some terms may not be used.

____ 1. A class of stock that pays a fixed dividend but has no voting rights

____ 2. Price for which stock is bought and sold in the marketplace

____ 3. An assigned dollar value to each share of stock

____ 4. A type of stock that has a history of paying high dividends

____ 5. Money paid to stockholders from earnings of a corporation

____ 6. A written authorization to vote for a stockholder

____ 7. Those who own shares of stock

____ 8. Stocks of large, well-established companies

a. blue chip stock

b. common stock

c. dividends

d. growth stock

e. income stock

f. market value

g. par value

h. preferred stock

i. proxy

j. stockholders

CHECK YOUR UNDERSTANDING

9. In what two ways can you make money from owning stock?

10. How is an income stock different from a growth stock?

11. Why do stockholders want to know a corporation's earnings per share?

APPLY YOUR KNOWLEDGE

12. Investing in blue chip stocks is said to be a conservative choice. Can you list several well-known stocks that are considered blue chip, besides the two mentioned in the text? (Hint: Read through the listing of stocks in the financial pages or online and mark the stocks you recognize.)

THINK CRITICALLY

13. If you had some money to invest, what stock would you choose? Why? Explain how you would make your stock choice(s). In other words, what criteria would you use to evaluate a potential stock purchase?

14. Why should young people (just starting their long-term investment strategy) invest in growth stocks rather than income stocks? Explain how these two types of stock are different and what that means to you, as a young person.

Buying and Selling Stock

THE SECURITIES MARKET

The securities market consists of the channels through which you buy and sell *securities* (stocks and bonds). To purchase common or preferred stock, you need a trading agent. Your agent will buy or sell for you in a securities marketplace, which is either a securities exchange or the over-the-counter market.

SECURITIES EXCHANGES

A **securities exchange** is a marketplace where brokers who are representing investors meet to buy and sell securities. The largest organized exchange in the United States is the New York Stock Exchange (NYSE). The smaller American Stock Exchange (AMEX) is also in New York City. Regional exchanges are located throughout the country. To have a stock listed with the NYSE or AMEX, a company must meet a minimum number of public shares and dollar market-value requirements.

In the NYSE building, the trading floor (where stocks are bought and sold) is about two-thirds the size of a football field. Around the edge of the trading floor are booths with computer terminals and room inside for a dozen or more floor brokers. *Floor brokers* buy and sell stocks on the exchange. Only brokers who are members of the exchange may do business there.

Spaced at regular intervals around the trading floor are trading posts, which are horseshoe-shaped counters, each occupying about 100 square feet on the floor. Behind each counter are *specialists*—the brokers to the

© Photodisc/Getty Images

What does a floor broker do?

floor brokers. All buying and selling is done around trading posts. About 90 different stocks are assigned to each post. Post display units above each counter show which stocks are sold in each section, the last price of that stock, and whether that price represents an increase or a decrease from the previous price.

Orders received at a brokerage firm or discount brokerage are phoned or sent by computer to that firm's booth at the exchange. A message is printed out and is given to the floor broker to carry out. When the transaction is completed, the brokers who bought and sold the stock report back to their respective brokerage firms. The buyer and seller can then be advised that the transaction has been concluded.

The exchange is a form of *auction market* where buyers and sellers are brought together to trade securities. Stock trading happens auction-style because in every transaction, stock is sold to the highest bidder (buyer) and bought from the lowest offeror (seller). Securities listed with the NYSE are traded only during official trading hours—9:30 a.m. to 4 p.m. New York time, Monday through Friday (except holidays).

OVER-THE-COUNTER MARKET

When securities are bought and sold through brokers but not through a stock exchange, the transaction is over-the-counter (OTC). The OTC *market* is a network of brokers who buy and sell the securities of corporations that are not listed on a securities exchange. Brokers in the OTC market do not deal face-to-face with other brokers. Their marketplace is as large as the number of brokers at work that day. Trades with other brokers are completed by telephone, and a computerized system displays current price quotations on a terminal in a broker's office. Brokers operating in the OTC market use an electronic quotation system called NASDAQ. (The letters were originally an acronym for the National Association of Securities Dealers Automated Quotation System.) With nearly 3,200 companies listed, NASDAQ has more trading volume in a day than any other stock exchange in the world.

BULL AND BEAR MARKET CONDITIONS

The stock market goes through cycles. For a period of time, stocks go up in value. Then the market corrects itself as people sell (to make a profit) and stock prices decrease. A **bull market** is a prolonged period of rising stock prices and a general feeling of investor optimism. Confidence in the country's economy also serves to drive up stock prices.

A **bear market** is a prolonged period of falling stock prices and a general feeling of investor pessimism. It develops when investors become negative about the overall economy and start to sell stocks. In bear markets, stock prices may fall 20 percent or more. Bear markets are usually short and savage. The average bull market often lasts three to four times as long as a bear market.

Whether the stock market in general is bullish (on an upward trend in prices) or bearish (on a downward trend in prices) influences your decisions about when to buy stocks and which stocks to buy. To make a profit, you need to buy stock when the price is low and sell when the price is high. However, nobody knows, including brokers, when a stock is at its lowest price or whether or not the price will rise.

INVESTING STRATEGIES

You can approach investing with either a short- or long-term strategy. Generally, if you buy and sell stock within a short period of time, you are a *speculator* or *day trader*. If you hold your investment for a long period of time (a year or more), you are an investor.

▌SHORT-TERM TECHNIQUES

When you buy and sell stocks for quick profits, you are "playing the stock market." The goal is to buy a stock that will soon increase in value. Then, when the price rises, you sell the stock. Many investors make short-term gains through processes called buying on margin and selling short.

Buy on Margin

You can borrow money from your broker to buy stock if you open a margin account and sign a contract called a *margin agreement*. To establish a margin account, you must deposit a minimum of $2,000 in cash or eligible securities (securities your broker considers valuable collateral) with a broker. Let's assume you have $2,000 in your margin account. You want to buy 100 shares of XYZ Corporation at $20 per share ($2,000). You could use $1,000 from your margin account and borrow $1,000, with interest, from your broker. This strategy is called **leverage**—the use of borrowed money to buy securities. You use less of your own money and therefore can buy more stocks with less cash. You would still have $1,000 in your margin account to use toward another purchase on margin.

With a margin purchase, you are betting that the stock will increase in value. If it does, you sell the stock, repay the loan with interest and commission, and take your short-term profit. Figure 12.2 shows how margin buying works.

FIGURE 12.2   *Buying on Margin*

Buying on Margin

Example: You buy $2,000 worth of stock with $1,000 of your own money and $1,000 borrowed from your broker at 6% annual interest. The stock increases in value, and you sell it after 60 days for $2,800. Your broker's commission to buy and sell is $200.

Computing Profit:

Interest cost: $1,000 borrowed $\times$ .06 annual interest $\times \left(\dfrac{60 \text{ days}}{360 \text{ days in a year}} \right)$
= $10 interest on the 60-day loan

Costs: $1,000 from margin account + $1,000 borrowed
+ $10 interest + $200 commission = $2,210 total cost

Profit: $2,800 selling price − $2,210 cost = $590 total profit

Computing Return on Investment:

$\dfrac{\$590 \text{ profit}}{\$2,210 \text{ cost}}$ = 26.7% ROI

Unfortunately, if the value of the stock does not increase, you will have to make up the difference. When the market value of a margined stock decreases to approximately one-half of the original purchase price, the investor will receive a *margin call* from the broker. This means the investor must pledge additional cash or securities to serve as collateral for the loan.

Sell Short

Short selling is selling stock borrowed from a broker that must be replaced at a later time. To sell short, you borrow a certain number of shares from the broker. You then sell the borrowed stock, knowing that you must buy it back later and return it to the broker. You are betting that the price will drop, so that you can buy it back at a lower price than you sold it for, thus making a profit. However, if the stock price increases, you will lose money because you must replace the borrowed stock with stock purchased at a higher price. Figure 12.3 shows how selling short works. There is usually no broker fee for selling short. The broker receives a commission when the stock is bought and sold.

LONG-TERM TECHNIQUES

As you may already suspect, investing in the stock market for short-term gains can be extremely risky. You cannot beat the market all of the time, but you can make some healthy profits if you study and follow the market carefully. However, most financial consultants advise you to invest for the long term. Records have shown that, over a long time, stock investments have consistently beaten rates for savings accounts, CDs, and other conservative options.

FIGURE 12.3 **Selling Short**

Selling Short

Example: You borrow 100 shares of stock of XYZ Corporation from your broker. You then sell 100 shares of XYZ at $28 per share and pay a $100 commission.

Income from sale: 100 shares × $28 per share − $100 commission
   = $2,700 initial income

Two weeks later, the stock price drops to $22 per share. You buy 100 shares to return to the stockbroker and pay a $100 commission.

Cost of buying back the shares: 100 shares × $22 per share +
   $100 commission = $2,300 cost

Profit from selling short: $2,700 income − $2,300 cost = $400 profit

Return on Investment: $\dfrac{\$400}{\$2,300} = 17.4\%$ ROI

Buy and Hold

Most investors consider stock purchases as long-term investments. All stocks go up and down, but over a number of years, the overall trend of non-speculative stocks is moderately up. Remember, a profit or loss occurs only when you sell the stock. If you "buy and hold" stocks for many years, you can ride out the down times. When you are ready to sell years later, most likely your stock will have gained value. In addition, many stocks pay dividends, so you are earning income while you hold the stock.

A stock split can also add to the value of the stock over time. A **stock split** is an increase in the number of outstanding shares of a company's stock. When a company increases its number of outstanding shares, it lowers the selling price in direct proportion. For example, if there were 1,000 shares outstanding with a market value of $60, then a 2:1 (two for one) stock split would result in 2,000 shares outstanding selling for $30. You will notice that the stock is still worth a total of $60,000. A stock split lowers the selling price of the stock, making the shares more affordable and encouraging investors to buy more. As investors buy more stock at the lower price, the share price often rises. If you held the stock before the split, then this price increase makes your stock worth more.

Dollar-Cost Averaging

The *dollar-cost averaging* technique involves the systematic purchase of an equal dollar amount of the same stock at regular intervals. The result is usually a lower average cost per share. To calculate the average cost per share, divide the total amount invested by the total number of shares purchased, as shown in Figure 12.4. In this figure, the investor purchased $100 worth of stock every quarter for one year. Over that time, the average price of the stock was $8. However, by investing at regular intervals over the time period, the investor's average cost per share was lower: $7.41.

Investors use this technique so they don't have to worry about timing their investment purchases. A regular purchase over a year's time will usually average

---

FIGURE 12.4   *Dollar-Cost Averaging*

Dollar-Cost Averaging

Quarterly Investment Amount		Share Price ($)		Number of Shares
$100	÷	10	=	10
$100	÷	7	=	14.29
$100	÷	5	=	20
$100	÷	10	=	10
$400		$32		54
Total $ invested				Total number of shares

Average share price = $8
$32 ÷ 4

Your average cost per share = $7.41
Total $ invested ($400) ÷ Total number of shares (54)

Ending value = $540
Last share price ($10) × Number of shares (54)

In May 2007, a Saudi Arabian company bought a plastic manufacturer in Massachusetts; in November, a French company bought a new factory in Michigan (adding 189 automotive jobs); in December a British company bought a New Jersey maker of cough syrup. Foreign investors buy businesses in America when the U.S. dollar is weak. At the same time, they make inroads to the world's largest market. In 2007, foreign investors poured $414 billion into American companies, factories, properties, and publicly traded stock, up 90 percent from the previous year. In the first part of 2008, foreign businesses invested another $22.6 billion. As the dollar continues to drop in value, more surge of foreign investment is expected. The weak dollar has made it easier for foreign companies to invest in the United States.

THINK CRITICALLY

In November 2007, a German company broke ground for a $3.7 billion stainless steel plant in Alabama based on the ability to reach millions of consumers. They cited NAFTA, a trade agreement which allows goods to flow into Mexico and Canada. How can this type of investment help America?

out to a reasonable price per share. With dollar-cost averaging, the investor makes a profit when the selling price per share is higher than the average cost per share.

Direct Investment

You can save money using **direct investment**, or buying stock directly from a corporation. By buying directly, you avoid brokerage and other purchasing fees. You may also be able to obtain shares at prices lower than on open exchanges. Direct investment is often available to existing stockholders who may have the privilege of buying additional shares at fixed prices that are at or below market value.

Reinvesting Dividends

You can also save money by reinvesting your dividends. **Dividend reinvestment** means using dividends previously earned on the stock to buy more shares. Buying stock this way avoids a broker fee and other costs that apply, such as taxes, when you receive cash dividends on the stock.

READING THE STOCK LISTINGS

To make wise investments in the stock market, it is a good idea to track the progress of your chosen investments to see how they are performing. Whether you are reading *The Wall Street Journal* or following your stocks online, you should see a listing similar to Figure 12.5. Follow along in this figure as you read the following explanation of each column.

- *Columns 1 and 2.* These columns show the highest and lowest price this stock sold for during the year. For the ExeB stock in Figure 12.5, the high for the last 52 weeks was 57.00 and the low was 32.00. This means the stock sold for $57 a share at one point (high) and $32 a share at another (low), though it may have sold for many prices in between during the year.

FIGURE 12.5 *Reading the Stock Listings*

Excerpt from stock exchange listings:

| 52 wks | | | | | P/E | Sales | | | | Net |
High	Low	Stock	Div	Yld%	Ratio	100s	High	Low	Close	Change
1	2	3	4	5	6	7	8	9	10	11
58.75	44.00	Enger	2.20	4.8	12	109	46.38	45.50	46.00	−.50
45.00	23.00	Eng pf	2.25	8.9	10	25	26.25	24.00	25.38	+.38
10.50	9.00	Entld	.10	1.0	3	8	10.13	9.50	10.00	----
24.00	16.00	Epsco	1.00	5.0	7	12	21.00	19.00	20.00	+.88
6.38	4.00	Exlab	----	----	15	300z	5.75	5.12	5.50	----
57.00	32.00	ExeB	2.50	5.7	11	48	46.00	43.00	44.00	+1.00

- *Column 3.* This column lists stocks alphabetically by name. You will notice that stock names are abbreviated. This abbreviated name is called the stock's *ticker symbol.* You may see additional abbreviations, such as "pf" (which means "preferred stock"), beside the name of the stock. There will be a legend at the bottom of the page that explains what these abbreviations mean. For example, a small "s" means that the stock has recently split. When a stock splits, each share owned is traded for additional shares. A 2:1 split would double your shares. If you owned 10 shares worth $50 each, you would now own 20 shares worth $25 each.
- *Column 4.* This column shows the cash dividend per share for the year, listed in dollars and cents. For the ExeB stock, 2.50 means that if you owned 100 shares of this company, you would have received a dividend of $250 for the year.
- *Column 5.* Yld % stands for percent yield, or the percentage of the current price the dividends represent. In other words, divide the amount of annual dividends (Column 4) by the closing price (Column 10).
- *Column 6.* The P/E ratio (price/earnings ratio) is the price of a share of stock divided by the corporation's earnings per share over the last 12 months. For example, if XYZ Corporation's stock is selling for $50 per share and XYZ's earnings per share are $10, the P/E ratio is 5 ($50/$10 = $5). The price/earnings ratio is a key factor that serious investors use to evaluate stock investments. A low P/E may indicate a solid investment, and a high P/E may indicate higher risk.
- *Column 7.* This column shows sales in hundreds of shares from the previous day—how many round lots of stock were bought and sold. Multiply the number by 100 to get the number of shares.
- *Columns 8, 9, and 10.* These columns show the highest, lowest, and closing price for this stock on the previous day. The closing price is the final price at the end of trading for the day.
- *Column 11.* This column, called net change, compares the closing price today with the closing price of the day before. A minus means the price has gone down. A plus means the price has risen. Stocks that have a price change of more than 5 percent may be set in boldface in some financial listings.

How can you track your stock holdings?

© Photodisc/Getty Images

Keeping track of your stock portfolio (or stock holdings) can be as simple as checking the closing prices periodically. Some people check their investments only once a year to see if they should make changes to their portfolio. Investors might buy additional shares, sell, or choose a different type of stock after checking their portfolios.

The stocks shown in Figure 12.6 have been tracked for ten days straight. As you can see, some stocks have done better than others in terms of market value as of a certain date. But remember, this chart does not take into account dividends received or the appreciation in value since a stock was purchased. The stock progress chart is merely a device for monitoring changes in the closing prices of stocks.

Many financial Internet sites enable you to follow stock prices. Using a stock's ticker symbol, you can find the stock's price up to the minute. If you want stock quotes sent to your computer automatically, you can sign up for the service with your Internet service provider. Most sites will allow you to specify the stocks you want to follow.

You can even buy and sell stocks online. Most major stockbrokers maintain web sites that allow online transactions. All you have to do is set up an account, deposit some money, and you're on your way!

FIGURE 12.6   *Stock Progress Chart*

Stock Progress Chart

Stock Names	Closing Prices for 10 Days										Total Change (+ or –)
	1	2	3	4	5	6	7	8	9	10	
1. Enger	28	28.12	29	28	27	28	28.50	29	29.50	30	+2
2. Glastn	38	40	41	41.50	--	40	39	38	38	38	0
3. Karbr pf	61	61.25	61.13	61	61.38	61	62	62.38	61	61.13	+.13
4. Maxln	50.13	49	50	50.25	51	51	51.13	52	52	53.50	+3.37
5. Totlmb	10	11	11.13	11.50	11	10.88	10	9	8	8.50	–1.50

ISSUES IN YOUR WORLD

INFLATION: WHO GETS HURT?

Inflation *is an increase in the general level of prices. It is measured yearly to see how much prices are rising. The* consumer price index (CPI) *is the instrument most often used as a measure of rising prices. The CPI measures price changes for a "market basket" of goods and services typically purchased by consumers. Inflation is also evident in rising interest rates. Interest rates reflect the cost of lending and borrowing money. As prices increase, interest rates go up as well.*

Some people get hurt by rapidly rising prices and interest rates. People who are more likely to be impacted by inflation include the following:

- People on fixed incomes. *Many retired people live on a fixed monthly retirement check. When prices rise, their fixed income stays the same. Thus, they are unable to maintain the same standard of living in inflationary times.*

- People with a lot of debt. *During inflationary times, interest rates charged for loans are rising. Thus, creditors (lenders of money) can charge higher interest rates. This makes it hard for people with a lot of debt to pay off their loans. More of each month's payment goes toward interest rather than paying off the debt.*

- People who have to borrow. *If you need to borrow money, you will pay higher interest rates in times of inflation. As a result, your monthly payments will be higher or you will have to make payments for a longer time to pay off the loan.*

- People working as employees. *As an employee, you work for a salary or wage. Although you may get a yearly raise, it may not be enough to keep up with price increases, such as the rising cost of gasoline. Price increases (inflation) hit immediately, and you must adapt by making changes in your lifestyle. This lowers your standard of living as rapidly rising prices erode your purchasing power.*

To prepare for periods of inflation, save so you will have resources during hard times. Then you can be a lender rather than a borrower.

THINK CRITICALLY

1. *Using the keyword "inflation," conduct Internet research and compare interest rates and rising prices in the United States to those in other countries, such as Brazil, Mexico, or France. Look at the rates over a three-year or five-year period of time. Report your findings.*

2. *Have you noticed goods or services you buy frequently increasing in price? How have prices of those goods or services affected your lifestyle?*

Assessment

KEY TERMS REVIEW

Match the terms with definitions.

_____ 1. Buying stock directly from a corporation, avoiding costs of purchasing

_____ 2. A prolonged period of falling stock prices

_____ 3. Selling borrowed stock that must be replaced at a later time

_____ 4. A marketplace where brokers meet to buy and sell securities

_____ 5. The use of borrowed money to buy securities

_____ 6. A prolonged period of rising stock prices

_____ 7. An increase in the number of outstanding shares of stock

_____ 8. Using earned dividends to buy more shares of stock

a. bear market

b. bull market

c. direct investment

d. dividend reinvestment

e. leverage

f. securities exchange

g. short selling

h. stock split

CHECK YOUR UNDERSTANDING

9. What are two kinds of markets where securities are bought and sold?

10. Why is buying on margin risky?

11. How do you save money by reinvesting dividends?

APPLY YOUR KNOWLEDGE

12. Search the Web for investment advice. In no more than one page, summarize what the experts are saying about which stocks are hot right now and which are not. Do the experts seem to agree or disagree with each other? Some sites you might try include Forbes, MSN Money, CNN Money, Fortune, Kiplinger, and Barron's.

THINK CRITICALLY

13. How can you save money by direct investment? Is this a good idea for long-term investing? Why or why not?

14. Use the Internet or library resources to research the history of bull and bear markets. List the years when each type of market occurred during the 1980s and 1990s. Which type of market is evident today? Why is it important to understand bull and bear market trends?

Chapter Assessment

SUMMARY

12.1

- *Stockholders profit through dividends and capital gains.*

- *Because preferred stock pays a fixed dividend, it is less risky than a company's common stock, but generally earns a lower return.*

- *Corporations that issue income stocks pay profits to stockholders as dividends, while corporations that issue growth stocks reinvest profits in the business so it can grow.*

- *Emerging stocks are issued by young companies and have a higher overall risk.*

- *Blue chip stocks provide a relatively safe but moderate return.*

- *Defensive (non-cyclical) stocks remain relatively stable during good and bad economic times.*

- *Cyclical stocks do well when the economy is growing but do poorly during recessions.*

- *The par value printed on the stock certificate has nothing to do with the market value investors actually pay for the stock.*

- *Stock price depends on company performance, general level of interest rates, the market for the company's products, and the company's earnings per share.*

- *Both dividends and capital gains are used to determine the ROI.*

12.2

- *You can buy and sell securities through a securities exchange (physical place) or over-the-counter (by phone or computer).*

- *Stock prices are rising during a bull market and falling during a bear market.*

- *Short-term investors are speculators who try to make a quick profit by buying on margin or selling short.*

- *Long-term investment strategies are buy and hold, dollar-cost averaging, direct investment, and reinvestment of dividends.*

- *You can track your stock's progress by reading the stock listings in print publications and online.*

- *You can find information, set up an account, track your stocks, and buy and sell securities online.*

APPLY WHAT YOU KNOW

1. If you own 100 shares of common stock, which you purchased for $28 a share, and the company declares a cash dividend of $.88 for the quarter, how much will you receive in dividends?

2. Assume a company has issued the following stock: 2,000 shares of 5 percent preferred stock at $50 per share and 18,000 shares of common stock at $22 per share. A cash dividend of $1.30 per share is declared for common stock, after preferred stockholders have received their 5 percent dividend. Compute your total cash dividends for the year if you own (a) 100 shares of preferred stock; (b) 100 shares of common stock; (c) 50 shares of preferred stock and 50 shares of common stock. (Hint: To calculate preferred stock dividends, you must multiply 5 percent by the total cost of the number of shares of stock owned.)

3. Suppose you purchased 100 shares of stock in January for $48 a share. You received dividends of $1.25 per share on April 1 and July 1 and $.95 per share on September 1. You sold the stock in December for $50 a share. What would be the stock's return on investment for the year? Assume a broker commission of 3 percent on the purchase and 3 percent on the sale of the stock. (Hint: Use the formula in Figure 12.1.)

4. You have $2,500 in cash in a margin account. You decide to buy stock on margin. You buy 50 shares of stock selling at $100 per share. Assume that the stock rises in value, and 30 days later you sell the stock for $110 a share. Interest on the amount borrowed is 7 percent. The total commission charged is $150. What is the total return on investment? Explain why buying on margin is a risky practice. (Hint: Use the formula in Figure 12.2.)

MAKE ACADEMIC CONNECTIONS

5. **History** The Securities and Exchange Commission (SEC) was formed in 1933 to protect investors from corporations that would deceive them into buying stock. Visit the sec.gov web site and write a report describing the role of the SEC in the past and today. What do they do to protect investors? What kinds of reports do corporations file with the SEC that are made available to the public online at the SEC web site?

6. **Economics** Explain the relationship of the economy as a whole to the stock market. For example, stock prices are rising (bull market) when the economy is growing. Why is this true? Write a one-page report explaining how business cycles affect stock prices and what it means to you as an investor.

7. **Math** You wish to sell short. You arrange to borrow from your broker 100 shares of stock in XYZ Corporation on January 2. You immediately sell 100 shares of XYZ at $60 per share. On April 1, you instruct your broker to purchase 100 shares of XYZ at $53 per share. You return 100 shares of XYZ stock to your broker. Assume the commission was $200. What is your return on investment for this transaction? (Hint: Use the formula in Figure 12.3.)

SOLVE PROBLEMS AND

EXPLORE ISSUES

8. Suppose you decided to buy stock using dollar-cost averaging. You purchased $200 worth of stock every quarter for one year. You paid the following share prices. Quarter 1: $5; Quarter 2: $10; Quarter 3: $8; Quarter 4: $4. Using Figure 12.4 as a guide, calculate these values: (a) average share price; (b) your average cost per share; (c) ending value. Did you benefit from dollar-cost averaging? Explain.

9. Your friend Janice is considering investing in stocks. She has an extra $5,000 that she wants to invest. She won't need the money for five years, when she hopes to start medical school. Would you recommend common or preferred stock? Explain why.

10. Mr. and Mrs. Nelson are in their late fifties and plan to retire within the next three to five years. They would like to put some of their money into the stock market because interest rates on savings accounts are low. Which of these options would you recommend to them: Income or growth? Emerging stocks or blue chip? Defensive or cyclical? Give a brief reason for each choice.

11. Lucia and Carlo are married and are considering buying some stock to have a "nest egg" for their future children. Carlo prefers to buy stock in a local company that is small and just getting started. Lucia prefers to buy the stock of a well-known company that is listed on a major exchange. Discuss with them the pros and cons of each course of action.

12. Choose three stocks to follow for a week: one listed on the NYSE, one on the AMEX, and one on the NASDAQ. Pretend that you invested $1,000 in each stock. On the Internet, find the closing price for these stocks on the day you "purchased" them and at the end of every day for one week. At the end of the week, prepare a stock progress chart (see Figure 12.6) showing the closing prices for each day for all three stocks. Analyze your findings. Which stock price varied the most? Which had the highest high? The lowest low? Which had the most consistent upward trend? If you sold the stocks at the end of the last day, how much would you have gained or lost on each one?

EXTEND YOUR LEARNING

13. **Ethics and Legal Issues** In 2001, Enron Corporation and Arthur Andersen (accounting firm) were involved in a massive stock fraud scheme. Enron's stock plummeted, and it filed bankruptcy. Stockholders lost their entire investment. Prepare a history of the Enron scandal. What ethics issues were involved? Discuss reforms that were put in place as a result of the Enron stock scandal, such as the Sarbanes-Oxley (SOX) Act of 2002. How does SOX enhance corporate responsibility and protect you as an investor?

For related activities and links, go to *www.cengage.com/school/pfinance/mypf*

13

Investing in Bonds

13.1 *Evaluating Bonds*

13.2 *Buying and Selling Bonds*

Consider **THIS**

Brenda is a conservative investor. She wants to be certain her money is safe and that it will be available to her in two years when she needs it to start her business.

"I want to get a better return than I can get for a certificate of deposit," she told her investment adviser. "I'm thinking about investing my money in bonds. I read in the financial section of today's paper that there are some tax-free municipal bonds that are paying 5.5 percent. I'm also considering a high-grade corporate bond that pays 7 percent. While the rate is higher on the corporate bond, interest earnings are taxable. What would you advise?"

Evaluating Bonds

GOALS

- Discuss the features, types, and earnings on corporate bonds.
- Describe the different types of government bonds.

TERMS

- face value, *p. 283*
- callable bond, *p. 284*
- debenture, *p. 284*
- secured bond, *p. 284*
- convertible bond, *p. 285*
- zero-coupon bond, *p. 286*
- municipal bond, *p. 287*
- revenue bond, *p. 287*
- general obligation bond, *p. 287*
- agency bond, *p. 288*

CORPORATE BONDS

While a corporation may use both bonds and stocks to finance business activities, there are important distinctions between the two. First, bonds are loans (debt) that must be repaid at maturity. Stocks are shares of ownership (equity) in the corporation, not loans. Second, corporations must make the semiannual interest payments on their bonds. Corporations are not required to pay dividends on stocks. The board of directors decides whether or not to pay stock dividends.

Bondholders (those who invest in bonds) receive interest twice a year. When the bond matures on its maturity date, it is repaid. Bond maturities typically range from 1 to 30 years. **Face value** is the amount the bondholder will be repaid at maturity. Face value is also referred to as par value because the face value is the dollar amount printed on the certificate.

FEATURES OF CORPORATE BONDS

Corporate bonds are sold on the open market through brokers, just like stocks. Prices asked for bonds appear daily in *The Wall Street Journal* and the financial pages of other major newspapers. However, only a small fraction of the bonds issued are listed in the newspaper.

Bonds are known as "fixed-income investments." *Fixed-income investments* pay a specified amount of interest on a regular schedule. A bond's interest does not go up and down, like stock dividends do. A bond's *contract rate* (also called its interest rate) is the percentage of face value that the bondholder will receive as interest each year. Usually, payments of half the annual interest are

© Comstock Images/Jupiter Images

How are bonds different from stocks?

made twice a year. For example, a $1,000 bond might pay 5 percent, or $50 a year. The bondholder would receive two $25 payments during the year. Interest received on corporate bonds is taxable, and it must be reported as ordinary income on your tax return.

The process for collecting the interest on your bond depends on whether it is a registered bond or a coupon bond. A *registered bond* is recorded in the owner's name by the issuing company. Interest checks for registered bonds are mailed semiannually, directly to the bondholder. A *coupon bond* (also called a *bearer bond*) is not registered by the issuing company. To collect interest on a coupon bond, bondholders must clip a coupon and then cash it in at a bank, following the procedures outlined by the issuer. Today, most bonds are registered.

A major disadvantage for individual investors is the cost of bonds. Very few corporate bonds are sold in units of less than $1,000. Bonds are commonly sold in $5,000 units.

A bond may be issued with a call provision. A **callable bond** is a bond that the issuer has the right to pay off (call back) before its maturity date. The date when a bond can be called is identified at the time it is offered for sale. For example, a ten-year bond issued in 2008 with a maturity date of 2018 may be callable in the year 2013. If interest rates fall, corporations may choose to call the bonds because they can re-issue them at a lower interest rate. Generally, it is cost-effective for corporations to pay the costs of calling and re-issuing when interest rates drop by 2 percent or more. Corporations usually agree not to call bonds for the first five years after issuance. When the corporation does exercise its right to call the bond, it generally pays the bondholders a small premium—an amount above the face value of the bond. For example, a $1,000 bond may be called for $1,020.

▌ TYPES OF CORPORATE BONDS

For corporations, bonds are a primary way of raising money. The money raised pays for expansion, new technology, and long-term operating expenses. There are three basic types of corporate bonds: debentures, secured (mortgage bonds), and convertible bonds.

Debentures

A **debenture** is a corporate bond that is based on the general creditworthiness of the company. The issuer does not pledge any specific assets to assure repayment of the loan. Because of this, debentures are considered unsecured bonds. An investor relies on the full faith and credit of the issuer of the bond for repayment of the interest and principal. When issued by reliable companies, debentures are usually relatively safe investments.

Secured Bonds

A **secured bond**, also called a *mortgage bond*, is backed by specific assets which serve as security to assure repayment of the debt. If the corporation fails to repay the loan as agreed, the bondholder may claim the property used as security for the debt. The asset most often used for security is real estate, a building, or some other type of property.

Convertible Bonds

A **convertible bond** is a corporate bond that can be converted to shares of common stock. The bondholder has the option of switching to a stock investment. If the bondholder converts to common stock, the bond is no longer due and payable at maturity. Convertible bonds can be exchanged for a certain number of common shares at a specific price per share. For example, say you purchase a $1,000 corporate bond which is convertible to 50 shares of the company's common stock. You should convert the bond to stock whenever the price of the company's common stock is $20 ($1,000/50 shares) or higher. Assume the company's stock is selling for $22. In this situation, you would have an investment worth $1,100 ($22 × 50 shares) on conversion.

EARNINGS ON CORPORATE BONDS

All corporate bonds are issued with a stated face value and fixed contract rate. Figure 13.1 shows interest payments on a $10,000, ten-year, 6 percent corporate bond. Let's assume that the bond was issued on January 1, 2008, and interest payments are due on June 30 and December 31 of each year. The maturity date of the bond is the date when the principal (face value) must be repaid in full. This ten-year bond would have a maturity date of January 1, 2018, or ten years from the date of issue.

The return on the bond in Figure 13.1 is 6 percent per year. The yield is also 6 percent. In other words, there is no compounding. Half the annual amount of simple interest is paid every six months.

While the interest rate on your bond is fixed, the market price (what you could sell it for) can change. For example, a $10,000 bond may sell for more than $10,000 if interest rates are falling. People would be willing to pay more for the bond because it pays an interest rate higher than the current market rate. When bonds sell for more than their face value, they are selling at a *premium*. A $10,000, 6 percent bond selling for $10,000 is at 100 percent of

FIGURE 13.1	Earnings on a Ten-Year 6% Corporate Bond	
Year	June 30 Interest	December 31 Interest
1	$300.00	$300.00
2	300.00	300.00
3	300.00	300.00
4	300.00	300.00
5	300.00	300.00
6	300.00	300.00
7	300.00	300.00
8	300.00	300.00
9	300.00	300.00
10	300.00	300.00
January 1, 2018: $10,000 principal is repaid		

its face value, or "1." But if the bond sold for "104," it would have a premium of 4 percent. At 104, the market price would be $10,400.

$$\$10,000 \times .04 = \$400 \text{ premium}$$
$$\$10,000 + \$400 = \$10,400 \text{ market price}$$

In this case (buying at a premium), the buyer's yield would be lower than 6 percent because the buyer had to pay more than face value to buy the bond.

Bonds can also sell below face value. Investors are not willing to pay face value for a bond yielding 6 percent when current interest rates are higher than 6 percent and rising. Therefore, the bond may have to be sold at a *discount*, or for an amount lower than face value, to attract buyers. If a bond sold for 96, it was sold at a 4 percent discount. The purchaser of the bond would pay only $9,600 for a $10,000 bond.

$$\$10,000 \times .04 = \$400 \text{ discount}$$
$$\$10,000 - \$400 = \$9,600 \text{ market price}$$

In this case (buying at a discount), the buyer's yield would be higher than 6 percent because the buyer paid less than the face value for the bond.

Figure 13.2 shows how to compute the yield on bonds when they are issued at a premium or at a discount. Yield is not the same thing as the contract rate of interest.

ZERO-COUPON BONDS

Another type of corporate bond is a zero-coupon bond. A **zero-coupon bond** is sold at a deep discount, makes no interest payments, and is redeemable for its face value at maturity. These bonds may also be issued by the U.S. government or municipalities. They are sold at as much as 50–75 percent below the face value of the bond. As the bond progresses toward maturity, it may appreciate, or increase in value. The bondholders make money by selling the bonds before maturity at a price higher than they paid for them. Or, they can hold the bonds to maturity and receive the face value and interest.

With a zero-coupon bond, you must pay taxes on any "interest" you gained each year (even though you don't actually receive it) until the bond is paid at maturity. Interest on zero-coupon municipal bonds, however, is not subject to taxation. Prices on zero-coupon bonds can fluctuate widely. Should you need to sell the bond before maturity, you may face a loss.

FIGURE 13.2	Yield on a 6% Corporate Bond

$$\frac{\text{Annual interest dollar amount}}{\text{Market price}} = \text{Yield}$$

	Annual Interest/Market Price = Yield	
If you buy the $10,000 bond at face value	$600/$10,000 =	6%
If you buy the bond at 104	$600/$10,400 =	5.8%
If you buy the bond at 96	$600/$9,600 =	6.3%

The national debt consists of borrowing by the federal government. Each year, the national deficit (excess of spending over revenue collected) is added to that debt. In 2008, the national debt was near $10 trillion. In historical times, the national debt was used to finance wars. Currently, it is still used to fund the military, but it is also applied to funding recommendations outlined in the annual federal budgets. The national debt is represented by Treasury notes, bills, and bonds. Many people feel the debt is overwhelming and represents obligations that must be paid by future generations. Others feel the national debt is needed to fund spending requirements, such as tax rebates to stimulate the economy, tax cuts, government programs to aid disaster relief, and so on.

THINK *CRITICALLY*

Which side do you agree with? Enter the keywords "national debt" online and find out the current amount of the debt. What should the country do about the national debt?

GOVERNMENT BONDS

In addition to loaning money to corporations, you can also loan money to the government. Government bonds are issued by the federal as well as state and local governments. There are four major types of government bonds: municipal, savings, Treasury, and agency bonds.

MUNICIPAL BONDS

A bond issued by state and local governments is called a **municipal bond**. The minimum investment in a municipal bond is usually $5,000, although brokers often ask for a multiple of this amount as a minimum investment. Municipal bonds, also known as "munis," can be backed by specific projects, or by the general taxing authority of a governmental unit.

A **revenue bond** is a municipal bond issued to raise money for a public-works project. The revenues (income) generated by the project are used to pay the interest and repay the bonds at maturity. Major projects financed by revenue bonds include airports, hospitals, toll roads, and public housing facilities.

A **general obligation bond** (or GO) is a municipal bond backed by the power of the issuing state or local government to levy taxes to pay back the debt. For example, school districts issue bonds to finance construction of new buildings. A city may issue bonds to pay for a new police or administrative center. States may issue bonds to pay for a new college campus or a new road system. A GO bond is repaid with the government's general revenue and borrowings. In contrast, a revenue bond is repaid from the revenue generated by the facility built with the borrowed funds. Cities pay off the GO bonds using city income and sales taxes collected, fees, fines, and other sources. Schools and colleges pay off the bonds with property taxes, tuition, fees, state funding, and other sources.

Municipal bonds generally pay a lower interest rate than corporate bonds. However, the interest is exempt from federal taxes (and often state and local taxes as well), so the effective rate is higher than the stated rate. As Figure 13.3 on the next page shows, the tax advantage of municipal bonds sometimes makes them a better deal than a corporate bond paying a higher interest rate. Figure 13.3 calculates net interest on both kinds of bonds for an investor in the 28 percent tax bracket.

FIGURE 13.3	*Comparing Taxable and Tax-Exempt Bonds*	
	Corporate Bond	**Municipal Bond**
Face value (Principal)	$10,000	$10,000
Rate of interest	6%	5%
Amount of annual interest	$ 600	$ 500
Tax on interest earned (28%)	$ 168	$ 0
Net interest	$ 432	$ 500

SAVINGS BONDS AND TREASURY SECURITIES

You can buy U.S. savings bonds from commercial banks, through payroll deduction plans, or directly from a Federal Reserve Bank. You can buy up to $20,000 worth of these bonds a year. Series EE bonds are sold at one half of their face value. Investors who buy these bonds often hold them to maturity. These bonds are issued with maturity values that range from $50 to $10,000. Series I bonds are sold at face value and have fixed plus variable rates of return that increase as general interest rates rise. This helps protect you from the effects of rising prices (inflation).

Treasury securities (Treasury notes, bills, and bonds) are no longer issued as engraved certificates as are many stocks and corporate bonds. Instead, they are kept "electronically," and the investor receives a statement of account. Thus, these investments exist as bookkeeping entries in the records of the U.S. Treasury Department itself or in the records of commercial banks. Treasury securities are virtually risk-free, since they have the backing of the U.S. government. They are taxable at the federal level but are exempt from state and local taxes and are usually not callable.

AGENCY BONDS

In addition to the U.S. Treasury, other federal agencies issue debt securities. Federal agencies that issue bonds include the Federal Home Loan Mortgage Corporation (Freddie Mac), Federal National Mortgage Association (Fannie Mae), Federal Housing Administration (FHA), and Student Loan Marketing Association (Sallie Mae). When you purchase an **agency bond**, you are loaning money to one of these agencies. The agencies use this funding to provide low-cost financing to certain groups of people. Although agency bonds are basically risk-free, they offer a slightly higher yield than securities issued by the Treasury. In 2008, the federal government took over the administration of the Fannie Mae and Freddie Mac lending programs. This adds further stability and provides more protection against risk when buying these bonds. They can be bought directly through banks or from brokers. Agency bonds are usually exempt from state and local taxes, but not federal tax.

What is the purpose of an agency bond?

© Digital Vision/Getty Images

Police detectives at the local level, state level, and federal level investigate crimes of all types. FBI agents investigate crimes including white-collar crimes, such as insider trading.

Federal officers, which include FBI agents and U.S. Marshals, investigate more than 200 areas of federal laws, including national security issues in the Department of Homeland Security.

State law enforcement agencies exist in every state except Hawaii. Many work as investigators, perform court-related duties, and carry out other assignments.

Investigators conduct interviews, examine records, and observe activities of suspects in order to gather evidence for criminal trials. They often specialize in areas such as white-collar crime.

Employment Outlook

- Average rates of growth are expected, with higher than average demand and competition for state and federal jobs.

Job Titles

- FBI agent
- Deputy sheriff
- U.S. Marshal
- Detective

Needed Skills

- High school diploma and law enforcement training/program are required.
- College-level coursework and/or degree are preferable.

What's it like to work in... *Law Enforcement*

Jay is a senior compliance officer with the Securities and Exchange Commission (SEC). His job involves investigating complaints from employees, stockholders, and other stakeholders in publicly held companies. When someone accuses a publicly held company of impropriety, such as reporting inaccurate or misleading information regarding its financial position, Jay starts the process of verifying the validity of the claim.

Jay completes audit work both offsite and onsite, examining ledgers and records, talking to key employees and executives, and verifying information with inside and outside sources. If Jay agrees that a crime has been committed, he works with the attorney general's office of the Department of Justice to bring criminal charges.

Jay's schedule is varied. Sometimes he works at a computer station while other times he observes behavior and examines records. He would describe his job as challenging, interesting, and creative.

What About You?

Do you like conducting investigations to determine how things happened? Would you enjoy interviewing people and studying records and data? Would you consider a career in law enforcement?

Assessment

KEY TERMS REVIEW

Match the terms with the definitions. Some terms may not be used.

_____ 1. A corporate bond that can be exchanged for common stock

_____ 2. A bond issued by a federal agency

_____ 3. A corporate bond backed by the general creditworthiness of the company

_____ 4. The amount the bondholder is paid at bond maturity

_____ 5. A bond that is backed by specific assets as collateral

_____ 6. A bond issued by a state or local government

_____ 7. A bond that can be paid off early

_____ 8. A bond backed by the power of a government unit to levy taxes to repay the debt

a. agency bond
b. callable bond
c. convertible bond
d. debenture
e. face value
f. general obligation bond
g. municipal bond
h. revenue bond
i. secured bond
j. zero-coupon bond

CHECK YOUR UNDERSTANDING

9. What is a callable bond? Does this feature make the bond more attractive to the investor?

10. Under what conditions would bonds sell at a premium?

11. What is a major advantage of buying government and municipal bonds?

APPLY YOUR KNOWLEDGE

12. Why might an investor choose to buy bonds rather than stocks? As a bondholder, would your investment in a corporate bond be more secure than a stockholder's investment? Why or why not?

THINK CRITICALLY

13. Why might an investor choose a secured bond rather than an unsecured bond? Why would an investor prefer a convertible bond?

14. Explain why you might choose a municipal bond paying 5 percent over a corporate bond paying 7 percent.

15. Why would investors choose a zero-coupon bond? Explain why zero-coupon bonds are often considered to be the riskiest form of bond investment.

Buying and Selling Bonds

GOALS

- Explain how to buy and sell bonds, considering both risk and return.
- Explain how to read the bond listings of financial pages.

TERMS

- bond redemption, p. 292
- hedge, p. 292
- bond rating, p. 292
- bond default, p. 292
- investment-grade bonds, p. 293
- junk bond, p. 293
- bond fund, p. 293

OWNING BONDS

Full-service brokers can assist you in buying and selling all kinds of bonds. The broker will charge you a commission or a flat fee for this service. You also can use a discount broker to buy and sell bonds. A discount broker charges a smaller fee or commission, but you will receive no advice in your decisions to buy or sell. Also, many banks provide brokerage services to help you buy and sell bonds.

You can buy and sell U.S. savings bonds and Treasury securities through the Federal Reserve System. There are 12 Federal Reserve Banks and 25 regional branches spread across the nation. Although the Federal Reserve Banks do not provide walk-in service, they will mail you an application form. You can send your check or money order with the application directly to the Federal Reserve.

The Federal Reserve uses a system called *TreasuryDirect* to record and store data about Treasury securities and their owners. You can even buy securities through TreasuryDirect online at www.treasurydirect.gov. Interest (and principal when the bonds mature) is deposited directly into your bank account. Also, by using TreasuryDirect, you can reinvest in Treasury securities automatically when existing securities mature. U.S. government securities also may be purchased through banks or brokers, but you will pay a commission.

U.S. savings bonds can also be purchased online through TreasuryDirect. Some employers enable you to buy savings bonds through their payroll deduction plan. They will withhold money from your paycheck, and when your withholdings are sufficient, the bond will be purchased and sent to you. This process takes longer because your employer processes the money through a bank, which in turn purchases the bonds and returns them through your employer. It is often quicker to deal directly with a bank in your area.

How can you buy U.S. Treasury securities, such as savings bonds?

© Digital Vision/Getty Images

You can buy state and municipal bonds through banks or brokers. In most states, you can set up a bank account to buy and sell municipal bonds. Often, you are purchasing a bond from the inventory your bank has on hand. Banks buy large blocks of municipal bonds and make them available to their customers. There is a fee for this service, although it may be incorporated into the price of the bonds.

Most bonds sell for a minimum investment of $1,000. Only savings bonds can be purchased with small, regular payments. When you have a large sum of money to set aside, you can consider larger purchases of $5,000 or $10,000.

▍ RETURN ON BONDS

Investors can earn a return on bonds in three ways.

- Bondholders earn interest for each day they own the bond.
- Bondholders can redeem the bond for its face value at maturity. **Bond redemption** occurs when it is paid off at maturity. The issuer of the bond pays back the original amount that was borrowed.
- Bondholders can sell a bond before maturity. Bonds often appreciate in value, especially when interest rates are dropping, and bondholders may be able to sell the bond before maturity for a price higher than they paid for it.

Bonds are a safer investment than many other choices because they have a fixed interest rate and represent a loan that the issuer must repay. Bonds play an important role in a diversified portfolio of investments. Bond prices tend to remain steadier than do stock prices. Also, bond prices tend to react in the opposite direction of stock prices. When stock prices are generally falling, bond prices tend to rise, and vice versa. As a result, bond investments serve as a hedge to help offset the risk of the stocks in your portfolio. A **hedge** is any investment or action that helps offset against loss from another investment or action. Hedging is a tactic used to reduce overall risk.

▍ RISK ON BONDS

Like all investments, bonds also have risk. But the risk is not the same for all bonds. To help investors evaluate the risk level of different bonds, independent rating services rate bonds according to their safety. A **bond rating** tells the investor the risk category that has been assigned to a bond. Bond rating services such as Moody's and Standard & Poor's base their ratings on the financial condition of the issuing corporation or municipality. The highest rating is AAA, or triple A. The lowest rating is a D. A D rating indicates that the bond is in default. **Bond default** means that the bond issuer cannot

NET Bookmark

The 2001 scandal involving the Enron Corporation is probably the best known example of a company distorting apparent debt so that its portfolio did not consist primarily of junk bonds. By hiding much of its debt, Enron received higher ratings than it would otherwise have earned. Enron quickly went bankrupt after the company's financial misrepresentation came to light, and thousands of investors lost billions of dollars. What lessons can an investor learn from the Enron scandal? Access www.cengage.com/school/pfinance/mypf and click on the link for Chapter 13. Read the article and discuss which "lessons for investors" you think are most important.

www.cengage.com/school/pfinance/mypf

meet the interest and/or principal payments. Because bonds are not insured, investors can lose their money if the corporation or municipality defaults.

A bond with a rating of Baa or higher in Moody's, or BBB or higher in Standard & Poor's, is considered an investment-grade bond. **Investment-grade bonds** are considered the highest-quality, lowest-risk bonds. These bonds are considered safe because the issuers are stable and dependable. For example, U.S. Treasury bonds provide maximum safety because these securities are backed by the federal government itself. Lowercase letters in a bond rating indicate more risk than capital letters. The letters stand for company stability, bond security, and general industry risk. Unfortunately, the higher the bond's rating, the lower the interest rate you will earn.

A **junk bond** has a low rating, or no rating at all. Any bond with a rating of Ba/BB or lower is called a junk bond. Because of its low or no rating, this type of bond is highly speculative. Junk bonds have higher yields and at times appear to have reasonable levels of risk. However, in most cases, interest rates on junk bonds are high because they are high risk, since the companies issuing them are not financially sound. Carefully explore junk bonds before buying, and don't buy junk bonds at all if you can't afford to lose your investment.

To lower risk in owning bonds, many investors choose to buy into investment pools of various types of bonds rather than buying individual bonds. A **bond fund** is a group of bonds that have been bundled together and sold in shares (like stock) to investors. Typically, a bond fund would contain some investment-grade bonds along with bonds of some newer companies, foreign bonds, and a few junk bonds as well. Mutual funds, brokers, and investment services at financial institutions offer bond funds to their customers as a method of hedging against the risk of loss from other investments.

READING BOND LISTINGS

One main factor has a real effect on bond prices—interest rates. When interest rates rise, the value of bonds decreases. The bonds are paying less in comparison to other fixed-rate investments. Conversely, when interest rates drop, fixed-rate bonds will become attractive because they are "locked in" at higher rates.

GLOBAL *View*

Uruguay's economic situation deteriorated significantly following its neighbor and trading partner Argentina's financial crises in 2001. Uruguay lost its investment-grade risk rating in early 2002, and the withdrawal of foreign investors resulted in a banking crisis. With help from the International Monetary Fund (IMF), an international organization that provides temporary financial assistance to countries, Uruguay returned to the international capital markets in late 2003 through the issuance of bonds. Its economy has now greatly improved, and it has been able to repay part of the IMF loan sooner than required.

THINK *CRITICALLY*

Why do you think the involvement of IMF was necessary to aid Uruguay's financial recovery? Why would Uruguay's economy be a global issue?

To track bond prices, you need to understand the bond price listings in the financial section of your newspaper. Not all local newspapers contain bond quotations, but *The Wall Street Journal* publishes complete information on bond transactions. Many web sites such as www.yahoo.com or the user home page offered by Internet service providers enable users to track securities prices. Users can key in the names of the securities they wish to track, and the home page will display the updated prices each day.

Purchases and sales of corporate bonds are reported in tables similar to the one shown in Figure 13.4. In bond quotations, prices are given as a percentage of face value, which is usually $1,000.

- *Column 1.* The first column lists the name of the bond, abbreviated.
- *Column 2.* This column indicates the type of bond it is and its rating. The small letter "a" stands for a senior bond, a "b" stands for split coupon, a "c" stands for zero-coupon bond, a "d" is an unsecured bond, and an "e" is a secured bond. The bond rating can range from AAA (highest) to C (junk bonds).
- *Column 3.* This column shows the coupon rate of the bond (the guaranteed, fixed interest rate that will be paid annually on the bond). There may also be a volume column that lists the number of shares traded that day, in hundreds.
- *Column 4.* This column shows the maturity date. A date of 12/08 means December, 2008.
- *Column 5.* This column tells you what the final closing bid for the day was for this bond. It is similar to the closing price for stocks. For AK Steel, for example, the 3 p.m. price was 98½, which translates into $985.00 on a $1,000 bond, or 98.5 percent of the face value.
- *Column 6.* The net change column compares the last price paid for the bond today with that paid on the previous day. "Unch" means "unchanged"; the price has not changed from the previous day.
- *Column 7.* The yield column states the current yield for the bond. The current yield is computed by dividing the bond's coupon rate by its average current market value (not its closing value). This yield figure varies as market interest conditions change, and thus the yield may be above or below the actual coupon rate.

FIGURE 13.4 *Reading Corporate Bond Listings*

Excerpt from stock exchange (bond) listings:

Name	Type/ Rating	Coup.	Mat.	3 P.M. Bid	Net Chg.	Yld
1	2	3	4	5	6	7
AK Steel	a/BB	9.125	12/08	98½	unch	9.46
Allied Waste	b/B+	10.000	8/11	102	unch	9.57
Am Std	a/BB+	7.375	2/10	98½	−1¼	7.56
Chanclr	b/BB+	8.125	12/09	103	unch	7.36
Echostar	a/B	9.375	2/11	101¼	unch	9.52

ISSUES IN YOUR WORLD

TAX STRATEGIES

When choosing investment options, investors must keep one important consideration in mind—taxability. Some investments are fully taxable, while others are tax-free. There are numerous options in between. The choice of an investment might hinge on its tax status.

An investment is tax-exempt when there is no tax due on the interest income earned, either now or in the future. Tax-exempt investments include municipal bonds sold by state and local governments. However, to be free from both federal and state taxes, you must live in the state where the bond is issued. For example, if you live in California and own a municipal bond issued in the state of Oregon, the bond will be tax-free in Oregon but will be subject to state income taxes in California.

An investment is tax-deferred when income will be taxed at a later time. Tax-deferred investments include annuities, which will be discussed in Chapter 15. While earnings are credited to your account now, you do not pay taxes on the earnings until you withdraw them. At that time, your tax rate may be lower, so you will owe less tax.

Taxes also are deferred on assets that appreciate in value. Capital gains, the profits from the sale of assets such as stocks, bonds, or real estate, are not taxed until the asset is sold. For example, if shares of stock you own are currently worth more than you paid for them, you will owe no taxes on the gain until you sell the stock.

Income and deductions can be shifted by postponing them to the following tax year, or by accelerating them forward into a current year, when they will be more beneficial. If your income is higher this year than usual, you can shift some deductions to help offset this increased income.

Taxes can be avoided by selling securities on which you lost money to offset gains on the sale of other securities. You can deduct losses to reduce capital gains on securities you sold at a profit. This strategy is not the same as tax evasion, which is the use of illegal actions to reduce your taxes.

THINK CRITICALLY

1. Why is it important to consider tax consequences when choosing investment alternatives?
2. What type of investor would likely choose a tax-exempt investment? What type of investor would choose tax-deferred?
3. Why should you seek professional advice when shifting income and avoiding taxes?

Assessment

KEY TERMS REVIEW

Match the terms with the definitions. Some terms may not be used.

_____ 1. A category that tells an investor the risk assigned to a bond

_____ 2. A bond that is considered of the highest quality

_____ 3. When the bond is paid off at maturity by its issuer

_____ 4. A group of bonds that have been bundled together for investment purposes

_____ 5. A bond that has a low rating or no rating at all

_____ 6. When a bond issuer cannot meet the interest or principal payment on a bond

a. bond default

b. bond fund

c. bond rating

d. bond redemption

e. hedge

f. investment-grade bond

g. junk bond

CHECK YOUR UNDERSTANDING

7. How can you purchase savings bonds?

8. How are bonds rated?

9. What is the main factor that affects bond prices? Why?

APPLY YOUR KNOWLEDGE

10. What is a junk bond? Why might an investor buy a junk bond?

THINK CRITICALLY

11. When buying Treasury bonds, which would you choose: full-service broker, discount broker, or TreasuryDirect? Why?

12. You have the choice of buying a municipal bond with a rating of Aaa paying 4 percent or a corporate bond with a rating of Ba paying 8 percent. Which bond would be your choice? Explain why.

13. Explain how a bond fund lowers the risk of owning bonds, which is already considered safer than stock.

Chapter Assessment

SUMMARY

13.1

- Bonds are loans that a corporation or government body must repay at face value, with interest.

- Bonds are a fixed-income investment. They pay a specified interest at regular intervals.

- A callable bond may be "called" (paid off) by the issuer before maturity.

- Debentures are unsecured bonds. Secured bonds (such as mortgage bonds) are secured by a specific asset.

- Owners of convertible bonds can exchange their bonds for common stock if they wish.

- Bonds whose interest rates are higher than the current market rate will sell at a premium. Bonds whose interest rates are lower than the current market rate will sell at a discount.

- Zero-coupon bonds sell at a deep discount and make no interest payments. Holders make money by selling them at a profit before maturity or redeeming them at face value at maturity.

- Municipal bonds generally are tax-free. Revenue bonds are issued to raise money for public projects. General obligation municipal bonds are backed by the power of the issuing government unit to levy taxes.

13.2

- You can buy bonds through a broker, discount broker, financial institution, or the Federal Reserve System (TreasuryDirect).

- Investors can earn a return on bonds from interest, by redeeming the bonds for their face value at maturity, or by selling them before maturity for a price higher than they paid for them.

- Rating services rate bonds based on the financial condition of the issuing corporation or municipality. Investment-grade bonds are the highest-quality, lowest-risk bonds. Junk bonds have a low rating or no rating.

- When interest rates rise, the values of bonds fall, because bonds are paying less in comparison to other fixed-rate investments. When interest rates drop, fixed-rate bonds become attractive because they are "locked in" at higher rates.

- Bond listings in the financial section of the newspaper provide information about price fluctuations, yield, and maturity dates.

APPLY WHAT YOU KNOW

1. You bought a $10,000, 6 percent corporate bond at face value that matures in five years. What would be your total earnings during that five-year period?

2. A new bond you are considering buying has a face value of $1,000, an interest rate of 5 percent, and a maturity date eight years away. The bond is currently selling at 104. What is the current yield? What amount of interest would you earn in that time period?

3. Visit TreasuryDirect online at www.treasurydirect.gov and find the answers to these questions:

    a. What are STRIPS?

    b. What is the current national debt figure?

    c. How can you replace a lost, stolen, or destroyed savings bond?

4. Visit the Federal Reserve System online at www.federalreserve.gov, and go to the consumer information section. Read one of the consumer information articles that interests you. In no more than a page, summarize, in your own words, what you learned from the article.

5. Three $1,000 bonds have the following closing prices: 95³⁄₈, 103¼, and 99. What are the prices of the bonds in dollar amounts?

MAKE ACADEMIC CONNECTIONS

6. **Math** Marsha Clarke has just purchased a $10,000, 7.5 percent corporate bond that will pay interest semiannually for the next eight years. Prepare a chart showing how much interest she will receive for the next eight years (total interest payments are 16).

7. **Research** Choose a corporate bond listed on the New York Stock Exchange. Use Moody's Industrial Manuals (available at many public libraries) or Moody's online at www.moodys.com to answer the following questions about this bond.

    a. What is Moody's rating for the bond?

    b. What is the purpose of the bond?

    c. Does the bond have a call provision?

    d. What collateral, if any, has been pledged as security for the bond?

    Based on the information studied, would the bond be a good investment for you? Why or why not?

8. **Economics** The Federal Reserve System, known as the Fed, engages in monetary policy to help the economy grow without high inflation. One form of monetary policy is called "open market transactions" where the Fed buys and sells U.S. securities (Treasury notes, bills, and bonds). Go to the Federal Reserve System's web site to learn more about these kind of transactions. Explain how this monetary policy helps the economy expand or contract (grow or shrink).

SOLVE PROBLEMS AND

EXPLORE ISSUES

9. Your friend Jason has just inherited $10,000. He considers the stock market too risky. He wants to preserve the safety of the principal he invests. Explain to him why buying a bond would be a safer investment than buying a stock.

10. Jason now asks you if he should consider a corporate bond. Explain to him how bond investing works and the difference between the types of corporate bonds. What type of corporate bond would you recommend? Why?

11. Les has chosen to buy a 5.5 percent, $1,000 corporate bond. The bond currently sells for 106. Compute his current yield on the bond, and explain to him why it is not the same as the stated interest rate.

12. Tatanya is considering purchasing a $10,000 corporate bond yielding 9 percent. She also found that she could buy a $10,000, 7 percent municipal bond. Her federal income tax rate is 28 percent. Determine her net interest. Show your work.

13. Brian has narrowed his choice of bond purchases to two: MelMac is a $10,000, 7 percent corporate bond selling for 102; BrgPort is a $10,000, 5 percent municipal bond selling for 95. Compute the current yield of each bond and advise him about which bond to choose.

14. Blake is considering using payroll deductions to pay for a Series EE savings bonds. If he could set aside $10 per month, how long would it take to buy a $500 EE bond? Explain to him how savings bonds work.

15. Susanne has $10,000 to invest. She is considering buying investment-grade corporate bonds because interest rates on bonds are somewhat higher than on CDs. She has rejected stocks because of the risk involved. Susanne feels that interest rates will rise, but in the meantime, she needs a relatively safe place for her money. Explain to Susanne how bond prices are affected by interest rates. Is she making the right decision? Explain.

EXTEND YOUR LEARNING

16. **Legal Issues** It is illegal for firms selling bonds to mislead or defraud investors. Investment firms have an obligation to inform their customers about the risks associated with the bonds. The Financial Industry Regulatory Authority (FINRA) is the largest non-governmental agency that regulates bonds (and stocks). Use the Internet to learn more about FINRA. How does it help enforce federal securities laws and protect investors?

For related activities and links, go to **www.cengage.com/school/pfinance/mypf**

Chapter 14

Investing in Mutual Funds, Real Estate, and Other Choices

14.1 *Investing in Mutual Funds*

14.2 *Investing in Real Estate and Other Choices*

Consider **THIS**

Patrick works 20 hours a week, lives at home, and can save $100 a month. He doesn't have a large lump sum to invest, but he's sure that he can set aside this amount permanently.

Patrick told his financial adviser, "I've thought about several kinds of investments. I researched several mutual funds online, and I think I'm ready to buy shares in a fund that specializes in growth stocks. The one I'm most interested in has averaged a 12 percent annual return over the last 15 years. That's good, considering the ups and downs of the stock market. An important benefit I'll have is the ability to check my account daily, if I want, by logging onto the fund's web site. I can transfer my money from one fund to another electronically if I see that this would be a wise thing to do. And, once I buy in, I'm guaranteed to be able to keep buying shares of the fund, even if the fund is closed to new investors later on."

Investing in Mutual Funds

EVALUATING MUTUAL FUNDS

A *mutual fund* is a professionally managed group of investments bought using a pool of money from many investors. Individuals buy shares in the mutual fund. The fund managers use this pooled money to buy stocks, bonds, and other securities. The kinds of securities they buy depend on the fund's stated investment objectives. For example, some mutual funds specialize in aggressive growth stocks. Others specialize in more conservative investments, such as bonds or money market securities.

Most mutual fund companies offer a *family of funds*, which is a variety of funds covering a whole range of investment objectives. You can choose the family member or members that best match your own goals. You are allowed to move back and forth among the company's funds. You can purchase one type of fund (such as a stock fund) and later switch to another (such as a bond fund), all within the same family of funds.

Professional mutual fund managers perform the following duties:

- Research individual stocks and bonds
- Interpret market conditions, financial statements, industry trends, and other market data
- Buy and sell individual stocks, bonds, and other financial instruments
- Match good investments to meet their investors' objectives

Fund investors share in any profits made by the mutual fund. They receive profits as dividends and as capital gains, both of which may be reinvested in the fund or distributed to

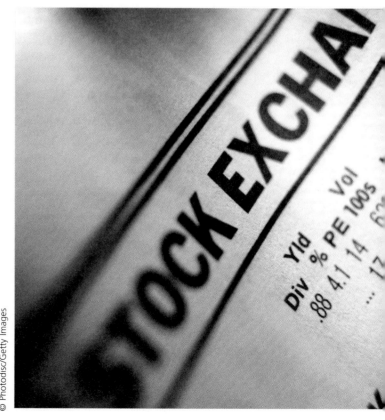

© Photodisc/Getty Images

Is a family of funds a good investment? Why or why not?

investors as cash payments. *Capital gains* come from the profits made when the managers sell some of the fund's securities for more than they paid for them.

For most mutual fund investing, you will have to make an initial purchase of $500 to $3,000 or more. Once you buy into a fund, you can make additional purchases as often as you like. Many people make regular purchases of $50 to $100 a month. To take money out of your fund, you simply call the company and place an order to sell your shares or make your request online at the company web site.

ADVANTAGES OF MUTUAL FUNDS

Investors often choose mutual funds for several good reasons.

- *Professional Management.* When you hire someone who knows how to invest, you don't have to worry about following stock and bond markets or looking for hot new investments. Professionals are doing the work for you.
- *Liquidity.* You can get your money quickly if you need it, though there is some risk of loss if the fund's price is low when you choose to sell.
- *Diversification.* When you invest in mutual funds, you are *diversifying* because mutual funds purchase a variety of stocks and bonds. When you have enough money to invest in more than one fund, you can further diversify by buying shares in funds with different investment objectives. In the same way that you would diversify individual stock purchases, you can buy some shares in riskier, aggressive mutual funds and limit the risk by also purchasing shares in more conservative funds.
- *Small Initial and Ongoing Purchases.* Another advantage of mutual funds is that you need not have a lot of money to invest. Many funds require only a small minimum investment. Also, through pooling your money with other investors in the fund, you can own, for example, part of a $10,000 government bond without having $10,000 to buy the whole bond yourself.

MUTUAL FUND RISK

Individual funds within a family have different investment goals and risk levels. In their publications and on their web sites, investment companies describe the investment goals and level of risk for each fund. You can choose funds that match your goals and risk tolerance. As with any investment, the greater the potential return, the higher the risk. Figure 14.1 shows the general risk/return profiles for general categories of mutual funds.

Growth Funds

A **growth fund** is a mutual fund whose investment goal is to buy stocks that will increase in value over time. To do this, the fund's managers select stocks in companies that reinvest their profit in the company rather than distribute it to investors as dividends. Investors in growth funds earn their return through capital gains rather than through dividends. An aggressive growth fund invests in stock of new or out-of-favor companies and industries that the fund managers think will achieve above-average increases in value. The philosophy behind aggressive growth funds is to accept high risk of loss in exchange for a chance to earn high returns. Other growth funds follow a less risky philosophy. They

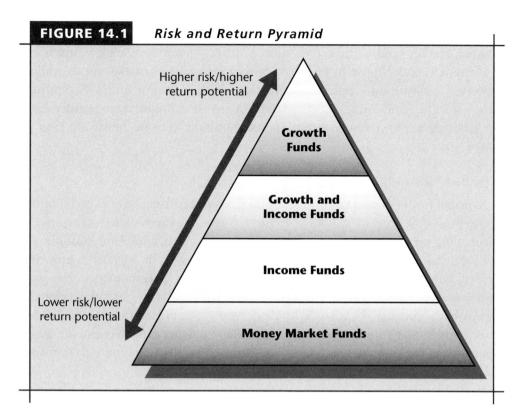

FIGURE 14.1   *Risk and Return Pyramid*

Higher risk/higher
return potential

**Growth
Funds**

**Growth and
Income Funds**

Income Funds

Lower risk/lower
return potential

Money Market Funds

invest in more stable companies that the fund managers expect to increase in value but at a slower, steadier rate than the stocks of aggressive growth funds.

Income Funds

An **income fund** is a mutual fund whose investment goal is to produce current income in the form of interest or dividends. At times, these investments will also share money with investors in the form of capital gains distributions. In this case, the investor receives a check or deposit to his or her account. Investors in income funds are looking for income from their investments now rather than capital gains later. Income funds are considered to be of low-to-moderate risk and less risky than growth funds. Some income funds specialize in tax-exempt bonds. Their goal is to provide tax-free income for investors. Tax-exempt bond funds appeal to investors in high-income tax brackets.

Growth and Income Funds

A **growth and income fund** is a mutual fund whose investment goal is to earn returns from both dividends and capital gains. Managers of these funds try to select stocks that pay dividends as well as stocks that increase in market value over time. The risk level of this type of fund is moderate—between the riskier growth funds and less risky income funds, as you can see in Figure 14.1.

A **balanced fund** is a mutual fund that seeks both growth and income but attempts to minimize risk by investing in a mixture of stocks and bonds rather than stocks alone. Like growth and income funds, the goal of a balanced fund is to earn returns from current income and capital gains. Balanced funds have moderate risk. They are a little less risky than growth and income funds that invest only in stocks.

Money Market Funds

A **money market fund** is a mutual fund that invests in safe, liquid securities, such as Treasury Bills and bonds that mature in less than a year. These short maturities provide modest current income with little risk. The goal of any money market fund is the preservation of principal and very high liquidity.

Many investors choose to put their money into money market funds while they are "waiting out" unfavorable market conditions. For example, returns from income funds may be dropping. An investor might then transfer his or her balance to a money market fund until the income funds are rising once again.

Global Funds

A **global fund** is a mutual fund that purchases international stocks and bonds as well as U.S. securities. Global funds fall into a variety of risk categories, depending on the investment objective of the individual fund. For example, a global fund can be very risky if its goal is to invest in aggressive growth international stocks. A global fund that invests in a conservative mix of international stocks and bonds would be less risky. However, most global funds have risks that U.S. stock funds do not have. Fluctuations in currency exchange rates and political instability in other countries can affect the value of global stocks. These uncertainties make global funds generally more risky than U.S. stock funds.

Index Funds

An *index* is an average of the price movements of certain selected securities. Investors use indexes as benchmarks for comparison to judge how well their investments are doing. An **index fund** is a mutual fund that tries to match the performance of a particular index by investing in the companies included in that index. For example, an index fund might invest in companies included in the Standard & Poor's 500 index or the Dow Jones Industrial Average index. The risk level of an index fund depends on the index to which it is tied. Since the Dow includes only blue chip stocks, funds tied to this index would be relatively low risk. The NASDAQ Composite Index, on the other hand, averages stocks of some volatile high-tech companies. Funds tied to this index could be relatively risky.

BUYING AND SELLING MUTUAL FUNDS

There are thousands of mutual funds covering the whole range of investment objectives and risk levels. To choose the mutual fund that is right for you, you must know your own investment objectives and risk tolerance. Do you want income from your investments now, or can you wait for capital gains in the future? Do you need a tax-free or tax-deferred investment to reduce your current income taxes? Are you comfortable with risking your investment for a chance at big returns, or do you prefer a safe but lower return? Once you know your own requirements, you can read about the objectives and risk profiles of different funds and find one that matches your requirements.

NET ASSET VALUE

Unlike stocks, mutual fund prices are not determined by what people are willing to pay for them. They are determined by net asset value (NAV). The **net asset value** tells you the market price for a share of a mutual fund. The NAV is the total value of a fund's investment portfolio minus its liabilities, divided by the number of outstanding shares of the fund.

$$\text{NAV} = \frac{\text{Value of Portfolio} - \text{Liabilities}}{\text{Number of Shares}}$$

For example, suppose the value of all stocks in a fund's portfolio is currently $100,000. The fund has $90,000 in liabilities and has sold 500 shares of its fund to investors. The price for one of its shares, or its net asset value, would be $20 at this time.

$$\frac{\$100,000 - \$90,000}{500} = \$20$$

Because the value of the portfolio changes as the stocks and other securities are traded throughout the day, the NAV is calculated at the end of each business day. Thus, the value of your investment depends on that fund's performance in the securities market.

Although a mutual fund provides professional management, you should monitor your fund's performance. Some funds consistently outperform the average among those with the same objective and risk. For example, if you own an income fund, you can compare its performance to that of other income funds.

THE PROSPECTUS

By law, investment companies must provide detailed information about their funds. A mutual fund company must provide a prospectus for each fund offered. The **prospectus** is a legal document that offers securities or mutual fund shares for sale. It must contain the terms, a summary of the fund's portfolio of investments, its objectives, and financial statements showing past performance. You can usually find this information on the investment company's web site as well. Before choosing a mutual fund, read the prospectus carefully. Compare the fund's objectives with your own, and compare its past performance with that of other funds you are considering.

COSTS AND FEES

If you buy a mutual fund through a broker, you will likely have to pay a sales fee, called a **load**. The broker's commission comes from this fee. A *front-end load* is a sales charge paid when you buy an investment. Sometimes you pay

VIEW *Points*

Some investors believe that once you have selected a mutual fund or other type of long-term investment, you should check on it only periodically and resist making changes. Others believe that it is important to check your account balances almost daily. These investors frequently move their balances from one fund to another as they constantly look for choices that pay higher returns.

THINK *CRITICALLY*

Which view do you agree with? The Internet provides a very convenient way to check balances. How often should you check your balances?

this fee on reinvested dividends as well. A *back-end load* is a sales charge paid when you sell an investment. Either way, loads can range from 2 to 8 percent of the value of the shares purchased.

In some cases, you can buy mutual funds directly from the investment companies. This kind of fund, called a *no-load fund*, does not charge a sales fee when you buy or sell because no salespeople are involved. You buy directly from the company by telephone, mail, or through the company's web site.

Mutual funds make money by charging fees to their customers for the professional services provided. Funds often charge an annual management fee, which averages about 1 to 1½ percent of a fund's total assets. This charge is for the services of professional fund managers and for maintaining your account. The fund may also charge a "12b-1 fee" to cover the costs of marketing and distributing a mutual fund. These fees are part of the fund's *expense ratio*, which is expressed as a percentage of assets deducted each year for fund expenses. Mutual funds publish their expense ratios with their fund descriptions. When you consider investing in mutual funds, compare expense ratios as part of your evaluation.

THE MUTUAL FUND COMPANY

The most important decision you will make with mutual fund investing is selecting the right mutual fund company or companies. You can read about a fund in its printed material. You can compare its costs and fees. You can research published comparisons about funds of the same type. But, you still have no guarantees that a mutual fund will make money or that the mutual fund company itself will not fail. To reduce these risks, choose a mutual fund company that has the following characteristics:

- It has been in business for 20 or more years
- It has a solid track record of returning good solid returns to its investors
- It is a large company that manages investments for millions of investors
- It is a well-known company that is highly respected among investment advisers and experts
- It exists both in brick-and-mortar and in cyberspace
- It is customer friendly and responsive to customer questions and needs
- It provides customers with easy-to-read statements and reports and offers daily online access

SOURCES OF MUTUAL FUND INFORMATION

Financial publications, such as *Forbes*, *Fortune*, and *Money*, regularly review and rank mutual funds. They compare one-year, five-year, and ten-year performances of various funds with similar objectives. They also show the expense ratios of each one, so that you can make comparisons. Occasionally, entire sections of business magazines are devoted to listing, describing, and ranking mutual funds.

You can also find a great deal of information online. For example, the Morning Star web site issues reports that compare mutual funds. You can also search for the sites of fund families by name, such as Vanguard, Fidelity, and Dreyfus. At their sites, you can find detailed descriptions, including risk/return profiles for all funds in their fund families. At the Yahoo! Finance web site, you can search for fund information by its ticker symbol. Another good web site for educational information on mutual funds is the Mutual Fund Investors Center.

ISSUES IN YOUR WORLD

HOW TO READ THE MUTUAL FUNDS LISTINGS

Mutual Fund Quotations

1	2	3	4	5	6	7	8
	Inv.		Offer	NAV		Return	
	Obj.	NAV	Price	Chg.	YTD	26 Wks.	4 Yrs.
Ables Fund:							
AciBt1A	GRO	9.63	10.11	...	0.0	−0.1	NA
BiClo	BND	1.51	NL	−.01	−2.9	−1.6	+8.9
CoxDli	SML	8.61	NL	+.01	+1.6	+1.5	+18.6
DrixLt	G&I	26.54	NL	−.07	+6.1	+4.0	+18.0
BB&B Fund:							
Globl B	WOR	6.25	6.25	−.03	−4.3	−4.3	+2.7
MtgLtd	MTG	2.80	2.80	+.02	−2.3	−1.4	−1.0

- Column 1. *The sponsoring mutual fund company's name is listed first. Its funds appear below in alphabetical order.*
- Column 2. *The investment objective of the fund family is identified here. These companies offer investors a choice of growth (GRO), bond (BND), small company growth (SML), growth and income (G&I), global (WOR, for "world"), and mortgage (MTG) funds.*
- Column 3. *NAV stands for net asset value. It is the dollar value of one share of the fund, based on closing quotes.*
- Column 4. *The offer price reflects the net asset value plus sales commission, if any. An "NL" indicates a no-load fund.*
- Column 5. *NAV change indicates the gain or loss in the price for a share of the fund, based on the previous NAV quotation.*
- Column 6. *YTD stands for "year to date." It tells you how much this fund has gone up or down since January 1 of the current year.*
- Column 7. *Total return, 26 weeks, shows the average earnings the fund has returned to investors in the last six months, stated as a percentage return on investment.*
- Column 8. *Total return, 4 years, shows the average earnings the fund has returned to investors for the last four years, stated as a percentage return on investment.*

THINK CRITICALLY

1. *Which of the mutual funds in the listing seems to be the best investment as compared to the other choices given? Why?*
2. *Why is it important to know the investment objective?*

Assessment

KEY TERMS REVIEW

Match the terms with the definitions. Some terms may not be used.

_____ 1. A mutual fund whose investment goal is to produce current income in the form of interest or dividends

_____ 2. A mutual fund that invests in safe, liquid securities

_____ 3. A mutual fund that tries to match the performance of a particular index

_____ 4. A mutual fund that purchases international stocks and bonds as well as U.S. securities

_____ 5. The sales fee charged for buying mutual funds

_____ 6. A mutual fund whose goal is to buy stocks that increase in value over time

_____ 7. A mutual fund that minimizes risk by investing in a mixture of stocks and bonds

_____ 8. The legal document that offers securities or mutual fund shares for sale

_____ 9. The market price for a share of a mutual fund

a. balanced fund

b. global fund

c. growth and income fund

d. growth fund

e. income fund

f. index fund

g. load

h. money market fund

i. net asset value

j. prospectus

CHECK YOUR UNDERSTANDING

10. Why might you choose a mutual fund over investing directly in stocks?

11. What is NAV, and how is it computed?

APPLY YOUR KNOWLEDGE

12. Describe the type of investor (in terms of goals and risk tolerance) who would be interested in each of the following types of mutual funds: (a) growth funds, (b) income funds, (c) growth and income funds, and (d) money market funds.

THINK CRITICALLY

13. Where is a good place for young and inexperienced investors to start buying mutual funds?

14. How can you lower risks while choosing mutual funds?

15. Why is it important to choose a mutual fund company that has been in business for a long time?

Investing in Real Estate and Other Choices

GOALS
- Explain real estate investing, both direct and indirect.
- Describe other investments, including metals, gems, collectibles, and financial instruments.

TERMS
- real estate, *p. 309*
- duplex, *p. 310*
- condominium, *p. 310*
- mortgage, *p. 312*
- depreciation, *p. 313*
- precious metals, *p. 314*
- gems, *p. 314*

REAL ESTATE INVESTING

When you invest in **real estate**, you are buying land and any buildings on it. Investing in real estate is considered a good way to combat inflation, because it usually increases in value over the years at rates equal to or higher than inflation. However, real estate is one of the least liquid investments you can make, since a property can take months or even years to sell. Also, some real estate investments are speculative and can result in a substantial loss.

Commercial property is land and buildings that produce lease or rental income. Such property includes office buildings, stores, hotels, duplexes, and multi-unit apartments.

You can invest in real estate directly or indirectly.

BUYING REAL ESTATE

There are many types of real estate properties you can buy directly, such as vacant land, single-family houses, duplexes, apartments, condominiums, and recreation or retirement property. With direct *investments,* the investor holds legal title to the property.

© Photodisc/Getty Images

Why would you invest in a vacant lot?

Vacant Land

Vacant land, or unimproved property, is usually considered a speculative investment. Investors hold the property expecting it to go up substantially in value over time. Other people purchase a vacant lot with plans for building a house on it later, either when they can afford it or at retirement. In either case, you will likely have to pay cash for vacant land. Because it is considered speculative, banks are often unwilling to make loans on vacant land.

Single-Family Houses

In addition to owning your own home, you might wish to purchase a single-family house and rent it to others. Because the property is not owner-occupied, you may find banks reluctant to grant you a mortgage loan to buy a house as rental property. As a condition for a loan, you may have to make a larger down payment or pay a higher interest rate. When a renter takes possession of your house, you still have responsibilities. For example, as the owner, you must maintain the premises in a livable condition. You must provide running water, electricity, sewer or septic hookups, and normal repairs and maintenance. If the roof leaks or a pipe breaks, it is your responsibility to fix it.

Rental Properties

There are several other types of *rental properties*, or real estate designed for owners to rent to tenants.

- A **duplex** is a building with two separate living quarters. A duplex may be side-by-side living quarters with separate entrances, or it may be upper and lower floors of the building.
- A *triplex* (three units) and a *quad* (four units) are buildings with three or four individual housing units. They often have common walls and surrounding areas.
- An apartment complex is a group of many apartments with common facilities such as recreation areas, clubhouses, and parking lots.
- A **condominium**, or *condo*, is an individually owned unit in an apartment-style complex with shared ownership of common areas. The owner of a condo owns the individual apartment as well as a proportional share of common areas, such as the lobby, yard, and hallways.

Condo owners usually pay a monthly fee for the upkeep of the common areas, such as for mowing the lawn and maintaining a shared swimming pool. Condos are generally less expensive than single-family houses because they have less land and private areas and share roofs, walls, plumbing, and so on.

By pooling your cash with that of other investors, you can afford to buy larger and more expensive pieces of property. For example, if you and three others formed a partnership to buy an eight-unit apartment building, each of you would have to pay only one-fourth of the total costs of buying and maintaining the property.

Recreation and Retirement Property

Many people buy second homes for vacations or for their retirement years. Often, the owners rent these properties out to others to generate income during the times when they are not using them. Of course, rented property will not be in brand-new condition when the owner retires to live there full time.

Recreation property includes beach and mountain cabins and even vacant land near vacation sites such as rivers, lakes, or an ocean. The owner can use and enjoy the property on weekends and during vacations, and at other times rent out the property. However, absent owners may need to arrange for someone to take care of the property and manage the rental process. Real estate companies in popular vacation areas often provide these services for absent owners for a fee.

INVESTING INDIRECTLY

With *indirect investing*, investors have a third person do the actual buying and selling of property. A *trustee* is an individual or institution that manages assets for someone else. The trustee holds the title to the property. Real estate syndicates, real estate investment trusts, and mortgage pools (in the form of participation certificates) are examples of indirect investments using a third-party trustee.

Real Estate Syndicates

A *real estate syndicate* (often called a limited partnership) is a group of investors who pool their money to buy high-priced real estate. This is a temporary association of individuals organized for the purpose of raising a large amount of capital. The organizer of the syndicate is called the general partner or syndicator. The people who contribute the capital are called limited partners.

In a real estate syndicate, the general partner forms a partnership and assumes unlimited liability for all the obligations (debts) of the partnership. By assuming

unlimited liability, the general partner's responsibility extends beyond the initial investment to his or her personal assets if the investment incurs debt. The general partner then sells participation units to limited partners whose liability is limited to the amount of their investment. This means that the limited partners can lose no more than they invested if the investment fails. Limited liability is especially important in real estate partnerships because the mortgage acquired to purchase real estate often exceeds the net worth of the individual partners.

A real estate syndicate often owns several properties for diversification. The commercial properties acquired are usually professionally managed.

Real Estate Investment Trusts (REITs)

A *real estate investment trust* (REIT) is similar to a mutual fund. It is a corporation that pools the money of many individuals to invest in real estate. Like a mutual fund, the REIT makes all buy-and-sell decisions

© Digital Vision/Getty Images

Why might an investor choose an indirect real estate investment?

for properties. You can buy and sell REIT shares at will. REITs are traded on stock exchanges or over the counter. Like stocks, REIT shares fluctuate with market conditions, and dividends are paid when the real estate investments do well. There are many types of REITs, investing in everything from rental properties for monthly income to mortgages for long-term income. REITs are found in the financial section of the newspaper along with stock, bond, and mutual fund price quotations.

Participation Certificates

A *participation certificate* is an investment in a pool of mortgages that have been purchased by a government agency. Participation certificates are sold by federal agencies such as the Government National Mortgage Association (Ginnie Mae), the Federal Home Loan Mortgage Corporation (Freddie Mac), and the Federal National Mortgage Association (Fannie Mae). At one time, you needed $25,000 to invest in these certificates. However, many mutual funds invest entirely in them, making it possible to buy shares for as little as $1,000.

▮ BUYING AND OWNING RENTAL PROPERTY

When buying real estate, most people make a down payment and get a mortgage to pay the balance. A **mortgage** (also called a trust deed) is a loan to purchase real estate. Most people borrow money to buy property because large sums of cash are needed. Borrowing money to buy an investment is called *leverage*, which means only a small amount of the purchase price is your own money. For example, if you buy a duplex for $300,000 and make a down payment of $60,000 (a 20 percent down payment is usually required for rental property), you are borrowing $240,000 from the bank. As the property gains in value, the mortgage remains fixed. When you eventually sell the property, you keep the difference between the sales price and the mortgage. This difference is the *equity*, or ownership interest.

Monthly Payments

As your tenant makes rent payments, you make the mortgage payments to the bank. You would use the difference between the amount of rent collected and the mortgage payment to pay property taxes and the cost of upkeep on the property. If you have money left over after paying these expenses, you have a *positive cash flow*. If, however, you cannot collect enough rent to pay the mortgage, property taxes, repairs, and maintenance, then you have a *negative cash flow* and must make up the shortfall from your own pocket.

Monthly Management

To manage your property, you can be a resident landlord or hire a resident landlord or property manager. A *resident landlord* lives at the rental site, takes care of all repairs and maintenance, collects the rent, and assures suitable living conditions. A *property manager* collects rent, hires and pays people to make repairs and maintain the property, charges a fee for his or her services, and remits the difference to the owner of the property. Property managers do not live on site, but usually manage a large number of rental properties at the same time.

Tax Advantages

Depreciation is the decline in the value of property due to normal wear and tear. Even though your property may be increasing in overall value, you can deduct depreciation expense on your rental property using Schedule C of the Form 1040 tax return. In addition, property taxes and other expenses of maintaining rental property can be deducted to help reduce the taxes you have to pay on your rental income.

Selling Rental Property

When you sell your property, you will have to pay taxes on the capital gain. Real estate can be difficult to sell. During slow economic times when people have difficulty obtaining low-interest loans, you may have to lower the price of your property substantially in order to sell it.

Risks of Owning Rentals

You should consider the risks of owning and renting property. Renters can damage or destroy your property to a degree far exceeding what a security deposit can cover. When your units have vacancies, your rental income will decline, yet you still have to pay the mortgage and other expenses, thus cutting into your profits.

Real estate is also subject to zoning laws and other local use restrictions. Cities have laws that regulate what type of structure (for example, single-family residence, apartment complex, office building) can be built in each area of the city. Before buying property, you should check the applicable zoning laws to make sure you will be allowed to use the property as you intend.

OTHER INVESTING CHOICES

You may be willing to invest your money in just about anything you think will bring you a return in value over time or some other form of income. Often these choices depend on personal values and tastes.

METALS, GEMS, AND COLLECTIBLES

Investments in this category are often speculative. They can return large profits or losses when sold. In some cases, the enjoyment of having the investment will far exceed any resale value. Although not inexpensive, precious metals, gems, and collectibles are easy to purchase. However, they can be very difficult to sell in a hurry and do not provide any current income in the

© Photodisc/Getty Images

Why are gems considered risky investments?

form of interest or dividends. So be cautious when making this type of investment.

Precious Metals

Gold, silver, and platinum are examples of precious metals. **Precious metals** are tangible metals that have known and universal value around the world. They are usually natural substances that people value. However, prices of precious metals can swing widely over time. These swings are what make investments in precious metals very risky.

You can buy gold and silver as coins, medallions, jewelry, and bullion. Storing precious metals safely may be a problem because of bulk and weight. Instead of storing your investment yourself, you can buy gold and silver in the form of a certificate stating how much you own of the metal being stored for you. You also can own gold indirectly by investing in gold-mining stocks or in mutual funds specializing in these stocks. Other metals in which you can invest include aluminum, tin, copper, lead, nickel, and zinc. Prices for metals can be found in the financial section of newspapers and online.

Gems and Jewelry

Gems are natural, precious stones, such as diamonds, rubies, sapphires, and emeralds. Their prices are high and subject to drastic change. Precious metals and gems have their greatest value as jewelry. However, when you purchase jewelry at retail prices, you are paying markups of 50 to 500 percent or more. Prices must increase substantially in the world market before you can recover the cost and make a profit from reselling your jewelry.

The biggest disadvantage of investing in gems is the risk that you won't be able to resell them. The gems market can be very small and unpredictable. No ready market may exist when you decide to sell. Often you have to go out on your own to find a buyer, such as selling on the Internet or advertising in the paper. The process of buying and selling can also be hazardous, as most such transactions require the use of cash.

Collectibles

Collections of valuable or rare items, such as antiques, art, baseball cards, stamps, and comic books, are called *collectibles*. They are valuable because they are old, no longer produced, unusual, irreplaceable, or of historic importance. Coins are the most commonly collected items. Silver coins (rather than today's alloy coins) often are worth more than 20 times their face value.

COMMUNICATION *Connection*

Review the collectibles section(s) in your local newspaper's classified ads. You will find all types of things offered to buy, sell, and exchange. These often represent items people and families have collected for years. Sometimes you find these items at swap meets or other types of collectible shows. They attract a certain type of "investor."

What types of items are offered for sale? In contrast, what items are people looking to buy? Prepare a summary of your findings to share in a class discussion.

People like to collect favorite items, from porcelain figures to hubcaps, and hope that someday their collection will be valuable. Collecting can be a satisfying hobby. Unfortunately, collectibles can be hard to sell and may not increase in value. You may find it difficult to locate a buyer who is willing to pay you the value of your collection, even when the value is well known. If you want to be a collector, buy what you can personally appreciate and enjoy through the years, knowing that your collection may or may not result in a profit when you decide to sell it.

NETBookmark

Buying comic books as an investment is relatively new. Most people buy comics for the enjoyment of reading them. As they have grown more and more popular, some comics have become quite valuable. A single, mint-condition issue of *Action Comics #1*, which introduced the world to Superman, is worth over $1 million. Access www.cengage.com/school/pfinance/mypf and click on the link for Chapter 14. Read the article about comics collecting. List the three factors that determine a comic's value. According to the author, where are good places to find investment-grade comics? What does the author seem to think is the best way to sell comics?

www.cengage.com/school/pfinance/mypf

FINANCIAL INSTRUMENTS

Futures are contracts to buy and sell commodities or stocks for a specified price on a specified date in the future. *Commodities* include farm products (such as wheat, corn, and cattle) and metals (such as gold and silver). Commodity prices are volatile because supply and demand for commodities are disrupted by all kinds of mostly unpredictable situations, from political upheaval to the weather.

Commodities may be sold for cash (the local farmer's market) or traded in the futures market. For example, a farmer could sell a futures contract to deliver 5,000 bushels of wheat one year from today. The futures market was created for those who want to know in advance what they will be paid. Farmers enter the futures market only for protection against volatile prices. Futures contracts are like an insurance policy against changes in prices. In this case, the farmers like knowing in advance what they will be paid for their wheat.

An *option* is the right, but not the obligation, to buy or sell a commodity or stock for a specified price within a specified time period. A *call option* is the right to buy shares of stock at a set price by a certain expiration date. You can exercise the right at any time before the option expires. A *put option* is the right to sell stock at a fixed price until the expiration date. An investor who thinks a stock's price will increase during a short period of time may decide to purchase a call option. On the other hand, an investor who feels a stock's price will decrease during a short period of time may purchase a put option to safeguard the investment. Options are risky business and not for the inexperienced investor. Options also apply to the purchase and sale of futures contracts.

Investors who choose to buy and sell financial instruments are taking very high risk. While large gains are possible, the investor must be prepared to take losses as well as gains. It is feasible that you could lose your entire investment. Over time, those who specialize in financial instruments make profits, because their gains exceed their losses.

Planning a Career in... Stock Brokerage

The most common type of securities sales agent is the stockbroker. These are the people who sell securities to everyday people, called investors. Stockbrokers provide investing advice and help their clients buy and sell at the right times to maximize their profits.

Beginning stockbrokers spend much of their time finding clients and building a customer base. They rely on networking and social contacts to build their business. They join civic organizations and social groups to expand those networks.

After stockbrokers are established, they do most of their business through referrals. A referral is a recommendation from an existing customer. Stockbrokers work for commission income. They earn commissions each time they buy or sell a security.

Employment Outlook

- A much faster than average rate of employment growth is expected.

Job Titles

- Securities broker
- Floor broker
- Independent stockbroker
- Investment banker

Needed Skills

- A bachelor's degree in business, finance, accounting, or economics is required; an MBA is preferred and required for higher-level positions.

- Intensive on-the-job training is required for entry-level employees.
- Brokers must be licensed and pass a licensure exam.
- Maturity and ability to work independently are critical.

What's it like to work in... *Stock Brokerage*

Alysha is a stockbroker who works for a top investment company that has a seat on the New York Stock Exchange. She works in a regional office, has more than two dozen clients, and is responsible for brokerage accounts worth more than $5 million.

Alysha works hard to help her clients meet their investment objectives. She advises clients about mutual funds and other investment options to help them attain the risk level and the returns they desire. When clients have selected stock in which to invest or sell, Alysha makes the transactions.

Alysha is at the office daily before the stock market opens. She talks with her clients mostly by phone but sometimes meets with them for consultations.

What About You?

Would you like working independently and on commission? Do you enjoy social groups, civic organizations, and other networking events? Would you consider a career as a stockbroker? Why or why not?

Assessment

KEY TERMS REVIEW

Match the terms with the definitions.

_____ 1. A loan to purchase real estate

_____ 2. Tangible metals that have known and universal value worldwide

_____ 3. Land and the buildings on it

_____ 4. The decline in the value of property due to normal wear and tear

_____ 5. Natural, precious stones, such as diamonds, rubies, sapphires, and emeralds

_____ 6. An individually owned unit in an apartment-style complex with shared ownership of common areas

_____ 7. A building with two separate living quarters

a. condominium
b. depreciation
c. duplex
d. gems
e. mortgage
f. precious metals
g. real estate

CHECK YOUR UNDERSTANDING

8. What are some advantages of owning real estate as an investment?

9. Why are collectibles risky investments?

10. Explain how futures contracts work.

APPLY YOUR KNOWLEDGE

11. Describe what it would be like to be a landlord (your responsibilities and duties) if you owned: (a) a single-family house rented to a family, (b) a second home on the beach that you rented to vacationers, and (c) an eight-unit apartment building where you were the resident landlord.

THINK *CRITICALLY*

12. Owning rental property involves receiving enough money to pay expenses as you go along. Explain the concept of leverage and the need for a positive cash flow.

13. Price changes for precious metals can be very unpredictable. Why would anyone want to invest in these items?

14. Name some collectible items you have seen, collected, or read about that have increased substantially in value over the years. What do/would you like to collect?

Chapter Assessment

SUMMARY

14.1

- Mutual funds use money pooled from many investors to buy securities that fit the fund's stated objectives.

- Investors choose mutual funds for the professional management, liquidity, diversification, and relatively small minimum investment required.

- Growth funds focus on stocks expected to earn future capital gains, while income funds invest to provide current income in the form of interest and dividends.

- Growth and income funds and balanced funds seek current income and capital gains.

- Money market funds invest in safe, liquid securities, while global funds invest in more risky international as well as U.S. securities.

- Index funds try to match the performance of a particular index.

- NAV is calculated as the total value of the fund's investments minus its liabilities, divided by the number of outstanding shares.

- To evaluate a fund, examine the prospectus, fees, and published comparisons among funds of the same type.

14.2

- If you invest in real estate directly, you own legal title to it. If you invest indirectly, a trustee holds legal title on behalf of the investor group.

- You can invest in real estate indirectly through real estate syndicates, REITs, or federal agency participation certificates.

- If your rental income from rental property exceeds your mortgage payment, property taxes, and upkeep expenses, then you have a positive cash flow.

- As the owner of rental property, you benefit from tax advantages for depreciation and other expenses. However, it may be difficult to resell, and when sold, you will have to pay taxes on the capital gain.

- Investments in precious metals, gems, collectibles, futures contracts, and options are very risky and not for the novice investor.

- Gems have their greatest value as jewelry. The retail price has a huge markup, and the resale market is small and unpredictable.

- Collectibles can be very profitable or worthless, depending on the changing tastes of consumers.

APPLY WHAT YOU KNOW

1. Why should a new investor read the prospectus of a mutual fund carefully before investing in the fund?

2. Why would a person choose a front- or back-end load fund over a no-load mutual fund?

3. Why would you wish to buy a piece of vacant land? Describe what your plans might be for the property in 10 or 20 years, including where you would buy such a lot and its potential uses.

4. Describe investors who might buy a second home, such as a cabin in the woods. Why should they purchase the property now rather than in the future, when they plan to use it full time for retirement?

5. Explain how leverage applies to buying real estate. Why is it desirable to have a positive cash flow from rental property you own?

6. What is the meaning of the statement "Real estate is an illiquid investment"?

7. The Internet has provided a new way for buyers and sellers of collectibles to find each other. Search the Internet for sites dealing with a collectible that interests you. How is this item bought and sold online? Is there an association or club for your collectible? If so, how does the site help collectors?

MAKE ACADEMIC CONNECTIONS

8. **Communication** Mutual funds are often the best choice for young investors and those wishing to get started investing for the first time. Suppose a person had $500 to invest initially and planned to invest $50 a month thereafter. Write a one-page paper explaining why mutual funds might be a better way to invest this money than collectibles (such as buying Barbie dolls or baseball cards). Explain the advantages of investing in mutual funds.

9. **Research** Visit the web site of an investment company that offers a family of mutual funds (such as Vanguard or Fidelity). Select five of the company's funds that are very different from each other. Describe the investment objective(s) and risk level for each of the five funds. Draw a graphic that visually displays risk level, going from least risky to most risky. On the graph, identify the most risky fund you selected and the least risky fund. Then place the three other funds at their appropriate risk levels in between the two extremes. In a paragraph, summarize what you learned about mutual funds and risk.

10. **Economics** Gold is a commodity. Most of the U.S. gold supply is stored at Fort Knox. Also stored at Fort Knox is the gold supply of many foreign countries. What is meant by "the gold standard"? Do we have a gold standard today? How much gold does the United States have? Prepare a brief history of the importance of gold to the United States economy.

SOLVE PROBLEMS AND

EXPLORE ISSUES

11. Tony and Barbara have been married for three years and have managed to save some money to invest. They have decided on mutual funds but don't want to take too much risk. Still, they would like to have some additional income now and also be able sell the shares for a good profit in five to ten years. Suggest to them some types of mutual funds that might fit their investment goals and risk tolerance.

12. Obtain a prospectus for a specific mutual fund. You can write to an address provided in an ad in the financial pages of your local newspaper or The Wall Street Journal, obtain one from a brokerage firm or financial adviser, or locate the information at an investment company's web site. Read the prospectus and report on your findings regarding the objectives (goals) of the fund, risk profile, tax or tax-exempt status, and performance of the fund over the last year and last five years.

13. Alena has decided to invest in real estate. She can't decide whether to buy a vacant lot for $25,000 or a one-fourth interest in a four-unit apartment building selling for $400,000. Explain to her the pros and cons of both of these alternatives.

14. Your grandmother has a wonderful collection of crystal, gold coins, diamond jewelry, and silver dating back to the early nineteenth century. When purchased, it cost very little, but today it could be worth a great deal of money. Explain to your grandmother, using a current issue of the newspaper or Internet resources, what today's prices are for silver, gold, gems, and other valuables.

15. Your friend Georgia wants to buy a ruby ring at a local jewelry store. She believes that it will be an excellent investment for the future because she intends to sell the ring and make a profit. Explain to her the pros and cons of this type of investment.

16. Rick is worried that the money in his savings account is not earning enough interest to keep up with inflation. He has been reading about commodities and thinks that trading in commodities might be a great way to make some quick money. Explain to him the risks involved in trading commodities.

EXTEND YOUR LEARNING

17. **Legal Issues** Every state has requirements for becoming a licensed real estate broker. What are the requirements to become a licensed real estate broker in your state? Why do you think those requirements are necessary? What other laws or regulations exist that aim to protect consumers in real estate transactions? If these laws didn't exist, what legal issues might arise?

For related activities and links, go to **www.cengage.com/school/pfinance/mypf**

Retirement and Estate Planning

15.1 Planning for Retirement

15.2 Saving for Retirement

Consider **THIS**

"My grandparents say the time to think about retirement is when I get my first job," Susan told her coworkers. "But this isn't really my first job; it's just a part-time job while I go to school. When I get my first career-type job, then I'll start thinking about saving for retirement."

"Your grandparents are right," replied Andrew. "I have a great uncle who is getting Social Security benefits. He barely has enough money to buy his groceries and pay the rent. Every time prices go up, he gets stressed out because, in his words, he 'won't get a pay increase to make up for it.' I'm already thinking about the time when I won't be able to work. I think it's important to have enough money to live comfortably."

Planning for Retirement

GOALS

- Describe retirement needs for most individuals and families.
- Discuss estate planning documents and methods to minimize taxes on estates.

TERMS

- reverse mortgage, *p. 323*
- heir, *p. 323*
- estate, *p. 325*
- will, *p. 325*
- codicil, *p. 325*
- trust, *p. 325*
- power of attorney, *p. 327*
- estate tax, *p. 329*
- inheritance tax, *p. 329*
- gift tax, *p. 329*

RETIREMENT NEEDS

When you get ready to retire, you will want to have enough financial resources to live comfortably. At that point, many people also want to be able to afford to do the things they didn't have time for while they were working. Social Security and a company-sponsored retirement plan may not be enough to cover the costs of living. Inflation (increasing prices) will decrease the purchasing power of your retirement savings.

Why is it important to save for retirement during your work life?

HOW MUCH INCOME WILL YOU NEED?

Many financial advisers suggest that you will need between 75 and 85 percent of your preretirement income to live comfortably. This percentage may seem high. You may wonder how you can have that kind of income when you are no longer working. To have a comfortable retirement, most people need to limit current spending and start saving at the beginning of their work life.

There will be times when you won't have much cash to set aside. You may be paying for a college education, cars, houses, furniture, and so on. But it is important to save when you can. As your expenses go down, you can save more. With regular saving and investing, your nest egg will grow.

KEEP THE HOUSE OR MOVE?

Once their children are adults, many couples choose to sell their family home and find something smaller and easier to maintain. Current tax law allows married couples to sell the house they have lived in at least two years without paying taxes on the profits up to $500,000. (For single people, the tax-free profit limit is $250,000). Thus, you will have the opportunity to sell the family home and keep the proceeds.

Other people choose to keep their house because it is paid off. Before moving, they must consider the negative aspects. Moving can be expensive. Also, if you move far away, you will be leaving friends and family behind.

Equity in a house is the property's value minus the mortgage balance. As you make mortgage payments over the years, the equity in your home increases while the mortgage decreases. However, equity is not income. It is money "tied up" in property. There is a way to turn equity into current income without selling your house. It's called a reverse mortgage.

A **reverse mortgage** is a loan against the equity in the borrower's home. The lender makes tax-free monthly payments to the borrower. It works the opposite of a mortgage. Instead of making payments to the lender, the lender pays you. This is a loan, however, and it must be repaid in the future. Also there is a limit on the loan amount. Most reverse mortgages are a percentage of equity.

Equity can be computed as the difference between the balance remaining on the loan on the property (mortgage) and the current market value, assessed value, or appraised value:

- *Current market value* is the amount for which you could sell your home now.
- *Assessed value* is what the county or taxing authority has determined your property is worth for tax purposes.
- *Appraised value* is what a real estate appraiser believes your property is worth compared to similar properties that have recently sold in your area.

The appraised value is most often used by mortgage lenders in determining the amount of equity a homeowner has and, thus, the mortgage amount the homeowner can borrow. With a reverse mortgage, the monthly payments to you will continue until they add up, together with interest, to the amount of equity (loan amount).

Once the full loan amount has been reached, you may have to sell the home or get a regular mortgage to pay off the loan. If you die during the term of the loan, your heirs will have to pay it off. An **heir** is a person who will inherit property from someone who dies. Typically, heirs are spouses and children. If the property has to be sold in order to pay off the mortgage, the property will not pass to heirs.

WHAT TYPE OF INVESTMENT STRATEGY?

Retired people view investments from a different perspective than when they were younger. Because monthly income is often their main need, retirees may want to take dividends rather than reinvest them. Rather than saving for the future, investors at this stage are trying to preserve their financial position— that is, safeguard principal while earning a reasonable return. Fixed-income (low-risk) investments become a more practical choice. As people approach retirement, they often move some of their money out of growth stocks, which earn capital gains in the future, and into income stocks and bonds that produce interest and dividends now. Many also move more of their investment into low-risk options, trading high-potential earnings for lower but more certain earnings.

REVERSE MORTGAGE AMOUNT AND PAYMENTS

A couple owns a home that is worth $200,000 (appraised value) and the unpaid mortgage balance is $40,000. With a reverse mortgage that allows them to borrow up to 80 percent of the equity, they could borrow $128,000 ($160,000 × .80). Amortized over their life expectancy of 20 years and at 7 percent interest, how much could they receive in monthly payments? (*Hint:* Find a mortgage payment calculator online and plug in the years and interest rate to determine payment.)

Solution: As determined by using a mortgage payment calculator and inserting the inputs shown here, they would receive monthly payments of $992.38.

Mortgage Payment Calculator

Principal: 128,000

Interest: 7

Number of Years: 20

[Calculate]

HOW MUCH INSURANCE?

When you retire, your insurance needs also change. While your need for life insurance has decreased, your need for other types of insurance has increased.

For retired people, the crucial need for insurance falls in the area of health—being sure that an illness or injury will not wipe out a lifetime of saving and investing. When you qualify for *Medicare*, government-sponsored health insurance for the elderly, you will likely still need supplemental insurance to cover expenses not covered by Medicare.

The rapidly rising cost of prescription medications may be a major obstacle, along with extremely high payments for health insurance coverage. If there is an interim period between your retirement and the start of your Medicare coverage, you will have to pay for your own health insurance. Also, retired people may need coverage for long-term care in a nursing facility.

HOW DO YOU BEAT INFLATION?

The probable loss of buying power due to inflation is one reason that planning for retirement is so important. As you will recall, inflation is a general increase in prices. Because of inflation, the cost of living goes up over time. Price increases reduce buying power. If prices are increasing at 8 percent while your retirement income is increasing at only 3 or 4 percent, you'll have to cut out something from your budget or dip into your principal to maintain your living standard. Therefore, budgeting must continue throughout retirement. Seniors often work part time because they enjoy it, but many do so to earn more income to offset inflation.

ESTATE PLANNING

An **estate** is all that a person owns, less debts owed, at the time of the person's death. When people die, their possessions pass to other people, either as directed by the person who died (called the *decedent*) or by the laws of the state in which the person died. The estate may be taxed by the federal and/or state governments. *Estate planning* involves preparing a plan for transferring property during one's lifetime and at one's death. Your goals in estate planning should be to minimize taxes on the estate, to make known how you want your possessions distributed, and to provide for a smooth transfer of your possessions to your loved ones upon your death.

ESTATE PLANNING TOOLS

To provide for proper disposal of assets and to avoid taxes whenever possible, there are a number of good estate planning tools. These include wills, trusts, joint ownership of assets, and powers of attorney.

Wills

A **will**, *or testament* is a legal document that tells how an estate is to be distributed when a person dies. In your will, you name an *executor* (also called a personal representative) to carry out your wishes when you die. Any person who is 18 or older and of sound mind can make a legally valid will. The person who makes the will is called the *testator*.

A *simple will* is a short document that lists the people whom you want to be your heirs and what you want each to receive. Simple wills take a short time to prepare, and they are fairly standard documents. If your estate is relatively uncomplicated, you can prepare a will yourself, using an inexpensive kit or software purchased online or at an office products or software store. Whether or not you use a lawyer, you will need witnesses to your signature. Usually the witnesses must be two people not mentioned in the will. They must be 18 or older, not related to you, and able to attest to your mental competency at the time you signed the will. An example of a simple will is shown in Figure 15.1.

A *holographic will* is written in a person's own handwriting. A handwritten will is legally valid in 19 states and should be witnessed, like other wills. Because a handwritten will is often easier to contest (question), a typed will is better.

When people die without a will, they are said to be *intestate*. In that event, the person's property is distributed according to the laws of the state where the decedent died. By having a valid will, you can control who gets what, rather than allowing the state to make those decisions. Property reverts to the state when a person dies without heirs.

A person can make a will and later make small changes with a document called a codicil. A **codicil** is a legal document that modifies parts of a will and reaffirms the rest. A will cannot be legally amended by crossing out or adding words, by removing or adding pages, or by making erasures. A codicil is drawn by an attorney and is executed and witnessed the same as a will.

Trusts

A **trust** is a legal document in which an individual (the *trustor*) gives someone else (the *trustee*) control of property, for ultimate distribution to another person (the *beneficiary*). The trustee may be a financial institution or a person. A trust

FIGURE 15.1 *Simple Will*

LAST WILL AND TESTAMENT OF ANTHONY JOHN HINTON

I, Anthony John Hinton, of the city of Dayton and state of Ohio, do make, publish, and declare this to be my Last Will and Testament in manner following:

FIRST: I direct that all of my just debts, funeral expenses, and the cost of administering my estate be paid by my personal representative hereinafter named.

SECOND: I give, devise, and bequeath to my beloved daughter, Carol Hinton Campbell, now residing in Englewood, New Jersey, that certain piece of real estate, with all improvements thereon, situated in the same city and at the corner of Hudson Avenue and Tenafly Road.

THIRD: All the remainder and residue of my property, real, personal, and mixed, I give to my beloved wife, Kimberly Sue Hinton, personal representative of this, my Last Will and Testament, and I direct that she not be required to give bond or security for the performance of her duties as such.

LASTLY: I hereby revoke any and all former wills by me made.

IN WITNESS WHEREOF, I have hereunto set my hand this tenth day of October, in the year two thousand --.

Anthony John Hinton
_____
Anthony John Hinton

We, the undersigned, certify that the foregoing instrument was, on the date thereof, signed and declared by Anthony John Hinton as his Last Will and Testament, in the presence of us who, in his presence and in the presence of each other, have, at his request, hereunto signed our names as witnesses of the execution thereof, this tenth day of October 20--; and we hereby certify that we believe the said Anthony John Hinton to be of sound mind and memory.

Vilbin Schaenbar	residing at	251 Wonderly Avenue Dayton, Ohio 45419-2521
Samuel Vance	residing at	3024 James Hill Road Kettering, Ohio 45429-2454
Irene Vasilhous	residing at	423 Goldengate Drive Centerville, Ohio 45459-2459

can exist during the lifetime of the trustor. This type of trust is called *inter vivos*, or a "living" trust. You simply transfer some property to a trustee, giving him or her instructions regarding its management and disposition while you are alive and after your death. The other type of trust is called a testamentary trust, or *trust will*. It takes effect upon the death of a trustor. Such a trust can be valuable if your beneficiaries are minor children or if you wish to avoid high estate taxes.

In order for money and property to be left to a minor child, the child must have a legal guardian who makes accountings of the child's property and money. Parents of small children typically create trust wills to provide for their children's education and living expenses. Then the balance of the estate is given to the children at some later age, such as 25 or 30, when all of them have reached adulthood.

The purpose of a trust is twofold. First, trusts provide for beneficiaries who might not be able to effectively manage assets for themselves. The trustee is held accountable for how money is spent and how the trust is administered. The trustee must file papers yearly with the court, reporting on how the trust is progressing. Also, the trustee typically receives a fee for these services. Second, a trust can minimize inheritance or estate taxes and avoid probate. *Probate* is a court-supervised process of paying your debts and distributing your property to your heirs upon your death. An attorney is required to complete the probate process. The estate pays the costs of probate before heirs receive any property. Property held in a trust is not subject to probate. Therefore, the property can pass to beneficiaries quickly without a prolonged court proceeding and without the costs of probate.

Joint Ownership

There are several ways to hold title to property. By putting property in joint ownership, two or more people own an undivided interest in the property. Joint ownership of property between spouses is very common. Joint ownership may also exist between parents and children, other relatives, or any two or more people. If you and your spouse own property as joint tenants with right of survivorship (JTWROS), the ownership is split 50-50 for estate tax purposes. If one spouse dies, the surviving spouse automatically becomes the sole owner of the property. No legal action is necessary to transfer title. This form of ownership is commonly used for land, automobiles, residences, bank accounts, and securities. *Joint tenancy* is a convenient and automatic way to pass property. It is perhaps the most widely used property ownership arrangement.

Two or more people can own property without survivorship. As joint tenants without right of survivorship, when one person dies, his or her interest in the property passes to his or her heirs, not to the remaining owners.

When a person holds ownership singly, with no joint owner or named beneficiary, that asset becomes part of the person's estate upon death and will be distributed according to the terms of the will. Joint ownership is an effective way to avoid probate and inheritance taxes in some states.

Power of Attorney

At some time in your life, you may become incapacitated and unable to make your own decisions. A **power of attorney** is a legal document authorizing someone to act on your behalf. For example, if you become incapable of caring for yourself, the power of attorney gives your appointed person the power to use money from your savings to pay your bills and hire people to care for you. The power of attorney may be limited or general in time or in scope. A limited power of attorney may be good for 30 days or a year, or it may pertain to a particular transaction. A general power of attorney gives another person the right to act for you completely. When you give a power of attorney to another person, you give that person the power to do anything you could have done. Of course, you must fully trust the person to whom you give this legal right.

Figure 15.2 shows a power of attorney form. You can hire a lawyer to write your power of attorney, or you can do your own, using a kit or software designed for creating legal documents. Often software packages for writing wills, such as Quicken® WillMaker and Kiplinger's WILLPower, also contain templates for creating powers of attorney and other common legal documents.

FIGURE 15.2 *Power of Attorney*

GENERAL POWER OF ATTORNEY

I, [YOUR FULL LEGAL NAME], residing at [YOUR FULL ADDRESS], hereby appoint
_____ of _____, as my Attorney-in-Fact ("Agent").

    I hereby revoke any and all general powers of attorney that previously have been signed by me. However, the preceding sentence shall not have the effect of revoking any powers of attorney that are directly related to my health care that previously have been signed by me.

    My Agent shall have full power and authority to act on my behalf. This power and authority shall authorize my Agent to manage and conduct all of my affairs and to exercise all of my legal rights and powers, including all rights and powers that I may acquire in the future. My Agent's powers shall include, but not be limited to, the power to:

1. Open, maintain or close bank accounts (including, but not limited to, checking accounts, savings accounts, and certificates of deposit), brokerage accounts, and other similar accounts with financial institutions.

2. Sell, exchange, buy, invest, or reinvest any assets or property owned by me. Such assets or property may include income producing or non-income producing assets and property.

3. Purchase and/or maintain insurance, including life insurance upon my life or the life of any other appropriate person.

4. Take any and all legal steps necessary to collect any amount or debt owed to me, or to settle any claim, whether made against me or asserted on my behalf against any other person or entity.

5. Enter into binding contracts on my behalf.

6. Exercise all stock rights on my behalf as my proxy, including all rights with respect to stocks, bonds, debentures, or other investments.

7. Maintain and/or operate any business that I may own.

    My Agent shall be entitled to reasonable compensation for any services provided as my Agent. My Agent shall be entitled to reimbursement of all reasonable expenses incurred in connection with this Power of Attorney.

    My Agent shall provide an accounting for all funds handled and all acts performed as my Agent, if I so request or if such a request is made by any authorized personal representative or fiduciary acting on my behalf.

    This Power of Attorney shall become effective immediately, and shall not be affected by my disability or lack of mental competence, except as may be provided otherwise by an applicable state statute. This is a Durable Power of Attorney. This Power of Attorney shall continue effective until my death. This Power of Attorney may be revoked by me at any time by providing written notice to my Agent.

Dated _____, 20-- at _____, _____.

[YOUR SIGNATURE]
_____
[YOUR FULL LEGAL NAME]

[WITNESS' SIGNATURE]   [WITNESS' SIGNATURE]
_____   _____
[WITNESS' FULL LEGAL NAME]   [WITNESS' FULL LEGAL NAME]

STATE OF _____, COUNTY OF _____, ss:

The foregoing instrument was acknowledged before me this _____ day of _____, 20-- by [YOUR FULL LEGAL NAME], who is personally known to me or who has produced _____ as identification.

_____
Signature of person taking acknowledgment

_____
Name typed, printed, or stamped

_____
Title or rank

_____
Serial number (if applicable)

▌ TAXATION OF ESTATES

Federal and state governments levy various types of taxes that must be considered in planning your estate, including estate, inheritance, and gift taxes.

Federal Estate Taxes

The federal government levies an **estate tax**, which is a tax on property transferred from an estate to its heirs. An estate must be worth more than a certain amount ($3.5 million in 2009) to be subject to this tax. The federal estate tax is scheduled to be removed completely in 2010. The estate tax is paid from the assets of the estate, before anything can be distributed to heirs. An estate may have to sell property or investments in order to pay this tax.

State Death Taxes

The state **inheritance tax** is imposed on an heir who inherits property from an estate. The difference between an estate tax and an inheritance tax lies in who pays the tax. The estate tax is deducted from the value of the estate before distribution to heirs, but the heirs pay inheritance taxes on property received. The amount of tax is based on the value of the property in the estate. In states where inheritance taxes are imposed, laws vary widely as to the rate of taxation and the treatment of property to be taxed.

Federal Gift Taxes

Gifts are a popular way of distributing some property to loved ones before death to avoid estate and inheritance taxes. However, you would not want to give away property you need in order to live comfortably. One way to retain possession is to create a life estate. A *life estate* allows you to pass title to real property to a loved one but retain your right to live on the premises for as long as you live. This means that your children cannot evict you even after the property is in their names.

A **gift tax** is applied to a gift of money or property. It is paid by the giver, not the receiver, of the gift. In 2008, you could have given up to $12,000 per person per year without having to pay a gift tax. For gifts that exceed the limit, there is the unified gift tax credit, which basically allows a person to give away up to $1 million during his or her lifetime. Gifts to your spouse or to a charity are exempt from the gift tax. Also, gifts from a husband or a wife to a third party are considered as having been made in equal amounts by each spouse. Therefore, in 2008, a husband and wife together could have given as much as $24,000 per year to anyone, tax free.

The timing of the gift also matters. Any gift given within three years of death is usually considered a "gift in contemplation of death." In this event, the estate still must pay taxes on the value of the gift, and the one receiving the cash or property would have to pay inheritance taxes.

Federal/State Income Taxes

When someone dies, income taxes must be paid on the income the decedent earned that year and on any income earned by the estate while its assets remain undistributed (such as interest or dividends). The executor or attorney representing the estate must file this tax return and pay the taxes from the estate before the estate can be distributed to heirs.

Estate planners and financial advisers help people get ready for retirement. Their advice includes both analysis and guidance in making investment choices to meet their clients' long-term objectives and to suit their income and lifestyles. Many planners are accountants who specialize in estate tax laws.

Estate planners use their knowledge of investments, tax laws, and insurance to recommend options for individuals. They help clients with retirement choices as well as provide tax advice and sell life insurance. They develop a comprehensive plan that identifies problem areas, makes recommendations for improvement, and selects investments compatible with the client's goals.

Yearly updates keep clients and accounts protected from economic conditions and market changes. Most advisers also sell financial products, such as securities and insurance. They make fees based on the sales.

Employment Outlook

- A much faster than average rate of employment growth is expected.

Job Titles

- Estate planner
- Financial adviser
- Wealth manager
- Personal financial analyst

Needed Skills

- A bachelor's or master's degree is required, with emphasis in finance, business, or accounting.
- A license is typically required by the FINRA for those selling securities to investors.
- A CFP (certified financial planner) certification is needed for estate planners.
- Excellent math, analytical, and problem solving skills are required.

What's it like to work in... *Estate Planning*

Ruth has a group of 15 clients that she works with to maintain retirement portfolios. Most of her clients are already retired. Some of them are middle aged, and a few are in their mid-30s. She provides financial planning advice for her clients, based on their age, life stage, and financial goals.

Ruth works independently and is an insurance broker. She has a CFP and a stock broker's license, enabling her to sell securities to investors.

Today she is meeting with new clients who were referred to her by a retired couple. She accepts new clients by referral only. Her days consist of reviewing client accounts, watching financial and market conditions, and making recommendations for changes.

What About You?

Would you like working with people to help them achieve their lifelong goals? Do you enjoy working with financial analysis and numbers? Would you like to be an estate planner?

Assessment

KEY TERMS REVIEW

Match the terms with the definitions. Some terms may not be used.

_____ 1. A legal document that modifies parts of a will and reaffirms the rest

_____ 2. Person who will inherit property

_____ 3. A federal tax on property transferred from an estate to its heirs

_____ 4. All that a person owns, less debts owed, at the time of the person's death

_____ 5. A loan against the equity in the borrower's home in which the borrower receives monthly payments

_____ 6. A legal document authorizing someone to act on your behalf

a. codicil
b. estate
c. estate tax
d. gift tax
e. heir
f. inheritance tax
g. power of attorney
h. reverse mortgage
i. trust
j. will

_____ 7. A state tax on an heir who inherits property from an estate

_____ 8. A legal document in which an individual gives someone else control of property for ultimate distribution to another person

CHECK YOUR UNDERSTANDING

9. Why should you think about retirement when you are just beginning your work career?

10. Why is it important to have a will?

11. How does owning property jointly avoid probate?

APPLY YOUR KNOWLEDGE

12. At what age would you like to retire? Briefly describe your plans for retirement, such as travel and recreation. What things should you consider in the near future in order to meet your retirement goals?

THINK CRITICALLY

13. Why are many young people often reluctant to plan for retirement?

14. Explain how you might invest your money to be sure your income keeps up with inflation. Currently, the only income you expect upon retirement is Social Security.

15. What is a trust will? Why is it important? Explain how it is used in estate planning.

Saving for Retirement

PERSONAL RETIREMENT PLANS

Personal or individual retirement accounts are the best way to set aside money for the future. You can select from tax-sheltered plans, such as individual retirement accounts (IRAs), Keoghs, and simplified employee pensions (SEPs) if you qualify, as well as annuities. You should also include some savings on which you have already paid taxes.

INDIVIDUAL RETIREMENT ACCOUNTS (IRAS)

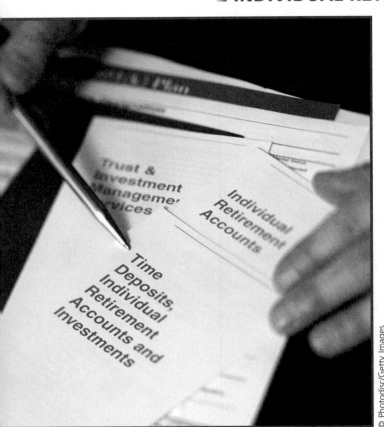

An **individual retirement account (IRA)** is a retirement savings plan that allows individuals to set aside up to a specified amount each year and delay paying tax on the earnings until they begin withdrawing it at age 59½ or later. In 2008, the contribution limit was $5,000 per year (or $10,000 for a married couple filing jointly). People not covered by a retirement plan at work may contribute the full amount per year, if they wish. Those who do participate in a retirement plan at work can also contribute to an IRA, but they may not be able to contribute the maximum, depending on their income.

With a **traditional IRA**, you can deduct your contribution each year from your taxable income. This allows you to delay paying tax on that income and the earnings it accumulates until you withdraw the money at retirement. At that time, your income will likely be lower than it was while you were working. As a result, you would be in a lower tax bracket and would pay less tax.

A **Roth IRA** is a type of IRA where contributions are taxed, but earnings are not. With a Roth IRA, you pay tax on your income before you put it into the account. After a five-year holding period, and

What is the value of contributing to a traditional IRA?

© Photodisc/Getty Images

at age 59½, you can begin making tax-free withdrawals. This is the opposite of a traditional IRA, for which you pay tax on the earnings as well as the contributions when you withdraw the money at retirement.

For early withdrawals of IRAs (before age 59½), a 10 percent penalty is imposed on the amount withdrawn. This penalty can amount to a lot of money, so you should avoid withdrawing money early. In addition, the money you withdraw is subject to federal and state income taxes in the year of withdrawal.

You can also set up an *education IRA* if you have children under age 18. Contributions to an education IRA are not deductible. It is a trust created for the purpose of paying higher education expenses. Withdrawals for qualified expenses, such as tuition, books, fees, and supplies, are not taxable when withdrawn. This is similar to how a Roth IRA works.

KEOGH PLANS

A **Keogh plan** is a tax-deferred retirement savings plan available to self-employed individuals and their employees. In 2008, Keogh contributions were restricted to $46,000 or 25 percent of earned income in any one year, whichever is less. Earned income is your net income after subtracting business expenses, including contributions to the plan for employees. Employees must be covered in the plan in a nondiscriminatory manner. Thus, the contribution rate set by the employer must be applied uniformly to all employees.

The amounts an employer contributes are fully tax deductible. Earnings on Keogh plans are also tax-deferred. Withdrawals cannot be made before age 59½ without penalty, and withdrawals must begin by age 70½. Keogh plans must be administered by a trustee, such as a financial institution.

SIMPLIFIED EMPLOYEE PENSION (SEP) PLANS

A **Simplified Employee Pension (SEP)** plan is a tax-deferred retirement plan available to small businesses. SEPs were authorized by Congress to encourage smaller employers to establish employee pension plans with IRAs as a funding method. Although SEPs were not exclusively designed for self-employed individuals, they can use them and often do because they are easier to set up than Keogh plans. Each employee sets up an IRA at a financial institution. Then the employer makes an annual tax-deductible contribution of up to 25 percent of the employee's salary or $46,000 (in 2008), whichever is less. Employees also can make contributions up to a $2,000 limit. Employee contributions to these plans are also tax-deductible.

ANNUITIES

An **annuity** is income from an investment paid in a series of regular payments made for a set number of years. Annuities are usually provided through insurance companies. You can buy an annuity for a lump sum or make regular payments into it. In recent years, *tax-sheltered annuities (TSAs)* have become popular because of

NETBookmark

Access www.cengage.com/school/pfinance/mypf and click on the link for Chapter 15. Study the chart that summarizes options, key details, and the advantages/disadvantages of various retirement plans for self-employed individuals. What is the best plan for sole proprietors who want to make the largest contribution possible? Which plan allows an individual to make the largest annual contribution toward retirement? Of all the plans listed, which makes the least sense for a self-employed person?

www.cengage.com/school/pfinance/mypf

the tax-free buildup of interest or dividends during the time the annuity contract remains in effect. Such annuities are often used by younger people to save money toward retirement.

■ PRETAXED SAVINGS

Not all of your retirement savings should be in tax-deferred plans. Some should be savings and investments made with pretaxed income (income on which you have already paid tax). Most financial advisers recommend that at least half of your retirement savings be pretaxed. You will be able to withdraw these funds at any time, without tax consequences. Since there is no penalty for withdrawing these funds before retirement, you will have to restrain yourself from spending this part of your nest egg, so that it will be there for you when you retire.

EMPLOYER-SPONSORED RETIREMENT PLANS

Another source of retirement income may be the retirement plan offered by your company. With employer-sponsored plans, you and often your employer contribute to your tax-sheltered retirement savings. Contributions and earnings on employer-sponsored plans accumulate tax-free until you receive them.

■ DEFINED-BENEFIT PLANS

Many larger employers provide defined-benefit plans or pensions for their employees. A **defined-benefit plan** is a company-sponsored retirement plan in which retired employees receive a set monthly amount based on wages earned and number of years of service. The employer may make the entire contribution to the plan. To become *vested*, or entitled to the full amount in the plan, you may have to work for the company for a specified number of years.

Employees who are vested but leave the company before retirement may withdraw the account balance in cash or "roll it" (transfer it) to an IRA. In this situation, most people choose to roll the money into an IRA to delay paying taxes on it until retirement. If they take it as cash when they leave the company, they will have to pay tax on the full amount that year plus a 10 percent penalty if they are under age 59½.

Each retirement plan has different rules and options. You should read the plan documentation to understand your choices.

If a company goes bankrupt or experiences serious financial difficulties, your plan may be protected by law. The Employee Retirement Income Security Act of 1974 (ERISA) sets minimum standards for pension plans in private industry and protects millions of workers from inadequately funded pension plans.

■ DEFINED-CONTRIBUTION PLANS

A **defined-contribution plan** is a company-sponsored retirement plan in which employees can receive a periodic or lump-sum payment based on their account balance and the performance of the investments in their account. These contributions are often tax-deferred (not taxed until withdrawn at retirement). The employer may or may not contribute to the employee's account as well. Each company's plan specifies the percentage of salary that an employee may contribute to his or her own account each year.

The plan also specifies the amount the employer will contribute, if anything, but does not promise any particular benefit. When a plan participant retires or otherwise becomes eligible for benefits, the benefit is the total amount of money accumulated in the employee's account, including investment earnings on amounts put into the accounts. Two defined-contribution plans are 401(k) and 403(b) plans.

401(k) Plans

A **401(k) plan** is a defined-contribution plan for employees of companies that operate for a profit. Under a 401(k) plan, employees choose the percentage of salary they want to contribute to their account. The employer deducts this amount from their paychecks and puts it into the employees' individual accounts. This amount is not part of the employees' taxable income for the year, so they do not have to pay taxes on it until they withdraw the money at retirement. An investment company manages the accounts and invests the money. Usually employees may select the types of investments they want from among several options offered by the plan.

Why are 401(k) plans a wise investment choice?

Frequently, employers match employee contributions by some percentage. For example, for every $1 of salary employees contribute to their account, the employer may add 50 cents (a 50 percent match). Companies usually set limits on how much they will match of an employee's salary.

Withdrawal restrictions and penalties apply when money is withdrawn early, except in the event of death, disability, or financial hardship. A 401(k) is usually an excellent investment for employees, particularly if the employer also contributes. The employer's contribution is pure profit to the employee. In the example above, the 50 percent match is the same as making an immediate 50 percent return on your investment!

403(b) Plans

A **403(b) plan** is a defined-contribution plan for employees of schools, non-profit organizations, and government units. Under a 403(b) plan, employees contribute a percentage of their salary toward this tax-deferred account. While the rules may vary slightly, the 403(b) plan operates like a 401(k). These plans have been called tax-sheltered annuities because originally these were the only type of investment permitted by law. Today, 403(b) plans can choose other investments, such as mutual funds. Investment options are still fewer than under a 401(k) plan, however.

Earnings are tax-deferred, and early withdrawal penalties apply. Should an employee leave his or her employer, the 403(b) funds can be rolled into an IRA.

GOVERNMENT-SPONSORED PLANS

You may be entitled to government benefit checks—in the form of Social Security, military retirement, or veterans' benefits. Many state, county, and city governments also operate retirement plans for their employees.

SOCIAL SECURITY BENEFITS

When you retire, you will be eligible for Social Security benefits if you paid Social Security taxes during your lifetime. The amount of your benefit is based on your earnings and contributions to Social Security. Remember, these withholdings from your paychecks were matched by your employer(s).

Social Security is designed as a safety net, or supplement to an individual's own retirement savings. It was never intended to fully support people in retirement. To retire comfortably, you must have accumulated your own nest egg apart from Social Security.

Once you have started paying into the system, you can request a Social Security statement, which you will receive each year thereafter. This statement shows a record of the income on which you paid Social Security taxes and an estimate of the benefits you will receive at retirement. Some federal government employees and railroad employees are not covered by Social Security retirement benefits. They have a different benefit plan that includes a retirement annuity. However, recent federal employees are now paying into the Social Security system.

Maximum Social Security retirement benefits are available at age 65 for many people. However, the government is raising the retirement age, so the age when you can receive the maximum benefits will likely be later than age 65. You can retire early, at age 62, and receive reduced benefits. If you were married for 10 years or more, you may be entitled to receive Social Security benefits based on your spouse's income, even if you are divorced.

Remember, too, most or all of Social Security retirement benefits are taxable if your total income from all sources exceeds maximum limits that are adjusted from time to time. In addition, several states currently tax Social Security benefits as income.

MILITARY BENEFITS

Retired military personnel receive pensions after 20 years of active duty in the U.S. armed forces. Pensions are payable in full regardless of other sources of income and are subject to income taxes. In addition, military retirees may have special privileges, such as the ability to purchase goods through military posts. These benefits can be very attractive, especially for people who retire from the military in their early forties and continue working in different jobs for another 15 or 20 years.

The Veterans Administration provides regular pensions for survivors of men and women who died while in the armed forces and disability pensions for veterans who were permanently injured while in the armed forces. Veterans may also be entitled to additional benefits, such as low-interest mortgage loans, college tuition, and low-rate car, home, and life insurance. Veterans should check to see what benefits are available to them—both now and at retirement.

ISSUES IN YOUR WORLD

YOUR RETIREMENT INCOME

During your work life, you may set aside money in a retirement savings plan, such as a 401(k) or a 403(b). Money you set aside is tax-deferred; that is, you do not have to pay income tax on it until you receive it and are able to spend it. Then it is taxed as ordinary income at your tax rate when you are retired.

Tax-deferred investments provide a "tax shelter" benefit during your work years. They reduce your taxable income, and thus you pay less in taxes at that time. But when you retire and withdraw the money, you must claim it as income and pay taxes. Thus, retirement investments should consist of more than just tax-deferred options. Otherwise, all income received at retirement will be subject to tax.

Retirement income should provide enough money to pay your living expenses and other costs (such as medical care and prescriptions), as well as allow you to enjoy some travel and leisure activities. At least part of that income should be from money set aside while you were working that will not be subject to tax (you paid taxes on it as you went along). Consider the following recommended income plan:

Source of Income	Percent of Total Retirement Income
Social Security/government pensions (contributions withheld from paychecks)	25%
401(k) or 403(b) savings plans during work years	25%
Employer-provided retirement accounts (you do not contribute to this)	15%
Private money you save that is not tax-deferred and will not be taxed at retirement	35%

With this plan, you depend on yourself more than on any other source. Income you set aside will be yours to take as you wish, without tax consequences. Because Social Security benefits become taxable after you earn a certain level of income, you should consider it as a part of the taxable portion of your retirement.

THINK CRITICALLY

1. How much money will you need for a secure retirement? What is the ideal combination of savings for retirement to meet those needs?

2. Why is it important to set aside money that is not tax sheltered? How much of your retirement money should be tax sheltered?

Assessment

KEY TERMS REVIEW

Match the terms with the definitions. Some terms may not be used.

____ 1. A type of IRA where contributions are taxed, but earnings are not

____ 2. Income from an investment paid in a series of regular payments

____ 3. A tax-deferred retirement plan for the self-employed

____ 4. A tax-deferred retirement savings plan that allows individuals to set aside up to a specified amount per year

____ 5. A defined-contribution plan for employees of companies that operate for a profit

____ 6. A company-sponsored retirement plan in which retirees receive a set monthly amount based on wages earned and years of service

a. 401(k) plan

b. 403(b) plan

c. annuity

d. defined-benefit plan

e. defined-contribution plan

f. individual retirement account (IRA)

g. Keogh plan

h. Roth IRA

i. simplified employee pension (SEP)

j. traditional IRA

____ 7. A company-sponsored retirement plan in which employees receive a periodic or lump-sum payment based on their account balance

CHECK YOUR UNDERSTANDING

8. How is a traditional IRA different from a Roth IRA or an education IRA?

9. How is a 401(k) different from a 403(b)?

10. Who is eligible to collect Social Security retirement benefits?

APPLY YOUR KNOWLEDGE

11. Do a search for an online retirement calculator and input reasonable numbers into the required fields. Work several examples, changing only one number each time. Keep track and compare results. What did you learn about retirement planning?

THINK CRITICALLY

12. Explain why personal retirement plans are better and safer for your financial security than employer- or government-sponsored plans.

13. Suppose your employer offers a 401(k) plan with 50 percent matching. How would contributing to this plan affect your current income? Future income? Do you think participating in this plan is a good idea? Explain.

Chapter Assessment

SUMMARY

15.1

- Social Security benefits alone will not provide a comfortable retirement. You must start building your nest egg now with regular saving and investing.

- The equity you build in your home can be a source of retirement income with a reverse mortgage.

- As you near retirement, you may want to switch to less risky investments that emphasize current income over future capital gains.

- Plan your estate to minimize estate and inheritance taxes, to make known how you want your possessions distributed after your death, and to provide a smooth transfer of your assets to your loved ones.

- A will specifies how to distribute your assets. A codicil can be used to specify small changes to a will.

- Transferring property through a trust can help ensure one's wishes are carried out and avoid high estate taxes.

- Joint ownership with right of survivorship transfers property at death without the costs and time involved in probate.

- A power of attorney empowers someone else to act on your behalf.

15.2

- A traditional IRA allows you to delay paying income tax on the contributions until you withdraw the money at retirement age.

- On a Roth IRA, you pay taxes on the contributions but pay no taxes on withdrawals at retirement.

- A Keogh plan is a tax-deferred plan for self-employed people.

- SEP plans are tax-deferred plans for employees of small businesses.

- An annuity is a tax-sheltered investment sold by insurance companies that provides regular payments after retirement.

- Under a defined-benefit plan, retired employees receive a specified amount based on wages earned and years of service.

- Defined-contribution plans, such as 401(k) and 403(b), allow employees to contribute part of their salary to tax-deferred investments. Employers may or may not contribute matching funds.

- You will be eligible for Social Security benefits at retirement if you paid Social Security taxes during your lifetime.

APPLY WHAT YOU KNOW

1. Visit the Nolo web site, which offers legal information for consumers and small businesses. Follow the links to wills and estate planning. Select an article that interests you. Write a paragraph summarizing the key points of the article.

2. Prepare a simple will for yourself, following Figure 15.1. What would happen to your property if you did not have a will?

3. If you had minor children, you might create a trust to provide for them if you died while they were still young. Explain why a trust fund is important for managing the financial needs of minors.

4. What are some advantages of owning property jointly with another person? Why would people own property as joint tenants with the right of survivorship?

5. Suppose you gave a $20,000 gift to a friend. Would you pay a gift tax on $20,000 if you were single? If so, how much of the gift amount would be taxed?

6. Use the Internet to learn more about Roth IRAs. From the information you find, write a paragraph about Roth IRAs. Who would choose them and why?

7. Explain the difference between an IRA and a Keogh account. Explain who can have these types of accounts.

MAKE ACADEMIC CONNECTIONS

8. **Math** The Andersons, a retired couple, own their house free and clear. It has been appraised at $280,000. They are considering a reverse mortgage with a loan of 80 percent of appraised value. How much could they borrow? What would they receive in monthly income, for a period of 20 years (12 payments per year) at an assumed interest rate of 5 percent? 6 percent? 7 percent? (Hint: Use an online mortgage calculator.)

9. **Communication** Retirement and estate planning is a field of study, with many professionals making a career of providing advice in this area. Some advisers charge fees for their services; others make money based on the retirement tools they sell to customers. Research the types of retirement and estate planning experts who are available to consumers. Report your findings in a two-page paper, citing your sources of information and briefly evaluating each source. Include private sector as well as government-provided resources.

10. **Economics** Inflation is a major consideration for those on fixed incomes such as retirees. As prices rise, their incomes remain flat. What can retired people do to preserve their purchasing power? Use the Internet to do research on the history of inflation in the United States (enter the keyword "inflation" or go to a government web site). Prepare a one-page report that summarizes your findings and explains the best ways to protect your retirement income from the effects of inflation.

11. **Research** When people die, they often leave their estates (assets) to beneficiaries. To learn more about inheritances, financial implications, and investment options, access www.school.cengage.com/pfinance/mypf, click on the link for Chapter 15, and read the article. What is the difference between estate taxes and inheritance taxes? What are some of the financial implications and investment options if you receive a large inheritance?

SOLVE *PROBLEMS* AND

EXPLORE *ISSUES*

12. Mr. and Mrs. Owens are getting older. Their children are grown and through college. Their home is nearly paid off. In five more years, they both plan to retire. Explain to them how their investment strategies today should probably be different from when they still had children to support.

13. Mrs. Rameriz is a widow. She has an employer-paid pension of $300 a month, together with Social Security benefits of $600 a month. She owns her home free and clear but has high medical bills. Explain to her how she can use her house equity to generate monthly income for her retirement years.

14. Renee and Ryan own a new car jointly with right of survivorship. Can Renee leave her share of the car to another person when she creates her will? Why or why not?

15. Tanya is self-employed. Every year, she has extra money she could save, but instead spends it on trips and jewelry. She earns above-average income from her business, putting her in a high tax bracket. Explain to her why she should strongly consider a Keogh plan or SEP plan for her retirement years.

16. Bob works and earns under $25,000 a year. He has never had an IRA because he thinks Social Security will be enough for retirement income. Explain to him how an IRA works, and why he should consider one.

17. Jackson has worked for over 45 years. He served in the military for 20 of those years. He is qualified to retire next year when he reaches age 65. Explain to him what types of benefits he might expect to receive.

18. Assume you are 21 years old and have no savings yet, but you have a good job and can start saving. You think you can retire comfortably at age 65 on $30,000 a year for 20 years (based on a life expectancy of 85). On average, you think you can earn 8 percent on your savings. Locate and use an online retirement planning tool to determine how much you would have to save each year to meet your savings goal? How much would you have to save each year if you didn't start until age 35?

EXTEND YOUR LEARNING

19. **Legal Issues** Senior citizens often fall victim to scams. One such scam was reported in California. A real estate broker searched for unoccupied homes with delinquent taxes, many of which were owned by senior citizens staying in nursing homes. The broker paid the delinquent taxes and fraudulently transferred the property to his name without the owners' consent. He then rented the homes and kept the money. This crook defrauded homeowners of more than $5 million. How can elderly people protect themselves and their property from scams?

For related activities and links, go to **www.cengage.com/school/pfinance/mypf**

Ben S. Bernanke

In 2006, Ben Bernanke was appointed by the President to be the 14th Chairman of the Board of Governors of the Federal Reserve System (The Fed). He was born December 13, 1953, in Augusta, Georgia, and grew up in Dillon, South Carolina. He was a high-achieving pupil in high school. He taught himself calculus, edited the school newspaper, and was class valedictorian. Upon taking the SAT, he achieved the highest score in his state that year, scoring 1,590 out of 1,600 points.

© AP Photos/Susan Walsh

Bernanke attended Harvard University and graduated with a BA in economics (1975). He earned a PhD in economics from MIT (1979). He taught at Stanford University from 1979 to 1985 and then went on to become a tenured professor at Princeton University. He became a member of the Board of Governors in 2002.

Through his role on the Board of Governors, Mr. Bernanke helps set U.S. monetary policy, which has an impact on the lives of all U.S. citizens in many important ways. He brings changes in interest rates, money supply, and open-market transactions with the goal of stabilizing the economy and promoting economic growth accompanied by low inflation. Mr. Bernanke believes in the power of saving money and the need for financial responsibility. He understands how inflation erodes purchasing power and believes the government as well as individuals should take all steps possible to guard against it.

The Fed lowers interest rates when the economy is slowing down. The lower rates make money easier to borrow and help the economy to expand. Alternatively, it raises rates when the economy seems to be expanding too rapidly. Mr. Bernanke's actions (whether lowering or raising interest rates, or just making comments about the economy) have an immediate and often dramatic effect on the stock market. Investors and traders make decisions based on anticipated changes in the economy due to Federal Reserve policies.

THINK *CRITICALLY*

1. *Explain how Mr. Bernanke, or the Chairman of the Federal Reserve System, can affect your life personally.*

2. *What can you do when interest rates are rising? Falling?*

3. *How do interest rates affect your investments, whether they are stocks, bonds, mutual funds, real estate, gold, or other choices?*

Assessing Your Financial Security

Overview

At the end of Unit 2, you began financial planning with a careful examination of your financial position. Now you will continue to build your plan. You can protect your financial security through savings, investments, and retirement and estate planning.

YOUR SAVINGS PLAN

Money you set aside today (savings) will allow you to make purchases later. In Chapter 10, you learned how to calculate interest on savings deposits. When money is deposited in savings, it gains interest until some point in the future when it is withdrawn and spent. *Future value* is the final compounded value of a deposit or series of deposits. Using future value tables (which are built into financial calculators), you can determine how much money you need to set aside today in order to reach a future goal.

Figure U3.1 shows the future value (compound sum) factors to use when computing interest earned at numerous interest rates and allowed to compound for a number of compounding periods. Rather than compute interest for each period and add it to the previous balance, you can use this table. For example, if

© Creatas/Getty Images

Period	Percent								
	3%	**4%**	**5%**	**6%**	**7%**	**8%**	**9%**	**10%**	**11%**
1	1.03000	1.04000	1.05000	1.06000	1.07000	1.08000	1.09000	1.10000	1.11000
2	1.06090	1.08160	1.10250	1.12360	1.14990	1.16640	1.11810	1.21000	1.23210
3	1.09273	1.12486	1.15723	1.19102	1.22504	1.25971	1.29503	1.33100	1.36763
4	1.12551	1.16986	1.21551	1.26248	1.31080	1.36049	1.41158	1.46410	1.51807
5	1.15927	1.21665	1.27628	1.33823	1.40255	1.46933	1.53862	1.61051	1.68506
6	1.19405	1.26532	1.34010	1.41852	1.50073	1.58687	1.66710	1.77156	1.87042
7	1.22987	1.31593	1.40710	1.50363	1.60578	1.71382	1.82804	1.94872	2.07616
8	1.26677	1.36857	1.47746	1.59385	1.71819	1.85093	1.99256	2.14359	2.30454
9	1.30477	1.42331	1.55133	1.68948	1.83846	1.99901	2.17189	2.35795	2.55804
10	1.34392	1.48024	1.62890	1.79085	1.96715	2.15893	2.36736	2.59374	2.83942
11	1.38423	1.53945	1.71034	1.89830	2.10485	2.33164	2.58043	2.85312	3.15176
12	1.42576	1.60103	1.79586	2.01220	2.25219	2.51817	2.81266	3.13843	3.49845
13	1.46853	1.66507	1.88565	2.13203	2.40985	2.71962	3.06581	3.45227	3.88328
14	1.51259	1.73168	1.97993	2.26090	2.57853	2.93719	3.34173	3.79750	4.31044
15	1.55797	1.80094	2.07893	2.39656	2.75903	3.17217	3.64248	4.17725	4.78459
16	1.60471	1.87298	2.18288	2.54035	2.95216	3.42594	3.97031	4.59497	5.31089
17	1.65285	1.94790	2.29202	2.69377	3.15882	3.70002	4.32763	5.05447	5.89509
18	1.70243	2.02582	2.40662	2.54035	3.37993	3.99602	4.71712	5.55992	6.54355
19	1.75351	2.10685	2.52695	3.02560	3.61653	4.31570	5.14166	6.11591	7.26334
20	1.80611	2.19112	2.65330	3.20714	3.86968	4.66096	5.60441	6.72750	8.06231
25	2.09378	2.66584	3.38636	4.29187	5.42743	6.84848	8.62308	10.83471	13.58546
30	2.42726	3.24340	4.32194	5.74349	7.61226	10.06266	13.26768	17.44940	22.89230
35	2.81386	3.94609	5.51602	7.68608	10.67658	14.78534	20.41397	28.10244	38.57485
40	3.26204	4.80102	7.03999	10.28572	14.97446	21.72452	31.40942	45.25926	65.00087
45	3.78160	5.84118	8.98501	13.76461	21.00245	31.92045	48.32729	72.89048	109.53024
50	4.38391	7.10668	11.46740	18.42015	29.45703	46.90161	74.35752	117.39085	184.56483

you deposit $5,000 at 8 percent and leave it for five years, compounded semiannually, you would use the table as follows: 8 percent a year is 4 percent per compounding period (8 ÷ 2). Five years, compounded semiannually, is 10 compounding periods (5 × 2). In the table, the factor for 4 percent and 10 periods is 1.48024. Multiply $5,000 by 1.48024, and the account total will be $7,401.20 after 5 years, at 8 percent interest, compounded semiannually.

When you make regular payments (rather than deposit a lump sum at irregular intervals) to your account, you can use another table to shortcut the calculations. Figure U3.2 shows the future value (compound sum) factors used to compute future value of an annuity. (You will recall that an annuity is a sum of money set aside regularly, such as monthly, for the future.) Instead of calculating interest, adding a deposit, calculating interest, and so on, the table shown in Figure U3.2 simplifies the procedure. For example, assume you deposit $1,000 per year for 12 years, earning 6 percent interest a year. In the table, the factor for 6 percent and 12 periods is 16.86994. Multiplying $1,000 by 16.86994, you get $16,869.94, which is the value of the deposits at the end of 12 years.

Using the two tables shown in Figures U3.1 and U3.2, complete Worksheet 1 (Future Values) provided for you in the *Student Activity Guide* and also presented for reference on the next page.

Period					Percent				
	3%	**4%**	**5%**	**6%**	**7%**	**8%**	**9%**	**10%**	**11%**
1	1.00000	1.00000	1.00000	1.00000	1.00000	1.00000	1.00000	1.00000	1.00000
2	2.03000	2.04000	2.05000	2.06000	2.07000	2.08000	2.09000	2.10000	2.11000
3	3.09090	3.12160	3.15250	3.18360	3.21490	3.24640	3.27810	3.31000	3.34210
4	4.18363	4.24646	4.31013	4.37462	4.43994	4.50611	4.57313	4.64100	4.70973
5	5.30914	5.41632	5.52563	5.63709	5.75074	5.86660	5.98471	6.10510	6.22780
6	6.46841	6.63298	6.80191	6.97532	7.15329	7.33593	7.52334	7.71561	7.91286
7	7.66246	7.89829	8.14201	8.39384	8.65402	8.92280	9.20044	9.48717	9.78327
8	8.89234	9.21427	9.54911	9.89747	10.25980	10.63663	11.02847	11.43589	11.85943
9	10.15911	10.58280	11.02656	11.49132	11.97799	12.48756	13.02104	13.57948	14.16397
10	11.46388	12.00611	12.57789	13.18080	13.81645	14.48656	15.19293	15.93743	16.72201
11	12.80780	13.48635	14.20679	14.97164	15.79360	16.64549	17.56029	18.53117	19.56143
12	14.19203	15.02581	15.91713	16.86994	17.88845	18.97713	20.14072	21.38428	22.71319
13	15.61779	16.62684	17.71298	18.88214	20.14064	21.49530	22.95339	24.52271	26.21164
14	17.08632	18.29191	19.59863	21.10507	22.55049	24.21492	26.01919	27.97498	30.09492
15	18.59891	20.02359	21.57856	23.27597	25.12902	27.15211	29.36092	31.77248	34.40536
16	20.15688	21.82453	23.65749	25.67253	27.88805	30.32428	33.00340	35.94973	39.18995
17	21.76159	23.69751	25.84037	28.21288	30.84022	33.75023	36.97371	40.54470	44.50084
18	23.41444	25.64541	28.13239	30.90565	33.99903	37.45024	41.30134	45.59917	50.39594
19	25.11687	27.67123	30.53900	33.75999	37.37897	41.44626	46.01846	51.15909	56.93949
20	26.87037	29.77808	33.06595	36.78559	40.99549	45.76196	51.16012	57.27500	64.20283
25	36.45926	41.64591	47.72710	54.86451	63.24904	73.10594	84.70090	98.34706	114.41331
30	47.57542	56.08494	66.43885	79.05819	94.46077	113.28321	136.30754	164.49402	199.02088
35	60.46208	73.65223	90.32031	111.43478	138.23688	172.31680	215.71076	271.02437	341.58956
40	75.40126	95.02552	120.79977	154.76297	199.63511	259.05652	337.88245	442.59257	581.82607
45	92.71986	121.02939	159.70016	212.74351	285.74931	386.50562	525.85874	718.90484	986.63856
50	112.79687	152.66708	209.34800	290.33591	406.52893	573.77016	815.08356	1163.90853	1668.88115

WORKSHEET 1
Future Values

Directions: For numbers 1–4, use Figure U3.1 to compute the value of each deposit at the rate given. For numbers 5–8, use Figure U3.2 to compute the value of each annuity at the given rate.

Future Value (Compound Sum) of $1

Deposit	Time	Annual Rate	Value
1. $5,000 Compounded quarterly	4 years	12%	$_____
2. $1,000 Compounded semiannually	10 years	6%	$_____
3. $7,500 Compounded annually	8 years	8%	$_____
4. $3,850 Compounded semiannually	2 years	8%	$_____

Future Value (Compound Sum) of an Annuity

Deposit	Time	Annual Rate	Value
5. $500/year	5 years	6%	$_____
6. $100/year	10 years	9%	$_____
7. $900/year	2 years	8%	$_____
8. $250/year	10 years	5%	$_____

For your own personal savings plan, you should set aside a predetermined amount each month. It is often more difficult to set aside lump sums. However, should you inherit money, receive a large refund, or earn a large bonus, you can always make lump-sum deposits. Complete Worksheet 2 (Your Savings Plan) in the *Student Activity Guide*, which is also presented for reference below, to see how funds set aside now can grow larger in the future.

INVESTMENTS AND RISK

After you have provided for savings, you can then begin investing. Investments can bring higher returns than savings, but they also carry higher risk. When choosing investments, you should first determine your risk comfort level. Complete Worksheet 3 (Risk Aptitude Test) provided for you in the *Student Activity Guide* and also presented for reference on the next page. The worksheet

---

WORKSHEET 2
Your Savings Plan

Directions: In the spaces, project what you could save presently (either lump sum or monthly payment), and calculate the future value in 5, 10, and 20 years at the interest rate shown. Then project what you would like to be able to save (lump sum or monthly payment) in 5,10, and 20 years.

Savings Amount	Interest Rates	Future Value
$_____ What you could set aside today	6% per year, compounded annually, in 5 years	$_____
	6% per year, compounded annually, in 10 years	$_____
	6% per year, compounded annually, in 20 years	$_____
$_____ What you want to be able to save 5 years from now	8% per year, compounded annually, in 10 years	$_____
	6% per year, compounded semi-annually, in 20 years	$_____
$_____ What you want to be able to save 10 years from now	5% per year, compounded annually, in 20 years	$_____
	6% per year, compounded semi-annually, in 5 years	$_____

Make a plan for the amount of money you will set aside now and in the future.

Directions: In the spaces below, write when you will set aside money, how much you will set aside and how often, your goal amount, and the future purpose of the amount saved.

Date	Amount Set Aside/How Often/Goal	Future Purpose of Saved Amount
_____	$ _____ / _____ / _____	_____
_____	_____ / _____ / _____	_____
_____	_____ / _____ / _____	_____

---

will help you assess your tolerance for risk. If you find that you are risk averse, you should choose low-risk investments to avoid stress. If you determine that you are a risk taker, you can take maximum risks and enjoy the excitement of uncertainty. Most people fall somewhere in the middle and should try to balance their investments. After completing Worksheet 3, write a paragraph summarizing what you have learned about your risk tolerance.

WORKSHEET 3
Risk Aptitude Test

Directions: Answer the following questions, recording your answers in the spaces provided. Then compute your risk aptitude score as shown.

_____ 1. You have an extra $100 left over from your year-end bonus. Would you rather (a) put it all in savings, (b) spend some and save a little, (c) bet it on a lottery.

_____ 2. You are ready to buy a new car. Will it be a (a) small economy car, (b) conventional, standard car with a variety of options, (c) sports car emphasizing speed, style, or performance.

_____ 3. You have won a weekend trip of your choice. Will you (a) take cash instead, (b) go on a cruise or sightseeing trip, (c) fly to a mountain lodge for skiing.

_____ 4. You are considering a job offer. Which of these is most important to you? (a) job security (permanent employment), (b) higher salary with moderate security, (c) higher pay and less job security.

_____ 5. You are betting on a horse race. Which wager will you make? (a) bet on the favorite, even though winnings will be small, (b) select a horse with a good chance of winning and moderate payback if it does, (c) pick a long shot with high payback.

_____ 6. You have a mortgage on your home. Will you (a) make regular payments, paying off the loan on schedule, (b) repay the loan quicker than required so you can save interest, (c) refinance the loan and use the extra cash for other investments.

_____ 7. You are considering changing jobs. Which sounds best? (a) joining a well-established firm and doing similar work, (b) associating with a new company in a newly created position, (c) going into business for yourself.

_____ 8. You have a schedule conflict. The following three events are all scheduled for the same day and time. Which will you choose? (a) attending a seminar, (b) working on a committee, (c) giving a speech to a group of students.

_____ 9. Your dinner is "on the house." Which will you choose? (a) cold turkey sandwich and salad, (b) enchilada with hot peppers, (c) rare sirloin with fries.

_____ 10. You have a delayed flight, and your plane will be four hours late. Will you (a) read a book and wait, (b) take in a short sightseeing trip, (c) book another flight.

Scoring: Give yourself 1 point for each question you marked (a); 3 points for each (b); and 5 points for each (c). Scores 40 and above indicate willingness to take risk (you are a risk taker); scores between 25 and 40 indicate a willingness to take moderate risk; and scores below 25 show high risk aversion. A score of 30 is average.

Analyzing Your Score:

Based on your score, what are some investments that have the amount of risk you are willing to take? (See Chapter 11.)

INVESTMENT STRATEGY

An *investment strategy* is a plan that examines potential returns and rates investments according to desirability. To measure investment potential, two standards apply: the rate of inflation and the overall performance of the stock market. Inflation may be averaging 4 to 6 percent, and if your investment matches or exceeds that rate, you've done well. To estimate the return you're getting, follow the formula in Figure U3.3.

Suppose that four years ago you purchased ten shares of stock at $35 each. The stock is now trading at $38.50 per share. You have received dividends of $0.50 per share for four years. Computation of the average rate of return is shown in Figure U3.4.

If inflation averaged less than 3.9 percent during those four years, your investment was worthwhile. However, if the inflation rate was higher than your average return of 3.9 percent, you should sell that investment and buy something else.

Now you can use this same formula to evaluate and rank a group of investments. Complete Worksheet 4 (Investment Analysis) provided for you in the *Student Activity Guide* and also presented for reference on the next page.

FIGURE U3.3   *Average Rate of Return Formula*

Current market value of investment	$ _____	A
Less: Original price paid for investment	_____	B
Gain (loss) (A − B)	$ _____	C
Plus: Dividends, interest, and other revenue you've received from the investment	_____	D
Total gain (loss) (C + D)	$ _____	E
Average yearly gain (E ÷ years owned)	$ _____	F
Average rate of return (F ÷ B)	$ _____%	G

FIGURE U3.4   *Example Calculation of Average Rate of Return*

Current market value ($38.50 × 10 shares)...................	$ 385.00	A
Less: Original price ($35.00 × 10 shares).......................	−350.00	B
Gain...	$ 35.00	C
Plus: Dividends ($0.50 × 10 shares × 4 years)..............	20.00	D
Total gain..	$ 55.00	E
Average yearly gain ($55.00 ÷ 4 years).........................	$ 13.75	F
Average rate of return ($13.75 ÷ $350.00)...................	3.9%	G

YOUR INVESTMENT PLAN

A good investment plan is to begin slowly, choosing low-risk, predictable, and stable options. Then, as your comfort level increases and you have more money to risk, expand into moderate and high-risk ventures with greater potential profits (and losses). Complete Worksheet 5 (Investment Plan) provided for you in the *Student Activity Guide* and also presented for reference on the next page. You may wish to refer to Chapters 12–14 to examine your options as you plan for future investments.

YOUR RETIREMENT PLAN

The time to begin planning for retirement is now—at the beginning of your work career. Because people are living longer and healthier lives, it is important to consider those post-working years. With adequate financial resources, retirement can be fun, satisfying, and enjoyable.

The most difficult part of retirement planning is estimating your post-retirement income and needs. Generally, living expenses decrease following retirement. Bureau of Labor statistics show that retired couples are able to maintain a similar standard of living with about half the spendable income needed by the average family of four. Some financial advisers recommend that retiring individuals have 75 to 85 percent of their current income to maintain their preretirement lifestyle. The types of expenses will also change. Health care can become a major budget item, while house payments disappear as mortgages are paid off. Other expenses, such as utilities and property taxes, do not change significantly.

```
┌─────────────────────────────────────────────────────────────┐
│                        WORKSHEET 5                            │
│                       Investment Plan                         │
│                                                               │
│  Directions: Complete the following worksheet by listing your │
│  investment and how much you expect to invest, how long you   │
│  will keep the investment, and your potential return.         │
│                                                               │
│  Investment Choice   Initial Cost   Time Kept  Expected Profit│
│  Example:  Time CD      $1,000        1 year        $80        │
│                                                               │
│  Initial Investments                                          │
│                                                               │
│      1. _____│
│                                                               │
│      2. _____│
│                                                               │
│      3. _____│
│                                                               │
│  Systematic Investments                                       │
│                                                               │
│      1. _____│
│                                                               │
│      2. _____│
│                                                               │
│      3. _____│
│                                                               │
│  Speculative Investments                                      │
│                                                               │
│      1. _____│
│                                                               │
│      2. _____│
│                                                               │
│      3. _____│
└─────────────────────────────────────────────────────────────┘
```

Between today and the day you retire, inflation will likely continue to be an issue. However, your investments and savings should grow at a slightly faster pace. Therefore, when planning for retirement needs, prepare a budget based on today's dollars. Complete Worksheet 6 (Retirement Plan) provided for you in the *Student Activity Guide* and also presented for reference on the next page.

Completing the retirement plan in Worksheet 6 should convince most people of the need for multiple sources of income. You cannot rely on Social Security benefits alone. Keep in mind that some income sources will have a tax advantage and others will not. For example, when you make withdrawals from a traditional IRA or other tax-deferred account, such as a 401(k) or 403(b), you will pay income taxes on the withdrawn amounts as current income. When computing the future monthly income to be derived from such sources, be sure to subtract the taxes (25 percent, for example).

ESTATE PLANNING

You learned about many aspects of estate planning in Chapter 15, but there are additional matters to consider. If you become ill and incapacitated or die, your loved ones will have many decisions to make and expenses to pay on your behalf. These decisions and expenses fall into two categories: final directions and health care decisions.

FINAL DIRECTIONS

The costs involved when a person dies can range from a few hundred dollars to several thousand dollars. These expenses include final medical and hospital charges, the funeral and a casket (or other desired arrangements), and burial. By preparing instructions and making provisions for these costs in advance, you spare your loved ones the emotional decision-making process. Survivors who are grieving the loss of a loved one often are unprepared to make the many decisions involved in planning a funeral. At such an emotional time, a family may incur excessive expenses neither they nor the estate can afford.

Traditional funeral services may be performed in a church or in a funeral home. The cost can be $2,500 to $10,000 or more, which includes cremation and urn or a casket, embalming, preparations, music, printed remembrances, and newspaper notices. All decisions about these matters must be made in a relatively short period of time.

Cremation is an alternative to burial. It is less expensive than casket burial, but there are special requirements. When a body is not cremated within a certain time span, usually two days, it must be embalmed or otherwise prepared for burial. These costs must be paid, even though cremation is later chosen.

Many funeral homes have prearranged plans available at guaranteed costs. Money for the funeral is placed into an account that is insured by the FDIC or NCUA and earns interest. Although the money is for the funeral, it can be withdrawn in an emergency. Written instructions will save the family from overspending at the time of death, minimize emotional and financial distress, and assure the family that the type and cost of the funeral is as desired by the loved one.

A typical letter of final instruction is shown in Figure U3.5. It outlines a person's wishes and helps others to implement them. Prepare Worksheet 7 (Letter of Instruction) provided for you in the *Student Activity Guide*, or simply prepare a Letter of Instruction using a word processing program.

HEALTH CARE DECISIONS

One final detail remains to be handled—your wishes in the event you should be unable to make medical decisions on your own behalf. The *physicians' directive*, also known as a health care directive or living will, is a legal document

---

FIGURE U3.5   *Letter of Instruction*

Date: _____

To my family,

This is a list of my last wishes and arrangements I have made which I hope will make decisions easier for you.

1. I wish to be cremated. I have prearranged services at the Bennet Funeral Home. These arrangements include the details of announcements, selection of urn, etc. I have prepaid these services, and the receipt is attached to this document.

2. I do not wish to be an organ donor. Please do not sign forms to indicate otherwise.

3. My Last Will and Testament is in my safe-deposit box at First Independent Bank, Main Branch, this city. A copy is also in my attorney's office (Anderson & Anderson, this city).

4. I have the following accounts and policies which should be included in my estate:

   Checking Account ....First Independent Bank
   Savings Account ....First Independent Bank
   Life Insurance Policy ($100,000) ....New York Life
   Mortgage Insurance ....Veterans Services

5. My safe-deposit box contains deeds to property I own, past tax returns, and lists of credit and charge accounts I hold.

_____

J. B. Adams

that declares your intent in the event you are unable to tell doctors and other providers your wishes. It is binding upon doctors and must be presented at such time as it is needed. Thus, you would give the signed original document to your designated person. You should also keep copies at home and give them to doctors as well. Your designated person should be listed as your contact person on all medical forms.

Figure U3.6 is a sample physicians' directive. It can be typed or handwritten. Everyone should prepare this type of directive so that there is no question about his or her wishes should the unthinkable occur.

In addition, you may wish to sign a *health care power of attorney*. This document names a person to represent you in the event you cannot make your own medical decisions. Your representative must be willing to serve and also be willing to respect your wishes. Then, when you become incapacitated, your representative can step in and make decisions for you in the manner in which you discussed them beforehand. The health care power of attorney is non-specific in the decisions your representative will make. Unlike the physician's directive, it leaves some discretion to your representative.

FIGURE U3.6 *Physician's Directive*

PHYSICIAN'S DIRECTIVE

To My Physicians and Health Care Providers:

In the event that I become incapacitated and unable to make my own choices, I specifically make the following directive(s) regarding my health care (I have checked all that apply):

_____   If I am in a continuous state of nonresponsiveness for a period of a week or longer and two or more doctors have determined that I will not recover, then I wish to have all life support services removed within 24 hours of such determination.

_____   If I am in a continuous state of nonresponsiveness for a period of a week or longer and two or more doctors have determined that I will not recover, then I wish to have nutrition and comfort services only.

_____   If I am in a continuous state of nonresponsiveness for a period of a week or longer and two or more doctors have determined that I will not recover, then I wish to have all efforts continue to be made until one month or 30 days have passed. If I continue to show no signs of responsiveness, then I request that all life support be removed within 24 hours of such determination.

_____   I specifically request a do-not-resuscitate (DNR) order. Take no extraordinary measures to revive me through CPR should I suffer a condition that causes my heart and breathing to stop.

Date: _____   Signature: _____

4

Credit Management

Unit 4 begins with a general introduction to what credit is and why it is important to you as a consumer in the American economy. Credit has many advantages for those who use it wisely, but it can also be a trap.

In Chapter 17, you will learn about credit bureaus, ratings, and reports, and your rights and responsibilities as a credit user. You will also discover the many credit laws that have been enacted to protect consumers.

In Chapter 18, you will study the responsibilities associated with consumer credit along with the high costs of credit. You will also explore ways to minimize those costs and manage credit wisely.

Finally, in Chapter 19, you will learn about credit problems and ways to avoid them, both when getting started and as a final resort.

16

Credit in America

Consider **THIS**

It was two days before the spring festival, and Jasmine still hadn't purchased the supplies she needed in order to make her costume. She had been saving her money for four months and was still $50 short of her goal.

"I'll just have to borrow the rest," she told her friends. "Otherwise, I won't be able to get the costume completed and that means I'll have let down the team. I really wanted to pay cash and not go into debt, but in this case, it can't be helped. Credit is serious because it's money I'll have to pay back in the future. I probably should have used credit a little sooner. Now I'll have to work all night in order to get this costume completed. I learned an important lesson. There's a time and a place for using credit."

Credit: What and Why

GOALS
- Discuss the history of credit and the role of credit today.
- Explain the advantages and disadvantages of using credit.

TERMS
- credit, *p. 357*
- debtor, *p. 358*
- creditor, *p. 358*
- capital, *p. 358*
- collateral, *p. 359*
- finance charge, *p. 359*
- line of credit, *p. 359*
- deferred billing, *p. 360*

THE NEED FOR CREDIT

When you borrow money or use a charge account to pay for purchases, you are taking advantage of the most commonly used method of purchase in the United States: credit. Over 80 percent of all U.S. purchases are made with credit rather than cash. **Credit** is the use of someone else's money, borrowed now with the agreement to pay it back later.

The need for credit arose in the United States when the country grew from a bartering and trading society to a currency exchange economy. During the 1800s, the Industrial Revolution started a new economy. Items were manufactured in mass for sale to others. People no longer produced everything exclusively for their own use. With their earnings, they were able to buy the things they previously had to make for themselves. Soon the need developed for sources of credit to help families meet their financial needs. Consumer credit had begun.

EARLY FORMS OF CREDIT

One of the earliest forms of credit was the account at the general store. Wage earners or farmers would pick up supplies and put the amount due "on account." When the borrowers received a paycheck or sold a harvested crop, they would pay their account in full, and the charging process would begin again. The store rarely charged interest. Credit was a convenience that storeowners provided for customers they knew well and trusted. The customers paid off their accounts as soon as they could.

As the use of credit expanded, individual purchasing power also increased. Because credit increased people's ability to buy more goods and services, the American economy grew at a healthy pace. People bought luxuries as well as necessities with the help of credit, and the average American's standard of living rose. Both businesses and consumers benefited from credit.

Between 1920 and 1990, buying on credit became the American way of life. No longer was credit saved for emergencies. Many different forms of credit developed to meet changing consumer needs and wants.

In the 1990s, record numbers of people declared bankruptcy. Overuse of credit cards was one of the main reasons. With the economic prosperity of the decade,

How did the use of credit get started in this country?

people were optimistic and willing to spend their income well into the future. But this overspending brought enormous credit debt.

CREDIT TODAY

Credit today is a way of life. Merchants encourage consumers to use credit to buy all kinds of goods and services. Banks, stores, and credit card companies offer credit in the form of cards, loans, and lines of credit. Both short-term and long-term financing is available.

Some transactions are difficult to make without a credit card, such as reserving a hotel room, renting a car, or making an online purchase. It's no longer "How can I get credit?" but "How can I wisely manage credit?"

Millions of Americans are overextended with credit. They have adopted a lifestyle that is dependent on the use of credit to make ends meet. The average American has more than $5,000 in credit card debt.

Some people are living beyond their means and are abusing credit. They are barely able to make the minimum payment on outstanding debt and resort to tactics such as using one credit card to pay another credit card. This technique of "robbing Peter to pay Paul" results in ever-increasing credit card debt.

Many people have no savings, no emergency fund, and no way to support themselves if they should lose their job or experience a financial downturn. These people often turn to credit. For them, credit becomes a burden, an enemy, and something to avoid.

THE USE OF CREDIT

A **debtor** is a person who borrows money from others. This money, called *debt*, must be repaid. A **creditor** is a person or business that loans money to others. Creditors charge money for this service in the form of interest and fees. A debtor must be qualified to receive credit.

Qualifying for Credit

To qualify for credit, you must have the ability to repay the loan. Qualifications are based on three things: income, financial position, and collateral.

Income   You need to have a job and earn an income in order to make loan payments. Income can also come from other sources, such as interest, dividends, alimony, royalties, and so on. Income represents cash inflow. When your earnings exceed your expenses, you have the capacity to take on debt.

Financial Position   Your financial position is based on capital. **Capital** is the value of property you possess (such as bank accounts, investments, real estate, and other assets) after deducting your debts. Having capital tells the creditor that you have accumulated assets, which indicates responsibility. Your debt represents cash outflow and will be compared to your cash inflow (income).

Collateral   To borrow large amounts of money, creditors often want more than just your promise to repay; they want collateral. **Collateral** is property pledged to assure repayment of a loan. If you do not make your loan payments, the creditor can seize the pledged property. For example, when you buy a car on credit, the car serves as collateral. If you do not repay the loan, the car can be *repossessed*. The lending institution can take possession of the car and sell it to repay the loan.

Making Payments

Once you have completed a credit purchase, you owe money to the creditor. The *principal* (amount borrowed) plus interest for the time you have the loan is called the *balance due*. You generally will make monthly payments until you repay the balance due in full. The payments include both principal and interest, and with each payment, the amount you owe is reduced. The **finance charge** is the total dollar amount of all interest and fees you pay for the use of credit. It is the price you pay for the privilege of using someone else's money to buy goods and services now.

Credit card or store account statements usually specify a *minimum payment*. This is the least amount you may pay that month under your credit agreement, though you may pay more to further reduce your debt. All credit payments are due by a specific due date. Typically, you will be given 10 to 25 days from the date you receive a bill in which to pay. If you do not pay within the time allowed, you are likely to be charged a late fee, which is added to the balance due. In addition, your interest rate may go up as a result of late payments.

For particularly expensive purchases, you may have to sign a loan agreement. You agree to make regular payments for a set period of time. At the end of that time, you will have repaid the entire debt. This is a type of *secured loan*, because the goods you purchased with the loan serve as collateral for the money loaned.

ADVANTAGES AND DISADVANTAGES OF CREDIT

Some people use credit extensively while others pay cash as much as possible. Many people get into trouble each year by not using credit carefully. Credit can have several advantages, but you must not lose sight of its disadvantages.

ADVANTAGES OF CREDIT

Used correctly, credit can greatly expand your purchasing power and raise your standard of living. For example, credit allows you to purchase expensive items now that you do not currently have enough cash to buy, and then pay for them over time. As a result, you can enjoy items like furniture and a car earlier in your life. Making your payments on time helps you establish a good credit record that will help you get loans in the future.

Credit can also provide emergency funds. A sudden need for cash can be solved by a **line of credit**, which is a preestablished amount that can be borrowed on demand with no collateral. To establish a line of credit, you fill out the application with a lender. Lenders examine your income and financial position and approve an amount that they believe you can repay. With a line of credit, money is always available should you need it.

Traditionally, consumers in Thailand preferred to use cash when purchasing goods and services. This conservative attitude toward cashless transactions hindered consumer credit expansion. As of 2002, it was estimated that only 10 percent of the Thai population had a credit card. Major card issuers then began aggressive marketing campaigns and promotional offers to entice new customers. With extensive incentives for consumers and a low minimum income threshold for credit card eligibility, many card issuers witnessed considerable growth in their customer numbers. Today many consumers in Thailand rely on credit.

THINK *CRITICALLY*

What consumer benefits as well as problems might result from the boom in credit card use in Thailand? How can consumers avoid the disadvantages of credit as it grows in popularity?

Credit is convenient. Credit customers often get better service. If there is a problem with a purchase, cardholders can withhold payment until it is resolved. Regular charge customers of a department store, for example, receive advance notices of sales and special offers not available to the general public, such as deferred billing. **Deferred billing** is a service available to charge customers whereby purchases are not billed to the customer until much later than the standard billing time. For example, merchandise purchased in October might not be billed until January, with no payment due until February.

Consumers also have more leverage when using credit rather than cash or other methods of purchase. With credit, the money remains to be paid, giving the consumer more power in the event of a dispute. With a debit card, check, or cash, money has already been paid for the purchase, which may make it more difficult to settle a dispute and get a refund. Finally, carrying a credit card is safer than carrying large sums of cash.

DISADVANTAGES OF CREDIT

Use of credit also has disadvantages. For instance, credit purchases may cost more than cash purchases. Merchants must pay fees, which are usually a percentage of credit card sales, to credit card companies, and they often pass this cost on to customers in the form of higher prices. In addition, an item purchased on credit and paid for over time costs more because of the finance charges. A finance charge of 18 percent a year is 1½ percent a month. On a $1,000 balance, the finance charge would be $15 a month. The larger your balance and the longer you take to pay it off, the greater the finance charges.

When you use credit, you tie up future income. You have committed to making payments. During that time, those funds are not available to you for buying other products you may need. This situation can put a strain on your budget.

Buying on credit can lead to overspending. Because no cash leaves your bank account, you may not realize how much money you are really spending. You can get into trouble with credit if you buy more than you can pay back comfortably. At the end of the month, when the bills come in, you may be surprised at how much you have really spent. Using credit too much can result in debts so high that you can never pay them off, and it may even lead to bankruptcy.

Loan Processing

Marketing

Nearly 90 percent of all loan processors work in banks, savings banks, credit unions, and other financial institutions. For most people, taking out a loan is the only way they can pay for a house, a car, or a college education.

Businesses also depend on credit to start their companies, buy inventory, and expand. Loan processors guide their clients through the process of applying, qualifying, and executing loan documents. This process involves getting credit reports and verifying other information, such as employment history, capital, and collateral. Loan officers must also be sure that loan applicants are able to meet the requirements of the underwriter—the company that provides the loan funding.

Loan processors often specialize in consumer, commercial, or mortgage loans. They earn commissions based on the loans that are closed (completed).

Employment Outlook

- An average rate of employment growth is expected.

Job Titles

- Loan consultant
- Loan processor
- Loan collection officer
- Mortgage loan specialist

Needed Skills

- A bachelor's degree in finance, economics, or a related field is desirable.

- Training and licensing requirements vary by state.
- Good communication skills and high motivation are needed.

What's it like to work in... *Loan Processing*

Blake works as a consumer lending specialist for a credit union. He helps customers obtain loans for cars, boats, and major appliances. Blake works with customers to help them obtain the financing option that best meets their needs.

Each day, Blake keeps up with the latest financial market news. He knows when interest rates are rising or falling. He knows the best rates he can offer his customers and what it takes to qualify for them. When customers ask for his assistance, he must be able to give them good estimates of what a loan will cost them and how long it will take to process and close on the loan.

Blake's office is comfortable and complete with all he needs to facilitate the loan process, including a high-speed Internet connection.

What About You?

Would you like working with people of various backgrounds to help them obtain financing so that they can meet their goals? Do you like advising people to ensure they make knowledgeable decisions? Is a career as a loan processor right for you?

Assessment

KEY TERMS REVIEW

Match the terms with the definitions.

_____ 1. Property pledged to assure repayment of a loan

_____ 2. A service whereby purchases are not billed to the customer until much later

_____ 3. A person who borrows money

_____ 4. The value of property you possess

_____ 5. The total dollar amount of interest and fees you pay for the use of credit

_____ 6. A person or business that loans money to others

_____ 7. The use of someone else's money, borrowed now with the agreement to pay it back later

_____ 8. A preestablished amount that can be borrowed on demand with no collateral

a. capital

b. collateral

c. credit

d. creditor

e. debtor

f. deferred billing

g. finance charge

h. line of credit

CHECK YOUR UNDERSTANDING

9. Compare the use of credit today to its use in this country's early years.

10. Why is it important to make credit card payments on or before the due date?

APPLY YOUR KNOWLEDGE

11. Credit can be very beneficial or it can lead to financial ruin. Discuss the advantages of credit in terms of purchasing power. Discuss how credit can become a trap and lead to overspending and other problems.

THINK CRITICALLY

12. Individuals and families must make choices regarding credit—how much credit, when is it appropriate, and so on. How does your family make use of credit? Do you see credit use in your family as a good or bad thing? Explain your answer.

13. In the early part of our nation's history, we had no credit. People used coins or paper money to make purchases. Today, we are moving toward a paperless and cashless society. Would it be possible to live without ever using coins, paper money, or even checks? Explain how people might live on credit alone.

Types and Sources of Credit

TYPES OF CREDIT

You will likely use several forms of credit throughout your life. Different types of credit are designed to meet different consumer needs.

OPEN-END CREDIT

Credit card accounts are an open-end form of credit. **Open-end credit** is where a borrower can use credit up to a stated limit. As payments are made, the limit allows for more use of credit. The borrower usually has a choice of repaying the entire balance within 10 to 25 days or repaying it over time while making at least minimum payments. Open-end credit can be used again and again, as long as the balance owed does not exceed the credit limit.

Charge Cards

In a *charge card* agreement, a consumer promises to pay the full balance owed each month. Travel and entertainment cards, such as American Express and Diner's Club, are examples of charge cards. On all charges, the balance must be paid in full when the bill is received. A 25-day billing period is common. These cards are widely accepted nationwide and overseas, usually have high or no credit limits, and provide instant purchasing power.

© Banana Stock/Jupiter Images

Why would anyone want to use a charge card if the balance has to be paid in full when billed?

Charge cards often include rewards or rebates based on purchases. These rewards can be a percentage of dollar purchases or gift items of value. You benefit in two ways—you do not incur interest charges, and you receive a payback (such as a reward or rebate) based on card usage.

Revolving Accounts

With a *revolving account*, the consumer has the option each month of paying in full or making payments at least as high as the stated minimum. The minimum payment is based on the amount of balance due. Most all-purpose credit cards, such as Visa, MasterCard, and Discover, as well as store accounts, are revolving credit agreements. Retail store cards, such as department store and gasoline company cards, are also based on revolving credit. Many of these credit cards also offer rewards or rebate programs. Figure 16.1 shows a credit card statement for a revolving credit account.

Credit Card Agreements

Credit card companies keep a record of transactions made on your account and send you a bill at the end of each billing period. If you pay off the total each month, you probably can avoid a finance charge. But remember—a credit card is a form of borrowing and usually involves interest and other charges. Before selecting a credit card, be sure to compare the following terms that will affect the overall cost of the credit you will be using.

- *Annual Percentage Rate.* The **annual percentage rate (APR)** is the cost of credit expressed as a yearly percentage. The Truth-in-Lending law requires lenders to include all loan costs in the APR. The APR must be disclosed to you when you open the account and must be noted on each monthly bill you receive. Usually the APR is a variable rate, and it can be very high on credit cards.
- *Grace Period.* The **grace period** is a timeframe within which you may pay your current balance in full and incur no interest charges. The grace period may be from 10 to 25 days, and to qualify, you must have had no balance carried forward from the previous period. If there is no grace period specified, the card issuer will impose an interest charge from the date you use your credit card.
- *Annual Fees.* Many credit card issuers charge an annual fee. The fee can range from $15 to $35 or more, and you must pay it whether or not you use the card.
- *Transaction Fees.* If you use a credit card check, pay by phone, or request a balance transfer, you may be charged a transaction fee. These fees may run from 3 to 10 percent of the transaction amount.
- *Penalty Fees.* If you go over your credit limit or make your payment late, you are likely to be charged a flat penalty fee, such as $30 to $50.
- *Method of Calculating the Finance Charge.* If you pay for purchases over time, it is important to know how the card issuer will calculate your finance charge. The method used can make a difference, sometimes a big difference, in how much finance charge you will pay. Examples of these methods will be shown in Chapter 18.

FIGURE 16.1 *Credit Card Statement*

McAdams

Account Number	Payment Due Date	New Balance	Minimum Payment Due	Indicate Amount Paid
779 19 9171	05/24/--	$244.61	$20.00	

70

0 7 7 3 4 2 7 0 4 2 0 0 0 0 2 4 4 6 1 0 0 0 0 2 0 0 0 4

ADDRESS CHANGE

ll·l·l·l·ll·l·l·l·l·ll·lll····ll·ll·ll·l···ll·ll···ll·ll

_____ ADDRESS

ELIZABETH SANCHEZ
3410 MAIN STREET
VANCOUVER WA 98684-0129

_____ CITY/STATE/ZIP

(AREA CODE) PHONE   5008440

Please return this portion
with your payment. Detach here ▼

- -

Account Number	779 19 9171	To avoid additional **FINANCE CHARGES** being applied to your current purchases on next month's statement, pay the new balance on this statement in full by the due date.	Page [1] of [1]

Date	Store	Reference	Description	Charges	Payments Or Credits
3/28	021	108475936	SPECIAL CARE TREATMENT COSMETICS	60.00	
4/07	021	108476335	COSMETICS CLEANSERS, TONERS, MOISTURIZERS	80.00	
4/12	311	071070078	PAYMENT-THANK YOU		189.16
4/24	097		FINANCE CHARGE	4.61	

ANNIVERSARY TO DATE PURCHASES $1,853.39
ANNIVERSARY TO DATE DIVIDEND $5.96
YOU WILL EARN A 1% DIVIDEND ON MCADAMS PURCHASES
MADE PRIOR TO YOUR NEXT BILLING.
DIVIDEND WILL BE CREDITED ON YOUR JUNE 19-- STATEMENT.

Previous Balance	+ New Charges	− Payments Or Credits	Average Daily Balance (For Finance Charge Only)	+ FINANCE CHARGE (50¢ Minimum)	+ Late Payment Fee	= New Balance
289.16	140.00	189.16	307.19	4.61		244.61

Billing Date This Month	Payment Due Date	PERIODIC RATE	ANNUAL PERCENTAGE RATE	Credit Line	Amount Past Due	Minimum Payment Due
04/24/--	05/24/--	1.50	18.00	2,000		20.00

McAdams

Payments or credits received after payment due date will appear on next month's statement. For customer service inquiries, please call 1-800-555-6200. **AMOUNTS DUE HEREUNDER MAY BE ASSIGNED.** **NOTICE: SEE REVERSE SIDE FOR IMPORTANT INFORMATION.**

▌CLOSED-END CREDIT

To pay for very expensive items, such as cars, furniture, or major appliances, consumers often use closed-end credit. **Closed-end credit** is a loan for a specific amount that must be repaid in full, including all finance charges, by a stated due date. Often called *installment credit*, closed-end agreements do not allow continuous borrowing or varying payment amounts. The borrower takes out a closed-end loan for a particular amount and then repays it with fixed payments, or installments, that include principal and interest.

The contract for closed-end credit tells, among other things, the amount loaned, the total finance charge, and the amount of each payment. Sometimes a down payment is required. The product purchased with the loan becomes collateral to assure repayment.

▌ SERVICE CREDIT

Almost everyone uses some type of service credit. **Service credit** involves providing a service for which you will pay later. Your telephone and utility services are provided for a month in advance; then you are billed. Many businesses—including doctors, lawyers, hospitals, dry cleaners, and repair shops—extend service credit. Terms are set by individual businesses. Some of these creditors do not impose finance charges on unpaid account balances, but they do expect regular payments to be made until the bill is paid in full. Others, such as utility and telephone companies, expect payment in full by a specified due date. However, they usually offer a budget plan as well, which allows you to average bills to get lower monthly payments.

SOURCES OF CREDIT

The extension of credit is a service to consumers. It is not free—consumers must pay for it, the same as they would pay for any other purchased service. As with other things you buy, it pays to shop around to get the best deal.

▌ RETAIL STORES

Retail stores sell goods directly to consumers. Examples include department stores, discount stores, and specialty stores. Many retail stores offer their own credit cards. These cards are accepted only at the issuing store. Store credit customers often receive discounts, advance notice of sales, and other privileges not offered to cash customers or to customers using bank credit cards.

Most retail stores also accept credit cards issued by major credit card companies. Accepting credit cards helps retail stores attract customers, because people like to shop where they can buy on credit.

▌ CREDIT CARD COMPANIES

You may receive credit offers directly from credit card issuers, such as Visa, MasterCard, American Express, and Discover. These all-purpose cards are generally accepted nationwide and even internationally. You can also get an all-purpose credit card through your financial institution or other organizations.

Affinity cards are credit cards sponsored by professional organizations, college alumni associations, and some members of the travel industry. Although these cards may show the name of the organization, they are actually issued and serviced by a credit card company. The affinity card issuer usually donates a portion of the fees and/or a percentage of the purchases made with the card to the sponsoring organization.

With an all-purpose credit card, you have an automatic line of credit up to the limit of the card. Some cards even allow you to take a *cash advance*, which is money borrowed against your line of credit. You can access this money at a teller machine, at a customer service desk in your bank, or by writing an access check against the credit card account. *Access checks*, which are supplied by the credit card company, look just like regular checks and are treated by the credit card company as a purchase. You must pay back the cash advance in the same way that you pay for credit card purchases. There is often a transaction fee for this service in addition to interest charges, which may or may not be the same rate as purchases made with the card.

Some companies (like American Express) offer both charge cards, where the balance must be paid in full each month, and credit cards, where you are required to pay only a portion of the balance each month. It's important to read the terms carefully, so you are sure which type of account you are getting.

BANKS AND CREDIT UNIONS

In addition to offering credit cards, commercial banks and credit unions make closed-end loans to individuals and companies. They loan money to consumers for specific purchases, such as a home, car, or vacation. Interest on closed-end loans tends to be lower than on credit cards, usually because there is collateral used as security on the loans.

Credit unions make loans to their members only. Interest rates are sometimes lower than those charged by banks because credit unions are nonprofit and are organized for the benefit of members. Credit unions may be more willing to make loans because the members who are borrowing also have a stake in the success of the credit union.

© Photodisc/Getty/Images

What types of credit do banks and credit unions offer?

FINANCE COMPANIES

A **finance company** is an organization that makes high-risk consumer loans. In many cases, people who are turned down by banks and credit unions can get loans at finance companies. These high-risk loans are usually accompanied by high interest rates. Finance companies are second only to banks in the volume of credit extended.

There are two types of finance companies:

- Consumer finance companies
- Sales finance companies

A *consumer finance company* makes most of its loans to consumers who are buying durable goods. *Durable goods* are items expected to last several years, such as automobiles, appliances, and electronics. Well-known consumer finance companies include HSBC.

A *sales finance company* makes loans to consumers through authorized representatives, such as car dealerships. For example, GMAC Financial Services finances General Motors automobile dealers and their customers. Both types of finance companies borrow money from banks and lend it to consumers at higher rates.

Finance companies take more risks than banks. Therefore, they must be more careful to protect their loans. If you do not make your payments when due, you can expect a call from someone at the finance company who will ask for an explanation. The company will stay in constant contact with you until you make your payments as agreed. You can expect phone calls, letters, and even personal visits if you deviate even slightly from the agreed-upon payment schedule.

High interest rates are another form of protection for finance companies. The high income from interest makes up for the percentage of loans that become uncollectible.

The growth of finance companies is partially the result of efforts to eliminate **loan sharks**, which are unlicensed lenders who charge illegally high interest rates. Nevertheless, it is difficult to eliminate such practices, which take advantage of the poorest members of society—those who can least afford to pay.

A **usury law** is a state law that sets a maximum interest rate that may be charged for consumer loans. In states where usury laws exist, finance companies charge the maximum rate allowed. Where no usury laws exist, finance companies charge as much as the customer is willing to pay. When an emergency or other extreme need arises, consumers feel forced to pay these higher rates to get the money they need.

▌ PAWNBROKERS

A **pawnbroker (or pawnshop)** is a legal business that makes high-interest loans based on the value of personal possessions pledged as collateral. Possessions that are readily salable (such as guns, cameras, jewelry, radios, TVs, and collector's coins) are usually acceptable collateral. The customer brings in an item of value to be appraised. The pawnbroker then makes a loan for considerably less than the appraised value of the item. Some pawnshops give only 10 to 25 percent of the value of the article. Most give no more than 50 or 60 percent.

For example, if you have a ring appraised at $500, you could probably borrow between $50 and $300 with the ring as collateral. You would turn the ring over to the pawnbroker and receive a receipt and

© Digital Vision/Getty Images

What do pawnbrokers usually accept as collateral? Why?

a certain length of time—from two weeks to six months—to redeem the ring by paying back the loan plus interest. If you do not pay back the loan and claim the ring, the pawnbroker will sell it in the pawnshop and keep the proceeds. Property acquired by a pawnbroker is considered collateral for the loan because it is something of value that may be sold if you fail to pay off the loan.

PRIVATE LENDERS

One of the most common sources of cash loans is the private lender. Private lenders might include parents, other relatives, friends, and so on. Private lenders may or may not charge interest or require collateral. Those who loan money to friends and relatives should take special steps to be sure their interests are protected. For example, rather than loaning cash to someone based on oral promises, they should get the agreement in writing with a formally signed note or other document that will serve as evidence of the debt.

OTHER SOURCES OF CREDIT

Other sources of credit include the following:

- Life insurance policies
- Borrowing against a deposit
- Borrowing against an asset

Life insurance policies that build cash value can be used to borrow money. The loan does not have to be repaid, but interest will be charged. The loan amount will reduce the value of the policy. You will learn more about life insurance policies in Chapter 27.

If you have a certificate of deposit (CD) or retirement account with a financial institution, you might be able to borrow money against it. A loan against this type of account usually has a good interest rate because of the collateral providing safety. In addition, borrowing an amount against such a deposit allows you to avoid the penalties for early withdrawal. However, you should consider the drawbacks to this type of loan. If you do not repay the loan, the bank or other lender can collect the account balance. Also, you are slowing down the growth of your savings plan by withdrawing money from it. Thus, this type of loan should be considered a last resort.

You may also borrow against an asset, such as your car. If you own a vehicle free and clear (no loan against it), you can take the title to your credit union or bank and ask for a loan. They will use the car title as collateral for the loan. Usually the car must be fairly new—five years old or less—for this type of loan.

NET Bookmark

A payday loan is a small, short-term loan that is intended to cover a borrower's expenses until his or her next payday. Typical loans are between $100 and $500 and are due in two weeks, with interest rates of up to 400% APR. On a two-week loan, fees average $15 for each $100 lent. In 2008, the state of Ohio passed a law to more closely regulate payday lending. Access www.cengage.com/school/pfinance/mypf and click on the link for Chapter 16. Read the article and then answer the following questions: What did the Ohio law do? Why did the Ohio legislators think the law was needed? What does the payday lending industry say in response? What is your opinion about the Ohio law?

www.cengage.com/school/pfinance/mypf

ISSUES IN YOUR WORLD

CREDIT CARD TRAPS

Credit offers may sound good, but you must read the fine print carefully. There are many traps to avoid. What may appear to be a great deal can be a very expensive lesson that hurts your credit rating. Watch for the following signs that the credit offer is not as good as it sounds:

Low Introductory Rate. Interest rate offers may be as low as 0 percent for six months. The fine print may tell you that if you are late by even one day in making a payment, the rate will rise to 25 to 30 percent or more! This introductory rate may be subject to change without notice.

Fixed Percentage Rate. The offer may say the interest rate is fixed, which should mean that it will not go up. But the fine print may tell you that the fixed rate is subject to change without notice and that it can be "adjusted" (raised) at the option of the creditor.

Closed Account Rate. You may see fine print that says "closed account rate." This is the rate you will be assessed if you close your account. These rates are often very high—25 to 30 percent or more! This tactic is used by credit card issuers to keep you from closing your account when they raise your interest rate. Without this clause, consumers could reject a change in terms regarding interest rates, close the account, and continue making payments based on the original agreement until the balance is paid off. But if the agreement specifies a closed account rate, you won't be able to "lock in" the lower rate you had previously agreed to pay.

Late Fees. Most credit card issuers charge late fees if you do not pay your account within the time specified. Often this timeframe is only 10 to 25 days. These late fees are bad enough, but you may also discover that if your account is "late," the issuer will also raise your interest rate. On credit reports, your late payment(s) can make you appear to be a high risk, so other creditors may also raise your interest rates.

Over-the-Limit Fees. Card issuers will charge you a fee for exceeding your credit limit. This fee is added to your balance, and it will take even more money to pay the account down (remember, interest charges are increasing your balance daily). Fine print may tell you that if you go over the limit, your interest rate will increase.

Transaction Fees. Some credit card companies allow you to transfer balances from other credit cards. They may also provide you with access checks where you can borrow money without preapproval. There may be very high transaction fees for these types of borrowing, such as 3 to 10 percent of the transaction amount, in addition to flat fees, such as $30.

To avoid being taken advantage of, read the credit offers carefully and compare them to offers by known lenders, such as your credit union or bank. Ask questions and be sure you understand the terms and conditions.

THINK *CRITICALLY*

1. *Look for a credit card offer in your mail. Then read the fine print. Make a list of all the potential "traps" you find.*
2. *Discuss credit offers with parents and other adults and ask about their experience with credit offers. Write a paragraph about what you learn.*

Assessment

KEY TERMS REVIEW

Match the terms with the definitions. Some terms may not be used.

_____ 1. The providing of a service for which you will pay later

_____ 2. A timeframe within which you may pay your balance in full and incur no interest charges

_____ 3. A legal business that makes high-interest loans based on the value of personal possessions pledged as collateral

_____ 4. State law that sets a maximum interest rate that may be charged for consumer loans

_____ 5. An organization that makes high-risk consumer loans

_____ 6. The cost of credit expressed as a yearly percentage

a. annual percentage rate (APR)

b. closed-end credit

c. finance company

d. grace period

e. loan sharks

f. open-end credit

g. pawnbroker

h. service credit

i. usury law

CHECK YOUR UNDERSTANDING

7. What is a revolving credit agreement?

8. Why might it be better to get a bank loan rather than a loan from a finance company?

APPLY YOUR KNOWLEDGE

9. How is open-end credit different from closed-end credit? What are the advantages and disadvantages of each? Which of these is most likely to have a lower annual percentage rate? Why?

THINK CRITICALLY

10. Do you think it is unfair that some consumers get "free credit" by taking advantage of the grace period on credit cards? Give reasons for your answer.

11. One major advantage of credit is that it helps consumers deal with emergencies. How does this advantage have special meaning where service credit is concerned?

12. If you were going into business for yourself, you would have to decide whether or not to accept credit cards from customers. Explain the points in favor of both positions.

Chapter Assessment

SUMMARY

16.1

- Credit began as the United States grew from a bartering society to a currency exchange economy with mass-manufactured products available to consumers. Today, credit has become a way of life.

- The person who borrows money is called the debtor; the person or business that loans money is called the creditor.

- To qualify for credit, your ability to repay will be assessed based on your income, financial position, and collateral.

- For the privilege of using credit, you will pay a finance charge, which includes interest and fees.

- A line of credit can be preestablished to provide for emergency funds.

- Advantages of credit are the ability to buy now and pay later, a source of emergency funds, deferred billing, and the safety of not having to carry a lot of cash.

- Disadvantages of credit are higher product prices, finance charges, decreased ability to spend in the future, and the tendency to overspend.

16.2

- Open-end credit allows you to borrow again and again, up to a set limit.

- The annual percentage rate is the cost of credit expressed as a yearly percentage.

- With a grace period, you can avoid interest charges so long as you pay your balance in full every month by the due date.

- Closed-end credit is a one-time loan for a specific amount that must be repaid in full by a specified due date. Lenders generally require payment in monthly installments.

- Many service providers, such as your utility company, provide service credit, allowing you to pay for services a month or more after their use.

- Sources of credit include retail stores, credit card companies, banks, credit unions, finance companies, pawnbrokers, private lenders, and life insurance policies.

- Loan sharks are unlicensed lenders who charge illegally high rates and prey on people who can least afford to pay.

- Usury laws in some states protect consumers from unfairly high interest rates.

APPLY WHAT YOU KNOW

1. Give an example of a situation in which you would use collateral when making a purchase on credit. What would be the advantage to using collateral with a closed-end loan over making the purchase with your credit card?

2. Companies and organizations that offer credit cards compete for your credit card business by offering low introductory rates. Search the Internet for offers of a special deal. What is the "low introductory rate"? Read the fine print. What will the rate be after the introductory period? At the regular rate, how much finance charge would you have to pay on a $1,000 balance each month? How does this compare to the introductory rate?

3. How are consumer finance companies different from sales finance companies? Why do finance companies charge high interest rates?

4. Why might credit unions offer lower interest rates on loans than do commercial banks or credit card companies?

5. Does your state have a usury law? You can find out by consulting your state's web site, a current almanac, or other library resources. Identify the maximum finance rate that your state allows. Then identify the maximum rates allowed by neighboring states.

6. What is the purpose of a pawnshop? What kind of merchandise can you find at a pawnshop?

MAKE ACADEMIC CONNECTIONS

7. **Communication** Write a one-page paper about credit—the good and the bad of how it has affected you, what it means to your family, and what it means to retailers and other businesses. Explain in a neutral tone how credit is both positive and negative for the economy as a whole.

8. **Research/History** Do library and/or Internet research about the Industrial Revolution in this country and how it changed the lives of Americans. How did people adapt? Specifically, explain how people changed their buying and spending habits.

9. **Economics** When citizens in an economy save money, their deposits provide money that can be loaned to others. This increases the supply of money and lowers its cost to borrowers. Research the economic concepts of average propensity to save (APS) and marginal propensity to save (MPS). Explain what these concepts are, how they are computed, and why they are important to the economy as a whole.

10. **International Studies** Choose another nation in the world and research the use of credit in that country. Compare it to the United States. How different is the standard of living enjoyed by its citizens? Prepare a one-page report of your findings.

SOLVE PROBLEMS AND

EXPLORE ISSUES

11. Suppose that your elderly neighbors have never used credit. When they were young, their families lost their life savings during bad economic times. As a result, they don't have much trust in financial institutions and prefer to use only cash. What types of problems can result from not using credit? What would be your advice to them, knowing that they have a good income and have no need to buy on credit?

12. Interview three or four adults about credit. Ask them the following questions: (a) How do you feel about the use of credit? (b) Do you think interest rates charged on credit cards and accounts are reasonable? (c) Do you prefer to make purchases using credit or cash? Why? Prepare a short report from what you learn.

13. Find three credit card offers. You can find them in junk mail, e-mails (spam), bill enclosures, advertisements, credit card web sites, and even kiosks found in shopping areas. Analyze and compare the provisions of the offers, such as the introductory rates, regular rates (variable or fixed), grace periods, annual fees, and so on. Prepare a report of your findings.

14. Do you feel that the advantages of using credit outweigh the disadvantages? How would you advise a young person just starting out about credit? Write a paper giving reasons for your opinions.

15. A friend of yours wishes to buy a new car but has only enough money to make a down payment. She asks your advice about where she can finance the balance of her loan for $10,000. What will you tell her? Explain.

16. Your cousin Tyler needs $100 immediately. He has a portable stereo worth at least $800 and wants to take it to a pawnbroker. Explain to him how much he might be able to borrow against the stereo and what can happen when using pawnbroker credit.

EXTEND YOUR LEARNING

17. **Ethics** The wide use of credit can lead to abuses. Some people take out more credit than they can repay. Then they refuse to pay back what they have borrowed. When merchants get stuck with unpaid balances, they pass along that cost to other customers in the form of higher prices. Thus we all pay for people who overuse credit. Is it ethical for people to overextend their credit, knowing or suspecting that they will not be able to repay it? What can we all do to keep the cost of products and services at reasonable levels?

For related activities and links, go to **www.cengage.com/school/pfinance/mypf**

17

Credit Records and Laws

| 17.1 | *Establishing Good Credit* |

| 17.2 | *Evaluating Credit and Laws* |

Consider **THIS**

Renae is a full-time student and works part time on weekends and during the summer. She has been able to save a little money. She has just turned 16 and is learning to drive.

"I'd like to buy my own car," she told her friend Bradley. "That way I can drive myself to work. If I had my own car, I could work after school, too, and I'd have a way to get to more school activities. As it is, I depend on my mom to take me everywhere. She works, so she isn't always available to take me places. To get a car, I'll have to get a loan. My mom says I'll establish credit by getting a loan, but because I don't have any credit already, she'll probably have to cosign for me to get my first car loan."

Establishing Good Credit

CREDIT RECORDS

Before granting you credit, a creditor will check into your past credit performance: Did you pay your bills on time? How much total credit did you receive? How much do you owe now and how large are your payments? Your **credit history** is the complete record of your borrowing and repayment performance. This record will provide answers to these questions and thus help the creditor determine your ability to pay new debts.

YOUR CREDIT FILE

Every person who uses credit has a credit history on file at a credit bureau. A **credit bureau** is a business that gathers, stores, and sells credit information to other businesses. Maintaining credit files is big business. Credit bureaus assemble and distribute detailed credit information concerning an estimated 150 million consumers.

When you open a new credit account, a person at the business submits information from your application to the credit bureau. Each time you use credit or make a payment, the business records the transaction. About once a month, the business electronically transmits the data about your borrowing and repayments to one or more of the three big national credit bureaus listed below.

- TransUnion, www.transunion.com
- Experian, www.experian.com
- Equifax, www.equifax.com

The credit bureau enters the information into your file and stores it under your Social Security number for identification. Local and regional credit bureaus hook into the Big Three's computer networks, making everybody's files widely accessible.

Credit bureaus issue credit reports about consumers. A **credit report** is a written statement of a consumer's credit history, issued by a credit bureau to businesses. You can order a copy of your credit report online at the credit bureau's web site or by writing to the bureau. You can check your local telephone book for the names and addresses of credit bureaus in your area that can also provide a credit report about you. Ordinarily, a credit bureau will charge $15 or more to give you your credit file information. When you are denied credit, you can get a free credit report if you ask within 30 days of being denied. In addition, there are other services available related to your credit files, including credit guard services and credit freezing services.

Credit Guard

Credit guard services are available to consumers who wish to hire a company to monitor their credit files at the three credit bureaus. With this type of service, you receive an annual copy of each credit report. You are notified whenever anyone accesses your credit file for any reason. The fee charged for this service ranges from $15 a month to $50 a month, depending on the degree of

What kind of information is stored in your credit file?

"protection" provided. For example, you can supply a list of your credit cards, and if one or more is lost or stolen, the service will have it canceled and notify the credit bureaus on your behalf.

Some credit card companies offer this service to their customers. Independent credit guard companies also provide this service. As a consumer, you should recognize that you can do anything that these companies can do; you are paying for the convenience of having someone else do it for you.

Credit Freeze

Many states have passed laws allowing consumers to "freeze" their credit reports and files. A *credit freeze* is a consumer request that requires the credit bureaus to deny all access to a consumer's credit information or files. Thus, new credit applications are blocked and loan solicitation information cannot be given out by the credit bureau. Consumers that choose a credit freeze can unfreeze their credit files when they wish to obtain new credit, and then refreeze them when they are ready. Credit bureaus can charge a reasonable fee (such as $15) for each of these activities.

Credit freezes have come about as a result of credit fraud and identity theft. When another person opens credit in your name or uses your credit without your permission, this can cause a significant drop in your creditworthiness. Most experts agree that credit freezes are an important protection tool for consumers.

■ HOW INFORMATION IS GATHERED AND USED

Credit bureaus gather information from businesses, called **subscribers**, that pay a monthly fee to the credit bureau for access to this information. Each subscriber supplies information about its accounts with customers—names, addresses, credit balances, on-time payment record, and so forth. Credit bureaus also gather information from many other sources. Public records are searched for information to add to a file. When someone applies to a business for credit, the business (subscriber) asks the credit bureau for the applicant's credit report. Information in the credit report is then used as the basis for granting or denying credit. Usually credit grantors (banks and retail businesses), employers, landlords, and insurance companies have an interest in credit reports. Before entering into a financial agreement with someone, they want evidence that the person is financially responsible.

■ TYPES OF INFORMATION STORED

Any public information becomes part of your credit record. For example, if you fail to pay your property taxes, file for bankruptcy, file for a divorce, or apply for a marriage license, this information will appear in your credit record. Birth announcements published in newspapers, job promotions, lawsuits, and other visible activities are recorded. When you fill out a credit application, information requested such as occupation, length of employment, spouse's name and occupation, residence, length of occupancy, number of children and other dependents, and other related data is sent to the credit bureau by the subscriber.

CREDITWORTHINESS

Before potential creditors will grant credit to you, they must determine whether you are a good risk—that you are **creditworthy**. A person who is considered creditworthy usually meets five basic qualifications, called the five Cs of credit: character, capacity, capital, conditions, and collateral.

■ CHARACTER: WILL YOU REPAY THE DEBT?

Character is a responsible attitude toward honoring obligations, often judged on evidence in the person's credit history. If you have character, you pay your bills on time, and your credit history will show it. Creditors often use stability as a measure of character as well. For example, a person who has moved six times during the past year might not be considered a good credit risk.

■ CAPACITY: CAN YOU REPAY THE DEBT?

The financial ability to repay a loan with present income is known as **capacity**. Before lending you money, creditors want to make certain that your income is sufficient to cover your current expenses each month plus the payments on the new loan.

■ CAPITAL: DO YOU HAVE SUFFICIENT ASSETS TO SUPPORT THE DEBT?

Capital refers to financial assets (bank accounts, investments, and property) you possess that are worth more than your debts. In other words, when you add up all that you own (assets) and subtract all that you owe (liabilities), the difference (net worth or capital) should be sufficient to ensure payment of your debt.

CONDITIONS: WHAT AFFECTS YOUR ABILITY TO REPAY THE DEBT?

There may be "external" conditions that affect your ability to repay a debt. For example, if the economy is slowing and many people in your geographic area are losing their jobs, creditors may be less willing to loan to you. If you lose your job, you may not be able to meet your payments. Therefore, creditors want to know the following: How secure is your job? How secure is the firm for which you work? How is the employment situation in your geographic location and in your occupation?

COLLATERAL: WHAT ASSETS ARE PLEDGED TO SUPPORT THE DEBT?

Collateral is property pledged to assure repayment of a loan, such as the house, car, or furniture being purchased. Collateral protects creditors, making them more willing to lend to you. If you do not repay your debt as agreed, they can sell the collateral to collect on the debt.

GETTING STARTED WITH CREDIT

Establishing a good credit record is a slow process. It can take several years of responsible money management to prove your creditworthiness.

BEGIN WITH A SAVINGS ACCOUNT

Open a savings account. Start at a financial institution that will not charge you a monthly fee when your savings account balance is small. Credit unions and some banks allow minors to establish accounts with small balances and waive normal fees charged to other depositors. Also, choose a financial institution that has full services available as you prove yourself: checking accounts, loans, and credit cards. Each month or pay period, make a deposit to your savings account. Keep your account growing through regular saving.

OPEN A CHECKING ACCOUNT

As soon as you have enough money in your savings account to allow you a little "cushion," open a checking account. This will provide a convenient method of paying your bills when you have credit accounts and will serve as a record-keeping system for your budget. Choose the checking plan that is the least expensive and most convenient for you. Then carefully manage your

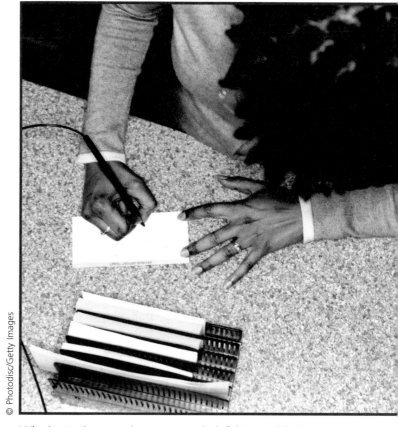

© Photodisc/Getty Images

Why is starting a savings account helpful in establishing your creditworthiness?

checking account. Do not write checks when your account contains insufficient funds to cover them. Bouncing checks will tarnish your creditworthiness. Record all your transactions immediately in your checkbook register and balance your checkbook as soon as you receive your statement. In this way, you will always know how much is in your account, so that you won't bounce a check accidentally.

OPEN A STORE CREDIT ACCOUNT

Your parent or guardian may need to serve as cosigner to help you open your first credit account. A **cosigner** is someone who promises to pay if the borrower fails to pay. Many stores will allow you to open a small account with a responsible adult as a cosigner. Make small purchases on your new account and pay the bills promptly, using your checking account. Be sure to make your monthly payments on or before the due date. If you mail your payment, allow sufficient time for your payment to arrive before the due date. Never pay late!

GET A SMALL LOAN

Take out a small loan from the credit union or other financial institution where you have your savings and checking accounts. Use the money to buy something you really need. Then pay back the loan as agreed. Make early payments if possible. A six-month loan is sufficient. Again, you may need to rely on your parents or another adult with a good credit record to cosign your first loan.

APPLY FOR A CREDIT CARD

With credit established for a couple of years, a part-time job, and a few credit references, you might now be eligible for a major credit card, such as a Visa or MasterCard. Check the application carefully and ask about the income requirements. If you do not make enough money to qualify for the card, do not apply until you do.

It's often easier and usually safer to apply for a card with your credit union or bank. Because you have a savings and checking account with them, they already know you. They may give you a smaller credit limit to get started, but they will raise that as you continue to manage your account wisely.

Banks and other financial institutions will have brochures explaining the terms and conditions of their credit cards. You will be less likely to be hit with high interest rates or fees than if you apply to a credit card company online or respond to an unsolicited credit card offer.

Once you have your first credit card and you make the payments without fail, you will find it easy to obtain additional credit. It's good to have credit available in case you need it, but don't take out too much credit. Two or three credit cards should be sufficient at any given time.

Issues in Your World

TEENAGE CREDIT

Many businesses are finding it financially rewarding to offer credit to teenagers. The logic is simple! Teenagers have a lot of money to spend, whether it is earned or supplied by parents. Because teenagers make many buying decisions, from clothing to automobiles, they are a market worth targeting.

Retail businesses that sell merchandise to teenagers are the first to admit that their teenage customers are important to them. By extending credit to teens, they are winning loyalty and at the same time helping teens get established with credit.

A typical teenage credit account might begin at age 16. The applicant (teenager) should have some steady source of income, whether it is from a part-time job or from parents. In most cases, the teenager needs parental permission. Permission is expressed in the form of a parent's signature as cosigner on the account. Otherwise, the teen would be turned down if he or she applied for credit alone. A parent's signature on the credit application allows the credit grantor to rely on the parent's credit rating at first. If the teenager fails to make the payments, the parent, as cosigner, is responsible for the amount owed.

Why would parents consider such a deal? Many parents want their teenagers to be able to do some shopping on their own, to learn responsibility, and to get their own credit record established.

Typically, teen credit accounts also have a low credit limit, or maximum amount that they can spend on credit. However, even a $300 credit limit would allow a teenager to charge purchases, pay them off responsibly, and build a good credit record. By keeping the credit limit low, merchants and parents are assured that young people just beginning to use credit won't get carried away and get into debt trouble.

THINK CRITICALLY

1. Do stores in your area extend credit to teenagers? If so, under what conditions?

2. Would you like to get established in credit early? How would you pay for the purchases you make?

3. Pick several stores where you would like to have a credit account. Why did you choose these stores?

Assessment

KEY TERMS REVIEW

Match the terms with the definitions. Some terms may not be used.

_____ 1. *Businesses that supply information to credit bureaus about their customers*

_____ 2. *Someone who promises to pay if the borrower fails to pay*

_____ 3. *Complete record of your borrowing and repayment performance*

_____ 4. *A business that gathers, stores, and sells credit information*

_____ 5. *A determination that you are a good credit risk*

_____ 6. *A written statement of a consumer's credit history*

_____ 7. *The financial ability to repay a loan from present income*

a. *capacity*

b. *character*

c. *cosigner*

d. *credit bureau*

e. *credit history*

f. *credit report*

g. *creditworthy*

h. *subscribers*

CHECK YOUR UNDERSTANDING

8. *How do credit bureaus gather information for your credit file?*

9. *What does "creditworthiness" mean?*

10. *Why is it important to make payments on time?*

APPLY YOUR KNOWLEDGE

11. *As a teenager, you would like to get started in establishing a good credit history. Based on your personal situation and the stores and banks in your area, prepare a plan that you might follow in getting started using credit.*

THINK *CRITICALLY*

12. *As a consumer, you have the right to see what is in your credit files at the three major credit bureaus. Why is it important for you to check the content of your credit files at least once a year?*

13. *Are credit guard companies a good deal for consumers? Why or why not?*

14. *Why would a person want to freeze his or her credit?*

Evaluating Credit and Laws

EVALUATING CREDIT

Credit bureaus evaluate each consumer based on his or her credit history, amount of credit, and ability to take on additional debt. There are two major classifications used to evaluate consumers—their credit rating and their credit score.

CREDIT RATING

Your **credit rating** is a measure of creditworthiness based on an analysis of your credit and financial history. This process rates consumers according to how reliably they pay back money borrowed or charged. Credit bureaus can analyze data and supply a rating, or they can supply credit files (names of customers, account balances, and payment records) to which subscribers can apply their own rating systems. Many large businesses prefer to prepare their own ratings. Consumers may earn ratings such as excellent, good, fair, or poor.

To earn an *excellent credit rating*, sometimes called an **A-rating**, a customer pays bills before the due dates. If a payment is due on the fifth of the month, it is received before the fifth. An A-rating also means that credit is well established (used successfully for many years), there are no missed payments, and debts are paid off early.

To earn a *good credit rating*, which is designated a **B-rating**, a customer pays

© Image Source/Jupiter Images

How can you earn an excellent (A-rating) credit rating?

bills on the due date or within a ten-day grace period. A payment due on the first of the month is received no later than the tenth of the month. (When a bill is paid within ten days of its due date, this is considered an *automatic grace period.*) A good customer pays around the due date, but never outside the grace period, and does not miss any payments.

A *fair credit rating* is earned by a customer who usually pays all bills within the grace period, but occasionally takes longer. Late charges are sometimes applied, but normally no reminder is needed. This person is often described as slow in paying but fairly dependable.

People with a *poor credit rating* are usually denied credit because their payments are not regular. They miss some monthly payments, and they must be reminded frequently. In many cases, they have failed entirely to pay back a debt, have filed for bankruptcy, or have otherwise shown that they are not a good credit risk.

▌CREDIT SCORE

Credit bureaus as well as some larger creditors have point systems on which credit ratings are based. In a **point system**, the credit bureau assigns points based on factors such as amount of current debt, number of late payments, number and types of open accounts, current employment, amount of income, and so on. When your points are added up, they result in a **credit score** that tells potential creditors the likelihood that you will repay debt as agreed. The higher your score, the greater the chance you will be a good credit risk. Business subscribers then use these scores as part of their decision to grant or deny credit. Your score is based on data provided to credit bureaus. If the data is wrong, so is your score.

Your FICO Score

FICO (Fair Isaac and Company) scores are the credit scores most lenders use to determine credit risk. Each person has three FICO scores, one for each of the three credit bureaus. As information changes, your scores change as well. FICO scores affect loan terms, such as interest rate, that you will be offered.

To calculate a FICO score, you must have at least one account open for at least six months. Your FICO scores may be different at each of the credit bureaus because of varying information collected and slight differences in the way the rating system is applied.

FICO scores are calculated based on five categories: payment history (35%), amounts owed (30%), length of credit history (15%), new credit (10%), and types of credit used (10%).

1. *Payment history* is rated based on how you pay your debts; the presence of bankruptcy, liens, or collections; and whether accounts are past due or paid as agreed.
2. *Amounts owed* is rated based on the amounts owed on accounts, amounts owed on specific types of accounts, lack of balances, and proportion of credit line used.
3. *Length of credit history* is rated based on the oldest account opened and the average age of all accounts. Accounts that have been open for a long period of time reflect positively on your score.

4. *New credit* is rated based on the number of recently opened accounts and the number of recent credit inquiries.
5. *Types of credit used* is rated based on the mix of credit accounts, such as credit cards, retail accounts, installment loans, mortgages, and so on.

Figure 17.1 is a credit score point system that would be typical for a credit bureau or other creditor.

How Errors Are Made

When a credit report contains errors, it often is because it is incomplete or contains information about someone else. For example, a clerical error in reading or entering a name or address, an inaccurate Social Security number, or loan payments that are applied to the wrong account can cause errors.

Credit Inquiries

A credit inquiry is an item that indicates a business with a "permissible purpose" has requested a credit check. Businesses can make an inquiry without your permission or knowledge, but usually these don't count toward your score. When you apply for a loan, mortgage, or other credit, you authorize the lender to check your credit. These inquiries, which are prompted by your own actions, will affect your FICO score. For example, if you are *rate shopping* at various financial institutions to get the best loan, you will have many credit inquiries. These inquiries are an indicator that you are looking to increase your debt.

Improving Your FICO Score

To raise your FICO score takes time and patience. Pay your bills on time. If you have missed payments, get current and stay current. Keep balances low on credit cards and revolving credit. Pay off debt rather than moving it around. Open accounts slowly—not a bunch at a time. Some experts suggest that too many open accounts, even unused, can hurt your credit score because of the potential for obtaining more available credit than you are able to handle.

FIGURE 17.1	*Credit Scores*
SCORE	**EXPLANATION**
800 – 950	*Excellent. Has used credit wisely; has considerable capital but low revolving debt. Pays off credit monthly; rarely carries credit balances other than home mortgage loan.*
700 – 799	*Good. Has good credit payment record; good, solid income and the ability to repay debts. Pays monthly credit obligations on time and pays more than the minimum.*
500 – 699	*Fair. Has considerable debt and is making obligations within the grace period; makes minimum payments; income is adequate; may have some small credit discrepancies.*
Below 500	*Poor. Not able to take on much debt; some credit history but not well established; income may be questionable; has had some credit problems in the past.*

CREDIT REPORTS

Credit files are updated continuously, and information stays in the file for seven years. Bankruptcy information stays in the file for ten years. Credit reports are requested for credit applications, employment applications, and insurance reasons. Reports from different credit bureaus may be arranged differently, but they all contain sections similar to those shown in Figure 17.2, described as follows.

- *Summary of Information.* This first section is a summary of negative and positive items. It tells the subscribers what to look for as they go through the information that follows. Negative items could harm your ability to get credit. Accounts in good standing are favorable to your credit.
- *Public Record Information.* This section lists information found in public records. You would expect to find any lawsuits, judgments, bankruptcy, property purchase and sale, marriage, divorce, adoption, and other public information available to anyone who searches public records.
- *Credit Information.* This section lists credit accounts, including those with department stores, credit card companies, and other loans, that have been reported to credit bureaus. It reports details such as each account's high balance since the account was opened and the current payment status.
- *Account Detail.* This section shows the monthly balances of accounts. It also lists the credit limits that have been reported.
- *Requests for Credit History.* This section lists every business that has sought information from your credit file. It includes requests by potential employers, creditors, insurance companies, and others, along with requests that you may have made to inspect your own credit records.
- *Personal Information.* This section lists the personal information that you have given when applying for credit or that is available through public records. It includes your name and previous names, your contact information, whether you own or rent, your date of birth, your Social Security number, your driver's license number, your spouse's name, and your employers and salaries.

Why should you check your credit report for errors?

© Digital Vision/Getty Images

CREDIT LAWS

The government has passed a number of laws to protect consumers from unfair credit practices. Each law was intended to remove some of the problems and confusion surrounding the use of credit. Together, these laws set a standard for how individuals are to be treated in their daily credit dealings. Several of these laws are summarized on the following pages.

FIGURE 17.2   *Credit Report*

PERSONAL CREDIT REPORT

Prepared for	*Report Date*	*Report Number*	**Summary of Information:**	
Jane Smith	June 1, 20--	108881	Potentially negative items:	
			Public records	2
			Accounts with creditors	2
			Accounts in good standing:	3

Public Record Information:

Source	Date Filed	Responsibility	Liability Amount	Comments
1. Jess County Courthouse	3/2007	Joint	$5,000	District Court complaint (defendant)
2. U.S. District Court	6/2004	Joint	$85,000	Bankruptcy discharged 11.01

Credit Information:

Source	Date Opened Last Report	Responsibility	Type/ Payment	High Amount	Status
3. Fidelity Bank (VISA)	6/2003	Individual	Revolv. $100 min.	$5,000	Late 2 pmts
4. CC & C Credit	10/2004	Individual	Install. $200/mo.	$8,500	Late charges-3
5. U.S. Finance Co.	3/2008	Joint	Install. $350/mo.	$18,000	Current

Account Detail:

Source	Date/Balance
6. U.S. Finance Co.	3/2008 $0 4/2008 $17,850 5/2008 $17,700 6/2008 $17,500 7/2008 $17,250 8/2008 $17,000
7. Merlo's Dept. Store	5/2007 $0 6/2007 $500 6/2007 $850 7/2007 $700 8/2007 $900 9/2007 $1,000 10/2007 $800 11/2007 $900 12/2007 $1,000 1/2008 $900 2/2008 $700 3/2008 $500 4/2008 $300 5/2008 $100 6/2008 $0

Between 5/2007 and 6/2008 your credit limit was $2,500.

Others Who Have Requested Your Credit History:

11/2007 Bill's Frame Shop (employment check)
2/2008   ABCD Mortgage Co. (related to real estate offer)
8/2008   Art's Motors (car loan application)

Requests Initiated by You:

5/2008   Credit report for denial of credit

Personal Information:

Names: Jane L. Smith   *Social Security Number*: 999-00-9999
           Jane Louise Smith
           J. L. Smith

Residences: 123 Main Street   Single-family house (owned)   4488 West Melody Lane   Condominium (rental)
               Clio, CA 90001   Brighton, NJ 02411

Date of Birth: 9.23.1971   *Driver's License Number*:   CA0948X23
Telephone Numbers: 503.555.3331
                       253.555.4441

Spouse's Name: John B. Smith
Employers: Cranston Bakery (Partner) $48,000 salary, reported 3/2/2008
                  4480 West Palm Beach
                  Clio, CA 90022

                  McGraw School District $37,000 salary, reported 2/1/2003
                  42 Maple Wood
                  Clinton, NY 00442

VIEW *Points*

Some people believe that credit bureaus are too powerful and do not adequately safeguard consumer information. For example, there are many errors contained in credit files. Information is gathered and shared without the knowledge or consent of consumers. Credit bureaus sell information about consumers and provide lists of consumers who meet certain criteria. This information is often used by businesses to send out unsolicited credit offers.

Consumer privacy advocates believe that consumers should have more control over their private and personal information contained in credit files. Rather than being allowed to "opt out" of having information supplied at will, they believe that credit bureaus should have to get written permission of consumers (called opt-in) before they can sell and distribute information about them. Credit bureaus disagree and believe the information is their property and that of their subscribers. They believe they need to have free access to it and be able to share it in order to generate business profits.

THINK *CRITICALLY*

With which position do you agree? Why? Would you choose to opt-in if this was an option? Explain why or why not.

■ CONSUMER CREDIT PROTECTION ACT

The *Consumer Credit Protection Act,* also known as the Truth-in-Lending Law, requires lenders to fully inform consumers about all costs of a credit purchase before an agreement is signed. Lenders must disclose the *finance charge,* which is the total dollar amount of all costs of the credit, including interest, service fees, and any other costs. Lenders must also state the annual percentage rate (APR), which is the yearly percentage of interest charges that must be calculated the same way by all lenders. Consumers can use the APR to compare costs from different lenders. In addition, the law requires a grace period of three business days in which purchasers can change their mind about a credit agreement. The law also limits the consumer's liability to $50 after the consumer reports a credit card lost or stolen. There is no liability if the card is reported lost prior to its fraudulent use.

■ FAIR CREDIT REPORTING ACT

If you are denied credit based on a credit report, inaccurate information in your file may be the cause. Under the *Fair Credit Reporting Act,* you have a right to know what is in your file and who has seen your file. A listing of requests made for your file for credit purposes in the last six months, and for employment purposes in the last two years, must be available to you. You may see your credit file at no charge within 30 days of a credit denial. A small fee may be charged in the event you want to see your file at any other time for any reason. You have the right to have inaccurate information investigated, corrected, and deleted from your file and have a new report furnished to creditors. Or, if potentially damaging information in the file is essentially correct, you can write a statement giving your side of the story. Your statement must be added to the file.

FAIR CREDIT BILLING ACT

Under the *Fair Credit Billing Act*, creditors must resolve billing errors within a specified period of time. A *statement* is an itemized bill showing charges, credits, and payments posted to your account during the billing period. Suppose your monthly statement showed purchases you did not make. Perhaps a company billed you for merchandise you ordered but did not receive. Creditors are required to have a written policy for correcting such errors.

If you believe your bill contains an error, act immediately. Write a letter giving a complete explanation of why you believe there is an error. Be specific about the amount in dispute, when you noticed the error, and any details relevant to the disputed amount. Figure 17.3 shows an example of what you might say. Include your account number and your contact information.

FIGURE 17.3   *Letter Reporting Billing Error*

P.O. Box 4848
Milwaukee, WI 40412-4848
April 10, 20--

Melon Visa Bank
Customer Service Center
24 Chambers Street
New York, NY 02040-3112

RE: ACCOUNT # 4902 3818 4783 1783
     Disputed Amount: $289.00 Melvin's, 3/21/--

As stated in my telephone conversation with Melanie at your 800 number on April 9, 20--, I am hereby disputing the above charge.

Copies of the invoice and other documentation for the purchase I made on March 21 at Melvin's Auto Repair are enclosed. I am disputing the amount listed because the service provided was unsatisfactory. I was charged $589, but within a week, the same operational problem occurred. I asked Melvin's to correct the problem, but the manager said it was not the company's responsibility and that I would be charged an additional $200 in parts and labor. As you can see, I then went to Barlow's and had the defective part fixed for $300. Therefore, I believe that of the $589, which is the fair market value of the product, I should not have to pay more than $289 to Melvin's.

You can reach me at (201) 555-2372 on weekdays. My e-mail address is listed below. Please let me know if you need any further information.

Thank you,

Jackie B. Chen

JACKIE B. CHEN
Jackiebc@starnet.com

Enclosure

Your complaint must be in writing and mailed within 60 days after you receive the statement. The creditor must acknowledge the complaint within 30 days. Within 90 days, the creditor must either correct the error or show why the bill is correct. You are not liable for the amounts in dispute while the error is being investigated. However, you must still make payments on all other amounts. Figure 17.4 is an example of a written policy for handling billing errors.

EQUAL CREDIT OPPORTUNITY ACT

The *Equal Credit Opportunity Act* was designed to prevent discrimination in the evaluation of creditworthiness. **Discrimination** is treating people differently based on prejudice rather than individual merit. There are many legitimate reasons for denying an applicant credit. Some reasons, however, are considered discriminatory. The act specifies the following:

- Credit may not be denied solely because you are a woman, single, married, divorced, separated, or widowed.

FIGURE 17.4	*Error-Correction Policy*

IN CASE OF ERRORS OR INQUIRIES ABOUT YOUR BILL:

The Fair Credit Billing Act requires prompt resolution of errors. To preserve your rights, follow these steps:

1. Do not write on the bill. On a separate piece of paper, write a description as shown below. A telephone call will not preserve your rights.

   a. Your name and account number.
   b. Description of the error and your explanation of why you believe there is an error. Send copies of any receipts or supporting evidence you may have; do not send originals.
   c. The dollar amount of the suspected error.
   d. Other information that might be helpful in resolving the disputed amount.

2. Mail your letter as soon as possible. It must reach us within 60 days after you receive your bill.

3. We will acknowledge your letter within 30 days. Within 90 days of receiving your letter, we will correct the error or explain why we believe the bill is correct.

4. You will receive no collection letters or collection action regarding the amount in dispute; nor will it be reported to any credit bureau or collection agency.

5. You are still responsible for all other items on the bill and for the balance less the disputed amount.

6. You will not be charged a finance charge against the disputed amount, unless it is determined that there is not an error in the bill. In this event, you will be given the normal 25 days to pay your bill from the date the bill is determined to be correct.

- Credit may not be denied specifically because of religion, national origin, race, color, or age (except as age may affect your ability to perform or your ability to enter into contracts; for example, minors cannot be held liable for their contracts because they are not considered competent parties).
- Credit may not be denied because you receive public assistance (welfare), unemployment, Social Security, or retirement benefits.
- Credit applications may be oral or written. However, a creditor is prohibited from asking certain questions, either orally or in writing, such as: Do you plan to have children? What is your ethnic origin? What church do you attend?
- A creditor may not discourage you, in writing or orally, from applying for credit for any reason prohibited by the act (such as being divorced).

Why do you think creditors are prohibited from asking certain questions?

In addition to these prohibitions, the act states that creditors must notify you of any action taken on your credit application within 30 days of submission. If you are denied credit, the denial must be in writing and must list a specific reason for the denial. After a denial of credit, the creditor must keep for 25 months all information used to determine the denial and any written complaint from you regarding the denial. You have the right to appeal, and the creditor must give you the name and address of the federal agency that enforces compliance with the law.

Also, the act requires new accounts to reflect the fact that both husband and wife are responsible for payment. In this way, both spouses establish their own credit histories. Existing accounts should be changed to assure that both the wife and husband receive credit for the payment record.

FAIR DEBT COLLECTION PRACTICES ACT

The *Fair Debt Collection Practices Act* was designed to eliminate abusive collection practices by debt collectors. A **debt collector** is a person or company hired by a creditor to collect the overdue balance on an account. The fee charged by the debt collector is often half of the amount collected. The law prohibits use of threats, obscenities, and false and misleading statements to intimidate the consumer into paying. It also restricts the time and frequency of collection practices, such as telephone calls and contacts at place of employment. Debt collectors are required to verify the accuracy of the bill and give the consumer the opportunity to clarify and dispute it.

Business Management & Administration

Almost one in four debt collectors works for a collection agency. Others work for banks, retail stores, government agencies, doctors' offices, hospitals, and other creditors. Bill or debt collectors keep track of accounts that are overdue and attempt to collect payments.

Investigation plays a role as collectors locate and notify consumers of overdue accounts. Most contacts are made by phone. Collectors may need to obtain information about debtors from phone companies, employers, credit bureaus, and neighbors. When a person has moved, they must try to locate them. Finding a new address is called "skip tracing." New computer systems assist in tracking customers who change address or other contact information on any open accounts.

Collectors try to convince consumers to pay. If they are unsuccessful, legal steps will follow. In an office environment, debt collectors often must meet targets (quotas) for debt recovered within a certain period (such as a month).

Employment Outlook

- A higher than average rate of employment growth is expected.

Job Titles

- Debt collector
- Bill collector
- Collection manager
- Collection agent
- Recovery specialist
- Medical collector

Needed Skills

- High school education is required; post-secondary training is preferred.
- Persistence and patience are a must.
- Good communication and negotiation skills are required.

What's it like to work in... *Debt Collection*

Jan works as a debt collector for a local collection agency. When a customer has failed to pay for 30 days beyond the due date of a loan or account payment, accounts are referred to Jan for a preliminary contact. If customers do not respond, formal collection procedures begin.

Each day, Jan keeps track of accounts and payments. She makes sure people are paying as agreed. She works with customers to create special payment plans to help accommodate their budgets. She follows up with phone calls for those who need reminding. She is on the phone six or more hours a day talking to people and trying to reach an agreement for repayment of debt.

Jan has her own collection accounts, but she compares notes with other collectors to stay current on different collection techniques.

What About You?

Are you good at negotiation and persuasion, yet patient and persistent? Are you willing to work with a strict set of rules of what you can and cannot do? Could a career as a debt collector be right for you?

Assessment

KEY TERMS REVIEW

Match the terms with the definitions.

____ 1. A method of evaluation in which points are assigned by a credit bureau based on several factors

____ 2. An excellent credit rating

____ 3. A good credit rating

____ 4. Treating people differently based on prejudice rather than individual merit

____ 5. A measure of creditworthiness based on an analysis of your credit and financial history

a. A-rating

b. B-rating

c. credit rating

d. credit score

e. debt collector

f. discrimination

g. point system

____ 6. The total of assigned points used to determine the likelihood that you will repay debt as agreed

____ 7. A person or company hired by a creditor to collect the overdue balance on an account

CHECK YOUR UNDERSTANDING

8. What are some things you can do to maintain a good credit rating?

9. Why might a credit report be requested by individuals and businesses?

10. What should you do if you believe there is an error on your credit card statement?

APPLY YOUR KNOWLEDGE

11. Explain the purpose of credit ratings and credit scores. Who uses them and why?

THINK CRITICALLY

12. How is an excellent (A-rating) different from a good (B-rating)? What can you do to improve your credit rating or score?

13. Credit reports contain personal, financial, and other private information. Why is it important for you to monitor the contents of your credit file?

14. Why should you follow up and get a free credit report if you are denied credit? What can you do?

Chapter Assessment

SUMMARY

17.1

- *Your credit history is a complete record of your experience with credit.*

- *Credit bureaus collect information about consumers' credit transactions from businesses and prepare credit reports about individual consumers for their business subscribers.*

- *Businesses use a consumer's credit report to decide whether to grant credit.*

- *Businesses judge your creditworthiness based on the five Cs of credit: character, capacity, capital, conditions, and collateral.*

- *To start building a good credit history, follow these steps: open a savings account, open a checking account, open a store credit account, get a small loan, and apply for a credit card.*

- *You may need a cosigner to get started with credit. A cosigner guarantees that payments will be made.*

17.2

- *Your credit rating, such as an A-rating (for excellent) or a B-rating (for good), is a measure of your creditworthiness based on an analysis of your credit and financial history.*

- *Many credit bureaus rate consumers' creditworthiness on a point system, assigning points based on debt, payment history, income, and other factors. Assigned points are totaled to determine your credit score.*

- *Credit reports provide information about individual consumers, including public record information, credit information, account details, and personal information.*

- *The Consumer Credit Protection Act (Truth-in-Lending Law) requires full disclosure of all costs of credit, including finance charge and APR.*

- *The Fair Credit Reporting Act gives you the right to inspect your credit file and to make changes or dispute information contained in the file.*

- *The Fair Credit Billing Act requires creditors to resolve billing errors within a reasonable time.*

- *The Equal Credit Opportunity Act prohibits discrimination in judgment of creditworthiness.*

- *The Fair Debt Collection Practices Act prohibits abusive collection practices by debt collectors.*

APPLY WHAT YOU KNOW

1. Visit the web site of one of the three major credit bureaus listed in Lesson 17.1. In no more than one page, summarize what the bureau includes in its credit reports and outline the procedure you would have to follow to get a copy of your own report.

2. What kinds of credit do you think you will be using in five years? How will you establish a good credit rating to be eligible for increasing credit limits and privileges?

3. Assume you have a well-established credit history and have filled out an application for credit at a local department store. The store has notified you that it cannot give you credit because you have a poor credit rating. What are your rights, and what are some things you should do? You have not missed any payments or made any late payments, and you have paid off previous debts as agreed. Suppose there is an error. What responsibilities does the credit bureau have to you?

4. The Federal Reserve System has a publication entitled "Consumer Handbook to Credit Protection Laws." Search for this publication online. Choose one of the sections to read and summarize the main points in a one-page report.

5. Describe what you must do if you believe a statement you receive from a creditor contains an error. Describe the process for error correction, including your responsibilities and time limits and the responsibilities and time limits of your creditor.

MAKE ACADEMIC CONNECTIONS

6. **Communication** Write a two-page paper about credit reports, credit ratings, and credit scores. Explain what they are, how they work, and how everyone is affected by them. Give both favorable and unfavorable analyses of how consumer information is gathered and used.

7. **History** Conduct library and Internet research about credit bureaus—what they are, when they began, how they are regulated, and the opposition to their practices by consumer privacy advocates. Cite your sources and give direct quotes where possible. Give a historical perspective to the need for credit bureaus.

8. **Research** Using online sources such as the Federal Trade Commission's web site, find out how your personal information can be revealed through a procedure called pretexting. Explain how it works. Countering pretexting are organizations such as EPIC (Electronic Privacy Information Center). Explain what it does.

9. **Careers** Explore what it would be like to work in the Consumer Protection Division of a state attorney general's office or for a federal agency such as the FTC (Federal Trade Commission). How are consumers able to make/file complaints? What does the government agency do to help them? What would be your role as a government employee?

SOLVE PROBLEMS AND

EXPLORE ISSUES

10. Obtain a credit application from a local merchant or national credit card company. On a separate piece of paper, create two columns. List each question on the form in the left column. In the right column, indicate whether each question is (a) a personal question, (b) a payment record question, (c) an employment stability question, or (d) an income question.

11. Your friend Krista has just been turned down for credit. She works part time and would like to obtain a credit card from a local department store. The department store stated lack of credit history as the reason for credit denial. Is there anything Lisa can do?

12. You have just received your monthly Visa bill. There is a charge on your bill of $42, but you have a receipt showing the amount should have been $24. You made the purchase at a local clothing store one month ago. You returned to the store to try to resolve the problem, but the store manager was of no help. Write a letter to the local bank that issued the Visa card and explain the error.

13. Obtain a written error policy supplied by a local or national credit card company or other creditor. Companies that sell over the Internet should state their policy at their web site. Compare the policy statement with Figure 17.4 and describe the similarities and differences.

14. Your friend Enrique was denied credit, so he asked for a copy of his credit report from one of the national credit bureaus. On examination of the report, he discovered several errors. For example, the report showed a previous employer and account that he never had. It also showed a previous address in another state that was not correct. What can Enrique do about this incorrect information?

15. Evaluate your creditworthiness based on the five Cs of credit: character, capacity, capital, conditions, and collateral. What do you conclude?

EXTEND YOUR LEARNING

16. **Legal Issues** Your neighbor recently purchased a refrigerator on credit but was unable to continue making payments because he lost his job. In the last week, he has received abusive telephone calls at home from a debt collector. Your neighbor has volunteered to return the refrigerator, but the debt collector refuses and threatens him with public humiliation. The collector has now come to your house looking for him and has made false and degrading comments about the neighbor's character. Are the debt collector's actions legal? Why or why not? What advice would you give to your neighbor? Are there any laws that protect him?

For related activities and links, go to **www.cengage.com/school/pfinance/mypf**

Chapter 18

Responsibilities and Costs of Credit

| 18.1 | **Using Credit Wisely** |
| 18.2 | **Costs of Credit** |

Consider **THIS**

Mike was well on his way to managing credit and taking the next steps, such as buying a house and making a commitment to long-term payments.

"I learned the hard way that all credit isn't created equal," he thought. "Some credit cards have annual fees, and others charge very high interest rates. I switched from credit accounts that didn't meet my needs. Now I have a group of cards and accounts that have no annual fees, low fixed interest rates, and the kinds of rebates that benefit me. I keep my accounts paid off and use credit cards mainly for emergencies and convenience. It wasn't always so easy, though. When I wasn't careful, I ended up spending a lot of money impulsively that I could have used later to buy something I wanted more."

Using Credit Wisely

GOALS

- Describe the responsibilities of consumer credit.
- Discuss how to protect your credit accounts from fraud.
- Explain how you can reduce or avoid credit costs.

TERMS

- comparison shopping, p. 398
- impulse buying, p. 398
- garnishment, p. 399
- encryption, p. 401
- phishing, p. 401
- unused credit, p. 401
- rewards program, p. 402
- rebate plan, p. 402

RESPONSIBILITIES OF CONSUMER CREDIT

Once you have established credit, you have the responsibility to manage it carefully. Failure to take this responsibility seriously can result in having your credit limited or, in some cases, withdrawn. Because using credit is important to your financial future, you should be aware of your responsibilities to yourself and to creditors. In return, creditors have responsibilities to you, their customer.

RESPONSIBILITIES TO YOURSELF

As a credit user, you have a responsibility to yourself to use credit wisely and not get into debt beyond an amount you can comfortably repay. Never having enough money and always scrambling to make your next payment is a stressful way to live.

You are also responsible for checking out businesses before making credit purchases. Better Business Bureaus and Chambers of Commerce have information about businesses and complaints that have been filed against them.

You owe it to yourself to comparison shop. **Comparison shopping** involves checking several places to be sure you are getting the best price for equal quality. When you check prices in various stores, it will help you to avoid impulse buying. **Impulse buying** occurs when you buy something

What responsibilities do you have to yourself as a user of credit?

© Digital Vision/Getty Images

without thinking about it and making a conscious decision. It's important to take the time to evaluate the product and your other options before buying. Be sure you are buying for the right reasons—because you have a need rather than because you want to impress people. Tying up future income should be done with careful planning to maximize your purchasing power and quality of life.

Comparison shop for credit as well. Compare features, costs, and availability of credit, and make wise choices. Become familiar with billing cycles, annual percentage rates (APR), and any special charges related to each credit account. Learn about state and local laws regarding the use of credit.

Finally, as a credit user, you should have the right attitude about using credit. Enter into each transaction in good faith and with full expectation of meeting your obligations and upholding your good credit reputation.

If you can't make your payments, a creditor may take you to court to have your wages garnished. **Garnishment** is a legal process that allows part of your paycheck to be withheld for payment of a debt. Your employer sends the amount directly to the creditor.

RESPONSIBILITIES TO CREDITORS

When you open an account, you are entering into a relationship with a store, bank, or credit card company. You are pledging your honesty and sincerity in the use of credit.

You have the responsibility to limit your spending to amounts that you can repay according to the terms of the credit agreement. By signing a credit application, you agree to make all payments promptly, on or before the due date. In addition, you are responsible for reading and understanding the terms of all agreements, including finance charges, what to do in case of error, late fees, over-the-limit fees, and any other provisions of the agreement.

It is your responsibility to contact the creditor immediately when you find a problem with the bill or discover that the merchandise is defective. If an emergency prevents you from making a payment, you should contact the creditor to make arrangements to pay at a later date.

CREDITORS' RESPONSIBILITIES TO YOU

Creditors also have responsibilities to consumers to whom they grant credit. These responsibilities include the following:

- Assisting consumers in making wise purchases by honestly representing goods and services, including all their advantages and disadvantages.
- Informing customers about all rules and regulations (such as minimum payments and due dates), interest rates, credit policies, and fees.
- Cooperating with established credit reporting agencies, making credit records available to the consumer, and promptly fixing mistakes in records when they occur.
- Establishing and adhering to sound lending and credit policies that do not overburden or deceive customers. This includes setting reasonable guidelines for credit use to avoid extending additional credit to customers who cannot afford it.
- Using reasonable methods of contacting customers who fail to meet their obligations and assisting them whenever possible with payment schedules and other means for solving credit problems.

PROTECTING YOURSELF FROM CREDIT CARD FRAUD

Credit card fraud costs businesses and consumers millions of dollars each year. The most common type of fraud is the illegal use of a lost or stolen credit card or of credit card information intercepted online. While the credit card holder's liability is limited to $50, the merchant is not protected from loss. Consequently, merchants often raise their overall prices to cover such losses.

■ SAFEGUARDING YOUR CARDS

It is your responsibility to protect your cards and credit accounts from unauthorized use. Here are some common sense tips for doing so.

- Sign and activate your cards as soon as you receive them.
- Carry only the cards you need.
- Keep a list of your credit card numbers, their expiration dates, and the phone number and address of each card company in a safe place.
- Notify creditors immediately by phone when your card is lost or stolen and follow up with a letter so that you have written evidence of the notification.
- Watch your card during transactions and get it back as soon as you can.
- Tear up old receipts no longer needed that contain account information.
- Do not lend your card to anyone or leave it lying around.
- Destroy expired cards by cutting them up.
- Don't give credit card numbers and expiration dates by phone or online to people or businesses you don't know.
- Keep your sales receipts and verify all charges on your credit card statements promptly. Use the procedure printed on your statement to question charges that you think are in error.

■ PROTECTING YOUR ACCOUNTS ONLINE

Buying on the Internet has opened new avenues for criminals to steal credit card information for illegal use. Software makers and online organizations are fighting back by constantly developing new ways to offer secure electronic transmission of customer information. There are some steps you can take as well to help protect your credit card and personal information during online transactions.

- Deal only with companies online that you know and trust. If the retailer also has a physical "bricks-and-mortar" store, then it is likely to be safer than an unknown merchant that exists only in cyberspace.
- When making an online transaction, always look for your browser's symbol that indicates a secure site before entering your personal information. For example, the Internet

© Photodisc/Getty Images

What are some ways you can protect your credit when completing transactions online?

Explorer and Netscape browsers display a small closed-lock symbol on the bottom of your screen when you have entered a secure web page. The symbol should appear whenever a web site asks you to enter credit card and other personal information to make a purchase. Among other security measures, this symbol means that the information you enter will be encrypted. **Encryption** is a code that protects your account name, number, and other information. When information is encrypted, it is made unreadable to others trying to read it. If you don't see the secure site symbol, it isn't safe to enter your information.

- Legitimate online merchants clearly state their *privacy policy*, explaining how they use the information you provide and how they protect your privacy. Review the policy to make sure you are comfortable with it before dealing with that company.

- Many sites offer assurance by displaying the seal of a nonprofit watchdog group, such as the Better Business Bureau (BBB) or TRUSTe. Sites that follow the privacy principles set forth by these organizations are allowed to display their seal. This kind of oversight is not fully developed yet, so not all legitimate merchants display seals.

- **Phishing** (pronounced "fishing") is a scam that uses online pop-up messages or e-mail to deceive you into disclosing personal information. "Phishers" send messages that appear to be from a business that you normally deal with, such as your bank or Internet service provider (ISP). They ask you to verify your bank account number, password, credit card number, or other personal information. They may direct you to a web site that looks like the real company site but isn't. Do not respond to e-mail requests for personal information or pop-up offers; report them to your ISP and bank or other real provider. Initiate all transactions yourself at sites you trust.

AVOIDING UNNECESSARY CREDIT COSTS

Credit can be helpful if you use it wisely. Before deciding whether to borrow money, ask yourself these three critical questions: Do I need credit? Can I afford credit? Can I qualify for credit? If you can answer "yes" to these questions, then follow these guidelines to minimize the cost of credit.

- *Accept only the amount of credit you need.* Although having credit available when you need it may be comforting, unused credit can count against you. **Unused credit** is the remaining credit available to you on current accounts; it is your credit limit minus the amount you already owe. For example, if the limit on your credit card is $1,000 and you owe $200, your unused credit is $800. Other creditors may be reluctant to lend you money because you could at any time access the other $800, thereby increasing your debt and reducing your ability to repay their loan.

- *Make more than the minimum payment.* Minimum payments will result in maximum cost and will keep you in debt for a long time. For example, if you owe $5,000 on a credit card at 18 percent APR, make no further purchases, and pay only the minimum payment (often 2 percent or less of the balance owing), it will take you 33 years to pay off the debt, and you will end up paying total interest of nearly $12,000 on a loan of $5,000.

Many credit card companies market their services aggressively to college students. As a result, the number of college students with credit card debt has increased significantly. Some colleges and universities require students to have debit/credit cards as their student identification (provided at enrollment). Not only can they purchase books, supplies, and tuition with the cards, they can also buy general merchandise.

These cards often carry high interest rates and fees. Students graduate owing large balances on their accounts.

THINK *CRITICALLY*

Do you think it should be easy for students to get credit cards? What qualifications should students fulfill to qualify? Do you think it's a good idea to use debit/credit cards as identification cards? Why or why not?

- *Do not increase spending when your income increases.* Instead of spending the income, use it to pay off credit card debt or put it in savings. Avoid the trap of spending more when your income rises.

- *Keep your credit accounts to a minimum.* Most credit counselors recommend carrying no more than two or three credit cards. The more cards you have, the greater the temptation to buy without thinking. A major credit card (Visa or MasterCard) is good at most businesses, which eliminates the need to have multiple credit accounts.

- *Pay cash for small purchases.* For many people, purchases under $25 represent daily commitments. You shouldn't charge these unless you can pay them off at the end of the month. By paying as you go, you'll avoid financing your current expenses. Paying cash will also help you realize how much you are spending. Thus, you may buy less and purchase only those items you really need.

- *Understand the cost of credit.* Think about the finance charges, the monthly payments, and the length of time you will be committed to paying off credit card debt. Consider how this will affect your lifestyle and your budget for months or even years to come.

- *Shop for loans.* The type and source of loans can make a big difference in cost. Compare the cost of credit from different sources, such as banks, credit unions, finance companies, and credit card companies. Plan your purchases accordingly. Avoid making big purchase decisions without long and careful thought. When computing your costs and making choices, do it at home and not in a lender's or seller's office where you will feel pressured.

- *Take advantage of credit incentive programs.* There are two major types of credit incentive programs: rewards and rebates. With an account that has a **rewards program**, you will receive a payback in the form of points that can be redeemed for merchandise or airline tickets. With a **rebate plan**, you get back a portion of what you spent in credit purchases over the year. For example, you may get a one percent rebate in the form of a credit to your account balance, a check that you can cash, or a Visa gift card that you can spend. Some programs are designed for a specific purpose, such as the GM MasterCard with 3 percent of charge purchases redeemable toward the purchase of a new GM vehicle. However, these kinds of programs often have annual fees and/or high interest rates on unpaid balances.

ISSUES IN YOUR WORLD

MAXING OUT THE CARDS

A credit card is "maxed out" when you have reached your credit limit and there is no room in your account for additional charges. You cannot buy anything else on credit until you pay down the current balance. Maxing out is not a good idea. Here's why:

- *When you get really close to the top, it is very easy to "go over." Most credit card companies will allow a purchase to go through and then charge you a fee for exceeding the card's credit limit. This fee may be $35 or more. These fees can add up quickly, increasing your debt. Going over the limit also gives credit card issuers a reason to raise your interest rate.*

- *In some cases, the credit card company will not honor charges that exceed the credit limit. It can be very embarrassing to try to use your credit card, only to have it rejected by the verification machine.*

- *When your cards are maxed out, you are paying maximum interest and maximum monthly payments. At the same time, you cannot use the card because the balance is going down very slowly and a single charge might take the card over the top once again.*

- *Having maxed-out credit cards does not look good on your credit report. It tells potential creditors that you are already overextended and unable to pay down existing debts.*

- *Having the credit card offers no advantages when you cannot use it for current purchases. You must be very careful not to use it until you have created enough room for additional charges.*

- *People with maxed-out credit can fall prey to "easy access" credit, such as payday loans, no-credit-check loans, bad-credit-okay loans, and pawnshops. These forms of credit have very high rates of interest and put you in a cycle of borrowing beyond your means.*

- *When you pay down your charges regularly, credit card companies will be more willing to raise your credit limit. But when the card is maxed out, the credit card company will not likely extend additional credit if you need it for a major purchase.*

For all these reasons, avoid the practice of maxing out your cards.

THINK CRITICALLY

1. *How might maxing out your credit card affect your lifestyle?*
2. *If you were a creditor and someone with maxed-out cards asked you for a loan, would you grant it? Why or why not?*

KEY TERMS REVIEW

Match the terms with the definitions. Some terms may not be used.

_____ 1. A legal process that allows part of your paycheck to be withheld to pay a debt

_____ 2. Checking several places to be sure you are getting the best price for equal quality

_____ 3. The remaining credit available to you on current accounts

_____ 4. A code that protects your account number and other information

_____ 5. A payback in the form of points that can be redeemed for merchandise

_____ 6. Buying something without thinking about it

_____ 7. A scam that uses online pop-up messages or e-mail to deceive you into disclosing personal information

a. comparison shopping
b. encryption
c. garnishment
d. impulse buying
e. phishing
f. rebate plan
g. rewards program
h. unused credit

CHECK YOUR UNDERSTANDING

8. List three responsibilities you have to your creditors.

9. List three responsibilities that creditors have to you.

10. List three things you can do to help avoid credit card fraud.

APPLY YOUR KNOWLEDGE

11. You want to buy a new $100 jacket. You can pay for it with cash or by check, debit card, or credit card. Which method is the least expensive? What possible costs might be associated with these payment methods?

THINK CRITICALLY

12. Comparison shopping isn't just for goods and services. Credit should be considered carefully. Explain why you might choose a credit card with a high interest rate that has an attractive rewards program. How could you use this card effectively?

13. Why is it important to keep your credit card in sight at all times? For example, why shouldn't you give your credit card to a sales clerk who takes it away and then brings it back later with a charge slip?

14. Explain why it is usually not a good idea to use credit to pay for day-to-day expenses, such as meals and groceries. If you do use credit for such purchases, how can you make credit work to your advantage?

Costs of Credit

- Explain why credit costs vary.
- Compute and explain simple interest and APR.
- Compare methods of computing finance charges on revolving credit.

- prime rate, *p. 405*
- fixed-rate loans, *p. 406*
- variable-rate loans, *p. 406*
- simple interest, *p. 406*
- principal, *p. 406*
- rate, *p. 406*
- time, *p. 407*
- down payment, *p. 409*

WHY CREDIT COSTS VARY

Several factors determine how much you will pay for the use of credit. One important factor is the method used to compute finance charges, explained later in the chapter. Other important factors include the following:

- *Source of credit.* Some lenders offer better credit plans than others.
- *Amount financed and length of time.* The more money you borrow and the longer you take to pay it back, the more you will pay in finance charges.
- *Ability to repay debt.* The greater your ability to repay (creditworthiness), the better your chances of getting credit at reasonable rates.
- *Collateral.* When you buy an item that serves as collateral (security), you are taking out a secured loan. Secured loans generally have fixed interest rates that are lower than other forms of credit.
- *Interest Rates.* The interest rates charged for the use of credit are most often affected by the prime rate. The **prime rate** is the interest rate that banks offer to their best business customers, such as large corporations. Individuals pay higher rates because the risk is greater to the lender. Generally, if the prime rate is 5 percent, consumers will pay 8 or 9 percent.
- *Economic conditions.* Borrowers pay more for the use of credit during inflationary economic periods. When prices are rising (inflation), then money is more in demand in order to buy higher-priced goods and services. Because people need to borrow more money (greater demand), lenders can charge higher interest rates.

What factors determine the cost of credit?

- *Type of credit or loan.* **Fixed-rate loans** are loans for which the interest rate does not change (up or down) over the life of the loan. With **variable-rate loans**, the interest rate goes up and down with inflation and other economic indicators. Creditors can raise the rates as they wish. Most borrowers find that rates go up faster during periods of rising prices than they go down during periods of falling prices. Sometimes variable-rate card agreements will state that the interest rate will rise and fall with the prime rate.
- *The business's costs of providing credit.* Businesses pass along their costs for providing credit to consumers in the form of higher finance charges and higher product prices. These costs are related to delinquent accounts (overdue, but still collectible), bad debts (probably uncollectible), and bankruptcy. Other costs of issuing credit include printing and mailing monthly statements, electronic authorization of credit charges, and salaries and facilities for a credit department. When businesses accept Visa, MasterCard, or other general-purpose credit cards, they are charged a fee each time a customer uses the card. In turn, businesses often raise prices as a way to pass along their cost of offering credit to customers.

COMPUTING THE COST OF CREDIT

Determining the cost of credit is easy using the formula for simple interest. The formula for calculating the total cost of installment credit is somewhat more complicated.

SIMPLE INTEREST FORMULA

In Chapter 10, you learned that *interest* is money paid for the use of someone else's money. In the case of savings, interest is the amount the financial institution pays you for the use of your deposit. In the case of a loan, interest is the money you pay the business or financial institution for the use of its money.

Simple interest is interest computed only on the amount borrowed (or saved), without compounding. The simple interest method of calculating interest assumes one payment at the end of the loan period. The cost is based on three elements: the principal, the rate, and time. The formula for simple interest is:

$$\text{Interest (I)} = \text{Principal (P)} \times \text{Rate (R)} \times \text{Time (T)}$$

Principal

In Chapter 10, you learned that *principal* is an amount in a savings account on which interest accrues. The term has a similar meaning when referring to a loan. A loan's **principal** is the amount borrowed, or the unpaid portion of the amount borrowed, on which the borrower pays interest. If you borrow $10,000 to buy a car, that $10,000 is the principal, or amount of the loan. Part of each payment you make goes toward paying down the principal. The rest of the payment is interest. After several payments, the principal on your loan may drop to $8,000, which is the unpaid portion of the amount you borrowed.

Rate

The **rate** is the percentage of interest you will pay on a loan. The higher the rate, the higher is the cost of the loan.

Time

Time is the period during which the borrower will repay a loan; it is expressed as a fraction of a year: 12 months, 52 weeks, or 360 days. (In most transactions, the standard practice is to use 360 as the number of days in a year for computing simple interest.) For example, for a six-month loan, the time is expressed as ½, because 6 months is half a year. If money is borrowed for 3 months, the time is expressed as ¼ (one-quarter of a year). When a loan is for a certain number of days, such as 90, the time is expressed as 90/360, or ¼.

Figure 18.1 contains a simple interest problem showing the dollar cost of borrowing. In this problem, a person has borrowed $500 and will pay interest at the rate of 12 percent a year. The loan will be paid back in 4 months.

FIGURE 18.1   Simple Interest

$I = P \times R \times T$

To multiply by a percent, first change it to a decimal: drop the percent sign, and then move the decimal point two places to the left.

$I = ?$
$P = \$500$
$R = 12\%$
$T = 4$ months

$\begin{aligned} I &= \$500 \times .12 \times \tfrac{4}{12} \\ &= \$500 \times .12 \times \tfrac{1}{3} \qquad \text{(Four months is } \tfrac{4}{12} \text{ or } \tfrac{1}{3} \text{ of a year)} \\ &= \$60 \times .3333 \\ &= \$20 \end{aligned}$

The simple interest formula also can be used to find principal, rate, or time when any one of these factors is unknown. For example, in Figure 18.2, the interest rate is 18 percent. The borrower paid a total of $26 in interest and repaid the loan in 18 months. What was the principal?

FIGURE 18.2   Simple Interest (Principal)

$I = P \times R \times T$

Or change the formula to read:

$I = \$26$
$P = ?$
$R = 18\%$
$T = 18$ months

$P = \dfrac{I}{R \times T}$

$\begin{aligned} \$26 &= P \times .18 \times \tfrac{18}{12} \\ &= P \times .18 \times \tfrac{3}{2} \, (1.50) \\ &= P \times .27 \end{aligned}$

$= \dfrac{\$26}{.18 \times 1.50}$

$\begin{aligned} P &= \$26 \div .27 \\ &= \$96.30 \end{aligned}$

$= \dfrac{\$26}{.27}$

$= \$96.30$

To find a missing rate, you can use the same formula. See Figure 18.3 for an example. As shown in Figure 18.2 and 18.3, you either plug the numbers into the formula or rearrange the formula. Either way, you use simple mathematics.

FIGURE 18.3   *Simple Interest (Rate)*

I $= P \times R \times T$

I $= \$18$
P $= \$300$
R $= ?$
T $= 240$ days

$\$18 = \$300 \times R \times {}^{240}/_{360}$
$= \$300 \times {}^{2}/_{3} \times R$
$= \$200 \times R$

R $= \$18 \div \$200$
$= .09$ or 9%

Or change the formula to read:

$$R = \frac{I}{P \times T}$$

$$= \frac{\$18}{\$300 \times {}^{2}/_{3}}$$

$$= \frac{\$18}{\$200}$$

$$= .09 \text{ or } 9\%$$

ANNUAL PERCENTAGE RATE FORMULA

Consumers often use an installment plan to pay for major items such as boats, cars, and furniture, making regular payments over time. To determine the APR for installment plans, in which the borrower repays the loan with more than one payment, use the formula in Figure 18.4. Work through the problem in the Math Minute to see how to apply the formula.

FIGURE 18.4   *Annual Percentage Rate*

To calculate the finance charge, use the following formula:

Finance Charge = Total Price Paid − Cash Price

Where:
Total Price Paid = (number of payments × amount of each payment) + down payment
Cash Price = the total price you would have paid if you had paid in cash rather than with a loan

Then use the finance charge in the following formula to calculate the approximate annual percentage rate:

$$APR = \frac{2 \times n \times f}{P(N+1)}$$

Where:
n = number of payment periods in one year
f = finance charge
P = principal or amount borrowed
N = total number of payments to pay off amount borrowed

MATH *Minute*

Computing the Finance Charge and APR

The Smiths are buying a new sofa. The cash price is $800. They decide to pay for it with an installment loan rather than with cash. They put $100 down and borrow $700. They will pay off the loan in 12 monthly payments (in a year) of $66 each. To determine their APR, you must first use the formula in Figure 18.4 to calculate their finance charge:

Total Price Paid = (12 Payments $\times$ $66) + $100 Down Payment = $892

Finance Charge = $892 Total Price – $800 Cash Price = $92

Then use the finance charge in the APR formula from Figure 18.4:

$$APR = \frac{2 \times 12 \text{ payments} \times \$92 \text{ finance charge}}{\$700 \text{ principal } (12 \text{ payments} + 1)} = \frac{\$2,208}{\$9,100}$$
$$= .2426 = 24.26\%$$

Following the above example, solve for finance charge and APR in the following case:

Mark and Diane bought a new refrigerator. The cash price was $1,200. They paid $49 down and borrowed $1,151, which they will repay in payments of $49 per month for the next 27 months.

Solution:

Total Price Paid = (27 Payments $\times$ $49) + $49 Down Payment = $1,372

Finance Charge = $1,372 Total Price – $1,200 Cash Price = $172

$$APR = \frac{2 \times 12 \times \$172}{\$1,151(27 + 1)} = \frac{\$4,128}{\$32,228} = .1281 = 12.81\%$$

An installment contract requires a **down payment**, which is part of the purchase price paid in cash up front. The down payment reduces the amount of the loan. When you buy a car, you will probably have to pay at least 10 percent of the purchase price in cash. If you trade in your old car, the dealer will likely use the value of your trade-in as your down payment rather than give you cash for your old car.

In the Math Minute, notice that the total price paid is more than the cash price. The total price includes all *installment payments* plus the down payment. Each payment includes principal and interest. The difference between the total price paid and the cash price is the finance charge.

By law, installment contracts must reveal the finance charge and the

NETBookmark

Consumers receive 0% APR credit card offers in the mail every day. Before you decide if this is a good deal, you must understand the pros and cons of such an offer. Access www.cengage.com/school/pfinance/mypf and click on the link for Chapter 18. Read the article about sneaky credit card tricks. Explain how a credit card company can offer 0% APR? Why should you check the "fine print" before signing up for such an offer? What questions should you ask about the offer?

www.cengage.com/school/pfinance/mypf

APR. There are two ways to calculate APR: the APR formula and the APR tables. The APR tables are more precise; the formula only approximates the APR. APR tables can be found on many web sites by doing an online search using the keywords "annual percentage rate tables."

CREDIT CARD BILLING METHODS

The cost of using an open-end (revolving) credit account, such as a credit card, varies with the method the creditor uses to compute the finance charge. Creditors must tell you the method of calculating the finance charge. Finance charges are usually calculated based on the monthly billing cycle. Purchases made up to the closing date are included in the monthly bill. Finance charges are computed on the unpaid balance after the billing date. Creditors must tell you when finance charges begin on your account, so you will know how much time you have to pay your bills before the finance charge is added. Most creditors offering revolving credit give you a 10- to 25-day grace period to pay your balance in full before imposing a finance charge. Creditors may calculate finance charges on open-end credit accounts using the adjusted balance method, the previous balance method, or the average daily balance method. The way the creditor determines the finance charge can make a big difference in the size of your credit card bills.

■ ADJUSTED BALANCE METHOD

When creditors use the *adjusted balance method*, they apply the finance charge only to the amount owed after you've paid your bill each month. For example, suppose your previous month's balance was $400 and you paid $300. If the creditor uses the adjusted balance method, you will pay additional finance charges only on the unpaid balance ($400 – $300 = $100). As you can see in Figure 18.5, the adjusted balance method results in the lowest finance charge.

FIGURE 18.5	*Three Billing Methods for Computing the Finance Charge*

The adjusted balance method, the previous balance method, and the average daily balance method produce different results. This example is based on an APR of 18% and a billing period of 30 days.

	Adjusted Balance Method	Previous Balance Method	Average Daily Balance Method
Monthly Interest Rate	1.5%	1.5%	1.5%
Previous Balance	$400	$400	$400
Payments	$300	$300	$300 (on the 15th day)
Finance Charge	$1.50	$6.00	$3.75
	($100 × 1.5%)	($400 × 1.5%)	(average balance of $250 × 1.5%)*

*To figure average daily balance:

$$\frac{(\$400 \times 15 \text{ days}) + (\$100 \times 15 \text{ days})}{30 \text{ days}} = \$250$$

To calculate the finance charge for this month, first determine the monthly rate by dividing the annual rate (18 percent) by 12 months. In this case, the monthly rate is 1.5 percent. Then multiply the balance due of $100 by 1.5 percent or .015 to determine the finance charge of $1.50. Then add the finance charge to the balance to determine the new account balance for the next billing cycle ($101.50).

PREVIOUS BALANCE METHOD

When creditors use the *previous balance method*, they impose the finance charge on the entire amount owed from the previous month. This method allows no deductions for payments made. As shown in Figure 18.5, this method applies the monthly rate to the entire $400 (previous month's balance). The finance charge is added, and then the payment is deducted to arrive at the new balance ($400 + $6 − $300 = $106), which will be the amount used to calculate the finance charge for the next month. This is the most expensive way to figure the finance charge for the credit user.

AVERAGE DAILY BALANCE METHOD

Most creditors use the *average daily balance method* for computing finance charges. Using this method, creditors calculate your balance on each day of the billing cycle. They then compute average daily balance by adding together all daily balances and dividing by the number of days in the billing cycle (usually 25 or 30). Payments made during the billing cycle are used in figuring the average daily balance. Because payments made during the period reduce the average daily balance, this method often results in a lower finance charge than does the previous balance method.

TWO-CYCLE BILLING

Many credit card companies are using a new, more costly method of calculating average daily balance called *two-cycle billing*. This method calculates the finance charge on the average daily balance over the last two billing periods (typically 2 months) rather than just one. For example, suppose you start with a zero balance. You make a credit purchase on March 10. When the bill arrives on March 30, you make a partial payment. On April 30, you pay it off. With two-cycle billing, even though you paid off the balance, on your May bill, you would still owe interest on the balance you carried in March and April. The result is higher interest and no grace period. You are paying interest from the date of purchase. It's best to avoid credit cards that use two-cycle billing.

© Brand X Pictures/Jupiter Images

How does the billing method affect what you ultimately pay for charged purchases?

Credit authorizers, checkers, and clerks review credit history and get the information needed to determine creditworthiness of individuals applying for credit. Their research includes checking with credit bureaus and verifying information contained on an application.

Credit authorizers approve charges against existing accounts. Computers approve most charges automatically. However, when accounts are past due, overextended, or some other irregularity appears, the credit authorizer may manually override a block or other computer action.

Credit scoring has made the work of credit checkers and clerks much easier. A computer program can assess and assign a score. This is very effective unless the information entered contains errors, is incomplete, or is out of date.

Employment Outlook

- A moderate (8 percent) decline in employment opportunities is expected due to computerization.

Job Titles

- Credit authorizer
- Credit checker
- Credit clerk
- Credit investigator

Needed Skills

- A high school education or its equivalent is required along with formal on-the-job training.

- Good communication, etiquette, and computer skills are needed.

What's it like to work in... *Credit*

Brad is a credit checker at a large financial corporation. Businesses use the services of Brad's company to run credit checks on customers and to provide credit reports. He spends much of his day on the telephone and on the Internet obtaining information from credit bureaus, employers, banks, credit institutions, and other sources.

Today, Brad is completing background checks on loan applicants. In addition to assessing the applicants' credit scores and ratings, he must verify employment history and complete a criminal background check.

Brad usually works a 40-hour week, although he may work overtime during holiday seasons and recruitment periods when stores are actively seeking new credit customers. Brad is organized and good with numbers and details. He enjoys the investigative function of his job and takes pride in producing accurate credit reports for his clients.

What About You?

Are you responsible, organized, and skilled in communication? Do you like completing research and verifying data? Would you enjoy making telephone calls and spending time on the Internet much of the day? Is a career in credit right for you?

Assessment

KEY TERMS REVIEW

Match the terms with the definitions. Some terms may not be used.

_____ 1. Interest computed only on the amount borrowed, without compounding

_____ 2. The interest rate that banks offer to their best business customers

_____ 3. Part of the purchase price paid in cash up front

_____ 4. The percentage of interest you will pay on a loan

_____ 5. Loans for which the interest rate goes up or down with economic conditions

_____ 6. The period during which the borrower will repay a loan

_____ 7. The amount borrowed, or the unpaid portion of the amount borrowed, on which the borrower pays interest

a. down payment

b. fixed-rate loans

c. prime rate

d. principal

e. rate

f. simple interest

g. time

h. variable-rate loans

CHECK YOUR UNDERSTANDING

8. Explain how economic conditions affect the cost of credit.

9. Why is a grace period important to you?

APPLY YOUR KNOWLEDGE

10. Given the following information, compute interest using the simple interest formula: (a) principal is $500, rate is 18%, and time is 6 months; (b) principal is $1,000, rate is 13.5%, and time is 8 months; (c) principal is $108, rate is 15%, and time is 3 months; and (d) principal is $89.50, rate is 8%, and time is 9 months.

THINK CRITICALLY

11. Explain the difference between a fixed-rate loan and a variable-rate loan. Which is better for most purchases? Why?

12. If two credit card offers were identical except for the billing method, which of these would you choose: adjusted balance method, previous balance method, or average daily balance method? Explain.

13. Rather than have their own credit department to process store accounts, many retailers accept major credit cards (Visa and MasterCard) instead. They pay fees amounting to 3 to 5 percent of the charged sales. How might adopting this policy benefit the retailer?

Chapter Assessment

SUMMARY

18.1

- *Your credit responsibilities to yourself include not going into debt beyond what you can comfortably repay, checking out businesses before you buy, comparison shopping, avoiding impulse buying, and using credit with the attitude that you will meet your obligations.*

- *Your responsibilities to creditors involve limiting your spending to amounts you can repay, understanding the terms, and contacting the creditor if an emergency prevents you from making a payment.*

- *Creditors are responsible for assisting consumers in making purchases, applying fair credit policies and informing them of the rules, and dealing fairly with credit problems.*

- *Protect your credit card. Keep account information in a safe place. Notify creditors immediately of a lost or stolen card. Do not lend your card.*

- *To protect your cards online, deal only with companies you trust, enter personal information only if you see the browser's symbol of a secure site that uses encryption, check the site's privacy policy, and don't respond to e-mail or pop-up requests for personal information that could be phishing scams.*

- *To reduce your credit costs, accept only the credit you need (avoid high amounts of unused credit) and make more than the minimum payment each month. Keep no more than two credit cards and pay cash for small purchases. Take advantage of reward programs and rebate plans that will pay you for using the card.*

18.2

- *Factors that determine the cost of credit include the source, amount and length of time financed, ability to repay, economic conditions, type of credit (fixed- or variable-rate loan), prime rate, collateral, and the business's costs of providing credit.*

- *The simple interest formula does not involve compounding: Interest (I) = Principal (P) × Rate (R) × Time (T).*

- *The annual percentage rate (APR) formula calculates the costs of installment credit. It includes the down payment and all monthly payments in the total price. The difference between the total price and the cash price is the finance charge.*

- *Most creditors calculate finance charges by the adjusted balance method, the previous balance method, or the average daily balance method. Finance charges vary depending on the method used.*

APPLY WHAT YOU KNOW

1. Using the simple interest formula, solve for the missing elements, rounding to the nearest penny: (a) Find principal when interest is $8, rate is 12%, and time is 60 days; (b) Find principal when interest is $54, rate is 18%, and time is 18 months; (c) Find rate when interest is $510, principal is $2,100, and time is 2 years; (d) Find rate when interest is $36, principal is $108, and time is 18 months.

2. Using the process illustrated in Figure 18.4 and the Math Minute, determine the APR in the following cases: (a) A $700 purchase requires a down payment of $60 with the balance to be paid in 12 monthly payments of $60 each. (b) A $2,000 purchase requires a down payment of $100 and 24 monthly payments of $90.

3. Using the previous balance method, complete the following chart, using a calculator and rounding to the nearest penny. The APR is 12 percent. What is the total finance charge paid after three months? (Hint: the new balance becomes the previous balance for the next month.)

Previous Balance	+	Finance Charge	−	Payment	=	New Balance
$100		_____		$20.00		_____
_____		_____		20.00		_____
_____		_____		20.00		_____
Total Finance Charge		$ _____				

4. Suppose you decide to pay off your $100 credit card debt by making only the minimum payment of $10 each month. Your APR is 12 percent, and your lender uses the previous balance method. On a separate sheet of paper, complete a chart like the one in question 3 above. Extend the chart until the debt is completely paid off. How many months would it take to pay off the debt if you make only the minimum payment? What total finance charge would you pay?.

MAKE ACADEMIC CONNECTIONS

5. **Technology** Search the Internet for current articles about Internet security. You might find an article about "phishing," about efforts to enhance online security, or about how to shop safely online. Prepare a written report that includes a bulleted list of the key points in the article.

6. **Research** Visit an online shopping site and follow links to the company's privacy policy. Write a one-page paper, analyzing the key points of the policy. In what ways does the company safeguard privacy? In what ways will customers give up some privacy if they buy from this company?

7. **Consumerism** Visit the Federal Reserve System online at www .federalreserve.gov and click on the "Consumer Information" link. Select an article about consumer credit and read it. Based on what you learn, create a presentation using visual aids to present the tips you found most useful.

SOLVE PROBLEMS AND

EXPLORE ISSUES

8. Your friend Leanna is proud of her ability to have and use credit. She buys lunch every day on credit, and at the end of the month she pays only the minimum balance due. When she reaches the limit on one credit card, she switches to another credit card. She thinks she can just go on charging forever. Do you see any problems with this behavior? Explain to Leanna how she is incurring finance charges.

9. Your cousin is considering whether to buy a new sound system. She can use installment credit at the store (18 percent APR), or she can put the purchase on her credit card. Her credit card has a variable rate, which is 9.9 percent right now, but is likely to increase in the next few months. What is your advice?

10. Jason's aunt gave him a loan for $200 and asked him to repay it in 9 months at 5 percent annual interest. How much will Jason owe his aunt 9 months from now?

11. You are considering buying a used piano. The cash price of the piano is $600. The company selling the piano is willing to sell it to you for $50 down plus 12 monthly payments of $50. What is the total price? What is the finance charge?

12. If you were to purchase a major appliance and pay for it this year, borrowing $800 at 18 percent for 8 months, how much would you pay to finance this purchase?

13. You buy a new car that sells for $14,000 by trading in your old car and using the trade-in allowance of $2,000 as a down payment. You pay the balance at $295 a month for 48 months. What is the APR?

14. Logan ran up a credit card debt of $1,000. He decided that he would not put any more purchases on the card until he paid off the debt. He can pay $50 a month, and the interest rate is 18 percent. On the Internet, locate a loan planner tool to find out how many monthly payments Logan will have to make to pay off his debt. How many years will he be paying on the debt?

EXTEND YOUR LEARNING

15. **Ethics** Creditors who make variable-rate loans are quick to raise interest rates when economic conditions change. Many people complain that when the prime rate rises by .25 percent, their loan rates go up by 3 percent or more. Lenders claim they have the legal right to raise rates, because the credit agreements allow for them to do so. Often those who can least afford to pay extra charges are hurt the most. Discuss the ethics of variable-rate loans. Why would consumers accept the terms of a variable-rate loan? Should restrictions be placed on creditors?

For related activities and links, go to **www.cengage.com/school/pfinance/mypf**

Chapter 19

Problems with Credit

| 19.1 | *Solving Credit Problems* |
| 19.2 | *Bankruptcy as an Option* |

Consider **THIS**

Ann Marie has income of $1,500 per month, but when she totals her expenses, she has over $2,100 per month in bills to pay.

"I'm ready for some type of debt relief," Ann Marie told her credit counselor. "My income just doesn't cover my expenses. I didn't overspend, either. Last year I had to have extensive dental work. I also had to get a different car because my old one was costing too much in repairs each month. And then my dog had to have surgery. The end result is that I'm buried. I have more expenses than income!"

Solving Credit Problems

GOALS

- Discuss good credit management rules and warning signs that you are overextended.
- List sources of credit advice.
- Explain how to avoid credit scams.

TERMS

- credit management, *p. 418*
- 20/10 Rule, *p. 418*
- credit payment plan, *p. 420*
- credit counseling, *p. 421*
- debt management plan (DMP), *p. 421*
- debt negotiation program, *p. 422*
- debt adjustment, *p. 422*
- credit repair, *p. 423*

CREDIT MANAGEMENT

One major disadvantage of credit is that it can lead to overspending. Many people get into trouble with credit every year, and they represent all levels of income and social standing.

Credit problems often do not happen suddenly. Certainly, emergencies can and do occur, causing people to get buried in debt. Typically, however, credit problems arise after months and years of poor planning, impulse buying, and careless budgeting. If you recognize early enough that you are falling into excessive debt, you can take steps to fix the problem.

Exercising good **credit management** means following an individual plan for using credit wisely. It involves recognizing your limits and planning your use of credit. There are steps to good credit management, beginning with following the 20/10 Rule.

THE 20/10 RULE

Credit counselors often suggest use of the 20/10 Rule. The **20/10 Rule** is a plan to limit the use of credit to no more than 20 percent of your *yearly* take-home pay, with payments of no more than 10 percent of *monthly* take-home pay. Mortgage loans and monthly payment commitments for housing are not included in these limits. However, all other types of borrowing are included in the limits of the 20/10 Rule.

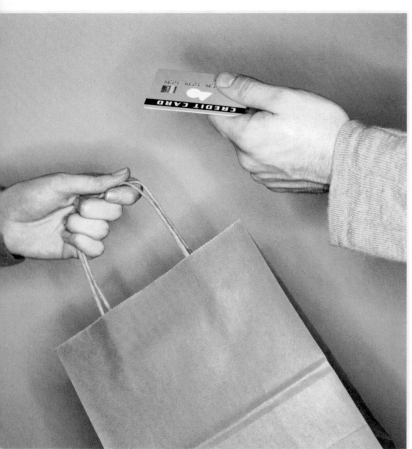

What is meant by credit management?

© Digital Vision/Getty Images

MATH *Minute*

USING THE 20/10 RULE

Take-home pay is roughly 70 percent of gross pay. If your annual salary is $30,000, then your take-home pay (after taxes) is $21,000 ($30,000 × .70). If your annual salary is paid in 12 equal monthly payments of $2,500, your monthly take-home pay is $1,750 ($2,500 × .70).

Using the 20/10 Rule, your total borrowing should not exceed 20 percent of annual take-home pay:

$21,000 × .20 = $4,200 maximum borrowing

Your monthly credit payments should not exceed 10 percent of monthly take-home pay:

$1,750 × .10 = $175 maximum monthly credit payments

Following the 20/10 Rule can help you keep your debt within your means to repay.

Now, assume you have an annual salary of $42,000. Apply the 20/10 Rule to determine your maximum borrowing and monthly credit payments.

Solution:

$42,000 × .70 = $29,400; $29,400 × .20 = $5,880 maximum borrowing

$29,400 ÷ 12 = $2,450; $2,450 × .10 = $245 maximum monthly credit payments

DANGER SIGNS

Another part of credit management is recognizing when you are headed for trouble. It's easy to get caught up in spending—enjoying vacations, purchasing clothes, and eating out with friends and family. Watch for these early warning signs that you are overextending your credit.

- You pay for everything with credit.
- You often pay late or at the end of the grace period.
- You often pay one credit card by shifting the balance to another.
- You worry about how you will be able to pay your bills.
- You recognize that if an emergency arises, you would have inadequate unused credit to take care of it.
- Your credit cards are all near the limit.
- Your credit card companies are raising the interest rates on your accounts because of late payments and charges that have exceeded your credit limit.
- You must time your payments carefully because otherwise you would not have enough income to pay your bills.
- You skip some payments in order to make other payments.
- Your credit rating is falling because you have too much credit.

A CREDIT PAYMENT PLAN

Nobody knows your situation better than you do. Before getting outside help, there are some things you can do first to help yourself. You can sit down with your most recent credit card bills and design a credit payment plan.

A **credit payment plan** is a record of your debts and a strategy for paying them off. Figure 19.1 is an example of what a person's current debt might look like. Listed are all debts, with enough information to analyze which ones should be paid off first. Generally, accounts with the highest interest rates should be first priority. Focus on paying one off at a time, while making only minimum payments on others. As one gets paid off, shift your focus to the next priority.

Once you've listed and analyzed your debt, you can prepare a plan to pay off the balances. Assume you have the debt listed in Figure 19.1, and you have disposable income of $200 per month with which to pay credit card bills. When you add up the minimum monthly payments in Figure 19.1, it totals $125. This leaves $75 ($200 – $125) to add to the minimum payment of the card having the highest priority. Figure 19.2 illustrates the credit payment plan.

FIGURE 19.1   *Current Debt Schedule*

Credit Card/ Account	Current Balance	Credit Limit	Interest Rate	Minimum Monthly Payment	Priority
1. Visa #1	$ 850	$900	18%	$ 55	2
2. Visa #2	450	500	22.9%	15	1
3. Store #1	300	200	14.9%	10	3
4. Store #2	600	400	11.9%	25	4
5. MasterCard	500	300	9.99%	20	5
Totals	$2,700			$125	

FIGURE 19.2   *Credit Payment Plan*

Credit Card/ Account	Current Balance	Monthly Payment	No. of Months Required	New Minimum Monthly Payment
1. Visa #2	$450	$90*	6**	$110***
2. Visa #1	850	145****	7	55
3. Store #1	300	155	3	45
4. Store #2	600	180	4	20
5. MasterCard	500	200	4	0
Total			24	

*$15 (Visa #2 minimum monthly payment) + $75 ($200 − $125) = $90.
**$450 ÷ $90 = 5 months + 1 (additional month to allow for added interest) = 6.
***$125 (total minimum monthly payment) − $15 (Visa #2 minimum monthly payment) = $110.
****$90 (monthly payment that was being paid to Visa #2) + $55 (Visa #1 minimum monthly payment) = $145.

Once Visa #2 is paid off, you can take the $90 you were paying on it and add it to the minimum monthly payment of Visa #1 (the next highest-priority card). You can continue this pattern until the cards are paid off. With this credit payment plan, you will have all of your accounts paid off in 24 months.

In creating the credit payment plan, you should use the original balances for estimation purposes, because by making minimum payments, balances will go down very slowly as interest continues to accumulate. Also, the number of months required to pay off the debt will not be exact, because you are adding one extra month to allow for accumulating interest charges. Finally, the credit payment plan works best when you are responsible and do not incur new debt.

SOURCES OF CREDIT ADVICE

If you find you still need help to get back on your feet, credit advice is available from several reliable sources. Be aware, however, that some sources will try to take advantage of you and leave you worse off than you were before.

CREDIT COUNSELING

Credit counseling is a service to help consumers manage their debt load and credit more wisely. It is available from nonprofit, government-sponsored, or commercial credit counseling services. These organizations can help you redeem your credit and manage your credit better in the future. Services begin with in-depth credit advice.

You may receive free advice and help, or you may be charged fees for the services provided. Much of what is done by a credit counselor you can do for yourself. A counselor will help you set up a realistic budget and will give advice about how to stay within your budget.

You cannot get a loan from a credit counseling service. A counselor can work with your creditors to reduce interest rates and set up a payment plan that you can afford. You could contact creditors and ask for reduced payments and interest rates on your own behalf. However, creditors are often more willing to work with a credit counselor.

When your financial situation is serious and needs immediate action, your credit counselor may suggest you enroll in a debt management plan. A **debt management plan (DMP)** involves giving money each month to a credit counseling organization. The organization uses your money to pay your unsecured debts (such as credit cards) according to the payment plan the counselor develops with you and your creditors. Typically, the creditors have agreed to lower your interest rates and waive fees. These concessions may be available only through a credit counseling organization. Usually debt management plans take 48 months or longer to complete. You also must agree not to use credit while the plan is underway.

You can find consumer credit counseling services in the *Yellow Pages* or through an Internet search. Your local Consumer Credit Counseling Service (CCCS) is a nonprofit organization affiliated with the National Foundation for Credit Counseling (NFCC). Anyone overwhelmed by credit obligations can contact a CCCS office. The NFCC web site will help you find a CCCS office near you. You may even be able to work with a CCCS counselor over the Internet. Some churches, private foundations, universities, military bases, credit unions, and state and federal housing authorities provide similar services.

ONLINE CREDIT ADVICE

There are good online sources of credit advice, both to help you get out of trouble and to stay out of trouble. For example, at the Federal Trade Commission (FTC) web site (www.ftc.gov), you will find consumer information about credit traps to avoid. At the MyMoney web site (www.mymoney.gov), you can find information on credit, credit repair, and current rip-offs against consumers.

DEBT NEGOTIATION

Debt negotiation programs are not the same as debt management or credit counseling. With a **debt negotiation program**, a company you hire will call your creditors on your behalf and negotiate reductions in the amounts you owe. Some advertise that they can negotiate a deal to lower your debt by 10 to 50 percent. These programs are not free and, in some cases, are costly. If you choose debt negotiation, be sure to check with the Attorney General's office of your state to verify that the company you want to hire is legally in business.

What are some sources of good credit advice?

© Photodisc/Getty Images

And be prepared—while your debts may be lowered, your credit rating is likely to fall as well.

DEBT ADJUSTMENT

People who are in deeper credit trouble than advice can solve often go to a finance company for debt adjustment. **Debt adjustment** is the formal process of taking over your debt situation for a period of time, after which you will be free of debt. There are two types of debt adjustment: a debt adjustment service plan and a debt consolidation loan.

Debt Adjustment Service Plan

With a *debt adjustment service plan*, a finance company takes over your checkbook, your paycheck, and your bills. This is similar to a debt management plan (DMP), except you hand over complete control of your finances to a counselor. You are given only a small spending allowance. The counselor uses your checkbook to make the payments on your unsecured and revolving credit accounts for a period of three to five years, after which time your checkbook is returned to you. To be eligible for a debt adjustment plan, you need to maintain a monthly income, and that income must be sufficient to pay off your bills in three to five years. Typically, this service involves a five-step plan. A counselor will do the following:

1. Take your paycheck and checkbook and make debt payments for you
2. Counsel you so that you understand how you got so far in debt and how to avoid doing so again in the future
3. Work with you to create a reasonable budget with which you can live
4. Take away your credit cards and give them back slowly as the counselor becomes certain that you understand how to use them wisely
5. Supervise your budget and help you make any needed changes or adjustments

Debt Consolidation Loan

With a *debt consolidation loan*, the finance company loans you money to pay off your debts. You then make a monthly payment to the finance company, instead of to your creditors, until the debt is repaid. To qualify for a consolidation loan, you must have some type of collateral, such as a house, that secures the payment of the debt. If you make payments as agreed, the second mortgage on your house is released. If you fail to make payments as agreed, the house is foreclosed. *Foreclosure* is a legal process where property used as collateral is sold to pay off a debt.

CREDIT REPAIR

After the damage is done and your credit rating is poor, you can take steps to repair it. **Credit repair** is the process of reestablishing a good credit rating. You can obtain copies of your credit reports, challenge incorrect information, and respond to disputes. For a fee, a credit repair company will complete these steps for you. Beware of credit repair companies that "guarantee" to reestablish your credit and cleanse your record—credit bureaus do not sell this service; it must be earned.

If your credit rating is poor for good reasons, you can begin to repair your record by using credit responsibly from this point on. Start by paying off your debts through credit counseling or debt adjustment. Then begin the repair process by making small purchases on your credit card and paying off the balance in full each month. Credit repair is a slow process. It may take several years of responsible credit management to raise your rating enough to enable you to get a loan when you need one.

The Federal Trade Commission offers advice to consumers with credit problems. Access www.cengage.com/school/pfinance/mypf and click on the link for Chapter 19. Read the tips, and answer the following questions: What is the only way to assure the removal of accurate negative information from your credit report? Can you get out from under debt by inventing a new credit identity by using an Employer Identification Number? Why is it a good idea for all consumers to periodically review their credit reports?

www.cengage.com/school/pfinance/mypf

CREDIT SCAMS

Credit counseling, debt adjustment, and repair scams abound. You may receive e-mail or pop-up messages, see TV ads, or get calls from telemarketers promising to repair your credit record "instantly." They may offer to reduce

What red flags should alert you to a credit scam?

your debt if you pay a fee up front or sign your house over to them. Such promises are warning signs of a scam.

PROMISES AND GUARANTEES

Paying off a large debt and repairing a poor credit record take time—often several years of responsible credit management. Beware of offers that do the following:

- Require you to pay a fee before they perform any service
- Do not tell you your legal rights
- Suggest that you start a "new" credit report by applying for a new Social Security number or Employer Identification Number (EIN)
- Recommend that you do not contact the credit bureau or creditors yourself

By law, credit-assistance companies may not charge you until they have performed the promised services. They must give you a copy of the "Consumer Credit File Rights Under State and Federal Law" before you sign a contract. They must provide a written contract that shows the organization's name and address and spells out the payments, total cost, and services to be performed. Every state has legitimate nonprofit credit counseling services that charge little or no fee. Your local bank or government consumer protection office can supply a list of reputable organizations.

GOLD AND PLATINUM CARDS

Be wary of some gold and platinum cards that promise to improve your credit rating. While they may look like general-purpose credit cards, they often permit you to buy only goods from special catalogs. The promises that these cards will lead to future credit offers, larger credit lines, and better credit reports are usually false. These cards are examples of "easy access" credit. Watch for promotions of gold and platinum cards that:

- Charge upfront fees of $50 or more, and then charge additional fees to cover the costs of catalogs and other items.
- Use 900 or 976 telephone exchanges. You will be charged for phone calls with these prefixes, and the costs can be high.
- Misrepresent prices and payments. Often you are not allowed to charge the total amount; you must make a cash deposit. For example, if the catalog price is $200, you might be allowed to charge only $150, with the remaining $50 to be paid in cash.
- Promise to improve your credit. The cards you may be offered will be "secured," which means you'll have to maintain a savings account as security for your line of credit. This deposit requirement makes the offer, in fact, not credit.

Lawyers, also called attorneys, are both advisors and advocates. As advisors, they counsel clients about their legal rights and duties, suggest courses of action, and prepare legal documents. As advocates, they represent clients at trial, both civil and criminal.

Attorneys also specialize. Trial lawyers communicate well and specialize in litigation—courtroom actions. Other areas include bankruptcy, probate, divorce, real estate, and contract law, to name only a few.

About one-fourth of lawyers are self-employed. Most work in private practice. Bankruptcy attorneys practice law in federal district trial courts. They represent individuals and businesses that are experiencing severe financial difficulties.

Employment Outlook

- An average rate of employment growth is expected.

Job Titles

- Trial lawyer
- Attorney at law
- District attorney
- U.S. attorney
- Bankruptcy attorney

Needed Skills

- Must have a bachelor's degree followed by a J.D. (doctorate in jurisprudence).
- Must be licensed by the state(s) in which law is practiced, requiring passage of the state's bar exam.
- Must have excellent communication and negotiation skills.

What's it like to work in... *Law*

Celia is an attorney specializing in bankruptcy. She spends considerable time talking to potential clients about their options involving bankruptcy. She has an initial consultation with them in which she discusses the clients' financial situation. Once Celia has a better grasp of clients' debts and obligations, she works with them to explore their options, such as the various types of bankruptcy. In some cases, bankruptcy is not the best option.

Today will begin with two initial consultations followed by a court appearance. Celia's court appearance will be the final hearing for a client who has completed an intensive debt repayment program for some of his accounts. Today her client will have the remainder of his debts discharged.

Celia enjoys helping people and giving them advice and encouragement to improve their financial health. Many of her clients are overwhelmed with debt and need immediate relief from debt collection.

What About You?

Would you like to learn about legislation and apply it to help others in need? Are you interested in a career that involves communicating effectively in a courtroom environment? Would you consider a career as an attorney?

Assessment

KEY TERMS REVIEW

Match the terms with the definitions. Some terms may not be used.

_____ 1. *The process of reestablishing a good credit rating*

_____ 2. *A service to help consumers manage their debt load and credit more wisely*

_____ 3. *Following an individual plan for using credit wisely*

_____ 4. *Hiring a company to call your creditors to negotiate reductions in the amounts owed*

_____ 5. *The formal process of taking over your debt situation for a period of time, after which you will be free of debt*

_____ 6. *A plan to limit the use of credit to no more than 20 percent of yearly take-home pay, with payments of no more than 10 percent of monthly take-home pay*

_____ 7. *A record of your debts and a strategy for paying them off*

a. 20/10 Rule

b. credit counseling

c. credit management

d. credit payment plan

e. credit repair

f. debt adjustment

g. debt management plan (DMP)

h. debt negotiation program

CHECK YOUR UNDERSTANDING

8. *Does the 20/10 Rule apply to all types of credit? Explain your answer.*

9. *How is credit counseling different from debt adjustment?*

10. *How can you avoid credit counseling scams?*

APPLY YOUR KNOWLEDGE

11. *What are some warning signs that you are overusing credit and will soon have credit problems? What choices do you have (in the order you would pursue them) to help you solve your credit problems?*

THINK *CRITICALLY*

12. *Explain how the 20/10 Rule is helpful as an individual manages his or her use of credit. Why is it important for consumers to consider credit management?*

13. *Why should individuals try a credit payment plan before seeking other types of credit advice?*

14. *Explain the two types of debt adjustment plans. Which one do you think is better? Why?*

Bankruptcy as an Option

GOALS

- List and describe the types of bankruptcy.
- Discuss the major causes of bankruptcy.
- Explain the advantages and disadvantages of declaring bankruptcy.

TERMS

- bankruptcy, *p. 427*
- involuntary bankruptcy, *p. 428*
- voluntary bankruptcy, *p. 428*
- discharged debts, *p. 428*
- Chapter 7 bankruptcy, *p. 428*
- Chapter 13 bankruptcy, *p. 429*
- reaffirmation, *p. 429*
- exempted property, *p. 431*

WHAT IS BANKRUPTCY?

When a person gets into serious and irreversible debt and cannot pay the bills, the final and most serious step is bankruptcy. **Bankruptcy** is a legal process that relieves debtors of the responsibility of paying their debts or protects them while they try to repay. When you declare bankruptcy, you are said to be *insolvent*. This means you have insufficient income and assets to pay your debts. Bankruptcy is a second chance, but it carries serious consequences.

BANKRUPTCY LAWS AND THEIR PURPOSE

Bankruptcy law in the United States has two goals. The first is to protect debtors by giving them a fresh start, free from creditors' claims. The second is to give fair treatment to creditors competing for debtors' assets. Many creditors complain that the bankruptcy code requires them to tighten credit policies because it is too easy for people to give up their debts rather than accept responsibility for them. On the other hand, bankruptcy casts a long, dark shadow over an individual's credit record.

What are the two main purposes of bankruptcy law?

Bankruptcy laws treat two general classes of debt: secured and unsecured. As you learned in Chapter 18, *secured loans* are backed by specific assets that the debtor pledged as collateral to assure repayment. If the debtor does not pay, the creditor can take possession of the pledged asset. *Unsecured debt* is a loan that is not backed by pledged assets. In bankruptcy, most of the debtor's resources may be used to repay unsecured debt.

▌ TYPES OF BANKRUPTCY

Bankruptcy can be voluntary or involuntary. **Involuntary bankruptcy** occurs when creditors file a petition with the court, asking the court to declare you, the debtor, bankrupt. If the court agrees, it takes over your assets to pay off as much of your debt as possible. Involuntary bankruptcy does not occur very often, because most creditors would prefer to be repaid in full over a period of time rather than settle only for a portion of your remaining assets.

Voluntary bankruptcy, the most common kind, occurs when you file a petition with a federal court asking to be declared bankrupt. The court notifies your creditors of the pending bankruptcy. Once notice is given, creditors may file claims. The court decides how much debt you will pay, what assets you can keep, and what debts will be canceled. Usually the value of all the bankrupt debtor's assets is not enough to pay off all the debts. The court trustee sells the assets and gives each creditor a share.

Discharged debts are debts erased by the court during bankruptcy proceedings. Creditors can no longer seek payment for these debts. Some debts are not discharged and must still be paid. These include child support, alimony, income taxes and penalties, student loans, and court-ordered damages due to malicious or illegal acts. Once declared bankrupt, an individual cannot file for bankruptcy again for several years (based on the type of bankruptcy).

The bankruptcy process deals with debtors in one of two ways: liquidation or reorganization. Under *liquidation*, the court sells the debtors' assets and uses the proceeds to pay as much of the debt as possible. The remaining debt is then discharged. Under *reorganization*, debtors may keep their property but must submit a payment plan to the court for repaying a substantial portion of their debts.

The types of bankruptcy can be distinguished by which of these methods is used. *Chapter 11 bankruptcy* is a reorganization form of bankruptcy for businesses that allows them to continue operating under court supervision as they repay their restructured debts. The two kinds of bankruptcy available to individuals are Chapter 7 and Chapter 13.

Chapter 7 Bankruptcy

Commonly called *straight bankruptcy*, **Chapter 7 bankruptcy** is a liquidation form of bankruptcy for individuals. It wipes out most debts in exchange for giving up most assets. Some assets that are considered necessary for survival may be retained. The advantage of Chapter 7 bankruptcy is immediate debt relief—large debts are wiped out as well as any payments on the debt. All collections must stop as soon as bankruptcy is filed. Debtors have a clean slate to start over. However, recent bankruptcy laws make it more difficult for a person to qualify for straight (liquidation) bankruptcy.

Chapter 13 Bankruptcy

Chapter 13 bankruptcy is a reorganization (payment plan) form of bankruptcy for individuals. It allows debtors to keep most of their property and use their income to pay a portion of their debts over three to five years. Debtors work out a court-enforced repayment plan. Under Chapter 13, often referred to as the *wage-earner's plan*, some debts are totally discharged, while others are paid off as agreed within the payment period.

Chapter 13 bankruptcy may seem better for the debtor in terms of reestablishing credit. However, the blemish on the debtor's credit record caused by any form of bankruptcy is hard to overcome for many years.

LEGAL ADVICE

A person considering bankruptcy should seek good legal advice. In most states, it is possible to file for bankruptcy without an attorney. But the law is complicated, and a good bankruptcy attorney can help you navigate through the details. The attorney can also assist you in deciding which bankruptcy plan will work best to help you solve your credit problems.

© Photodisc/Getty Images

Why is it best to seek legal advice if you are filing for bankruptcy?

REAFFIRMATION OF DEBTS

Creditors may ask debtors to agree to pay their debts, even after bankruptcy has discharged them. **Reaffirmation** is the agreement to pay debts that have been legally discharged. You may choose to reaffirm a particular debt if a friend or family member cosigned the loan and you don't want to burden this person with the debt. Also, you may choose to reaffirm rather than allow the collateral, such as a car, to be repossessed. Reaffirmation requires a court hearing, and debtors have 30 days to change their minds about promising to repay. A creditor is prohibited from harassing debtors to reaffirm after the court proceedings are over.

MAJOR CAUSES OF BANKRUPTCY

Bankruptcy is a last-resort solution to credit problems. Common reasons why individuals file for bankruptcy are job loss, emotional spending, failure to budget and develop a good financial plan, and catastrophic injury or illness.

Some businesses, such as credit card companies, believe that consumers abuse credit laws and take advantage of creditors. They believe bankruptcy laws are too lenient and make it possible for people to run up debts and then walk away from them. These businesses believe that credit is a privilege and not a right, and people should be held accountable for their decisions.

Others believe that credit laws are designed to protect consumers from unscrupulous businesses that would take advantage of them.

Bankruptcy is the ultimate protection to give consumers a new start when they get buried in debt that they can never repay. Those holding this viewpoint believe that creditors use deceptive practices to lure people into buying things they cannot afford. Then they raise interest rates and minimum payments, trapping consumers into a cycle of debt.

THINK *CRITICALLY*

With which side do you agree? What is your attitude toward credit laws, such as bankruptcy protection for consumers?

■ JOB LOSS

According to Consumers Union, two-thirds of people in bankruptcy have been unemployed for a period of time before the filing. While you cannot control unexpected events in life, such as a layoff, you can plan and save for them. Rather than spend all your income, save a portion each month to help you get through rough financial times. Avoid overuse of credit, locking you into high payments. If unemployment causes your income to fall, these payments could push you into bankruptcy.

■ EMOTIONAL SPENDING

Consumers often get into trouble because of purchases based on emotion rather than reason. Buy to meet your needs, not to impress people and not for recreation. Impulse purchases can quickly add up to more debt than you can afford.

■ FAILURE TO BUDGET AND PLAN

Many people who go bankrupt neither have nor follow a budget. Many do not know how to set up a budget and are not willing to ask for help in solving their credit problems. Bankruptcy is not a condition limited to poor people. Poor planning can occur at any income level. No matter what your financial position, you must keep your spending and borrowing in proportion to your income. Most causes of bankruptcy can be avoided by careful planning and decision making, based on good financial judgment, advice, and goals.

■ CATASTROPHIC INJURY OR ILLNESS

Medical care costs a great deal. Many people are uninsured or underinsured. Some insurance policies have high deductibles, holes in coverage, and dollar limits for major illnesses. While not all catastrophic injuries or illnesses result in bankruptcy, they often damage a person's finances for many years. For example, a person hospitalized for a long time with a critical illness could easily owe $100,000 a month for medical care, drugs, room charges, and other fees. If the person has no insurance, his or her savings can be wiped out in the first month. Many people with this type of debt try to pay it back at a rate they can afford. It may be years, even decades, before this type of debt can possibly be repaid, if ever.

BANKRUPTCY: FRIEND OR FOE?

Bankruptcy has its pluses, but it also comes with its downside. A person considering bankruptcy should carefully weigh the advantages and disadvantages of declaring bankruptcy.

ADVANTAGES OF BANKRUPTCY

For individuals whose debt situation seems hopeless, bankruptcy offers a solution. While this solution is not without a price, bankruptcy does offer the following advantages:

- *Debts are erased.* Bankruptcy offers a fresh start. It reduces or eliminates overwhelming bills, and the debtors can start over. With good financial planning and counseling, they can avoid future credit problems. However, future credit may be more difficult to obtain and much more costly for anyone who has filed bankruptcy.

- *Exempted assets are retained.* While Chapter 7 bankruptcy requires debtors to give up most of their assets in order to erase their debts, they can keep certain amounts and types of **exempted property**, or those assets considered necessary for survival. Exempted property includes a limited amount of equity in a residence, interest in a vehicle, personal property and furnishings, clothing, some jewelry, and tools of the trade, including books and equipment. Exempted items allow the debtor to start over and have a base with which to begin.

- *Certain incomes are unaffected.* Bankruptcy will not affect certain types of income a debtor may have, such as Social Security, veterans' benefits, unemployment compensation, alimony, child support, disability payments, and payments from pension, profit-sharing, and annuity plans. These sources of income need not be considered even in a Chapter 13 bankruptcy, in which a required payment plan is established.

© Photodisc/Getty Images

What is exempted property? Why is it important?

- *The cost is small.* Attorneys' fees and court costs in bankruptcy are relatively small in comparison to the amount of financial relief provided. On the first visit to an attorney's office, a debtor will be given total cost estimates and information about the options available in bankruptcy proceedings.

■ DISADVANTAGES OF BANKRUPTCY

While bankruptcy offers debt relief, it carries serious consequences. Bankruptcy should be considered a last resort. Some of the disadvantages of bankruptcy include the following:

- *Credit is damaged.* A bankruptcy judgment destroys your credit record for a long time. This judgment remains on your credit records for seven to ten years. During that time, you could find it very difficult or impossible to obtain credit. If you did get credit, it would be at a very high interest rate because you would be considered a very high risk. For example, credit card interest rates often exceed 25 percent for people who have filed bankruptcy. Bankruptcy is a red flag to creditors and others that you were at one time unable or unwilling to meet your financial responsibilities. Depending on the circumstances that caused the bankruptcy, people may continue to mistrust you in business affairs for well beyond the ten years.
- *Property is lost.* Most of your property will be taken away and sold to pay your debts. You may not even be able to keep exempt assets. Assume that you own a house worth $120,000 that has a mortgage of $90,000 against it. Your equity is $30,000. While the bankruptcy code (2007) allows you to keep the first $20,200 of equity in your home, you may be required to sell the home. You will be allowed to keep $20,200, and the remaining amount must be used to pay off creditors. Or, if you own a car valued at $5,000 and you owe $2,800 on it, your equity is $2,200. Since this amount is less than the allowance for a car according to bankruptcy law, ($3,225 in 2007) you will not have to sell the car. However, if you own a car valued at $9,000 with a loan of $5,000, your equity is $4,000. You are allowed only equity of $3,225. In this case, you will probably have to sell the car and use all proceeds over $3,225 to help pay off your creditors.
- *You may not qualify for liquidation.* Recent bankruptcy law changes make it difficult for people to file for Chapter 7 (straight) bankruptcy. Thus, they will be required to complete a three- or five-year payment plan.
- *Some debts continue.* Regardless of the type of bankruptcy selected, all debt is not erased. Certain obligations, such as for child support and alimony, will remain after bankruptcy. Income taxes and related penalties that are less than three years old, student loans, and other debts at the discretion of the bankruptcy court will also remain. Also, if a lender can prove that there was any type of false representation on the debtor's part in connection with a debt, the debt will not be discharged.
- *Some debts can be reaffirmed.* You may feel the need to reaffirm some debts to protect your cosigners or avoid losing an important asset. However, by reaffirming, you will not get the fresh start that you probably need.
- *Cosigners must pay.* After you have been declared bankrupt under Chapter 7, your cosigners must repay the loans they cosigned. Cosigners are likely to be your close friends or family members. Leaving them saddled with the debt can damage your personal relationships.

ISSUES IN YOUR WORLD

WHEN BANKRUPTCY IS THE BEST CHOICE

Ben and Michelle were married less than two years when she became pregnant with their first child. He was working full time and had good health insurance that paid 80 percent of all charges that were reasonable and necessary. The pregnancy appeared to be normal until shortly before the expected delivery date. At that time, it was discovered that the baby would be born with serious health problems, including a hole in her heart, birth defects that would leave her deaf, and underdeveloped organs that would require considerable medical attention.

Six months later, the baby came home, having survived six weeks in the hospital, three surgeries, and a poor prognosis. She would have to undergo several more surgeries in order to repair the damage and birth defects. During that time, Ben had to change jobs so he could have better coverage (most medical policies have maximum amounts they pay out on one individual). In addition, many procedures were considered "experimental" for which the insurance company would not pay. Still, the couple wanted their daughter to live, so they pledged their house and all other assets to secure medical care.

Medical technology has come a long way. When the baby was a year old, she had her last operation. It both repaired her hearing loss and allowed for the removal of feeding tubes so that she could, for the first time, eat on her own. When the final medical bills came in, the couple found themselves owing more than $300,000 to hospitals, doctors, labs, and surgeons.

Faced with payments that were overwhelming, the couple elected bankruptcy. It was the best choice for several reasons. First, even by spreading out payments over ten years, they would be unable to meet other financial obligations. Second, the debt would prevent them from moving forward with a financial plan for the future of their child as well as their own financial security. Third, bankruptcy allowed them the debt relief they needed to avoid the stress of overwhelming debt.

THINK CRITICALLY

1. *Do you agree that filing bankruptcy was the best option for Ben and Michelle? Explain why or why not.*

2. *Do you know someone who has faced a financial disaster for which bankruptcy was (or might yet be) the best solution? Explain why. Or, describe a situation in which you think bankruptcy would be the best solution.*

3. *Assume you know someone who is facing bankruptcy because of overspending, careless planning, or greed. What advice would you give this person?*

Assessment

KEY TERMS REVIEW

Match the terms with the definitions. Some terms may not be used.

_____ 1. Debts erased by the court

_____ 2. The agreement to pay debts that have been legally discharged

_____ 3. A legal process that relieves debtors of the responsibility of paying their debts or protects them while they try to repay

_____ 4. A reorganization (payment plan) form of bankruptcy for individuals

_____ 5. Assets considered necessary for survival that a bankrupt debtor is allowed to keep

_____ 6. Bankruptcy that occurs when creditors file a petition with the court against a debtor

_____ 7. A liquidation form of bankruptcy for individuals

a. bankruptcy

b. Chapter 7 bankruptcy

c. Chapter 13 bankruptcy

d. discharged debts

e. exempted property

f. involuntary bankruptcy

g. reaffirmation

h. voluntary bankruptcy

CHECK YOUR UNDERSTANDING

8. What kinds of spending are most likely to get you into credit trouble? What can you do to avoid these dangers?

9. Do you believe that advantages of bankruptcy outweigh the disadvantages? Explain.

APPLY YOUR KNOWLEDGE

10. List the four major causes of bankruptcy for individuals. Next to each one, explain what you could do to avoid bankruptcy caused by these events.

THINK CRITICALLY

11. How is Chapter 7 bankruptcy different from Chapter 13 bankruptcy? Which do you think is the best form for a person with enormous debts?

12. Explain why bankruptcy may be the best option for some consumers, giving advantages and reasons for choosing a form of bankruptcy.

13. Explain the disadvantages of bankruptcy and explore reasons why it should be a person's last resort.

Chapter Assessment

SUMMARY

19.1

- Consumers should have a responsible credit management plan. The 20/10 Rule suggests that your total debt not exceed 20 percent of yearly take-home pay and that your monthly payments not exceed 10 percent of your monthly take-home pay.

- Danger signs that you are overextended include buying everything with credit, paying late, using one account to pay another, worrying about debt, having inadequate unused credit to meet emergencies, reaching card limits, skipping payments, and having a falling credit rating.

- Consumers should manage their credit with a credit payment plan, which is a strategy to pay off the most expensive debt first.

- Credit counseling services provide budgeting advice and work with your creditors to create a payment plan you can afford.

- With a debt management plan, you give money each month to a credit counseling organization that uses it to pay off your debt.

- Debt negotiation involves hiring a company that will work with creditors to reduce the balances owed.

- Debt adjustment involves either a debt adjustment service plan, in which you hand over control of your finances, or a debt consolidation loan.

19.2

- Bankruptcy laws are designed to help people get a fresh start and to provide fair treatment to creditors competing for the debtor's assets.

- Bankruptcy may be voluntary (filed by debtor) or involuntary (filed by creditors against the debtor).

- Chapter 7 bankruptcy is a liquidation form in which debtors must give up most of their assets in exchange for having debts discharged.

- Chapter 13 bankruptcy is a reorganization form in which debtors may keep most of their property and repay a portion of their debts following a court-enforced repayment plan.

- Common causes of bankruptcy are job loss, emotional spending, failure to budget, and catastrophic injury or illness.

- Advantages of bankruptcy include that debts are erased, exempted assets are retained, certain incomes are unaffected, and the cost is small.

- Disadvantages of bankruptcy include that credit is damaged, property is lost, you may not qualify for liquidation, some debts continue, some debts can be reaffirmed, and cosigners must still pay.

APPLY WHAT YOU KNOW

1. Search the Yellow Pages, business directories, and the Internet, and list several of the following: (a) nonprofit credit counseling services, (b) finance companies that offer debt adjustment services, (c) attorneys specializing in bankruptcy, (d) classes or other credit counseling services provided in the community, either for a fee or free. Visit the web site of one organization of each type and write a brief summary of the kinds of information and services it provides.

2. Search the Internet for advice on staying out of credit trouble. Make a list of at least five tips that you find helpful. Note the URL of the web sites.

3. Mark and Julie have the following debts:

   - Credit Card #1: $2,000 balance, 18% interest, minimum payments of $30 per month

   - Credit Card #2: $1,000 balance, 15% interest, minimum payments of $20 per month

   - Credit Card #3: $3,000 balance, 24.99% interest, minimum payments of $50 per month

   - Store Account #1: $800 balance, 21% interest, minimum payments of $40 per month

   Prepare a credit payment plan. How many months will it take to pay off their credit cards if they have $200 per month to make credit payments?

4. Check the classified section of your newspaper for bankruptcy notices every day for one week. Answer these questions: (a) How many total bankruptcies were filed in the seven-day period? (b) What is the lowest amount of debt claimed? (c) What is the highest amount of debt claimed? (d) What was the lowest amount of property claimed as exempt? (e) What was the highest amount of property claimed as exempt?

5. Search for articles online or in print publications for information on the most recent bankruptcy laws in your state. List the exempted amounts for the most current year for (a) homestead, (b) personal property, (c) jewelry, (d) motor vehicles, (e) tools of trade, and (f) wild card—any property.

MAKE ACADEMIC CONNECTIONS

6. **History** Look up the original federal Bankruptcy Act of 1898 in a reference book or online and write a report covering the following: (a) provisions of the law (in outline form), (b) exempted items allowed and types of income excluded, and (c) procedures or steps involved in filing bankruptcy. Write a report about your findings.

7. **Economics** Although bankruptcy is used by consumers to get a "fresh start," it has other effects on businesses and the economy. Research the impacts of bankruptcy on our economy and prepare a short report.

8. **International Studies** Choose another nation in the world. Conduct Internet research and prepare a presentation on bankruptcy law in that country. Compare it to U.S. bankruptcy law. How is it different? How is it similar? Which one is better? Why?

SOLVE PROBLEMS AND

EXPLORE ISSUES

9. Your friend Al has trouble paying his bills. He has taken a second job in order to make all his payments, but the long hours and hard work are causing him health problems. What suggestions do you have in helping him manage his credit problems?

10. Mark and June have decided to get help with their credit problems rather than declare bankruptcy. They want to extend the time for repaying loans, but they don't want to hand over their checkbook and credit cards to a finance company. What other options do they have?

11. Betty owns a small store. The store has been losing money for some time. Because she is the sole owner of the business, her personal assets are at risk. Explain to Betty the differences among Chapters 7, 11, and 13 bankruptcy.

12. Dan is considering bankruptcy. He has the following assets: $34,000 equity in home, $5,000 equity in motor vehicle, $500 in personal items and clothing, $2,000 in appliances and furnishings, $2,000 in tools of the trade, and $8,000 in jewelry. Using the table below, how much (total) will he be allowed in exempted items?

Federal Bankruptcy Exemptions, Effective April 1, 2007:

Homestead	$20,200
Life insurance	10,775
Personal property	525 per item, up to $10,775
Jewelry	1,350
Motor vehicle	3,225
Tools of trade, books, or equipment	2,025
Wild card	1,075 of any property

EXTEND YOUR LEARNING

13. **Legal Issues** *Willfully hiding assets (in storage units or other places) so that they won't be used to pay off debts is called* bankruptcy fraud. *It is a federal crime. It is also illegal to transfer title to assets to relatives or friends so that they won't be part of the bankruptcy estate. The bankruptcy trustee must be able to access a debtor's full assets in order to fairly distribute lawful amounts to creditors. Why do people try to hide and transfer assets? How could they get caught? What are the penalties for this type of crime? Do you think the penalties are fair? Why or why not?*

For related activities and links, go to **www.cengage.com/school/pfinance/mypf**

Suze Orman

Born Susan Lynn Orman in Chicago in 1951, Orman came from a working class background and says she "did not grow up with money." She has a BA in social work from the University of Illinois, but she began her working life as a waitress at the Buttercup Bakery in Berkeley, California (1973). In 1980, a long time customer gave her a $50,000 loan to use toward her dream of opening her own restaurant. She tried investing the money but was swindled by a stockbroker. Orman took it as a hard lesson and decided to learn more about financing and investing. She went to work for Merrill Lynch and

© Chris Haston/NBCU Photo Bank via AP Images

completed training to become an account executive. She stayed there until 1983 and then moved on to the position of vice president of investments with Prudential Bache Securities. In 1987 she opened her own financial planning company. In 1997, she stepped down from Suze Orman Financial Group to write books and pursue her television personality goals.

Orman has written several books including *The Courage to be Rich*, *The Road to Wealth*, and *Women and Money: Owning the Power to Control Your Destiny*. She has a Q&A advice section in *O, The Oprah Magazine*, writes a biweekly column entitled "Money Matters" on the Yahoo! Finance web site, and contributes articles to magazines such as *Costco Connection* and *Your Business At Home*. Orman hosts a weekend financial planning show on CNBC called *The Suze Orman Show* and a TV program on QVC called *Suze Orman's Financial Freedom*. As of 2008, Orman's personal net worth was more than $10 million.

Orman has a straightforward approach, telling it as she sees it. She believes that people use too much credit and that overuse of credit is irresponsible. She advises people to get out of debt and save for the future. She explains that credit is a trap, and it's easy to get caught. Financial freedom is based on having money to spend, not tying it up on purchases you really cannot afford. She advises consumers to act responsibly and to not spend more than they can comfortably pay back.

THINK *CRITICALLY*

1. *How did writing books help Orman achieve success?*

2. *Explain what Orman means by "credit is a trap."*

3. *Will you follow Orman's advice regarding how to achieve financial independence? Why or why not?*

Managing Credit and Debt

Overview

Previous unit projects focused on examining your financial position, building and protecting your savings and investments, and planning your retirement and estate. In this project, you will learn more about credit and debt load and how to protect yourself from credit card fraud.

YOUR USE OF CREDIT

Credit will enable you to enjoy a standard of living that otherwise would not be possible. Nearly everyone uses credit. Wise consumers analyze their use of credit annually, comparing sources, interest rates, minimum payments, and other features (such as rebates). Understanding your current credit and planning future credit purchases is a part of good credit management. To analyze your use of credit, complete Worksheet 1 provided for you in the *Student Activity Guide* and also presented for reference on the next page.

When examining your use of credit, you may want to keep control sheets for tracking your progress in paying off debts. A sample control sheet is shown in Figure U4.1. You can make similar sheets for each credit account and track the monthly payments. At the end of the year, you can total the finance charges.

Keeping the control sheets will help you see the true cost of your credit card purchases. It will also encourage you as you see the debt going down.

© Comstock Images/Jupiter Images

WORKSHEET 1
Credit Analysis

Directions: List each type of credit you have and its features. Then complete the analysis to determine what action can and should be taken.

	Monthly Payment	No. of Payments Left	Outstanding Balance	APR	Special Features	Ranking
Installment credit:	_____	_____	_____	____	_____	_____
Personal loans:						
Automobile	_____	_____	_____	____	_____	_____
Home improvement	_____	_____	_____	____	_____	_____
Other:_____	_____	_____	_____	____	_____	_____
_____	_____	_____	_____	____	_____	_____
Charge accounts:						
1._____	_____		_____	____	_____	_____
2._____	_____		_____	____	_____	_____
3._____	_____		_____	____	_____	_____

Total debt outstanding................................ $_____

Average APR... _____

How long will it take to pay off the outstanding debt? (Total outstanding debt divided by total monthly payments)

_____

Which debts do you feel comfortable with? _____

_____

Which debts will you pay off first (those with highest rates/priority ranking)? _____

_____

_____

What are some anticipated future debt needs?_____

_____

_____

Which credit sources will you use for future debt (those with lowest rates)?_____

_____

_____

FIGURE U4.1 *Control Sheet*

Control Sheet: VISA Account

(1) Date	(2) Previous Balance	(3) Payments (Credits)	(4) New Charges (Debits)	(5) Finance Charge	(6) New Balance (2 − 3 + 4 + 5)
1/1	$280.63	$35.00	$20.00	$7.22	$272.85
2/3	272.85	35.00	0	7.01	244.86
3/2	244.86	35.00	15.00	6.88	231.74
3/4	231.74	35.00	0	6.55	203.29

YOUR DEBT LOAD

A *debt load* is the amount of outstanding debt at a particular time. Whether your debt load is acceptable to you will depend on your ability to meet the regular payments, your ability to pay off the debt quickly if necessary, and your level of comfort with the amount of debt you owe.

One rule says that installment debt should not exceed 20 percent of yearly take-home pay. Another holds that you should be able to pay off all installment debts in one year at your current monthly payments. Still another says that you should be able to pay off your debts within 30 days if absolutely necessary (with all the cash you can raise).

Complete your debt-load analysis, using Worksheet 2 provided for you in the *Student Activity Guide* and also presented for reference below. Compute your self-score. Assessing your debt load will help you determine the severity of your debt problem so that you can take corrective action if necessary.

WORKSHEET 2
Your Debt Load

Directions: Answer the following statements with a "Yes" or "No." Then read the information following the statements to make an assessment of your debt load.

1. You pay only the minimum amount due each month on charge and credit accounts.   YES   NO

2. You make so many credit purchases that your debt load (total debts outstanding) never shrinks.   YES   NO

3. You are usually not able to make it until the end of the month and must borrow from savings.   YES   NO

4. You have borrowed from parents or others and do not have plans to repay the debt.   YES   NO

5. You are behind on one or more of your payments.   YES   NO

6. You worry about money often and are discouraged.   YES   NO

7. Money is a source of arguments and disagreements in your family.   YES   NO

8. You often juggle payments, paying one creditor while giving excuses to another.   YES   NO

9. You really don't know how much money you owe.   YES   NO

10. Your savings are slowly disappearing, and you are unable to save regularly.   YES   NO

11. You've taken out loans to pay off debts or have debt consolidation loans.   YES   NO

12. You are at or near the limit of your credit lines on credit and charge accounts.   YES   NO

13. You worry more about the amount of the payment than the amount of interest (interest rate) you are paying on loans.   YES   NO

ASSESSMENT: Total number of "Yes" answers _____

If you answered yes to 8 or more statements, you need to take immediate action to correct your debt load. If you answered yes to 4–7 statements, you should seek to remedy the defects in your debt load soon. If you answered yes to 1–3 statements, you are in pretty good shape and can solve your debt problems. If you answered no to all the statements, congratulations—keep up the good work!

Debt represents future earnings already spent. Unfortunately, many people never assess how much future income they have already committed to debt and whether the types and sources of credit they use are most advantageous to them. You can avoid this trap by periodically making a careful assessment of your debt load throughout your life.

PROTECTING YOURSELF FROM CREDIT FRAUD

The cost of credit fraud exceeds $3 billion a year. Maybe you will never be a victim, but everyone pays for credit fraud through higher interest rates and membership fees and in other ways in which the costs are passed along to consumers. To protect yourself, do the following:

1. Shred unneeded statements and credit documents before pitching them so that account numbers cannot be read.
2. Do not allow store clerks to write your Social Security number, credit card number, expiration date, or other sensitive information on checks or other documents.
3. Pay cash in cases where you suspect your credit information may not be secure.
4. Never give credit information over the telephone or on the Internet to a person or company you do not know.
5. When shopping online, check for your browser's security icon to make sure your transaction will be encrypted.
6. Never sign blank credit slips, and draw a line through blank spaces when you sign.
7. Verify your monthly statements promptly upon receipt.
8. Notify creditors in advance of an address change.
9. Never lend your credit cards to anyone.
10. Never put your account number on the outside of an envelope or on a postcard.
11. Use a separate credit card with a low credit limit for purchases from merchants you don't know and for use on the Internet. This way you minimize the fraud that could occur.
12. Keep a list of credit accounts with their 1-800 contact numbers. In the event an account is compromised, report it immediately.
13. Freeze your credit if you suspect there is unauthorized activity.
14. Monitor all of your credit accounts, even those with zero balances. Most businesses have online account access that allows you instant contact.
15. Carefully examine all credit offers, reading the fine print and comparing them to other offers.

You can probably think of many more ways to protect yourself from credit fraud. One bad experience will convince you that it's worth your time to take precautions.

CREDIT SCAMS

There are many credit scams that sound like great deals. For example, you may see advertisements that guarantee you a loan, claiming that "bad credit or no credit" is not a problem or that "no applicant is ever turned down." In reality, these advertisements are for *advance-fee loans*. In this scam, the applicant fills out an application and pays an upfront fee. The fee is often substantial—from $25 to $200—and there may be other monthly service charges and fees in addition to interest. A legitimate lender does not charge a fee for applying for open-end credit, nor will the lender guarantee that you will qualify for credit. Whenever it seems too easy, there is likely a good reason to be suspicious.

Other scams may look like credit restoration or repair services. For example, a prepaid credit card is one where you have a "savings" balance that is as much or greater than the credit card spending limit. Maintenance fees and other charges are added to your account, so that you are making payments even when you aren't using the card. These deals make money for the scam artists but do nothing to help rebuild credit for the consumer. Legitimate credit card companies do not follow these practices.

ETHICAL DECISIONS

Ethics are principles of morality or rules of conduct. Ethical behavior conforms to these rules; unethical behavior violates them. You may have many opportunities to take advantage of other people. When these opportunities come your way, stop and think how you might feel if you were victimized. Worksheet 3 lists some circumstances involving credit. Think about how you might react to each circumstance. To develop skill in analyzing ethical issues, complete the situational analysis using Worksheet 3 provided for you in the *Student Activity Guide* and also presented for reference below.

WORKSHEET 3
Situational Analysis

For each situation described below, explain how you would respond and why. What are the ethical issues involved in each decision?

1. You walk by an ATM in a mall. You see a bank debit card that was left there by a previous user. You look around and there is no one nearby to claim the card. If you leave it there, someone else may find it. What would you do?

2. You make a payment on your credit account at a customer service center. The worker, who is new and in training, accidentally credits your account for more than you paid. For example, you gave her $25 and she credited your account twice, totaling $50. What would you do?

3. Someone you know returns merchandise to a store and gets a credit on his charge account, knowing that he purchased the merchandise elsewhere. What would you do?

4. Your friend frequently buys clothing on credit, wears it to a special event, and returns it to the store before the account is due, claiming the garment is damaged or dirty. She then receives a credit or a refund for the merchandise. What would you do?

Unit

5

Resource Management

Unit 5 begins with personal decision making. You will learn how to make good decisions based on your needs and wants.

When you leave home for the first time, you will have many housing options from which to choose. There is much to consider when deciding to rent or buy a residence.

Buying a car takes thought and preparation. You'll consider all the costs—from depreciation to accessories—and you'll learn ways to maintain your car's resale value.

The chapter on family decisions covers a wide range of topics. You will begin with marriage and learn about joint or group decision making. From there, you will examine family financial responsibility and some of life's uncertainties. Finally, we'll explore the process and cost of divorce, and conclude with the financial costs and process of dealing with death and its many dimensions.

445

Chapter 20

Personal Decision Making

20.1 *Making Better Decisions*

20.2 *Spending Habits*

Consider **THIS**

Basheer is preparing to go to college in the fall and isn't sure what he'll do with his summer. He can work full time and save more money, or he can go out with his friends and enjoy the break between high school and college.

"Making this decision is really tough," Basheer thought. "I'd like to have a fun summer with my friends. On the other hand, if I work, I can set aside more money. This would help reduce my student loans and make college less stressful in terms of financing. For me, it's a toss-up. Most of my friends are taking the summer off, and I could join them for one last time. Part of me says that's the right thing to do, but then part of me says it would be more responsible to set money aside for the future."

Making Better Decisions

THE DECISION-MAKING PROCESS

To make better purchase decisions, a rational, step-by-step process leads you through defining your needs and evaluating alternatives before making a final choice. This process will help you decide how to use your money in ways that will benefit you most.

STEP 1: DEFINE THE PROBLEM

The first step in the decision-making process is to define the problem or a goal you wish to achieve. Once it is identified, you can look for ways to resolve it in a manner that fits your financial resources now and in the future.

Defining the problem or solving a need is not as easy as it sounds. For example, let's say you want to get a laptop computer. First, consider exactly what purpose the computer would fulfill for school, for home, for work, and other reasons. How will it benefit you?

Are there special features or programs that the computer must have for you to be proficient in doing your job, doing your homework, and planning your personal schedule? Are some features more important than others? Because your resources are limited, you may have to make a **tradeoff**, which involves giving up one option in exchange for another. Ultimately, you will have to make the decision that resolves the problem in the best way possible.

© Digital Vision/Getty Images

Why should you approach purchase decisions with a step-by-step process?

If you can't define the problem or goal (what the laptop would be solving), then perhaps purchasing it would not be a good decision. Could it be that you are buying on impulse? How badly do you really need a laptop computer?

▌ STEP 2: OBTAIN ACCURATE INFORMATION

Once you have defined the problem or goal, gather information on all possible solutions. (How else could you be more proficient—without buying a laptop?) List all alternative solutions and the cost of each. In this example, you might list these possible solutions:

- Use a computer at school (on campus) or at a public library
- Rent a computer when needed at a copy center or technology store
- Buy a used laptop
- Buy a new laptop

To use the computer at school or at a library, identify where computer labs are located. You may be charged a lab fee. Also consider mileage (gas) and the time involved. Most libraries have computers available for the public to use, complete with Internet access. Or you could go to a full-service copy center or technology store that rents computers for an hourly fee.

Do not consider sunk costs. A **sunk cost** is an expense that occurred in the past for which money was spent and cannot be recovered. For example, maybe you already have an old computer. It may be slow, not capable of running new programs, or obsolete. Assume you paid $400 for it three years ago. If you added more memory to your old computer, would it solve the problem? If not, then the $400 cost is sunk. Sunk costs are not relevant because they cannot be recovered.

Keep a written record of the information you collect on choices of products and services. By doing so, you can compare alternatives and costs more easily. Figure 20.1 shows information collected for comparison purposes.

FIGURE 20.1	*Comparison Shopping Data*	
	Per Month	**Per Year**
Option 1: Use library/school lab		
Time: 5 hours/weekend	20 hours	240 hours
Gas: 6-mile round trip/weekend	$ 8.00	$ 96.00
Lab fee: $15 per year	1.25	15.00
	$ 9.25	$ 111.00
Option 2: Rent a computer at copy center		
Time: 5 hours/weekend	20 hours	240 hours
Gas: 20 mile roundtrip/weekend	$ 26.00	$ 312.00
Fee: $8 per hour	160.00	1,920.00
	$186.00	$2,232.00
Option 3: Buy a used laptop		
From private person (one-time cost)		$ 300.00
High-speed/wireless Internet access	$ 45.00	540.00
	$ 45.00	$ 840.00
Option 4: Buy a new laptop		
Cost: $900.00 or $974.88 financed		
Payments on one-year loan at 15%	$ 81.23	$ 974.76
High-speed/wireless Internet access	45.00	540.00
	$126.23	$1,514.76

■ STEP 3: COMPARE CHOICES

When you make choices, they often involve getting something in return for giving up something else (tradeoff). The tradeoff results in an **opportunity cost**, which is the value of your next best choice—what you are giving up. For example, in the chapter-opening scenario, Basheer's resources (time and money) are limited, so he has to make a tradeoff between spending time with his friends and working. Both options have opportunity costs. Suppose Basheer could earn $1,000 by working over the summer. If he decides to spend the summer with his friends, the opportunity cost of his choice is the $1,000 income he gives up. If he decides instead to work, the opportunity cost of that choice is the value to him of the time he could have spent with his friends. Part of comparing choices is considering the value of the options that would be given up.

When comparing total costs, consider time and convenience too. In some cases, convenience may be more important than cost, as long as the cost is reasonable. Using the laptop example, you may decide that the convenience of having your own computer is worth the extra dollar cost. You may also decide that even though the cost of buying a new laptop will be greater, you prefer to avoid the uncertainty of possible repairs on used equipment. Finally, as your computer skills increase, you may find home and work uses for a computer. Either way, if convenience is highly valued, then buying is a better decision than renting.

■ STEP 4: MAKE A DECISION

If you follow the steps outlined in the preceding paragraphs, the decision you make will be based on careful consideration of the problem, thorough information gathering, and analysis of that information. The wise decision in any situation is the one that best meets your needs, is within your budget, and gives you the most value for your dollar investment. Take the time you need to carefully evaluate the information you gathered about each choice before you make a decision, especially for expensive or complex products.

■ STEP 5: TAKE ACTION

After you make a decision, then take action to implement your chosen solution. Because you have made a thorough analysis of choices for solving your problem, you can be sure that you have made the best decision you could with the available information.

■ STEP 6: REEVALUATE

After several months have passed, revisit your decision. Are you happy with the choice you made? If not, what could you do differently next time to make a better decision? Should you do something different now? If your needs have changed or your initial decision isn't working out, go through the decision-making process again to decide whether to make a change.

NETBookmark

Comparing prices of a product in advance before shopping for the best bargain is called comparison shopping. Web sites such as Pricegrabber and My Simon make comparison shopping a breeze. Access www.cengage .com/school/pfinance/mypf and click on the link for Chapter 20. Search for prices for a Wii console. What is the price range of this item? How many online sellers offer the product? Can you think of any reasons why a consumer might not choose the lowest-priced seller?

www.cengage.com/school/pfinance/mypf

Reflect on decisions you have made in the past. Do you now regret some of your decisions? If so, did you use the decision-making process or did you act on impulse? While using a decision-making process won't make every decision perfect, it will help you make better decisions in the important aspects of your life.

ECONOMIC WANTS AND NEEDS

Basic needs are the items necessary for maintaining physical life. They include food, water, shelter, clothing, and basic medical care. You might also add safety and security to this list. Until these basic needs are met, there is little need for other enhancements.

Life-enhancing wants are items beyond basic needs that add to your quality of life. They include, but are not limited to, the following:

- Food, clothing, and shelter beyond what are necessary for biological survival
- Medical care to improve the quality and length of life
- Education to achieve personal goals, both social and economic
- Travel, vacations, and recreation to improve personal enjoyment of life
- Luxury items (like a jet ski or central air conditioning) to make life more fun or comfortable

You may have decided that many life-enhancing wants are necessary for your happiness. But you must admit that they are really wants, not needs. You do not need them for your physical survival.

What is the difference between basic needs and life-enhancing wants?

© Photodisc/Getty Images

▌ INDIVIDUAL WANTS

Beyond the basics, you decide what you "want" based on factors such as your values, personal preferences, income, and leisure time. Your wants, in turn, drive your buying decisions. The "best" choice is not the same for everyone. These factors vary among individuals and societies. They also change throughout your life.

Values

Each person has his or her own set of values. *Values* are the principles by which a person lives. Different people value things differently. One person may highly value education. Someone else may highly value time with family. You make economic choices based on your values. For example, if you highly value education, you will probably decide to save a large portion of your income for college. The person who highly values time with family may choose to save toward a family vacation.

Personal Preferences

Personal preferences or *tastes* are your likes and dislikes. One person may enjoy a weekend alone in the mountains hiking, while another would choose a visit to Disneyland. Based on personal preferences, we all make economic choices. We spend money for things consistent with our personal tastes.

Income

The amount you earn will influence the choices you make. As you learned previously, *discretionary income* is the money left over after you have paid your necessary expenses. This is the money you can spend or save as you wish. The more discretionary income you have, the higher the quality and quantity of products you can consider. The ability to afford goods and services to fulfill the wants you consider important will affect your satisfaction with employment, your personal life, your goals, and other personal factors such as self-esteem. For example, if owning a lot of expensive "things" is important to you, then you may wish to pursue career goals that will lead to a high-paying job.

Leisure Time

The amount of free time you have and the kinds of activities you enjoy also affect how you choose to spend your discretionary income. *Leisure time* is the time you get to spend doing things you like and enjoy. It isn't just for retired folks. Leisure time allows opportunities for rest, relaxation, and enjoyment of life. Some people use it to develop hobbies and an *avocation*, or side career that is meaningful to them. Leisure time gives you access to the time, energy, and availability of a variety of activities.

COLLECTIVE VALUES

Collective values are things that are important to society as a whole. All citizens share in their costs and in their benefits. Society also influences our values, goals, and choices because it demands social responsibility from its citizens. For example, owning a vehicle that is fuel efficient or uses an alternate energy source benefits everyone by reducing air pollution and our dependence on foreign oil.

COMMUNICATION *Connection*

Prepare a list of the top five "wants" in your life today and briefly describe each one. Place them in order of 1 to 5, assigning 1 to the most important and 5 to the least important item. Then answer these questions: How long have you wanted each of the five items? What is the cost of each choice (including opportunity costs)? How might your list be different ten years from now?

Legal Protection

In a market economy it is important to preserve legal and personal rights. Private property ownership and the freedom to make individual choices are important American values and part of our legal rights as U.S. citizens. Laws and their enforcement are the result of our desire to have and protect these freedoms. We pay for legal protection through taxes. We value the U.S. Constitution and its amendments. The first ten amendments, called the Bill of Rights, give us individual freedoms and rights of citizenship.

Employment

Most people who are able will work because it is expected in order to satisfy needs and life-enhancing wants in this society. Most of us are aware of this subtle, yet very real, pressure to perform in the work arena. Therefore, we strive to do the best we can and to get a job that pays well for the effort we put forth. In this way, we can be personally satisfied with our productivity and, at the same time, satisfy society's demand for citizens who are contributing members.

Progress

The relative state of *progress* of the country in which you live (its technological advances and perceptions about the importance of those advances) will affect your purchase decisions. The United States is technologically advanced and places a high value on innovations. **Innovations** are new ideas, products, or services that bring about changes in the way we live. If you are like most Americans, you will likely buy products that offer the latest innovations. They are often fun and entertaining, and they also add to the quality of life. This quality may be the result of time savings, effort or work savings, and cost savings.

Quality of Environment

Natural resources are of great value and concern because they are limited and some cannot be replaced. Because of our collective priority of preserving a quality environment for future generations, our society supports activities such as land-use planning, recycling, preserving natural beauty and wildlife, and establishing air pollution standards. We also expect producers to minimize the environmental damage caused by the production of their products and services. Environmental quality is important to society as a whole, and individuals respond to this concern by acting and purchasing accordingly.

Public Goods

Our country is organized to be "of the people, by the people, and for the people." We have a highly advanced and intricate system of government made up of the people, performing services for the people, with money contributed (through taxes) by the people. Money collected through taxes is then redistributed to those who need it. Americans place high value on government-provided services for all citizens, from police protection to public parks. **Public goods** are the goods and services provided by government to its citizens. They are provided by government because private business could not do so efficiently. For example, national defense is necessary to protect our country from those who would do us harm. Each state, family, or business cannot reasonably provide for its own defense.

Planning a Career in... Advertising

arketing

Marketing strategy is critical to the financial success of any company. How its product is packaged and sold determines financial success. Advertising executives oversee in-house departments, and in many cases, corporate executives contract with outside professional advertising agencies to provide this crucial service.

Advertising professionals are responsible for creating and expanding markets to sell products and services. They prepare overall promotion plans, which include types of media (such as television and radio) and how and when they are most effectively used.

Advertising professionals work in a dynamic, changing, and stressful environment. Long hours, evenings, and weekends are common. This is offset with high earnings, substantial travel, and high visibility.

Employment Outlook

- An average rate of employment growth is expected.

Job Titles

- Advertising manager
- Marketing manager
- Sales manager
- Public relations manager

Needed Skills

- A bachelor's or master's degree with an emphasis in marketing is required.
- Specialized knowledge in consumer behavior, market research, and sales is needed.

- Excellent communication skills, especially speech and presentation skills, are a must.
- Talent in creative arts is helpful.

What's it like to work in... *Advertising*

Rich is creating artistic examples of an advertising campaign for a new technology product. He is also preparing computer simulations to depict uses of the product. The examples and simulations will be used in television infomercials, a key ingredient of the overall marketing plan. Rich is working throughout the weekend to finish his presentation for Monday's meeting with team members. The team will go over each part of the presentation and coordinate topics and presenters.

Rich is the team leader for Monday's campaign proposal. His target audience is young adults who typically use hi-tech gadgets. The appeal will be emotional by creating a "must-have" image for consumers who want to be on the cutting edge of technology. The promotion will stress how the benefits outweigh the cost of the product. The campaign is expected to result in robust sales.

What About You?

Do you enjoy a creative, changing environment? Are you artistic and intuitive? Would you consider a career in advertising?

Assessment

KEY TERMS REVIEW

Match the terms with the definitions. Some terms may not be used.

_____ 1. Giving up one option for another

_____ 2. The value of your next best choice—what you are giving up

_____ 3. Your tastes, or likes and dislikes

_____ 4. New ideas, products, or services that bring about changes in the way we live

_____ 5. An expense that occurred in the past for which the money cannot be recovered

_____ 6. The goods and services provided by government to its citizens

_____ 7. Items beyond basic needs that add to your quality of life

_____ 8. Items necessary for maintaining physical life

a. basic needs
b. collective values
c. innovations
d. life-enhancing wants
e. opportunity cost
f. personal preferences
g. public goods
h. sunk cost
i. tradeoff

CHECK YOUR UNDERSTANDING

9. How can the Internet help you gather information about different purchase options?

10. What should you consider in addition to dollar cost when comparing the costs of alternative solutions?

APPLY YOUR KNOWLEDGE

11. Reflect on the last time you made a major purchase, such as a cell phone or iPod. Did you go through the six-step decision-making process? Was the decision a good one? Would you buy something different today if you had it to do over again?

THINK CRITICALLY

12. Explain how individual choices are dependent on values and personal preferences.

13. How have you and your family been affected by collective values of our society? List three things your family has done or purchased in order to meet societal goals and values.

14. Explain why public goods cannot be produced by individuals and private businesses. In some cases, they could be done quicker and at less total cost, so why do we leave that role to government?

Spending Habits

FACTORS THAT INFLUENCE SPENDING

Consumer purchasing decisions are influenced by personal factors and outside factors that encourage or discourage spending. When planning a major purchase, you should examine your motives. You should buy for the right reasons (to meet your needs and wants), instead of being swayed by outside influences that are not in your best interests.

PERSONAL FACTORS

Personal factors are things that influence your consumer spending choices. They include such things as personal resources; position in life; customs, background, and religion; and values and goals.

Personal Resources

Personal resources include time, money, energy, skills and abilities, and available credit. The more you possess of any one of these factors, the greater your purchasing power. For example, the amount of time you have available to compare prices and options before purchasing a product will affect your ability to make better buying decisions. The job skills you possess will affect the amount of money you can earn and, consequently, your purchasing power.

Position in Life

Your position in life includes such factors as age, marital status, gender, employment status, living arrangements, and lifestyle. Spending patterns of single people are different from those of married couples and families. New parents buy baby products. Women buy different kinds of clothes than men or teens.

Customs, Background, and Religion

A **custom** is a long-established practice that takes on the force of an unwritten law. Families may be faithful to customs that they have followed for generations. Cultural as well as religious and other groups share common customs.

How do goals affect spending decisions?

© Photodisc/Getty Images

For example, people of a cultural or religious group may observe special holidays that are not observed nationally. The customs of the groups to which you belong are likely to influence your buying patterns.

Values and Goals

Values are intrinsic, commonly understood, and slow to change, but they do change over time. Goals change often. When you accomplish one goal, you move on to others. Your value system may change as your goals in life are met or not met. Individual and family values and goals are expressed through choices of entertainment, literature, sports, luxuries, and so on. These choices are reflected in decisions to purchase goods and services, use of time, and attitudes toward accumulating possessions.

▋ OUTSIDE FACTORS

Factors outside yourself and your family also affect your spending patterns. These include the economy, technological advances, the environment, and social pressures.

The Economy

The **economy** refers to all activities related to production and distribution of goods and services in a geographic area. Economists measure economic activity to describe the financial well-being of the region or the nation. The general condition of the economy affects everyone. For example, when interest rates on car loans are high, fewer people buy new cars. When the price of fuel skyrockets, we drive less and buy fewer luxuries. When the economy is strong and growing, people travel more, dine out more, and buy more goods and services. We are always at some point in the *business cycle*, where the economy is growing or slowing. If we feel safe and secure, we are said to be optimistic and we spend more freely. When we feel threatened or insecure (in our jobs and income sources), we cut back and save more.

Technological Advances

You may be fascinated with new electronic games. Or you may be interested in the world's first mass-market electric-powered car. Perhaps you want to add a new solar heating device to your home to make it more energy efficient. Many Americans place a high value on new technological advances. Many people want to have the newest, most convenient, and interesting gadgets. As new goods and services are created to raise our standard of living, many consumers willingly purchase them.

The Environment

Concern for the environment can affect buying decisions. Citizens are concerned with home projects, community activities, and statewide programs to beautify and preserve, recycle, and protect existing resources and the environment. Thus, this interest in the environment affects consumers' actions and also their product preferences. People are buying more products that are ecologically safe, biodegradable, recyclable, and organic.

Social Pressures

Social pressures often induce consumers to buy goods and services beyond their ability to pay for them. Your friends, relatives, and coworkers all influence your buying decisions. The media (radio, television, newspapers) also act as sources of social pressure for consumers. Through advertising, the media convince consumers to buy goods and services designed to keep them young, active, good-looking, healthy, and happy.

PLANNING MAJOR PURCHASES

Major purchases generally tie up future income or take a big bite out of accumulated savings. Ask yourself these questions, take time to reflect on your answers, and then make a final decision based on a rational—not emotional—perspective.

1. Why do I want this product?
2. How long will this product last?
3. What substitutes are available and at what cost?
4. By postponing this purchase, is it likely that I will choose not to buy it later?
5. What types of additional costs are involved, such as supplies, maintenance, insurance, and financial risks?
6. What are the tradeoffs and opportunity cost of this purchase? (Do I want this item more than any other choice I could make?)
7. What is the total cost of this product (cash price, deferred price, interest, shipping charges, and so on)?

CASH OR CREDIT?

Major purchase decisions also involve the choice of whether to pay cash or use credit. Even though you may have the cash available, you should not automatically pay cash for all purchases. If you do, your cash reserves will dwindle, or you may have to do without many conveniences you could have now with wise use of credit.

On the other hand, just because you have unused credit available doesn't mean you should charge it. Examination of your credit choices will lead you to your best options for each type of purchase. For example, you may choose a store financing plan that offers zero percent interest for two years (installment credit) rather than using a credit card that charges 18 percent.

Figure 20.2 shows a comparison of various options available for buying a refrigerator, with positive and negative consequences.

	FIGURE 20.2	**Cash or Credit?**	

Item	Cash	Credit
Refrigerator		
Price	$800 + $15 delivery charge	$50/month ($900 total) + $15 delivery charge
Total cost	$815	$915
Used refrigerator		
Price	$400 + $15 delivery charge	$30/month for 15 months + $15 delivery charge
Total cost	$415	$465
Considerations	Ties up cash; cannot make other purchases. No monthly payments. Reduced savings balance. No interest charges.	Allows for budgeting; ties up future income. Can make other purchases. Establishes credit. Interest charged.

RESEARCH BEFORE BUYING

Comparison shopping will allow you to determine whether you are getting the best quality for the price. The same brand often sells at considerably different prices at different retailers, depending on the sellers' markups. By shopping at various retail outlets you may be able to save money. In addition, many stores offer sale prices at various times of the year or at regular intervals. Before making a major purchase, monitor prices for awhile to see if it goes on sale.

Take advantage of store policies that will refund part of your purchase price if the item you buy goes on sale within the next two weeks or months. This policy, together with a liberal return policy, should affect your choice of merchants. For example, a store that allows you to return a purchase within a reasonable period of time (a month or more) is much better than a store that will not accept returns or give refunds.

QUALITY AND PRICE

The fact that you are paying a high price does not necessarily mean you are getting the best quality merchandise. It pays to be aware of what is good quality and what you should expect from the merchandise. Consumers Union is a nonprofit organization that tests the quality of many products and compares different brands. It publishes the results in its *Consumer Reports* print and online magazine. You can also find product reviews in specialty magazines and web sites. For example, *Backpacker* magazine reviews outdoor equipment. However, keep in mind that reviews by for-profit organizations could be influenced by the manufacturers that advertise in the magazine or on the web site. For major purchases, check reviews in several sources before making your choice.

MARKETING STRATEGIES INFLUENCE SPENDING

Numerous marketing strategies lure us into stores to buy goods and services. Many of these strategies are subtle, and we are often unaware of their impact on our buying patterns.

ADVERTISING

The primary goal of all advertising is to create within the consumer the desire to purchase a product or service. Some advertising is informational and valuable; other advertising is false and misleading.

Advertising appears in a variety of media (billboards, television, radio, Internet, newspapers, magazines, leaflets, balloons, and t-shirts), all carefully coordinated to reach specific consumer groups. Advertising agencies create colorful and attractive campaigns, often appealing to emotion rather than reason. They hire celebrities, compose catchy jingles, develop slogans, design colorful logos, and choose mascots to identify their products. There are three basic types of advertising: product, company, and industry.

Product Advertising

Advertising intended to convince consumers to buy a specific good or service is called **product advertising**. Advertisers often repeat the product name several times during commercials to help consumers remember it. Many ads feature famous athletes, actors, or other celebrities. Advertisers hope that your positive feelings for the celebrity will carry over to the product. Testimonials from people who have used the product, giveaways, and other promotional gimmicks are used to persuade consumers to buy. Ads are carefully planned to appeal to certain types of consumers.

VIEW *Points*

When does the gathering and use of information about individuals constitute an invasion of privacy? For example, the main purpose of an Internet "cookie" is to identify a web site's users and prepare customized offers and services for them. The web site may gather and store information about you, such as your name, address, interests, spending patterns, where you go on the web site, and other personal data you volunteer.

Some web sites will not allow you to use their services without signing in and establishing an "account" with them. They are providing you with services, such as allowing bill payment, shopping, research, price comparisons, and custom orders. These businesses are unable to provide specific types of products or services without information that allows them to target your needs.

THINK CRITICALLY

Do you object to information being gathered about you on web sites? Why or why not? Do you feel that consumers should have control over how their personal information is collected and used? Do you think that new privacy protection laws are needed to regulate the use of information in the computer age?

A **target market** is a specific consumer group to which the advertisements are designed to appeal. Television advertisers consider the day of the week, time of day, and type of program when placing their product ads. Products advertised during football games differ from products advertised during daytime soap operas because the target markets are different.

Company Advertising

Advertising intended to promote the image of a store, company, or retail chain is known as **company advertising**. This type of advertising usually does not mention specific products or prices. Instead, it emphasizes the overall quality and reliability of the company and its products. For example, a company ad might feature company-sponsored community projects. A store ad might talk about the store's friendly employees or wide selection. These ads are designed to promote a favorable attitude toward the company so that you develop a loyalty to the store and shop there frequently.

Industry Advertising

Advertising intended to promote a general product group without regard to where these products are purchased is called **industry advertising**. For example, the dairy industry emphasizes the nutritional value of milk and other dairy products. Consequently, the whole dairy industry benefits when people drink more milk and eat more dairy products. Often, industry ads stress concern about energy conservation or environmental protection. General health and safety ads are often presented in industry campaigns, such as ads by the tobacco industry that discourage teen smoking.

PRICING

The price of merchandise depends on several factors. Supply and demand determine what will be produced and the general price range. The cost of raw materials and labor, competitive pressures, and the seller's need to make a profit are some of the factors that determine the price of a product. But there is more to pricing than adding up the production costs and including a profit.

Retailers understand the psychological aspects of selling goods and services and use pricing devices to persuade consumers to buy. For example, if buyers believe they are getting a bargain or think they are paying a lower price than they really are, they are more inclined to buy the product or service. **Odd-number pricing** is the practice of setting prices at uneven amounts rather than whole dollars to make them seem lower. For example, the price tag might read 99 cents instead of $1.00. Because the price is under a dollar, it seems lower. Consumers perceive a price of $5.99 to be significantly lower than $6.00. As a result, they are more likely to buy the product at $5.99 than at $6.00.

Discounts are often available for buying in large quantities. However, you cannot assume that because you are buying the large economy size you are actually paying less per ounce than if you bought a smaller size. Compare unit prices on all sizes.

Some stores sell larger quantities only—such as multiple packages. While the cost per unit may be lower, you aren't really saving money if you are unable to use all of the product before it spoils. In this case, you are actually paying more rather than less, especially if you pay a membership fee to shop at that store.

SALES

Stores advertise end-of-month sales, anniversary sales, clearance sales, inventory sales, holiday sales, pre-season sales, and so on. They may mark down merchandise substantially, slightly, or not at all. To be sure that you are actually saving money by buying sale items, you must practice comparison shopping and know the regular prices. When an ad states that everything in the store is marked down, check carefully for items that only appear to be marked down.

A **loss leader** is an item of merchandise marked down to an unusually low price, sometimes below the store's cost. The store may actually lose money on every sale of this item because the cost of producing the item is higher than the sale price. However, the loss leader is used to get customers into the store in the hope that they will buy other products as well. Profits from the sale of other items are expected to make up for the loss on the loss leader. There is nothing illegal or unethical about a loss leader as long as the product advertised is available to the customer on demand.

A customer who buys only loss leaders is called a *cherry picker*. Retailers rely on customers to buy other products to make up for the loss on loss leaders, so they are not fond of cherry pickers.

How can you be sure you are actually saving money by purchasing "sale" items?

PROMOTIONAL TECHNIQUES

To lure customers into their stores, retailers may use promotional techniques, such as displays, contests and games, frequent-buyer cards, coupons, packaging, sampling, and micromarketing.

Displays

Retail stores often use window displays and special racks of new items to entice customers. Products are arranged attractively, and the promotion may carry a theme centered on the nearest holiday—Halloween, Thanksgiving, or Christmas, for example. Color schemes, decorations, music, and special effects often set off the products in a way that will attract attention.

Contests and Games

Retail stores that depend on repeat customers often use contests and games to bring customers into the store. The possibility of winning something or getting something free is appealing. Large and small prizes are offered to get customers to come back and buy more—so they can get more game cards, have more chances to win, and receive some of the minor prizes. Careful reading of the rules on the game card or other token reveals the customer's chances of winning. Usually, the chances of winning a major prize are very small.

Coupons

Manufacturer coupons offer a lower price on specific products and may be redeemed wherever the product is sold. *Store coupons* offer discounts on specific products, usually for a short period of time, and only at a specific store. Manufacturer and store coupons may be inside or outside the package, in newspapers or magazines, on a store shelf, or even online. This is a form of *mass marketing*—an attempt to reach large numbers of consumers at once.

Frequent-Buyer and Customer-Loyalty Cards

Some stores use *frequent-buyer cards* that are punched with each purchase. Customers who accumulate enough punches or points may receive some type of reward, such as gift certificates or free merchandise. They are used to build customer loyalty and repeat business for future purchases. *Customer-loyalty cards* enroll consumers in a program in which they receive lower prices, rebates, or other valued services. Each time they buy at the store, their card is scanned. The cards allow the store to track individual purchasing patterns and target advertising accordingly.

Packaging

Packages do more than just protect the product inside. They are also promotional tools. Manufacturers design packaging to appeal to the eye as well as to provide the necessary consumer information. Packaging emphasizes special features, such as "fat free," "organic," "green," "new and improved," and many others. Size and shape of packages also attract attention. Containers that appear to hold more of the product or are reusable as storage devices appeal to consumers. Coupons may be included inside or on the package.

Sampling

Many companies promote their products through sampling. Free sample-size packages of a product may be sent directly to households or included with newspapers delivered to homes. Sometimes samples are given out in a store or shopping center. When a new product is first introduced, sampling enables potential customers to try it. Some companies advertise in magazines and newspapers, with offers for free samples by mail or online request.

Micromarketing

Many companies buy information about consumers in order to target promotions to those who are most likely to buy their products. Information about a person's lifestyle, marital status, family, age, and buying habits is known as *psychographics*. This information is gathered from purchases, customer-loyalty cards, public information, Internet shopping, and other sources provided by the government, postal service, banks, and credit bureaus. **Micromarketing** is a marketing strategy designed to target specific people or small groups who are likely to want certain products. For example, when a couple has their first child, they are likely to receive ads, samples, and coupons for baby products because the birth record of the child is public information. Targeted (micromarketing) promotions are efficient. Rather than pay the cost of mailing samples of baby products to everyone, baby product manufacturers can send samples only to consumers with babies.

Issues in Your World

MICROMARKETING, INTERNET-STYLE

When you purchase a product from an online retailer, you will likely register with the site and provide some information about yourself. The next time you visit, the site may present you with product recommendations. The products may be companions to your previous purchase or products similar to items you are currently browsing at the site. How does the web site know who you are and what you like?

When you register with an online retailer—and sometimes even when you don't—the site places a cookie, or small data file, on your computer. The next time you visit the site, the cookie sends the stored information about you back to the site. This way, the site can recognize its returning customer. It also recognizes your specific computer. As you travel around the site, the cookie keeps track of the product pages you visit. The online retailer is building a database of your preferences. This is micromarketing, Internet-style. The advertising targets you—a target market of one customer. This custom-tailoring service benefits you in that the ads you see really might interest you. It benefits the retailer by increasing the chances of making another sale to you.

With your e-mail address provided in your registration, the retailer can also send you advertising by e-mail. By knowing your product interests, the retailer can inform you of special offers on related products.

Internet micromarketing has its dark side—privacy concerns. Many companies that collect customer information online sell their customer databases to other companies. Also, the same technology that allows legitimate retailers to personalize their site for you can be used by criminals to steal information from you. Cookies can contain spyware. This is a program installed on your computer without your knowledge that constantly collects data about you and uses your Internet connection to send it to advertisers. Although spyware is not illegal, the potential for abuse is cause for concern. Consumers have no control over the data collected or its use. There are many anti-spyware programs on the market that enable you to detect and remove these programs from your computer.

THINK *CRITICALLY*

1. *Suppose you bought a music CD at an online music store. The next time you visited the web site, a list of similar music CDs popped up for your consideration, including some at a special low price. Is this kind of service worth the possible loss of privacy to you? Explain.*

2. *Would you like to receive e-mail advertising? How is this kind of advertising like or unlike advertising delivered by U.S. mail?*

Assessment

KEY TERMS REVIEW

Match the terms with the definitions. Some terms may not be used.

_____ 1. Advertising intended to promote the image of a store, company, or retail chain

_____ 2. The practice of setting prices at uneven amounts to make them seem lower

_____ 3. A marketing strategy designed to target specific people or small groups who are likely to want certain products

_____ 4. A long-established practice that takes on the force of an unwritten law

_____ 5. Advertising intended to convince consumers to buy a specific good or service

a. company advertising

b. custom

c. economy

d. industry advertising

e. loss leader

f. micromarketing

g. odd-number pricing

h. product advertising

i. target market

_____ 6. A specific consumer group to which the advertisements are designed to appeal

_____ 7. All activities related to production and distribution of goods and services in a geographic area

CHECK YOUR UNDERSTANDING

8. How do social pressures affect your buying habits?

9. Why do companies use micromarketing?

APPLY YOUR KNOWLEDGE

10. You are considering making a major purchase that will involve a large amount of cash and/or credit. What questions will you ask yourself before making such a commitment? Why is it important to make rational, rather than emotional, decisions regarding large purchases?

THINK *CRITICALLY*

11. Does your family have unique customs or cultural values that affect your spending choices? Explain how your values affect your decisions.

12. Advertising creates demand. List the types of advertising you experience and explain how you are affected in terms of spending choices.

13. If you were chosen as a target customer for a micromarketer, what characteristics about you would be targeted? Is there a particular industry or company to which you would like to be linked for frequent promotions?

Chapter ⟨Assessment⟩

SUMMARY

20.1

- The decision-making process typically involves six steps: (1) define the problem or goal, (2) obtain accurate information, (3) compare choices, (4) make a decision, (5) take action, and (6) reevaluate your choice.

- Giving up one option in exchange for another is called a tradeoff. The opportunity cost is the value of what you give up. Sunk costs should not be considered.

- Basic needs include food, clothing, shelter, and basic medical care. Life-enhancing wants add to the quality of life.

- Individual wants are shaped by such factors as values, personal preferences, income, and leisure time.

- Collective values that affect spending habits include the desire for legal protection, employment, progress (innovations), quality of environment, and public goods.

20.2

- Personal factors that influence individual spending habits include personal resources; position in life; customs, background, and religion; and your individual values and goals.

- Factors outside yourself and your family that affect your spending habits include the economy, technological advances, the environment, and social pressures.

- When planning major purchases, make sure you want the product for rational rather than emotional reasons. Research and compare before you buy.

- Advertising seeks to create more consumer demand to purchase goods and services. Product advertising promotes a specific product to its target market. Company advertising promotes a positive company image. Industry advertising promotes a general product group to benefit all sellers in that industry.

- Pricing plays a large role in purchasing decisions. Consumers perceive odd-number pricing as being lower than it actually is.

- Loss leaders lure customers to the store, hoping they will buy other more profitable products while they are there.

- Promotional techniques to increase spending include displays, contests and games, coupons, frequent-buyer cards, attractive packaging, sampling, and micromarketing.

APPLY WHAT YOU KNOW

1. *Using the steps in the decision-making process, make a decision that will satisfy your desire for an iPhone, gaming system, or other new technology product you've been wanting.*

2. *Use a search engine to find and select a price comparison web site. Request a price comparison for a product in which you are interested. What is the range of prices for the product? What other features does the site offer to help you research and select products?*

3. *What community and national environmental concerns do you have? What can you do as a single concerned citizen to help preserve the quality of the environment?*

4. *How do your spending patterns differ from those of your parents? What things do you buy that your parents also purchase? Can you trace any of these purchases to a strong family custom, background, or religion?*

5. *Spend an evening viewing television. List the jingles, key words, and slogans used in each commercial. How many commercials can you automatically sing along with? Also list the celebrities you saw in the ads and the products they promoted. Why do you think each celebrity was chosen for that particular product? Explain the emotional appeal behind each advertising slogan or campaign.*

6. *Browse the Internet and view the different types of online advertising. What kinds of things can advertisers do on the Web that they cannot do in a print magazine? Do you think Internet advertising is as effective as television advertising at getting customers to buy a product? Why or why not?*

MAKE ACADEMIC CONNECTIONS

7. **Economics** *Write a one-page paper about the economy of your geographic region and what is happening now. Explain how the economy affects spending decisions of consumers. How has your family been affected by rising (or falling) prices?*

8. **Advertising** *What advertisements appear on the web pages you visit frequently? Do they seem to target you? Why do you think the companies chose to advertise their products on a specific web site? Write a paper reporting your findings.*

9. **Communication** *Think of a problem that you need to resolve, such as a purchase you want to make or an issue at school or work that you need to resolve. Use the decision-making process to help make a rational decision. Outline the process in a graphic format. For example, you could create a flow chart that includes each step of the decision-making process and a short description of your actions. Be creative.*

10. **Technology** *List three or four new technological advances in the last five years. Explain how they have changed lives. What new technology is expected soon? Explain how it will benefit individuals and society.*

SOLVE PROBLEMS AND

EXPLORE ISSUES

11. Decide on a product or service you would like to buy. Do comparison shopping by checking with at least three different retailers. Which seller offers the best value for your money? Support your conclusion.

12. Watch a television program for one hour anytime during the day. Determine the program's target audience (teenagers, children, home-makers, sports fans, families). Pay close attention to all commercials shown during the hour and then do the following: (a) List all the commercials and categorize them as product, company, or industry advertising. (Count public-service and political advertisements as industry advertisements.) (b) Rate each commercial as good, fair, or poor, depending upon how well it is directed to the television program's target audience. (c) Explain which ads you think were most effective and why.

13. Bring to class an advertising insert from a newspaper. Write your answers to these questions on a separate piece of paper: (a) How many items show odd-number pricing? (b) Does the ad mention how much money the buyer will save or what the regular price is? (c) Are there coupons or references to coupons? (d) Does it mention frequent-buyer cards, games, or special incentives? (e) Did you see any loss leaders?

14. Describe a store display built around the theme of the most recent major holiday. Describe colors used, products displayed, product arrangement, location in the store, and other aspects. Were there price reductions?

15. List any stores in your area that use one or more of the following promotional techniques. Beside each store name, describe the specific techniques used: (a) contests and games, (b) frequent-buyer or customer-loyalty cards, (c) coupons, (d) sampling, and (e) other (be specific).

16. Find an appealing advertisement on the Internet and click on it. Then answer the following questions: (a) What product or service is the advertiser selling? (b) How does the arrangement of the advertiser's site help you learn more about the product or service? (c) How can you order the product or service? (d) Would you buy this product or service?

EXTEND YOUR LEARNING

17. **Ethics** Since pharmaceutical companies can now advertise prescription drugs to consumers directly via television ads, the sale of expensive drugs has increased dramatically. Sometimes these drugs help consumers, but in many cases, the side effects and long-term health consequences are severe and unpredictable. Many people feel these ads are misleading and emotional, rather than rational. Do you think it's a good idea to present these ads directly to consumers? Do the benefits outweigh the risks? How would you change advertising laws to regulate such ads?

For related activities and links, go to **www.cengage.com/school/pfinance/mypf**

21

Renting a Residence

Consider **THIS**

Anisa was finishing her sophomore year in college, and at age 20, she was ready to make new housing choices. During her first two years, she had lived in university housing, as was required by the university.

"We have lots of important decisions to make," she told her roommate. "We could stay right here in the dorm, but that may not be our best bet. Living off-campus has advantages, but there are also some variables that we haven't been concerned about while living here. For example, we'll have to pay separate utility bills, and we'll need transportation to get to class. Parking is limited on campus too. To afford to rent a house, we'd have to take in another roommate. But this is also pretty exciting, and I'm looking forward to the change."

Housing Choices

GOALS	TERMS
■ List and describe several rental housing alternatives. ■ Discuss potential living arrangements. ■ Explain how to plan a successful move into a rental property.	■ dormitory, *p. 469* ■ co-op, *p. 470* ■ studio apartment, *p. 471* ■ townhouse, *p. 471* ■ duplex, *p. 471* ■ condo, *p. 471*

Additional terms: ■ security deposit, *p. 473* ■ furnished rental, *p. 473* ■ unfurnished rental, *p. 473* ■ rent-to-own option, *p. 473* ■ bundling, *p. 476*

HOUSING ALTERNATIVES

You will soon have many important choices to make. One is where to live. You may choose to get a job, live at home with your parents, and move out later. You may decide to commute to college or live on campus. Or, you may choose to work and move away from your parents' home. Of all these options, it is usually less expensive to commute to school or work from your parents' home than to live on your own.

ON-CAMPUS HOUSING

Many college students prefer to live on campus. Advantages of *on-campus housing* include closeness to classes and campus activities, access to campus resources such as the library and health center, and a feeling of being part of campus life. If you choose to live on campus, you will have several choices: dormitories, sorority or fraternity housing, housing cooperatives, or married student housing.

Dormitories

A **dormitory** is an on-campus building that contains many small rooms that are rented out to students. The rooms usually come furnished with beds, dressers, and study tables. Some will have their own bathrooms, and some may require that units share a bathroom.

© Digital Vision/Getty Images

When you first leave home, what are some housing alternatives open to you at a college campus?

You might have a roommate, or for an extra charge, you might be able to have your own private room. Most dormitories have centrally located lounges for watching television and group activities. Most have shared kitchen and laundry areas as well. Meals at the college cafeteria may also be included with the cost of the room (room and board). Although individual rooms are small, with limited space for living and studying, the cost per school term may be less than most other housing alternatives.

Sororities and Fraternities

Many colleges have sororities and fraternities that provide on-campus housing. A *sorority* is a social organization of female students who share a residence, while a *fraternity* is a similar organization for male students. Sorority and fraternity houses are usually elegant, mansion-type buildings that can comfortably house 20 or more people. To live in one of these buildings, you have to become a member of the sorority or fraternity in a process called *pledging*. Typically, sororities and fraternities seek new members with goals, abilities, and ideals similar to those of the organization. For example, some require a certain grade point average. Others look for an interest in community service. The cost is usually higher for these facilities; however, you are living with people with similar values and goals to your own.

Housing Cooperatives

Housing cooperatives, known as co-ops, are also available on many large campuses. When you live in a **co-op**, you get a room similar to one in a dormitory at lower cost but with added responsibilities. In addition to keeping your room clean and usable, you share in cooking, cleaning, and maintaining the building. In exchange, your monthly cost is less because you help provide services for yourself and the group.

Married Student Housing

Some students will be married when they choose to go to a four-year college or university. Many large campuses have housing for married couples only. In these apartment-style facilities, you will find amenities for families.

OFF-CAMPUS HOUSING

Some colleges and universities (known as *residential campuses*) will not allow freshmen or students under the legal age to live off campus. Other colleges and universities (known as *commuter campuses*) do not provide on-campus housing options. When you live off campus, you have several choices, including apartments, duplexes, condominiums, and houses.

Apartments

If you don't attend college, or if you choose to live off campus, then your first residence away from your parents will likely be an apartment. An *apartment* is a separate living facility that exists among many other similar units. An *apartment complex* is a large building or group of buildings that contain many units, often as many as a hundred or more.

At this stage of your life, your resources will probably be tight. *Rent* is the monthly charge you will pay to live in an apartment. The amount of rent you will pay is based on the size and quality of the apartment and facilities provided, as well as the distance to downtown jobs, college campuses, and shopping centers. You can find apartments in your chosen area in brochures, newspaper ads, and apartment guides (printed booklets and online).

A **studio apartment**, also known as an *efficiency apartment*, has one large room that serves as the kitchen, living room, and bedroom. Studios have less living space than other apartments, but they are less expensive. Larger apartments with separate living, dining, and sleeping areas are available in a variety of floor plans. A **townhouse** is a living space that has two or more levels. Typically, living and dining space is on the ground level and bedrooms are upstairs.

Apartment facilities may include a laundry room, storage area, swimming pool, tennis courts, and clubhouse. In addition, all or part of the utilities (heat, electric, and garbage service) may be included in the rent. In some cases, you may have a washer and dryer in your apartment.

Apartment living provides independence and flexibility but also requires responsibility and good judgment. Most apartment buildings have rules that make close living more enjoyable for all.

Duplexes and Multiplexes

A **duplex** is a building with two separate living units. Usually both living areas are the same with separate entrances. Duplexes usually offer more space than apartments and more privacy, with only one close neighbor. They may include a garage or carport, private laundry facilities, and other privileges and responsibilities similar to a house.

A *multiplex* is a building or group of buildings, such as a four-plex (two sets of duplexes) or four units that are together. An eight-plex contains eight units that are connected. There are many different types of combinations. For example, a *quad* is a housing choice that has four bedrooms connected to a single kitchen that is shared by the occupants.

Condominiums

A *condominium* or **condo** is an individually owned unit in an apartment-style complex with shared ownership of common areas. If you are renting a condominium, you will have the same responsibilities for upkeep as the owner. Some condo owners rent them, and then upon retirement, the condo becomes their residence.

Houses

Rental houses offer many attractive features. However, they are usually more expensive to rent. You are paying for neighborhood living, often garage space and more living area, privacy, and the other comforts of home ownership. But you are also likely to find many of the same restrictions as with other rentals, such as no pets allowed. Because rented houses are investment properties that people buy and sell, the property may be shown to prospective new owners while you are living there. You may be asked to move if a new owner is purchasing it for private use rather than as a rental. Also, because you are living in a neighborhood, you have more responsibilities, such as maintaining the lawn and garden areas.

LIVING ARRANGEMENTS

To share expenses, you may wish to have a roommate. Choosing a roommate can be difficult. Just because you like someone doesn't mean that you can successfully live together. Your living habits may be very different. Be sure you are compatible with your potential roommate before you move in together. Discuss possible areas of disagreement that may cause trouble if not settled in advance. Some questions that each of you should answer include the following:

- Do you smoke or drink? How do you feel about others who do?
- Do you like a clean living area at all times, or are you easygoing and casual about your environment?
- Do you have steady employment or another source of income to ensure that you can pay your share of expenses?
- What are some of your goals? Do you want to continue your education, work full time, or travel?
- What are your leisure activities? What activities will you share with (or impose on) your roommate?
- What type of transportation do you have? Will you share transportation? If so, what are the costs and how will you divide them?

You might also consider having more than one roommate. The more personalities involved, however, the more difficult it becomes to have problem-free relationships. Matching similar personality types will increase the chances for a successful living arrangement.

It is a good idea to get to know each person before moving in together. The more you know about each potential roommate, the better you will be able to get along and work out problems. Roommates need not be completely alike to get along. But they do need to be aware of, and be able to accept, each other's personality traits, habits, and differences.

WHERE TO LIVE

The decision of where to live will depend largely on finances. For college students who choose on-campus housing, many of the decisions will be predetermined. Renting in the community involves more planning. You must determine how much rent you can comfortably pay. Then you can begin shopping for the housing option that best meets your needs. There are some additional considerations to think about as you decide where to live.

1. *Deposits and fees.* A **security deposit** is a refundable amount paid in advance to protect the owner against damage or nonpayment. If you take care of the property and pay your rent on time, you should get the security deposit back when you move. Utility companies (such as the power company) may require you to make a security deposit when you first open an account. *Fees* are nonrefundable charges, usually for a service provided. For example, the cable company may charge a one-time installation fee.

2. *Length of time you plan to live in the residence.* If you sign a lease for six months, you have made a commitment to remain for that length of time. You may face penalties if you wish to move sooner. Usually, the shorter your commitment, the higher the monthly rent.

3. *Distance from work or school.* Your proximity to work and school and access to public transportation are important considerations, especially if you do not own or have to share a vehicle.

4. *Distance from services.* You will need access to laundry facilities, shopping areas, gas stations, and other frequently used services. Your means of transportation can make a difference as to how close you need to live to these services.

5. *Repairs and maintenance.* As a renter, you may have responsibilities to maintain the property in minor ways, such as replacing light bulbs, mowing lawns, and repairing damages (such as broken screens) that you have caused.

© Digital Vision/Getty Images

What factors might influence your decision of where to live?

Most financial experts advise allotting 25 to 35 percent of your total budget for housing. At first, you may need a roommate to share costs. Later, you may be able financially to carry the burden of living alone.

WHAT TO TAKE

Rental housing can come furnished or unfurnished. A **furnished rental** means that the basics are provided—bed, dresser, sofa, chairs, lamps, dining table and chairs, and essential appliances. An **unfurnished rental** may or may not include basic kitchen appliances such as a stove and refrigerator. Usually the fewer the items furnished, the lower the rent. If you have enough furnishings or can acquire the essentials for an unfurnished residence, you can save a considerable amount in rent.

You can buy or rent furnishings. Compare purchase and rental payments carefully before you make a decision. For example, with a **rent-to-own option**, you rent furniture with an option to buy. At the end of the rental period (usually six months or longer), you have the option to buy the furniture at a reduced price. However, rent-to-own options can be more expensive than making payments on furniture you purchase outright with an installment plan. Renting furniture and appliances may be a good idea, however, for those who will be moving long distances in the near future and don't want to take the furniture.

Basic household and personal items necessary for setting up housekeeping include the following:

- Towels, wash cloths, sheets, and cleaning cloths
- Cleaning supplies (mops, brooms, buckets, vacuum cleaner, detergent, and cleansers)
- Personal items (shampoo, cosmetics, soap, and other personal hygiene items)
- Clothing, shoes, and other apparel
- Dishes, silverware, pots, and pans
- Lamps, clothes hangers, clocks, radio, television, and decorations

You may also need to provide rugs, drapes, shower curtains, and mirrors. You or your roommates may have some of these items, or you may decide to buy them. Make a list of things to be purchased jointly. If you buy some things jointly and one of you decides to move, you must then divide the purchases. Before moving in, it's a good idea to agree on who will get what joint items when you move out. To avoid arguments later, keep written records.

PLANNING YOUR MOVE

Begin planning your move several months in advance. Others who have experienced a similar move can help you with advice and contributions of household items. Here are some ways to prepare:

1. *Have savings.* Set aside savings to cover the security deposit, first and last months' rent, fees, and initial expenses. If you have a pet, you may have to pay an additional security deposit or fee.
2. *Have income.* Have a reliable source of income to pay rent, utility bills, and shared expenses. Expect that your landlord will run a credit report to verify your ability to pay the rent. You will have to fill out an application that requires personal and financial information.
3. *Have supplies.* Gather what you need to live independently, such as clothing, towels, sheets, pillows, small appliances, and dishes to minimize the items you need to buy when you move.
4. *Think ahead.* Plan the move with your career goals in mind. If your goal is to finish college, then your living plan should help you achieve this goal. For example, if you are planning to go to college in September and live on campus, it would probably not be wise to move out on your own for the three summer months. The expenses would be too high, and you would be better off saving your money to help meet college expenses.
5. *Make reservations.* Make arrangements for transporting furnishings. Professional movers can be expensive and must be reserved in advance. If you instead enlist friends to help you move, you may need to rent a truck that you reserve in advance. Also, plan to provide refreshments or a meal for your friends if the move will take several hours.

A good way to organize your preparations is to make a household needs inventory, such as the one shown in Figure 21.1. Decide with your roommates what you will need and check off each item as you fulfill the need. As you can see, it may take several months to get ready for the move.

FIGURE 21.1   *Household Needs Plan*

What Is Needed	Date Needed	Cost	Date Completed
1. Dishes/towels	October 1	$100	_____
2. First and last months' rent	October 1	$1,400	_____
3. Security deposit	October 1	$100	_____
4. Moving-in fees	October 1	$250	_____
5. Car (share of expenses)	September 1	$150	_____
6. Job (part-time)	August 1		_____
7. Household budget	September 1		_____
8. Plan with roommates	June 1		_____
9. Plan with parents	May 1		_____

GROUP FINANCIAL DECISIONS

All roommates are responsible for meeting the obligations to which they agree. For example, each person must pay his or her share of the rent, so that the total rent is paid on time. You will probably share utilities equally, as well as garbage service, cable TV, Internet, phone, and group activity expenses. Long-distance phone calls and cell phone charges should be paid for individually. But expenses such as gasoline or groceries might be divided according to percentage of use. Laundry services usually are an individual expense.

Group budgeting allows for the careful allocation of expenses, so that each person pays his or her share. The budget should be prepared and put into writing following a good discussion. It's important for each person to understand and agree to his or her responsibilities. Figure 21.2 is an example of a group budget.

FIGURE 21.2   *Group Budget*

Expense	Monthly Cost	Robert's Share	Carlos's Share	Ken's Share
Rent	$900	$300	$300	$300
Utilities (average)	150	50	50	50
Cable TV and Internet access	45	15	15	15
Gasoline/insurance /repairs	120	40	40	40
Groceries	600	200	200	200
Household supplies	90	30	30	30
TOTALS	$1,905	$635	$635	$635

The division of responsibilities and financial obligations can leave roommates at odds. Some roommates believe that, since they are now living away from home and enjoying their freedom, they can do anything they want. Some roommates may feel they are being taken advantage of. For example, some people are neat and clean and keep things tidy. It is unsettling for them to see food, clothing, and personal property scattered around. Others are not at all concerned about these things—their definition of clean and presentable may be very different. Some people may be very precise about paying obligations, while others wait until the last minute and are often late or short on money.

THINK *CRITICALLY*

How would you describe your living habits? How would you feel about having a roommate who has very different living habits? How can roommates avoid these kinds of misunderstandings?

To pay group expenses, each person could have a separate account for individual expenses, and the group could have a joint account to pay shared expenses. Each person could make a deposit into the joint account by a certain date each month. Then roommates could take turns writing checks to pay for rent, utilities, and other expenses incurred throughout the month.

MOVING COSTS

Moving costs include the time and money spent in packing, loading, transporting, unloading, and unpacking. Professional movers charge according to the amount you have to move, the distance traveled, and whether or not they do the packing. You can save money by doing your own packing.

You can save even more by renting a truck or trailer and using your own labor for loading, driving, and unloading. If you are just moving across town, the rental will likely be cheaper if you can return the vehicle to the place where you rented it. However, for a longer move, you can rent a truck or trailer one way and return it to the rental agency's branch in the new city. One-way rental fees are usually a flat rate plus mileage, gasoline, and security deposit.

INSTALLATION CHARGES

When you move into a new residence, you will pay some installation charges, such as for telephone, Internet, and cable TV services. You may be able to save money if you can bundle these services. **Bundling** is combining services into one package. For example, one company can provide telephone (local and long distance), Internet service, and cable TV for a price that is lower than what you would pay if you used three different companies. You may also find special offers and other types of discount plans.

You must also arrange to turn on the electricity and other utilities. Many utility companies charge new customers a refundable security deposit. Other companies, such as the telephone company, may charge a one-time nonrefundable fee. If you have a landline, monthly rates vary according to services. If you have a cell phone, your plan should include enough minutes to call home as desired, or you may want a plan that allows unlimited calls to family members. Some cell phone plans include Internet access and other special features at a cost.

Planning a Career in... Property Management

Business Management & Administration

Property managers take care of real estate for its owners. Some property managers reside on site at the apartment building or housing complex. These managers maintain office hours during which they show rental units to prospective tenants, take applications, assist residents, and arrange for maintenance, repairs, and general upkeep of the premises.

Some property managers are responsible for multiple properties, from houses and duplexes to commercial buildings. Well-managed property is a source of income, growing real estate values, and tax advantages for owners. Property managers are hired when the owners do not have the time or expertise for the day-to-day logistics of real estate rentals.

Property managers also handle the financial operations, ensuring that rent is collected and maintenance bills are paid on time. Managers of large complexes may be supervisors of other office staff and of maintenance personnel. They also must be experts in landlord/tenant laws and make sure that the laws are followed.

Employment Outlook

- A faster than average rate of employment growth is expected.

Job Titles

- Asset manager
- Resident manager
- Real estate manager
- Property manager
- Off-site manager

Needed Skills

- A bachelor's degree in business is often preferred.
- Licensure is required for public housing subsidized by the federal government.
- Real estate knowledge and skills are desirable.
- Excellent communication and people skills are helpful.

What's it like to work in... *Property Management*

Kelly works for a property management company that specializes in residential real estate. Kelly is responsible for 11 houses and 6 duplexes. She takes calls from renters reporting problems and repair needs. She reviews and signs contracts with plumbers, electricians, and other contractors who provide the repairs and maintenance. She also prepares quarterly reports to owners, itemizing rents collected and expenses incurred. For any expense that is out of the ordinary, she must contact the owner for prior approval, as per their agreement.

Kelly works a normal 40-hour work week, except under unusual circumstances, such as severe weather. She must make sure that her tenants are safe and that any damages are promptly addressed.

What About You?

Would you like managing property for others, collecting rent, and overseeing maintenance? Would you consider a career in property management?

Assessment

KEY TERMS REVIEW

Match the terms with the definitions. Some terms may not be used.

_____ 1. *A refundable amount a renter pays in advance to protect the owner against damage or nonpayment*

_____ 2. *A room similar to one in a dormitory at a lower cost but with added responsibilities*

_____ 3. *A building with two separate living units*

_____ 4. *An apartment with one large room that serves as the kitchen, living room, and bedroom*

_____ 5. *Combining services into one package*

_____ 6. *A living space that has two or more levels*

_____ 7. *An on-campus building that contains many small rooms that are rented to students*

a. bundling

b. condo

c. co-op

d. dormitory

e. duplex

f. furnished rental

g. rent-to-own option

h. security deposit

i. studio apartment

j. townhouse

k. unfurnished rental

_____ 8. *A rental unit in which basic furnishings—bed, dresser, sofa, chairs, lamps, and so on—are provided*

CHECK YOUR UNDERSTANDING

9. *Discuss some considerations to think about as you decide where to live.*

10. *What questions should you and your potential roommate ask each other before deciding to live together?*

APPLY YOUR KNOWLEDGE

11. *Your chosen university requires you to live on campus. Which type of on-campus housing will you choose? Why? After two years, you are able to move off campus. Which type of housing will you choose then? Why?*

THINK *CRITICALLY*

12. *Duplexes, condos, and houses are located in residential neighborhoods. As a resident, your obligations are different than if you lived in an apartment complex. Explain how they are different.*

13. *Why is it important to know a person well and have an agreement, both in terms of financial obligations and in terms of sharing responsibilities, before you become roommates? Give three reasons.*

14. *Give examples of why you need to have considerable savings when planning to move out on your own.*

The Renting Process

RENTING A PLACE TO LIVE

Living in an apartment, duplex, or other housing has many good points. Often it is your first experience after leaving your parents' home. It is an exciting experience to be on your own for the first time.

Most people begin their independent lives as renters. **Renting** is the process of using another person's property for a fee. A **landlord** is the owner, or owner's representative, of rental property. A person who rents property is called a **tenant** or renter. Because renting offers many advantages, it is a popular choice, especially among young people just getting started on their own.

ADVANTAGES OF RENTING

Renting has several advantages over other forms of living choices.

1. *Mobility.* Many people prefer to rent because of the ease and speed with which they can move when a good job opportunity comes along elsewhere. If you are unsure about whether or not you will stay in the same location for a long period, then renting a residence is a wise choice.
2. *Convenience.* Many landlords provide a number of conveniences for their tenants. For example, rental properties often have laundry and recreational facilities. Also, rental units are often located near major shopping areas, downtown, or business centers.
3. *Minimum Responsibilities.* Renting usually relieves you of many of the responsibilities of home ownership, such as costly repairs and maintenance of the grounds.

What are some advantages of renting?

4. *Social Life.* Apartments offer the opportunity to meet others and socialize informally, especially where recreational facilities are provided.

5. *Lower Cost.* Apartment rent is usually lower than the cost of buying a house. Sharing expenses with roommates lowers individual costs even more.

▊ DISADVANTAGES OF RENTING

Renting can have drawbacks as well.

1. *Noise.* Residents usually share common walls with neighbors above, below, or beside them. Consequently, music, conversations, and other activities of neighbors can be overheard. Strange hours or unusual habits of neighbors can be very irritating.

2. *Lack of Privacy.* Because conversations and other activities can be overheard through common walls, tenants often feel a lack of privacy. Problems associated with shared facilities—laundry and recreation, for example—can also be annoying.

3. *Small Living Space.* The typical apartment is smaller than most other housing choices. Five hundred to 800 square feet of living space is typical for a studio or one- or two-bedroom apartment. Condos and houses typically have more living space.

4. *Lack of Storage Space.* The small size of many apartments also means little cabinet and closet space. A few rental complexes offer additional storage space for rarely used items, but they may charge an extra fee for its use.

5. *Scarcity of Parking.* Many rental properties do not provide garages or off-street parking, especially in city centers. In complexes that provide parking lots, visitor parking is often very limited. Parking spaces may also cost extra, especially when they are covered or reserved.

RENTAL CONTRACTS

Whenever you rent a place to live, you will have to fill out a *rental application.* The purpose of the application is to allow the landlord to verify your income, previous rental experience, credit rating, and so on. The landlord does this to assure that you are a good risk—that you will likely pay your rent and be a good tenant. The landlord may refuse to rent you property because of your past rental history, employment record, or credit rating. Rental may not be denied, however, solely on the basis of race, religion, national origin, sex, or marital status. Some states have passed laws to prohibit denial of rental to tenants with small children. Figure 21.3 shows information asked on a typical rental application.

▊ LEASES AND MONTH-TO-MONTH AGREEMENTS

Basically there are two types of rental contracts: leases and rental agreements. A **lease** is a written agreement that allows a tenant to use property for a set period of time at a set rent payment. The landlord is called the **lessor**, or person responsible for the property. The tenant is called the **lessee**, or person who will take possession of the property.

FIGURE 21.3 *Rental Application*

RENTAL APPLICATION

Date _____

Section 1. Personal Information

Applicant:
Name _____
Current Address_____
_____
Phone_____
Landlord _____
Landlord's Phone_____
Previous Address _____
_____
Previous Landlord _____
Landlord's Phone_____

Co-Applicant:
Name _____
Current Address_____
_____
Phone _____
Landlord _____
Landlord's Phone_____
Previous Address _____
_____
Previous Landlord_____
Landlord's Phone_____

Section 2. Employment

Employer _____
Address_____
_____
Phone_____
Monthly take-home pay $_____
Years employed at this job _____

Employer _____
Address_____
_____
Phone_____
Monthly take-home pay $_____
Years employed at this job _____

Section 3. Credit

Bank _____
___ Checking ___ Savings/Investment

Companies through which you have credit
cards or charge accounts:
_____
_____
_____

Bank _____
___ Checking ___ Savings/Investment

Companies through which you have credit
cards or charge accounts:
_____
_____
_____

Section 4. Personal References

Name _____
Phone_____
Relationship to applicant_____

Name_____
Phone_____
Relationship to applicant_____

I hereby swear that the above information is true and complete. I understand that incomplete or
inaccurate information on this application may result in denial and/or eviction.

Applicant Signature:
_____ Date: _____

Co-Applicant Signature:
_____ Date: _____

You may sign a lease for six months, a year, or longer. During this time, rent remains constant. If you decide to move before the lease expires, you are still responsible for the remaining rent. Before the lease expires, the landlord will inform you of any rent increases. If you do not wish to stay beyond the lease period, you can notify the landlord as specified in the lease. Often leases require 30-days' written notice of rent increases and tenant departures. Figure 21.4 is an example of a lease agreement.

A **rental agreement** is a written agreement that allows you to leave anytime as long as you give the required notice. These are often called *month-to-month agreements*. The agreement does not bind you to pay rent for a period of time longer than a month, as a lease does. However, renting by the month also does not establish the rent amount for more than one month. The landlord can raise the rent anytime or ask you to leave anytime.

Still, the ease of moving in and out is an advantage of renting month to month. If your plans are very uncertain and you need maximum flexibility, then month-to-month rental may be a good option for you.

Both a lease and a rental agreement will include provisions for security deposits and their return, termination of rental, rent payments, tenant and landlord responsibilities, and various other matters. If you do not understand any part of the agreement, ask the landlord to explain. If the answer is not satisfactory, get a legal interpretation or refuse to sign the agreement and go elsewhere. Both a lease and a month-to-month rental agreement are legally binding when signed.

■ RENTAL INVENTORY

If you live in a rental property, you are expected to leave it as you found it. Normal wear and tear is expected and accepted. However, anything broken or misplaced is not acceptable. Therefore, to assure that you are not accused of such acts as breaking, damaging, or taking furnishings, prepare an inventory of the premises at the time you move in.

The **rental inventory** is a detailed list of current property conditions. Noted are such things as broken windows, missing window screens, holes in walls, torn or stained carpeting, plumbing problems, and so on. You and your landlord should tour the property together to take the inventory, so that you both agree on its contents. Then you or the landlord should make a copy for each of you. When you move out, you and your landlord should once again take an inventory. The comparison between this inventory and the initial one will often determine whether or not you get your security deposit back.

If your landlord does not do or require a rental inventory, you as tenant should do one anyway. Take pictures of any conditions that exist. Prepare the inventory and provide a copy to the landlord, even if the landlord does not ask for it. Figure 21.5 on page 484 shows an inventory and condition report that can be used in a variety of rental situations.

Why is it important to complete a rental inventory before you move in to a rental property?

© Photodisc/Getty Images

FIGURE 21.4 *Lease*

RESIDENTIAL LEASE AGREEMENT
AND SECURITY DEPOSIT RECEIPT

THIS INDENTURE, made this __29th__ day of __October__ , 20 __--__ , between

__Brendan Martin__ , hereinafter designated the Lessor

or Landlord, and __Teresa Thomas__ , hereinafter designated the Lessee,

WITNESSETH: That the said Lessor/Landlord does by these presents lease and demise the residence

situated at __614 Dundas Street__ in __Cincinnati__ City,

__Hamilton__ County, __Ohio__ State,

of which the real estate is described as follows:

> 614 Dundas Street, Cincinnati, Ohio,

upon the following terms and conditions:

1. **Term:** The premises are leased for a term of __one (1)__ years, commencing the __1st__ day of __November__ , 20__--__, and terminating the __31st__ day of __October__ , 20 __--__ .

2. **Rent:** The Lessee shall pay rent in the amount of $ __$600.00__ per month for the above premises on the __1st__ day of each month in advance to Landlord.

3. **Utilities:** Lessee shall pay for service and utilities supplied to the premises, except __None__ which will be furnished by Landlord.

4. **Sublet:** The Lessee agrees not to sublet said premises nor assign this agreement nor any part thereof without the prior written consent of Landlord.

5. **Inspection of Premises:** Lessee agrees that he has made inspection of the premises and accepts the condition of the premises in its present state, and that there are no repairs, changes, or modifications to said premises to be made by the Landlord other than as listed herein.

6. **Lessee Agrees:**
(1) To keep said premises in a clean and sanitary condition;
(2) To properly dispose of rubbish, garbage, and waste in a clean and sanitary manner at reasonable and regular intervals and to assume all costs of extermination and fumigation for infestation caused by Lessee;
(3) To properly use and operate all electrical, gas, heating, plumbing facilities, fixtures and appliances;
(4) to not intentionally or negligently destroy, deface, damage, impair, or remove any part of the premises, their appurtenances, facilities, equipment, furniture, furnishings, and appliances, nor to permit any member of his family, invitee, licensee or other person acting under his control to do so;
(5) Not to permit a nuisance or common waste.

7. **Maintenance of Premises:** Lessee agrees to mow and water the grass and lawn, and keep the grass, lawn, flowers, and shrubbery thereon in good order and condition, and to keep the sidewalk surrounding said premises free and clear of all obstructions; to replace in a neat and workmanlike manner all glass and doors broken during occupancy thereof; to use due precaution against freezing of water or waste pipes and stoppage of same in and about said premises and that in case water or waste pipes are frozen or become clogged by reason of neglect of Lessee, the Lessee shall repair the same at his own expense as well as all damage caused thereby.

8. **Alterations:** Lessee agrees not to make alterations or do or cause to be done any painting or wallpapering to said premises without the prior written consent of Landlord.

9. **Use of Premises:** Lessee shall not use said premises for any purpose other than that of a residence and shall not use said premises or any part thereof for any illegal purpose. Lessee agrees to conform to municipal, county and state codes, statutes, ordinances, and regulations concerning the use and occupation of said premises.

10. **Pets and Animals:** Lessee shall not maintain any pets or animals upon the premises without the prior written consent of Landlord.

11. **Access:** Landlord shall have the right to place and maintain "for rent" signs in a conspicuous place on said premises for thirty days prior to the vacation of said premises. Landlord reserves the right of access to the premises for the purpose of:
(a) Inspection;
(b) Repairs, alterations or improvements;
(c) To supply services; or
(d) To exhibit or display the premises to prospective or actual purchasers, mortgagees, tenants, workmen, or contractors. Access shall be at reasonable times except in case of emergency or abandonment.

12. **Surrender of Premises:** In the event of default in payment of any installation of rent or at the expiration of said term of this lease, Lessee will quit and surrender the said premises to Landlord.

13. **Security Deposit:** The Lessee has deposited the sum of $ __600.00__ , receipt of which is hereby acknowledged, which sum shall be deposited by Landlord in a trust account with __Citizens__ bank; savings and loan association, or licensed escrow, __Cincinnati__ branch, whose address is __201 Main Street, Cincinnati, Ohio__

All or a portion of such deposit may be retained by Landlord and a refund of any portion of such deposit is conditioned as follows:
(1) Lessee shall fully perform obligations hereunder and those pursuant to Chapter 207, Laws of 1973, 1st Ex Session or as may be subsequently amended.
(2) Lessee shall occupy said premises for __one (1)__ months or longer from date hereof.
(3) Lessee shall clean and restore said residence and return the same to Landlord in its initial condition, except for reasonable wear and tear, upon the termination of this tenancy and vacation of apartment.
(4) Lessee shall have remedied or repaired any damage to apartment premises;
(5) Lessee shall surrender to Landlord the keys to premises;
Any refund from security deposit, as by itemized statement shown to be due to Lessee, shall be returned to Lessee within fourteen (14) days after termination of this tenancy and vacation of the premises.

IN WITNESS WHEREOF, the Lessee has hereunto set his hand and seal the day and year first above written.

/s/ *Brendan Martin*   /s/ *Teresa Thomas*
LANDLORD   LESSEE
610 Dundas Street

Cincinnati, Ohio

ADDRESS   (Acknowledgment)

LANDLORD AND TENANT RESPONSIBILITIES

Most states have passed landlord/tenant laws. Both landlords and tenants should understand their legal rights and obligations.

FIGURE 21.5 *Rental Inventory*

INVENTORY AND CONDITION REPORT

Use this report to record the contents and condition of your unit when you move in and before moving out. If you mark anything as being either dirty or damaged, describe it fully on an additional sheet. Use the blank before each item to indicate how many there are. Ask the landlord to sign your copy.

	Dirty Yes* No	Damaged Yes* No		Dirty Yes* No	Damaged Yes* No
Living Room					
___ Couch 1	☐ ☐	☐ ☐	___ Oven racks 43	☐ ☐	☐ ☐
___ Chair. 2	☐ ☐	☐ ☐	___ Broiler pan 44	☐ ☐	☐ ☐
___ End table 3	☐ ☐	☐ ☐	___ Working refrigerator ... 45	☐ ☐	☐ ☐
___ Easy chair 4	☐ ☐	☐ ☐	___ Ice trays 46	☐ ☐	☐ ☐
___ Floor lamp 5	☐ ☐	☐ ☐	___ Working sink 47	☐ ☐	☐ ☐
___ Table lamp 6	☐ ☐	☐ ☐	___ Working garbage disposal .. 48	☐ ☐	☐ ☐
___ Coffee table 7	☐ ☐	☐ ☐	___ Counter tops 49	☐ ☐	☐ ☐
___ Light fixture 8	☐ ☐	☐ ☐	___ Range hood w/working fan .. 50	☐ ☐	☐ ☐
___ Rug or carpet 9	☐ ☐	☐ ☐	___ Working dishwasher 51	☐ ☐	☐ ☐
___ Floor.................... 10	☐ ☐	☐ ☐	___ Hot and cold running water.. 52	☐ ☐	☐ ☐
___ Walls 11	☐ ☐	☐ ☐	___ Drawers 53	☐ ☐	☐ ☐
___ Ceiling 12	☐ ☐	☐ ☐	___ Dinette table 54	☐ ☐	☐ ☐
			___ Dinette chairs 55	☐ ☐	☐ ☐
Bedroom			___ Light fixture 56	☐ ☐	☐ ☐
___ Bed frame(s) 13	☐ ☐	☐ ☐	___ Floor 57	☐ ☐	☐ ☐
___ Headboard(s) 14	☐ ☐	☐ ☐	___ Walls 58	☐ ☐	☐ ☐
___ Mattress 15	☐ ☐	☐ ☐	___ Ceiling 59	☐ ☐	☐ ☐
___ Mattress cover 16	☐ ☐	☐ ☐			
___ Bed springs 17	☐ ☐	☐ ☐	**Bathroom**		
___ Dresser 18	☐ ☐	☐ ☐	___ Towel racks 60	☐ ☐	☐ ☐
___ Nightstand 19	☐ ☐	☐ ☐	___ Tissue holder 61	☐ ☐	☐ ☐
___ Drapes or curtains 20	☐ ☐	☐ ☐	___ Mirror 62	☐ ☐	☐ ☐
___ Mirror 21	☐ ☐	☐ ☐	___ Medicine cabinet 63	☐ ☐	☐ ☐
___ Light fixture 22	☐ ☐	☐ ☐	___ Counter top 64	☐ ☐	☐ ☐
___ Rug or carpet 23	☐ ☐	☐ ☐	___ Working sink 65	☐ ☐	☐ ☐
___ Floor 24	☐ ☐	☐ ☐	___ Working tub 66	☐ ☐	☐ ☐
___ Walls 25	☐ ☐	☐ ☐	___ Working shower 67	☐ ☐	☐ ☐
___ Ceiling 26	☐ ☐	☐ ☐	___ Working toilet 68	☐ ☐	☐ ☐
			___ Toilet seat 69	☐ ☐	☐ ☐
Bedroom			___ Shower curtain 70	☐ ☐	☐ ☐
___ Bed frame(s) 27	☐ ☐	☐ ☐	___ Cabinet 71	☐ ☐	☐ ☐
___ Headboard(s) 28	☐ ☐	☐ ☐	___ Light fixture 72	☐ ☐	☐ ☐
___ Mattress 29	☐ ☐	☐ ☐	___ Hot and cold running water.. 73	☐ ☐	☐ ☐
___ Mattress cover 30	☐ ☐	☐ ☐	___ Floor................... 74	☐ ☐	☐ ☐
___ Bed springs 31	☐ ☐	☐ ☐	___ Walls 75	☐ ☐	☐ ☐
___ Dresser 32	☐ ☐	☐ ☐	___ Ceiling 76	☐ ☐	☐ ☐
___ Nightstand 33	☐ ☐	☐ ☐			
___ Drapes or curtains 34	☐ ☐	☐ ☐	**Miscellaneous**		
___ Mirror 35	☐ ☐	☐ ☐	___ Door key 77	☐ ☐	☐ ☐
___ Light fixture 36	☐ ☐	☐ ☐	___ Windows............... 78	☐ ☐	☐ ☐
___ Rug or carpet 37	☐ ☐	☐ ☐	___ Window screens 79	☐ ☐	☐ ☐
___ Floor 38	☐ ☐	☐ ☐	___ Mailbox 80	☐ ☐	☐ ☐
___ Walls 39	☐ ☐	☐ ☐	___ Mailbox key 81	☐ ☐	☐ ☐
___ Ceiling 40	☐ ☐	☐ ☐	___ Thermostat 82	☐ ☐	☐ ☐
			___ Other 83	☐ ☐	☐ ☐
Kitchen			___ 84	☐ ☐	☐ ☐
___ Working stove 41	☐ ☐	☐ ☐	Do all the windows work?_____		
___ Working oven 42	☐ ☐	☐ ☐	Does the heat work properly? _____		

_____
Tenant

_____
Witness

_____
Date

_____
Landlord

_____
Date

*Describe fully on an additional sheet.

LANDLORD OBLIGATIONS

Housing laws in most states require that landlords provide a dwelling that is habitable (livable) at all times. A dwelling is considered habitable if:

- The exterior (including roof, walls, doors, and windows) is weatherproof and waterproof.
- Floors, walls, ceilings, stairs, and railings are in good repair.
- Elevators, halls, and stairwells meet fire and safety regulations. Smoke detectors are required in each unit in most states. (Tenants are responsible for testing the alarms, replacing batteries, and reporting any defects.)
- Adequate locks are provided for all outside doors, working latches are provided for all windows, and exits meet fire and safety regulations.
- Plumbing facilities comply with local and state sanitation laws and are in good working condition.
- Water supply provided is safe and adequate.
- Lighting, wiring, heating, air conditioning, and appliances are in good condition and comply with local and state building and safety codes.
- Buildings and grounds are clean and sanitary; garbage receptacles are adequate. (Tenants may be responsible for garbage removal charges.)

TENANT OBLIGATIONS

Tenant obligations usually are stated specifically in the lease or month-to-month agreement. Even when not stated, tenants are responsible to:

- Read, understand, and abide by the terms of the rental contract.
- Pay the rent on or before the due date. (Failure to make a rent payment as stated in the rental contract may result in late fees, termination of the contract, or eviction.) **Eviction** is the legal process of removing a tenant from rental property. It is often reported to credit bureaus, reflecting poorly on one's creditworthiness and making it difficult for a person to rent property again in the future.
- Give at least 30-days' notice of intent to move. This notice will prevent the loss of the security deposit and allow the landlord time to find another renter before you leave.
- Keep the premises in good, clean condition to prevent unnecessary wear and tear or damage to the unit.
- Use a rental unit only for the purpose for which it is intended. For example, if you've rented the property as your residence, you cannot use it for a retail business or manufacturing facility.
- Allow the landlord access to the living unit to make repairs or improvements.
- Obey the rules specified in the rental contract for the residents of the rental community, covering such things as quiet hours, use of recreational facilities, use of laundry facilities, and parking regulations.

NET Bookmark

Tenants and landlords both have certain rights and responsibilities, but many tenants are not aware of their legal rights. Access www.cengage.com/school/pfinance/mypf and click on the link for Chapter 21. Read the "Tips for Tenants" article. Under what circumstances can a tenant withhold rent? What procedure should a tenant use to request repairs to the living area? Why should a tenant purchase renter's insurance?

www.cengage.com/school/pfinance/mypf

ISSUES IN YOUR WORLD

READ THE LEASE BEFORE YOU SIGN

Many owners of rental property would rather lease space to you than rent it to you on a month-to-month basis. A lease gives both the lessor (the landlord) and the lessee (the tenant) the security of knowing the property is committed for a fixed period of time. But the lease can be a trap if you don't understand its provisions before you sign.

For example, many lessors offer "specials" to those who sign leases for a year or more. These specials may include reduced monthly rent, reduced deposits and fees, and other concessions. But in most cases, if you need to terminate the lease before the agreed-upon time, there can be enormous consequences.

In a typical "special" lease offer, the lessor states that regular monthly rent is $800 per month. If the lessee signs a one-year lease, the rent is reduced to $750 and the move-in fee is also reduced from $500 to $300. The savings are significant. But the lease also states that if the lessee terminates the agreement prior to one year, he or she must repay the entire rent reduction and the balance of the reduced fee.

Suppose you are the lessee and you must move out early, say at the beginning of the eighth month. You would have to pay back seven months' worth of reduced rent ($50 × 7) plus the additional $200 move-in fee, for a total of $550. In addition, you are still obligated to pay the remaining five months' rent (at the higher rate) unless the lessor can find another tenant to take your place. This type of "deal" can be very, very expensive.

Before you sign the lease, be sure to read it carefully and understand your commitments. You may be able to negotiate better terms at the beginning, before you sign the lease.

THINK *CRITICALLY*

1. *Check your newspaper or online listings for rental housing in your area. Do you see any lease specials? Describe them.*

2. *Do you know someone who is leasing property? Ask to see the person's lease agreement. What potentially expensive provisions does it contain?*

Assessment

KEY TERMS REVIEW

Match the terms with the definitions. Some terms may not be used.

_____ 1. The landlord, or person who is responsible for the property

_____ 2. A person who rents property

_____ 3. The process of using another person's property for a fee

_____ 4. The legal process of removing a tenant from rental property

_____ 5. The owner, or owner's representative, of rental property

_____ 6. The tenant, or person who will take possession of the property

_____ 7. A detailed list of current property conditions

_____ 8. A written agreement that allows a tenant to use property for a set period of time at a set rent payment

a. eviction

b. landlord

c. lease

d. lessee

e. lessor

f. rental agreement

g. rental inventory

h. renting

i. tenant

CHECK YOUR UNDERSTANDING

9. How is a lease different from a rental agreement?

10. Explain the purpose of a rental inventory prepared when you first move into rental property and when you move out.

APPLY YOUR KNOWLEDGE

11. Explain the advantages and disadvantages of renting. Do you believe the advantages outweigh the disadvantages? Why or why not?

THINK _CRITICALLY_

12. The rental application asks many private and personal questions, and a potential landlord is likely to run your credit report. What does a credit report tell a landlord about a prospective tenant? Why is it necessary?

13. A lease gives you (the tenant) more protection than a month-to-month rental agreement. Why? How can a lease also be to the tenant's detriment?

14. Some landlords keep renters' deposits without proper justification. What can you do to help protect yourself from this practice?

Chapter Assessment

SUMMARY

21.1

- On-campus housing options include dormitories, fraternity or sorority houses, housing cooperatives, and married student housing.

- Duplexes, condominiums, and houses usually offer more space than studio, regular, or townhouse apartments but are also generally more expensive and require tenants to be responsible for some maintenance.

- To live together successfully, roommates must have compatible living habits and work out responsibilities in advance.

- When deciding where to live, consider required security deposits and fees, length of time you plan to live there, distance from work or school, distance from services, and required maintenance responsibilities.

- Prepare to move by accumulating needed items, saving to cover initial expenses, and making truck reservations in advance. You will need to accumulate less for a furnished rental than for an unfurnished rental.

- When you move in, you will have to pay fees to have utilities installed or turned on. The bundling of some services may save you money.

21.2

- Advantages of renting include mobility, convenience, minimal maintenance responsibilities, social opportunities, and lower costs.

- Disadvantages of renting include noise from close neighbors, lack of privacy, small living space, lack of storage space, and scarcity of parking.

- Landlords use the rental application to determine if you are a good risk as a tenant.

- If you lease, you (the lessee) agree to rent the space for a set period of time at a set rent payment. During this time, the landlord (the lessor) cannot raise the rent, but there are penalties if you leave early.

- If you enter a rental agreement, you can leave at anytime with proper notice, but the landlord can also raise the rent or ask you to leave at anytime.

- To protect yourself from being held responsible for pre-existing problems, complete a rental inventory when you move in.

- Landlords are responsible for providing a safe and habitable place for tenants to live.

- Tenant responsibilities include paying rent on time, obeying the rules, and taking reasonable care of the property. Failure to meet obligations could result in eviction.

APPLY WHAT YOU KNOW

1. List two advantages of on-campus housing and two disadvantages. Explain why living with parents and commuting to college is often the best alternative.

2. Compare and contrast apartment living to living in a duplex, condo, or house. What are the pros and cons of both types of renting?

3. Ask two people separately to answer the questions in the "Living Arrangements" section on page 472. Based on the answers, would the three of you make a compatible living group? List the problems you would have to work out to live together successfully. Then get together and role play a discussion in which you work out these problems. Record your agreements in writing.

4. What possessions have you accumulated that you would need in order to set up housekeeping in an apartment?

5. What basics would you have to acquire to live independently? Which of these would you have to buy and which could you borrow to save money? Would you consider having a roommate with whom to share ownership of these items? Why or why not?

6. Make a list of things you should do before moving out on your own.

7. To move your possessions from your present home to a new residence, what types of transportation are available to you? What is the best and least expensive option for you?

MAKE ACADEMIC CONNECTIONS

8. **Research** Conduct research of the rental housing market in your area. Compare today's prices to those of ten years earlier. Write a report explaining how rentals have changed: How many new rental properties are in the area? Have rental properties been sold as condominiums? Are there more or fewer houses for rent?

9. **Economics** Do research to find out if the housing market is a leading, lagging, or coincidental indicator of the state of the economy. For example, what do rental prices and availability say about the housing market and the current state of the economy? Write a report to explain your findings.

10. **Communication** Write a roommate-wanted ad. Then write a paper explaining what you are looking for in a roommate. Include requirements you would impose and the habits of a roommate you would reject.

11. **International Studies** Do Internet research to find out about renting in other countries. Choose a country that interests you and find the types of rental properties that are available, their features, and their prices. How do they compare to most rentals in the United States? Convert foreign currency into U.S. dollars for comparison purposes.

SOLVE PROBLEMS AND

EXPLORE ISSUES

12. Prepare a table or chart comparing the rental prices and availability of similar-sized apartments, duplexes, condominiums, and houses in your area. Also, note how many are presently available in each category, the high and low prices, and the average rental prices.

13. Your friend has decided to move from his apartment to a condo that is available for rent. The condo is in a large building; most of the owners are retired or mid-life professionals without children. Explain how a condo is different from an apartment and how expectations will change.

14. Select a large city in another state in which you might like to live. Search the Internet for apartments to rent in that city. Select a moderately priced apartment and print out or write down the description of it. Be sure to note the rent. Then find a similar apartment in a smaller town. What is the rent for this apartment? What can you conclude about the cost of living between these two locations based on apartment rents?

15. Renee and Brittany are best friends. They have a lot in common, but they also have very different lifestyles. Renee's room at home is neat and organized; Brittany's room is messy and cluttered. Renee balances her checkbook to the penny every month; Brittany pays cash for everything. Explain to Renee and Brittany what they should do now before becoming roommates so that their experience will be successful.

16. Using the community resources in your area, find out the installation fees and security deposits required for the following services: (a) telephone, (b) electricity, (c) cable or satellite TV, and (d) water. Are any of these fees and deposits refundable? If so, under what conditions?

17. You will be moving out of your parents' home and will need your own cell phone. Find out what it would cost you to buy a cell phone and a service plan (most companies require a contract) that would allow you (a) text messaging; (b) 500–1000 minutes per month, including day minutes, night minutes, and anytime minutes; (c) Internet access; and (d) a hands-free device to use while driving.

EXTEND YOUR LEARNING

18. **Legal Issues** *Landlord/tenant laws require that landlords provide a written explanation for any deposits that are withheld from renters when they move out. Deposits cannot be withheld without proof of damages and repairs that were made. Many tenants believe they have been charged for damage they did not cause. How can they prevent this from happening? If landlords keep deposits but do not provide explanations within a reasonable time period (usually 30 days), what legal recourse do tenants have?*

For related activities and links, go to **www.cengage.com/school/pfinance/mypf**

Chapter 22

Buying a Home

22.1	*Why Buy a Home?*

22.2	*The Home-Buying Process*

Consider **THIS**

Scott and Trisha have been married for five years, and they have managed to save money toward buying their own home.

"I think we have enough money saved to put a down payment on a four-bedroom home, though we really need only two bedrooms right now," Scott said to his wife.

"I'm not sure we have as large a down payment as you think," Trisha replied. "We'll have to pay other costs as well, such as closing costs and moving expenses."

"Okay," Scott agreed. "Let's start out with a smaller house that meets our needs and has potential for improvement. We can sell and move to another house when we start our family. By then we'll have built up some equity."

Why Buy a Home?

GOALS

- Discuss the advantages of home ownership.
- Describe the costs and responsibilities of buying and owning a home.

TERMS

- market value, *p. 492*
- appraised value, *p. 492*
- assessed value, *p. 492*
- equity, *p. 493*
- conventional loan, *p. 494*
- FHA loan, *p. 495*
- trust deed, *p. 495*
- escrow account, *p. 495*
- discount points, *p. 495*
- loan origination fee, *p. 495*
- closing costs, *p. 495*

ADVANTAGES OF HOME OWNERSHIP

Because the purchase of a home may be the most expensive decision you will ever make, you should carefully weigh the advantages, costs, and responsibilities.

VALUE AND EQUITY

There are four valuation methods commonly used in real estate:

1. *Market Value.* The **market value** of a home is the highest price that the property will bring on the market. It generally means what a ready and willing buyer and a ready and willing seller would agree upon as the price.

2. *Appraised Value.* Real estate appraisers can prepare an **appraised value** by examining the structure, size, features, and quality as compared to similar homes in the same geographic area. The recent selling price of a similar home in your area is a good estimate of the current value of your home.

3. *Assessed Value.* For purposes of computing property taxes owed against your home, the city or county in which you live sets an **assessed value**. It is often computed based on the cost to build, the cost of improvements, and the cost of similar properties. It is usually a percentage of market value. Computer programs, rather than visual inspection, are often used to determine assessed value.

4. *Estimated Value.* Real estate agents also estimate the value of homes to help sellers establish a list price. To do this, they compare your house and its features to those of comparable properties that have recently sold in a close geographic area. Using these comparable properties, or *comps*, may not be exact, but it gives a general idea of a property's value and establishes a point at which to begin negotiations.

The value of most homes *appreciates*, or increases in market value, over time. For example, if you buy a home for $150,000 and two years later you could sell it for $160,000, then your property has appreciated by $10,000. Appreciation is one way that the equity in your home increases. **Equity** is the difference between the market value of property and the amount owed on it.

Equity also increases because each loan payment you make decreases your debt. Equity turns to cash when you sell your home. For example, if you purchase a home valued at $150,000 and have a loan of $120,000, your initial equity is $30,000. Suppose that when you decide to sell, the market value has increased to $170,000 and your loan debt is down to $100,000. Your equity would be $70,000 (the $170,000 market value minus the $100,000 owed).

QUALITY OF LIFE

Home ownership generally offers more privacy, more space, and more personal freedom not available to renters. In your own home, you can make the changes you choose to accommodate your own needs and personal style. Knowing that the home is yours to do with as you wish can be very satisfying. Owning a home also provides a feeling of security and independence. No one can raise your rent or tell you that you have to leave. You also get a sense of stability and belonging to your community. You have "put down roots," so you care about what happens in your neighborhood.

Neighborhood living involves responsibilities to neighbors, but the homeowner also has a voice in helping to set the tone of the neighborhood. *Neighborhood associations* are groups of homeowners in geographic areas that meet and work to set quality-of-life standards for the area. They work with local government groups to be sure the area is being provided with needed services, from street lighting and speed bumps to safety patrols.

© Photodisc/Getty Images

What kinds of quality-of-life advantages do homeowners enjoy?

TAX SAVINGS

The interest you pay on your home loan, along with the property taxes, is tax-deductible. These deductions lower the cost of home ownership. Because of these tax savings, owning real estate is a *tax shelter*. Typically, renters cannot deduct any part of their rent payments from their income taxes. Even though your equity in your home may be increasing each year, you do not pay tax on the equity until you sell your home. Even then, you may be able to legally avoid taxes on the gains from the sale if the property was your primary residence.

COMPUTING EQUITY IN A HOME

Suppose you bought a home for $200,000. Your lender required a 20 percent down payment. Therefore, your down payment amount was:

$$\$200,000 \times .20 = \$40,000$$

Your initial loan amount (ignoring other costs) was:

$$\$200,000 - \$40,000 = \$160,000$$

Now let's say that you have been making payments on your house for two years, reducing your debt (principal) by $8,000. Therefore, you now owe $160,000 – $8,000 = $152,000.

Your house has been appreciating at 5 percent per year for two years. As a result, the current market value is:

$$\$200,000 \times 1.05 = \$210,000 \text{ after year 1}$$

$$\$210,000 \times 1.05 = \$220,500 \text{ after year 2}$$

Your equity is now:

$$\$220,500 \text{ market value} - \$152,000 \text{ remaining debt} = \$68,500$$

Based on the preceding example, compute the amount for the (a) down payment, (b) initial loan, (c) current debt, (d) current market value, and (e) current equity in the following situation:

Martin and Jamie bought a house two years ago for $175,000. They put 15 percent down. Their payments have reduced their debt by $6,000. Houses in their area have been appreciating at 4 percent per year.

Solution:

(a) Down payment = $175,000 × .15 = $26,250

(b) Initial loan = $175,000 – $26,250 = $148,750

(c) Current debt = $148,750 – $6,000 = $142,750

(d) Current market value = ($175,000 × 1.04) × 1.04 = $189,280

(e) Current equity = $189,280 – $142,750 = $46,530

COSTS AND RESPONSIBILITIES

Home ownership carries significant costs and responsibilities. Before deciding to buy a home, you must make sure that you can financially handle the costs and that you are personally ready to accept the responsibilities.

▌ DOWN PAYMENT

Mortgage lenders usually require that borrowers pay a certain amount down toward the purchase price. Then they will provide a loan for the balance of the price. A **conventional loan** is a mortgage agreement that does not have government backing and that is offered through a commercial bank or mortgage broker. This type of loan often requires a 10 to 30 percent down payment. For example, if you are purchasing a home for $150,000, you will need from $15,000 (10 percent) to $45,000 (30 percent) for the down payment. For many people, saving enough money for the down payment takes a number of years.

An **FHA loan** is a government-sponsored loan that carries mortgage insurance. In other words, borrowers pay a monthly insurance premium and their loan payments are guaranteed through the FHA (Federal Housing Administration) insurance program, making it less risky for banks to lend the money. FHA loans may require down payments of as little as 3 percent. Government-backed lending programs are often available for first-time home buyers, veterans, and low-income buyers.

■ MORTGAGE PAYMENTS

A loan to purchase real estate is called a *mortgage*. A **trust deed** is similar to a mortgage; it is a debt security instrument that shows as a lien against property. Payments on a mortgage or trust deed are made over an extended period, such as 15 or 30 years.

Monthly loan payments include principal and interest. If the borrower is required to have an escrow account, then the monthly payment will also include property insurance and property taxes. An **escrow account**, also called a *reserve account*, is a fund where money is held to pay amounts that will come due during the year. For example, if your property taxes were estimated to be $2,400 per year, an additional $200 per month would be added to your loan payment. This amount would be held in escrow monthly so that when the bill arrives for property taxes, it can be paid from the escrow account.

Mortgage lenders often allow borrowers to buy **discount points**, which are used to lower the mortgage interest rate. Typically, one point equals 1 percent of the loan amount. For example, 3 points on a $100,000 loan would be $3,000. Points are essentially extra interest that borrowers must pay at closing (time of purchase). They increase the cost of the loan. However, lenders usually offer lower interest rates in exchange for higher points. Whether or not this tradeoff is a good deal depends on how long you plan to keep your house. A lower interest rate will result in lower monthly payments. Over many years, the lower payments may make up for the cost of the points and save you money. But since points are paid up front, you could lose money if you keep your house for only a few years. When you compare loan rates, be sure to consider the points. Points paid are tax-deductible.

Points are often charged in addition to a loan origination fee. A **loan origination fee**, also called a *mortgage loan fee*, is the amount charged by a bank or other lender to process the loan papers. This fee compensates the loan officer or broker for the time spent in qualifying buyers, preparing paperwork, and working with loan underwriters.

■ CLOSING COSTS

Closing costs, also referred to as *settlement costs*, are the expenses incurred in transferring ownership from buyer to seller in a real estate transaction. Closing costs may add another $3,000 to $5,000 to the purchase price of your home. The buyer usually pays for a title search to make sure the seller is the legal owner and that no one else has a claim on the property. The buyer may also pay for a credit report, loan origination fee, loan assumption fee (to take over someone else's mortgage), closing fees (fees for preparing the paperwork), recording fees, and his or her share (called a *proration*) of taxes and interest currently owed on the property.

■ PROPERTY TAXES

The real estate property tax is a major source of funding for local governments. Homeowners pay property taxes based on the *assessed value* of land and buildings. A local taxing authority determines the assessed value of property, usually a percentage of the market value. A home worth $200,000 might have an assessed value of $180,000 (or 90 percent of its market value). If the property tax rate is $15 per thousand of assessed value, you will pay $2,700 (180 × $15) in property taxes per year. Property taxes are tax-deductible.

■ PROPERTY INSURANCE

A homeowner must have property insurance covering the structure. This is usually a requirement of the loan agreement to protect the interests of the mortgage lender as well as the homeowner. Standard homeowner's insurance includes both fire and liability protection. A more detailed explanation of homeowner's insurance is presented in Chapter 26.

■ UTILITIES

Because most homes are larger than apartments or other rental units, the utility bills are usually higher. The homeowner pays for all utilities and garbage services, whereas a renter may pay for some but not all of these services. Utilities may include water and sewer charges, storm drain (watershed) assessments, lighting fees (for neighborhood light poles), gas, and electricity. In addition, when repairs are needed to water or sewer lines on their property, homeowners are fully responsible for the costs.

VIEW *Points*

In 2007, the housing market was severely hurt when the economy slowed down and many people were unable to make their mortgage payments. In the years leading up to 2007, many loans with zero down payments were made; these were risky to lenders. Borrowers were assured that their equity would grow and that over time they would make money on their investment. Unfortunately, with a market slowdown, borrowers found themselves owing more money than their property was worth. This is called an upside down equity position.

Many of the mortgage agreements also allowed for adjustable interest rates. As interest rates on the loans increased in subsequent years, the required monthly payment also increased significantly. As a result, many people—especially those who lost their jobs—also lost their homes to foreclosure. Many people think that these borrowers should have known better; they made bad financial decisions. Others believe that lenders took advantage of borrowers with loans that had rapidly increasing interest rates and payments.

THINK *CRITICALLY*

With which side do you agree? Why? How could making a greater down payment have provided a measure of prevention to the situation in which many borrowers found themselves?

CCRs

Many housing subdivisions or planned unit developments have *covenants, conditions, and requirements (CCRs)* that were agreed upon when the subdivision was built. CCRs are rules designed to maintain property values and protect the interests of all property owners. CCRs include things such as maintaining your lawn, specifying where cars and RVs can and cannot be parked, controlling the kinds of fences or storage buildings that can and cannot be built, specifying the type of roof that can and cannot be installed, and so on.

© Photodisc/Getty Images

As a potential home buyer, what kinds of CCRs and zoning laws might you be expected to follow?

ZONING LAWS

As a homeowner, you must obey all *zoning laws* and local ordinances. These are laws passed by local governments to preserve the quality of life for all people in the community. They include rules such as obtaining a building permit when you add to or modify your home, following *setback* requirements that force buildings and improvements to be set back a minimum number of feet from streets and other properties, and adhering to restrictions regarding the kinds and types of buildings that can be constructed in the area. For example, you would not be allowed to build a commercial warehouse in a residential zone.

MAINTENANCE AND REPAIRS

As a homeowner, you will be responsible for maintenance and repairs inside and outside of your home. Before you choose to buy, make sure you are willing to spend the time and money needed to keep your home in good condition. For example, yard landscaping, fencing, and other features may be needed to meet neighborhood standards.

Ongoing maintenance includes such tasks as painting, mowing, weeding, and fixing things that break or wear out from normal use. You would incur not only the costs but also the responsibility for doing these tasks or arranging to have them done.

In addition to ongoing maintenance, you will occasionally have to make very expensive repairs or improvements to your home. For example, a roof lasts only about 15 years. The furnace, water heater, stove, and other appliances may also need replacing in about that length of time. There are numerous other expenses that come with owning a home.

arketing

Whenever residential or commercial property is bought or sold, one or more real estate sales agents and brokers will most likely facilitate the transaction. These professionals know the real estate market, real estate laws, and real estate finance. They help buyers and sellers navigate the complicated real estate laws that exist in every state.

Real estate listing agreements are used to input data about properties for sale. The listing is then made available to all local real estate sales persons, both locally and worldwide. Sales associates show houses to prospective buyers, hold open houses, work with buyers to be sure they are qualified to buy real estate, and present offers to sellers.

Brokers and agents often work evenings and weekends, and they are often on call to meet the needs of their clients. Compensation is based on sales commissions; if a property does not sell, the agent does not earn a fee.

Employment Outlook

- An average rate of employment growth is expected.

Job Titles

- Real estate agent
- Real estate broker

Needed Skills

- A license is required in all 50 states.

- Educational coursework is required before an applicant can take a license exam.

What's it like to work in... *Real Estate Sales*

Adam works for a real estate company in a small Midwestern city. He has had his license for three years and works under the supervision of a real estate broker.

Adam specializes in residential houses located in suburban areas. He also sells condos, duplexes, and other forms of rental residential property. Adam is meeting with prospective buyers who have been prequalified for a mortgage loan. Today they will be viewing six properties, and they wish to choose one of them by the end of the day. The buyers are being transferred to the area because of a job promotion.

Adam works long hours when clients' needs require it. He often does preliminary work, such as searching for houses on the market that meet buyers' wants and needs. Adam enjoys his work because he helps people find their dream homes.

What About You?

Would you like helping people navigate their way through the home-buying process? Would you enjoy the challenge of working for commission-based income and keeping up with complex real estate laws? Would you consider a career in real estate sales?

Assessment

KEY TERMS REVIEW

Match the terms with the definitions. Some terms may not be used.

_____ 1. A fund where money is held to pay amounts that will come due during the year

_____ 2. Home value determined by examining the structure, size, features, and quality as compared to similar homes

_____ 3. A government-sponsored loan that carries mortgage insurance

_____ 4. The highest price that the property will bring on the market

_____ 5. A fee charged by a lender to process the loan papers

_____ 6. Difference between the market value of property and the amount owed on it

a. appraised value

b. assessed value

c. closing costs

d. conventional loan

e. discount points

f. equity

g. escrow account

h. FHA loan

i. loan origination fee

j. market value

k. trust deed

_____ 7. The expenses incurred in transferring ownership from buyer to seller

_____ 8. Mortgage agreement that does not have government backing and that is offered through a commercial bank or mortgage broker

_____ 9. Value set by the city or county that is used to compute property taxes

CHECK YOUR UNDERSTANDING

10. Why do people choose to buy a house rather than rent a residence?

11. What responsibilities come with home ownership?

APPLY YOUR KNOWLEDGE

12. If you were trying to decide how much a piece of property was worth for the purpose of making an offer to purchase it, what types of value would you consider? Which valuation method is the best? Why?

THINK _CRITICALLY_

13. Owning real estate is often described as a tax shelter. What does this mean? Explain the tax advantages of owning real estate.

14. If you don't make a substantial down payment, you may be required to pay into an escrow account from which property taxes and insurance will be paid when due. Why would you want to avoid this requirement?

15. Explain how CCRs and zoning laws help ensure the quality of neighborhoods and thus enhance property values.

The Home-Buying Process

FINDING AND BUYING A HOME

When buying a home, factors to consider include location, accessibility, nearness to employment, type and quality of construction, cost and effort of maintenance, and personal likes and dislikes. Before starting your search, it's a good idea to list the features you want your home and neighborhood to have and the price range you can afford. Prioritize the list according to what features are most important to you. Decide what you want most before you begin to look.

Why is it a good idea to work with a real estate agent when buying your first home?

© Photodisc/Getty Images

WORKING WITH A REAL ESTATE AGENT

Before selecting a home to buy, look at many houses. You can look by yourself or work with a real estate agent. Agents know the market, can help you find the right home, and will assist you with the purchasing, financing, and closing processes.

One of the first things an agent will have you do is go to a mortgage lender and *prequalify* for a real estate loan. In other words, you fill out an application to see how much money you would be qualified to borrow. This will guide you and your real estate agent to look for houses in your price range.

Real estate agents earn commission income. The commission is a percentage of the home sale price, usually between 5 and 7 percent. The seller pays the commission, and the agents working for the buyer and seller split it. As the purchaser, you do not pay the agents' commission. If you are buying directly from an owner without the assistance of an agent, you might be able to negotiate a lower price because the seller would not have to pay this fee. However, you should still seek advice from a professional, such as a lawyer, to be sure your interests are protected.

You can find homes for sale online or in the newspaper classified ads, including those that the owners are selling themselves without a real estate agent. A big advantage of having an agent, however, is to gain access to the multiple listings. The *Multiple Listing Service (MLS)* is a real estate marketing service in which agents from many real estate agencies pool their home listings and agree to share commissions on the sales. Sellers gain wide exposure for their properties. Buyers can sift through the large pool of property descriptions to select those they want to visit.

As a consumer, you can visit multiple listing web sites online. You can also visit the web sites of individual real estate agencies to view properties they have listed for sale. In many cases, you can take a "virtual tour" of the house, which will show you the layout of the house and the room-by-room features.

After you have narrowed your choices to a small number of homes in your price range that match your criteria, you should visit the homes with your agent. Take notes, both pro and con, on the features of each house and neighborhood. Do not make a decision on the spot.

MAKING AN OFFER

To let the homeowner know of your interest in buying the home and the price you are willing to pay, you will sign an agreement called an offer. An *offer* is a serious intent to be bound to an agreement. In real estate, when you make an offer to buy property, it is called an **earnest-money offer**. The offer is accompanied by a deposit (usually a check) called the earnest money. It generally is a percentage of the sales price. For example, in an offer to buy a house selling for $200,000, the earnest-money deposit could be $2,000 (1 percent) or more. This money is held in escrow until the transaction is completed.

Earnest money protects the seller in case you fail to meet the terms of the agreement. If you and the seller have agreed on the transaction, the seller will take the house off the market until the deal is completed. During that time, the house cannot be sold to anyone else. If you later back out of the deal, you will likely forfeit your earnest money to the seller. One way to avoid losing your money is to make your offer *contingent* (dependent) on obtaining financing and the property passing an inspection. That way, if you do not qualify for a mortgage on this property or an inspection reveals major flaws in the house, you will not have violated the contract, and you will get your earnest money back.

The seller may or may not accept your initial offer. When the seller agrees to your offer exactly as stated, you have an acceptance. An *acceptance* is a formal agreement to the terms of an offer, forming a contract between the parties.

NETBookmark

Zillow.com is an online real estate service that provides buyers with information about homes that are for sale all over the country. Access www.cengage.com/school/pfinance/mypf and click on the link for Chapter 22. Enter your current ZIP code (or a ZIP code where you would like to live) into the search engine to generate a map and list of houses for sale. What is the price range of houses for sale in this area? Scroll through the list of available houses and read about a few. Which of these homes is the most attractive to you? Why?

www.cengage.com/school/pfinance/mypf

Write a one-page paper about your ideal house. What would it look like? In what city? How many bedrooms? Describe your house in terms of type or style, number of square feet, size and shape of lot, and other distinguishing features. Include pictures (from magazines, newspapers, or the Internet) or draw diagrams to help illustrate the features you desire. How is your choice of house different from that of your parents? How will your choice of house likely be different in the future?

You may withdraw your offer before the seller accepts it, but once accepted, the offer becomes a binding contract.

If the seller wants to change any part of the offer, he or she makes a counteroffer. A **counteroffer** is a rejection of the original offer with a listing of what terms would be acceptable. In effect, it is a new offer made back to the buyer. For example, if you offered to buy at a lower price than the seller was willing to accept, the seller may make a counteroffer with a different price. Usually, a buyer's initial offer is lower than the price for which the house is listed. The seller then counteroffers a price below the initial listing but higher than the buyer's first offer. The buyer and seller negotiate until they either agree on mutually acceptable terms or decide not to complete the transaction.

REAL ESTATE LOANS AND TITLE

After you have come to an agreement with the seller, you will have to arrange for your loan. To finance your purchase, you must have funds for a down payment and closing costs, meet certain requirements of your lending institution, and select the type of mortgage you want.

DOWN PAYMENT SOURCES

The most common sources of down payment money are personal savings and informal loans from parents or relatives. Most lending institutions will not allow mortgage applicants to formally borrow their down payment. In other words, you must invest a substantial amount of your own cash in the property. Because the down payment can be $5,000 to $10,000 or more, many first-time home buyers have difficulty saving the money and must "borrow" it informally from parents or relatives.

QUALIFYING FOR A MORTGAGE

To qualify for a mortgage, you must complete an extensive loan application. The financial institution will check your credit history, employment, and references. You must prove to the lender that you are capable of making the monthly payment. The lender will look for evidence that you can meet your current bills. The lender will also look at the type and amount of your current debts, the amount and source of your income, and your creditworthiness. The lender will judge if you can handle the monthly mortgage payments, which as a general rule, should not exceed 25 to 35 percent of your take-home (net) pay.

The lender will also require a real estate appraisal by a certified real estate appraiser. This is to assure the lender that the property is worth more than the loan it is making.

■ TYPES OF MORTGAGES

There are two basic types of mortgages: fixed-rate mortgages and adjustable-rate mortgages. A **fixed-rate mortgage** is a mortgage on which the interest rate does not change during the term of the loan. An **adjustable-rate mortgage (ARM)** is a mortgage for which the interest rate changes in response to the movement of interest rates in the economy as a whole.

The rate for an ARM usually starts lower than the current rates for a fixed-rate mortgage. The lender then adjusts the ARM rate based on the ups and downs of the economy. The lender may decrease the ARM's rate, but usually the rate goes up. For example, at a given time, fixed-rate loans may be offered at 7 percent. This rate would remain unchanged for the 30-year term of the loan. At the same time, adjustable-rate mortgages may be offered at 5 percent. The tradeoff for this low initial rate is its variability. The lender may raise the rate over time to 10 or 12 percent as interest rates go up in the economy. Many adjustable-rate mortgages specify maximum rate increases (such as 2 or 3 percent a year) and ceilings (such as a top of 12 percent) to which the interest rate can rise.

■ TAKING TITLE TO PROPERTY

After you and the seller have reached an agreement and you have arranged your financing, the next step is to prepare for the closing. An *escrow closer* is an independent person who gathers and verifies information. The closer also prepares the closing statement (which lists what you owe and what credits will be applied to you).

© Photodisc/Getty Images

Which type of mortgage would you prefer—fixed-rate or adjustable-rate? Why?

You will meet with the closer to sign documents and pay the balance you owe. Once the sellers receive their money, the escrow closer makes sure that title passes to you. **Title** is legally established ownership. A **deed** is the legal document that transfers title of real property from one party to another.

Before you take ownership, you will want to make sure that the title is clear—that is, free of any liens. A **lien** is a financial claim against property. For example, if the previous owner used the home as collateral for a loan other than the mortgage, then that lender has a financial claim or lien on the property. This claim must be paid before ownership of the property can be transferred.

To ensure that a property has clear title, the escrow closer orders a title search. A *title search* is the process of searching public records to check for ownership and claims to a piece of property. When the title insurance company confirms that title is clear and all is as represented, it will issue title insurance. A **title insurance** policy protects the buyer from any claims arising from a defective title. Most lenders also require title insurance to protect the lender's interests. Buyers and sellers often negotiate who will pay the title insurance fees.

Before the closing, the lending institution prepares the loan papers and sends them to the escrow closer. If any problems arise, the closer or the lender will notify the buyer and seller. For example, some deeds may carry restrictions that limit the kind of building that can be erected and the use of the property. Inspections, such as termite examinations, must be carried out. Any repairs required by the terms of the sale must be completed.

When all these procedures are completed, the buyer and seller will be notified of the closing date. In this meeting, you and the seller sign the papers and pay all related closing costs, such as those shown in Figure 22.1. If you have a real estate agent, the agent will attend the meeting with you and help you through the process. At the closing, the ownership of the home is transferred from the seller to the buyer.

FIGURE 22.1 *Typical Closing Costs*

REAL ESTATE CLOSING COSTS

Type of Cost	Typical Amount	Who Pays
Credit report (on buyer)	$50 to $100	Buyer
Property appraisal fee	$350 to $500	Buyer
Pest/damage inspection	$250 to $500	Buyer
Electrical/plumbing/ water inspection report	$250 to $500	Buyer
Mortgage loan fee	Varies; often 1% of loan amount	Buyer
Points	Varies; often 1% of loan amount	Buyer
Loan assumption fee	Varies, often $500 to $1,500	Buyer
Escrow closing fee	Depends on selling price of property; usually $750 to $1,500	Buyer and Seller
Notary and filing fees	$50 to $150	Buyer and Seller
Title search and title insurance	Depends on selling price of property; usually $750 to $2,000	Buyer and Seller
Survey	$500 to $1,500	Seller
Home warranty (optional)	Depends on selling price of property; usually $300 to $1,000	Seller
Real estate commission	Percentage of sales price of home; usually between 5 and 7 percent	Seller
Attorney's fees	Varies; depends on services provided, such as preparing contract	Buyer and Seller
Prorated interest and taxes	Depends on date of possession and when title passes	Buyer and Seller
Transfer taxes and fees	Varies by state	Seller

ISSUES IN YOUR WORLD

A 15-YEAR OR 30-YEAR MORTGAGE?

Lenders typically offer mortgages that run for a term of 15 years or 30 years. Before choosing a loan term, consider the differences. A 15-year mortgage has significant advantages.

- *Because the loan term is shorter, lenders consider a 15-year mortgage less risky. Thus, 15-year loans have lower interest rates than 30-year loans. For example, if a 30-year fixed-rate mortgage has a rate of 6.375 percent, you could likely get a 15-year fixed-rate mortgage for 5 percent or less. Thus, you will pay much less total interest over the life of the loan.*

- *Also because a 15-year mortgage is considered less risky, the borrower may receive more favorable loan costs, such as lower loan origination fees, lower closing costs, and easier loan qualification requirements.*

- *You will pay off a 15-year mortgage in half the time of a 30-year mortgage, enabling you to enjoy the payment-free status sooner.*

But 15-year loans also have disadvantages that make a 30-year loan more attractive to many home buyers.

- *Because the loan will be paid off in 15 years rather than 30, the monthly payments will be significantly higher. Many home buyers do not earn enough income to qualify for a 15-year loan because of the payment size.*

- *The 15-year loan will often require a much higher down payment at closing. In other words, the home buyer must have more cash up front, such as 20 percent or more of the cost of the property.*

- *The 15-year loan payment may put a strain on your budget, even though you are paying off the house at a faster rate. The payment may take such a large bite out of your paycheck that you would not have enough left over to live comfortably. If so, choose a 30-year loan instead.*

The loan term is an important consideration for home buyers. Your choice will affect your budget in a major way.

THINK CRITICALLY

1. *Which mortgage term (15 or 30 years) sounds better to you? How does your choice relate to your age?*

2. *Do you know someone with a 15-year mortgage? If so, ask why he or she chose the shorter term. If not, use the Internet to research additional advantages and disadvantages of a 15-year mortgage.*

Assessment

KEY TERMS REVIEW

Match the terms with the definitions.

_____ 1. *A mortgage for which the interest rate changes in response to the movement of interest rates in the economy as a whole*

_____ 2. *A financial claim against property*

_____ 3. *A rejection of an offer with a listing of what terms would be acceptable*

_____ 4. *Legally established ownership to property*

_____ 5. *An offer to buy property accompanied by a deposit*

_____ 6. *A mortgage on which the interest rate does not change*

_____ 7. *A policy that protects you from any claims arising from a defective title*

_____ 8. *The legal document that transfers title of real property from one party to another*

a. adjustable-rate mortgage (ARM)

b. counteroffer

c. deed

d. earnest-money offer

e. fixed-rate mortgage

f. lien

g. title

h. title insurance

CHECK YOUR UNDERSTANDING

9. *What are the advantages of the Multiple Listing Service?*

10. *What is the difference between a fixed-rate loan and an ARM?*

APPLY YOUR KNOWLEDGE

11. *Describe the steps in the home-buying process. If you were in the market for a new home, would you use a real estate agent to help you through the process? Why or why not?*

THINK *CRITICALLY*

12. *The Internet makes it possible for buyers to take virtual tours of a property without ever seeing it in person. Explain why it is still important to do an in-person walk-through before making an offer.*

13. *It's very difficult to save up enough money to make a sizeable down payment. Why is it important to make a large down payment when you buy a house? Where will you get the money?*

14. *Explain what is meant by a title search. Why is it important? Explain how homeowners as well as mortgage lenders are protected by title insurance.*

Chapter (Assessment)

SUMMARY

22.1

- *There are several valuation methods used in real estate, including market value, appraised value, assessed value, and estimated value.*

- *Financial advantages of home ownership include increasing equity as property values increase and the loan balance is paid down.*

- *Quality-of-life advantages for homeowners, as compared to renters, generally include more privacy, more space, more personal freedom, and a sense of belonging to a community.*

- *Real estate is considered a tax shelter because mortgage interest and property taxes on primary residences are tax-deductible.*

- *A conventional loan requires a 10 to 30 percent down payment, while an FHA loan with government backing requires as little as a 3 percent down payment but also requires the borrower to carry mortgage insurance.*

- *Home ownership involves costs such as a down payment, points, loan origination fee, closing costs, mortgage payments, property taxes, property insurance, utilities, and ongoing repairs and maintenance.*

- *Homeowners must abide by CCRs and local zoning laws.*

22.2

- *Before starting your house search, prioritize a list of the features you want and determine the price range you can afford. Search the multiple listings for homes that meet your criteria. Once you have narrowed your choices, visit these homes and note their good and bad points.*

- *Real estate agents' commission is a percentage of the sales price, paid by the seller.*

- *Once you have selected a home, you will make an earnest-money offer to buy it. The seller may accept your offer or make a counteroffer.*

- *Once you have agreed on a price and terms of the sale, the offer becomes a contract.*

- *To obtain financing, you must fill out an application and meet the lender's requirements. You can apply for a fixed-rate or an adjustable-rate mortgage.*

- *Prior to closing, you will want to have the title verified as free of any liens. Title insurance will protect the buyer and lender from a defective title.*

- *At the closing, you will sign papers and money will change hands. Then the deed will transfer title to you.*

APPLY WHAT YOU KNOW

1. Go to the library or search the Internet to find out the annual rate that houses are appreciating in your area. If you bought a house for $150,000 now, how much would it be worth five years from now at the current rate of appreciation?

2. With your instructor's permission, arrange to visit a real estate agent at work. Discuss with the agent the process of purchasing a house, including the steps, length of time, and costs involved. Ask the agent to show you what the multiple listings look like. If possible, ask the agent if you can accompany him or her while showing a house to a prospective buyer. Write a brief paper summarizing what you have learned.

3. Because of the complexities of real estate transactions, it is often wise to engage the services of a professional real estate agent. Find out through research or an interview with one or more real estate agents at least five services that a professional can provide when you are buying a home.

4. With your instructor's permission, visit a title insurance company in your area and ask people there what they do, how they gather information, and how they are able to insure titles. Briefly summarize your notes in one page or less.

5. Obtain the home mortgage rates from a local bank, savings and loan association, credit union, and online lender. Compare these rates and other loan terms such as the down payment, loan costs, points, and loan length. Compare the types of loans offered as well. Determine which lender makes the best financing offers.

MAKE ACADEMIC CONNECTIONS

6. **Technology/Research** Search the Internet for the multiple listings in your area. If you cannot gain access without a subscription, go to the web site of a large real estate agency that operates in your area. Create a bulleted list of the types of information supplied in the house listings. Look at the listings for several houses in your neighborhood. Write a brief summary of the kinds of houses available near you, including their price range, house styles, internal features, and acreage.

7. **Math** You bought your home last year for $130,000. You made a down payment of 20 percent. Through your mortgage payments, you have reduced your debt by $2,000. The annual appreciation rate for homes in your area has averaged 3 percent. Determine (a) the amount of your down payment, (b) the initial loan amount, (c) the amount you owe now, (d) the current market value of your home, and (e) the amount of equity you have in the home.

8. **Communication** Assume you have been appointed president of your homeowners' association. Create a brochure to be distributed to new homeowners that explains their responsibilities as a homeowner in your neighborhood. Include suggestions on how to be a good neighbor and how to maintain the quality of life and property values in the area. Be creative and make the brochure as attractive as possible.

SOLVE *PROBLEMS* AND

EXPLORE *ISSUES*

9. Your friend is considering buying a house, but she is not sure how to determine the property's value. Explain to her the difference between market value, appraised value, assessed value, and estimated value. Which value should she use when making an offer on real estate?

10. If you buy a house for $225,000, how much down payment will you have to make if the lender requires a down payment of (a) 10 percent, (b) 15 percent, (c) 20 percent, or (d) 25 percent?

11. Suppose you accept a mortgage for $150,000. What finance charge will you have to pay at closing if the lender charges (a) 1 point, (b) 2 points, or (c) 3 points?

12. Suppose your local taxing authority requires you to pay property taxes at the rate of $16 per thousand. Your house is assessed at $210,000 by the county. How much property tax will you owe each year?

13. Use the description of your ideal house that you created in the Communication Connection activity on p. 502. Prioritize your list of features in order of importance to you. Select a moderate price range for homes in your area. Search listings for houses in that price range that meet your criteria. Clip or print out the listings for three houses that you would like to tour if you were in the market for a home. Which of your criteria do these houses meet and which do they not meet?

14. Using the closing costs specifically stated in Figure 22.1, list the total maximum cost that a buyer might expect to pay for a $180,000 home, assuming the buyer pays 1 point. What is the total maximum cost the seller might expect to pay?

15. Search the Internet for a loan planner tool to solve this problem. To buy a home, you will have to borrow $100,000 at 7 percent interest for 30 years or 360 monthly payments. What will your monthly payment be?

EXTEND YOUR LEARNING

16. **Ethics** Some people feel that when they own property, they should be able to do with it as they wish. Many neighborhood associations enforce strict guidelines of what residents in an area can and cannot do with their property. Who is morally correct? Discuss whose rights are being violated and protected with each extreme. If you agree that neighborhood associations should have the right to create and enforce guidelines, at what point would you draw the line?

For related activities and links, go to **www.cengage.com/school/pfinance/mypf**

Buying and Owning a Vehicle

23.1 *Buying a Vehicle*

23.2 *Maintaining a Vehicle*

Consider **THIS**

Patrick works part time and attends school full time. He lives at home with his parents, and his take-home pay is over $600 a month.

"I'm ready to buy a car," he told his parents. "It says here in the paper that with just $100 down, I can finance the purchase of a brand new car. I'd have to make 60 payments of $350 each. I make nearly twice that much each month, so I can afford the car. But I'm not sure I want that particular car. I'm wondering if I can get the same deal through my credit union. How can I get the best deal?"

Buying a Vehicle

GOALS
- List and explain the steps of the car-buying process.
- Explain vehicle financing choices, including leasing.
- Discuss consumer protection laws for new- and used-car buyers.

TERMS
- preapproval, *p. 512*
- vehicle identification number (VIN), *p. 513*
- vehicle emission test, *p. 514*
- sticker price, *p. 514*
- invoice price, *p. 514*
- car-buying service, *p. 515*
- dealer add-ons, *p. 515*
- lemon laws, *p. 517*
- lemon, *p. 517*
- FTC Rule, *p. 518*

THE CAR-BUYING PROCESS

Most people are really excited when they buy their first car. Because it is a large purchase, buying an automobile should also involve taking the time to make a good decision—one that you won't regret later. Following a decision-making model, such as the one presented in Chapter 20, may help you make better choices as you get ready to buy a car.

IDENTIFY YOUR NEEDS AND WANTS

Buying a car starts with identifying your needs (not just your wants). Start by asking yourself some basic questions, such as the following:

- What do I need to do with a car?
- How much will I drive? (Fuel efficiency may be an important consideration.)
- Do I plan to haul a number of people or gear?
- Will I take the car off-road?
- What features would I like to have on the vehicle?

After you have made your list of wants and needs, decide which ones are most important. Prioritizing helps you identify what you must have and what you can give up if necessary to keep the price affordable.

DECIDE WHAT YOU CAN AFFORD

Before you start shopping for a car, determine how much you can afford to spend. One general guideline is that you can afford monthly payments of no more than 20 percent of the money you have left after paying all your regular monthly expenses, such as rent, utilities, credit card payments, and so on. Also figure into your budget the costs of maintaining your car as well as the costs of fuel and auto insurance.

IDENTIFY AND RESEARCH YOUR CHOICES

Select several types of cars that would meet your needs. In the library or online, research the features of each possibility. Print and online magazines such as

What needs and wants will your vehicle meet?

Consumer Reports or *Car and Driver* offer an abundance of information on different car models. Look for articles about performance, repair records, safety records, fuel economy, and prices.

Compare the features of the models you are considering against your list of wants and needs. Note the pros and cons for each model. Use your list and price range to narrow your choices to just a few that best fit you. When comparing prices, be sure to compare models that have the same options.

DECIDE WHETHER TO BUY NEW OR USED

A primary decision is whether to buy a new car or a used one. Cost is a major factor in this decision. A new car is much more expensive. Can you afford the high price of a new car? Also, a new car loses much of its market value as soon as you drive it off the lot. A car can lose as much as 20 percent of its value in its first year. Buying a well-maintained used car can save you money.

On the other hand, a used car is likely to need more repairs. Even if you have a mechanic check the car's overall condition before you buy it, a used car is still a bit of an unknown. You could be buying someone else's problems. A dealer may offer a used-car warranty that you would not get from an individual seller, but a dealer will typically charge more for the used car.

DECIDE HOW YOU WILL PAY FOR IT

Find out how much money you will be qualified to borrow before visiting car dealers. **Preapproval** is the process of getting a new- or used-car loan prearranged through your bank or credit union. Preapproval separates financing from the process of negotiating the price of the car. It also allows you to compare total costs of buying, including credit rates. You may or may not actually take the preapproved loan, but at least you will know how much you can spend and the interest rate you can get before you shop for a car.

To get preapproved, visit your credit union or bank and fill out an application. Based on the information you supply, the loan officer will determine how much the institution would be willing to lend you. The loan officer will then give you a form stating this preapproved amount and rate. Typically, the preapproval will expire in 30 or 60 days, after which time you must reapply if you want the loan.

CHECK INSURANCE RATES

Check out the insurance rates on your vehicle choices. If a car is rated as a "sports car," the cost of insurance may be much higher than for vehicles rated higher for safety and other features. A call to your insurance agent to get this information helps rule out choices that may result in insurance that is too high.

SEARCH FOR AVAILABLE VEHICLES

Search your newspaper's classified ads and the Internet for cars available from dealers and from individual sellers in your area. Many areas offer a free print publication, such as *Auto Trader*, dedicated to used-vehicle listings. If your area has such a publication, you can probably find it in the lobby of car parts stores and various other neighborhood stores and restaurants. Many web sites allow you to search electronically for specific models, both new and used. Most will even get price quotes for you.

Make a list of the available cars that match your criteria, including their features and prices. These are your finalists—the cars that you think are worth your time to investigate further.

TEST DRIVE VEHICLES

Sometimes descriptions are quite different from the actual car. Test drive the cars of interest to you. Compare ride, handling, braking, features, and cost. Try all the features to see how well they work. Play the radio to judge the sound, but then turn it off so that you can hear the sounds of the car as you drive. Is the engine quiet? Especially when evaluating used cars, listen for noises that might indicate a problem. When you accelerate, look for dark smoke from the exhaust. This is a sign that the car is burning oil, which would require an expensive repair. Look for rust and mismatched paint that might mean the car has been in an accident.

Take your time. Don't be in a hurry when shopping for a car. Some salespersons will try to pressure you into buying right away. Resist that temptation. You will enhance your bargaining position with patience and knowledge of the car you are planning to buy. Experts recommend never buying a vehicle on your first visit to a dealership, and before buying, check the dealer's reputation. A call to the Better Business Bureau will give you valuable information about the number and types of complaints consumers have made about this dealer.

CHECK THE HISTORY OF A USED VEHICLE

You can learn the history of any used vehicle. A **vehicle identification number (VIN)** is an alphanumeric number that identifies each vehicle manufactured or sold in the United States. This number is available on vehicle documents and on the dashboard on the driver's side. It is visible through the front windshield.

Get the VIN from the used vehicle you are considering and enter it into the online search tool at CARFAX. A detailed history for one vehicle costs approximately $25, and you can get reports on several vehicles for around $30. The full report provides information such as whether the vehicle has been in a serious accident, how many times the vehicle has been sold, and the mileage readings each time it was sold so that you can check for odometer rollbacks.

NET Bookmark

Access www.cengage.com/school/pfinance/mypf and click on the link for Chapter 23. The NADA Guides web site is one of the most comprehensive vehicle information sites on the Internet. By clicking the "Build Your New Car with Options" link on the NADA Guides home page, you can easily find a new car that matches your needs. Follow this link to build yourself a vehicle. What did you come up with? How much does it cost? Explain why the features you selected are important to you.

www.cengage.com/school/pfinance/mypf

GET THE VEHICLE CHECKED MECHANICALLY

After the used vehicle has passed the VIN check and you've decided you'd like to buy it, have it checked out by a mechanic. You'll want to know whether the engine is in good shape. A *compression test* can tell you if the head gasket is about to go out. You'll also want to be sure the transmission is okay. If the vehicle passes these two critical tests, then ask for a complete check to see what repairs might need to be made in the near future and their cost. For example, you'll want to know if the engine is sound, how much longer the brakes will last, whether it needs new tires, and so on. A vehicle inspection may cost around $150. Be sure to ask how much the inspection will cost before you have the vehicle checked.

Many states require vehicles to pass a **vehicle emission test**, which verifies that a vehicle meets the minimum clean-air standards. The fee for the test is usually about $15 to $30. However, the repairs needed if it fails the test may cost much more. Before deciding to buy a car, ask the seller for the record showing that it passed the most recent vehicle emission test. If the seller cannot produce the record, ask the seller to have the vehicle tested before you buy.

DETERMINE A FAIR PRICE

Decide what price you feel is fair before you make any offer for a car. Kelley Blue Book publishes a popular pricing guide for all models and years. You can find the publication in the library or online. By looking up the model and year of the car you are considering, you can find an estimated fair price for it. You can also get a feel for a fair price by checking other ads for cars of the same model and year to see what other sellers are charging.

For a new car, the **sticker price**, or *manufacturer's suggested retail price (MSRP)*, is the price shown on the tag in the car's window. A fair price for a new car usually lies somewhere between the sticker price and the price the dealer paid for it, called the **invoice price**. Many car-buying web sites can give you the dealer's invoice price. According to the American Automobile Association (AAA), the dealer's invoice is approximately 90 percent of the sticker price for compact and subcompact vehicles. It is approximately 84 to 87 percent of sticker price for luxury vehicles. Depending on the vehicle's popularity and the number currently on the market, a fair price is likely to be 3 to 6 percent above invoice. Arm yourself with this knowledge before making an offer.

NEGOTIATE THE PRICE

Make up your mind that you will not be pressured into paying more than you think is fair. Stick to facts and don't reveal emotions to sellers. For example, don't make statements like, "This car is just what I want." This type of information can weaken your bargaining position. Make your initial offer lower than your top price. Then be prepared to negotiate.

Sometimes, you will have a car that you want to trade in when buying a new car. To prevent confusion in determining the true price of the new car, negotiate the price for it separately from the price for your trade-in. After you have settled on a fair price for the new car, ask how much the dealer will give you for your old car. If the dealer does not offer an amount close to the trade-in value quoted for your car by Kelley Blue Book, then plan to sell your old car yourself rather than trade it in. Selling the car yourself can be a hassle, but you will likely get more money for it that way.

If you are uncomfortable negotiating the price of a vehicle, you may wish to use the services of a professional. Through your automobile club, a wholesale membership such as Costco, your credit union, or an online car-buying service, you can get a price based on cost to the dealer. A **car-buying service** allows you to choose the vehicle features you want, and a professional car buyer takes over the price negotiation for you. Once you know exactly what car you want, the service will locate the car, negotiate the price, and arrange for its delivery. This service may not be free, but it can potentially save you money.

© Photodisc/Getty Images

What are some tips for successfully negotiating the price of your car?

If you do your own negotiating, be aware of common dealer negotiating practices. For example, the salesperson might initially act positive toward your offer and allow you to get your heart set on the car. Then the salesperson may say that he or she needs approval from the sales manager, leave you for several minutes, and then return to say your low offer just isn't acceptable. Be polite but don't be intimidated. If the price you are discussing is still below the maximum you set for yourself as the fair price, then make a counteroffer that is a little higher but still no higher than your top price. Walk away from the deal if you feel you are being pressured or the dealer won't come down to a price you feel is fair.

DEALER ADD-ONS

After you have agreed on the price from a vehicle dealership, the dealer may try to increase the purchase price with **dealer add-ons**—high-priced, high-profit dealer services that add little or no value. For example, dealer preparation is nothing more than cleaning the car and checking the air in the tires and the oil in the engine. These services should be provided without extra charge. Other common dealer add-ons include protective wax or polish, rustproofing, and extended warranties. Rarely are these special services worth the cost.

FINANCING YOUR CAR

The best way to buy a car is with cash. You won't have to pay any interest that way. Unfortunately, most people don't have enough money to make such a large purchase without financing a portion of the cost. They need a means of transportation now and cannot wait until they have saved enough cash for the purchase.

■ FINANCIAL INSTITUTIONS

Banks, credit unions, and even insurance companies offer vehicle loans for 36, 48, 60, or 72 months. Longer terms mean lower monthly payments but higher total interest paid because you are using the money for a longer period of time. In many cases, your local credit union will offer the best car loan. Often, a credit union will finance more of your purchase (requiring less of your own cash), have lower interest rates, and require smaller monthly payments. Compare rates and terms before selecting a loan.

■ CAR DEALERS

Most new-car dealers offer financing. On particular models and at particular times of the year, they may offer you better terms than those available from other sources. These special deals are sponsored by the manufacturers or their financing agencies to stimulate sales or to promote a particular model. GMAC Financial Services is an example of a finance company that makes loans on cars through dealerships. Ford, Chrysler, and most other manufacturers offer similar programs. Although you finance through the dealer, you will make your payments to the finance company. Use caution with this type of financing. Don't allow a special promotional loan rate to influence you to buy a more expensive car.

■ LEASING A CAR

Rather than purchasing a new car, you might consider leasing. A car lease is similar to an apartment lease. It is a written agreement that allows you to use the property (in this case, a car) for a specified time period and monthly payment. You do not own the car. You are simply renting its use. However, at the end of the lease period, you usually have an option to buy the car for a price specified in the lease agreement. The selling price specified in the lease is based on the expected value of the car at the end of the lease term.

Because interest on car loans is tax-deductible only for some people (such as small business owners), auto leasing may be a popular option. Individuals can afford to lease a more expensive car than they could buy on credit. Leasing provides an alternative—no large down payment or trade-in to worry about. Just drive away for a set monthly payment! On the other hand, remember that after making all of the payments, you still own nothing. Also, you may have to pay penalties if you return the car with excessive wear and tear or too many miles as defined in your lease agreement. Make sure you understand all the details before you sign. Not all auto manufacturers offer leasing, so if interested, you may have to shop around to find a participating auto dealer.

CONSUMER PROTECTION FOR CAR BUYERS

As you learned in Chapter 8, a *warranty* is a written statement about a product's qualities or performance that the seller assures are true. A warranty clearly states what the manufacturer will do if the product does not perform as it should. A new-car warranty provides a buyer with some assurance of quality. Car warranties vary in the time and mileage of the protection they offer and in the parts they cover. The main aspects of a warranty are the coverage of basic parts against manufacturer defects and the coverage of the power train for the engine, transmission, and drive train.

Sometimes, however, being aware of warranty provisions is not enough. Some cars have so many problems (or such hard-to-fix problems) that warranty coverage is of little comfort to their owners. As a result of consumer frustration, many states have enacted lemon laws.

LEMON LAWS

Lemon laws exist in many states and protect consumers from the consequences of buying a defective car. A lemon is a car with substantial defects that the manufacturer has been unable to fix after repeated attempts. You have a lemon if, in the first year of ownership or 12,000 miles, (a) you've taken the car into the dealer for four or more unsuccessful attempts to repair the same substantial defect or (b) your car has been out of service for a total of at least 30 days. Lemon laws allow you to get a new car or your money back. Unfortunately, this protection is not automatic. You need to have good documentation and be prepared for a long process. A proceeding called *arbitration* and a possible lawsuit may be necessary to enforce your state's law. Figure 23.1 indicates what to do if you buy a lemon.

| FIGURE 23.1 | *What to Do If You Buy a Lemon* |

Here are some things you can do to protect yourself in the event you end up with a lemon.

1. When you take the car in for repair, give the dealer a written list of problems. Make sure these problems are in the dealer's repair records. Keep copies of each list and the repair receipts you are given.

2. Any time you are returning to have the same item repaired, point it out to the dealer. Make the dealer aware that the problem is continuing and not new. Again, keep copies of each list and their attempted repairs.

3. If your car qualifies as a lemon, tell the car dealer. Bring copies of your records. If the dealer is not responsive, contact the manufacturer's zone office. Talk to someone in the consumer relations office, or go all the way to their national headquarters if necessary. Follow up the conversation with a letter and copies of your records. Be sure you keep your own copy of the letter and the original documentation.

4. If the defect is serious and the car is dangerous to drive, file for arbitration immediately. Make sure you fill out all necessary forms. State the problem clearly and, once again, provide copies of your documentation.

5. Demand a quick hearing date. Remind the arbitrators that under Section 703 of the Magnuson-Moss Warranty Act you are entitled to an arbitration decision within 40 days of filing.

6. You are under no obligation to accept a prolonged hearing. You can demand that the arbitration panel meet and make a decision.

7. If you are not satisfied with the arbitrator's decision or the process, you might want to contact a lawyer who specializes in lemon-law cases. The Center for Auto Safety in Washington, D.C., may be able to help you.

THE FTC USED-CAR RULE

People who buy a used car must be concerned about whether it has some hidden defects or potentially expensive repairs ahead. The Federal Trade Commission's "Used-Car Rule," called the **FTC Rule**, requires that dealers fully disclose to buyers what is and is not covered under warranty for the used vehicle. The FTC Rule is designed to protect used-car buyers. This rule does not guarantee that the car has no problems. However, it does require used-car dealers to inform consumers prior to purchase about who will be responsible for paying for certain repairs if they occur after the sale.

The rule requires dealers to place a sticker, called the "Buyer's Guide," on all used cars they offer. Figure 23.2 illustrates this sticker. If the "as is" box is checked, the buyer must pay all repair costs. If the "Warranty" box is checked, the dealer pays for the items listed for the specified period of time. Cars bought from a private seller do not carry this warranty. While you may save money by buying directly from the previous owner, you cannot expect the previous owner to make repairs or stand by the condition of the vehicle. For this reason, a pre-purchase mechanical check is crucial when buying from an individual or when buying from a dealer displaying an "as is" sticker.

FIGURE 23.2   *Buyer's Guide (FTC Rule)*

BUYER'S GUIDE

IMPORTANT: Spoken promises are difficult to enforce. Ask the dealer to put all promises in writing. Keep this form.

Ford	Focus	2006	A0A085C147961
VEHICLE MAKE	MODEL	YEAR	VIN NUMBER

T6204B
DEALER STOCK NUMBER (Optional)

WARRANTIES FOR THIS VEHICLE:

☒ AS IS – NO WARRANTY

YOU WILL PAY ALL COSTS FOR ANY REPAIRS. The dealer assumes no responsibility for any repairs regardless of any oral statements about the vehicle.

☐ WARRANTY

☐ FULL   ☐ LIMITED WARRANTY. The dealer will pay ___% of the labor and ___% of the parts for the covered systems that fail during the warranty period. Ask the dealer for a copy of the warranty document for a full explanation of warranty coverage, exclusions, and the dealer's repair obligations. Under state law, "implied warranties" may give you even more rights.

SYSTEMS COVERED: DURATION:

_____   _____
_____   _____
_____   _____
_____   _____

☒ SERVICE CONTRACT. A service contract is available at an extra charge on this vehicle. Ask for details as to coverage, deductible, price, and exclusions. If you buy a service contract within 90 days of the time of sale, state law "implied warranties" may give you additional rights.

PRE-PURCHASE INSPECTION: ASK THE DEALER IF YOU MAY HAVE THIS VEHICLE INSPECTED BY YOUR MECHANIC EITHER ON OR OFF THE LOT.

SEE THE BACK OF THIS FORM for important additional information, including a list of some major defects that may occur in used motor vehicles.

Issues in Your World

HOW TO SELL A USED CAR

If you decide to sell your old car yourself, here are some steps that will help you make a quicker sale:

1. *Wash and polish the outside, vacuum and clean the inside, and shampoo the upholstery. Remove all personal property. Check fluid levels and tire pressure, and make certain all lights are functioning. A car that appears well cared for will bring a higher price.*

2. *Set a reasonable price. Check a recent National Automobile Dealers Association (NADA) or Kelley Blue Book publication (in print or online) for estimates of fair market value. Check the classified ads in your newspaper to be sure this price is within the range advertised by other people selling the same model and year as your car.*

3. *Advertise your vehicle in local newspapers. Weekend ads are usually most effective. If possible, also advertise in a used-car listing publication in print and online.*

4. *Present the truth to prospective buyers—what's good about the car as well as its weaknesses. Disclose the last time you had a tune-up, and allow prospective buyers to check maintenance records.*

5. *Go along when the potential buyer test drives your car. Give the buyer a chance to think about and evaluate your car. Observe any inspections performed by a mechanic.*

6. *Always ask for cash or a cashier's check as payment. Remove the license plates if they cannot be transferred.*

7. *Make sure that you have the title, registration, and other documents that are required to sell the car. Meet the buyer at the Bureau of Motor Vehicles and transfer title when you receive the cash or cashier's check. Never let a new owner drive away with a car that is still in your name.*

8. *During the time you are attempting to sell your car, be sure to maintain at least the minimum insurance coverage (usually liability) required in your state. Notify your insurance company immediately when you have sold the car.*

After you sell the car, remove all registration and other documents that contain your name and address. Only the bill of sale and the new owner's insurance information are needed for the car to be driven legally.

THINK *CRITICALLY*

1. *Why should you tell the truth about your car when you are trying to sell it? What consequences might you face if you don't?*

2. *Do you think it's best to go along on a potential buyer's test drive? Why or why not?*

3. *If you were selling your car, what kind of payment would you accept? Explain your answer.*

Assessment

KEY TERMS REVIEW

Match the terms with the definitions. Some terms may not be used.

_____ 1. Requires that dealers fully disclose to buyers what is and is not covered under warranty for the used vehicle

_____ 2. An alphanumeric number that identifies each vehicle manufactured or sold in the United States

_____ 3. A test to verify that a vehicle meets the minimum clean-air standards

_____ 4. A car with substantial defects that the manufacturer has been unable to fix after repeated attempts

_____ 5. The process of getting a new- or used-car loan prearranged through your bank or credit union

_____ 6. The manufacturer's suggested retail price (MSRP) shown on the tag in the car's window

_____ 7. High-priced, high-profit dealer services that add little or no value

a. car-buying service

b. dealer add-ons

c. FTC Rule

d. invoice price

e. lemon

f. lemon laws

g. preapproval

h. sticker price

i. vehicle emission test

j. vehicle identification number (VIN)

CHECK YOUR UNDERSTANDING

8. Why should you not play the radio the whole time you are test driving a car?

9. Why is it important to know the dealer invoice price before making an offer on a new car?

APPLY YOUR KNOWLEDGE

10. Describe the vehicle that would be your first choice, based on identifying your wants and needs. Describe the process you would use in researching your choices.

THINK CRITICALLY

11. Being able to negotiate a fair price for your vehicle is an important skill. What are some tactics you must learn to be a better negotiator? Do you know someone who is very good at negotiations? Describe what he or she does.

12. How will you decide how much you can afford to pay for a car?

13. What can you do to protect yourself from predatory sales techniques?

Maintaining a Vehicle

GOALS

- Identify the costs of owning and operating a car.
- Describe methods for extending the life of your car and maintaining its resale value.

TERMS

- hybrid, *p. 521*
- classic cars, *p. 522*
- car title, *p. 522*
- car registration, *p. 522*
- oxidize, *p. 525*
- polishing compound, *p. 525*
- car detail, *p. 525*
- upholstery, *p. 525*

COSTS OF OWNING A CAR

Most people spend more of their income on transportation than on any other item except housing. Costs of owning a car include the monthly car payment and car insurance (to be discussed in Chapter 26). Other costs associated with owning and operating your car include fuel, depreciation, registration and title fees, vehicle emission fees, maintenance and repairs, and the cost of accessories.

FUEL

Most engines today are gas powered. Gasoline is a *fossil fuel* that is refined from crude oil taken from the earth. The cost of gasoline depends on world supplies of crude oil, political conditions, and world energy markets. The amount of gasoline you consume depends on your car's fuel efficiency, the number of miles you drive, and your driving habits.

In an effort to reduce fuel costs and reduce air pollution from exhaust fumes, you may wish to buy a hybrid or alternate-energy vehicle. A **hybrid** is a type of vehicle that uses alternate energy sources, such as natural gas or battery power, in addition to gasoline. Hybrids can get high miles per gallon while cutting the cost of operation substantially. As technology improves, you will see vehicles developed that use other types of energy, from electricity (with cars that recharge when plugged into your home outlets) to natural gas or eco-fuels that are environmentally friendly. By cutting fossil-fuel emissions from cars, air quality is preserved and enhanced. Alternate sources of energy will also help reduce our dependence on foreign oil and the volatile prices that go with it.

© Digital Vision/Getty Images

Why is fuel efficiency an important factor when shopping for a car?

HOW TO CALCULATE MILES PER GALLON (MPG)

Because of rising fuel prices, fuel efficiency is more important than ever. Determining how many miles your car gets per gallon, or its MPG, is very useful. You can calculate MPG as follows:

1. Go to the gas station and fill up your tank. It doesn't matter if it's empty or half-full before doing so.
2. Record the mileage on your odometer before leaving the gas station.
3. Drive your normal route until your tank is almost empty.
4. Return to the gas station, record the mileage on your odometer, and fill up your tank again. Look at the pump to see how many gallons of gas were needed to fill up your tank.
5. Subtract the first odometer reading from the last odometer reading. Then divide this number by the number of gallons needed to refill your tank to calculate the MPG.

Suppose you filled up your tank and had an odometer reading of 11,300. After driving your normal route all week, you refill your car, which now has an odometer reading of 11,725. It takes 12 gallons of gas. What is your MPG?

Solution:

$11{,}725 - 11{,}300 = 425$ miles $\div$ 12 gallons = 35.4 MPG

DEPRECIATION

Depreciation is a decline in the value of property due to normal wear and tear. As a car ages, the number of miles driven increases, the physical condition begins to deteriorate, and mechanical difficulties arise. Also, styles and consumer tastes change over time. All these factors usually cause cars to lose market value. However, not all cars depreciate. Older vehicles called **classic cars**, which are in excellent condition, may *appreciate*, or increase in value, if people value them as collectors' items.

Depreciation is the single greatest cost of owning a car. The cost of gasoline comes second. In most cases, the age of a car is the most important factor in determining its resale or trade-in value. Other factors include mileage, mechanical condition, model popularity, size, and color. A car will retain more of its value over time if it is well maintained and has low mileage at the time of sale. Popular models depreciate more slowly than other models.

REGISTRATION AND TITLE

All states charge fees for title and registration. A **car title** is a legal document that establishes ownership of the vehicle. A car title lists the legal owner (usually the lending institution) and the registered owner (you). You must pay title fees and sales taxes only at the time you buy the car. In addition, you must also pay an annual **car registration** or *license tag* fee. The license plate on your vehicle carries a sticker that shows you have paid the current year's renewal registration fee.

VEHICLE EMISSION FEE

In many states, you are required to have your car tested to be sure it is meeting environment standards for vehicle emissions. Vehicle emission tests are often required every two years once the car is four or more years old.

MAINTENANCE AND REPAIRS

The owner's manual will tell you what services your car needs and how often. Typically, you can expect to change the oil every few thousand miles, have a major engine tune-up every 20,000 to 30,000 miles, and perform other maintenance at scheduled intervals. Car systems that you should monitor and maintain include emissions control, air conditioning, brakes, and transmission.

You should also plan for unscheduled repairs. Such things as flat tires, broken belts, and leaky hoses happen from time to time, and the repairs can be costly. Saving money for car repairs should be part of your monthly budget. As your car gets older, repair costs will increase. You should expect to replace relatively inexpensive parts such as fan belts, hoses, battery, and muffler, but also plan for occasional expensive repairs such as replacing the alternator. You will also need new tires at some point. Tires can cost from $50 to $200 apiece.

ACCESSORIES

Many people choose to add certain features to make their vehicles safer, more functional and attractive, or more efficient. These items include GPS systems, DVD players, snow tires, wheel covers, striping and paint features, alarm systems, and sound systems. In some cases, these accessories will add to the value of the vehicle. In other cases, they will subtract from it. Some devices, such as portable DVD players, are personal property and can be easily removed from the vehicle when you sell it.

VIEW *Points*

Many states have passed laws making it illegal to use a hand-held cell phone while driving. They usually allow a hands-free system, which may include earphones, a Bluetooth, a mounted cell phone, or a cell phone speaker through the sound system. These laws are based on safety. Some laws specifically target teenagers. When people are talking on the phone, especially inexperienced drivers, they become distracted, which can be dangerous. Their driving skills are also impaired when they have only one hand available to drive. For example, they often fail to signal when changing lanes.

Many motorists believe, however, that a cell phone is no more dangerous than speaking to a passenger, using a GPS, eating, or any other distraction. Cell phones are a great convenience and help people get where they need to go. On long trips or traffic jams, they can save time and allow for multitasking.

THINK *CRITICALLY*

With which side do you agree? Why? Do you think that vehicles should contain features such as game systems and DVD players? Why or why not? Do you think laws targeting teenagers are discriminatory? Explain your answer.

EXTENDING THE LIFE OF YOUR CAR

Because a car is expensive, you will get your best value (cost versus benefit) if you take care of your investment. By performing routine maintenance, taking care of the interior and exterior, and practicing good driving habits, you can keep your car running well and looking good.

MAINTAIN FLUID LEVELS

Many newer cars claim to run 7,000 or more miles between oil changes. But most mechanics believe that changing oil more frequently can add years of life to a car. Oil lubricates the moving parts of the engine and keeps it clean. Oil must be changed to eliminate accumulated dirt and sludge. Your individual driving habits will dictate how often you should change the oil. For example, the frequent starting and stopping of city driving use up oil sooner than do long expressway trips.

Experts advise changing oil every 3,000 miles, or every three months, whichever comes first, for city driving. You should replace the oil filter when you change the oil. The filter helps clean the oil circulating through the engine. Lubrication, oil change, and oil filter replacement (called "lube, oil, and filter") should cost from $20 to $35, depending on the size of the engine.

You should also regularly check and maintain the proper fluid levels for your transmission, power steering, window washer, radiator, and brakes. These car functions must have fluid to work properly.

PERFORM ROUTINE MAINTENANCE

Don't wait for trouble before checking fluid levels and inspecting belts, hoses, and tire pressure. Inspect tires for wear and replace them before tread wear puts you in danger of a blowout. Most car owners find that by replacing parts periodically, they can avoid major problems. These ongoing routine checks and fixes should cost $150 to $300 a year but will save you major repairs in the long run. The owner's manual will tell you mileage or time intervals for certain checks and maintenance services.

KEEP YOUR CAR IN A GARAGE

If possible, keep your vehicle in a garage. Using a garage protects the vehicle from theft and vandalism. It also protects it from weather, which can damage or destroy the vehicle's finish and even affect its mechanical condition. Low temperatures, for example, affect almost every component. The engine is harder to start, and the battery is weaker. Thus the starter has to work harder, and the charging system is stressed.

PRESERVE THE EXTERIOR

It's important to keep your vehicle clean. When water sits on the surface of metal, it can cause rust. Cleaning off road grime occasionally will protect the shiny finish. Apply protective wax to guard your paint from the damaging rays of the sun and from snow-melting chemicals spread on streets in cold climates. If you live near the coast, wax is essential for protecting the car's finish from the salty spray of ocean breezes.

Wax the paint twice a year—before the cold and rainy winter and before the hot and dry summer. Once the paint has begun to **oxidize** (permanently lose its color and shine because of chemical reaction with the air), it is very difficult to restore the original gloss. In most cases, a vehicle with oxidized paint must be repainted to restore its shine. A **polishing compound** is a substance that can smooth out surface scratches, scuffs, and stains. Polishing compounds, often called cleaners or pre-waxes, can be tricky to use. They often contain *abrasives*, which are coarse materials that scour or rub away a surface. Used gently, an abrasive can remove the top layer of paint and expose the shiny paint underneath. But rubbed too vigorously or too often, an abrasive will strip the paint right down to the primer.

© Photodisc/Getty Images

What can you do to preserve the exterior of your vehicle?

Many people choose to have their vehicles detailed. A **car detail** is a service provided by specialists who clean and polish the outside, along with cleaning and treating the interior. For example, high-shine polishes can help restore the shine to your vehicle paint job. Stains in the carpet can be removed, and carpet can even be dyed to cover damage. It generally costs from $150 to $250 to detail your car. Experts recommend the service twice a year (as seasons change from hot to cold and vice versa).

Just as important as washing and waxing is repairing dents and paint chips before rust has a chance to take hold. You can get a small amount of vehicle paint that matches your car's color from a dealer that sells your make of car. When something nicks your paint, such as a rock that hits your car when you drive, it's a good idea to touch up the ding. First clean the area with mild soap and dry it. Then apply the touch-up paint in very small amounts.

▌ PRESERVE THE INTERIOR

The condition of the inside of your vehicle is also very important for good resale value. The **upholstery** is the seat-covering material. Generally, cloth upholstery is more durable than vinyl. Although spills and dirt are more difficult to clean off of cloth upholstery, vinyl can crack and tear when it gets too hot or cold and can be punctured by sharp objects. Leather upholstery holds up best, but it is more expensive and requires regular cleaning and lubricating to keep it soft and to prevent cracking.

Floor mats will protect the carpeting and are a good investment. You can cover the interior of your trunk with an old blanket to protect it. Avoid eating messy foods in the car and vacuum frequently to keep your car's interior in good condition. Products are available to rub on vinyl dashboards and plastic interior surfaces to protect them from fading and cracking from exposure to the sun's rays. If you must park your car in the sun for long periods of time, you might consider covering the inside of your windshield with an inexpensive cardboard shade made for that purpose.

FOLLOW WISE DRIVING HABITS

Good driving habits can keep your vehicle running efficiently for years. Some new vehicles have a "break-in period," during which you may need to drive differently. It is best to check your owner's manual.

When the vehicle is new:

1. Don't drive for long stretches at a constant speed. Vary speed as driving conditions permit.
2. During the first 1,000 miles, drive progressively faster, accelerating gradually.
3. Avoid fast starts, sudden stops, sharp turns, and rapid gear changes to help break-in your brakes.
4. Drive at moderate speeds and around town, avoiding long trips, so your tires can get adjusted. You may need additional wheel balancing and front-end alignment.

For all vehicles:

1. Don't race a cold engine. Give it 10 to 15 seconds to warm up to allow the oil to start circulating. Then drive off gently as soon as the engine is running smoothly.
2. Keep coolants in the radiator during hot weather and antifreezes in it during very cold weather.
3. Check and maintain all fluid levels. Never drive a car when the "check engine" light is on. Take it in for service right away.
4. Make sure your brakes and tires are in good shape at all times. Having a flat tire can cause more than an inconvenience.
5. When driving a vehicle with a manual transmission, shift deliberately, pausing as you move through the neutral position.
6. Don't shift into a forward gear when your vehicle is rolling backward, or vice versa.
7. When stopped in traffic, hold the vehicle in place with the brakes rather than engaging the clutch to avoid excessive wear on the clutch.
8. Don't turn the steering wheel when the vehicle is motionless. This strains the front-end components. Turn the wheel only when the vehicle is moving.
9. Keep the windshield and back window free of ice, using a scraper rather than your wiper blades. Running wipers over a dry surface can scratch the glass and tear the blades.
10. Glance at gauges and warning lights as you drive. When your vehicle signals you to stop or to get something checked, do it right away. When your engine shows it's too hot, turn off the air conditioner and drive slower. If overheating is severe, pull over and stop the engine quickly. Open the hood, but do not unscrew the radiator cap (hot steam and fluid will gush out and burn you).
11. Follow a safe distance from other cars. Adjust your speed with weather conditions. For example, leave more space when it is raining because it will take longer to stop.
12. Keep up with new traffic laws; check the new driver's manual in your state at least every few years.
13. Drive courteously, sharing the road with others, including bicycles, motorcycles, and pedestrians. Yield the right of way even when it's not required.
14. Finally, always wear your seat belt. It can save your life!

*Transportation,
Distribution
& Logistics*

Automotive Service and Repair

Vehicles are not designed to run forever. They will require service and maintenance throughout their useful lives. Most newer models have complex computer systems and engines designed to burn new types of fuels. Automotive technicians must know how to take care of a wide range of vehicles, to diagnose problems, and to keep them running efficiently.

During routine service, technicians test engines. They repair or replace worn parts before they cause breakdowns and damage to the vehicle. They usually follow a checklist to ensure they do the right work. Belts, hoses, plugs, brake and fuel systems, and other potentially troublesome areas are watched closely.

Technicians in large shops often specialize in certain types of repairs, such as air conditioning. Most technicians work a standard 40-hour workweek, but overtime is often required to meet customer needs.

Employment Outlook

- Faster than average employment growth is expected.

Job Titles

- Service technician
- Automotive mechanic
- Transmission technician
- Air-conditioning specialist

Needed Skills

- High school plus career and technical education in automotive service technology is helpful.

- Automotive Service Excellence (ASE) certification is often required.

What's it like to work in...
Automotive Service and Repair

Janelle works for a large repair shop that services and repairs most models of cars. She specializes in warranty repairs as indicated by computerized system checking devices.

Janelle works a normal 8-hour shift. Once a month, she works on a Saturday and is paid a premium wage for the extra work. Because automobile technology changes frequently, she also attends training workshops to obtain certification.

She enjoys working with both older and newer cars. The older cars often require simple mechanical repairs. The newer cars have complex electronic systems, which require a different set of mechanical skills. Today, Janelle is waiting for a part to install in the computer module of a new car that has Internet access in the driver's panel. She will test the system before delivering the car to its owner.

Regardless of the type of car, she is expected to troubleshoot and fix problems rapidly for customers who often need their car back the same day.

What About You?

Do you have mechanical aptitude and like to work on cars? Would you like to work in auto repair?

Assessment

KEY TERMS REVIEW

Match the terms with the definitions. Some terms may not be used.

_____ 1. *A license tag fee that must be renewed annually*

_____ 2. *A service provided by specialists who clean and polish the outside as well as clean and treat the interior of a car*

_____ 3. *A type of vehicle that uses alternate energy sources in addition to gasoline*

_____ 4. *A substance that can smooth out surface scratches, scuffs, and stains*

_____ 5. *Older vehicles in excellent condition that appreciate if valued as collectors' items*

_____ 6. *A chemical reaction with air that causes paint to lose its color and shine*

_____ 7. *A legal document that establishes ownership of the vehicle*

a. car detail

b. car registration

c. car title

d. classic cars

e. hybrid

f. oxidize

g. polishing compound

h. upholstery

CHECK YOUR UNDERSTANDING

8. *Why do vehicles usually depreciate? What might cause a particular vehicle to appreciate?*

9. *Why should you avoid turning the steering wheel while the vehicle is not in motion?*

APPLY YOUR KNOWLEDGE

10. *List and explain the costs of owning a vehicle. Which of these costs will be the most expensive over time? How will you minimize the costs of ownership and extend the useful life of your car?*

THINK *CRITICALLY*

11. *Many items that people add to their cars add resale value, while other items do not. List an accessory that adds value and one that takes away value from a vehicle.*

12. *In Germany it is against the law to run out of gas on the autobahn. The violation costs $500. Give three reasons why it is important for vehicle owners to keep their cars running properly at all times, including avoiding flat tires and running out of gas.*

13. *As you observe other drivers, list several habits that are dangerous to the drivers and to others. What should they do differently? Explain.*

Chapter (Assessment)

SUMMARY

23.1

- The car-buying process begins with identifying and prioritizing your needs and wants. Then determine what you can afford. Identify affordable models that will meet your needs. Research and compare features, and narrow your choices to a few. Decide whether to buy new or used.

- If you determine you need to finance part of the cost, obtaining pre-approval at your bank or credit union will let you know how much you can borrow and at what rate before you commit to a purchase.

- Test drive your top choices. Before buying a used vehicle, check its history by looking up its VIN at CARFAX and have a mechanic check it.

- The fair price for a vehicle is somewhere between the sticker price and invoice price. Make your initial offer below your top price. Then negotiate, but be prepared to walk away if the seller pressures you or will not come down to a fair price. Resist purchasing dealer add-ons.

- If you are uncomfortable with negotiations, you can hire a car-buying service to negotiate the purchase for you.

- Leasing is renting the use of a vehicle, often with an option to buy at the end of the lease term.

- Lemon laws help consumers get a new car or their money back if the car they purchased has substantial, unfixable defects. The FTC Rule is designed to protect consumers who buy used cars from dealers.

23.2

- Costs of operating a vehicle include the down payment, car title, car registration, sales taxes, monthly loan payments, and insurance.

- The amount you spend for gasoline depends on the fuel efficiency of your engine, the number of miles you drive, and gas prices. A hybrid will reduce fuel costs and reduce air pollution.

- Most vehicles depreciate as they get older, wear out, and go out of style. A few classic cars may appreciate.

- You can extend the life of your car by maintaining fluid levels, performing routine maintenance as prescribed in your owner's manual, keeping your car in a garage, preserving the exterior with wax, preserving the interior, and following wise driving habits.

- Car paint can oxidize, so it's important to protect it with wax. A polishing compound with abrasives gently applied can restore shine. The interior can be preserved by regularly lubricating/cleaning upholstery and other interior surfaces. A car detail service can perform all these tasks for you.

APPLY WHAT YOU KNOW

1. *Make a list of car dealers in your area. Divide into groups to visit dealerships. Collect brochures on various car models and look at sticker prices. As a group, report on your findings and your experience at the dealer—characteristics of the cars in the dealer's product line, price ranges, how you were treated, and so on.*

2. *Choose a particular model of a used car. Find listings for this model for sale in your area, using an Internet car-buying site or your newspaper's classified ads in print or online. Write a paragraph about the cars you found. How many are for sale? What are their years and prices? How do the prices offered by dealers compare to those of private sellers?*

3. *Visit the Kelley Blue Book web site and look up the trade-in value of your car or your family's car. This is the estimated amount a dealer would give you for your car in trade for a new one. Now look up the used-car retail price for the same car. This is an estimate of a fair price that a buyer could expect to pay for the car. Now subtract the two figures. What is the difference? What does this number represent?*

4. *Prepare a budget that lists the potential costs a car owner may face. Ask someone who has owned a car for a long period of time to help you complete the list. In computing an average year's depreciation, look up the value of an older car of the same model using Kelley Blue Book or the classifieds. Deduct this from the purchase price of the car and divide by the age (number of years) of the car to determine the total cost of depreciation. Summarize in one or two paragraphs your findings about the costs of operating a vehicle.*

5. *Find out the costs of registration, title, driver's license fees, and vehicle emission tests in your county. You can get this information by calling or visiting the web site of your state's Bureau of Motor Vehicles (BMV). Or, you can visit the BMV's local office.*

MAKE ACADEMIC CONNECTIONS

6. **International Studies** *Perform online research to find out about speed limits and traffic laws in three other countries. Write a report comparing those laws to similar laws in your state. How are they different? How do auto accident rates compare among all three countries and your state?*

7. **Science** *Conduct a study about fossil fuels, including how much is still available and when they are expected to run out. Discuss other sources of energy that are more environmentally friendly and sound. What might these alternate sources of energy mean for our future?*

8. **Communication** *Write a one-page paper describing the car of your dreams, its features, its cost (including payments), and why you would want to own that particular vehicle. Present your choice to the class.*

9. **Technology** *List three or four new technological advances in vehicles in the past three to five years. Explain how they have improved safety, efficiency, and/or comfort for the owners.*

SOLVE *PROBLEMS* AND

EXPLORE *ISSUES*

10. Your friend Devon is considering buying a small older car. He works part time after school and on holidays. In the summer, he makes good wages but is saving for college. He visits a local dealer who suggests that buying an older car is not a good idea. The dealer points out that the car will likely cost a lot to maintain and wouldn't be dependable. Do you agree? What advice would you give Devon?

11. Your friend Grace has decided to buy a car. Because she is working at a regular job, she feels she can afford a new car. She isn't sure how much she can afford to pay for monthly car payments, and she doesn't know how much of a down payment she might need to make. How would you advise her to get started in the car-buying process?

12. To buy the new car Grace selected (from 11 above), she needs to finance $20,000. The dealer will finance the loan at 6.5 percent for 60 months. Use an online car loan calculator to determine the (a) monthly payment, (b) total payments, and (c) total interest.

13. Bella just purchased a new car. Now she faces a decision: Should she also purchase undercoating and rust protection, a polish shine application, and a three-year extended warranty? Altogether, these items will add almost $1,000 to the price of the car. She's considering it because the dealer told her that these items will add to the life of the car, and she plans to keep it for a long time. What is your advice?

14. You are buying a new car and are considering whether to trade in your old vehicle. The dealer tells you that you are paying $1,500 less on the new car because of your trade-in. You think that your car is worth more than $1,500 and that you should be able to get a reduction in price without the trade-in. Discuss the pros and cons of trading in your car versus selling it yourself.

15. Ryan just purchased a new car. He plans to drive the car at least 100,000 miles and then sell it to get as much money as he can for it. What advice can you give him about extending the life of the car and improving its resale value?

EXTEND YOUR LEARNING

16. **Legal Issues** Most states have traffic laws that require drivers to stay to the right except when passing. Yet some drivers believe that as long as they are driving the speed limit they have the right to drive in the left lane. Some states will ticket people for staying in the passing lane. Similarly, speed limits are set on interstate highways to enhance traffic flow, promote safety, and keep traffic moving. What are the laws in your state and local area regarding the use of the passing lane and speed limits? Do people obey those laws? Why are they needed?

For related activities and links, go to **www.cengage.com/school/pfinance/mypf**

Chapter 24

Family Decisions

24.1 **Family Plans**

24.2 **Life's Uncertainties**

Consider **THIS**

Aaron and Chloe have announced their engagement and plans to be married. They both have large families and want a formal wedding with all the trimmings.

"By waiting a year, we'll be able to plan this wedding thoroughly, and we'll both be finished with college," Aaron said to Chloe. "It also gives us time to save money, since we can't expect our parents to pay for all the costs of such a large wedding."

"You're right," replied Chloe. "There are a million details, and I'd like to enjoy this period of time. I think a year is just the right amount of time between the announcement and the wedding. We also need to plan the honeymoon. Do you want to hike in the mountains or relax on the beach?"

Family Plans

MARRIAGE AND COMMITMENT

Statistics show that people are waiting until later in life to get married and start families and that more are choosing to remain single. For those who choose to have a long and committed relationship, the preplanning process can be vastly rewarding and surprisingly complex.

ENGAGEMENT

When a couple decides to commit to a life together, they become **engaged**, or formally pledged to each other. An engagement or commitment ring, a symbol of this pledge, can cost between a few hundred and thousands of dollars. An engagement period of six months to a year allows the couple time to prepare for the wedding, make plans for the future, and set joint goals.

PREMARITAL COUNSELING

Assuming that a couple has the maturity and legal capacity (age 18 in most states) to get married, many honest discussions about goals and values should precede the wedding. For example, if one person feels that having children is a vital part of the couple's lives together while the other does not want children, this difference could present an insurmountable obstacle.

It's also important to discuss issues that may affect family life, such as career goals, political and religious beliefs, roles (such as who pays the bills), hobbies, vacations, and living preferences and habits.

© Photodisc/Getty Images

What is the purpose of premarital counseling?

Some religions require *premarriage counseling* sessions. The couple meets with a member of the clergy or designated counselor, together and separately, to discuss issues that will be vital to the success of the marriage. Topics most often discussed include areas that may cause conflict, such as money and budgeting, the meaning of the marriage commitment, in-laws, and religious aspects of marriage that are unique to the each partner's faith.

■ CEREMONY PLANS AND COSTS

Planning for the wedding ceremony should begin at least six months in advance. Figure 24.1 is a bride's budget worksheet, which shows the many preparations to consider. (A groom may use a similar worksheet.) This worksheet should be completed in rough-draft form as the wedding plans progress. As costs begin to add up, the bride and groom may decide to adjust their preferences to reduce expenses.

The bride and groom and each set of parents should prepare guest lists and then combine them. The number of guests and the size of the wedding party will determine the number of invitations needed, size of the church or facility, cost of the reception, and so forth. The **wedding party** consists of the people who are active participants in the wedding ceremony: the bride and groom, best man, maid or matron of honor, bridesmaids, ushers, flower girl, and ring bearer.

In the past, wedding expenses were paid by the bride's family. Today, the couple pays more of the expenses, and the groom's family may also contribute.

Typically, the following expenses belong solely to the groom:

- Bride's ring(s)
- Marriage license
- Wedding gift for the bride
- Gifts for the groom's wedding party
- The bride's bouquet, corsages for mothers and grandmothers, and boutonnieres for the men in the wedding party
- Cleric's or judge's fee
- Bachelor dinner (unless given and paid for by the best man)
- Lodging (if necessary) for out-of-town wedding party members
- Groom's special clothing, including clothing for rehearsal dinner, wedding, and honeymoon
- Delivery of wedding presents to new home

A number of print magazines and web sites offer helpful information for planning a wedding. The bride and groom usually plan the wedding jointly. Many couples participate in gift registries, whether in-store or online. A *gift registry* is a listing of the couple's choices of dishes, housewares, and other products. Having a gift registry helps prevent duplicate gifts and helps gift givers decide on what to buy.

The size of the wedding, time of day, location, and formality of the bride's dress determine the style of the wedding. A **formal wedding** may be held in the daytime or in the evening, and participants as well as guests wear formal attire (long gowns and tuxedos). A **semiformal wedding** usually is held

FIGURE 24.1   *Bride's Worksheet*

Engagement Party

Invitations . . . . $_____
Food . . . . _____
Beverages . . . . _____
Music . . . . _____
Rental fees . . . . _____
Decorations . . . . _____
Professional services. . . . _____
Gratuities . . . . _____

Total . . . . $_____

Stationery

Invitations . . . . $_____
Announcements . . . . _____
At-home cards . . . . _____
Personal stationery . . . . . _____
Stamps . . . . _____

Total . . . . $_____

Clothing

Wedding dress . . . . $_____
Headpiece/veil . . . . _____
Shoes . . . . _____
Accessories . . . . _____
Personal trousseau . . . . . _____

Total . . . . $_____

*Denotes expenses usually
shared by both families

GRAND TOTAL . . . . $_____

Bridesmaids' Luncheon

Invitations and
   place cards . . . . $_____
Food . . . . _____
Beverages . . . . _____
Rental fees . . . . _____
Decorations . . . . _____
Professional services. . . . _____
*Gratuities . . . . _____

Total . . . . $_____

Photographs

Engagement portrait . . . . $_____
Wedding portrait . . . . . . _____
Formal photos . . . . _____
Reprints . . . . _____

Total . . . . $_____

Wedding Ceremony

Sanctuary rental . . . . $_____
Music . . . . _____
Decorations . . . . _____
Flowers for attendants . . . _____
Aisle runner . . . . _____
Transportation
   to/from ceremony . . . . _____
*Gratuities . . . . _____
Miscellaneous . . . . _____

Total . . . . $_____

Reception

Hall rental . . . . $_____
Decorations . . . . _____
Music . . . . _____
Food . . . . _____
Beverages . . . . _____
Wedding cake . . . . _____
Favors . . . . _____
Professional services. . . . _____
*Gratuities . . . . _____

Total . . . . $_____

Other

Bridal consultant fees . . . $_____
Accommodations for
   out-of-town
   attendants . . . . _____
*Security guard . . . . _____
Sound recording of
   ceremony . . . . _____
*Insurance for
   wedding gifts . . . . _____
Bride's blood test
   (if required) . . . . _____
Groom's ring . . . . _____
Gift for groom . . . . _____
Gift for attendants . . . . . _____
Special effects . . . . _____
Other fees . . . . _____
   _____
   _____
   _____

Total . . . . $_____

---

during the afternoon or early evening, with less formal wear required of guests. While members of the wedding party may still dress as formally or informally as they choose, guests generally wear clothing normally chosen for special occasions. An **informal wedding** may be held outside, in a church, or almost anywhere. No special attire is required for the wedding party or guests. *Destination weddings*, in which the wedding party and the families of the bride and groom gather at a vacation destination for three or more days for the wedding festivities, are becoming increasingly popular.

Some couples prefer a **civil ceremony**, which is a wedding performed by a public official, such as a judge or justice of the peace, rather than a member of the clergy. This is a quick, inexpensive ceremony and requires the presence of two witnesses in most states.

THE HONEYMOON

Immediately following the wedding reception, the newly married couple often takes a *honeymoon* trip. Resorts and places that provide different types of entertainment are popular. Honeymoons may be inexpensive car trips, elaborate cruises, or flights to exotic islands. It may last from several days to several weeks and cost several thousand dollars. A couple generally plans the honeymoon together, carefully considering preferences and sharing costs.

FAMILY FINANCIAL DECISIONS

When people live together in a committed relationship, they form a new family unit. The family should make major decisions together, based on each person's needs and wants.

FAMILY GOALS

Couples should examine their needs and set goals for their future together. *Short-term goals* involve decisions about the near term, such as where to live, whether both partners will work, major purchases to make this year and next, and leisure activities. *Intermediate goals* are those the couple wants to pursue in the next five or so years: whether they want children, where the couple will put down roots, and training or education needs. *Long-term goals* are for the distant future. They include decisions about children's education (savings and investments), job changes, and retirement.

Financial goals should be:

- Specific (clearly stated actions you plan to take that will serve as the basis for various financial activities)
- Measurable (stated in terms of dollars and timelines)
- Realistic (based on income and life situation)

For example, the goal of "accumulating $10,000 in a mutual fund within five years" is more specific and measurable than just "saving money for future expenses."

THE FAMILY BUDGET

In Chapter 8, you learned the steps in creating a budget. You can follow these same steps in creating a budget for your family. Unlike an individual budget, a family budget should consider the needs and goals of each family member in allocating resources.

A *family budget* allocates spending, saving, borrowing, and investing of the family's pooled resources to meet future goals. Joint decisions can be difficult because more people are involved in the decision making. Nevertheless, family budgeting and communicating are essential parts of a successful marriage.

DIVIDING RESPONSIBILITIES

Maintaining a household entails ongoing responsibilities, many of them financial. For example, a couple may choose to have individual as well as joint checking accounts. If the family unit has only one checking account, managing the account will be easier if only one person writes the checks. Otherwise, accidental overdrawing can easily result.

Arranged marriages are common in the Indian subcontinent (India, Pakistan, and Bangladesh), even among those individuals in the educated middle class. Many people believe that these arranged marriages are more successful than marriages in Europe and the United States. They assert that romantic love does not necessarily lead to a good marriage and that real love comes from a properly arranged union between two individuals and their families.

THINK *CRITICALLY*

How might family decision making in the Indian subcontinent be different from the way it is in Western societies?

Many couples choose to have individual checking accounts, and each partner is responsible for part of the income and part of the bills. For example, the couple may decide that one will pay the utilities, groceries, and car payment, while the other will pay the mortgage or rent, insurance premiums, and other miscellaneous expenses. Then each partner is responsible for balancing his or her checking account each month and meeting his or her part of the budget.

Couples must divide other ongoing household tasks as well. Perhaps one person might take charge of preparing tax returns and doing the family grocery shopping. The other person might take responsibility for making vacation arrangements, planning social engagements, and arranging to have home repairs done. Housecleaning can be less distasteful if partners do the tasks they like best and share equally the tasks that neither likes to do. By agreeing on how to divide up household responsibilities, both partners can do their fair share and avoid resentment that may result from an unequal division of labor.

VACATION PLANNING

Vacations are an important part of life. Well-planned vacations maximize the time available for fun, while managing costs and timelines.

KIND OF VACATION

Apply the decision-making process to help you choose a vacation. First, define the problem: What does your family want most from a vacation—relaxation, excitement, travel, adventure, special events, time with relatives, or a combination of these items? Based on these vacation goals and the time and money available, identify your alternatives, as shown in Figure 24.2. Then gather information about each alternative, weigh the pros and cons of each, and make a final decision. A successful vacation depends on selecting the trip that will best satisfy family members, saving for it, and planning it carefully.

ITINERARIES

If you plan your vacation activities ahead of time, then you can use your vacation time to do them rather than wasting time finding hotels, figuring out transportation, and handling other practical details. Start your planning by writing out what will happen, when, at what cost, and how. An **itinerary** is a detailed schedule of events, times, and places.

FIGURE 24.2 Vacation Analysis

VACATION ANALYSIS

$500 or less	$500–$1,500	More than $1,500
Camping	Car trip	Car or plane trip
Visiting relatives	Sports (skiing, other adventure)	Tours/group travel
Sports events	Amusement parks	Varied entertainment options
Three days or less	Three to five days	Five days or more

List each day's activities, as shown in Figure 24.3, and build in flexibility. Bad weather or unexpected problems may require you to change your plans. You may want to list on your itinerary the time it takes to do certain activities, distances to and from activities, methods of transportation, and special notes, such as "bring camera." When designing your itinerary, be sure to leave enough time to do the planned activities in a relaxed way. Check on seasonal adjustments that may change operating days, fees, and opening or closing times. Before going on vacation, leave a copy of your itinerary with a neighbor or friend in case of emergency.

FIGURE 24.3 Itinerary

ITINERARY

Date	Time	Activity
Monday	8:00 A.M.	Arrive at airport (Flight 739 leaves at 9:05 A.M.).
	10:00 A.M.	Arrive at Los Angeles airport. Take hotel shuttle service; arrive at hotel by 10:45 A.M.
	12:00 noon	Lunch at hotel restaurant.
	1:30 P.M.	Disneyland for remainder of day. Dinner at Disneyland.
Tuesday	8:00 A.M.	Breakfast at Howard Johnson's.
	9:00 A.M.	Knott's Berry Farm (20-minute ride by tour bus). Spend day there; eat lunch there.
	7:00 P.M.	Leave Knott's Berry Farm; go to dinner at Bob's Big Boy.
	8:00 P.M.	Return to hotel.
Wednesday	8:00 A.M.	Breakfast at Pancake House.
	9:00 A.M.	Universal Studios. Tour begins at 10:00 A.M., lasts until noon.
	12:00 noon	Lunch at nearby restaurant. Catch tour bus at 1:30 P.M. to return to hotel.

RESERVATIONS

Make reservations whenever possible. A **reservation** is an advance commitment to receive a service at a specified later date. A room reservation guarantees that a hotel or motel room will be waiting for you when you arrive. Hotels and motels may be *booked up*, or full, well in advance of your vacation date. Therefore, make reservations early; a month or more before your vacation is not too soon. You can make reservations for airlines, buses, trains, boats, hotels, car rentals, and special events. You can get airline boarding passes and seat assignments a few days before your trip, even with ticketless travel. Confirm your flight reservations at least 24 hours before you leave because flights are often canceled or changed at the last minute.

Why should you plan your vacation ahead of time?

You may choose to use a **travel agency**, which is a business that arranges transportation, accommodations, and itineraries for customers. The agent can make plane and hotel reservations for you and can help you plan the whole trip if you like. Agents get their fee from the airlines and hotels you book.

You can book your flights and accommodations online by going to the web sites of specific airlines, hotels, car rental agencies, and entertainment centers or make all the reservations through a full-service travel site. If you enter your travel times and preferences, the search tool will present you with a list of available flights and/or hotel rooms that meet your criteria. You can even have them listed based on price levels. You can select a flight and pay for it online with your credit card.

Some airlines also assist with car rental and hotel reservations. Travel destinations (such as Disney) also provide package deals, offering flight, hotel, and amusement park tickets. You can save money by comparing your options.

AT THE AIRPORT

Flights today are often ticketless. You receive a reservation number when you book your flight. Most airlines also allow you to print your boarding pass from home within 24 hours of the flight. This process is quicker than waiting in line to check in, especially if you are traveling light with only carry-on bags. Carry-on bags, including your purse or computer case, are usually limited to two and must be under a specified size that will fit in the overhead compartment or under the seat. People who have large or additional bags to be stored in the plane's cargo bay may be charged a fee for each checked bag.

Bring a photo ID, such as your driver's license or passport. You will need it to get through airport security. FAA and Homeland Security regulations permit passengers to carry only specific types of items onto planes. For example, all liquid containers must fit into a one-quart plastic bag, and no individual container may have more than three fluid ounces. Open containers are not permitted in carry-on bags. Do not carry any sharp objects, such as a pocket knife or scissors, in your carry-on bags. A security officer will confiscate anything that could be used as a weapon. Pack such items in your checked luggage.

Arrive at the airport at least two hours before a domestic flight and three hours before an international flight. This gives you time to check in and pass through security. Also, most flights (other than first class) do not serve meals on planes, and you may be charged for the snacks and beverages that are available during the flight. Plan accordingly to eat at the airport immediately before your flight and pack snacks in your carry-on bags.

Often, airlines **overbook** flights, meaning they sell more reservations than they can fulfill. Airlines overbook flights expecting that some people will not show up for a scheduled flight. If more people show up for a flight than the plane can accommodate, the airline will ask people to give up their seats voluntarily in exchange for a future free ticket and a later flight. Passengers "bumped" (forced to miss a flight involuntarily) are usually entitled to compensation, often in the form of cash, a coupon, or a free flight. By arriving early to check in, you can decrease your risk of an overbooking problem.

By signing up for an airline's *frequent-flyer program*, you can earn credit toward a free ticket. You receive credit for miles traveled each time you fly with that airline. You may also receive frequent-flyer miles for staying at a participating hotel, renting from a participating car rental agency, booking online, or taking other actions the airline defines in its program. After you accumulate enough points, you earn a free flight or an upgrade (to first class), although the program often limits your flight options.

AT-HOME PREPARATIONS

Before leaving on your vacation, you should take care of a few things at home. Ask a neighbor to pick up your newspaper, or call the paper to stop delivery while you are gone. Fill out a form at the post office to have your mail held there rather than delivered. By stopping these deliveries, you avoid a buildup of mail and newspapers that may tip off burglars that you are away from home.

Arrange for someone to feed your pets, care for your plants, mow the lawn, and do other household duties that cannot wait for your return. Use an automatic timer for lights so that they come on in the evening and go off a few hours later, giving the appearance that you are home. Lock all doors and windows and close the curtains. It is also a good idea to ask a neighbor to keep an eye on things while you are away.

LAST-MINUTE DETAILS

Plan your packing so that you have everything you need, but don't overpack. Make a list of things you will need, such as cameras, special clothing, and personal items. Take only what you need in the smallest possible containers. Be sure to pack enough clothing to last the entire vacation without laundering (unless it is a very long vacation). Put medications and breakables in your carry-on baggage.

You may wish to take major credit cards. However, leave at home in a safe place all the cards you do not need. Take enough cash to pay the expenses that require cash only. Charge other expenses on a credit card. Because of the availability of ATMs across the country and around the world, you can obtain cash easily while on vacation.

ISSUES IN YOUR WORLD

ONLINE TRAVEL PLANNING

Have you ever considered doing all of your travel planning online? The Internet offers a number of travel-planning sites, and while there are some risks, the savings can be substantial.

At some web sites, you can do fare searches, check seat availability, book flights, and even book cruises, car rentals, and hotel rooms. For example, the CheapTickets web site offers discount fares and rates on reservations once you register online. You will need to give personal information including your credit card number to use this service.

At Priceline.com, you can check the availability of flights that are inexpensive and underbooked because they are scheduled at less desirable flight times—after 10 P.M. or before 8 A.M. Using this web site, you can also get substantial discounts on flights to "hot destinations." The downside is that you must be able to take the openings on short notice, which requires flexibility in travel plans.

Another popular site, TRAVEL.com, offers special advisories, airport and gate locations, ATM locations, embassy locations, flight information, and weather reports. This type of information can be very important when traveling to foreign countries or when time between flights is extremely tight.

Many sites, such as Travel-for-less.com, provide discount airfares and discount cruises. This type of site offers tickets on an auction basis. You bid on the tickets that are available, and the airline or cruise line will take the highest bid.

Often major attractions such as theme parks have their own travel agencies to help guests have a more pleasant stay. These services include hotel and flight reservations, park admission, and car rental arrangements.

Internet research when planning trips can save you both time and money. Even if you book your tickets by telephone, you can still benefit from the information and search-and-compare features of the Internet prior to booking your trip.

THINK CRITICALLY

1. *What distant vacation destination appeals to you most? Use the Internet to find the best airfare and motel rate for this destination. Do travel dates affect the cost?*

2. *What is the downside of using the Internet to make reservations and pay for flights?*

Assessment

KEY TERMS REVIEW

Match the terms with the definitions. Some terms may not be used.

_____ 1. A wedding held outside with no special attire needed

_____ 2. Being formally pledged or in a committed relationship

_____ 3. A detailed schedule of events, times, and places to visit

_____ 4. Active participants in a wedding ceremony

_____ 5. An advance commitment to receive a service at a specified later date

_____ 6. A wedding with long gowns and tuxedos worn by wedding party and guests

a. civil ceremony

b. engaged

c. formal wedding

d. informal wedding

e. itinerary

f. overbook

g. reservation

h. semiformal wedding

i. travel agency

j. wedding party

_____ 7. A business that arranges transportation, accommodations, and itineraries for customers

_____ 8. To sell more reservations than an airline can fulfill

CHECK YOUR UNDERSTANDING

9. Why is it important to have at least six months' time between the engagement and wedding?

10. What is an advantage of booking a flight online through a full-service travel agency or destination site?

APPLY YOUR KNOWLEDGE

11. Premarital counseling is available and, for some religions, is a required activity before marriage. Explain what you might learn with this type of counseling and why it is an important step before getting married.

THINK *CRITICALLY*

12. Family financial goals differ from individual plans because two people must merge their future plans. Explain the differences and discuss why the family budget can be both complicated and controversial.

13. Explain how vacation planning changes over time, beginning with a young couple and ending with a retired couple.

14. Traveling by airplane can be more inconvenient and complicated today than in the past. Explain why additional steps are needed and how you can avoid as much frustration and extra cost as possible.

Life's Uncertainties

GOALS
- Describe the costs and steps involved in a divorce.
- Explain what to do when a major illness or injury interrupts life unexpectedly.
- Discuss preparations for death, life's final plans.

TERMS
- dissolution of marriage, p. 543
- property settlement agreement, p. 543
- child support, p. 543
- spousal support, p. 543
- divorce decree, p. 544
- adult foster care facility, p. 545
- hospice, p. 546
- employee assistance plan (EAP), p. 546
- cremation, p. 548

DIVORCE

Regardless of what you plan, things will happen to you that you have not planned. While we all hope for the best, there are times when we must deal with the worst. Many marriages end in divorce each year. In all but a few states, a divorce is now called a **dissolution of marriage** or *no-fault divorce*, which means that irreconcilable differences have led to the breakdown of the marriage. One partner does not have to prove fault by the other to be granted a divorce. If one partner wants the marriage to be dissolved, it can be done.

COST OF DIVORCE

Expenses involved in divorce are high. They may include attorneys' fees, court costs and filing fees, child support and spousal support, division of property, and other settlement costs. The more issues there are to settle, the higher the attorneys' fees will be.

Often the divorcing couple can agree outside of court and enter into a **property settlement agreement**. This is a document specifying the division of assets agreed to by both parties and entered in court for the judge's approval. The more issues that the divorcing couple can settle out of court, the less the divorce proceedings will cost.

In divorce, the law assumes that both parents are responsible for supporting the children to the best of their ability. The *custodial parent*, or the parent with whom the children will live, fulfills most support obligations by taking care of the children every day. In most cases, the parent who is not granted custody will be required to pay **child support**—monthly payments to the custodial parent to help provide food, clothing, and shelter for the children. The amount of the payments will depend on the income of both parents and their ability to pay. Sometimes both parents share custody, and the children live part of the year with each parent.

Spousal support, also called *alimony*, is money paid by one former spouse to support the other. The money may be paid as one lump sum or monthly

What is the purpose of the property settlement agreement?

payments, usually for a set number of years, until the former spouse can become self-supporting. Spousal support is awarded in some cases when one spouse has been dependent on the other for a number of years and has little means of self-support. Child support and alimony are at the discretion of the court and become binding on the parties under the divorce decree. Amounts of child support and alimony can be modified only by another court order.

© Comstock/Jupiter Images

▌ STEPS IN DIVORCE

Dissolving a marriage is often a lengthy and unpleasant process. One party goes to an attorney, and the attorney prepares the documents and files them with the court. The other party is served with copies of the papers, called Petition for Dissolution of Marriage, and given a short time to appear (file papers) if there is a disagreement with the proposals set forth in the petition. The petition specifies how the first party proposes to divide property and award custody, amounts desired for any child support, visitation rights, and so on. If the second party fails to appear (defaults), then the first party is awarded whatever is asked in the petition. In most cases, the second party does appear, and a court date is set to decide the issues that cannot be settled between the parties.

Often it takes many months, even a year or more, for the case to be heard in court. Separate hearings may be held to establish temporary custody, child support, visitation rights of the noncustodial parent, and other matters. Many of these temporary provisions tend to become permanent. Often both parties agree in writing to property settlement and other matters prior to the court date. When the judge approves the agreement, it is entered as part of the **divorce decree**, which is a final statement of the dissolution decisions. A decree is final and binding on both parties until modified by the court.

If the parties cannot agree on a settlement, the case then goes to court. There is no jury in divorce cases. Both parties present their cases. In child-custody cases, witnesses may be called to determine which parent would be the better custodial parent. The judge's decision is based entirely on the best interests of the children. All other matters—property, alimony, amount of child support, and visitation rights—are also decided by the court. Once the decree is entered, the court usually imposes a waiting period before either party may remarry.

MAJOR ILLNESS OR INJURY

Accidents and illnesses happen. Such occurrences will interrupt finances and plans. But there are certain things to know and do that will ease the financial burden on the family.

ABSENCE FROM WORK

If you or a close family member suffers from a major illness or accident, it is often necessary to miss work. Some people can use their accumulated sick leave or personal leave. If they still need more time, the Family and Medical Leave Act will provide up to six months of unpaid time from work. When a wage earner's salary is lost, the house payment and other expenses continue, and health insurance generally only covers medical expenses. Additional forms of insurance are needed to cover lost wages.

Short-Term Disability

Many work-provided benefit plans provide for short-term replacement of a wage earner's salary, up to a percentage, such as 75 percent. This benefit usually lasts from a few weeks to a few months. If your employer does not have such a group plan, individual coverage can be provided through private insurance (covered in Chapter 27).

Long-Term Disability

When you are unable to return to work in the short term, you need long-term disability coverage (also covered in Chapter 27). This coverage will help you pay your bills for three to six months or longer. Individual plans are also available. Should the disability become permanent, long-term disability can bridge the gap between the injury or illness and retirement. *Long-term disability* coverage is available through the Social Security Administration for those who have a Social Security number and have paid into the program through employment taxes. Forms and paperwork along with detailed documentation must be provided. It often takes a year or longer to get approved and before monthly payments begin.

EXTENDED CARE EXPENSES

Some types of insurance policies provide coverage so people can remain at home and receive nursing care and other services when needed. When family members are unable to provide adequate care for the injured or ill person, an **adult foster care facility**, which is a shelter for adults who need care beyond what can be provided at home, may be required. Sometimes the care is temporary; other times, it is permanent. For example, a person who suffers a stroke may need physical therapy and recovery treatment for six months to a year. After that time, they may be recovered well enough to return home and resume their lives. Other people will not recover and must have ongoing care.

Private or group health insurance will cover some of these expenses, but there are limits, both in dollars and in time. Special kinds of insurance are needed to provide for these expenses (discussed further in Chapter 27). Many people use

Under what circumstances might an adult foster care facility be utilized?

savings and home equity extensively to pay for costs of treatment and recovery. Sometimes all of their money is used up, and public assistance is all that remains to help them.

There are private and nonprofit groups who seek to help families. For example, the Shriners help uninsured children get adequate eyeglasses and other essential services. St. Jude's Hospital was founded to help poor children receive life-saving care when they have diseases such as cancer. Ronald McDonald House is a program sponsored by McDonald's to help families of critically ill children. The Make a Wish Foundation also provides support services for very ill children.

Finally, organizations (usually nonprofit) help individuals and families deal with pending death and its costs and procedures. **Hospice** is a nonprofit agency that has trained, compassionate people who assist those who are dying and their families. They will visit the home where the dying person resides, provide pain medications, and make final arrangements for transporting the deceased person. This relieves the family of dealing with police and other governmental agencies when a person dies at home (because it is considered a planned death). In addition, a hospice provides counseling and grief recovery programs for those who have lost their loved ones.

■ MENTAL HEALTH SERVICES

Sometimes the impact of major illness or injury within a family creates the need for mental health services. Counseling may also be needed when individuals are dealing with a bad marriage or with depression, addiction, or dependency issues. An **employee assistance plan (EAP)** is a group benefit that allows employees and their families to seek counseling and other services. Often these plans are limited as to the types of services and number of appointments allowed. Thus, many families must bear the cost of continuing these services if they are needed for an extended period.

Outpatient services are more common and less expensive than inpatient programs. With *outpatient services*, those needing counseling or other services attend regular meetings (such as weekly) and complete self-directed plans. With *inpatient programs*, people move into residential facilities for a month to six months or longer to recover and make new life plans. Fees for these services, which are rarely paid by insurance, may range from a few hundred dollars to tens of thousands of dollars.

DEATH: A FINAL PLAN

Aging and death are part of living. Planning is needed to make the process easier for loved ones left behind. All adults should prepare for death to help ensure their final wishes are carried out.

SURVIVORS' BENEFITS

The surviving spouse and children are usually provided with some kind of death benefits. Survivors need to check to see what benefits have accrued through the years.

Life insurance benefits are not taxable to the recipients. Benefits from a life insurance policy can be obtained by mailing a copy of the death certificate, the original life insurance policy, and a claim form to the life insurance company. (Life insurance is described in detail in Chapter 27.)

The Veterans Administration pays a benefit to survivors of armed-service veterans. The benefit may include a grave marker, funeral service, and a small amount of cash. Children of veterans may also be entitled to scholarships and educational grant benefits.

The Social Security Administration also pays a death benefit to surviving families. The more the deceased person earned over his or her lifetime, the larger the payment. An estimated death benefit will appear on your annual Social Security statement. The administration also pays a one-time death benefit of $255 to the surviving spouse or minor children who qualify.

Many employer pension and retirement plans also pay lump-sum or monthly benefits to the surviving families. The family will probably have to apply to receive these benefits.

LAST EXPENSES

The costs involved when a person dies can range from a few hundred dollars to many thousands. These expenses include final medical and hospital charges, funeral expenses, casket, and burial. By preparing instructions and making provisions for these costs in advance, you spare survivors the emotional decision-making process at a time of vulnerability. Survivors who are grieving the loss of a loved one are often unprepared to make the many decisions involved in planning a funeral and burial. At such an emotional time, a family may incur elaborate final expenses that they or the estate cannot afford.

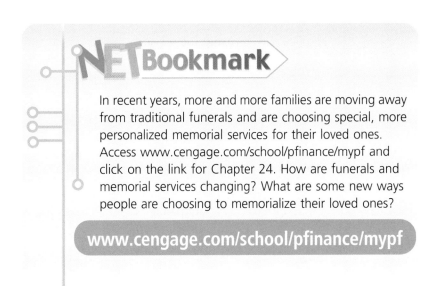

NETBookmark

In recent years, more and more families are moving away from traditional funerals and are choosing special, more personalized memorial services for their loved ones. Access www.cengage.com/school/pfinance/mypf and click on the link for Chapter 24. How are funerals and memorial services changing? What are some new ways people are choosing to memorialize their loved ones?

www.cengage.com/school/pfinance/mypf

Why should all adults plan their final arrangements and expenses?

Funerals

The cost of a funeral can range from $2,500 to $10,000 or more, depending on the type of casket and burial. Typical funeral charges include moving the body (to funeral home, church or synagogue, and cemetery), embalming and preparation for public viewing, casket, use of facilities, and funeral staff fees. They may also include the hearse, family limousine, escort to cemetery, obituary (newspaper death notice), clergy fees, printed memorial folders, memorial book, death certificate, and all necessary permits. The costs of a burial plot and marker are significant additional expenses.

Many funeral homes have prearranged plans available at guaranteed costs. Payments made in advance for the funeral are placed in a trust that earns interest. You should be able to get a full refund if you cancel the plan. Look over any "preneed" or prepayment plan you consider. It may lock you into using the services of a particular funeral home at uncertain future prices. If you move away or the funeral home goes out of business, you may have trouble getting your money back.

Cremation

Cremation is a process of reducing a body to ashes in a high-temperature oven. The ashes are then placed in an urn. The urn is presented to the family for safekeeping or burial. Cremation is a less expensive alternative to embalming and "cosmetizing" the body for public viewing. When a body is not cremated within a certain time span, usually two days, it must be embalmed or otherwise prepared for burial. Cremation, like immediate burial without a funeral, permits the survivors to hold a memorial service at any time or place, without having the body present. This procedure is less expensive and may be more comfortable for families and other mourners.

Nurses treat patients, educate patients, and provide advice and support to patients and their families. Nurses also record patients' medical histories and symptoms, perform diagnostic tests and analyze results, operate medical machinery, administer treatment and medication, and help with follow-up rehabilitation. They often work long, difficult shifts and deal with rapidly changing conditions.

More than half of all nursing jobs are in hospitals, but many nurses also work in home care, nursing facilities, medical offices, and clinics. Nurses are in contact with individuals who have infectious diseases. They must follow rigid procedures to avoid spreading germs.

Nurses spend considerable time walking, bending, stretching and standing. Nurses in hospitals may work nights, weekends, and even holidays and may need to be available on short notice. Nurses often face emotional situations involving very sick or dying patients.

Employment Outlook

- Much faster than average employment growth is expected.

Job Titles

- Registered nurse
- Emergency room nurse
- Surgical nurse
- Radiology nurse

Needed Skills

- Two-year associate's degree in nursing plus national license examination is required.
- Bachelor's degree for higher-level supervisory positions plus license examination is needed.

What's it like to work in... *Nursing*

Henri works in the cancer ward of a large local hospital. He works four 10-hour shifts a week. His time is often divided between the chemotherapy patient room and radiology services.

Today, Henri will spend his first four hours administering chemotherapy to patients as instructed by their doctors. He monitors patients throughout their treatment to ensure no problems arise. Many patients need reassurance, and Henri is always upbeat and friendly. He will also see patients for follow-up visits. Henri performs blood tests and then monitors them over a period of time to determine whether patients are adapting to the treatments.

Today, Henri is helping with a patient who has just completed a bone marrow transplant. He will provide close care for the first several hours after surgery. Afterward, Henri will work in the radiology unit by assisting patients who need X-rays.

What About You?

Do you want to learn and apply life-saving skills? Would you like to work in nursing?

Assessment

KEY TERMS REVIEW

Match the terms with the definitions. Some terms may not be used.

_____ 1. Monthly payments to the custodial parent to help provide food, clothing, and shelter for the children

_____ 2. A group benefit that allows employees and their families to seek counseling and other mental-health services

_____ 3. The breakdown of a marriage due to irreconcilable differences (no-fault)

_____ 4. A nonprofit agency that has trained, compassionate people who assist those who are dying and their families

_____ 5. Money paid by one former spouse to support the other

_____ 6. A shelter for adults who need care beyond what can be provided at home

_____ 7. A final statement of the dissolution decisions

_____ 8. A document specifying division of assets agreed to by a divorcing couple outside of court and submitted for the judge's approval

a. adult foster care facility

b. child support

c. cremation

d. dissolution of marriage

e. divorce decree

f. employee assistance plan (EAP)

g. hospice

h. property settlement agreement

i. spousal support

CHECK YOUR UNDERSTANDING

9. Can a person obtain a divorce without proving his or her spouse is at fault? Explain.

10. List the costs involved with planning and paying for a funeral.

APPLY YOUR KNOWLEDGE

11. Explain several reasons why it is better for a couple to reach a property settlement agreement and agree upon the child's visitation plan outside of court.

THINK CRITICALLY

12. Why is a waiting period imposed before a divorced person can remarry?

13. An adult foster care facility or nursing home may be required to meet the needs of a person who cannot care for himself/herself. Why do most individuals and families seek to avoid these arrangements?

14. Why do many people choose cremation rather than traditional burial?

Chapter Assessment

SUMMARY

24.1

- When a couple becomes engaged, they are formally pledged to each other. The engagement marks the time to begin planning the marriage ceremony, honeymoon, and living arrangements.

- Some religions require premarital counseling to prepare couples for a successful marriage.

- Planning the wedding begins with determining the size of the wedding party and number of guests. Weddings can be formal, semiformal, or informal, or you can choose a civil ceremony.

- Family financial decisions should be based on common goals, and a family budget should be agreed to by all family members.

- Vacation planning is based on time and money available, along with interests of all family members. Plan your itinerary and make reservations ahead of time, so that you can relax and enjoy your vacation.

- You can choose to use a travel agency or you can gather vacation information, compare prices, and make most reservations online.

24.2

- In most states, divorce is now called a dissolution of marriage and neither party needs to prove fault.

- Divorce can be expensive. Divorcing spouses can save on costs by reaching a property settlement agreement and child custody agreement outside of court. The noncustodial parent will be required to pay child support and possibly spousal support.

- Steps in getting a divorce include filing a petition, agreeing to a property settlement, attending a court hearing, and obtaining a divorce decree.

- Short- and long-term disability insurance can help cover lost wages resulting from injury or illness. If family members are unable to provide adequate care, an adult foster care facility may be required.

- Hospice is a nonprofit agency that has trained, compassionate people who assist those who are dying and their families.

- Mental health services are sometimes covered by health insurance policies or employee assistance plans (EAPs) but are often limited in scope.

- All adults should prepare for their death in order to make the process easier for their loved ones left behind. Last expenses include the costs of hospital and medical care, a funeral, and cremation or burial.

APPLY WHAT YOU KNOW

1. Describe the wedding you would choose for yourself, including the setting, type of ceremony, size of wedding party, total cost, and so on. Use three web sites to obtain information about wedding costs and planning. List the web site URLs and summarize the kinds of assistance they provide to couples who are planning to get married.

2. As couples set their future goals, they often include short-term, intermediate, and long-term goals. What types of goals would appear in each of these categories? Explain why families as a unit should set goals in addition to individual goals.

3. Design a three-day itinerary for a trip to a resort area within about 1,000 miles of where you live. Include all necessary information. Use the Internet to determine prices and availability of transportation, accommodations, and entertainment tickets.

4. Explain the purpose of child support and spousal support. Should a noncustodial parent be required by a divorce decree to provide child support while adult children achieve a college education? Why or why not?

5. Visit an adult foster care facility or nursing home in your area. Prepare a report on the kinds of services being provided, the living conditions for the patients, and how the use of the facility would affect family life and finances.

6. Interview a person whose employer provides an employee assistance plan (EAP). Write a report on the kinds of services provided and any limitations imposed.

MAKE ACADEMIC CONNECTIONS

7. **International Studies** Perform online research to find out about divorce laws in another country. Compare those laws to those in the United States. How does religion and culture play a part in the laws?

8. **History** Conduct a research study about the current divorce statistics, including rate of divorce, reasons for divorce, how the trend is changing over time, and how the divorce rate in this country compares to other countries. Why are these trends changing?

9. **Communication** After the wedding, it is important that the newly married couple express their appreciation for gifts received and other acts of kindness. Assume you are newly married. Compose a thank-you letter to someone who sent you a wedding gift or to a church member who helped with the preparations and decorations at the church.

10. **Technology** List new security devices and procedures being used in airports, train terminals, sports arenas, and other areas where many people gather. How do these protect large numbers of people? How much do they cost?

11. **Psychology** Conduct research to learn about factors that affect the success of a marriage. Use the Internet or interview a counselor or married couples to determine common characteristics that are present in successful relationships. Report your findings in a two-page report.

SOLVE *PROBLEMS* AND

EXPLORE *ISSUES*

12. Write a report describing different engagement ring options: (a) diamond solitaire with matching bands (compare costs of different diamond sizes), (b) gold and silver bands (compare quality, width, and costs), (c) costs of stones other than diamonds (rubies, emeralds, and sapphires in varying sizes), and (d) financing plans available.

13. Joshua and Larissa will be married in a month. Both are working now and plan to work at least five years before having children. They have asked for your opinion on how they should divide household duties, because both of them work eight-hour days, five days a week. Devise a plan for dividing financial responsibilities, including keeping the checkbook and managing the budget, as well as nonfinancial duties.

14. You and a friend have decided to take a trip. For each of the following situations, describe a trip you would take and list all of the costs that would be involved in each trip. (a) You each have $100 to contribute and could get away for a three-day weekend. You have one car that does not need maintenance or repairs. (b) You each have $500 to spend and could get away for three to five days. (c) You each have $1,500 to spend and could be away for seven to ten days.

15. What types of divorce/dissolution laws are in effect in your state? Are they no-fault or fault laws? What are the waiting periods? Describe the procedures for dissolution. (Hint: This information is probably available online through your state government web site.)

16. When a person experiences a major illness or injury, there are often privately funded or nonprofit agencies available that can help with the costs and the procedures. List three or more such agencies or groups in your area, together with the services they provide.

17. Divide into groups. With your instructor's permission, each group should arrange to visit a local funeral home. Ask someone there to walk you through preparations for a funeral, including the costs and decisions you would have to make. Present an oral report to the class.

EXTEND YOUR LEARNING

18. **Legal Issues** Most states have laws regulating nursing homes, home caregivers, and other services provided to people who cannot care for themselves. Although it is against the law, elder care abuse happens frequently. Relatives or others closely associated with an ill or aged person may take advantage of that person by stealing his or her money and other assets. They may abuse or neglect the person and not provide for his or her basic needs. What are some laws in your state regarding elder abuse? What can be done to prevent it? Are the laws working or are more restrictions needed?

For related activities and links, go to **www.cengage.com/school/pfinance/mypf**

Les Kelley

In 1918, Les Kelley was a young man with a bright future. He started his first used car lot with three Model T Fords and $450. The Kelley Kar Company would grow into the world's largest dealership and lead to a new publication and service for car buyers called the *Kelley Blue Book*.

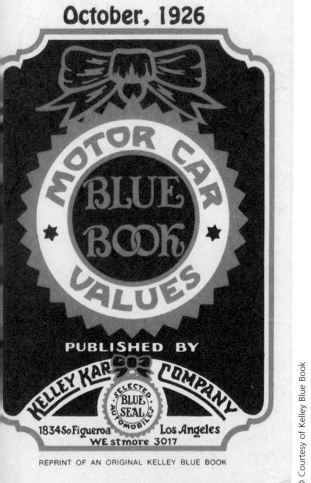

October, 1926

MOTOR CAR
BLUE
BOOK
VALUES

PUBLISHED BY
KELLEY KAR COMPANY
SELECTED
BLUE
SEAL
AUTOMOBILES
1834 So. Figueroa   Los Angeles
WEstmore 3017

REPRINT OF AN ORIGINAL KELLEY BLUE BOOK

© Courtesy of Kelley Blue Book

As a young person, Les learned how to care for his vehicle; he was good at auto mechanics. He was able to buy cars, fix them up, and sell them for a profit. He made enough money to put himself through college. With his younger brother Buster, he opened his first car lot, both selling and servicing automobiles. In the 1920s, Mr. Kelley distributed lists of cars he wanted to buy and the price he was willing to pay for them. He became known for his accurate assessment of what cars were worth. The automotive industry began to trust his lists to set the value for car prices. It wasn't long before Les Kelley realized he could provide an ongoing service for both car dealers and bankers who made loans for cars.

In 1926, Les Kelley published the first *Blue Book of Motor Car Values*. His publication listed both factory list price and cash value on thousands of vehicles. He chose the "Blue Book" as part of the title because people associated the words with information containing value. Even today, people will say, "What is the Blue Book value for this car?" which means they want to know what is the true value for resale or trade-in.

Kelley Kar Company was also known for innovative ways of selling cars. For example, the first automobiles were available in one color only—black. It was Buster Kelley who first painted a car pink, and it sold immediately. In those early days of the automobile, many people didn't know how to drive a car. When you bought a car through the Kelley Kar Company, it came complete with driving lessons.

By the 1960s, the Kelleys moved away from car sales and devoted their time totally to the *Kelley Blue Book,* by then an industry standard for determining prices. Les continued to be active in the business until his death in 1990.

THINK CRITICALLY

1. *How did Les find new ways to be innovative in his life?*

2. *How does the Kelley Blue Book help consumers of automobiles make better decisions and better use of their financial resources?*

3. *What can you learn about entrepreneurship from the life story of Les Kelley?*

Managing Resources

Overview

Unit 5 presented personal decision making (Chapter 20), renting or buying a home (Chapter 21 and Chapter 22), owning a car (Chapter 23), and family decisions (Chapter 24). This project will extend your knowledge into related areas.

PERSONAL DECISIONS: AVOIDING SCAMS

As you get started in life making a good, solid income and accumulating wealth, you will need to exercise caution to protect your assets. Home improvements, car purchases, and other major expenses are common areas in which scam artists take advantage of unsuspecting consumers. Let's look at some situations you may face in the future.

DON'T CALL ME, I'LL CALL YOU

A typical home-improvement fraud might work like this: Someone knocks on your door and compliments you on your well-maintained yard. The person notices that your house needs painting. The person assures you that he or she is qualified to perform the work and could do the job more quickly and cheaply than a large company. To get started, he or she will need payment up front to buy materials and cover expenses. After getting your money, the person may never do the work or may do such a poor job that you would have been better off without it. Figure U5.1 lists some tips for handling this type of pitch.

© Photodisc/Getty Images

When you are solicited at home:

1. Don't say "yes" today. Any agreement that is worthwhile can wait until you have time to think about it.

2. Don't give cash. When you give a check, you may have the option of stopping payment. But you must act quickly. It is better to avoid giving cash or check until you have had time to reconsider. Many states have laws (called "green river laws") that allow you three business days after a purchase over $25 with a check or credit card to change your mind and revoke the transaction.

3. Check it out. Ask the Better Business Bureau or your state attorney general's office for consumer complaints about the individual or company. Are they authorized to do business in your state? Are there consumer complaints on file against them?

4. Compare prices. Compare the prices for labor and materials with other sources. This may take several days but is worth it.

5. Don't hurry. If you didn't originate the sale, don't allow others to "create demand" for a product. Don't allow others to talk you in to something you don't want.

6. When in doubt, don't. Make this your motto. As the saying goes, "If something seems too good to be true, it probably is." Get all the information you need, and then evaluate it carefully. If you still have doubts, wait.

PROMISES, PROMISES

An "unconditional, lifetime, money-back guarantee" is only as good as the person or company that offers it. When the company goes out of business, the guarantee goes with it. Another common guarantee says, "Good as long as you own this car." The dealer offering this guarantee is counting on the fact that you won't keep the car more than a few years. When things start to go wrong, you will no longer be the owner. Remember: if it sounds too good to be true, it probably is!

ALL THAT GLITTERS

This investment scheme capitalizes on the desire to get rich quick, coupled with an attraction to beautiful and rare objects (from gold to diamonds). Thousands of counterfeit Krugerrands (gold coins) circulate across the nation. Investors have no idea they are fake until they try to resell them. By then the seller has vanished. Gold-painted lead also appears to be the real thing—gold bullion. Investors who pay up front, before verifying true value, get stuck with worthless lead. Junk gems are passed off as valuable rubies, sapphires, emeralds, and diamonds. They are advertised as rough stones that need polishing, but they are junk. When you purchase these items by mail, you may have little recourse. Complete Worksheet 1 (Before you Buy: Ripoffs and Warning Signals) provided for you in the *Student Activity Guide* and also presented for reference on the next page.

HOME LOAN PAYMENTS

First-time homebuyers need to know the anticipated monthly payment when they purchase a house. Many consumers also take out a second mortgage, or borrow money against their home equity. The monthly payment will depend on the type of loan: fixed rate or variable rate.

COMPUTING THE PAYMENT AMOUNT

The largest cost of home ownership is the house payment. Payments on second mortgages are in addition to the original mortgage. The total payment on either loan is based on the (a) loan amount (principal), (b) interest rate, and (c) length of time to repay the loan. As you learned in Chapter 22, the interest rate on a fixed-rate mortgage remains constant over the life of the loan. This is also true for a second mortgage, or equity loan against your home. Under a fixed-rate loan, the payment for a $50,000 loan at 8 percent spread over 15 or 30 years would be:

	30-Year Loan	15-Year Loan
Monthly payment:		
Principal and interest	$366.85	$477.68

Note that the above payment amounts do not include property taxes or insurance premiums, which some mortgage contracts require be included with your monthly payment.

While monthly payments are higher on the 15-year loan, your total interest would be lower over the life of the loan. For example, under the 30-year term, you would repay \$132,066 (\$366.85 × 12 payments per year × 30 years). Under the 15-year term, you would repay \$85,982 (\$477.68 × 12 payments per year × 15 years). This is a savings of \$46,084!

The interest rate on an adjustable rate mortgage (ARM) starts low but changes over time with changes in the economy. For example, for the first three or five years, the rate may be several percentage points below a similar fixed-rate loan. After that initial time period, the lender can raise the rate as much as two or three percent a year, with a cap or maximum rate that can be charged. Typically, when fixed mortgage rates are 8 percent, an ARM might start at 5 percent for three years but may increase to as much as 12 percent over the life of the loan. This type of loan is ideal for individuals who plan to move frequently and expect the market value of the house to increase in the short term. They can sell the house and move before it is time for a mortgage rate increase. The profit realized from the increased property value can cover the selling costs and moving expenses.

LOAN FEES

When financial institutions loan money to home buyers, they charge loan fees that pay the costs of setting up the loan. Loan fees may range from \$100 to \$2,500 or more, depending on the loan. In most cases, if the loan does not go through for some reason, the borrower forfeits the loan fees.

Mortgage lenders often charge points, or finance charges that the borrower must pay at the beginning of the loan. One point is 1 percent of the loan amount. Three points charged for a \$50,000 loan would be a 3 percent fee, or \$1,500 (\$50,000 × 3%). These fees are usually charged for original mortgage loans, but may be charged for second mortgages as well.

MORTGAGE PAYMENT AMOUNT

The chart below provides a simple way to estimate what your mortgage payment amount would be. The higher the interest rate, the higher your monthly payment. To estimate your monthly mortgage payment (for principal and interest only), complete the steps that follow the chart.

Monthly Mortgage Payment Factors (per \$1,000 of loan amount) Loan Rate	30 Yrs.	25 Yrs.	20 Yrs.	15 Yrs.
6.0%	5.94	6.40	7.16	8.40
6.5%	6.29	6.73	7.46	8.69
7.0%	6.64	7.06	7.76	8.98
7.5%	6.99	7.39	8.06	9.27
8.0%	7.34	7.72	8.36	9.56
8.5%	7.69	8.05	8.68	9.85
9.0%	8.05	8.39	9.00	10.14
9.5%	8.41	8.74	9.32	10.44
10.0%	8.78	9.09	9.65	10.75

1. In the chart above, find your mortgage interest rate in the first column.
2. Run your finger across that row until you reach the column for the length of your loan. This number is your monthly mortgage payment factor. For example, for a 7 percent, 30-year mortgage, the factor is 6.64.

3. Multiply this factor by the number of thousands in the mortgage principal. For example, in $50,000, there are 50 thousands. Multiply 6.64 times 50. Your monthly payment for a $50,000 loan at 7 percent for 30 years would be $332.

Complete Worksheet 2 (Computing Loan Payments) provided for you in the *Student Activity Guide* and also presented for reference below. Use it to estimate mortgage or loan payments for different rates and amounts.

WORKSHEET 2
Computing Loan Payments

Directions: Compute the following estimated mortgage amounts, using the chart supplied on page 558.

What is your estimated mortgage payment for:

1. A 30-year mortgage for $50,000 at 8%?

_____

2. A 25-year mortgage for $70,000 at 6%?

_____

3. A 15-year mortgage for $80,000 at 7.5%?

_____

4. A 30-year mortgage for $100,000 at 6%?

_____

5. A 25-year mortgage for $100,000 at 7%?

_____

6. A 15-year mortgage for $100,000 at 8%?

_____

7. A 30-year mortgage for $150,000 at 7.5%?

_____

8. A 25-year mortgage for $150,000 at 9%?

_____

9. A 15-year mortgage for $150,000 at 10%?

_____

HOUSING OPTION: BUILDING A HOME

When you decide to build a new home rather than buy an existing one, you hire a builder and the process begins. First, you must choose house plans for the size and style of the house you want. Often the builder has lots for sale, and you must select one of these lots. In other cases, you may own a vacant lot or purchase a lot and contract with the builder for only the house itself.

The first cost of building a house is the *architect's fee* for drawing up the house plans. Based on your desires and what you can afford, the architect prepares a house plan. The architect's fee ranges from $1,500 to $3,000 or more, depending on house size and value. The more complicated the floor plans, the higher the fee.

Once you and the builder (often called a *building contractor*) agree on the house specifications and price, the builder will have a building contract drawn. It specifies what is to be done, what materials are to be used, and a timetable for completion. You would probably have to make a large down payment so that the builder can purchase materials. Your loan will generally be approved only after the house is completed. Therefore, the builder may provide a construction loan that finances construction and is paid off when the house is completed. While you do not pay for the construction loan, the interest costs on the loan are a part of the builder's costs of operation and are included in the price of the house. Any changes in the original plans will increase your costs. Such a change requires a separate agreement to account for the added costs of this construction.

The government requires inspections of new construction at regular intervals for electricity, plumbing, and so on to make sure it meets building codes. While the builder is responsible for any required charges related to inspection (as a part of the total price), delays can result when construction must wait for inspectors to arrive. Closing costs are similar to those for buying a previously owned home. At closing, all *subcontractors* (companies and individuals contracted by the builder to do specific jobs, such as install plumbing or electrical wiring) and all expenses of construction will be paid.

To get an idea of the type of house you would like to build, complete Worksheet 3 (Building Your Dream Home) provided for you in the *Student Activity Guide* and also presented for reference on the next page.

AUTO REPAIR RIPOFFS

Overcharging and needless repairs cost motorists billions of dollars each year. Some states require repair shops to give written estimates. The final bill cannot be increased by more than 10 percent without your prior authorization. Many states require that the repair shop return replaced parts to you rather than discard them. This practice allows you to examine the part that has been replaced.

You should be wary when allowing others to check your car's engine, tires, belts, fluid levels, and the like. For example, you may go in for an oil change, but the mechanic reports that you should replace your water pump, hoses, valve covers, and other parts. These repairs may be needed, or maybe not. If the mechanic finds a number of problems, or one very expensive problem, be suspicious. Ask for evidence of the problem.

WORKSHEET 3
Building Your Dream Home

Directions: Answer the following questions and complete the research suggested to specify your dream home. Be sure to list your sources of information.

1. What style of house do you prefer? (two-story, ranch, Victorian, Tudor, and so on)

2. Attach a picture of a house that closely resembles the home of your dreams.

3. Prepare a floor plan that details the rooms and configuration, along with windows, doors, and so on.

4. What is the total square footage of your home?

   How many bedrooms?

   Bathrooms?

   Describe the kitchen and eating area(s).

   Describe the general layout of the house, starting at the front door and ending at the back door or on the second floor.

5. Describe the lot and landscaping, including lot size and shape.

6. Describe the block—what part of town, city or county, the neighborhood or region.

7. Based on today's costs of building real estate, what would it cost to build this house? (*Hint:* You need to consult newspaper or online ads that describe similar new properties or interview a builder or other reliable source.)

8. Prepare a report of your findings, including a cover page, drawings or exhibits, narrative of information, and list of sources of information.

Figure U5.2 shows a list of tips from New York City's Department of Consumer Affairs to help you know what to do when you experience car trouble. Complete Worksheet 4 (Ripoffs and Warning Signals for Your Car) provided for you in the *Student Activity Guide* and also presented for reference on the next page.

| FIGURE U5.2 | *When You Run into Car Trouble* |

Tips from New York City's Department of Consumer Affairs

- Look for a reliable mechanic before you are faced with an emergency. Ask friends for references.

- If you suspect your car needs repairs, have it checked before it becomes a big repair.

- For large repairs, get two estimates and compare the charges. Let the shops know you are comparison shopping.

- List all symptoms so you won't forget anything when you are talking to a mechanic. Give a copy of the list to the mechanic and keep a copy for yourself. Make sure all of the symptoms are taken care of before you accept the work for full payment.

- Don't authorize work unless you understand what is being done. Add-on work that does not apply to the reason for your repair should be suspect.

- Don't tell a mechanic to "get this car in good running order." This is a blanket opportunity for him or her to do anything whether or not it is essential.

- Don't sign a repair order unless you understand what is being done to your car. Question each line item.

- Keep itemized bills. Good records will help you in the event work is not satisfactory. Mechanics should stand behind their work. Be able to tell the mechanic, "I had this fuel pump replaced by you two months ago. It should be working." Have the documentation with you to prove it.

- If you suspect you are being overcharged, ask to see the supplier's parts price list.

- Find out which local and state government agencies have jurisdiction over auto repair complaints. Use the agency if necessary to get satisfaction.

WORKSHEET 4
Ripoffs and Warning Signals for Your Car

Directions: Read each of the following statements that could be a potential ripoff. Identify the warning signal (a point that makes you uncomfortable) and what you would do about it.

1. Your car is making pinging noises every time you accelerate to pass another car or go up a hill. You stop by a service station, and while your car is being filled with gas, you casually ask what could be wrong. The attendant replies that he would be happy to take a look at it when he gets off work, and that he could probably fix it in his spare time. Repairs could cost as little as $50 or as much as $250.

2. You are on vacation and driving the family car. You had it tuned up before you left, and your tires are fairly new. Along the way, you stop for gas. While checking the oil, the attendant notices that one of your hoses is loose. He fixes it (no charge) but then sees that you have an oil leak. He offers to make the repair within an hour for $100 plus parts.

3. You take your car in for its regular tune-up and maintenance. You take a list of things that need to be done. An hour later, you receive a telephone call and are asked to authorize extra repairs that total $500. These repairs are not related to the tune-up or regular maintenance. But when the car is up on the rack, the mechanic sees that the work needs to be done.

Unit

6

Risk Management

CHAPTERS

564

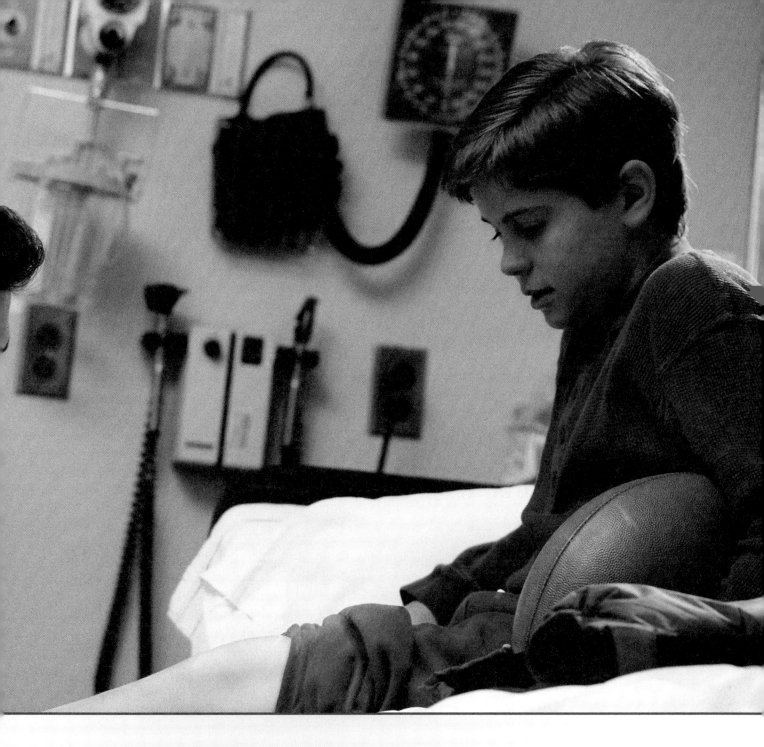

Unit 6 begins with risk—what it is and how it will affect you. In Chapter 25, you will examine different types of risks along with strategies to manage risks.

In Chapter 26, you will learn more about one type of risk management—buying insurance. You will study property insurance—how to protect your residence and personal possessions and how to protect yourself from liability as a result of your negligence or errors in judgment.

In Chapter 27, you will learn about rising health costs and the need for health insurance. Finally, you will learn about life insurance: who needs it, how it works, and the types available.

25

Introduction to Risk Management

25.1	*Understanding Risk*
25.2	*Managing Risk*

Consider **THIS**

Giang was visiting with her financial planner and discussing plans for purchases and investments in the future. Her planner asked about her risk management plan.

"I have basic insurance on my car," she answered, "but I don't really know whether it's adequate or too much. I hear a lot about life insurance, but I haven't bought a policy. At this point in my life, I can't afford a lot of money going toward payments. Still, I don't want to take chances that could drain my savings. You've mentioned having a risk management plan. What is that? Is that the same thing as insurance?"

Understanding Risk

GOALS

- Explain risk and the different types of risk.
- Explain the concept of insurance and how risks are spread.

TERMS

- pure risk, *p. 567*
- speculative risk, *p. 568*
- economic risk, *p. 568*
- insurance, *p. 569*
- insurable risk, *p. 569*
- insurable interest, *p. 569*
- personal risk, *p. 569*
- property risk, *p. 569*
- liability risk, *p. 569*
- premium, *p. 570*
- indemnification, *p. 572*

TYPES OF RISK

Chapter 11 described one type of risk (investment risk) as the chance of financial loss from a decline in an investment's value. There are many other types of risk you will face in your lifetime. *Risk* is a state of uncertainty where some of the possibilities may result in loss or another undesirable outcome. *Uncertainty* is the likelihood that something will or will not happen. In other words, there is more than one possibility. For example, you may hear that there is a 50 percent chance of rain.

PURE RISK

Pure risk is a chance of loss with no chance for gain. Pure risks are random (can happen to anyone) and result in loss (not gain). Examples of pure risk include the following:

- Accidents resulting in physical injury and damage to property
- Illnesses that people get throughout life, as a part of aging
- Acts of nature, resulting in damage to persons and property

However, it is possible to do things to help protect yourself from the consequences of these types of risk. Everyone should have a plan in place in the event of a pure risk because the consequences are often serious and can even be catastrophic, affecting both your life and your lifestyle.

© Comstock Images/Jupiter Images

What are some types of pure risk that we experience during our lives?

▌ SPECULATIVE RISK

In contrast, a **speculative risk** may result in either gain or loss. For example, if you buy gold, futures, options, or commodities, you could either make or lose money. Because speculative risks are not "accidental" or random, and may result in either gain or loss, you cannot protect yourself from losses in a traditional manner. While *hedging* (making an investment to help offset against loss) is a technique used to help reduce losses from such risky acts, it does not reduce the risk itself.

▌ ECONOMIC RISK

We all face risks due to the current state of the economy. **Economic risk** may result in gain or loss because of changing economic conditions. For example, when the business cycle is in a period of recovery or growth, most people and businesses are realizing gains in their financial position. However, the economy can slow down (and go into a recession if the slowdown lasts for very long). During this time, people lose jobs and are unable to buy goods and services. As a result, many businesses find themselves unable to meet their debts. Figure 25.1 is an illustration of the business cycle.

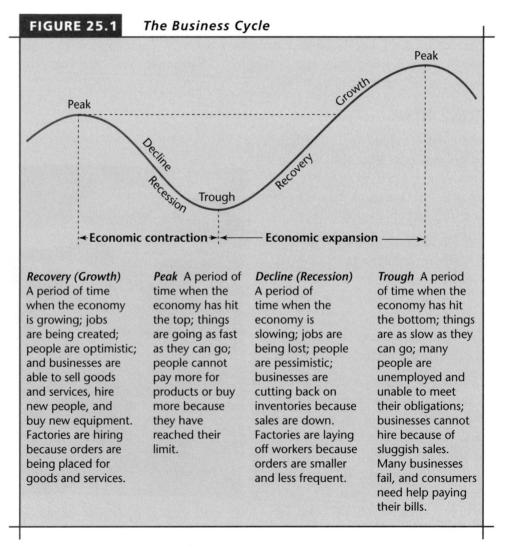

FIGURE 25.1   *The Business Cycle*

Recovery (Growth) A period of time when the economy is growing; jobs are being created; people are optimistic; and businesses are able to sell goods and services, hire new people, and buy new equipment. Factories are hiring because orders are being placed for goods and services.

Peak A period of time when the economy has hit the top; things are going as fast as they can go; people cannot pay more for products or buy more because they have reached their limit.

Decline (Recession) A period of time when the economy is slowing; jobs are being lost; people are pessimistic; businesses are cutting back on inventories because sales are down. Factories are laying off workers because orders are smaller and less frequent.

Trough A period of time when the economy has hit the bottom; things are as slow as they can go; many people are unemployed and unable to meet their obligations; businesses cannot hire because of sluggish sales. Many businesses fail, and consumers need help paying their bills.

INSURABLE RISK

You can reduce negative consequences of a pure risk by purchasing insurance. **Insurance** is a method for spreading individual risk among a large group of people to make losses more affordable for all. An **insurable risk** is a pure risk that is faced by a large number of people and for which the amount of the loss can be predicted. Insurance companies can make these predictions by examining the amount of loss incurred from past events, such as flooding.

To purchase insurance, you must have an insurable interest to protect. An **insurable interest** is any financial interest in life or property such that, if the life or property were lost or harmed, the insured would suffer financially. For example, you cannot buy insurance on someone else's house. Unless you own the house, you would not suffer a financial loss if it burned down. However, if you depend on your spouse's income to live, then you have an insurable interest in your spouse and can buy insurance on his or her life.

You face risks every day. From the moment you get out of bed, you take chances. You could slip and fall. You could have an accident in the kitchen. You could have your stereo stolen or injure another person or property while driving your car. There are three major insurable risks: personal, property, and liability. You should consider each of these risks as you make plans to protect your financial interests. Figure 25.2 gives examples of common risks and ways to protect yourself or to reduce their impact on you financially.

Personal Risk

A **personal risk** is the chance of loss involving your income and standard of living. You can protect yourself from personal risks by buying life, health, and disability insurance. In addition, insurance against personal risks protects others who are depending on your income to provide food, clothing, shelter, and the comforts of life.

Property Risk

The chance of loss or harm to personal or real property is called **property risk**. For example, your home, car, or other possessions could be damaged or destroyed by fire, theft, wind, rain, accident, and other hazards. To protect against such risks, you can buy property insurance.

Liability Risk

A **liability risk** is the chance of loss that may occur when your errors or actions result in injuries to others or damages to their property. For example, you could accidentally cause injury or damage to others or their property by your conduct while driving a car. Or a person could fall and break

© Comstock Images/Jupiter Images

What property risks do you face?

FIGURE 25.2   *Common Risks*

Risks	Causes (Perils)	Ways to Protect Yourself
1. Losing job (income)	Poor economy Company's financial condition Job-skills obsolescence	Unemployment insurance Learn new skills; make yourself more valuable
2. Illness or injury	On-the-job accident Chronic health condition or handicap	Health insurance Disability insurance Retraining programs
3. Death of wage earner	Dangerous activities including sports or job; illness	Life insurance Get training/lessons Take safety precautions
4. Liability for others' injuries	Careless driving Hazard at home/place of work	Liability insurance Signs, warnings, supervised uses
5. Loss of property to theft	Vehicle stolen Robbery	Property insurance Park in well-lit and secure places Locks/security devices

an arm because of your home's crumbling front steps. Liability insurance will protect you when others sue you for injuring them or damaging their property.

SPREADING THE RISK

There are many types of insurance, including life, health, homeowner's, and automobile. They all provide one important thing: the relief from fear of severe financial loss due to events beyond your control.

Here's an example of how insurance works. Suppose your textbook for this class costs $60. If you lose it, you will have to pay that amount to replace it. An average of 10 out of every 100 textbooks (or 1 out of every 10) is lost each school year. Based on this statistic, the expected losses in a class of 30 students would be 3 books, at a total cost of $180 (3 × $60). The class could establish an insurance company to help lower the cost of these expected losses to individual students. Every student would contribute $6 to the company. The total of $180 collected would be used to replace the books. The cost to each student would be relatively low ($6), and no one student would have to pay the full $60.

An insurance company, or *insurer*, is a business that agrees to pay the cost of potential future losses in exchange for regular fee payments. When people buy insurance, they join a risk-sharing group by purchasing a written insurance contract (a *policy*). Under the policy, the insurer agrees to assume an identified risk for a fee, called the **premium**, usually paid at regular intervals by the owner of the policy (the *policyholder*). The insurer collects insurance premiums from policyholders under the assumption that only a few policyholders will have financial losses at any given time.

Figure 25.3 illustrates the many insurance terms that all consumers need to understand.

FIGURE 25.3 *Insurance Terminology*

Actuarial table A table of premium rates based on ages and life expectancies

Actuary A specialist in insurance calculations and statistics

Beneficiary A person named on an insurance policy to receive the benefits from the policy

Benefits Sums of money to be paid for specific types of losses under the terms of an insurance policy

Cash value The amount of money payable to a policyholder upon discontinuation of a life insurance policy

Claim A policyholder's request for reimbursement for a loss under the terms of an insurance policy

Coverage Protection provided by the terms of an insurance policy

Deductible The specified amount of a loss that the policyholder pays before the insurer is obligated to pay anything; the insurance company pays only the amount in excess of the deductible

Exclusions Specified losses that the insurance policy does not cover

Face amount The amount stated in a life insurance policy to be paid upon death

Grace period The additional time after the premium due date that the insurer allows the policyholder to make the payment without penalty (usually 30 days)

Hazard A condition that creates or increases the likelihood of some loss; for example, defective house wiring can increase the likelihood of a fire

Insurance agent A professional insurance salesperson who acts for the insurer in negotiating, servicing, or writing an insurance policy

Insured The person or company protected against loss (not always the owner of the policy)

Insurer Insurance company who provides insurance coverage for a policyholder

Loss An unexpected reduction in value of the insured's property caused by a covered peril; the basis of a valid claim for reimbursement under the terms of an insurance policy

Peril An event whose occurrence can cause a loss; people buy policies for protection against such perils as a fire, storm, explosion, accident, or robbery

Probability The mathematics of chance, or statistical likelihood that something will happen

Proof of loss The written verification of the amount of a loss that must be provided by the insured to the insurer before a claim can be settled

Standard policy The contract form that has been adopted by many insurers, approved by state insurance departments, or prescribed by law (modifications are made to suit the needs of the individual)

Unearned premium The portion of a paid premium that the insurer has not yet earned because the policy term has not ended; the unearned premium is returned to the policyholder when a policy is canceled

Experts believe that in order to reduce teen driving accidents, the most effective tactic is to limit teens' driving risk exposure. For example, some states impose night driving and passenger restrictions for beginning drivers and require higher ages for initial licensure. Curfews that apply to late-night activities of 13- to 17-year-olds have also reduced crashes. At the same time, very few states have laws that regulate elderly drivers. This group often continues to drive after their vision, reflexes, hearing, and other skills necessary for safe driving have diminished.

THINK *CRITICALLY*

Do you think that stricter rules for teen driving are effective? Do they infringe on teens' rights? Do you think that restrictions should be placed on older drivers? What would you recommend? Explain your answer.

To make a profit, the insurer must collect more in premiums than it pays out for losses and operating expenses. In years when a catastrophic disaster occurs or when multiple major disasters occur, such as hurricanes, floods, and earthquakes, an insurer may pay out more in benefits than it receives in premiums.

Insurance is not meant to enrich—only to compensate for actual losses incurred. This principle is called indemnification. **Indemnification** means putting the policyholder back in the same financial condition he or she was in before the loss occurred.

Insurers set premiums based on statistical probability. In other words, they estimate the likelihood of potential losses. They gather and analyze large amounts of historical data to determine how many of a particular loss occurred, on average, in a population over a given time period. From this analysis they can predict approximately how many such losses to expect among their policyholders over a similar future time period, such as a year. For example, in a sample of 100,000 drivers under the age of 18, an insurer can predict approximately how many will have accidents in a given year.

The higher the probability of a loss occurring, the higher the premium for insuring against it. Remember that insurers deal in averages. They cannot predict which specific individuals will suffer losses.

© Photodisc/Getty Images

How can a major disaster affect an insurance company financially?

Planning a Career in...   Insurance

Insurance agents help people select insurance policies that provide the best protection for their lives, health, and property. Many insurance agents also offer financial planning services, such as retirement planning and estate planning.

Insurance agents also prepare reports, maintain records, and seek new clients. When their policyholders experience a loss, agents also help them settle their claims.

Insurance agents may work exclusively for one insurance company (captive agents), or they may represent a number of insurance companies (independent broker). Insurance brokers match clients' insurance needs with the companies that offer the best rates and coverages to meet those needs.

Insurance brokers typically work in small offices; however, much time may be spent outside the office. Agents usually set their own hours of work, depending on appointments and paperwork needs.

Employment Outlook

- An average rate of employment growth is expected.

Job Titles

- Insurance agent
- Insurance broker
- Claims adjuster
- Claims investigator

Needed Skills

- College graduates are preferred, especially with degrees in business or economics.

- Agents must obtain licenses in the states where they work; tests are required.

What's it like to work in... *Insurance*

Mylee has worked in insurance for several years following her graduation from college, where she earned a specialized certificate along with her bachelor's degree.

Mylee is an independent broker and manages her own workload. Today she is meeting with new clients, a young married couple who have just purchased their first home. She describes the kinds of risks they may face at this stage of their lives, including personal, property, and liability risks, and explains the types of coverages available that will help minimize their financial risk. She gathers information from the couple so she can put together an insurance policy that will meet their needs.

Later that afternoon, Mylee checks coverages and rates with several insurance companies to see which one offers the best policy for her new clients. After selling the policy, Mylee sets up a follow-up meeting with her clients to ensure they understand the deductibles, exclusions, and claim procedures outlined in the policy.

What About You?

Would you like to help people assess and plan for risks? Would a career in insurance be right for you?

Assessment

KEY TERMS REVIEW

Match the terms with the definitions. Some terms may not be used.

_____ 1. *A method for spreading individual risk among a large group of people to make losses more affordable for all*

_____ 2. *A risk that may result in either gain or loss*

_____ 3. *Putting the policyholder back in the same financial condition he or she was in before a loss occurred*

_____ 4. *The chances of loss or harm to personal or real property*

_____ 5. *A chance of loss with no chance for gain*

_____ 6. *A financial interest in life or property*

_____ 7. *The chances of loss that may occur when your errors or actions result in injuries to others or damage to their property*

_____ 8. *A risk that may result in gain or loss because of changing economic conditions*

a. economic risk

b. indemnification

c. insurable interest

d. insurable risk

e. insurance

f. liability risk

g. personal risk

h. premium

i. property risk

j. pure risk

k. speculative risk

CHECK YOUR UNDERSTANDING

9. *What is the purpose of insurance?*

10. *Explain the concept of an insurable risk.*

APPLY YOUR KNOWLEDGE

11. *Pure risk is the chance of loss but not of gain. List and explain three types of pure risk that you have encountered in the last month. Then explain how you or your family assessed and managed the risk.*

THINK *CRITICALLY*

12. *The economy is not under your control, but there are things you can do to prepare for changing economic conditions. What can an individual consumer do to be better prepared for times of recession?*

13. *Explain how a peril is different from a hazard. Explain why insurance companies charge higher premiums if property does not meet minimum standards of safety or quality, or is hazardous.*

14. *Insurance policies are based on statistical averages. Explain why teenage drivers pay the highest premiums for automobile insurance. How can teenagers and their families qualify for lower premiums?*

Managing Risk

RISK MANAGEMENT IS A PROCESS

While you cannot eliminate risk, you can manage it so that a loss does not become financially devastating. **Risk management** is an organized strategy for controlling financial loss from pure risks and insurable risks. It begins as soon as you have something to lose. In other words, as soon as you have assets, wealth, income, and anything that others could take from you, you must begin to think about how you can protect yourself from loss.

Risk management begins early in life and remains in effect throughout your life. Even after death, your estate can be vulnerable to attacks from those who would like to take part of your wealth from your heirs.

Risk management is more than buying insurance for every possible peril that could occur. Some risks are not serious enough to insure. Others are better handled by taking steps to avoid the risk or reduce the chances that the risk will occur.

RISK ASSESSMENT

Risk management begins with a systematic study of the risks that you face. It begins with **risk assessment**, or understanding the types of risk you will face and their potential consequences. Risk assessment is a three-step process, as illustrated in Figure 25.4.

Step 1: Identify Risks of Loss

Ask yourself what financial risks you take daily, such as when you drive a car, own a house, or plan

© Photodisc/Getty Images

What is the purpose of risk management?

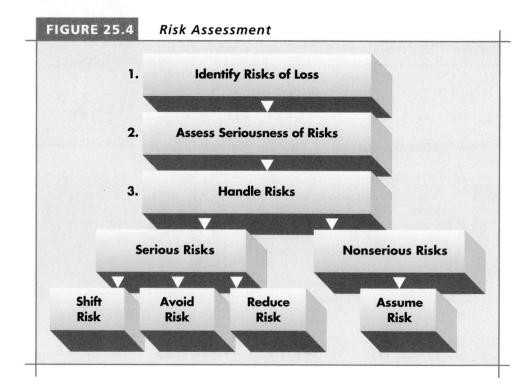

FIGURE 25.4   *Risk Assessment*

1. **Identify Risks of Loss**

2. **Assess Seriousness of Risks**

3. **Handle Risks**

Serious Risks

Nonserious Risks

Shift Risk   **Avoid Risk**   **Reduce Risk**   **Assume Risk**

a party. As you will see in later chapters, many potential losses could occur. Even though they may not happen as a result of your error or fault, you still can be held responsible for damages to others and to property.

Step 2: Assess Seriousness of Risks

Human activities and the ownership of property reflect a certain amount of risk. Some risks are high priority because they could have serious financial consequences. For example, when driving your car, you could destroy the property of others, injure others, or even kill someone. Because potential losses are very great, driving is a high-priority risk. Other types of risk may have a relatively low financial consequence or may have only a very small chance of occurring. These types of risk are therefore of a lower priority.

Step 3: Handle Risks

There are four techniques you can consider to handle risk: shifting, avoiding, reducing, or assuming risk. A good risk-management plan uses a combination of these strategies to balance risk, the cost of insurance, and your potential losses.

1. **Risk shifting**, also called *risk transfer*, occurs when you buy insurance to cover financial losses caused by damaging events, such as fire, theft, injury, or death. By making premium payments, you shift the risk of major financial loss to the insurance company.
2. **Risk avoidance** lowers the chance for loss by not doing the activity that could result in the loss. For example, instead of having a party at your house and risking damage, you could reserve a section of a restaurant. Instead of participating in a dangerous sport, you could go camping.
3. **Risk reduction** lowers the chance of loss by taking measures to lessen the frequency or severity of losses that may occur. For example, you may put studded snow tires on your car, install fire alarms or sprinklers in your home, or use seat belts. All these steps would lessen the financial risk of potential losses.

On December 26, 2004, an earthquake with a magnitude of 9.1 (the second largest ever recorded) had its epicenter off the west coast of Indonesia. The earthquake triggered a series of devastating tsunamis in the Indian Ocean, killing more than 225,000 people in eleven countries. Coastal communities were hit with waves more than 30 meters (100 feet) tall; it was one of the deadliest in history. Hardest hit were Indonesia, Sri Lanka, India, and Thailand. Many villages and towns along coastlines were destroyed. Residents and tourists alike were killed as the waves hit the beaches. Despite a lag of several hours between the earthquake and the impact of the tsunami, nearly all of the victims were taken by surprise. There were no warning systems in the Indian Ocean to detect tsunamis or to warn coastal communities.

THINK *CRITICALLY*

Is it possible to protect yourself against all types of risks? If you choose to do nothing, what costs can result? How do those costs compare with the cost of risk management?

4. **Risk assumption** is the process of accepting the consequences of risk. To help cushion your financial burden, you could establish a monetary fund to cover the cost of a loss. People who *self-insure* plan to absorb the costs of some risks themselves. This strategy can reduce the cost of insurance. In some cases, the cost of insuring against a particular risk may be too great, or the probability that the risk will occur may be too low, to justify paying an insurance premium.

Based on the nature and seriousness of the risks you identify, you should select the risk-management techniques that best address each risk. For example, suppose you own a car. Because driving a car is a serious risk, you buy auto insurance to shift most of the risk. (It's also required in most states.) You like bungee jumping, but since engaging in this activity would make your health insurance premium extremely high, you decide to avoid the risk and not do the activity. You know that your old house will probably need major repairs soon. You decide to assume this risk by starting a home-maintenance fund and contributing regularly to it.

THE RISK-MANAGEMENT PLAN

Everyone faces risks and the potential losses they bring. Some people choose to do nothing—but this is in fact a choice. When you allow events to control your life, they also drain your finances in unpredictable and expensive ways. To avoid possible financial disaster, create a risk-management plan, listing the risks you identified, your assessment of their financial impacts, and the techniques that you plan to use to manage each risk.

Figure 25.5 outlines a risk-management plan that a young person might develop. As you progress through different life stages, your priorities will change, and you will need to adjust your plan. For example, life insurance may become a higher priority when you have children who depend on your income.

FIGURE 25.5   *Risk-Management Plan*

Risk	Seriousness of Financial Impact	Method for Handling
1. Auto accidents	High	Collision and liability insurance Reduce risk—driver's education class
2. Theft or damage to personal property in apartment	Medium	Renter's insurance Reduce risk—add deadbolt lock to door
3. Theft or damage to personal property at work or in my car	Medium	Renter's/homeowner's standard policy Floater policy (for higher-priced items) Reduce risk—alarm in vehicle; keep items locked and out of sight
4. Injury to apartment visitors	Medium	Renter's insurance Low probability of occurring—assume risk above renter's insurance coverage
5. Personal illness and sports injuries	High	Health insurance Avoid some risk—stop bungee-jumping Reduce some risk—wear a helmet for mountain biking Reduce risk—get special training
6. Vision and dental needs	Low	Assume risk—contribute $10 a month to a fund to pay for new glasses and dental work when needed (self-insure)
7. Income protection	Medium/low (depending on life situation)	Life insurance (to protect dependents) Disability insurance (to provide income if I can't work) Insurance to make minimum payments when I am unemployed

A good risk-management plan uses a combination of techniques to lower overall risk. Insurance is an important part of any risk-management plan. In general, financial advisers say that a basic insurance plan should help reduce risk and protect against the following:

1. Potential loss of income due to the premature death, illness, accident, or unemployment of a wage earner.
2. Potential loss of income and extra expense resulting from the illness, disability, or death of a spouse or other family member.
3. Potential loss of real or personal property due to fire, theft, or other hazards.
4. Potential loss of income, savings, and property resulting from personal liability (injuring a person or damaging the property of others).

For each risk that you will face, you can find ways to reduce, avoid, or assume part of the risk yourself. However, when a risk is significant and can have drastic consequences, then shifting the risk by purchasing insurance is a good idea. In Chapters 26 and 27, you will learn more about types of insurance.

REDUCING INSURANCE COSTS

As you consider an insurance plan, think about the following ways to save on insurance costs.

- *Increase Deductibles*. A **deductible** is the specified amount of a loss that you must pay. The insurer's obligation to pay begins only after you have paid your full deductible. Generally, the higher the deductible, the lower the insurance premium. For example, premiums for a policy with a $100 deductible will be considerably higher than for a policy with a $500 deductible. To reduce your premiums, you can accept a higher deductible.

- *Purchase Group Insurance*. The premiums for group plans are usually considerably lower than for an individual plan, especially for health insurance. If group plans are available to you through your job, credit union, a social or professional organization, or other similar group, you will likely save money by enrolling in them.

- *Consider Payment Options*. How you pay premiums can save you considerable money over a short period of time. Monthly payments usually contain an extra charge, while semiannual payments do not. Some premiums are paid annually or semiannually. Agreeing to have your premiums automatically deducted from your checking account or paying electronically may also reduce your costs. Always compare payment options and weigh the differences in costs.

- *Look for Discount Opportunities*. Many insurance companies offer discounts for special conditions. For example, nonsmokers can get lower premiums on fire and health insurance. Taking driver's education courses and getting good grades can reduce automobile insurance costs for teenagers. Having more than one vehicle or more than one insurance policy with a company can result in multiple-policy discounts.

- *Comparison Shop*. Like many other things you buy, it pays to shop around for insurance. Get quotes from several insurers. Be sure to give each one the same information so you can compare exact coverage and costs. When getting cost estimates for many types of insurance, you need to know what your property is worth. Also, maintaining a good driving record is important when getting price quotes for automobile insurance. It's also important to know exactly what coverage you need—and don't need—before talking to insurers.

The financial strength of the insurer may be a major factor in keeping down insurance costs. You can find ratings for different insurers in print and online publications of the A.M. Best Company and Standard & Poor's. Ask people you know for recommendations about insurers they have used. Check with your state insurance commissioner to see what companies are legally doing business in the state and which companies have had complaints filed against them.

NETBookmark

Every year, more than 5,000 people die from injuries sustained on the job. Access www.cengage.com/school/pfinance/mypf and click on the link for Chapter 25. Read the article to find out who is most at risk, and why. Then select three of these risky occupations and suggest some ways workers might avoid or reduce their risk of being injured or killed on the job.

www.cengage.com/school/pfinance/mypf

ISSUES IN YOUR WORLD

SOFTENING THE BLOW

Since the Great Depression, the United States has had many programs designed to protect people from the harsh realities of risk in their lives. Transfer payments *are government grants to some citizens paid with taxes collected from other citizens. Essentially, the government uses taxes to transfer some wealth from those who have it to those who do not. Some transfer payments are made in cash. Others are made "in kind." That is, the government provides the needed item rather than cash. The following programs are available to U.S. citizens:*

In-Cash Payments

- Unemployment Compensation. *When workers are laid off, they are eligible to receive a percentage of their pay for a specified number of weeks, or until they get a new job (whichever comes first).*

- Disability Payments. *For injured workers, the disability portion of Social Security pays a monthly benefit until the workers recover, or for the rest of their lives if they remain disabled.*

- Temporary Assistance for Needy Families (TANF). *Low-income families with children can receive a monthly payment for a maximum of 4 years. To receive the benefit, adults in the family must work to gain the experience needed to become self-sufficient.*

In-Kind Payments

- Food Stamps. *People with insufficient money to buy food may qualify to receive food stamps, which are government vouchers that can be exchanged for food items.*

- National School Lunch Program. *Children from low-income families may receive free or low-cost lunches at school. The schools receive cash subsidies and donated food from the government.*

- Medicaid. *Medicaid is government-sponsored health insurance for people living in poverty who cannot afford private health insurance.*

These programs are temporary. They are designed to help sustain people while they are retraining, recovering, or working to get back on their feet financially. They are not permanent solutions.

THINK *CRITICALLY*

1. *What would you do if you lost your job and had no immediate source of cash for food and other necessities? How would you cope?*

2. *Visit your state government web site and list resources that are available to people in need.*

Assessment

KEY TERMS REVIEW

Match the terms with the definitions.

_____ 1. Lowering your chance of loss by not doing high-risk activities

_____ 2. Transferring risk by buying insurance to cover potential losses

_____ 3. An organized strategy for controlling financial loss from pure risks and insurable risks

_____ 4. Taking measures to lessen the frequency or severity of losses that might occur

a. deductible

b. risk assessment

c. risk assumption

d. risk avoidance

e. risk management

f. risk reduction

g. risk shifting

_____ 5. The specified amount of a loss that you (the insured) will have to pay

_____ 6. Understanding the types of risk you will face and their potential consequences

_____ 7. Accepting the consequences of risk by self-insuring to absorb the loss

CHECK YOUR UNDERSTANDING

8. Provide an example of risk avoidance, risk reduction, risk assumption, and risk shifting.

9. How can changing your deductible reduce your insurance premium?

APPLY YOUR KNOWLEDGE

10. Why is it important to perform a risk assessment before developing a plan to manage risk?

THINK CRITICALLY

11. Why is it important to handle risks in ways other than shifting, or buying insurance, to protect you from every financial loss? As a responsible adult, how will you handle the risks in your life?

12. Refer to the risk-management plan shown in Figure 25.5. How might this plan be different for a person with a spouse and children? How might it be different for a person nearing retirement?

13. What are some things you and your family can do now to reduce your overall automobile insurance premium costs?

Chapter Assessment

SUMMARY

25.1

- Pure risks are random and can result in losses, but not gains, while speculative risks may result in either loss or gain.

- Everyone is affected by what happens in the economy; economic risk is not avoidable, but there are ways to lessen its impact (such as to save during good economic times to help prepare for slow economic times).

- Insurance is a method of spreading risk across a large group, so that no one member must endure the full cost of a devastating loss. To be insurable, a risk must be a pure risk faced by a large number of people and for which the amount of the loss can be predicted.

- Insurable risks include personal risks (life and health), property risks (home and car), and liability risks (causing injury to others or their property).

- Insurers make a profit by collecting more in premiums than they pay out in losses and operating expenses.

- Insurance is not meant to enrich, but to provide indemnification, or return the policyholder to the same financial condition as before the loss occurred.

- Insurers analyze historical data to help predict how many losses to expect among their policyholders over a given time period. They base premiums on these statistical averages.

25.2

- Risk management is an organized strategy for controlling financial loss from pure, not speculative, risks.

- The risk-management process begins with assessing the risks you face through a three-step process: identifying risks, assessing the seriousness of the risks, and considering the techniques for handling the risks.

- You can choose to handle risks through (1) risk shifting (transfer), (2) risk avoidance, (3) risk reduction, or (4) risk assumption.

- A good risk-management plan uses a combination of techniques to lower overall risk.

- To reduce insurance costs, increase your deductibles, buy group plans, choose cost-effective payment options, take advantage of discounts, and comparison shop.

APPLY WHAT YOU KNOW

1. Prepare a list of insurers in your area. Include the types of insurance sold by each company. For each insurance agency, list the insurance companies represented.

2. Based on Figure 25.2, list any current or anticipated risks you or your family face or will face in the near future. Analyze your current personal, property, and liability risks. Then assume that you are now ten years older. Based on being where you would like to be and doing what your current goals dictate, analyze your personal, property, and liability risks for this stage in your life.

3. Using Figure 25.4 as a guide, identify your most significant risks and the perils that cause them. Then list ways that you can protect yourself by either reducing the financial impact of the risk or reducing its chances of occurring.

4. Visit your state insurance commissioner online. Download and print the complaint form if one is available, and write a paragraph about what recourse you may have when you feel an insurer is treating you unfairly.

5. Find Standard & Poor's in your library. Look up the financial strength ratings for particular insurance companies until you find two with different ratings. Then look up the meaning of these ratings. Which company did Standard & Poor's judge to be financially stronger? Why?

6. Using Figure 25.5 as a guide, prepare a risk-management plan for yourself. As an alternative, interview a person at a different life stage and ask for advice on an appropriate risk-management plan.

MAKE ACADEMIC CONNECTIONS

7. **Economics** Write a report about the business cycle (see Figure 25.1). Compare business cycles over time—for example, how long do slowdowns usually last? When was our last trough; how long did it last? Explain how to survive during the various business cycle stages.

8. **History** Using the Internet, search for the "Great Depression" and locate several sources of information, including Wikipedia. Write a paper presenting a narrative of what it was, how long it lasted, how people were affected, and what President Franklin D. Roosevelt did to help end the Depression and get people working again.

9. **Research** The design of the automobile has changed significantly throughout the years, with safety becoming a bigger factor in the design. Conduct research to learn about safety features that have been incorporated in the design of automobiles over the years. Present your findings to the class. Use visual aids to showcase the safety features.

10. **Technology** Describe how technology has affected the insurance industry. Discuss how consumers apply for insurance coverage, how insurance agents use the Internet, and how costs for premiums are affected because information is readily available online. Interview an insurance agent to discuss how his or her life has changed because of technology.

SOLVE PROBLEMS AND

EXPLORE ISSUES

11. Zoe and Ricardo are planning to get married next summer. They don't own a car and plan to rent an apartment. They intend to have children in the next few years. What advice can you give them about risk and risk management? When should they consider purchasing insurance?

12. Your cousin Jerry has decided to take up snow skiing. He has very minimal health insurance coverage, so he wants to avoid high medical bills. How can he minimize the risks and costs that could occur as a result of skiing?

13. A neighbor has asked for your advice regarding insurance. She is single, owns a car, and works full time. She is buying a home and has student loans and other debts to pay. She would like to know what risks she is facing and how to plan for them. Help her identify and assess her risks and develop a risk-management plan based on her situation. Include strategies for reducing insurance costs.

14. Jeremy made this statement: "I don't take any chances. Everything I own is insured, including my life and ability to provide money for my family. In fact, I pay so much in insurance premiums that there is little money left for entertainment. Am I doing something wrong?" What advice would you give to Jeremy?

15. Osami is single and under age 25. She just started her first full-time job, and group health insurance is available through her employer. She has a car and has had no accidents or traffic tickets. She has an apartment that contains furnishings and personal belongings. Prepare a list of the risks she may face. What types of insurance coverage may she need?

16. Interview an insurance agent. Find out what an agent can do to help you purchase various types of protection and save money.

EXTEND YOUR LEARNING

17. **Ethics** Government programs to help people through difficult times have existed since the 1930s. When the Great Depression began (1929) there was no Social Security, welfare, unemployment, or other safety nets to help people. Today, these programs continue to exist. Although they were not designed to be a person's sole or permanent refuge, many people—possibly millions—abuse the system to avoid working and providing for their own needs. As a result, the system is strained, leading to tax increases for employers and employees to fund these programs. Is it ethical to use the system long after you are able to support yourself? Do you think it's the government's responsibility to provide services to those in need? How does the government promote self-sufficiency?

For related activities and links, go to **www.cengage.com/school/pfinance/mypf**

26

Property and Liability Insurance

26.1 *Property Insurance*

26.2 *Automobile and Umbrella Insurance*

Consider **THIS**

Andy attends college full time and shares a rented house with two housemates.

"As renters, we have to insure our personal possessions, and we're responsible for what happens on the property, even though we're only renting," he told his housemates. "I've talked to my insurance agent about renter's insurance to protect us in case of theft, fire, or freezing pipes. The good news is that we won't have to pay very much—probably between $150 and $300 a year. That's about $50 to $100 per person for the year. I've included that item in our budget for monthly expenses."

Property Insurance

GOALS

- Explain the purpose and provisions of renter's insurance.
- Describe the need for and coverage provided by homeowner's insurance.

TERMS

- renter's policy, *p. 586*
- homeowner's policy, *p. 587*
- endorsement, *p. 588*
- co-insurance clause, *p. 588*
- personal property floater, *p. 589*
- liability coverage, *p. 590*
- uninvited guest, *p. 590*
- attractive nuisance, *p. 591*

RENTER'S INSURANCE

If you rent your residence, you don't have to worry about insuring the building. That is the landlord's responsibility. However, your personal possessions are your responsibility to protect—not the landlord's (the landlord has no "insurable interest" in your assets). You are also responsible for personal injuries that occur inside your home.

A **renter's policy** is insurance that protects renters from property and liability risks. A renter's policy will protect you from damage to personal property, liability for injuries to your guests, and loss of personal possessions you carry with you outside the home.

PERSONAL PROPERTY

Personal possessions inside the rental property can be damaged or destroyed by fire, smoke, water, moisture, freezing, or heat. For example, if you rent an apartment and there is a fire in the building, your personal property (couch, chairs, bed, clothing, and so on) may suffer damage. A renter's policy will cover the costs of repairing or replacing damaged or destroyed property.

LIABILITY

If someone is injured while in your rented home, you may be liable to pay his or her expenses. The landlord (owner) is not responsible for what happens inside the residence; that is your responsibility because you have control over those events. Your renter's policy will pay for medical costs incurred by your guests.

© Digital Vision/Getty Images

What protection is available through renter's insurance?

EXTENDED COVERAGE

A renter's policy will also protect your personal possessions while they are in your car or at work. If you have particularly valuable possessions at your home, in storage, or with you as you travel, you might need to buy special coverage for the items. For example, expensive jewelry beyond the policy's limits may need extended coverage based on an appraisal of value.

HOMEOWNER'S INSURANCE

A **homeowner's policy** is insurance that protects property owners from property and liability risks. It is similar to renter's insurance, except that it includes coverage for the building in addition to the owner's personal possessions inside the building. Homeowner's policies typically cover property owners' losses from these three types of risks:

- *Hazards*—fire, water, wind, and smoke that may cause physical damages.
- *Crimes*—criminal activity, such as robbery, burglary, arson, and vandalism.
- *Liability*—the cost of another person's losses for injuries at your property.

Homeowner's policies may be very basic or very broad in their coverage. Figure 26.1 lists common types of homeowner's policies. *Package policies* that include several types of coverage in a single contract usually carry a lower premium than you would pay for each coverage purchased separately.

HOW MUCH COVERAGE DO YOU NEED?

Generally, people insure the contents of their house for at least half the value of the building. For example, a building insured for $200,000 is likely to have contents covered for at least $100,000. This includes all types of personal possessions, from furniture and appliances to clothing and other personal property.

To be sure you are reimbursed for all damaged or destroyed property, you should complete a household inventory, as shown in Figure 26.2. This inventory is similar to the personal property inventory you prepared in Chapter 8, except that a homeowner's inventory usually needs to be more detailed. Your inventory should include documentation that shows proof of ownership and value. Some people keep receipts and take pictures or a home video. Keep this documentation in a safe place (such as a safe deposit box). Most insurance agents provide household inventory forms for their customers.

Typically, not every loss will be covered by property insurance. *Exclusions* are items that insurance policies specifically will not cover, as shown in Figure 26.3 on page 590.

Avoid *overinsuring*—that is, buying more insurance than is necessary. An insurer will pay no more than the actual replacement value of the house. The *replacement value* is the cost of replacing an item regardless of its actual cash (market) value. For example, if your house has a market value of $150,000, due to rising costs, it may cost $200,000 to rebuild it using material of similar quality if lost in a fire. If a house with a replacement value of $200,000 and contents worth $100,000 were totally destroyed, the insurer would pay no more than $300,000 ($200,000 + $100,000). If you owned a $400,000 homeowner's policy, you would still receive reimbursement of no more than $300,000. As you learned in Chapter 25, insurance follows the legal principle

FIGURE 26.1 Homeowner's Policy Coverage

HO-1	Basic coverage	Fire, lightning, windstorm, hail, explosion, riot, civil commotion, aircraft, nonowned vehicles, smoke, vandalism, malicious mischief, theft, and glass breakage. Limits apply, such as $500 or 5 percent of policy value.
HO-2	Broad Form	Broader list of perils; broader definition; still has restrictions and limits, such as fire from fireplaces being excluded; limit of $1,000 or 10 percent of policy value.
HO-3	Special Form	All-risk coverage on dwelling itself; a loss not specifically excluded (such as flood) is covered.
HO-4	Renter's	Insuring personal property on a broad-form basis with advantages of homeowner's policy (such as special coverage in event of flood or water damage).
HO-5	Comprehensive	Most complete coverage available; dwelling and contents are covered on all-risk basis.
HO-6	Condominium Owner's	HO-4 coverage for condominium owners (wording is adjusted to fit legal status of condominium owner).
HO-7	Mobile Homes	Protects owners of manufactured homes.
HO-8	Older Homes	Meets special needs of owners of older buildings with high replacement costs (actual cash value basis rather than replacement cost basis).

of *indemnification*. It will reimburse the actual cash value of a loss (which includes depreciation), unless your policy includes a replacement value clause, in which case it will reimburse the amount needed to restore you to your pre-loss financial position (up to the amount of insurance you purchased). Although insuring for replacement value is more expensive, it is often worth it.

Claims adjusters, also known as *insurance adjusters*, determine the value of the property destroyed or damaged by a covered hazard. Also, insurers employ *insurance investigators* who look for evidence of destroyed or damaged property. They also look into cases where people try to claim damages that did not occur. False insurance claims can result in criminal charges, fines, or both.

An **endorsement** is a written amendment to an insurance policy. Policy-holders often use endorsements to add coverage to their policy for an additional premium. For example, you can add flood or earthquake insurance as an endorsement to your homeowner's policy.

Most property insurance policies contain a **co-insurance clause**, a provision requiring policyholders to insure their building for a stated percentage of its replacement value in order to receive full reimbursement for a loss. The percentage is usually at least 80 percent. Insurers do not require 100 percent coverage because even if your property is completely destroyed, the land and the building foundation will probably still be usable. If you do not meet the co-insurance minimum coverage, you will receive less than the full amount of the damages.

FIGURE 26.2   *Household Inventory for Insurance*

HOUSEHOLD INVENTORY

Room	Type of Property	Replacement Cost	Receipt/Proof
Kitchen	Appliances:		
	Stove/oven	$ 600	Sears, 7/07
	Microwave	400	JC Penneys, 9/06
	Toaster	25	Gift
	Mixer/blender	125	Shaleys, 1/08
	Bread maker	250	K-Mart, 6/08
	Cabinets and contents:		
	Dishes	500	
	Pots and pans	500	
	Silverware	800	Oneida, 2/05
	Clock on wall	100	Gift
	Table and chairs	1,200	Dixons, 5/08
	Curtains	500	Wards, 8/07
Family Room	Bookcase, books	2,000	
	Couch and chair	1,000	Dixons, 2/08
	End tables/lamps	800	Dixons, 2/08
	Television	1,000	Mel's, 3/09
	Stereo	1,200	Mel's, 3/09
	Paintings	700	Dixon's, 2/08
Bedroom	Antique bedroom set	5,000	Appraisal
	Clothing	2,000	
	Jewelry	500	
	Picture/mirrors	800	Dixon's, 2/08
Garage	Lawn mower	900	Swath's, 3/07
	Garden tools	300	
	Camping equipment	800	Mel's, 3/09
	Bicycles	1,800	Jon's, 3/09
Utility Room	Washer/dryer	1,200	Sears, 3/07
	Cleaning supplies	100	

PHYSICAL DAMAGE COVERAGE

Hazards such as fire, wind, water, and smoke may damage or destroy your home or cause you to temporarily lose use of it. The main component of homeowner's insurance is protection against financial loss due to damage or destruction. Detached structures on the property, such as a garage or shed, as well as trees, plants, and fences are also covered. If damage from a covered hazard prevents you from using your property while it is being repaired or replaced, your homeowner's policy will pay for temporary housing for a limited time.

THEFT AND VANDALISM COVERAGE

Theft and vandalism coverage protects your personal belongings against loss from criminal activity, such as robbery and physical damage from vandals. It covers your property when it is in your home or with you when you are away. This coverage is commonly a part of homeowner's and renter's policies.

A **personal property floater** is insurance coverage for the insured's moveable property wherever it may be located. People often buy it to protect specific

FIGURE 26.3   *Exclusions from Homeowner's Insurance*

Items Not Covered by Most Homeowner's Insurance Policies:

- Articles insured separately (floater) such as jewelry, collections, and fine art

- Animals, birds, fish, and other pets

- Motorized land vehicles (licensed for use), except for lawn mowers and things used on the property exclusively

- Stereos, radios, CBs, cellular phones, or CD or DVD players in vehicles

- Aircraft and parts of aircraft

- Property of renters, boarders, and other tenants (unless they are related to the owner and not paying rent)

- Business property in storage, such as samples

- Business property pertaining to a business that is conducted at the residence (separate insurance is required)

- Business property away from the residence

items of high value, such as jewelry, coin and stamp collections, fine art, musical instruments, and the like. A standard homeowner's policy has limits on coverage of personal property. For example, your policy may pay up to $1,500 for computers and related technology, $5,000 for jewelry, and $2,000 for collections. If, in fact, you have personal property worth more than these minimum amounts, you can protect it with a floater.

LIABILITY COVERAGE

Liability coverage is insurance to protect against claims for bodily injury to another person or damage to another person's property. For instance, if a guest in your home falls and breaks a leg, you may be held liable for medical expenses. If you own a dog, you are responsible if the dog bites someone or another dog. If a child hits a baseball through a neighbor's window, parents are responsible for the damage.

Homeowners are responsible for acts occurring on their property, both for guests and for uninvited guests. A *guest* is someone you specifically ask to come to your house. An **uninvited guest** is presumed to have permission to be on your property, such as door-to-door solicitors or delivery people. In most cases, homeowners will not be held liable for damages by a *trespasser* (unlawful intruder).

COMMUNICATION *Connection*

Assume you work for an insurance company and have been asked to create a sales pamphlet of two or more pages that explains the need for homeowner's/renter's insurance and describes the different types of coverages. Put together an attractive ad piece, including a company logo. Add photos or other types of images if possible.

CALCULATING INSURANCE REIMBURSEMENT FOR A LOSS

The co-insurance clause in a homeowner's policy requires that you buy coverage equal to a stated percentage of the property's replacement value in order to receive full reimbursement for a loss. For example, an 80 percent co-insurance clause would require the following coverage on a $150,000 house:

$150,000 × .80 = $120,000 coverage required

Many homeowners believe they can save money by underinsuring. Say the owners of the home in our example decide to buy only $100,000 of insurance instead of the required $120,000, thinking that $100,000 will cover most losses. Then they have a fire that results in a loss valued at $50,000. They think their $100,000 policy will cover the loss, but that isn't the case. Because they did not meet the $120,000 requirement, the insurer will reimburse based on the percentage of coverage they do have:

$100,000 ÷ $120,000 = .833 or 83.3%

To determine the amount of reimbursement, the insurer will multiply the value of the loss by this percentage:

$50,000 × .833 = $41,650

Thus, for a $50,000 loss, the homeowners will receive only $41,650, or 83 1/3% of the loss.

Based on the preceding example, compute the insurance reimbursement in the following situation.

Daniel bought a house for $200,000. His co-insurance requirement is 85 percent. Daniel bought insurance for $120,000 to save money on insurance premiums. Last month, a storm caused $60,000 damage to his house. How much will the insurer reimburse?

Solution: $200,000 × .85 = $170,000 required coverage

$120,000 ÷ $170,000 = .706, or 70.6%

$60,000 × .706 = $42,360 reimbursement

An **attractive nuisance** is a dangerous place, condition, or object that is particularly attractive to children, such as a swimming pool. If a child sneaks into a private pool without permission and is hurt, the homeowner will be held liable for the child's injuries. The owner is usually responsible, even if he or she takes steps to prevent entry into the pool.

▌COMPARISON SHOP

Most large insurers have web sites where you can get information about the policies and premiums they offer. To compare the offerings of many companies, the Internet is a good resource. Entering the keyword "insurance" into an online search engine will lead you to many consumer-oriented sites, such as InsuranceMachine.com, NetQuote, and Insure.com. At these sites you can get insurance quotes for all types of insurance policies, along with a wealth of information to help you evaluate insurance options.

Claims adjusters work for insurance companies. They assess the amount of damages that will be paid for a claim. Although many adjusters, appraisers, examiners, and investigators have overlapping duties and may even perform the same tasks, each of these positions adds value to the claims process.

When a policyholder submits a claim, the adjuster processes the report. The adjuster investigates, negotiates settlement, and authorizes payment to or on behalf of the policyholder. The adjuster must be familiar with and abide by all state and federal laws in the claims process.

Appraisal skills are required to accurately estimate the extent of the current and future monetary damages suffered. The adjuster's estimate of repair costs is often lower than estimates provided by repair professionals.

Employment Outlook

- An average rate of employment growth is expected.

Job Titles

- Insurance adjuster
- Claims analyst
- Insurance investigator
- Damage appraiser

Needed Skills

- College degree preferred, including two- and four-year business degrees.

- Mechanic, legal, medical, and construction backgrounds are desirable.

What's it like to work in... *Claims Adjustment*

Nate is an experienced insurance adjuster. He has worked on automobile insurance claims for two different insurance companies for more than 15 years.

Nate spends most of his time in the office but often goes out to visually inspect vehicle damage. The vehicles may be sitting in salvage lots or at the insured's home. He talks to mechanics and repair specialists regularly, so he can keep current with techniques, trends, and costs in the industry. He completes reports, meets with claimants, discusses estimates, and negotiates when there are discrepancies. It's Nate's responsibility to be both accurate and fair.

Nate likes negotiating and working with insurance claims. He understands the need to give a quick and accurate assessment of damages so the company (his employer) and the policyholder (the consumer) are both satisfied with a fair resolution of the claim.

What About You?

Would you like to assess damages and claims in order to help individuals recover from a financial or property loss? Would you consider a career as a claims adjuster?

Assessment

KEY TERMS REVIEW

Match the terms with the definitions.

_____ 1. A written amendment to an insurance policy

_____ 2. A person presumed to have permission to be on your property

_____ 3. Insurance that protects renters from property and liability risks

_____ 4. A dangerous place, condition, or object that is particularly attractive to children

_____ 5. Insurance that protects property owners from property and liability risks

a. attractive nuisance
b. co-insurance clause
c. endorsement
d. homeowner's policy
e. liability coverage
f. personal property floater
g. renter's policy
h. uninvited guest

_____ 6. Insurance coverage for the insured's movable property wherever it may be located

_____ 7. A provision requiring policyholders to insure their building for a stated percentage of its replacement value to receive full reimbursement for a loss

_____ 8. Insurance to protect against claims for bodily injury to another person or damage to another person's property

CHECK YOUR UNDERSTANDING

9. Why do renters need insurance?

10. Why is it important not to overinsure your property?

APPLY YOUR KNOWLEDGE

11. Explain why liability insurance is necessary coverage for both renters and homeowners.

THINK CRITICALLY

12. Explain why homeowners have liability for injuries to invited and uninvited guests. What can they do to lower the risks?

13. Homeowner's insurance premiums are significantly higher than renter's insurance premiums. Why?

14. Explain why homeowners with an attractive nuisance should take extra precautions in addition to increasing their liability insurance coverage. Why do homeowners have such a responsibility?

Automobile and Umbrella Insurance

AUTOMOBILE INSURANCE

Most states require minimum automobile insurance. Automobile insurance covers costs of damage to the vehicle, its owner, and any passengers. It also covers costs of repairs to other vehicles, medical expenses of occupants in other vehicles, and property damage (shrubs, trees, and fences) caused by an accident. Standard policies also cover theft of the vehicle and/or its contents.

COST OF AUTOMOBILE INSURANCE

Automobile insurance is expensive. *Premiums* are based on a number of factors, such as:

- Model, style, and age of car
- Driver classification (age, sex, marital status, driving record)
- Location (city, county) of driver and car
- Distances driven
- Purpose of driving (such as work)
- Age, sex, and marital status of other regular drivers of the car

Premium discounts are available for certain conditions, such as more than one vehicle insured with the same company, driver's education training, and good grades in high school and college (usually a B average or better).

How are premiums set for car insurance?

© Photodisc/Getty Images

Driving Record

Your **driving record** includes the number and type of traffic tickets you've received for driving infractions and misdemeanors along with the number of accidents in which you've been involved. An *infraction* is a minor violation, punishable only by a fine, and includes such things as a parking violation, failure to come to a complete stop at a stop sign, or an improper left-hand turn. More serious offenses, called *misdemeanors*, may incur fines as well as jail time. Examples include speeding, driving without a license, or reckless driving. Very serious traffic violations, such as drunk driving, hit and run, or leaving the scene of an accident, can cause insurance premiums to rise dramatically. Many insurance companies use *point systems* to calculate premiums, For example, a traffic infraction might count as 1 point and a misdemeanor might count as 5 points. When you reach 3 points, your premiums rise. If you reach 10 points, your policy could be canceled.

What is the difference between an infraction and a misdemeanor?

Type of Car

Except for vintage (antique) cars, older cars should require less insurance than newer cars because older cars are worth less. New and expensive cars cost more to insure because they are worth more and would therefore be more expensive to repair or replace.

Statistics

As you learned in Chapter 25, insurers base their premiums on statistical probabilities. From their analysis, insurers determine that some drivers have a higher probability of getting into accidents than others. For example, young, single drivers are statistically more likely to be involved in an accident than married drivers over 25. Thus, young drivers pay higher premiums.

Similar statistics may cause insurers to charge higher premiums on sports cars than on family cars. Certain geographic locations (such as large cities) have had higher accident rates. As a result, insurers charge higher rates to drivers in these areas.

Other Factors

The farther you drive on a regular basis (such as to work), the higher your insurance premiums. Who will be driving the car is also a factor in setting premiums. Adding a teenage driver to an existing policy will increase premiums. Another important consideration is the number of claims filed. When you file too many claims, your premiums rise. Also, when you are in an accident that is your fault and your insurance company has to pay claims, you are likely to see a *surcharge*, which effectively increases your premium for three years or longer.

▮ TYPES OF AUTOMOBILE INSURANCE COVERAGE

There are five basic types of automobile insurance.

- Liability
- Collision
- Comprehensive
- Personal injury protection (PIP)
- Uninsured/underinsured motorist

When all of these types are purchased together in a single policy, it is known as *full coverage*. Figure 26.4 shows a comparison of coverages for automobile insurance.

Liability Coverage

Most states require all drivers to carry *liability insurance*. The purpose of liability coverage is to protect the insured against claims for bodily injury to another person or damage to another person's property. It pays nothing toward the insured's own losses, either personal injury or damage to the vehicle. However, if an accident is legally not your fault, the other driver's liability coverage will pay for damages to your car. If the accident is your fault and all you have is liability coverage, your insurance will not pay for the damages to your car.

Liability insurance coverage is usually described using a series of numbers, such as 100/300/50. These numbers mean that the insurer will pay up to $100,000 for injury to one person, $300,000 total for all people, and $50,000 for property damage per accident. Premiums charged for liability insurance vary according to the amount of coverage.

FIGURE 26.4	Automobile Insurance		
		Who Is Protected	
		Policyholder	**Other Persons**
Liability coverage:			
Personal injuries		No	Yes
Property damage		No	Yes
Collision coverage:			
Damage to insured vehicle		Yes	No
No-fault provision		Yes	No
Comprehensive coverage:			
Damage to insured vehicle		Yes	No
Personal injury protection:			
Medical payments		Yes	Yes
Pedestrian coverage		Yes	No
Uninsured/underinsured motorist coverage:			
Bodily injury		Yes	Yes

Collision Coverage

Collision coverage is automobile insurance that protects your own car against damage from accidents or vehicle overturning. This coverage will pay for the damage to your car in the event you are at fault and the other driver's liability insurance does not have to pay. Most collision coverage has a deductible. For example, you may have to pay the first $500 (or whatever deductible is specified by your policy) for repairs, and the insurer pays the rest. Many minor traffic accidents involve damage that costs less than the deductible. However, it may be wise to have a higher deductible and pay lower premiums to save money. In other words, paying the first $1,000 for each accident would be less expensive in the long run than having a $500 deductible and paying higher premiums.

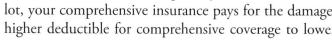
What is the difference between collision coverage and comprehensive coverage?

Comprehensive Coverage

Comprehensive coverage protects you from damage to your car from causes other than collision or vehicle overturning. The causes might be fire, theft, tornado, hail, water, falling objects, natural disasters, and acts of vandalism. For example, if your car is scratched while parked in a mall lot, your comprehensive insurance pays for the damage. You can also choose a higher deductible for comprehensive coverage to lower your premium.

Personal Injury Protection (PIP)

Also known as medical coverage insurance, **personal injury protection (PIP)** is automobile insurance that pays for medical, hospital, and funeral costs of the insured and his or her family and passengers, regardless of fault. If the insured is injured as a pedestrian or bicyclist, this insurance will pay the medical costs. To reduce costs for this kind of insurance, consider buying a car with airbags, antilock brakes, and other safety devices that lower the risk of injury.

Uninsured/Underinsured Coverage

Uninsured/underinsured coverage is automobile insurance that pays for your injuries when the other driver is legally liable but unable to pay. In other words, if the other driver is legally at fault for the accident but has no insurance or insurance that is insufficient to cover the costs, your insurer will pay your medical costs. This coverage also protects you as a pedestrian if you are hit by an uninsured vehicle.

NO-FAULT INSURANCE

Many states have passed no-fault insurance laws. These laws set up a system of compensation for auto accidents that does not require a legal determination of who was at fault before claims are paid. **No-fault insurance** is automobile insurance in which drivers receive reimbursement for their expenses from their own insurer, no matter who caused the accident.

The basic idea behind no-fault insurance is to avoid the years of legal battling required to settle a case and determine fault. Even then, drivers with no assets and no insurance would not be able to fix the other driver's car or pay for damages resulting from their negligence. It was also hoped that by reducing the number of lawsuits, more money could go to injured people in a timelier manner.

ASSIGNED-RISK POLICIES

If you have an accident that costs your insurer large sums of money, the insurer may cancel your policy. The number of traffic citations and fines on your record may also cause your insurer to drop you. If so, you may not be able to find another insurer willing to insure you.

Every state has an **assigned-risk pool** that consists of people who are unable to obtain automobile insurance due to the high risk they present. The state assigns these people to different insurers in the state. The insurers must then provide coverage. However, the insurance premiums may cost the insured several times the normal rate until the risky driver is able to re-establish a good driving record.

UMBRELLA LIABILITY INSURANCE

People who maintain required liability coverage on their automobile and residence can also purchase an umbrella policy that picks up where the other coverage leaves off. **Umbrella liability insurance** supplements your basic auto and property liability coverage by expanding limits and including additional risks.

Umbrella liability insurance would generally pay up to $1 million or $2 million for any accidental injuries caused to another person while you are driving or for an accident that occurred on your property or in the course of your employment. This type of policy protects you from *extraordinary losses*, which are extremely high claims because of unusual circumstances. For example, you may be involved in an automobile accident in which a person receives a permanent injury. Medical costs may exceed $500,000 with additional costs for many years to come. As long as you carry the required liability coverage on your automobile insurance, the umbrella policy will cover the rest.

NET Bookmark

SafeAuto Insurance Company sells auto insurance that meets the required minimum limits for the 14 states in which it offers its services. Access www.cengage.com/school/pfinance/mypf and click on the link for Chapter 26. Browse through the SafeAuto site, then answer: What type of customer do you think would most likely purchase auto insurance from a company like SafeAuto? Why? Do you think it is wise to purchase only the minimum amount of liability insurance required by law? Explain your answer.

www.cengage.com/school/pfinance/mypf

ISSUES IN YOUR WORLD

DRIVING UNINSURED

In most states, drivers are legally required to have liability insurance. This insurance protects others from loss when the accident is not their fault. Still, many people drive uninsured, even though it is against the law. For uninsured drivers, the following are some likely consequences:

- *They may be cited for failure to have insurance. The fine for this offense can be severe.*

- *Their citation may subject them to state financial responsibility laws. These laws would require them to file special forms with the state each year, proving they have insurance or the ability to pay for damages they may cause. Filing these forms will cause them to have even higher insurance rates.*

- *Because they do not have insurance, an accident may be deemed their fault automatically, requiring them to pay for damages.*

- *Continued lack of insurance, following a citation, can result in jail time, loss of driving privileges, and large fines.*

    Uninsured motorists also cause consequences to others on the road.

- *Because people drive without insurance, or without enough insurance, other drivers must carry uninsured/underinsured motorist coverage. This raises the cost of insurance for everyone.*

- *When insured drivers file claims that their insurance company must pay because the other driver was uninsured, this loss may be counted against the policyholders. Thus, another person's failure to have insurance can result in your premiums being increased.*

- *It may take longer to process claims and get your car repaired when an uninsured driver is at fault.*

    So, obey the law and carry the required insurance. You as well as everyone else will benefit.

THINK CRITICALLY

1. *Do you know of someone or have you read about a person who had an accident in which the party at fault had no insurance? What were the consequences?*

2. *What are the requirements for car insurance in your state? Does your state have a no-fault law? What is the penalty for those who disobey your state law?*

Assessment

KEY TERMS REVIEW

Match the terms with the definitions. Some terms may not be used.

_____ 1. *Automobile insurance that pays for your injuries when the other driver is legally liable but unable to pay*

_____ 2. *A supplement to your basic auto and property liability coverage that expands limits and includes additional risks*

_____ 3. *A group of people who are unable to obtain automobile insurance due to high risk*

_____ 4. *Automobile insurance that protects you from damage to your car from causes other than collision or vehicle overturning*

_____ 5. *Automobile insurance that protects your own car against damage from accidents*

a. *assigned-risk pool*

b. *collision coverage*

c. *comprehensive coverage*

d. *driving record*

e. *no-fault insurance*

f. *personal injury protection (PIP)*

g. *umbrella liability insurance*

h. *uninsured/ underinsured coverage*

_____ 6. *Automobile insurance in which drivers receive reimbursement from their own insurer, no matter who caused the accident*

_____ 7. *Automobile insurance that pays for medical, hospital, and funeral costs of the insured's family and passengers, regardless of fault*

CHECK YOUR UNDERSTANDING

8. *Why do young, single drivers generally pay higher automobile insurance premiums than do married drivers over 25?*

9. *What is the purpose of no-fault insurance laws?*

APPLY YOUR KNOWLEDGE

10. *Liability coverage (automobile insurance) is required in all states. What is the reasoning behind this requirement?*

THINK *CRITICALLY*

11. *What are some things you and your family can do now to reduce overall automobile insurance premium costs? What can you do to help?*

12. *Explain why comprehensive coverage is of lesser value to drivers of older (but not classic) cars. What type of risk management strategy is effective for owners of older cars?*

13. *Explain why a person who has substantial assets and income should consider adding an umbrella policy to his or her insurance coverage.*

Chapter (Assessment)

SUMMARY

26.1

- *Renter's insurance protects your possessions at home, in the car, and at work and pays medical costs if someone is injured in your rented home.*

- *Homeowner's insurance includes personal property and liability protections plus coverage for the building itself. It protects against three risks: hazards, crimes, and liability.*

- *Insurers will reimburse no more than replacement value, so overinsuring will result in higher premiums with no additional benefits.*

- *An endorsement is a written amendment to an insurance policy often used to add coverage.*

- *The co-insurance clause requires you to insure your building for a stated percentage of its replacement value to receive full reimbursement for a loss.*

- *A personal property floater covers valuable moveable property generally not covered by basic policies.*

- *Liability coverage protects you in the event that a guest, invited or uninvited, is injured on your property and for damage you cause to others' property. A homeowner is generally not responsible for losses to a trespasser, except in cases where the property has an attractive nuisance.*

26.2

- *Factors such as type of car, driver classification, driving record, coverage desired, distances driven, purpose of driving, and deductibles affect auto insurance premiums.*

- *Liability coverage protects others who may be injured or have property damage as a result of your actions or negligence.*

- *Collision coverage repairs damage to your vehicle when you are at fault in an accident.*

- *Comprehensive coverage protects your vehicle from noncollision losses, such as from theft, storms, and falling objects.*

- *Uninsured/underinsured motorist coverage protects you in the event the other driver is uninsured or does not have enough insurance.*

- *No-fault insurance laws require insurers to pay the losses of their own policyholders rather than requiring the at-fault driver's insurer to pay.*

- *Umbrella liability insurance may be purchased to expand coverage and reimbursement limits.*

APPLY WHAT YOU KNOW

1. Prepare a household inventory, listing only the contents of your room or another room in your home. Follow Figure 26.2 as an example. Next to each item, record its approximate value and indicate whether or not you have a receipt to prove its cost and a photo of each item.

2. Write a paper discussing the perils of overinsuring or underinsuring property. Be specific in the consequences that may result in either case. How can you be sure that you are insuring property for its appropriate replacement value?

3. Outline ways you can protect valuables from being stolen from your home or automobile. Research the cost of protection devices or services.

4. Get a price quote for full-coverage automobile insurance on the car of your choice. Determine ways to reduce premium costs through discounts or other methods. Write a paper reporting your results.

5. Visit your state government web site and gather information to answer these questions: What types and how much insurance coverage does your state require for all drivers? How are financial responsibility laws enforced? For example, is vehicle insurance tied to vehicle registration? What are the fines or penalties if a driver is caught without insurance?

6. Visit the web sites of two insurers and list the features of each insurer's basic automobile policy. How are their coverages alike or different? If possible, get a price quote from both companies for their auto policy. Which provides the best coverage for your premium dollar? What other factors should you consider when choosing an insurer?

7. Interview an insurance agent about the need for umbrella liability insurance in your state. Ask questions about coverage availability, maximum policy limits, and premium costs. Also ask about exclusions. What situations would not be covered by the umbrella policy?

MAKE ACADEMIC CONNECTIONS

8. **Math** Your friend owns a home that has a value of $180,000. Her insurance policy has an 80 percent co-insurance clause. She has the property insured for $140,000. Later that year, a tree falls on her house during a storm, causing damages of $25,000. Compute the reimbursement she will be able to collect.

9. **Communication** Write a paper about the type of insurance (property and vehicle) that you and your family need to have at this point. Explain how that will change over time, both for you and for your family. Include the reason why you have chosen insurance over some other form of risk management.

10. **Research** Do a comparative study of insurance laws in two or three states, or between two or three countries. Create a table or chart that outlines how they are similar and how they are different. Cite your sources of information.

SOLVE *PROBLEMS* AND

EXPLORE *ISSUES*

11. Megan is renting an apartment. She has nice furniture that she inherited from her grandparents. She mentions to you that last year the pipes burst in her apartment building and she was lucky that her valuable furnishings were not damaged. You ask if she has renter's insurance, and she says no. The landlord has insurance, though. How would you advise her?

12. As a first-time homebuyer, your friend Curtis is considering what type of insurance to buy. Describe the types of insurance that he might consider. (Refer to Figure 26.1.)

13. Your friend Luis is complaining about the high cost of car insurance. He would like to own his own car, but at age 19, he feels he can't afford the insurance premiums. Explain how he can reduce insurance premiums.

14. Your neighbor owns a valuable collection of antique plates. She estimates their value at more than $10,000. When talking about the plates, you learn that she has homeowner's insurance but no personal property floater for the plates. Explain to her the reason for a floater.

15. Tia has the following insurance coverages on her car:
    Comprehensive physical damage
    Bodily injury and property liability (100/200/25)
    Collision ($250 deductible)
    As a result of an accident in which she was negligent, the driver of the other car was awarded $9,800 for injuries and $2,100 in damages to his car. Tia's auto was damaged at a cost of $820. Her medical bills were $135. How much did the insurer have to pay in claims as a result of the accident? What is the maximum the policy would pay for injuries to the other driver?

EXTEND YOUR LEARNING

16. **Legal Issues** Tort lawsuits (person v. person) are civil (as opposed to criminal) actions that involve injuries caused to other persons. Negligence is a tort, and it is based on foreseeable risk. You have a duty of care to others when there is a foreseeable risk that your actions could cause injuries. Thus, even though you do not have intent to injure another, the fact that you have a duty of care that was breached and led to another's injury will make you responsible for their injuries. Unfortunately, a single event can be both a tort and a crime. You can also be held liable for criminal acts when your behavior causes injuries to others. Driving is a serious activity that has both civil and criminal liability. How can you reduce your civil and criminal liability? Why is it important for everyone to share the road and to act as a reasonable person at all times?

For related activities and links, go to **www.cengage.com/school/pfinance/mypf**

Health and Life Insurance

| 27.1 | **Health Insurance** |
| 27.2 | **Disability and Life Insurance** |

Consider **THIS**

Corrie wasn't feeling well and was sure it was strep throat. Because she had it before, she knew the symptoms.

"I need a doctor's appointment," she told her friend. "I'm insured under my mother's policy at work. I have an insurance card that allows me to see the doctor, but I have to pay a $30 copayment at the time I go to the clinic. The doctor will give me a test called a 'lab culture' to be sure that I have strep. I'll have to pay 20 percent of the cost of that test. Then I'll get a prescription, and I have a $20 copayment for that. Even with insurance, this illness will cost me $75 plus another $80 for time lost from work. Health care sure is expensive! Soon I won't be able to stay on my mom's policy any longer. That really worries me."

Health Insurance

GOALS

- Describe group and individual health insurance choices.
- Discuss common types of health insurance coverage.
- Discuss common types of health insurance plans.
- Explain Medicare and Medicaid coverage.

TERMS

- health insurance, *p. 605*
- group insurance, *p. 605*
- COBRA, *p. 606*
- coordination of benefits, *p. 606*
- Flex 125 Plan, *p. 606*
- basic health coverage, *p. 607*
- major medical coverage, *p. 607*
- stop-loss provision, *p. 608*
- HSA, *p. 609*
- HMO, *p. 609*
- PPO, *p. 610*

GROUP AND INDIVIDUAL HEALTH INSURANCE

The cost of medical care has escalated dramatically. (In 2008, it was remarked, that if the cost of gasoline had increased over the last 20 years like the cost of health care, gasoline would be more than $15 a gallon.)

People without health insurance provided through employment seek individual policies, but monthly premiums are often unaffordable. Tens of millions of Americans do not receive proper medical care because they have no insurance or because they have inadequate insurance.

Many states have implemented health care reform to meet the needs of vast numbers of uninsured people. At the same time, rising premiums have forced employers who provide health insurance for their employees to search for ways to control costs. Most are requiring employees to pay a larger share of the cost.

Health insurance is a plan for sharing the risk of high medical costs resulting from injury or illness. Like other forms of insurance, health insurance reduces individual risk by spreading it among many people. In exchange for regular premiums, the insurer promises to pay medical expenses for the treatments covered by the policy.

GROUP POLICIES

The most common type of health insurance is **group insurance**, in which all those insured have the same coverage and pay a set premium. It is most often obtained through employers. Because a group represents a large portion of

© Banana Stock/Jupiter Images

How has the rising cost of health care affected many Americans?

potential business for an insurer, a group can usually negotiate better coverage and lower premiums than individuals can get on their own.

Some employers pay the premiums as a benefit to their employees. More commonly, however, the two share the premium costs. Group plans make up over 70 percent of all health insurance issued. The insurer may not cancel the insurance of any individual group member unless the person leaves the group or the group plan itself is terminated.

COBRA

The *Consolidated Omnibus Budget Reconciliation Act*, or **COBRA**, is a law that allows people who leave employment to continue their health insurance under the company plan for a limited period of time (usually 18 months). During this period, former employees pay premiums individually for the same group coverage they had while employed. The purpose of this law is to give former employees time to obtain other insurance, either on their own or through a new employer.

Pre-Existing Conditions

The *Health Insurance Portability and Accountability Act of 1996* (HIPAA) limits the pre-existing conditions that group plans may exclude. It also makes it illegal for an insurer to deny coverage based on health status, though it does not limit the amount the insurer may charge for coverage. The purpose of the law is to increase your ability to obtain insurance when you start a new job and lower your chances of losing your current health insurance.

Double Coverage

If a family has more than one group insurance plan, the insurers will share the costs of a claim. **Coordination of benefits** is a group health insurance provision that specifies how the insurers will share the cost when more than one policy covers a claim. This provision assures that reimbursement will not exceed 100 percent of allowable expenses. For example, if a couple has two policies—one through the husband's employer and one through the wife's employer—then one policy may pay 80 percent of the medical expenses and the other the remaining 20 percent.

Flex Plans

A Section 125 Flex Plan, or **Flex 125 Plan**, is an employee benefit program that allows employees to set aside money, pretax, to help pay deductibles, copayments, and other health expenses during the year that are not covered by insurance. Many employers provide the Flex 125 Plan, but it has one significant disadvantage. If you don't use the money you set aside, you lose it (the employer keeps it).

NET Bookmark

Pre-existing conditions can make it difficult for some people to obtain health insurance. Access www.cengage.com/school/pfinance/mypf and click on the link for Chapter 27. Browse the article, then answer: What is the definition of *pre-existing condition*? Why do health insurance companies seek to exclude covering people with pre-existing conditions? According to Health Insurance Portability and Accountability Act (HIPAA) guidelines, what is the maximum amount of time that someone in a group insurance plan must wait in order to get coverage for his/her pre-existing condition? How can "credible coverage" reduce this waiting period?

www.cengage.com/school/pfinance/mypf

INDIVIDUAL POLICIES

People can also buy individual health insurance policies. The premiums are often high, depending on the type of coverage. Unlike group plans, many individual policies require a physical exam, and insurers may refuse to cover individuals with health problems (unless there are state laws prohibiting this practice). Also, individuals may have a waiting period of 30 to 90 days before coverage begins. (Members of group plans usually receive immediate coverage.)

Many states require insurers to make some type of individual policy available for purchase by individuals who do not have group policies. States may also have high-risk health insurance pools whereby people with pre-existing conditions (such as diabetes) can buy insurance. Unfortunately, the premiums can be very high, and placement on a waiting list can exclude people from coverage when they need it.

Sometimes medical costs can exceed the limits of a standard health policy. To protect against this risk, people can buy *supplemental health insurance*. This secondary policy is designed to pay high deductibles and copayments as well as medical fees that are higher than the insured's standard policy allows. For example, a standard plan may pay up to $450 a day for a hospital room, but the actual charges may come to $500 per day. A supplemental policy would pay the difference of $50 per day.

TYPES OF COVERAGE

Health insurance policies typically cover basic health expenses (medical, hospital, and surgical) and major medical costs. Some cover dental and vision needs for a higher premium. The main purpose of these kinds of coverage is to protect consumers from doctor and hospital bills that could ruin them financially.

BASIC HEALTH INSURANCE

Basic health coverage includes medical, hospital, and surgical costs. Medical coverage helps pay for physician care that does not involve surgery. This type of coverage pays for office visits and routine services, such as X-rays and laboratory tests. When the policy covers prescriptions, it often requires the use of generic rather than name-brand drugs. Hospital coverage pays hospital bills for room, board, and medication. Surgical coverage pays for part or all of a surgeon's fees for an operation. Usually, basic health insurance covers only necessary (not cosmetic or elective) surgery and excludes some types of surgery.

MAJOR MEDICAL INSURANCE

Major medical coverage provides protection against the catastrophic expenses of a serious injury or illness. Coverage is beyond basic health insurance and usually specifies a lifetime maximum, such as $1 million. For example, when a patient is admitted to the hospital for an organ transplant or some other major surgery, the cost can easily be $500,000 or more.

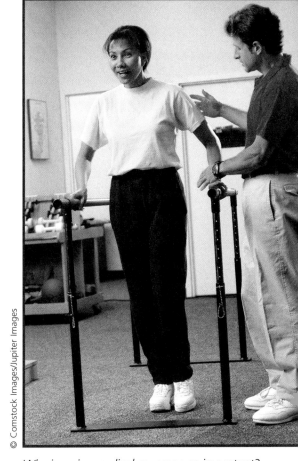

© Comstock Images/Jupiter Images

Why is major medical coverage so important?

Major medical coverage often has a co-insurance provision requiring the insured to pay some portion (such as 20 percent) of all bills. For a higher premium, a stop-loss provision could be included. A **stop-loss provision** is an insurance clause that caps or sets a maximum that the insured has to pay during any calendar year. For example, a $3,000 stop-loss means the insured would have to pay no more than $3,000 for copayments and deductibles in a year.

▮ DENTAL AND VISION INSURANCE

Some group plans also provide dental and vision coverage for an additional cost. *Dental insurance* covers basic dental services, such as exams, cleanings, X-rays, and fillings. Dental plans usually have low deductibles and co-insurance requirements of 20 percent or more. They often state upper limits, such as $1,500 per year per person. Insurers typically pay less (such as 50 percent) for some services, such as crowns or bridges.

In some cases, insurers cover only certain types of services. For example, the cost of an amalgam filling (metal) is far less than a porcelain filling. Most dental policies will pay only for amalgams except when the filling is in the front teeth. If you want a porcelain filling for a back tooth, you would have to pay the difference in cost. For instance, if your dentist charges $180 for a porcelain filling, and your insurance allows only $90, the insurance will pay 80 percent and you must pay 20 percent of the $90. In addition, you must pay the $90 difference between the dentist's fee and the allowable amount.

MATH *Minute*

CALCULATING COSTS OF SERVICES NOT FULLY PAID BY INSURANCE

John needs to have a root canal. His dental insurance will pay 80 percent of the cost. The policy sets an allowable limit for a root canal at $600. John's dentist bills his insurer for $800. How much will insurance pay? How much will Bill have to pay?

First, compute how much insurance will pay on the root canal:

$600 × .80 = $480 will be paid by insurance

Then subtract the amount paid by insurance from the total for the root canal:

$800 − $480 = $320 due from John

Based on the preceding example, compute the out-of-pocket expenses in the following situation.

Fran's dental insurance will pay 70 percent of the cost of a porcelain crown. The policy sets an allowable limit for a crown at $800. Fran's dentist bills her insurer for $1,000. How much will Fran have to pay?

Solution: $800 × .70 = $560 will be paid by insurance

$1,000 − $560 = $440 due from Fran

Vision insurance often pays for exams for eye disease as well as for prescription adjustments and lenses. Policies usually cover an eye examination on a regular basis—once every year or two—and the purchase of single-vision corrective lenses and frames. Some policies offer limited coverage for prescription sunglasses and contact lenses.

TYPES OF HEALTH PLANS

Employee or private health plans are grouped into two categories: unmanaged and managed.

UNMANAGED CARE

Unmanaged care (traditional fee-for-service) plans allow participants to choose any doctor and to be reimbursed for a portion of the expenses (usually 80 percent) incurred after a deductible is met. Deductibles often range from $100 to $1,000 per patient, or $500 or more per family. This plan is often the most expensive because control over costs and services is less strict.

A health savings account, commonly known as an **HSA**, is used in association with a medical plan that carries a high deductible ($1,100 or more). The insured basically takes the money that would have gone toward the premiums for basic health coverage and has it deposited into an HSA account. The account is then used to pay qualified medical expenses not covered by insurance, including deductibles and copayments. Contributions to the account are made pretax and are tax-deductible. If the HSA is sponsored through the employer, it may contribute to the account as well. Money withdrawn from an HSA to pay qualified medical expenses is tax-free. The remaining money in the account grows on a tax-deferred basis, like an IRA.

MANAGED CARE

Managed care plans rely on a network of health care providers. To receive maximum reimbursement, participants in a managed care plan must select doctors who belong to the network. The policy requires participants to obtain preapproval for any surgery or hospital admission and two or three doctors' opinions before allowing a major procedure to be performed. The insurer exercises significant control over the types of services provided and the maximum benefits allowed for those services. Health maintenance organizations (HMOs), preferred provider organizations (PPOs), and point of service (POS) plans are the most common types of managed care plans.

Health Maintenance Organization (HMO)

A *health maintenance organization*, commonly called an **HMO**, is a group plan offering prepaid medical care to its members. An HMO often has its own facilities and provides a full range of medical services. Patients must choose doctors on the HMO staff, including one doctor to be their *primary care physician (PCP)*, or main provider. To see a specialist, patients must get a referral from their PCP first. Otherwise, the insurance will not cover the visit to the specialist. In this way, the PCP acts as a "gatekeeper."

An advantage of belonging to an HMO is that *preventive care*, such as routine physical exams and vaccinations, are generally covered. The idea is to encourage people to come in for treatment before a minor ailment becomes a major (and expensive) problem. HMO patients usually make a copayment of $15 to $30 for an office visit. HMOs that are *capitated* (meaning "per person") receive a fixed monthly premium for each patient, regardless of whether the patient seeks medical care.

Preferred Provider Organization (PPO)

A *preferred provider organization*, commonly called a **PPO**, is a group of health care providers (doctors and hospitals, for example) who band together to provide health services for set fees. Patients can choose doctors from an approved provider list, but they can also go outside the plan for care. However, if they choose to do so, they will have to pay a larger percentage of the fee. You are not required to choose a primary care physician, and you do not need a referral to see a specialist, but the cost will be higher. There are limits on types of services that can be provided and fees that can be charged. Patients who stay within the network of providers usually must make a small copayment, such as $15 per office visit or per prescription. Because this type of plan is more flexible than an HMO, it is more expensive.

Point of Service (POS) Plan

Hybrid medical insurance plans are also available today. *Point of service (POS) plans* give people more choice and control over medical services. They combine the features of HMOs and PPOs. Like an HMO, patients must choose a primary care physician, but like a PPO, patients can choose to go outside the plan for health care. However, unless referred by the primary care physician, patients will pay more for going outside the plan than they would with a PPO. Although a POS gives you more flexibility than an HMO, its cost structure is designed to encourage participants to stay within the plan.

MEDICARE AND MEDICAID

Medicare is government-sponsored health insurance for people aged 65 or older. Medicare is run by the Social Security Administration and funded by employee payroll deductions. Like other plans, there are maximum benefits, exclusions, and other requirements. Retired people pay a monthly premium for Medicare insurance.

For an additional premium, people can buy *medigap* insurance (a supplemental private insurance policy) to pay the deductibles and copayments not covered by Medicare. These policies are available from traditional insurance companies.

Medicaid is government-sponsored health insurance for people with low incomes and limited resources. This program is designed to help families who live in poverty and are unable to afford private health insurance or medical care. Like Medicare, there are limitations and exclusions.

Also, many states have plans for their citizens who cannot afford insurance, are working but uninsured, or have been turned down by insurance companies. As with car insurance (Chapter 26), *high-risk pools* make it possible for people who are otherwise "uninsurable" to obtain some type of coverage. To find out what is available in your state, visit your state's web page or make an inquiry by phone.

ISSUES IN YOUR WORLD

UNINSURED AND UNDERINSURED IN AMERICA

All people need adequate health care to maintain a high quality of life. To have access to the quality of health care available in this country, health insurance is essential to help pay the high and rising costs. Yet Census Bureau statistics and the National Coalition on Health Care show that between 45 and 47 million Americans were uninsured in 2007. Eight in ten uninsured Americans come from working families, nearly 20 percent (8.4 million) are children, and young adults (age 18 to 24 years) are the least likely of any age group to have insurance. Every 30 seconds, an American files for bankruptcy after having a health problem. Many of these people have health insurance, but it isn't enough.

According to the Public Broadcasting Service, more than 25 million Americans were underinsured in 2007. Underinsured people spent more than 10 percent of their total income on out-of-pocket medical expenses. This rate has jumped 60 percent in the last four years. Over 6.8 million Americans spend more than a third of their total income on health care.

The United States spends nearly $100 billion per year to provide uninsured residents with health services, often for preventable diseases that physicians could have treated more efficiently with earlier diagnosis.

The United States spends a greater portion of gross domestic product on health care than any other industrialized country, yet it is the only industrialized country that does not have a national health care plan.

Lack of insurance results in poor health and shorter lives for many Americans. There are costs to society as well, such as:

- *Developmental deficiencies from insufficient health care during infancy*
- *Expenses for chronic health conditions not treated until they become emergencies*
- *Lost income due to reduced job productivity and employment*
- *Diminished overall health in the country due to low immunization and lack of access to preventive health care*
- *Health care expenses paid by taxpayers for uninsured patients*
- *Higher program costs (such as Social Security, criminal justice, and Medicare)*
- *Social inequality (with lower-income Americans being at a definite health disadvantage)*

Some say a single-payer, government-sponsored health plan is the answer. This is the type of system that exists in many other nations, such as Canada and most western European countries. Others say we can reform the system we have so that health insurance becomes portable—that is, you can take it with you from job to job. Whatever the answer, we as a country must find a way to provide access to affordable health care for all Americans.

THINK *CRITICALLY*

1. *Suppose you had no health insurance. How would this fact affect the decisions you make about your health care?*
2. *Conduct some Internet research about the problem of uninsured Americans. Is the problem getting better or worse? Explain.*

Assessment

KEY TERMS REVIEW

Match the terms with the definitions. Some terms may not be used.

_____ 1. A group plan offering prepaid medical care to its members

_____ 2. Health insurance obtained through employers in which all insured have the same coverage and pay a set premium

_____ 3. An insurance clause that caps or sets a maximum that the insured has to pay during any calendar year

_____ 4. A law that allows insurance to continue after employment ends

_____ 5. An employee benefit program that allows employees to set aside pretax money for deductibles and copayments

_____ 6. A plan for sharing the risk of high medical costs resulting from injury or illness

_____ 7. Coverage against catastrophic expenses of a serious injury or illness

_____ 8. Coverage for medical, hospital, and surgical costs

a. basic health coverage

b. COBRA

c. coordination of benefits

d. Flex 125 Plan

e. group insurance

f. health insurance

g. HMO

h. HSA

i. major medical coverage

j. PPO

k. stop-loss provision

CHECK YOUR UNDERSTANDING

9. Why is group insurance generally less expensive than individual policies?

10. What is the purpose of COBRA?

APPLY YOUR KNOWLEDGE

11. Why are more and more employers (group policies) and individuals switching to managed care plans? Explain the advantages and disadvantages of managed care.

THINK CRITICALLY

12. Why are more and more employers expecting employees to bear a greater portion of their health care costs?

13. Explain why people who are in good health might prefer to have high-deductible medical insurance with an HSA.

14. Explain the concept of capitation and how it may be contrary to patients' best interests.

Disability and Life Insurance

DISABILITY INSURANCE

Disability insurance is an insurance plan that makes regular payments (usually monthly) to replace income lost when illness or injury prevents the insured from working. This type of insurance is frequently referred to as *income protection*, because coverage compensates workers for loss of income resulting from serious illness or injury. Generally there are two types of disability insurance: short term and long term. Short-term disability insurance typically provides benefits for up to six months but can last as long as two years. Long-term disability insurance usually picks up where short-term disability leaves off and can provide coverage up to retirement.

Of all the types of insurance, disability insurance is the most overlooked. People think nothing can happen to them that will interrupt their earning power. Unfortunately, recovery from an accident or an illness can extend for weeks or even months. Yet while you are disabled (unable to perform your job), your regular living expenses go on.

Disability coverage requires a *waiting period*. Benefits don't begin the day you become disabled. The waiting period may be from 1 to 14 days for short-term disability or from 60 to 180 days for long-term disability. During this time, you would likely be on sick leave from work and would be collecting regular pay. Benefits begin after the waiting period and end as soon as you can return to work.

The maximum *duration of benefits* under most disability policies is until age 65 or early retirement if you qualify. A few policies pay benefits for life if you become permanently disabled. In addition, the maximum amount you can collect is usually 50 to 75 percent of your regular pay.

Guaranteed renewability of coverage will protect you against cancellation if your health declines. Without this provision, an insurer could refuse to renew your insurance. The premium for a policy with guaranteed renewability is higher, but the coverage may be worth the extra cost.

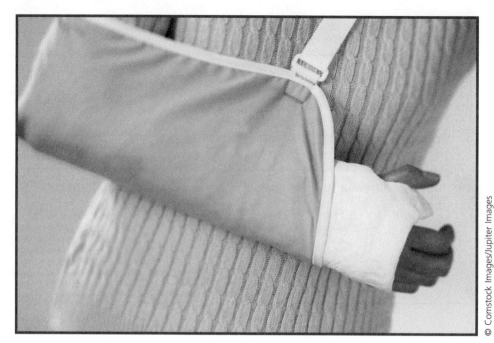

Why is disability insurance the most overlooked type of insurance?

© Comstock Images/Jupiter Images

GROUP DISABILITY INSURANCE

Group disability insurance plans are generally the least expensive option. In many cases, the employer pays for part or all of the plan. However, the insurance is good only as long as you work for the employer. If you leave the company, you lose all policy rights.

SOCIAL SECURITY DISABILITY INSURANCE

Most workers in the United States participate in the Social Security program. As you learned in Chapter 5, Social Security is more than retirement income. Social Security is OASDI (old age, survivors, and disability insurance) as well as HI (health insurance—Medicare). Because you have Social Security taxes deducted from your paycheck, you are entitled to disability payments from Social Security in the event you become disabled and cannot work. To qualify, you will have to prove the extent of your disability, fill out forms, and have medical exams as required by the Social Security Administration. Workers are considered disabled if they have a physical or mental condition that prevents them from doing any gainful work and the condition is expected to last for at least 12 months or result in death. Benefits are determined in part by your pay and in part by the number of years you have been covered under Social Security. The work requirement may be waived for certain individuals, including the blind, widows or widowers with disabilities, children with disabilities, and wounded military service members.

WORKERS' COMPENSATION INSURANCE

You learned in Chapter 5 that workers' compensation is insurance that covers your expenses if your injury or illness resulted from your job. If you are permanently disabled—partially or totally—workers' compensation will pay monthly benefits. This insurance also carries a death benefit. It provides a burial payment and an allowance for living expenses for survivors of people killed on the job. Like Social Security benefits, these benefits are determined by your earnings and your work history.

LIFE INSURANCE

Life insurance provides funds to the beneficiaries when the insured dies. Consider the financial needs that a family will face after the death of a wage earner—and how much income will be needed to pay the ongoing expenses of daily living. The purpose of life insurance, then, is to provide for those who depend on you as a source of income. Figure 27.1 shows a list of purposes that life insurance can fulfill. As you can see, some types of life insurance provide savings as well as death benefits.

Like all types of insurance, life insurance is based on risk sharing and probability. To predict the probability of death at different ages, insurers use *mortality tables*. These tables are based on statistics gathered about life expectancy and death rates among various groups of people. Insurers set premiums based on these tables. For example, older people have a higher probability of dying while the policy is in effect than do younger people. As a result, insurers generally charge older people higher premiums. Other factors enter the calculation as well. For example, smokers tend to die sooner than nonsmokers, and premiums reflect this. Someone with a serious health problem, such as heart disease, may not be able to buy an individual life insurance policy at all.

To buy individual life insurance policies, you will have to supply a detailed medical history. You may be required to have a medical examination, especially for large policies. You may be able to buy inexpensive group life insurance through your employer. A *group life insurance plan* insures a large number of people under the terms of a single policy without a medical examination. Employers often provide group life insurance as an employee benefit. Today, recent laws require that these policies be portable. **Portability** means that when you leave your employer, you are able to continue paying the premiums and convert your group policy into an individual policy.

FIGURE 27.1   *Purposes of Life Insurance*

Why You Should Purchase Life Insurance

- to provide cash to pay for a funeral
- to pay off a home mortgage and other debts at the time of death
- to provide a lump-sum payment to children when they reach a specified age
- to provide an education or income for children
- to make charitable bequests after death
- to provide for retirement income
- to accumulate savings
- to make estate and inheritance tax payments
- to take care of children's needs as they are growing up (including child care services in the event of the death of a parent)
- to provide cash value that can be borrowed

Why are younger people generally charged lower life insurance premiums?

© Image Ideas/Jupiter Images

■ PROVISIONS OF LIFE INSURANCE POLICIES

An important provision in every life insurance policy is the right to name your beneficiary. As you previously learned, beneficiaries are the people named in an insurance policy who will receive the benefits of the policy. The beneficiaries of a life insurance policy will receive the amount specified in the policy upon the death of the insured. Beneficiaries can be anyone; if children are minors, parents may name a trustee or guardian to handle the money on behalf of the children.

An **incontestable clause** is a provision of a life (or health) insurance policy stating that once the policy has been in effect for a stated period of time (usually two years), the insurer may no longer question items on the application in order to deny coverage. For example, an applicant may lie about their age or a previous medical condition. After the specified period, the insurer cannot dispute the policy's validity during the lifetime and after the death of the insured for any reason. A reason for this provision is that the beneficiaries should not be made to suffer because of acts of the insured.

A life insurance *rider* is a small insurance policy that modifies the coverage of the main policy. A rider usually adds or excludes some types of coverage or alters policy benefits. Insurers offer many riders, and the costs can add up. A *waiver of premium* rider allows you to stop paying premiums and keep your coverage in force if you become disabled and cannot work. This rider usually does not kick in until you've been disabled at least six months.

Guaranteed insurability riders give you the right to renew a policy or buy additional coverage regardless of changes in health. Many insurers also offer accidental death riders. In the case of accidental death, some riders provide for double indemnity. **Double indemnity** means that the beneficiary is paid double the face amount of the insurance policy.

■ TYPES OF LIFE INSURANCE

There are two main types of life insurance: temporary and permanent. **Temporary life insurance** lasts for a specified period, such as 20 years. After that time, it ceases to exist. *Permanent life insurance* lasts for life. It has stated premiums over time and cannot be canceled by the insurance company. Both types of life insurance have advantages and disadvantages.

Temporary Life Insurance

The most common form of temporary life insurance is term insurance. **Term life insurance** is a life insurance policy that remains in effect for a specified

An insurance agent's income is usually based on commissions. Some people believe that insurance agents will sell as much insurance as possible, with little regard to the actual needs of their customers. They will encourage people to buy permanent insurance with a high face value as an investment when, in reality, only temporary insurance is needed to meet temporary needs. These people believe that permanent insurance is a poor savings and investing plan. Others believe that people should carry large amounts of life insurance as a way to leave an estate for their heirs. They also feel that permanent insurance is a good investment because it forces you to save money.

THINK *CRITICALLY*

With which side do you agree? Why? How much insurance do you think is needed by the average person of your age?

period of time. If the insured survives beyond that time, coverage ceases with no remaining value. Term policies are sometimes called "pure" life insurance because they have value only if the covered risk (death) occurs while the policy is in effect. They have no savings component, as permanent life policies do. Parents often buy 15- or 20-year term policies to cover the financial needs of their children in case they should die while the children are still young. By the time the term policy ends, the children will be grown and out on their own, so the parents no longer feel a need to provide for their children.

With *decreasing term insurance*, the amount of coverage decreases each year while the premium remains the same. A 20-year decreasing term policy decreases in coverage each year until the value reaches zero at the end of 20 years. If the insured dies during the first year of the policy, it pays the full benefit (let's say $100,000). If the insured dies during the second year, death benefits decrease to, say, $95,000. So, the coverage of the policy decreases by a specified amount each year. In contrast, the death benefit on *level term insurance* remains constant from beginning to end. Although it can be used for any purpose, decreasing term insurance is often sold for the purpose of paying off a mortgage in the event of death. The value of decreasing term insurance decreases over time as does the principal in a mortgage.

Another type of temporary life insurance is *credit life*, or some version of it such as mortgage life insurance. This insurance can be used only to repay a specific debt should the borrower die before doing so. You can obtain this type of coverage through the lender. However, in most cases it would be cheaper to buy term insurance that can be applied to any debt.

Renewable term insurance gives the policyholder the right to renew each year, without having to pass a physical exam. Premiums increase with each renewal because the policyholder is older (and the risk of death greater), but the death benefits remain the same.

Term insurance policies can have additional features, such as optional conversion to a permanent life policy. Additional features generally raise premiums, however, and beyond a certain age, term insurance may not be renewable. The main advantage of term insurance is its low cost.

What added benefit does permanent life insurance provide?

Permanent Life Insurance

Permanent life insurance remains in effect for the insured's lifetime and builds a cash value. **Cash value** is the savings accumulated in a permanent life insurance policy that you would receive if you canceled your policy. You could also borrow using your policy's cash value as collateral. If you do not repay the loan, the policy will repay it out of the death benefit when you die.

Four common types of permanent life policies are whole life, limited-pay life, universal life, and variable life.

- *Whole life* (also known as straight or ordinary life) is a policy for which you pay fixed premiums throughout your life, and the policy pays a stated sum at death to your beneficiary. The amount of your premium depends primarily on the age at which you purchase the policy. The premiums are high enough to pay for the death benefit plus contribute to the policy's cash value.

- *Limited-pay life* is a policy on which premiums are limited to a specific number of years (such as 20 years) or until age 65. At the end of the payment period, the policy is considered "paid up." However, you remain insured for life, and the company will pay the face value of the policy at your death.

- *Universal life* combines a savings plan with a death benefit. However, unlike the others, the premiums and death benefit on a universal life policy are not fixed. The policyholder can choose to change the death benefit and the amount or timing of premiums during the life of the policy. Thus, the face value of the policy can be reduced or raised without rewriting the policy. The interest rate earned on the cash value varies with short-term rates in the economy.

- *Variable life* combines a death benefit with investment options. The insurer invests part of the premiums in securities chosen by the policyholder. Policyholders designate what portion of the net premium (the amount left over after paying for the death benefits) is to be invested in stocks, bonds, or short-term money market instruments. Both the death benefit and the cash value rise (or fall) with the investment results. While a minimum death benefit is guaranteed, there is no guaranteed cash value. With some variable life policies, policyholders pay fixed premiums. With others, the premiums can fluctuate because the interest earned on investments may be applied to the premiums, thus reducing the amount the policyholder pays.

Insurance companies write policies to protect consumers from financial loss. Underwriters decide if insurance will be provided to applicants and under what terms. They identify and calculate risk of loss, establish who receives a policy, determine the right premium, and write policies to cover the risk.

When underwriters underestimate the risk, the insurance company pays out excessive claims. When they overestimate risk, the insurance company loses customers. Using computers, the underwriters must do a careful analysis of risk factors to determine the end decisions.

Underwriters specialize in one type of insurance: life, health, mortgage, or property. Life and health underwriters specialize in group or individual policies. Any time an insurance policy is written, an underwriter has assessed the risk.

Employment Outlook

- Slower than average employment growth is expected.

Job Titles

- Insurance underwriters
- Property value analyst
- Group risk analyst

Needed Skills

- College degree preferred, especially in business and accounting.
- Good judgment and analytical and computer skills are essential.

What's it like to work in...
Insurance Underwriting

Stefanie is an experienced group health insurance underwriter. She knows how to analyze data for a group of similarly sized employers and develop a risk assessment that will be used to set their annual premiums.

Stefanie works mostly in her office at the computer. She uses the Internet to connect to large databases of information that help her analyze information on applications. She also spends time talking to industry representatives, attending meetings where the newest trends in data collection are discussed, and working with groups of other underwriters who share and compare techniques and results of previous analyses.

Stefanie is detailed oriented and takes the time to do a thorough and accurate job. She realizes the importance of assessing risk accurately so that premiums reflect a positive profitability ratio for her company. As an accounting major in college, Stefanie learned the many ways of preparing ratios and charting their statistical probabilities.

What About You?

Would you like to work with numbers and large amounts of data over time? Are you analytical, accurate, and detail oriented? Would you enjoy working as an insurance underwriter where you are able to assess and predict risk?

Assessment

KEY TERMS REVIEW

Match the terms with the definitions. Some terms may not be used.

_____ 1. The feature that allows a group policy to be converted into an individual policy

_____ 2. A life insurance policy that remains in effect for a specified period of time

_____ 3. The savings accumulated in a permanent life insurance policy

_____ 4. Insurance that provides funds to the beneficiaries when the insured dies

_____ 5. Life insurance that remains in effect for the insured's lifetime and builds a cash value

_____ 6. A provision that prevents denial of coverage after a period of time

a. cash value

b. disability insurance

c. double indemnity

d. incontestable clause

e. life insurance

f. permanent life insurance

g. portability

h. temporary life insurance

i. term life insurance

_____ 7. An insurance plan that makes payments to replace income lost when illness or injury prevents the insured from working

_____ 8. A rider that allows the beneficiary to be paid double the face amount of the insurance policy in the event of accidental death

CHECK YOUR UNDERSTANDING

9. Why do insurers use mortality tables?

10. How is universal life insurance different from other permanent life policies?

APPLY YOUR KNOWLEDGE

11. Life insurance is designed to protect those left behind when you die. How much life insurance do you need at this point in your life? How will your insurance needs change over your lifetime?

THINK CRITICALLY

12. Why is it a good idea for people to have disability insurance, even when it is not available through their employer?

13. Employers often provide group life insurance policies for employees. The policies are often portable, and employees are allowed to buy additional coverage. Explain why this is a good idea for many workers.

14. Why do financial advisers recommend term insurance instead of permanent insurance?

Chapter Assessment

SUMMARY

27.1

- Group health insurance policies provide broad coverage at lower rates than do individual policies.

- COBRA allows people who leave their jobs to keep their employer-provided health insurance for a limited time.

- HIPAA limits exclusions for pre-existing conditions and makes it illegal to deny coverage based on health status.

- A Flex 125 Plan allows employees to set aside money, pretax, to help pay deductibles, copayments, and other health expenses not covered by insurance.

- People without a group plan can buy individual health insurance, but they may have to pass a physical exam.

- Typical health insurance includes basic medical and major medical coverage. Some offer dental and vision coverage for a higher premium.

- Unmanaged care plans allow employees to select their own providers and be reimbursed a percentage of expenses after a deductible. An HSA may be used in association with a high-deductible medical plan.

- Managed care plans contract with a network of health care providers. With an HMO, patients must choose providers from within the network. A PPO is more flexible and allows patients to choose doctors outside the plan. A POS combines features from HMOs and PPOs.

27.2

- Disability insurance replaces your income if you are injured or ill and cannot work. Social Security and workers' compensation insurance provide some disability insurance benefits.

- Life insurance provides funds to beneficiaries when the insured dies.

- Insurers set life insurance premiums based on life expectancy and death rates compiled in mortality tables.

- Temporary life insurance remains in effect for a specified time. If the insured survives beyond that time, coverage ceases with no remaining value. Term life insurance is the most common type of temporary life insurance.

- Permanent life insurance remains in effect for the insured's lifetime and has a savings component (cash value) as well as a death benefit. Common types of permanent life policies are whole life, limited-pay life, universal life, and variable life.

APPLY WHAT YOU KNOW

1. Interview a person who has recently had surgery or been in the hospital for several days or longer. Ask this person about the type of services provided and the approximate cost per day of those services. Ask him or her how much of the cost was paid by insurance and how much (percentage or dollar amount) he or she will have to pay. Write a report on your findings.

2. Obtain a brochure describing the benefits of a group health insurance plan. If you don't know someone who belongs to this type of plan, your local library and the Internet will have information about group plans. Write a paper summarizing your findings regarding the types of coverage available and their provisions for deductibles, copayments, exclusions, and so on.

3. Search the Internet for information on Medicare. A good place to start is the government site for Medicare at www.medicare.gov. Find out what types of medical/hospital/surgical and major medical coverage it provides and how much of these costs the patients must pay. Then look into medigap insurance. Based on your findings, do you feel that medigap insurance is a good value for a person on Medicare?

4. Visit the AARP (American Association of Retired Persons) web site and describe the products and services it offers to its members, including supplemental health insurance. Do you see value to these services for someone who is 50 or older but not yet age 65 and retired?

5. Assuming that you are working full time, are married, and have one child, prepare an analysis of your disability needs. Select a career that you would like to have and use a realistic income figure for someone with one to three years of experience.

6. Examine the list of life insurance needs shown in Figure 27.1. Can you add anything to this list? Would you delete anything? Prepare a list of life insurance needs based on your personal situation as you imagine it will be in ten years.

MAKE ACADEMIC CONNECTIONS

7. **Math** Compute the out-of-pocket expenses in the following situation. Tom's medical insurance will pay 80 percent of the cost of a procedure. The policy sets an allowable limit for the procedure at $1,000. Tom's doctor bills the insurer for $1,300. How much will Tom have to pay?

8. **Communication** Write a paper about the uninsured and underinsured in this country. Conduct Internet research to get current statistics. What can be done to resolve the problem? How can we control medical costs and make medical care affordable to all citizens?

9. **Research** Choose a permanent life insurance policy that meets your needs and decide on the amount of coverage you want. Then, visit an insurer in person or online to find out more about the policy and its premiums. Write a report summarizing why you selected the policy and what you learned about it from the insurer.

SOLVE PROBLEMS AND

EXPLORE ISSUES

10. Your friend is considering two career opportunities—one in which she would be an independent contractor and have no benefits provided, and one in which she would work as an employee of a company and have full health insurance as well as other benefits. Explain to her the importance of having health insurance and how her options for insurance might differ, depending on which of the two career choices she makes.

11. A young couple is a dual-income family. Both have full medical coverage provided through their employers. They believe that this "double coverage" will pay off if they get injured or become ill because they can claim benefits twice. Explain to them the concept of coordination of benefits for group health insurance policies such as theirs.

12. Your cousin is working but cannot afford to buy an individual health insurance policy. His employer does not provide a group plan. Explain to him the importance of purchasing major medical coverage.

13. Your friend Devon is working full time at two jobs in order to make house payments and buy a new car. His wife Cara is working nights so she can care for the children during the day. Devon can purchase both short-term and long-term disability insurance for a small premium ($10 a month) through his employer's group insurance plan. Explain to them the importance of disability insurance.

14. As a young, unmarried person, you are contemplating college next year and the pursuit of a professional degree that will take six years or more to complete. A neighbor sells life insurance and wants you to buy a universal life policy with a $100,000 face value. Explain whether or not you would consider purchasing this policy. Would you consider purchasing a different type of policy?

15. You and your spouse are in your mid-twenties. You are expecting your first child. Both of you are presently working. You hope to buy your first house in the next few years. Discuss your need for life insurance and the type of life insurance you would purchase now and five years from now.

EXTEND YOUR LEARNING

16. **Legal Issues** *It is common practice today for employers to discontinue health insurance coverage when employees retire. If individuals are 65 or older, it isn't usually a problem—they can go on Medicare. But when people are forced to retire, or they must retire due to health or other conditions, they may be unable to pay the premiums for an individual health insurance policy. Thus many older Americans live in fear of incurring high medical expenses that would drain their savings. Should employers be required by law to keep retired employees on their group policies until they turn age 65? What are the likely consequences of such a law?*

For related activities and links, go to www.cengage.com/school/pfinance/mypf

Carl Michael Edwards, II

Born August 15, 1979 in Columbia, Missouri, Carl Edwards has a long and inspiring life in car racing. He grew up in Missouri watching his father (Carl Sr.) race. Carl Jr.'s career began in 1993 when he started racing four-cylinder mini-sprints at age 13. During 1994 and 1995, he won 18 races.

Carl attended the University of Missouri and completed his education degree. He was substitute teaching when he began racing in NASCAR. His big break came in 2002 when he competed in seven NASCAR Craftsman truck series events. In 2003, he was awarded NASCAR truck series Rookie of the Year. His Rookie of the Year award led to many other races and wins, followed by honors and points standings at the end of the racing seasons. His winning racing career continues today as a driver in the NASCAR Sprint Cup Series and Nationwide Series.

Edwards learned early the basic principles of risk management on and off the track. Although Carl was on his way to a successful car racing career, he realized the importance of an education and completed his degree. A good education provides a more secure future. On the track, Carl has learned ways to reduce risk. He is well trained and practices year round. His vehicle is checked repeated times to ensure it exceeds all safety standards. As an expert driver, he does not take unnecessary chances. Because his sport is physically demanding, Carl takes care of his health to reduce his chances of injury.

Carl is also practicing risk management when it comes to his future. His career path is on a dual track. He has a new record label, Back40 Records, a company he started in high school. His label helps local musical artists realize their dream. Carl is giving back to the community while helping to secure his financial future should he someday decide to end his car racing career.

© AP Photo/Terry Renna

THINK *CRITICALLY*

1. *What risk management strategies is Carl Edwards using on and off the track (risk shifting, risk avoidance, risk reduction, risk assumption)?*

2. *For those who have a high-risk career such as Carl Edwards, which types of insurance would you recommend? Explain why.*

3. *Do you think it's important for successful people to give back to the community? Why or why not?*

Managing Risk

Overview

In this project, you will apply risk and insurance concepts. You will also do some further exploring and assessing of your insurance needs. You'll learn how to compute the true cost of insurance, how to file an insurance claim, what to do if you have an accident, what you can do to reduce health insurance costs, how to use mortality tables, and how to build a good lifetime risk management plan.

You will also learn about workplace safety and emergency planning. Knowing what to do ahead of time will prevent injuries and lower overall risk to yourself and others.

THE TRUE COST OF INSURANCE

People buy insurance for protection against the risks of financial uncertainty and unexpected losses. The alternative—being uninsured—may represent large and undefined risks that can leave you feeling uncomfortable. Since the alternative of not being insured is often unacceptable, most people are covered by some type of insurance most of their lives.

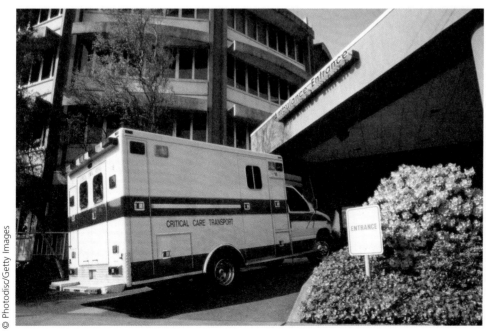

© Photodisc/Getty Images

Auto Insurance

Let's look at automobile insurance first. Your full-coverage policy might offer these coverages and annual costs:

Liability coverage, 100/300/50	$560
Collision coverage, $50 deductible	180
Comprehensive coverage, $50 deductible	90
Personal injury protection	80
Uninsured/underinsured motorist	60
Towing	15
Total annual cost	$985

If you were willing to increase the deductibles, your savings could be considerable. Let's assume that a $500 collision deductible would reduce the cost of the coverage in our example by $100 a year. Over a five-year period, your total insurance costs would be:

Full coverage, $50 deductible: $985 × 5 =	$4,925
Full coverage, $500 deductible: $885 × 5 =	4,425
Savings	$ 500

In five years, you would have saved enough in premiums to pay a $500 loss, should it occur. Check your options for saving on insurance premiums. Calculate the savings over time, and decide whether you would likely save more in premium reductions than you would likely pay out in losses.

You can also lower your premiums by reducing the limits of liability coverage from 100/300/50 to your state's minimum. This method of sharing the risk will save premium dollars, but you risk greater loss if you are at fault in an accident.

Figure U6.1 illustrates when it would be wise to reduce or drop collision coverage on your car to save on premiums.

FIGURE U6.1   *Reduce or Drop Coverage (Collision)*

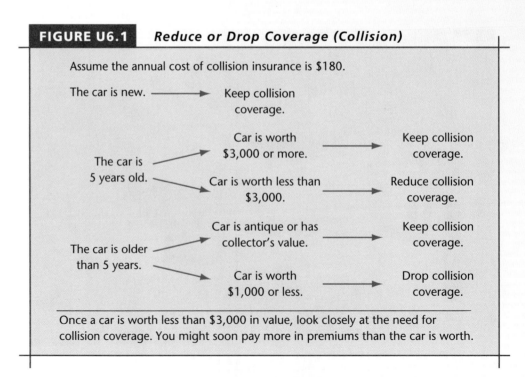

Assume the annual cost of collision insurance is $180.

The car is new. ──────▶ Keep collision coverage.

The car is 5 years old.
- Car is worth $3,000 or more. ──────▶ Keep collision coverage.
- Car is worth less than $3,000. ──────▶ Reduce collision coverage.

The car is older than 5 years.
- Car is antique or has collector's value. ──────▶ Keep collision coverage.
- Car is worth $1,000 or less. ──────▶ Drop collision coverage.

Once a car is worth less than $3,000 in value, look closely at the need for collision coverage. You might soon pay more in premiums than the car is worth.

Life Insurance

Let's now compute the cost of a whole life insurance policy and compare the results to the purchase of term insurance. To do this, we must use the time value of money concept—the fact that money will grow over time because it is earning interest.

Suppose you are age 25 and purchased a $100,000 face value whole life policy. The annual premium for this policy is $250. The policy will pay a guaranteed rate of 6 percent (on the policy's cash value) after the first year. At the end of the first year, there is no cash value. The entire premium is used to cover commissions and policy costs. After the first year, a portion of the premium covers the cost of insurance, and the rest is deposited in a savings plan. The amount deposited accumulates as cash value.

In the example on the next page, the death benefit remains at $100,000 over a five-year period. During this time, the cost of insurance rises slightly each year, leaving a smaller amount of the premium for savings. Assuming the 6 percent rate holds, the cash value of the policy after five years would be $634.95.

Whole Life Policy

Year	Premium	Insurance Cost*	Deposit	+	Interest	Cash Value at Beg. Year
			Savings Plan			
1	$ 250.00	$100.00	$ 0.00			$ 0.00
2	250.00	102.00	148.00	+	$ 0.00	148.00
3	250.00	104.00	146.00	+	8.88	302.88**
4	250.00	106.00	144.00	+	18.17	465.05
5	250.00	108.00	142.00	+	27.90	634.95
Totals	$1,250.00	$520.00	$580.00		$54.95	$634.95

* This amount represents only policy costs. Commissions are not included.

**Assume the full premium is paid at the beginning of each year. To compute the interest earned at the end of Year 2, multiply $148 by 6 percent. Then add the deposits of $148 and $146 to interest earned of $8.88 to derive the Year 3 cash balance of $302.88.

As an alternative, you could purchase term life insurance. Assume the term premiums are the same as the cost of the insurance alone in the whole life example: $100 (Year 1), $102 (Year 2), $104 (Year 3), $106 (Year 4), and $108 (Year 5). You deposit the difference between the whole life premium ($250) and the term premium at the beginning of each year in a 6 percent savings account. That is, you invest $150 in Year 1 ($250 − $100); $148 in Year 2 ($250 − $102); $146 in Year 3, and so on. With whole life insurance, the cash value is $634.95. With term insurance, the accumulated value of the savings account at the end of five years would be $873.79, as shown in the table on the next page. The difference is $238.84 ($873.79 − $634.95). In this case, you can achieve a higher savings balance through buying term insurance and saving on your own.

To practice computing the future value of savings between different policies, complete Worksheet 1 (Computing Future Value) provided for you in the *Student Activity Guide* and also presented for reference on the next page.

WORKSHEET 1
Computing Future Value

Assume that you purchased a whole life policy for $100,000 and your premiums were $300 a year, with $150 covering insurance and $150 directed to your savings plan. The insurance cost increases by $3 every year. You are guaranteed 5 percent interest on your savings for the first five years but will not earn interest until the end of the second year.

Required:

1. Prepare a table that lists how much total premium you will have paid in five years, total insurance cost for five years, and the balance in your savings portion at the end of five years for the whole life policy. (See table on page 627.)

2. How much would you have had in savings if you had bought a term policy for $150/year (for 5 years) and put the remainder in a savings account at your bank with interest compounding at the rate of 4 percent a year? (See table below.)

Invested Savings with Term Insurance Policy

Year	Beginning Balance	Deposit	Interest	Ending Balance
1	$ 0.00	$150.00	$ 9.00	$159.00
2	159.00	148.00	18.42	325.42
3	325.42	146.00	28.29	499.71
4	499.71	144.00	38.62	682.33
5	682.33	142.00	49.46	873.79*

*The total saved at the end of five years is $873.79.

HOW TO FILE AN INSURANCE CLAIM

When you have sustained a loss, such as fire damage to your home, you must file a claim. To receive compensation for the insured property, you must be organized before you file the claim. First, you should know your policy and its coverage, limitations, and exclusions.

Keep receipts and other documentation of value. If you own antiques, collectibles, or other items for which you have no receipt, have the items appraised so that you will have a certificate of authenticated value. Such an appraisal may cost $100 or more, but it will help you receive the full reimbursement due to you when you file a claim.

If property is stolen, call the police and fill out a report. Without evidence of a break-in or a police report as documentation, the insurance company has no way to verify that the incident took place. Also, you must take ordinary precautions against theft. If, for example, you leave your car unlocked, the insurer may not pay benefits for stolen property. You should have good notes about what was taken, witnesses, time of day, what you observed, and so on.

If property is damaged, you will need to get repair estimates—usually more than one. Contact your insurer right away and have documentation and notes ready. The insurance adjuster will take your report and ask you questions. It's important to be clear and accurate when supplying information. You must also take reasonable precautions to avoid further damage. For example, if a storm creates a hole in your roof, you must cover the hole as soon as possible with plastic or some other protective covering to avoid rain damage to your home's contents. If you do not act quickly to protect your property, the insurer may not pay for the extra damage.

Complete Worksheet 2 (Insurance Claim Form) provided for you in the *Student Activity Guide* and also presented for reference on the next page. It provides hypothetical information and a sample claim form, similar to one that your insurer would require you to complete to report property damage.

WHAT TO DO IF YOU HAVE A CAR ACCIDENT

Sooner or later, it is likely to happen to you. Either as a driver or as a passenger, you may be involved in an automobile accident. Most accidents are the result of human error. The higher the speed, the higher the likelihood of a serious injury and damage to property.

If you are involved in an accident, there are several things you must do. Figure U6.2 lists standard procedures to follow. Your state may have additional things you should do, or not do, following an accident. You will find

FIGURE U6.2   *What to Do If You're in an Accident*

If you are involved in a motor vehicle accident, standard requirements are as follows:

1. Stop your vehicle, turn off the ignition, and remain at the scene of the accident. If feasible, pull your car to the side of the road so you won't impede traffic.

2. Get the names and addresses of other drivers, passengers, and witnesses. Make notes of what happened, including time of day, weather conditions, roadway location, signal lights, and so on. Write down vehicle license numbers.

3. Fill out the necessary accident report forms within the time requirements in your state (usually 3 days). Give a copy of the report to your insurance company. Also obtain a copy of the police report, if any.

4. Provide assistance to persons who are injured; seek medical help if needed. Stay at the scene of the accident until all needed information is exchanged and all involved parties leave the scene.

5. Always have your insurance and vehicle registration information with you. Get insurance and vehicle registration information from the other driver; copy it from the documentation rather than taking it down orally.

6. Know the laws of your state. There may be additional requirements where you live.

WORKSHEET 2
Insurance Claim Form

Directions: Fill out the claim form below based on the following information. The insured is Mary B. Ownbey, who lives at 845 Oak Street, Wellington, Ohio 45887. Her phone number is (202) 555-0180. Her policy number is KN338-44-2281, and her agent is G. Smiley. Her home was broken into sometime between 8 p.m. and 2 a.m. (Friday evening) while she was away. The kitchen was vandalized (spray paint on the walls and eggs thrown on the floor); the carpeting in the dining room was stained as well. A police report was filed (Case 95-2288) by Officer K. Bridges. There were no witnesses. The walls in the kitchen must be scraped and painted; the carpeting must be cleaned or replaced if the stain cannot be removed. The value of the damage is estimated at $500. The house was painted last year ($100 for the kitchen walls); the carpet was new a year ago ($2,000 for the damaged carpeting). Both were purchased at Excel Interiors and she has a receipt. The property is located in the home at the above address. Use today's date.

Claim No. _____

Name of Insured _____

Address _____

_____Phone _____

Policy No. _____Agent _____

Describe what happened: _____

_____

_____

_____

Was a police report filed? _____Case No. _____
(Attach copy)

Police officer taking report _____

Were there any witnesses? _____ List their names and addresses:

_____

_____

Description of property damaged _____

Value of property _____

Date purchased _____Purchase price _____

Where purchased _____Receipt?_____

Where is property now located (for inspection)? _____

_____

_____   _____
Date   Signature of Insured

---

this information in your state's driver's manual or a similar publication from the motor vehicles division or licensing department. You should be familiar with this information before an accident occurs.

Your state has accident reporting forms. Get one and fill it out for a fictional situation. In most cases, you have only three days (72 hours) to fill out an accident report once you are in an accident.

HOW TO REDUCE HEALTH CARE COSTS

The best way to avoid high medical costs is to stay well. Corporations across America are realizing the importance of "wellness" programs in an attempt to keep their employees healthy. Here are some examples of ways to avoid illness and injury:

- Eat a balanced diet and keep your weight within reasonable limits.
- Avoid smoking.
- Don't drink to excess.
- Get sufficient rest and relaxation.
- Know your body's limitations; don't overdo it, including too much of a type of activity that could lead to injury.
- Never get in a vehicle where the driver's abilities are impaired by alcohol, anger, or any other condition.
- Don't drive if you have had anything that could impair your ability to drive, including over-the-counter and prescription drugs.
- Drive carefully; avoid and reduce risks where possible. For example, don't drive in freezing rain. If you must drive, use safety devices.

When you do use health care services, there are additional ways to minimize your costs and your insurer's costs. Figure U6.3 lists some methods of reducing health care costs and maximizing the benefit from services that you can use. Complete Worksheet 3 (Reducing Health Care Costs) provided for you in the *Student Activity Guide* and also presented for reference on the next page.

FIGURE U6.3   *How to Cut Health Care Costs*

When you are the patient, whether or not insurance is involved, you can maximize your health care dollars with the following actions:

1. Know your insurance coverage, limitations, and exclusions.

2. Take insurance information with you when visiting a hospital or doctor's office and when picking up prescriptions.

3. Take a list of questions with you to the doctor. Take notes so you will remember specific answers.

4. Give your doctor information needed to make correct diagnoses. Write down symptoms, relevant past history, what you have done or taken so far, and related information.

5. Ask the doctor about short- and long-term side effects of prescriptions. Read prescription directions and information supplied by a pharmacist and manufacturer.

6. Get second (and third) opinions for any type of surgery or medication with serious risks or potential side effects.

7. Predetermine fees for routine tests and services and look for less expensive providers. For example, have your cholesterol tested at a local clinic rather than the doctor's office.

8. Use generic medicines when possible.

9. Be cautious and ask lots of questions. Remember: You are in charge of your health, and the doctor is there to assist you, not the other way around. Take charge of your own life, nutrition, and lifestyle and know what it takes to stay healthy and strong.

LIFE EXPECTANCY AND MORTALITY TABLES

In a current edition of an almanac, you will find both life expectancy tables and mortality tables. For example, a person born in 2004 is expected to live 75.2 years (males) or 80.4 years (females). For a person who was 40 in 2004, life expectancy was another 38.0 years (males) or 42.1 years (females).

Another table shows life expectancies over time. For example, in 1920, the average life span was 54.1 years (53.6 for men and 54.6 for women). By 1970, the average life span had risen to 70.8 (67.1 for men and 74.7 for women).

Life expectancy and mortality tables are used by insurance actuaries in setting life insurance premiums. A mortality table matches age with a mortality rate and sets a premium accordingly. Figure U6.4 is part of a mortality table from the American Council of Life Insurance. Use this table to complete Worksheet 4 (Using Mortality Tables) provided for you in the *Student Activity Guide* and also presented for reference on the next page.

Age	Deaths per 1,000	Life Expectancy (Years)
25	1.11	59
30	2.33	48
40	3.21	37
45	4.58	33
50	5.86	28
55	8.44	21
60	12.88	18
65	17.22	15
70	26.10	13

WORKSHEET 4
Using Mortality Tables

Directions: Based on the mortality table above, answer the following questions:

1. At the bottom of the Life Expectancy column, what does the number 13 mean?

2. On average, people who are 50 years old now could be expected to live to be what age?

3. In the Deaths per 1,000 column, what does the number 1.11 mean?

4. In a group of 10,000 people, all age 40, an average of how many could be expected to die in the next year?

A PERSONAL INSURANCE PLAN

As you make choices about the type and amount of insurance you will buy, keep the following guidelines in mind:

1. To avoid billing fees, you can have premiums deducted automatically from your checking account. You may also be able to pay online. When you pay monthly, your fees are the highest (for most car insurance policies). If you can pay premiums quarterly or semiannually instead, you may be able to reduce or avoid those fees. For life insurance, premiums may be monthly, quarterly, or annually. Making annual payments may also reduce your cost.

2. Read the policy carefully. If you discover a clause you do not understand, call your agent for clarification.

3. Review your policies regularly to see if the coverage meets your needs. As your family situation changes, you might wish to modify your life insurance coverage. As your car gets older, you should consider dropping collision insurance.

4. Consider carefully the outcome of switching insurers or changing policies. If you do, be sure you are approved for the new insurance—and that it is correct as represented—before dropping your old insurance.

5. Get to know your insurance agent. Use his or her expertise. Ask lots of questions and be sure you understand all coverages, limitations, exclusions, and so on. Discuss your changing needs and get his or her recommendations, but make your own decisions.

6. Don't hold on to policies or companies for sentimental reasons. Be a wise comparison shopper. When you are certain you can do better with another company and have taken proper precautions, move forward to secure a new policy. For example, you may find better rates through a professional organization or other group, such as a credit union. For drivers over 50, AARP provides very competitive rates. It is able to do so because it represents such a large group of safe drivers.

7. Don't keep overlapping policies with the hope of making a quick profit off insurance claims. Group policies require coordination of benefits. Private policies that overlap coverage in a group policy can be very expensive.

8. Use deductibles wisely! By paying the first part of an expense yourself, you can save a bundle on insurance rates.

9. Keep your insurance up to date. Pay premiums promptly and take advantage of any discounts. Ask regularly about what new discounts, such as discounts for nonsmokers, are available to reduce premiums.

10. Consider risk management strategies of risk avoidance, risk assumption, and risk reduction. As you experience life changes, such as having a family, your risks, and thus your insurance needs, will change. For example, you might choose to save premium dollars by reducing your collision or comprehensive coverage on your car while increasing your coverage for term life insurance.

To review what you have learned about preparing a personal insurance plan, complete Worksheet 5 (Personal Insurance Plan) provided for you in the *Student Activity Guide* and also presented for reference on the next page.

WORKSHEET 5
Personal Insurance Plan

1. Explain the purpose of each of the following types of insurance.

   a. Homeowner's insurance

   b. Automobile insurance

   c. Liability insurance

   d. Health insurance

   e. Disability insurance

   f. Life insurance

2. Based on your current situation, what types of insurance do you currently purchase?

   a. Homeowner's insurance

   b. Automobile insurance

   c. Liability insurance

   d. Health insurance

   e. Disability insurance

   f. Life insurance

3. How do you anticipate that your need for each of these insurance coverages will change in the next five years?

   a. Homeowner's insurance

   b. Automobile insurance

   c. Liability insurance

   d. Health insurance

   e. Disability insurance

   f. Life insurance

4. List several guidelines for building a plan for purchasing all types of insurance.

WORKPLACE SAFETY

Americans spend a large percentage of their time at work, yet work is often one of the most dangerous places to be. Workplace injuries are common, and they are often caused by carelessness, lack of proper training, lack of proper equipment, and lack of understanding what to do when an emergency happens.

Preventing Work-Related Accidents

All workers are entitled by law to a safe place to work. This includes safe working methods and safety training. Workers' compensation costs are partially based on the safety record of the company. Having a safe workplace and reducing the number of accidents or injuries will benefit both workers and the company.

Safety begins with good work attitudes. Safety is part of everyone's job. All workers must understand safety needs and make safety a priority. Major work-related accidents, injuries, and illnesses are related to the following factors:

- Unsafe working conditions
- Hazards that can lead to injuries of some or all workers
- Tasks that require constant focus to prevent injuries
- Machinery, equipment, or other conditions that require well-developed skills and training
- Carelessness of workers
- Failure to use safety equipment
- Lack of awareness of dangers
- Not knowing how to avoid and reduce risks
- Lack of a practiced and workable emergency plan

Where potentially dangerous conditions exist, workers must know and appreciate the risks that are involved. Safety training should be required for all employees, even though they may not be directly involved with dangerous work.

An Emergency Plan

An *emergency plan* is a vital part of safety. An effective emergency plan provides for the safety of workers, employees, visitors, and others. A good emergency plan has the following components:

- Detailed steps to follow in an emergency
- A list of who is responsible for each activity
- A list of who has backup roles
- A secondary plan in case the first course of action fails
- A data backup system
- A process to communicate status inside and outside the company
- Practice drills so that everyone will know what to do in case of a real emergency

Emergency plans should be in writing and shared with everyone. If special training is required, it should be completed and practiced regularly.

Sometimes a safety committee draws up and tests the plan. A *safety committee* should have representatives for each part of the plan and from each part of the organization. For example, if the organization is a high school campus, every building, floor, or other subunit should have representation.

Emergency plans should include both "expected" events such as windstorms, fire, and freezing conditions and "unexpected" or nonroutine events such as bomb threats, explosions, shootings, or terrorist acts. When companies (as well as families) focus on what could happen, they can identify weak points and take needed steps to take all possible precautions.

Figure U6.5 is an emergency plan for a family in the event they lose power and can't go for help. It is suggested by FEMA (Federal Emergency Management Agency) that all families have such a plan and be able to survive on their own for at least a week.

FIGURE U6.5	*Emergency Plan (for Inclement Weather)*
Event:	• Weather or other event that leaves us without power (electricity or gas) for a week and also prevents us from driving or walking to get food and water.
What to do:	• Close up the house to preserve as much heat as possible. • Use blankets and a wood-burning fireplace for heat. • Move everyone into one room to share the warmth.
What to have:	• Food for seven days, to include canned food (tuna, beans, and other items that are not perishable) • Dry pet food in sacks • Water for seven days • Firewood; Pres-to-logs for fireplace fuel • Blankets • Flashlights, candles, and matches • Emergency supplies in case of injuries (bandages, antiseptic) • Battery-powered radio • Extra batteries
Notes:	• Food has to be rotated to make sure it is fresh and edible. • Batteries have to be rotated to be sure they are good.

Consumer Rights and Responsibilities

Unit 7 focuses on the role of consumers in a market economy. In Chapter 28, you will examine the three economic systems, how the market economy works, and the role of money. You will also explore wise buying practices and discover both your rights and your responsibilities within a market economy.

In Chapter 29, you will take a look at federal laws and agencies that have been formed to help protect you. You'll look at ways to protect yourself from deceptive practices and fraud. You will learn about things you can do to be a responsible consumer, how to shop effectively online, and how to stay informed. Finally, you'll examine ways you can gain redress when you have a complaint.

In Chapter 30, you will learn about the legal system of the United States. You'll discover the trial process, including the people, the paperwork, and the legal remedies available to you. You will also discover other methods of reaching redress, from the informal steps of alternate dispute resolution to small claims court and other forms of government assistance.

28

Role of Consumers in a Market Economy

| 28.1 | *Our Market Economy* |
| 28.2 | *Consumer Responsibilities* |

Consider **THIS**

Steven is a full-time student. He works part time at a gym to earn money during the school year.

He wants many things, but he doesn't have enough money for all of them. He just heard about a new electronic device that will be the latest and best for downloading, storing, and playing music and videos, but the price is very high. He doesn't have enough money, but he could use credit to purchase it.

"If I wait to buy this device until I can save enough money for it, I won't be able to enjoy it now while it's cutting edge. On the other hand, if I wait, the price will come down, and then I can afford it. By then, similar alternatives may be on the market. I'm not sure how the law of supply and demand works, but I do know that my resources are limited and I want to get the most for each dollar spent," he told his friend.

Our Market Economy

GOALS

- Describe and compare the three major types of economic systems.
- Discuss basic characteristics and parts of a market economy.
- Describe the role of money in a market economy.

TERMS

- communist economic system, *p. 641*
- socialist economic system, *p. 642*
- traditional economic system, *p. 642*
- capitalism, *p. 642*
- market economy, *p. 642*
- scarcity, *p. 643*
- competition, *p. 645*
- monopoly, *p. 645*
- money, *p. 646*
- fiat money, *p. 647*

ECONOMIC SYSTEMS

An *economic system* refers to the process used by a society to decide what to produce, how to produce it, and for whom (how to distribute it among the population). There are three major types of economic systems: hands-on, hands-off, and compromise.

HANDS-ON SYSTEMS

A *hands-on system* is one where the government or central authority controls most of the decisions involving what will be produced, how, and for whom. This type of system grew from the feudalism of the middle ages, where people grouped together for safety and to provide for group needs. Today, there are two basic types of hands-on economic systems: communism and socialism.

- *Communism.* Within a **communist economic system** (also known as a *command system*), the government owns and controls most, if not all, of the productive resources of a nation. Red China and the former USSR are examples of the communist, classless system. Based on the Marxist theories of sharing resources for the greater benefit of all, this system excludes most private property and ownership of resources; it also limits individual choices for the greater economic good of the society.

© Digital Vision/Getty Images

How is a hands-on economic system different from a hands-off system?

- *Socialism.* A **socialist economic system** (also called a *planned system*) is characterized by a large degree of government control of many of the decisions within the nation. Examples include Sweden, Germany, and other nations that have high tax rates but provide universal access to services, such as education and heath care, and guarantee jobs for all citizens. While there is private ownership of resources and property, many of the nation's choices are predetermined.

▊ HANDS-OFF SYSTEMS

A *hands-off system* is one where there is little or no role for government or a central authority. Decisions about what will be produced, how, and for whom are made by the people, acting as a whole rather than individually.

- *Traditional.* Within a **traditional economic system**, the people decide what decisions will be made and how they will be made. Often these systems are based on long-established traditions, religion, or cultural values. Japan, India, Middle-Eastern countries, and some small nations in Africa and Asia are organized as traditional economies.

- *Capitalist.* When our country first began, it started as a pure free-enterprise system, also known as capitalism. **Capitalism** is an economic system in which producers and consumers are free to operate and compete in business transactions with minimal, if any, government interference or regulation. Within a "laissez-faire" (hands-off) economy, the power to make decisions regarding resources belongs to individuals and businesses rather than society as a whole and without governmental interference.

- *Others.* There are other hands-off economic models, including anarchism, mutualism, and libertarianism. These models reject the role of government or other forms of "group-think," and instead embrace self-rule for all choices.

▊ COMPROMISE SYSTEMS

Most nations today have some form of *mixed economy*, which means it contains elements of more than one type of economic system. For example, over time a capitalist system can become a "survival of the fittest" society unless it accepts a growing need to protect those who would not otherwise survive. Our U.S. economy is considered a **market economy**, because both market forces (based on individual freedoms) and government decisions determine which goods and services are produced and how they are distributed. The government produces some goods and services, rather than leaving them to private enterprise.

In a market economy, the government also influences and controls some choices. For example, the government collects taxes and borrows money that it spends and redistributes according to its own priorities. Government is also able to impose price controls and other regulations. For example, a *price floor* is imposed on the market when government sets a minimum wage. Employers cannot pay less or below the floor. When government sets a *price ceiling*, then sellers cannot charge more. The government does this to protect some buyers. For example, the government might set a price ceiling on milk and insulin to protect young families and those with diabetes. Without these controls, many who need these items would be unable to afford them.

In our market economy, government influence also exists in the form of fiscal policy. *Fiscal policy* refers to actions of the government to stimulate or slow the

Many people in the United States feel that health care is a right, not a privilege. As such, they would like to have a single-payer, government-run, national health care plan similar to that found in most European countries. Other people feel that health care is best left to the free-enterprise system and that government control over health care or insurance is socialist, or moving away from the individual freedoms this country was based on. Congress has struggled with these issues for many years as it argues about ways to help the nearly 47 million Americans who are uninsured.

THINK *CRITICALLY*

Whose side do you agree with in this argument? Do you feel that health care is a right, not a privilege? Explain.

economy, such as tax increases or decreases and tax rebates. A market economy recognizes the need for such actions in order to protect consumers from adverse economic conditions.

Today, there are few if any pure economic systems. For example, a country may be a command system mixed with individual choices and ownership of some resources. Or, it may be a free-enterprise system mixed with some degree of governmental controls. The degree of those centralized or group decisions determines into which classification each country falls.

ELEMENTS OF A MARKET ECONOMY

In a market economy, both producers and consumers must play active roles. *Producers* are the manufacturers or makers of goods and services for sale. *Consumers* are the buyers and users of goods and services. Both producers and consumers engage in *self-interest behavior* that forces the wise use of scarce resources.

SCARCITY

In any economy, consumers' wants are unlimited, while the resources for producing the products to satisfy these wants are limited. This basic economic problem is called scarcity. A country's economic system determines what products will be produced with its limited resources. In our market economy, consumers play a key role in determining what businesses will produce.

Consumers' purchasing decisions act as votes. When consumers buy a particular product, they are casting their dollar votes for that product. After the "votes" are counted, producers know what consumers want. To make a profit, producers must provide goods and services that consumers will buy.

As an individual consumer, you have limited resources. You must decide what to buy with your limited income to achieve the greatest satisfaction or *utility* (measurement of something's usefulness). Your spending decisions and those of other consumers determine which products will succeed and which will fail and leave the market. Producers heed these cues from the marketplace to produce products that are profitable.

SUPPLY AND DEMAND

Supply is the quantity of goods and services that producers are willing and able to provide at various prices. *Demand* is the willingness and ability of consumers to purchase goods and services at various prices. You, along with other consumers, create demand for a product with your dollar "votes."

Generally, if enough consumers demand a product (are willing and able to buy it), producers are willing to produce and sell it. The system works like this:

1. Increased demand creates a situation in which the supply of the product is not sufficient to satisfy all consumers who want to buy it. As a result, producers can raise their prices.
2. The high prices bring large profits to the producers.
3. Large profits prompt current producers to make more of the product and attract other producers to start providing the product, thus increasing supply.
4. Supply then exceeds demand, and consumers can pick and choose. In order to entice consumers to buy their product instead of their competitors', producers must reduce their prices.
5. Reducing prices, in turn, lowers profits, and producers begin to produce less.
6. Eventually, the product reaches the *equilibrium price*. This is the price at which the quantity supplied equals the quantity demanded of the product. At this price, there is just enough of the product available for all consumers who want to buy it.

What is meant by consumer sovereignty?

CONSUMER POWER

Consumers have the ultimate power in a market economy; this is known as *consumer sovereignty.* Consumers determine what is produced and at what price. Collectively, consumer buying decisions direct the production of goods and services. When consumers purchase a good or service, they are casting dollar votes for its continued production.

If consumers refuse to buy a good or service, the price will drop. When the good or service still does not sell or sales do not generate a profit, producers will no longer provide it.

PRODUCER POWER

Producers also have power in a free-enterprise system because they can employ various techniques to influence consumer buying decisions. They use advertising and other marketing strategies to try to increase demand for their products. Advertising can be informative and provide important facts about the quality and features of products. Unfortunately, it can also be false and misleading, as you learned in a previous chapter.

PARTS OF THE ECONOMIC SYSTEM

Three essential parts of a market economy are: (1) competition, (2) purchasing power, and (3) informed consumers. If one of these parts is missing or not functioning properly, the system begins to fail. The economy gains strength when each component functions properly.

Competition

In order for prices to rise and fall with changes in supply and demand, competition must exist. **Competition** is the rivalry among sellers in the same market to win customers. There are three forms of competition in a market economy:

1. *Pure Competition*. With *pure competition*, there are many sellers and many buyers in the market, resulting in improved quality and lower prices. Because of the freedom of both producers and consumers to enter and leave the market, supply and demand are free to interact to set equilibrium prices.

2. *Oligopoly*. An *oligopoly* exists where there are only a few sellers producing a very similar product or service. Because the barriers to entry are high, it's difficult to simply start up this kind of business. For example, the automobile industry has only a few manufacturers. An oligopoly works properly when buyers shop carefully and negotiate prices effectively.

3. *Monopoly*. A **monopoly** is a market with many buyers but only one seller. Without competition, the one seller has no incentive to improve quality or lower prices. Sometimes a monopoly is necessary within a market economy. Examples of monopolies include power and utility companies. Monopolies must be controlled (by government) so they provide the lowest price to consumers.

© Digital Vision/Getty Images

What is competition like in an oligopoly market?

Illegal business practices can reduce competition and result in higher prices. *Price fixing* is an illegal agreement among competitors to sell a good or service for a set price. There is no real competition because prices have been predetermined, or fixed. Because price fixing prevents the forces of supply and demand from determining prices freely in the marketplace, it impedes free enterprise, and thus, the government has made it illegal.

Purchasing Power

How does the economy affect purchasing power?

For a market economy to operate, citizens must have the ability to buy. In the United States, most adults have income from their jobs that they can spend on goods and services. However, the purchasing power of the dollar goes up or down with the economy. *Purchasing power* is the value of money, measured in the amount of goods and services that it can buy.

In a period of *inflation*, when prices are generally rising in the economy, purchasing power decreases. For example, if the price of a soft drink rises from $1.50 to $2.00, then your income won't buy as many soft drinks. Your purchasing power has decreased. Purchasing power also declines during periods of *recession*, when production, employment, and income are declining. People who lose their jobs or have their wages reduced cannot buy as many goods. The result is an overall loss of purchasing power in the economy.

The government also shifts purchasing power among citizens by making *transfer payments*, which are government grants to some citizens paid with money collected from other citizens, generally through taxes. For the receivers, transfer payments are unearned income. They did not earn the income by working at a job. However, transfer payments provide purchasing power for needy people. Welfare, Social Security, and veterans' benefits are all transfer payments. Food stamps, reduced-price school lunches, and housing assistance also fall into this category.

Informed Consumers

A market economy must have informed consumers who know their rights and responsibilities in the marketplace. Informed consumers compare products and prices. When consumers make wise decisions, the system works to weed out inferior products and keep prices at acceptable levels. When consumers do not act in a responsible manner, prices increase.

THE ROLE OF MONEY

All economic systems use some form of money or medium of exchange. **Money** is anything that can be used to settle debt. It must be in a form where it can be readily divisible; it must be durable, and it must be recognizable as a store of value.

- *Divisibility.* In the United States, money, or *currency*, is divided into denominations for ease in completing transactions. The dollar bill is easily recognizable, and for sums less than a dollar, coins are used. The largest denomination produced for circulation is the $100 bill. In recent years, the Bureau of Engraving and Printing has added color and new security features to help prevent counterfeiting. When money is counted, it is divided into units. For example, 50 cents is one half of a dollar. Ten dollars is ten times one dollar. Because money is readily *divisible*, you can buy and sell goods, giving and receiving the exact "change" for your money.

- *Durability*. Money must be transferred from one person to another. Currency lasts a long time (durability) before it must be reissued. Coins are produced by the U.S. Mint; paper money is produced by the Bureau of Engraving and Printing. As money wears out, new coins and bills replace old ones, which are destroyed.

- *Store of Value*. To serve as a medium of exchange, money must have a *store of value*, or be recognized to represent that value. For example, a $5 bill is readily exchangeable for merchandise of that value. When you accept a $5 bill for something you have sold, you expect to be able to reuse that $5 bill when you wish to do so. Because you have confidence that our paper money can be used again, you will accept it in exchange for goods and services.

THE GOLD STANDARD

When our nation was young, our money was based on a gold standard. With a *gold standard*, each dollar bill was backed by that same amount of gold on store at a safe place. Much of the U.S. gold supply is stored at Ft. Knox, Kentucky. In its early days, a citizen could go into a bank and demand $20 of gold in exchange for a $20 bill. Banks issued their own money, called "gold certificates" or "silver certificates," because they were able to produce the gold or silver on demand.

Today our money is referred to as fiat money. **Fiat money** is not backed by gold, but by faith in the general economy and government of the country. You readily accept dollar bills and other currency because you are confident that you will be able to exchange them for other goods and services when you wish.

SUPPLY AND DEMAND OF MONEY

Like most other commodities, money is also subject to the forces of supply and demand. The Federal Reserve System controls our money supply. Using the reserve requirement, the Fed can increase or decrease the supply of money. The *reserve requirement* tells banks how much money can be loaned out

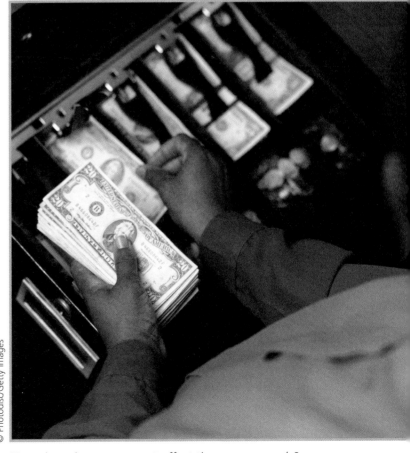

© Photodisc/Getty Images

How does the government affect the money supply?

from its transaction deposits (checking accounts) and how much must be kept "on reserve." For example, with a 20 percent reserve requirement, 20 percent of all demand account deposits must be retained by the bank in its vaults. Raising that percentage means the banks have less money they can lend. When they have less to lend, the price of borrowing (the interest rate) will rise.

The Fed also controls the discount rate and the federal funds rate. The *discount rate* is the interest rate charged to banks that borrow from the Fed. The *federal funds rate* is the interest rate at which banks are able to borrow from the excess reserves of other banks. As these rates increase, money supply shrinks. As the rates are lowered, more money can be borrowed by banks and used for loans. When more money is available, its price (rate) will be lower.

▌ THE MONEY MULTIPLIER

When banks are able to lend money they have on deposit from customers (transaction deposits), they are able to "create" more money. The *money multiplier* tells you how much more money can be created when banks can lend out a portion of each customer's deposit. The formula is as follows:

$$\text{Money Multiplier (MM)} = \frac{1}{\text{RR}} \text{ (reserve requirement)}$$

With a reserve requirement of 20 percent, the formula would work like this:

$$\text{MM} = \frac{1}{.20} = 5$$

Thus, if one customer deposits $100 in his or her checking account, the bank must keep 20 percent on reserve, or $20, and can lend the rest of the deposit, $80, to another customer, which creates a new deposit in another account. Of that new $80, 80 percent, or $64, can also be loaned to others, and so on. This will result in a multiplier of 5, or a maximum of $500 ($100 × 5) in additional money that can be created from the initial deposit.

If the Fed lowers the reserve requirement, the money multiplier gets larger. If the Fed raises the reserve requirement, the money multiplier gets smaller.

GLOBAL *View*

The World Bank provides financial assistance to developing countries around the world. It is owned by 185 member countries. One of its goals is to reduce poverty and improve living standards around the world. The World Bank does this through low-interest loans, interest-free credit, and grants to developing countries for education, health, infrastructure, communication, and other purposes. For example, it is providing financial support for suburban rail systems in Buenos Aires, Argentina. Improved transportation systems will improve the quality of life for the low-income population.

THINK CRITICALLY

Visit the World Bank online at www.worldbank.org. What has been accomplished by this international organization? Do you think its mission is worthwhile? Why or why not?

Planning a Career in... Government & Public Administration

Federal, state, and local governments all utilize professionals in the quest to provide consumer protections. Careers exist in planning, law, human resources, information technology, financial management, and public relations.

All forms of government require qualified people in the management and implementation of public services and programs. This includes public health, safety, finance, human resources, and public relations.

City, county, and state consumer agencies offer a variety of important services. They might mediate complaints, conduct investigations, prosecute offenders of consumer laws, license and regulate professional service providers, provide education materials, and advocate for consumer rights.

Employment Outlook

- Average to faster than average employment growth is expected.

Job Titles

- Urban and regional planner
- Building inspector
- Public relations officer
- Director of finance
- Public safety director
- Parks and recreation director

Needed Skills

- A bachelor's or master's degree in the desired discipline with an emphasis on community service is required.
- Creativity, high motivation, and strong problem-solving, communication, and people skills are needed.

What's it like to work in... *Government & Public Administration*

Jay has an office in the Municipal Building close to those of top city officials. He often works under pressure when schedules change and problems arise. He must meet deadlines and goals. He has to balance the needs of the city and its residents against the funds available in the budget. He has many people that look to him for solutions to their problems.

This morning, Jay is meeting with a concerned citizens group about the rising costs of water and waste management in the city. This afternoon, Jay is attending a meeting with the mayor to discuss a new program for low-income families in the city.

What About You?

Are you a problem solver? Can you handle several projects at the same time? Do you like working with a diverse group of people? Would you consider a career in government and public administration?

Assessment

KEY TERMS REVIEW

Match the terms with the definitions. Some terms may not be used.

_____ 1. A system in which the people decide what decisions will be made and how they will be made

_____ 2. A system characterized by a large degree of government control of many of the decisions within the nation

_____ 3. A situation in which consumers' wants are unlimited, while the resources for producing the products to satisfy those wants are limited

_____ 4. A system in which the government owns and controls most of the productive resources of a nation

_____ 5. Anything that can be used to settle debt

_____ 6. The rivalry among sellers in the same market to win customers

_____ 7. A market with many buyers but only one seller

a. capitalism

b. communist economic system

c. competition

d. fiat money

e. market economy

f. money

g. monopoly

h. scarcity

i. socialist economic system

j. traditional economic system

CHECK YOUR UNDERSTANDING

8. What group, as a whole, has the ultimate power to determine what will be produced and at what prices in a market economy?

9. What happens when the supply of a product exceeds the demand?

APPLY YOUR KNOWLEDGE

10. How is the market price of a good or service affected by (a) an increase in demand; (b) a decrease in demand; (c) an increase in supply; and (d) a decrease in supply?

THINK CRITICALLY

11. If you were given $100 to spend however you want, how would utility play a factor in what you would buy and how much you would spend?

12. Why do companies spend millions of dollars advertising their products? Provide an example of a product you purchased based solely on an advertisement.

13. Most economic systems today are compromise or mixed systems. Why is this the case?

Consumer Responsibilities

GOALS

- Describe deceptive practices used to defraud consumers.
- Discuss how to be a responsible consumer.

TERMS

- deception, *p. 651*
- bait and switch, *p. 651*
- fake sale, *p. 651*
- low-balling, *p. 652*
- pyramid schemes, *p. 652*
- pigeon drop, *p. 653*
- infomercial, *p. 654*
- identity theft, *p. 654*
- clearance, *p. 656*
- liquidation, *p. 656*
- redress, *p. 659*

FRAUDULENT AND DECEPTIVE MARKETING PRACTICES

The marketplace is full of deceptive and misleading promotions that induce consumers to buy goods and services of inferior quality or things they do not really need or want. **Deception** occurs when false or misleading claims are made about the quality, the price, or the purpose of a particular product. In many cases, little can be done once the consumer has been duped into making a purchase. Dishonest sellers quickly disappear or deny wrongdoing. In a market economy, consumers must educate themselves to recognize a potential fraud before they become victims. Prevention is still the best safeguard against financial misfortune.

BAIT AND SWITCH

Bait and switch is an illegal sales technique in which a seller advertises a product with the intention of persuading consumers to buy a more expensive product. The "bait" is the bargain product that gets customers into the store. When they arrive to purchase the advertised product, however, the salesperson then switches their interest to a more expensive product. In some cases, the bait is a poor-quality product that is placed next to high-quality merchandise. The poor-quality bait is advertised to be of better quality than it is, giving customers the idea that they are really getting a bargain. In other cases, when customers ask for the bait merchandise, they are told that it is sold out, but that comparable merchandise is available—for more money.

To avoid the bait-and-switch trap, educate yourself about products and prices. When a product is advertised at a special price, find out its quality and regular price. Shop around before making major purchases.

FAKE SALES

Probably the most common of all consumer frauds is the **fake sale**. A merchant advertises a big sale but keeps the items at regular price or makes the

What is a fake sale?

price tags look like a price reduction when there actually is none. Often the merchant increases the prices just prior to the sale and alters the price tags to show the so-called markdowns.

The best way for consumers to protect themselves from fake sales is to compare products and prices offered at other stores. Just because a flashy sign shouts "SUPER SAVINGS" does not mean that prices have been reduced. Only product and price knowledge can help you identify a real bargain.

© Digital Vision/Getty Images

▮ LOW-BALLING

Repair shops sometimes use a deceptive practice called "low-balling." **Low-balling** is advertising a service at an unusually low price to lure customers and then attempting to persuade them that they need additional services. For example, when repairpersons dismantle appliances, they discover other "necessary" repairs. If consumers refuse the offer of additional repairs, the shop charges extra fees for reassembly.

Another form of low-balling is applying pressure, either bluntly or subtly, to convince car owners that their cars need additional work for safe operation. For example, a repair shop may offer a special on brake relining. But when the mechanics inspect the brakes, they find several other "necessary" repairs. Customers may wind up with a front-end alignment, wheel balancing, or other repairs that are not really as urgent as they are led to believe.

To protect yourself from this type of low-balling, state that you want no repairs other than those agreed upon unless the repair shop informs you of the additional cost ahead of time and you choose to authorize the extra repairs. You should not pay for unauthorized work. Before having major work done, get a second opinion. Discuss major car repairs with someone you trust who knows about the mechanical aspects of cars. Find a mechanic you know and can trust. Don't take your vehicle to repair shops you know nothing about.

▮ PYRAMID SCHEMES

Pyramid schemes are mostly illegal multilevel marketing plans that promise distributors commissions from their own sales and those of other distributors they recruit. A cash investment of some kind is usually required to become a distributor. The pyramid consists of managers at the top and many middle and lower distributors arranging parties, recruiting new distributors, and selling products to friends and acquaintances. The managers at the top make big profits by selling the products to the distributors below them in the pyramid—not to the general public. However, most distributors lower in the pyramid never make a profit or recover their initial investment. Instead, they are left with a lot of low-quality products that their friends won't buy.

The best defense against pyramid sales schemes is to remember that you cannot expect to make big profits without hard work. Before committing to such a plan, investigate it. Talk to people who have purchased the products. Check with local consumer protection agencies. Think it through. What is the company's track record? Does the company have evidence to back up its claims? Who will buy this product? Will your commission depend on recruiting other distributors? Be skeptical if the company requires you to buy a "starter kit" of sales brochures and product inventory.

NETBookmark

The word *bunco* comes from the Spanish word *banco* (bank) and is used to describe a variety of fraudulent and deceptive practices against consumers. The National Association of Bunco Investigators provides details about several common bunco schemes reported by consumers. Access www.cengage.com/school/pfinance/mypf and click on the link for Chapter 28. Browse the site, and then explain how a bunco operator typically works. Finally, select a specific bunco scheme, describe it, and explain how consumers can protect themselves from it.

www.cengage.com/school/pfinance/mypf

PIGEON DROP

The term **pigeon drop** refers to any method used by experienced con artists to convince vulnerable people to invest in phony investments, swampland real estate, or other swindles. The pigeon is the unsuspecting consumer. Con artists often target trusting people who know little of such scams but have a source of money. For example, senior citizens become the targets of fast-talking "financial experts." The con artist may ask them to deposit their savings in an investment fund. These funds are then to be loaned out at high interest rates. The con artist promises the victims monthly payments for the use of their money. In some cases, the trusted adviser immediately disappears with the money. In other cases, the swindler maintains an outwardly healthy business and pays dividends to the victims until it is no longer advantageous to do so. Then the swindler disappears with the investments. By maintaining a supposedly legitimate business for a period of time, the swindler can gain additional victims—friends eager to get in on the deal at the recommendation of the original victims.

The best protection against this type of swindle is the local Better Business Bureau. The Bureau is equipped to investigate questionable schemes, so-called investment experts, and unsound businesses. If someone approaches you with a suspicious deal, insist upon seeing credentials, annual financial reports, and proof of past dealings. Invest only in established firms with a proven track record. Deposit your money only in financial institutions that are insured by the government.

FRAUDULENT REPRESENTATION

Telephone or door-to-door solicitations made by people who claim to represent well-known companies or charities are another type of swindle. Consumers buy products and then learn that the products have been rebuilt, stolen, or made of inferior quality with a reputable brand name label applied to them. In some cases, the product is worthless or unusable. One such scam involves the sale of a book of discount coupons to be used at numerous restaurants and businesses. When the buyers present the coupons for a discount or free merchandise, they discover that the merchant has not authorized the coupon.

Before giving money to someone claiming to represent a major company or charity, check with the organization to verify the person's identity. The local Better Business Bureau will have a record of solicitors who repeatedly engage in questionable practices.

■ HEALTH AND MEDICAL PRODUCT FRAUDS

A common type of swindle involves deceptive advertising for expensive "miracle" pills, creams, and devices to enhance the consumer's health and beauty. The ads are designed to appeal to the typical consumer's desire to be healthy and attractive. Usually, deceptive health and medical advertisements carry endorsements and pictures of people who have found success using the product. Magazines, newspapers, web sites, e-mail, and flashy tabloids often carry these advertisements. The manufacturers ask you to mail money to a post office box to receive the miracle product. Sometimes you pay your money but never receive the product. If you do receive the product, it is totally ineffective.

■ INFOMERCIALS

An **infomercial** is a lengthy paid TV advertisement that includes testimonials, product demonstrations, and presentation of product features. These programs usually last 15 to 30 minutes and target people with specific needs that are usually emotional—from weight loss to hair growth. While the product may be reputable, there is no guarantee, and claims about results may be greatly exaggerated. With infomercials, it is important to find out before you buy whether the business is reputable and the product works. Be cautious about giving credit card numbers over the telephone. Don't expect that because something "worked" for the paid actors describing the product on television that you will receive the same results. You must also beware of add-ons, such as high shipping and handling charges and club memberships. For example, you may get your initial shipment at a reduced price, but you may also be signing up for six more shipments or some other hidden commitment.

■ INTERNET FRAUD

When you are online, you will be bombarded by advertisements, from banners to e-mail. Some of these are legitimate; others are not. On the Internet, fraudulent businesses can appear genuine. Fake web sites can be designed to look just like their legitimate counterparts. Don't assume that a professional-looking web site means that the company is legitimate. You may order and pay for goods and never receive them. When you give credit card numbers and other personal information to these scam artists, you may become a victim of identity theft. **Identity theft** involves stealing personal information, such as credit card numbers and Social Security numbers, to gain access to a person's finances, often to make purchases with credit. Don't click on advertising links. Instead, look up the legitimate web addresses of reputable businesses with which you would like to do business. Report any look-alikes to the actual business.

TELEMARKETING FRAUD

Consumers lose billions of dollars each year to telemarketing fraud. One warning sign is the offer of a "free" prize if you pay shipping and handling. A truly free prize never requires that you pay a fee. Foreign lotteries are illegal, and sweepstakes requiring you to pay any money are not legitimate. Fake charities frequently ask for money around holidays and after disasters.

Fraudulent telemarketers will ask you to courier money to them or give a credit card number to claim your prize. Unsolicited calls from people who know a lot about you should ring an alarm. Promises of big prizes, wonderful vacations, and no-risk investments usually turn out to be fraudulent. They collect the tax, fees, delivery charges, and other "costs" from you, and that's the last you ever hear from them.

Many reputable companies use telemarketing to sell existing customers more products they do not need. You can protect yourself from these calls by saying "no, thank you" and hanging up. You can greatly reduce the number of unwanted telemarketing calls you receive by signing up with the government's National Do Not Call Registry. You can register for free online at www.donotcall.gov.

What kinds of telemarketing fraud might you experience?

BEING A RESPONSIBLE CONSUMER

Learning to identify various deceptive marketing tactics is the first step toward being a responsible consumer. Prevention is your best choice. After you have been swindled, it is difficult to undo the financial damage. To protect yourself, be alert for the warning signs of a scam. Educate yourself on products and prices, and seek redress when necessary.

IDENTIFY DECEPTIVE PRACTICES

When you hear unrealistic claims, be suspicious. Watch for warning signals in claims or offers made through advertising and by salespeople. Figure 28.1 lists common warning signals of possible deception that should catch your attention.

SHOP SMART

Our economy produces a large assortment of products from which to choose. Many products are complex, and the methods used to sell them are sometimes misleading. Internet shopping has added new dangers as well as helpful shopping tools. To make wise buying decisions, consider these ideas:

- *Shop at several stores. Comparative shopping* means comparing quality, price, and guarantees for the same products at several different stores. Use online price-comparison search tools to help you find the best deal.

FIGURE 28.1 *Warning Signals*

Watch Out When You Hear This:

- You can get something for nothing.
- You will receive a free gift if you reply now.
- You or your home has been specially selected.
- You can make high earnings with no experience or little effort.
- You have been selected to complete an advertising questionnaire.
- You may attend a demonstration with no obligation to buy.
- If you don't decide now, you will lose a golden opportunity.
- You may buy a high-quality product for an incredibly low price.
- To receive a product or service, you must first send money.
- To receive your prize, you must supply your credit card or checking account number.

- *Be aware of prices.* Know regular or "list" prices of common items. Terms often used in advertising, such as "manufacturer's list price" and "suggested retail price" and phrases such as "comparable value" or "value $40, you pay only $35," attract your attention, but the prices actually may not be reduced.

- *Understand sale terminology.* **Sale** means that goods are being offered for sale but not necessarily at reduced prices. **Clearance** means that the merchant wants to clear out all the advertised merchandise, but not necessarily at a reduced price. **Liquidation** means that the merchant wants to sell immediately to turn the inventory into cash. Again, prices may not be reduced.

- *Avoid impulse buying.* Take a list with you when you shop, and buy only what is on the list. Watch for displays of merchandise that attract your attention but are expensive and unnecessary. When shopping online, don't let an attractive web site or the ease of entering a credit card number lure you into buying something you don't need.

- *Plan your purchases.* Thoroughly research major purchases before making your choice. Read online and printed product information and comparative reviews. Do not make major purchases during periods of emotional stress or when your judgment is impaired. Ask questions so you are sure that you understand claims, features, prices, and terms. For example, the product may show net price after a mail-in rebate. You may not qualify for the rebate or it may have expired.

- *Compute unit prices.* Unit pricing is the cost for one unit of an item sold in packages of more than one unit. For example, to compare the price of a 15-ounce box with the price of a 24-ounce box, divide the total price of each box by the number of ounces in it. The result is the price per ounce of each box. The lowest unit price for products of comparable quality is the best buy.

- *Read labels.* Know ingredients and materials and what they mean. For example, a shirt that is 100 percent cotton may shrink, or if it is a dress shirt, it will probably have to be pressed each time you wear it. A product that says, "Dry Clean Only" will be more expensive to maintain.

COMPUTING UNIT PRICES

Which is better: 24 ounces for $2.59 or 15 ounces for $1.89? To determine which is better, you'll need to know the cost per unit. To compute cost per unit, divide the total cost by total units:

$$\$2.59 \div 24 \text{ ounces} = \$0.108 \text{ per ounce}$$

$$\$1.89 \div 15 \text{ ounces} = \$0.126 \text{ per ounce}$$

In this case, the 24-ounce container is the better buy.

Based on the previous example, determine which of the following is the better buy: 3 for $0.89 or 6 for $1.99?

Solution: $\$0.89 \div 3 = \$0.297$ each

               $\$1.99 \div 6 = \$0.332$ each

               Thus, 3 for $0.89 is the better buy.

- *Check containers carefully*. Be sure packages have not been opened or damaged. Occasionally, harmful substances have been injected into products. Report any suspicious openings in packages to the store manager.
- *Read contracts*. Read and understand contracts and agreements before signing.
- *Keep receipts and warranties*. Print out warranty statements and sales receipts from online purchases. For all major purchases, keep receipts along with warranties, guarantees, or other written promises for possible enforcement later.
- *Compute total cost*. Check the total cost of an item, including supplementary items (such as batteries), delivery charges, finance charges, and other add-on costs. In some cases, the base price may be lower than for similar products, but once you add up all the related charges, you will find that the total cost exceeds other choices.
- *Ask for references*. Ask for references from company representatives to be sure they really do represent the company. Call the company to check.
- *Be loyal*. Patronize online and bricks-and-mortar businesses that have good reputations and have served you well in the past. Tell others when you have a good experience, and ask others for recommendations of doctors, accountants, repair shops, and other service businesses.
- *Check up on businesses*. Check for valid certifications, licenses, bonding, and endorsements. Use your local Better Business Bureau and state records divisions to be sure you are getting service from qualified and reputable professionals.
- *Wait a day for major purchases*. Try waiting at least 24 hours before making a major purchase to be sure you are not making the purchase on impulse or being coerced into wanting the item. Many people change their minds after a "cooling-off" period. If you still want the product after further consideration, then you can feel sure you are buying for the right reasons.

ONLINE SHOPPING

You are responsible for protecting yourself if you shop online. Here are some tips to follow when shopping over the Internet:

- *Shop at secure web sites.* Look for "https" in the web address. The "s" indicates "secure."
- *Check the web site address, called the Uniform Resource Locator (URL).* A business address should be followed by .com; a government address should be followed by .gov, and so on. Be suspicious of URL addresses that are not in the approved domains.
- *Research the web site before you order.* Look for the business address and the telephone number.
- *Read the web site's privacy and security policies.* These policies are usually listed in a section entitled Privacy and Security. Determine if the site intends to share your information with a third party or another company. If the policies are not posted, do not trust the site.
- *Shop safely.* The safest way to shop on the Internet is with a credit card. If something goes wrong, you can protest the charge through your credit card company.
- *Share only the essentials when your order.* Never provide a Social Security number, date of birth, or other information that is not relevant to the purchase.
- *Print and keep the confirmation order.* Print at least one copy of what you have ordered as well as the page showing the company name, address, phone number, and legal terms.
- *Know shipping and return policies.* Check the web site for cancellation and return policies.
- *Use common sense.* If it seems too good to be true, it probably is!

STAY INFORMED

You are responsible for educating yourself about products and services before you buy. To protect yourself, actively seek consumer information in the following ways:

- Become familiar with sources of information on goods and services, such as *Consumer Reports*, consumer-oriented web sites, and local agencies.
- Read warranties and guarantees. Ask questions so that you can fully understand performance claims. Get written guarantees and warranties whenever possible.
- Read and understand care instructions before using a product.
- Analyze advertisements about products before buying. Know why you are interested in the product or service and decide what you want before you buy.
- Know the protections offered by consumer protection laws, and know how to seek a remedy to consumer problems.
- Inform appropriate consumer protection agencies of fraudulent or unsafe performance of products and services. Do not hesitate to make your dissatisfaction known to help others avoid the same problem and to prompt producers to improve their product or service.
- Report wants, likes, and dislikes as well as suggested improvements and complaints to retailers and manufacturers.

- Keep good records of complaints, defective products, actions taken, and so on. You will need these forms of evidence to support your claims.

SEEK REDRESS

When you have a complaint or need to solve a problem about a product or service, you have a right to seek redress. **Redress** is a remedy to a problem. When you have a consumer problem, you have a right to expect the business to work with you to resolve the problem. The remedy might be your money back, a repair, or some other compensation. Here are some suggestions for filing a complaint and resolving problems:

1. Take the product back to the store where you bought it. Calmly explain the problem to a salesperson there. If necessary, talk to a manager. If you bought the item online, then talk to a customer service representative on the phone. Explain the specifics about the problem and give evidence. Keep all warranties, sales receipts, and related material. If necessary, provide photocopies of necessary information to explain and support your position.

2. Stay firm but not angry. Say that you are dissatisfied and explain why. Be specific about the type of adjustment you want: refund, repair, replacement, or other action. Many consumer problems can be resolved simply by discussing them reasonably with the retailer.

3. If you are not satisfied with the manager's remedy, then put your complaint in writing to the store's owner or headquarters. If you do not receive satisfaction, write to the manufacturer or distributor and state your complaint. In any written correspondence, describe your previous interactions with store personnel and explain why you are dissatisfied with the result. Be specific.

4. Send photocopies of evidence, such as sales receipts, warranties, or anything else that will help you support your position. Be firm and again state the type of adjustment you want. Specify a reasonable time limit in which to resolve the problem.

5. If you are still dissatisfied with the result, file a complaint with the appropriate government agency for consumer protection. There may be more than one private or public agency to assist you in solving the problem.

6. Finally, you may need to seek legal recourse. Attorneys' fees are expensive, so it is better to try to resolve the issue yourself if possible. Small claims court and other legal remedies are discussed in detail in Chapter 30.

© Photodisc/Getty Images

Why do customers have the right to seek redress?

ISSUES IN YOUR WORLD

YOUR MOUSE TRACKS ON THE WEB

When you explore different web sites, be aware that you are not always anonymous. Some sites can immediately determine certain information about you when you visit that site, such as the type of computer system you use, the company you use to access the Internet, and the last web page you visited. You can find out what information your computer automatically transmits by visiting the Center for Democracy and Technology's privacy demonstration, which can be accessed at www.cengage.com/school/pfinance/mypf.

At some web sites you must log in, register, and/or give information about yourself. This information is saved and often shared with others. These "mouse tracks" enable others to determine whether you are a potential customer and what types of interests you have.

Some web sites electronically record information about your visit to their site by depositing a piece of information called a cookie onto your computer. Once a cookie is saved on your computer, that web site can keep track of information about your visit, such as which parts of the site you visit. This helps site operators determine the most popular areas of their site, and it helps them improve what they offer. Cookies also allow for more efficiency when revisiting a site because:

- Your preferences for visiting certain areas of the site are stored in your cookie file. The next time you return, the section you like best may already be displayed for you.

- You may be alerted to new areas of interest based on sites you have previously visited.

- Your past activity may be recorded in the cookie file so the site knows what you like and, thus, will offer you products and services tailored to your interests.

Some versions of browser software can be set to notify you before a web site places a cookie on your computer. Then you can choose to accept or reject the cookie. Some browsers will allow you to deactivate a cookie. You can also delete cookie files, but you would then lose the customizing offered by the sites.

THINK CRITICALLY

1. What web sites do you visit regularly? What information have you given them about yourself?

2. What are the advantages and disadvantages of having cookies stored on your computer?

Assessment

KEY TERMS REVIEW

Match the terms with the definitions. Some terms may not be used.

_____ 1. A remedy to a problem

_____ 2. Making false or misleading claims about the quality, price, or purpose of a product

_____ 3. An illegal sales technique in which a seller advertises a product with the intention of persuading consumers to buy a more expensive product

_____ 4. Intent of selling merchandise for cash as quickly as possible

_____ 5. A lengthy paid TV advertisement that includes testimonials, product demonstrations, and presentation of product features

_____ 6. Multilevel marketing plans that promise distributors commissions from their own sales and those of other distributors they recruit

a. bait and switch

b. clearance

c. deception

d. fake sale

e. identity theft

f. infomercial

g. liquidation

h. low-balling

i. pigeon drop

j. pyramid schemes

k. redress

CHECK YOUR UNDERSTANDING

7. What makes a sale a "fake sale?"

8. What is the first step toward being a responsible consumer?

APPLY YOUR KNOWLEDGE

9. Locate a product advertisement with an unusually low price or a claim to perform in extraordinary ways. Explain the appeal that leads to consumer deception.

THINK _CRITICALLY_

10. Have you ever gone to a store to purchase a product advertised on sale only to find that the product was not available, but another, more expensive product was available? What was your reaction? Did you purchase the other product? Why or why not?

11. Under what circumstances would you consider seeking redress for a consumer problem? What procedures would you follow before seeking legal advice?

Chapter (Assessment)

SUMMARY

28.1

- *Hands-on economic systems involve government controls over the way decisions are made. Examples are communism and socialism.*

- *Hands-off economic systems do not involve central authority; individuals make the choices. Traditional and pure capitalism are examples.*

- *Most economies today are mixed. A free-enterprise system with some governmental controls is today's market economy.*

- *All economies face the problem of scarcity because resources are limited but consumer wants and needs are not.*

- *In a market economy, consumers determine what products will be produced and at what prices. The interaction of supply and demand determines what will be produced, in what quantities, and at what prices.*

- *To function smoothly, a market economy needs competition, purchasing power, and informed consumers.*

- *All economic systems use some form of money or medium of exchange. Fiat money is backed by the faith in the general economy and government of the country.*

28.2

- *Bait-and-switch schemes lure customers into the store with advertised bargains and then switch customers to a more expensive product.*

- *Fake sales make customers think prices are reduced when they really aren't.*

- *Low-balling repair shops offer a repair at a low price and then discover several other "necessary" services to run up the price.*

- *Pyramid schemes depend on recruiting multiple levels of distributors.*

- *Pigeon drops lure trusting people into making phony investments with promises of extraordinary returns.*

- *Identity theft involves stealing personal information, such as credit card numbers and Social Security numbers, to gain access to a person's finances, often to make purchases with credit.*

- *To be a responsible consumer, learn to identify deceptive practices, follow wise buying habits, stay informed, and seek redress for consumer problems.*

APPLY WHAT YOU KNOW

1. Select a product that you are interested in purchasing, such as an iPod or digital camera. Using the Internet, search for retailers that sell this product and compare features and prices. Decide which features you want and where you would purchase the product. Write a summary of your findings and your decision to purchase the product.

2. Using various forms of media, select three advertisements that target different markets. Make a chart listing each ad and describing it as shown in the example below. Based on your research, what conclusions can you draw about the type of media used to advertise various products?

Type of Advertisement	Product Advertised	Target Market	Product Information Featured
Television	Blackberry	Students—back to school	Blackberry Pearl; $20 discount; pink or silver; use to get e-mail, surf the Web, and get directions

3. Search through magazines, newspapers, and the Internet for advertisements. Collect or print out ads that offer the following: (a) something for nothing, (b) bonus for early reply, (c) offers of gifts and prizes, and (d) very short time limit for response to get a special deal. Evaluate the authenticity of the ads.

4. Visit the web site of a retailer and check its prices and variety of products available online. Answer the following questions: (a) Does the site show pictures of the products? (b) Are you able to determine the full price, including shipping and other charges? (c) When can you expect to receive the goods ordered? (d) What are your payment options? (e) What types of personal information do you have to supply? (e) Does the site offer secure ordering and a privacy policy? (f) What is the return policy?

MAKE ACADEMIC CONNECTIONS

5. **Economics** Compare and contrast the three major ways economies can be organized. What type of economy exists in the United States? Do you think another type of economy would be better? Explain your answer.

6. **Research** Perform research to find a recent news story about a business that used deceptive marketing practices, such as price-fixing, bait and switch, fake sales, or another scam. Write a two-page report describing the deception and the final outcome.

7. **Social Studies** Conduct a survey of at least three people of varied ages based on the following question. "How is our economy impacting your life?" As a class, compare and discuss the results.

8. **International Studies** Using the Internet, compare the value of the dollar to the value of worldwide currencies. Find the value of the Japanese yen, British pound, Chinese yuan, Euro, Canadian dollar, and Mexican peso. Make a chart that shows the value of each compared to the U.S. dollar. What does this indicate about the current state of our economy?

SOLVE PROBLEMS AND

EXPLORE ISSUES

9. Compute unit prices for the following pairs and determine which of the two is the better deal: (a) 3 for $0.98 or 8 for $2.99, (b) 4 for $1.00 or 12 for $3.39, (c) 24 oz. for $1.98 or 36 oz. for $2.49, and (d) 2 lbs. for $2.19 or 5 lbs. for $5.89?

10. Copy the ingredients from the labels of the following products: (a) deodorant, (b) breakfast cereal, (c) liquid cleaning product, and (d) bug spray. Do any of the labels carry warnings? What types of precautions are suggested? Why is it important that customers are informed of product ingredients?

11. Read the warranty or guarantee for a household product that your family has purchased (examples: coffee maker, blender, or electronic device). What does the manufacturer agree to do? What exceptions are stated? What actions does the manufacturer state it will not agree to do?

12. Visit Consumer Reports online or obtain an issue from your library and answer the following questions: (a) Who publishes the magazine? (b) Who advertises in the magazine? (c) How are products tested and compared for quality? Then select a tested product and summarize three key findings that would influence your buying decision.

13. Assume you bought a new GPS navigation device at the store last week. It froze up while you were using it, and you were unable to reset it. Because the screen wouldn't turn off, you let the battery run down and then replaced the battery, but now the screen won't turn back on again. You returned to the store for help, but the manager told you that you would have to contact the manufacturer directly. Write a letter of complaint. For the purposes of this activity, make up information about the manufacturer, receipt, and warranty to include in your letter. Request a replacement or a refund.

EXTEND YOUR LEARNING

14. **Ethics** Some celebrities lend their names to products that later turn out to be ineffective or harmful to consumers. The celebrities are paid to endorse the product by claiming they have used it. But in many cases, the celebrities have not actually used the product and know very little about it. Some celebrities have been held legally liable because people relied on their claims. When a celebrity—whether entertainer or athlete—endorses a product or service, do you seek to buy it based on his or her opinion alone? Do you think this marketing tactic is ethical? Explain why or why not.

For related activities and links, go to **www.cengage.com/school/pfinance/mypf**

Chapter 29

Consumer Protection

29.1 *Consumer Rights and Laws*

29.2 *Consumer Agencies*

Consider THIS

Diego bought a computer at an online auction web site. He gave his credit card number and expiration date, along with his name and home address for shipping.

"I think you can get a pretty good deal when you buy online," he told his instructor, "but at the same time, I worry about giving personal information to a vendor that I don't know. When I checked with the Better Business Bureau online, I learned that this company meets its criteria and that there are no complaints filed against it. That makes me feel a little better, but I know I'm still taking a risk."

Consumer Rights and Laws

- Describe your rights as set forth in the Consumer Bill of Rights.
- Describe the protections provided by major federal consumer protection laws.

TERMS

- time-shifting, *p. 667*
- space-shifting, *p. 667*
- prudent layperson, *p. 668*
- flammability, *p. 668*
- recall, *p. 669*
- generic drugs, *p. 669*
- warning labels, *p. 669*
- care labels, *p. 670*

CONSUMER RIGHTS

For many years the consumer's position in the marketplace was known as "buyer beware." Consumers had little protection against unfair business practices. Since 1960, however, things have changed. As abuses have become apparent, new rights for citizens and consumers have arisen.

© Banana Stock/Jupiter Images

What are the basic provisions of the Consumer Bill of Rights?

CONSUMER BILL OF RIGHTS

One of the most important steps in the direction of consumer protection was the adoption of the *Consumer Bill of Rights*. This law was proposed by President John F. Kennedy in 1962 and later was expanded by Presidents Nixon and Ford. It outlines the following rights:

1. *The Right to Safety*: protection against products that are hazardous to life or health.
2. *The Right to Be Informed*: protection against fraudulent, deceitful, or grossly misleading practices and assurance of receiving facts necessary to make informed choices.
3. *The Right to Choose*: access to a variety of quality products and services offered at competitive prices.
4. *The Right to Be Heard*: assurance of representation of consumer interests in formulating government policy and of fair and prompt treatment in enforcement of laws.
5. *The Right to Redress*: assurance that buyers have ways to register their dissatisfaction and receive compensation for valid complaints.
6. *The Right to Consumer Education*: assurance that consumers have the necessary assistance to plan and use their resources to maximum potential.

AIRLINE PASSENGER RIGHTS

In 1999, it became apparent that airline passengers were being treated unfairly. Thus, a new bill of rights was needed to provide rights for airline passengers. These rights include the following:

1. *Confirmed Reservations.* When you have a confirmed reservation, you will be provided a seat on that flight. You cannot be denied boarding because you have no reservation "in the computer."
2. *Refunds.* If you cancel a ticket for a "nonrefundable fare," you can apply the fare toward a future flight, minus a cancellation fee. If you cancel a refundable ticket, your refund will be issued in the same manner as your purchase (if you used a credit card, the credit card will be credited).
3. *Delays and Cancellations.* Compensation is required if you are "bumped" from a flight that is oversold. The only exception to this requirement is if the airline can claim extraordinary circumstances, such as weather or security issues.

CONSUMER TECHNOLOGY BILL OF RIGHTS

As a result of technology and its widespread use by consumers, a new set of rights was needed to protect consumers. Provisions include the following:

1. *Time-Shifting.* Consumers have the right to time-shift. Consumers are **time-shifting** when they record video or audio for later viewing or listening. (For example, you can record a TV show and play it later.)
2. *Space-Shifting.* Consumers have the right to use content in different places. **Space-shifting** allows you to copy the contents of CDs and other media to portable devices, as long as the use is personal, not commercial.
3. *Backup Copies.* Consumers have the right to make backup copies of purchased CDs and other electronic media to protect against the event the original copy is destroyed.
4. *Platform of Choice.* Consumers have the right to listen to music on whatever device they choose. You can listen to music on your Rio MP3 player, watch TV on your iMac, and view DVDs on your Linux computer.
5. *Translation.* Consumers have the right to translate legally acquired content into a format that makes it more usable to them. For example, a blind person can modify an electronic book so it can be read out loud.

PATIENTS' BILL OF RIGHTS

Abuses in managed care and other related institutions created the need for the patients' bill of rights. These policies were adopted by the President's Advisory Commission on Consumer Protection and Quality in the Health Care Industry in 1998. Further rights were defined in 2001. Broadly, patients have the following rights:

1. *Information Disclosure.* Patients have the right to receive accurate, easily understood information to make informed health care decisions.
2. *Choice of Providers.* Patients have the right to choose their own doctors and other health care providers.

3. *Access to Emergency Services.* Patients have the right to access health care services how and where the need arises. A health plan must pay for costs that a **prudent layperson** (a reasonable, untrained person in a similar position) would reasonably expect the plan to cover. For example, your health plan may say you must use a particular hospital. But if a prudent layperson would go to the closest hospital to avoid death or serious consequences, then those costs must be covered.

4. *Treatment Decisions.* Patients have the right to fully participate in all decisions related to their health care.

5. *Respect and Nondiscrimination.* Consumers have the right to considerate, respectful care from all members of the health care system at all times.

6. *Confidentiality.* Consumers have the right to have the confidentiality of their individually identifiable health care information protected. Consumers have the right to review and copy their own records and to amend those records.

CONSUMER PROTECTION LAWS

Since the 1930s, Congress has passed many laws to protect consumers from unsafe products and unfair or deceptive business practices. These laws help ensure that consumers get quality goods and services for their hard-earned dollars.

FOOD, DRUG, AND COSMETIC ACT

In 1937, a Tennessee drug company marketed a new wonder drug that would appeal to pediatric patients. However, the solvent in this untested product was a highly toxic chemical similar to antifreeze. Over 100 people died, many of whom were children. The public outcry reshaped the drug provisions of a new law proposed that year to prevent such an event from happening again.

The *Food, Drug, and Cosmetic Act* of 1938 requires that foods be safe, pure, and wholesome; that drugs and medical devices be safe and effective; and that cosmetics be safe. The law also requires truthful labeling on these products, including the name and address of the manufacturer.

The FDA approves drugs before they can be sold. Requirements include years of research, testing, and proof of effectiveness and safety.

FLAMMABLE FABRICS ACT

The *Flammable Fabrics Act* of 1953 enabled the Consumer Product Safety Commission to set flammability standards for clothing, children's sleepwear, carpets, rugs, and mattresses. **Flammability** is the capacity for catching on fire. The law prohibits the selling of wearing apparel made of easily ignited

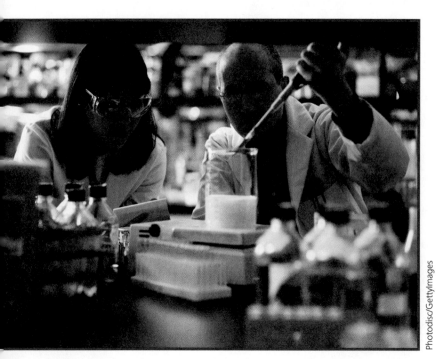

Photodisc/GettyImages

What are the advantages and disadvantages of the FDA's testing of drugs?

material. The flammability standard for children's sleepwear requires that the garment will not catch fire when exposed to a match or small fire. The flame-retardant finish must last for 50 washings and dryings. In 1967, Congress amended the Flammable Fabrics Act to expand its coverage to include interior furnishings as well as paper, plastic, foam, and other materials used in consumer products.

MEAT INSPECTION LAWS

The *Poultry Products Inspection Act* of 1957 requires poultry to be inspected for harmful contaminants. In 1967, the *Wholesome Meat Act* updated the Meat Inspection Act of 1906 and provided for stricter standards for processing facilities of red-meat products. Both of these acts protect consumers in the purchase of chicken and beef by standardizing inspection procedures.

HAZARDOUS SUBSTANCES LABELING ACT

The *Hazardous Substances Labeling Act* of 1960 requires that warning labels appear on all household products that are potentially dangerous to the consumer. In most cases, products found to be unacceptably hazardous must be recalled. A **recall** is a request for consumers to return a defective product to the manufacturer for a refund or repair.

KEFAUVER-HARRIS DRUG AMENDMENT

As a result of the *Kefauver-Harris Drug Amendment* of 1962, drug manufacturers must test drugs for safety and effectiveness before they are sold to consumers. This law was a reaction to the Thalidomide tragedy in which thousands of children were born with birth defects as a result of their mothers taking thalidomide for morning sickness during pregnancy.

This amendment also provides for the manufacture and sale of generic drugs. **Generic drugs** are medications with the same composition as the equivalent brand-name drugs, but they are generally less expensive. National brand names are expensive because of the costs of development and marketing. To allow drug companies to recoup the costs of developing new drugs, the law offers patent protection, which gives companies the exclusive right to market the drug for a number of years before competitors can sell the generic equivalents.

CIGARETTE LABELING AND ADVERTISING ACT

The *Cigarette Labeling and Advertising Act* of 1965 requires warning labels of health hazards from smoking. **Warning labels** advise consumers of risks and safety issues. Today these warning labels are even more specific. Original labels read: "Warning—Cigarette smoking may be hazardous to your health." Current labels read: "Surgeon General's Warning: Smoking causes cancer."

NATIONAL TRAFFIC AND MOTOR VEHICLE SAFETY ACT

The *National Traffic and Motor Vehicle Safety Act* of 1966 established national safety standards for automobiles and for new and used tires. The National Highway Traffic Safety Administration enforces provisions of the act. Its responsibilities include increasing public awareness of the need for safety devices, testing for safety, and inspecting vehicles for proper safety equipment.

CHILD PROTECTION AND TOY SAFETY ACT

The *Child Protection and Toy Safety Act* of 1966 bans the sale of toys and children's articles that contain hazardous substances or pose electrical, mechanical, or thermal dangers. Such products can be inspected and removed from the marketplace. The act requires special labeling for children's products, along with devices that make potentially dangerous products *childproof*, or resistant to tampering by young children.

FAIR PACKAGING AND LABELING ACT

The *Fair Packaging and Labeling Act* of 1966 requires product labels to contain accurate names, quantities, and weights. These rules apply to all types of products, such as groceries, cosmetics, cleaners, and chemicals. It is the responsibility of the consumer to compare weights and sizes of products available—a much easier job when accurate, standard information is available for comparison.

Amendments to the Fair Packaging and Labeling Act were passed in 1992. These laws require labels to include conversion of quantities into a metric measurement in addition to the U.S. system of weights and measures.

CARE LABELING RULE

The *Care Labeling Rule* of 1971 requires that clothing and fabrics be labeled permanently with laundering and care instructions. **Care labels** give instructions for cleaning, wash and dry temperatures, and other care needed to preserve the product. The labels must stay attached and be easy to read for the life of the garment.

This law was amended in 1984 to allow for exceptions to the rule for fabrics that may be damaged as a result of having a permanent label. These fabrics include leather, gloves, hats, and reversible clothing. In 1997, the law was updated to allow symbols to be used rather than written instructions.

TOY SAFETY ACT

The *Toy Safety Act* of 1984 permits quick recall of toys and other articles intended for use by children that might present a substantial risk of injury. Further revisions to the act are expected as a result of defective toys shipped to the United States from China in 2007.

GENERIC DRUG ACT

The Drug Price Competition and Patent Term Restoration Act of 1984 (also called the Hatch-Waxman Act or the *Generic Drug Act*) established the modern system of generic drugs. It speeds up the FDA approval process of generic versions of drugs. It attempts to protect the consumer more quickly than in the past by reducing roadblocks that would keep drug prices high.

NUTRITION LABELING AND EDUCATION ACT

The *Nutrition Labeling and Education Act* of 1990 requires detailed information on labels and standardization of descriptive terms, such as "low fat." The act requires that labels disclose the amount of specified nutrients in foods. Every covered food must have a uniform nutrition label disclosing the calories, fat, salt, and all other ingredients.

In 1993, the act was modified to require restaurants to comply with health claims appearing on signs, placards, and menus. Because of this act, consumers

Many people depend on properly labeled foods in order to maintain their health and weight and to prevent deadly reactions. For example, if you are gluten-intolerant, you cannot eat foods that contain any amount of wheat protein. If foods are not labeled properly with every ingredient, you are at risk. Foods that are produced in other countries and shipped to the United States do not have to meet the same standards, either in purity or in labeling. Some foods produced in the United States are shipped into Mexico for processing to avoid having to follow these requirements. Yet the labels say "Grown in the USA," leading people to believe that the food products meet U.S. standards. Some people feel that all foods, regardless of where grown or processed, should have to meet the same standards to be sold in the United States. Others believe that following these regulations only increases the cost.

THINK *CRITICALLY*

With which side do you agree? Why? How would you assure that pure food standards are met and that labels are accurate for all contents?

are more informed about food products in general and are better able to make choices about menu items and their true content.

CHILDREN'S ONLINE PRIVACY PROTECTION ACT

The *Children's Online Privacy Protection Act* of 1998 applies to the online collection of personal information from children under 13. Rules spell out what a web site must include in a privacy policy, when and how to seek verifiable consent from a parent, and responsibilities of the web site to protect children's privacy and safety online.

FAMILY AND EDUCATIONAL RIGHTS AND PRIVACY ACT (FERPA)

FERPA is a federal law that protects the privacy of student records. Parents and students over 18 have the right to inspect and review schools' education records. Errors or misleading information may be corrected. Schools must obtain written permission from the parent or student over 18 before releasing any information. Only directory-type information, such as name, address, and phone number, may be disclosed without consent. Parents and students may request that even this information not be disclosed. One important feature is the requirement that student ID numbers cannot be Social Security numbers.

HEALTH INSURANCE PORTABILITY AND ACCOUNTABILITY ACT (HIPAA)

In addition to the HIPAA health provisions discussed in Chapter 27, HIPAA also sets rules about who can see your health information. The law applies to doctors, pharmacies, hospitals, health insurance companies, employer group health plans, and Medicare and Medicaid. Protected information includes medical records, conversations, information about you stored in a computer system, and billing information. Consumers are allowed to have a copy of all their health records, make corrections, know how information is being used, and decide whether to give permission to share this information. Also as a result of HIPAA, Social Security numbers cannot be used as a personal identifier for patients.

Postal inspectors, airport security inspectors, testers, sorters, and weighers all work in careers where they make sure that rules are being followed, people are safe, and products meet safety and quality standards.

Most inspectors work in manufacturing companies, doing quality control. But following the acts of terrorism on 9/11 and the subsequent Homeland Security Act, positions at airports are also in demand.

Government agencies also employ inspectors, specifically health and safety specialists and technicians, to help prevent harm to workers, property, the environment, and the general public. They ensure that machinery and processes comply with safety regulations and laws.

If injury or illness does occur, inspectors help investigate and make recommendations for a remedy.

Employment Outlook

- Average employment growth is expected.

Job Titles

- Postal inspector
- Airport security inspector
- Product testers
- Quality assurance officer

Needed Skills

- High school education plus a specialized training program is required.
- On-the-job training and apprenticeship programs are often used for new hires.

What's it like to work in... *Inspection*

Bill works in airport security on a crew with six others. Every day is different. He meets interesting people, some of which are in a hurry and impatient. Bill must be courteous and observant as he completes his inspection duties. He screens passengers and watches for unusual behavior. He checks bags and other carry-on items to ensure passengers don't have items that aren't permitted because of potential harm to other passengers. He rotates from inspecting carry-on bags to running the scanning equipment and searching passengers who set off metal detectors.

Bill maintains contact with other security personnel through radio communications. If he requires assistance with an inspection, he may need to contact police, fire, or other emergency personnel.

Bill likes his job and plans to move into management where he can be a part of the overall security team for the airport. He is interested in homeland security and in finding ways to detect and prevent attacks on citizens. He believes his job offers a valuable service to the public.

What About You?

Are you observant? Would you like being responsible for the safety of others? Would you consider work as an inspector?

Assessment

KEY TERMS REVIEW

Match the terms with the definitions.

_____ 1. *A reasonable untrained person in a similar position*

_____ 2. *Labels that give instructions for cleaning*

_____ 3. *A request for consumers to return a defective product to the manufacturer for a refund or repair*

_____ 4. *Recording a video or audio for later viewing or listening*

_____ 5. *The capacity for catching on fire*

_____ 6. *Labels that advise consumers of risks and safety issues*

_____ 7. *Copying the contents of CDs and other media to portable devices*

_____ 8. *Less-expensive medications with the same composition as the equivalent brand-name drugs*

a. *care labels*

b. *flammability*

c. *generic drugs*

d. *prudent layperson*

e. *recall*

f. *space-shifting*

g. *time-shifting*

h. *warning labels*

CHECK YOUR UNDERSTANDING

9. *What are some ways that consumer laws protect you as a consumer?*

10. *Why should the online safety of young children be a consumer concern?*

APPLY YOUR KNOWLEDGE

11. *Which consumer protection law has the most significance for you? Describe how you and other consumers have benefited because this law was passed.*

THINK *CRITICALLY*

12. *Explain the need for consumer rights or bills of rights, such as the airline passenger rights. Why do we need these protections? Would you like to see additional rights added to the list? Explain.*

13. *In the early 2000's, the FDA lifted its ban on pharmaceutical companies and allowed them to advertise directly to consumers. Since then, targeted ads have appeared on television, and drug sales have soared. Do you think it was a good idea to lift the ban? Why or why not?*

14. *How has technology changed the way we view consumer rights and protection?*

Consumer Agencies

GOALS

- List and describe government and private sources of consumer assistance.
- Explain how to contact public officials to express opinions.

TERMS

- USDA, *P. 674*
- NIST, *P. 675*
- FDA, *P. 675*
- CPSC, *P. 675*
- FCC, *P. 675*
- FTC, *P. 676*
- USPIS, *P. 676*
- FAA, *P. 676*
- SEC, *P. 676*
- BBB, *P. 677*
- consumer advocate, *p. 677*

SOURCES OF CONSUMER PROTECTION

When you need assistance with a consumer problem, numerous federal, state, local, and private organizations are available to help you. These sources offer an abundance of helpful consumer information on their web sites. You can even file a consumer complaint online.

FEDERAL AGENCIES

Many federal government agencies provide information of interest to consumers. Some of these agencies handle consumer complaints, and others direct complaints to agencies or sources that address consumer issues. Most agencies can be easily located through the Internet.

What does the USDA do to help protect consumers?

Department of Agriculture

Within the **USDA** (United States Department of Agriculture), there are a number of agencies that exist to meet various consumer needs regarding the food supply in this country. The *Agricultural Marketing Service* inspects food to ensure wholesomeness and truthful labeling, develops official grade standards, and provides grading services. For example, eggs must meet specific standards to be classified as extra large, jumbo, large, medium, or small. The *Food and Nutrition Service* provides food assistance programs, such as the food stamp and school lunch programs, and information on diets, nutrition, and menu preparation. The *Cooperative Extension Service* provides consumer education materials (pamphlets and booklets) on such topics as budgeting, money management, food preparation and storage, gardening, credit counseling, and many more. Most of the materials are free and available online.

National Institute of Standards and Technology

The **NIST** (National Institute of Standards and Technology) is an agency within the U.S. Department of Commerce. One of its missions is to develop and reward standards of excellence in business. NIST sponsors the *Malcolm Baldrige National Quality Award* given each year to U.S. businesses that achieve high standards of quality in their business practices.

NIST also sets uniform standards of weights and measures. NIST is the reason that you don't have to shop with a tape measure or scale to make sure you get what you pay for. NIST sponsors a network of state and local agencies that set performance standards for measuring devices used to determine the costs and amounts of products sold to consumers. For example, agencies of the NIST network determine the amount of error that is acceptable for a gas pump or grocer's scale and establishes testing procedures for enforcing the standards.

Food and Drug Administration

One of the many agencies within the U.S. Department of Health and Human Services is the **FDA** (Food and Drug Administration). The FDA enforces laws and regulations preventing distribution of mislabeled foods, drugs, cosmetics, and medical devices. The FDA does the following:

- Requires testing and approval of all new drugs.
- Tests new and existing products for health and safety standards.
- Provides standards and guidelines for poisonous substances.
- Sets standards for identification, quality, and volume of food containers.
- Establishes guidelines for labels and proper identification of product contents, ingredients, nutrients, and directions for use.
- Investigates complaints.
- Conducts research and issues reports, guidelines, and warnings about substances found to be dangerous or potentially hazardous to health.

Consumer Product Safety Commission

The **CPSC** (Consumer Product Safety Commission) protects consumers from unreasonable risk of injury or death from potentially hazardous consumer products. The commission enforces standards for consumer products, bans products that are dangerous, arranges recalls, and researches potential hazards. In addition, the CPSC offers many publications on safety, which are available to consumers online.

Federal Communications Commission

The **FCC** (Federal Communications Commission) regulates interstate and international communications by radio, television, wire, satellite, and cable. The FCC's Consumer and Governmental Affairs Bureau is the consumer's one-stop source of information, including forms, applications, and current complaints and issues before the FCC.

What is the purpose of the USPIS?

Federal Trade Commission

The **FTC** (Federal Trade Commission) regulates unfair methods of competition, false or deceptive advertising, deceptive product labeling, inaccurate or obsolete information on credit reports, and concealment of the true cost of credit. The FTC's Bureau of Consumer Protection enforces federal consumer protection laws, helping to enhance consumer confidence. The FTC is also the federal clearinghouse for complaints of identity theft.

United States Postal Inspection Service

The **USPIS** (United States Postal Inspection Service) is a federal law enforcement agency that investigates consumer problems pertaining to illegal use of the mail. The USPIS enforces postal laws, protecting consumers from dangerous articles, fraud, pornography, and identity theft involving the mail. Through its Consumer Protection Program, USPIS resolves unsatisfactory mail-order transactions.

Federal Aviation Administration

The **FAA** (Federal Aviation Administration) is an agency of the U.S. Department of Transportation. It controls air traffic and certifies aircraft, airports, pilots, and other personnel. The FAA writes and enforces air safety regulations and air traffic procedures.

Securities and Exchange Commission

The main purpose of the **SEC** (Securities and Exchange Commission) is to protect investors and maintain the integrity of the securities markets. The SEC requires companies to disclose certain financial and other information so that investors can research investment options before buying. The SEC also oversees stock exchanges, brokers, and investment advisers to protect investors in their dealings with securities professionals. The SEC's Office of Investor Education and Advocacy serves investors who complain to the SEC about investment fraud or the mishandling of their investments by securities professionals.

■ STATE AND LOCAL ASSISTANCE

Most states have a consumer protection agency, or the state attorney general may handle consumer complaints. Many county and city governments also have consumer protection offices. Consumer leagues and public-interest research groups are also active at the state and local levels, with newsletters, pamphlets, handbooks, and web sites on current consumer issues.

At the local level, consumers have access to legal aid societies, newspaper and broadcast consumer action reporters, and consumer representatives on local utility or licensing boards. Independent consumer groups focusing on specific issues, such as food prices, may operate on the local level as well.

PRIVATE ORGANIZATIONS

There are many private organizations for consumers to access when they need to gather information or file complaints. They include the following:

- The **BBB** (Better Business Bureau) is a clearinghouse of information about local businesses. Complaints against local businesses may be filed with the BBB. Merchants are given an opportunity to respond to the complaint; if they do not, the BBB may advise consumers to seek another form of redress. You can request reports regarding the nature of complaints filed against local merchants from the BBB in your area or look up complaints at the BBB web site.

- The *Major Appliance Consumer Action Panel* (MACAP) is comprised of representatives of the home appliance industry. It provides assistance in resolving or minimizing consumer problems in the purchase and use of home appliances. The automobile and furniture industries, all of which produce goods that represent significant investments for buyers, have voluntary consumer-action panels.

- Consumers may also seek the support of a **consumer advocate**—a person who actively promotes consumer causes. Ralph Nader is the best-known consumer advocate. When he finds, through research and investigation, that an injustice or dangerous condition exists, he pursues it on behalf of all consumers. Consumer advocates may file lawsuits against companies to force them to meet safety standards, correct inequitable situations, or properly inform consumers of dangers in the use of their products.

- The *National Consumers League* (NCL) operates the National Fraud Information Center, established in 1992 to combat fraud. In 1996, the Internet Fraud Watch was created. Trained counselors will help you identify danger signs of fraud as well as help law enforcement agencies collect information quickly so they can respond quickly. These services are free.

- The *Federal Citizen Information Center* (FCIC) assists federal agencies in the development, promotion, and distribution of practical consumer publications. You can order free, or at very low cost, brochures on topics from how to apply for a passport to *The Consumer's Almanac*. You can order publications by mail, phone (toll-free), fax, or Internet.

- The *Consumers Union* is a not-for-profit organization. It has the largest consumer testing facility in the world. Through its monthly magazine, *Consumer Reports*, Consumers

NETBookmark

News stories about unsafe products have become commonplace, and staying on top of all those product recalls can be a full-time job! The Consumers Union has tried to make it a bit easier with its *Not In My Cart* page. Access www.cengage.com/school/pfinance/mypf and click on the link for Chapter 29. List at least five products that have recently been recalled, along with the reasons for the recall. Were you previously aware of the product recalls you listed? Do you think this service is helpful? Explain.

www.cengage.com/school/pfinance/mypf

Union gives test results and product ratings. To assure that all ratings are unbiased, Consumers Union buys all products it tests and accepts no advertising. *Consumer Reports* contains articles dealing with insurance, credit, and other items of consumer interest. The Consumers Union also publishes an annual *Buying Guide* that summarizes its reports of the previous year.

CONTACTING PUBLIC OFFICIALS

National elected officials include the President and Vice President and members of Congress. State elected officials include the Governor, secretary of state, treasurer, attorney general, superintendent of public instruction, labor commissioner, and state senators and representatives.

Each court (federal, state, and local) has at least one judge and several clerks of court to assist in filing and information gathering. County elected officials include the county administrator, district attorney, sheriff, and tax assessor, plus a number of commissioners. Other elected local officials include the mayor, city council members, and city manager. These officials are available at county and city office buildings and meet regularly or are available to the public by appointment. The phone book lists various officials separately by state and by county, with each department listed alphabetically.

If you wish to communicate with a public official about a consumer issue, there are several ways to do so:

1. *In Person.* You can make an appointment during regular office hours as well as attend meetings of government bodies, which are generally open to the public (except for executive sessions). Almost all hearings offer citizens the opportunity to speak.
2. *By Phone.* Brief calls at reasonable hours are generally effective. Your state may supply toll-free numbers for contacting public officials.
3. *By E-mail.* Legislators receive e-mail correspondence from their constituents (people who live in the areas they represent). You can get e-mail addresses of senators and representatives from their own web sites or from your state government web site links.
4. *By Letter.* To be effective, a letter written to the appropriate representative should state clearly the purpose of the letter, identify the proposed legislation or bill by proper name and number, refer to only one issue, and arrive while the issue is current. Give reasons for your position and avoid being emotional. Ask for specific relief—what you want the public official to do.

COMMUNICATION *Connection*

Assume you are unhappy with the service you received from a local business. Make up the name of the company and the type of service received. Write a letter of complaint about the business that you would send to the BBB. Be specific in your complaint, giving reasons for your dissatisfaction and asking for a specific remedy. What do you expect as a result of your complaint?

ISSUES IN YOUR WORLD

IDENTITY THEFT: PROTECTING YOURSELF

Skilled identity thieves can rob you of your identity despite your best efforts at managing your personal information. Stolen identification cards, debit cards, and credit cards can be used by thieves to run up charges. Mail stolen from your mailbox or garbage can be used to have fake checks printed based on your bank account information. Thieves posing as a landlord or employer can get a copy of your credit report and then open accounts to borrow money or make purchases.

To minimize your risk, here are some things you can do:

- *Do not give out personal information unless you have initiated the contact and know with whom you are dealing.*
- *Memorize your Social Security number and don't carry your Social Security card.*
- *Pay attention to billing cycles; follow up when bills are late.*
- *Guard your mail from theft. Use post office collection boxes for outgoing mail; promptly remove mail when it arrives or get a post office box.*
- *Minimize the number of accounts you have and cards you carry.*
- *Keep personal information safe; shred discarded copies.*
- *Order a copy of your credit report every year; be sure it is accurate.*

If your identity has been stolen, you should take the following four steps as soon as possible and keep a record of your actions and copies of correspondence.

1. *Place a fraud alert on your credit reports. A fraud alert will prevent anyone from opening any more accounts in your name.*
2. *Close the accounts you know have been tampered with or opened fraudulently. Ask for a letter verifying that the disputed account is closed and that the charges are being disputed and/or discharged. When you open new accounts, change your PIN and/or password.*
3. *File a complaint with the Federal Trade Commission (FTC). Their complaint form is available online; print a copy and keep it for your records. This record, together with a police report, will entitle you to certain protections, such as ensuring that debts will not reappear on your credit report.*
4. *File a report with your local police. Call the police department and ask to fill out a police report for the identity theft. File in person if possible and obtain a copy. If local police are reluctant to take your report, call the state police or your state attorney general's office to find the appropriate place to file the police report.*

For more information on identity theft and what to do if it happens to you, call 1-877-IDTHEFT (toll-free), or visit www.consumer.gov/idtheft.

THINK *CRITICALLY*

1. *What are some ways your identity could be stolen?*
2. *What precautions can you take to prevent identity theft?*
3. *What can you do after your identity has been stolen? Why is it important to take action?*

Assessment

KEY TERMS REVIEW

Match the terms with the definitions. Some terms may not be used.

____ 1. Develops and rewards standards of excellence in business

____ 2. Protects the food supply in the United States

____ 3. A private clearinghouse of information about local businesses

____ 4. Investigates consumer problems pertaining to illegal use of the mail

____ 5. Regulates unfair methods of competition, advertising, and labeling

____ 6. A person who actively promotes consumer causes

____ 7. Enforces laws and regulations preventing distribution of mislabeled foods, drugs, cosmetics, and medical devices

a. BBB

b. consumer advocate

c. CPSC

d. FAA

e. FCC

f. FDA

g. FTC

h. NIST

i. SEC

j. USDA

k. USPIS

CHECK YOUR UNDERSTANDING

8. What is the purpose of the CPSC?

9. Which government agency protects stock market investors? Explain how.

APPLY YOUR KNOWLEDGE

10. There are many federal agencies providing consumer protection services. Select one agency, describe what it does for you, and list several new things you would like to see the agency do for consumers.

THINK CRITICALLY

11. Why is it necessary for the FCC to regulate communications? Visit the FCC online and explain the agency's mission. Do you think this agency is adding value for consumers?

12. In recent years, small, private airplane crashes have increased significantly, and the FAA announced in 2008 that it would increase regulations of small aircraft. Do you agree that increased regulations are needed? Why or why not?

13. The National Consumers League is a private, nonprofit organization that promotes consumer protection. Research this organization and explain why its services are important to consumers.

Chapter Assessment

SUMMARY

29.1

- The Consumer Bill of Rights outlines basic rights that consumers should expect in the marketplace.

- Airline Passenger Rights outline the rights of paying passengers on commercial airlines.

- The Consumer Technology Bill of Rights outlines permissible reproduction and uses of purchased digital content.

- The Patients' Bill of Rights gives you more control over your medical decisions, treatments, and records.

- Some laws (such as the Food, Drug, and Cosmetic Act) set standards for product purity and safety.

- Many consumer laws (including the Fair Packaging and Labeling Act) set rules for product labeling.

- Several consumer laws (such as the Children's Online Privacy Protection Act) are designed to protect children from harm.

- FERPA and HIPAA are laws designed to protect privacy.

29.2

- The USDA (U.S. Department of Agriculture) inspects and grades food.

- The FDA (Food and Drug Administration) approves new drugs, tests products for safety, and sets labeling guidelines.

- The CPSC (Consumer Product Safety Commission) enforces product standards and bans or recalls hazardous products.

- The FCC (Federal Communications Commission) regulates communications by radio, television, wire, satellite, and cable.

- The FTC (Federal Trade Commission) regulates methods of competition, marketing practices, and credit reporting.

- The USPIS (U.S. Postal Inspection Service) investigates consumer problems pertaining to illegal use of the mail.

- The SEC (Securities and Exchange Commission) requires businesses to disclose financial information and oversees the securities markets.

- Private organizations, such as the BBB (Better Business Bureau), can assist consumers with incidents of unethical and illegal practices.

APPLY WHAT YOU KNOW

1. Select any garment from your closet. Read the care label. What kinds of information are on the label? How is this information helpful?

2. Cut the labels from three food products, such as soup, cereal, and snacks. List the different types of information—such as quantity per serving, ingredients, and vitamin and mineral content—you find on the label. Are there ingredients you do not recognize? Is the nutritional value what you expected?

3. Identify the law that protects consumers from each of the following abuses: (a) A box states that it contains 12 ounces of product when it actually contains only 9 ounces; (b) A doctor tells an employer that an employee has a potentially expensive medical condition. Rather than risk higher health insurance premiums, the employer fires the employee; (c) A company develops a new "miracle" drug. To get it on the market quickly, the company does not test it sufficiently; (d) A company develops an effective new cleaning product. However, the chemicals it contains are quite dangerous. To avoid scaring potential customers, the company does not mention the dangers on the label.

4. Visit the Federal Citizen Information Center's web site (www.pueblo.gsa. gov) and locate a news article that interests you. Write a bulleted list of the most important consumer information facts you found in the article.

5. Visit the Securities and Exchange Commission's web site (www.sec.gov). Follow the link to Laws and Regulations. Select one law or regulation and briefly summarize how it protects investors.

6. Go to the Better Business Bureau's web site (www.bbb.org) and look up the reports on two local companies. Write a brief summary of the kinds of information the reports provide about companies.

7. Visit the National Fraud Information Center's web site (www.fraud.org) and answer the following questions: What services are available to consumers who have complaints? What is the process of registering a complaint?

MAKE ACADEMIC CONNECTIONS

8. **Social Studies** Prepare a presentation to explain the role of government in consumer protection, why it is important, and how citizens pay for services that are provided for society as a whole. Use visual examples to explain the societal benefits of governmental consumer protection.

9. **Communication** Write a paper declaring a bill of rights in an area that concerns you. What rights would you like to have guaranteed to you as a citizen? Follow one of the bill of rights in Lesson 29.1 as an example.

10. **Research** Look up the Malcolm Baldrige National Quality Award online. Write a report explaining the history of the award, its recipients, and its purpose.

11. **International Studies** Select another country and research its consumer protection laws. How are they different from laws in the United States?

SOLVE PROBLEMS AND

EXPLORE ISSUES

12. List your state and local sources that can provide assistance with a consumer complaint.

13. Consult the Consumer Reports' Buying Guide for the most current year. Summarize the key points of three product reports that interest you.

14. Your local library contains much information about consumer problems and assistance. Visit the library and list in outline form what types of information are available for consumers.

15. Check your local newspaper for public notices of hearings by local government groups. List hearings that are scheduled. Which hearings are on issues affecting consumers? How would consumers be affected in each case?

16. Attend a public hearing on a local issue—land use or zoning, for example— and write a report on who was present, what was discussed, and the conclusion reached. Hearings are held in city hall or county buildings and are open to the public for testimony and input.

17. Check recent issues of newspapers, news magazines, or online news sources for reports of proposed laws and regulations affecting consumers. Choose an issue that concerns you and investigate it. Prepare an e-mail message to the appropriate official with your comments on the proposed law or regulation.

18. Why are the rights protected by FERPA important to you? What could happen if these rights were not protected?

19. Why should you consider buying generic drugs rather than brand-name drugs? What do you think would happen if drug development companies did not receive patent protection for a number of years before other companies could sell generic equivalents?

EXTEND YOUR LEARNING

20. **Ethics** Cable companies are essentially monopolies—customers have little if any choice in products available to them. Packaged plans contain features that consumers do not want, yet they have to buy the entire package to get the channels and programs they do want. This bundling raises costs for consumers. Satellite and other providers of similar services have the same bundling plans. To maintain profitability, these communications providers may also charge fees to replace obsolete equipment and to repair it when it breaks down or sell costly service contracts. Do you think these business practices are ethical? How can consumers fight back? What can the government do to help protect citizens from these predatory practices?

For related activities and links, go to **www.cengage.com/school/pfinance/mypf**

Chapter 30

Dispute Resolution

30.1 *The Legal System*

30.2 *Other Redress Solutions*

Consider **THIS**

Jim wanted to paint his apartment. The landlord promised to pay for the paint if Jim provided the labor. Based on this agreement, Jim painted the apartment. But when he asked the landlord for reimbursement, the landlord refused.

"I've tried everything," Jim told his sister. "I talked to him nicely and referred to our verbal agreement. He said that he never made such an agreement, and I have nothing in writing to prove it. Then when I moved out of the apartment, he refused to refund my deposit. He said that I painted the apartment without authorization, so he was entitled to keep my deposit. Together the paint and the deposit total $900! What can I do to get my money back?"

The Legal System

GOALS

- Describe the structure of the legal system in the United States.
- Explain legal procedures from complaint to judgment.

TERMS

- common law, *p. 685*
- civil case, *p. 685*
- criminal case, *p. 685*
- statute of limitations, *p. 688*
- complaint, *p. 689*
- plaintiff, *p. 689*
- defendant, *p. 689*
- counterclaim, *p. 689*
- deposition, *p. 689*
- verdict, *p. 690*
- judgment, *p. 690*
- appeal, *p. 690*

STRUCTURE OF THE LEGAL SYSTEM

The legal system in the United States is built on several sources of law, including constitutional law, statutory law (laws passed by Congress or state legislature), agency law (laws relating to commercial or contractual dealings), maritime law (laws governing the high seas), and common law. **Common law** is a system of laws based on decisions made in court cases. These decisions set legal *precedents*, which serve as models for deciding similar cases in the future. At the base of our common law legal system are the courts. The *court* holds judicial proceedings to hear and decide matters according to the law.

THE COURTS

There are many types of courts—federal, state, and local. Each court is empowered to decide certain types or classes of cases. This power is called *jurisdiction*, which is the legal authority to hear and decide a case. *Trial courts* are said to have *original jurisdiction* because they are the first court to hear a case. *Appellate courts* are said to have *appellate jurisdiction*, or the authority to review the judgment of lower courts.

COURT CASES

Legal matters are also classified as either civil or criminal. A **civil case** involves one person who has a dispute with another person or entity. For example, matters such as divorce, estate settlement, or torts (civil violations that result in damages or injuries to others) would be settled in a civil proceeding. A **criminal case** involves a government unit who is accusing an individual of committing a crime. When a law has been broken, a *prosecutor* files criminal charges against the accused person. In this country, a person is presumed innocent until proven guilty.

The losing parties may appeal the decision of a civil or criminal court if they believe the court made an error in applying the law. The appellate court reviews decisions of lower courts.

■ COURT PERSONNEL

Our federal and state court systems require many people to operate efficiently.

■ The *judge* is the presiding officer in the court and is either elected or appointed. Attorneys are usually selected by the parties in the dispute but are sometimes appointed by the court. For example, if you are accused of a crime and cannot afford an attorney, an attorney called a *public defender* will be appointed to help you present your case.

■ The *court clerk* enters cases on the court calendar and keeps an accurate record of the proceedings. The clerk also accepts, labels, and safeguards all items of evidence; administers the oath to witnesses and jurors; and sometimes approves bail bonds and computes the costs involved.

■ The *court reporter* keeps a word-by-word record of the trial, usually through the use of a special recording machine. These trial records are available to each attorney and are used for appeals.

■ The *bailiff* maintains order in the courtroom at the instruction of the judge. He or she also is the conduit between the judge and the jury and other members of the court.

■ The *jury* is a body of citizens sworn by a court to hear the facts submitted during a trial and to render a verdict. While a judge decides *issues of law*, the jury decides *issues of fact* (guilt or innocence). A trial jury consists of not more than 12 people. A juror must be of legal age, a resident, and able to see and hear. Jurors are chosen from a list of local citizens—usually from tax or voter rolls or from motor vehicle registration records.

■ THE THREE-TIERED COURT SYSTEM

Both the state and the federal levels have a three-tiered court system. It starts with the trial court level. Cases are then appealed to the appellate court level, and finally cases can be appealed to the supreme court level.

The Federal Court System

The authority of federal courts comes directly from the U.S. Constitution and the laws enacted by Congress. The federal courts hear matters that concern the nation as a whole. These matters pertain to constitutional rights, civil rights, interstate commerce, patents and copyrights, federal taxes, currency, and foreign relations. The federal courts may also hear a dispute between citizens of two different states, but only if it involves $75,000 or more.

The federal court system is a three-tiered system consisting of U.S. District Courts, U.S. Courts of Appeal, and the U.S. Supreme Court.

■ *U.S. District Courts.* These are the *trial courts* at the federal level. The United States is currently divided into 94 federal districts, with a court assigned to each. Each district covers a state or a portion of a state. Consequently, some states may be home to more than one federal district court. Every state has at least one U.S. District Court. U.S. District Courts are staffed by judges who hear cases individually, not as a panel.

Some issues are always considered federal issues, such as bankruptcy and crimes involving interstate commerce. Hijacking, kidnapping, bank robbery, and counterfeiting are all federal crimes and would be prosecuted in federal courts. This is called *exclusive jurisdiction* because trial for these issues must take place at a U.S. District Court (state courts may not hear these cases).

- *U.S. Courts of Appeal.* The United States is divided into 12 judicial circuits. Each circuit has a court of appeals. Each appellate court has a panel of judges who review final decisions of the district courts. The decisions of the courts of appeal can be appealed to the U.S. Supreme Court.

- *The United States Supreme Court.* The U.S. Supreme Court is the top court of the federal court system and is located in Washington, D.C. There are nine Supreme Court justices, including a *chief justice.* The President appoints the justices

© Comstock Images/Jupiter Images

What kinds of cases are heard by the U.S. Supreme Court?

to their positions for life. The U.S. Supreme Court is the only federal court expressly established by the U.S. Constitution. Appeals from federal appellate courts and from state supreme courts are considered by the U.S. Supreme Court, which chooses which cases it will hear. Only cases of the greatest importance and national consequence are accepted. Thousands of actions are appealed every year, but the Supreme Court accepts only a small percentage of them.

Special Federal Courts

Congress established special courts to hear only particular kinds of cases. These special federal courts include the Court of Claims, Customs Court, Court of International Trade, Tax Court, Court of Military Appeals, and the territorial courts. If you want to sue the United States, you would file a claim in a U.S. district or special federal court.

State Court Systems

The state court systems handle the greatest share of legal matters because the U.S. Constitution sets limits on the federal system. The Tenth Amendment to the Constitution grants each state the sovereign power to enact and enforce state laws.

A state's laws are contained in its state constitution and enacted by its own legislature (statutory law). These laws are binding upon the citizens of the state and must not violate the U.S. Constitution. Each state has the power to run its own court system to decide issues that involve state laws. Each state establishes its own set of court procedures, determines court names, divides areas of responsibility among the various courts, and sets limits of authority among the state courts. Some issues are tried exclusively in state trial courts, such as divorce, probate, and adoption. Issues that can be heard in either state or federal courts are said to be under *concurrent jurisdiction.* In such cases, the law allows you to choose where to file your case, in either a state or federal court.

Like the federal court system, state court systems also have three tiers.

- *District and Circuit Courts.* General *trial courts*, often called state district courts, circuit courts, or superior courts, decide matters that can be appealed to higher courts. These courts hear civil cases involving large sums of money, criminal matters with major penalties, and cases that are appealed from local courts whose decisions are questionable. Judges at this level are usually appointed by the state governor, although some may be elected on state or local ballots.
- *State Courts of Appeal.* Most states also have an appellate court level, where trials at the state level can be appealed. A panel of judges renders a decision or refuses to hear the cases, whereupon they may be appealed to the next level.
- *State Supreme Courts.* In most states, the highest court is the state supreme court, sometimes called the court of final appeal. Ordinarily, the state supreme court has appellate jurisdiction. The decision of a state supreme court is final, except in cases involving the federal Constitution, laws, and treaties. These decisions can be appealed from the state supreme court to the U.S. Supreme Court.

County and City Courts

The lowest state courts are found at the city or county level. These courts may also be called municipal or justice courts. Courts at this level have authority limited by geographic boundaries. Civil and criminal cases are heard at the local level. However, civil cases must be for small amounts only. At the local level, disputes usually are heard and decided by judges, not by juries. In very small areas, a judge may be called a justice of the peace, who is an appointed, part-time official. Justices of the peace in other areas are elected officials. Special courts at the local level may be called police courts, traffic courts, small claims courts, and justice-of-the-peace courts. Generally, the types of cases heard in special courts cannot be appealed to a higher level; the decision of the judge or jury is final.

COURT PROCEEDINGS

Filing a lawsuit involves many steps, costs, and possible outcomes. You would need an attorney who would advise you of your chances of winning your case, explain the laws pertaining to your case, and tell you what you need to do to prepare for trial. The services of a competent attorney can cost $200 an hour or more. Some attorneys will work on a *contingency-fee* basis, which means they receive fees only if you win the case. Your state bar association can supply names of attorneys who specialize in the area of your complaint. Your attorney will appear in court on your behalf and represent your interests.

All states have a **statute of limitations**, which is a legally defined time limit in which a lawsuit may be filed for various complaints. For example, in many states personal injury lawsuits must be filed within two years from the date of the injury. A lawsuit filed after the two-year limit will be dismissed.

Generally, a lawsuit involves the following four phases—pleadings, discovery, trial, and appeal.

PLEADINGS

In the *pleadings* phase, documents are filed with the court. The first document to be filed is the complaint. The **complaint** is a document outlining the issues of the case and the relief (damages) that the plaintiff requests. The **plaintiff** is the person who brings a lawsuit by filing the complaint. A copy of the complaint is *served* (presented) to the defendant named in the lawsuit. The **defendant** is the person against whom the lawsuit is filed. The local sheriff's department or a *process server* may be used to serve the defendant. Because the officials must present the papers to the defendant personally, the serving process may take several days. The defendant then has a specified amount of time in which to *appear* (file a response to the complaint). If the defendant does not appear, the plaintiff will win the case by *default judgment*.

The defendant usually discusses the case with an attorney. Then the defendant's attorney prepares and files an *answer* to the complaint. The defendant may choose to file a counterclaim. A **counterclaim** is an accusation that the plaintiff is at fault and should pay damages to the defendant. If a counterclaim is filed, the plaintiff then has a set time period in which to file a reply. After the *reply* (admission or denial) is filed, the pleadings phase is finished.

DISCOVERY

In the *discovery* phase, attorneys gather information, talk to witnesses, prepare legal arguments, take depositions, perform investigations, examine reports, and negotiate with the opposing party. The purposes of discovery are (1) to preserve evidence, (2) to eliminate surprise, and (3) to lead to settlement.

A **deposition** is a sworn statement of a witness that is recorded and often videotaped to preserve the memory of the issues at hand. Many cases are settled before going to trial because both parties realize the risk involved in a trial and because information gathered by both sides is known and shared. If the opposing parties can reach a settlement, they sign a formal agreement and the case is resolved. When a settlement cannot be reached, the parties then proceed to the next phase.

VIEW *Points*

In the United States, you can sue anybody for any reason. Of course, that doesn't mean that you will win. The court system is bogged down with millions of cases filed each year. Some of these cases are called frivolous lawsuits, which means they have no merit. Somebody may be suing another person just because they think they can get some money. For example, a person who has an argument with a celebrity (or other rich and famous person) may file a lawsuit even though the person suffered no injuries. If the court finds the lawsuit to be without merit (frivolous), it can award attorneys' fees to the winning party, which means the person filing the frivolous lawsuit must pay not only his or her own costs but also the legal costs of the winning party. Some people feel this practice is unfair and discourages the poor from filing legitimate lawsuits for fear of losing and having to pay exorbitant costs. Others feel that it is a fair practice to protect those being sued unjustly and to discourage frivolous lawsuits.

THINK *CRITICALLY*

With which side of the argument do you agree? Why? Do you think that people file lawsuits too quickly in this country?

TRIAL

The trial phase begins with the setting of a court date. The attorneys representing both sides have a pretrial conference with the judge to plan the trial itself. Defendants may be entitled to a *jury trial* (if they could go to jail), and often juries are provided, but the right to a jury is not automatic. If there is a jury trial, the first step is *jury selection*. Citizens have a duty to serve on a jury when called by the court. The court identifies a pool of potential jurors from voting records or motor vehicle registration records. Attorneys for both sides select jurors from the pool and may challenge jurors (have them dismissed) if they believe the jurors are biased. The process of jury selection is called *voir dire*.

The *trial* begins with *opening statements* from both sides. The plaintiff then presents evidence and witnesses; the defendant then does the same. Both sides attempt to prove their claims and to *discredit* evidence and witnesses presented by the other side. In the process of *direct examination*, witnesses are asked questions by the plaintiff's attorney. In *cross-examination*, the same witnesses are asked questions by the defense attorney. This process starts over when the plaintiff "rests" his or her case and the defense case is presented. Then the attorneys make *closing arguments*, and the judge instructs the jury on relevant points of law. The jury *deliberates*, or carefully considers the arguments of both sides. Then the jury reaches a decision, called the **verdict**.

In deciding civil cases, the burden of proof is called a *preponderance*, or superiority, of the evidence. In other words, one side convinces the jury that its side is more believable. This is sometimes called "clear and convincing evidence." In deciding criminal cases, however, the burden of proof required by prosecutors is called *beyond a reasonable doubt*. The defense attorneys must prove reasonable doubt of the guilt of the accused; they do not have to prove innocence.

Based on the verdict, the court enters a judgment. A **judgment** is the final court ruling that resolves the key issues and establishes the rights and obligations of each party. In a criminal case, the judgment is the ruling of the defendant's guilt or innocence and the consequences of guilt. In a civil case, the judgment typically establishes an amount that the losing party must pay.

APPEAL

The final phase begins if the losing party files an appeal. An **appeal** is a request to a higher court to review the decision of a lower court. Appeals are based on errors of law made at the trial court level that led to the verdict. For example, a judge may have failed to admit evidence that should have been admitted or may have granted a motion that should have been denied, and so on. Errors made by the judge in jury instructions can also be the basis of appeal.

Appellate courts may refuse to hear the case, which happens with more than 50 percent of all cases appealed. If heard, the appellate court may (a) *affirm* (agree with the lower court's decision), (b) *reverse* (change the lower court's decision), or (c) *remand* (send the case back for a new trial).

A case heard in a state trial court may be appealed to a court of appeals, after which it may be appealed to the state supreme court. Any matters involving national interests may be appealed to the U.S. Supreme Court, which may or may not choose to hear the case. In a civil lawsuit, the losing party may be required to pay court costs as well as the winner's attorney's fee.

Court reporters create verbatim transcripts of legal proceedings, depositions, and other legal events. They play a critical role in judicial proceedings and every other meeting where the spoken word must be preserved in its exact content.

The most common method of court reporting is stenography where reporters use a stenotype machine. Combinations of letters represent sounds, words, and phrases. These symbols are displayed as text in a process called computer-aided transcription (CAT). In real-time, these symbols can instantly appear as text on a screen.

Some court reporting is done with audio and video recording. Another type is voice writing where the court reporters speak into a voice silencer, which is a hand-held mask that contains a microphone.

Employment Outlook

- Much faster than average employment growth is expected.

Job Titles

- Court reporter
- Webcaster
- Real-time reporter (for hearing impaired)

Needed Skills

- Completion of one- or two-year program and state licensure is often required.
- Certification through the National Court Reporters Association is preferred.
- Excellent keyboarding skills are required along with good grammar and listening skills.

What's it like to work in... *Court Reporting*

Laura has worked in court reporting for many years. She is currently using a stenotype machine but is learning to use CAT technology that was recently purchased for the state court building where she works.

Laura is scheduled to work the civil and criminal cases in her county. She works four days a week recording testimony. She is responsible for ensuring a complete and accurate legal record of the court proceedings. After the trial, Laura prepares written transcripts, makes copies, and distributes them to the courts and attorneys. One day a week she performs retrieval and storage tasks needed to maintain the court's information systems. Judges and attorneys often rely on Laura to help them search for information they need contained in official records.

Laura prepared a customized law dictionary containing words and terminologies that are commonly used, and she updates it periodically to ensure she remains efficient in her job. She loves the many challenges presented by her job.

What About You?

Do you have an interest in the legal system? Are you able to listen carefully and process what you have heard? Would you consider a career in court reporting?

Assessment

KEY TERMS REVIEW

Match the terms with the definitions. Some terms may not be used.

_____ 1. The person who files a lawsuit

_____ 2. A sworn statement of a witness

_____ 3. Case that involves a government unit who is accusing an individual of committing a crime

_____ 4. The decision of the jury

_____ 5. A case that involves one person who has a dispute with another person or entity

_____ 6. The person against whom a lawsuit is filed

_____ 7. A legally defined time limit in which a lawsuit may be filed

_____ 8. The final court ruling

_____ 9. A document outlining the issues of the case and the relief (damages) that the plaintiff requests

_____ 10. An accusation that the plaintiff is at fault and should pay damages to the defendant

a. appeal

b. civil case

c. common law

d. complaint

e. counterclaim

f. criminal case

g. defendant

h. deposition

i. judgment

j. plaintiff

k. statute of limitations

l. verdict

CHECK YOUR UNDERSTANDING

11. What is common law?

12. Who can serve on a jury?

APPLY YOUR KNOWLEDGE

13. Describe the three-tiered court system of your state along with the federal system. Explain how a lawsuit might progress from the state trial level to the U.S. Supreme Court.

THINK _CRITICALLY_

14. The judge decides issues of law; the jury decides issues of fact. Explain why this separation of duties is a needed part of our legal system.

15. Why would a person who has a personal injury claim against another driver wish to enter into a contingency-fee agreement with her attorney?

16. The period of time between the pleadings phase and the trial is called discovery. Give examples of discovery and explain why it is an important part of the legal process?

Other Redress Solutions

GOALS
- Define remedies available to consumers other than individual lawsuits.
- Explain alternative dispute resolution (ADR) options.

TERMS
- disputing a charge, p. 694
- small claims court, p. 694
- class-action lawsuit, p. 695
- alternative dispute resolution (ADR), p. 697
- negotiation, p. 697
- mediation, p. 697
- arbitration, p. 697
- binding arbitration, p. 698
- unfair labor practice (ULP), p. 698

SELF-HELP REMEDIES

Lawsuits are lengthy, expensive, and emotionally draining. If you have a consumer problem, you should pursue a settlement yourself before deciding to sue. In many cases, when you approach the other person with your side of the dispute, you can resolve the issue without taking further action.

INFORMAL DISCUSSIONS

Whenever you have a dispute, start talking. Contact the retailer, seller, or other party with whom you have the dispute. Describe the situation and your proposed remedy. Listen carefully to the other side and look for ways to settle the argument so that both sides have their interests met.

If you buy a defective product, first seek an agreeable remedy with the merchant before pursuing legal remedies. Informal discussions that lead to settlement are much less expensive and easier to achieve than legal remedies. They are also less stressful. If the informal discussion process does not work, you can proceed to more serious steps, such as withholding payment, returning or refusing merchandise, or disputing a charge.

© Photodisc/Getty Images

Why should you try to resolve a dispute through informal discussions rather than simply filing a lawsuit?

Withholding Payment

As a consumer, you can withhold payment in a purchase dispute. This assumes you have the merchandise but have not yet paid for it. However, you must put your complaint in writing right away and explain the reason why you are withholding payment on the disputed amount. You cannot have double remedies; that is, you cannot both keep the merchandise and withhold payment.

Returning or Refusing Merchandise

You can refuse delivery or return merchandise to the seller. Even if the seller refuses to accept it back, you can leave it at the store or other business location. In some cases, you can mail it back or have it delivered back to the business. Be sure to get and keep any receipts or other evidence that the goods were returned. This is proof that you have not benefitted from having something for which you are refusing to pay.

Disputing a Charge

If you used credit for a purchase, you can call your credit card company and dispute a charge. **Disputing a charge** generally means that you are asking the credit issuer to reverse the charge on your account. To dispute a charge, you must follow procedures outlined by the credit issuer. The law requires the seller to respond to your complaint within a reasonable time limit. You should pay all other amounts due as agreed. Your credit should not be damaged if you follow the proper procedures for disputing credit charges.

When you buy merchandise with credit, you have more leverage than if you pay cash. You can instruct the credit card company to withhold payment to the merchant. If you follow the credit card company's procedure, the credit card issuer will help you resolve the problem with the merchant.

NETBookmark

If you purchase a product with your credit card and later have a dispute with the merchant because there is a problem with the product, your credit card company may be able to help. Access www.cengage.com/school/pfinance/mypf and click on the link for Chapter 30. Read the article, then answer: What should your first step be when you have a dispute with a merchant because you are unhappy with a purchase? If you do subsequently contact your credit card company about the disputed purchase, what information will you need to provide them?

www.cengage.com/school/pfinance/mypf

SMALL CLAIMS COURT

If the disputed amount is relatively small, you might consider taking the matter to small claims court. A **small claims court** is a court of limited jurisdiction. It decides small matters quickly with a minimum of cost, and the decision is final. You must represent yourself—no attorneys are allowed—and there is no jury. A judge decides the matter. Most states set a maximum amount of $2,000 to $5,000 in damages that can be recovered in a small claims court.

Small claims courts are easy to use. You can get an instruction sheet from your county courthouse that explains how to file a small claim. You must know the name and address of the

Assume that you purchased a television from a local retailer, using cash. When you plug it in at home, the television will not work. You want to return it, but unfortunately you didn't keep the receipt from the merchant. Role-play this situation with a classmate who acts as the store manager. What will you say to the manager? What are you willing to accept or do in order to achieve a favorable settlement?

person with whom you have a problem. You must know the amount in contention and make a short statement of why you are entitled to the money.

Once you file your claim, the court will serve a copy of it to the defendant. The defendant has ten days to appear. If the defendant contests (disagrees with) the claim, the court sets a hearing date. The hearing lasts about a half hour. You present your side of the case; the defendant does the same. You may bring in written statements and other evidence as well as witnesses. You should summarize your position on one page and present it to the judge.

No record is made of the small claims court hearing. It cannot be appealed. The judge's decision is final. The benefit of taking your dispute to small claims court is financial: you pay no attorneys' fees. Court filing fees are small, typically $50 to $150. The case is heard in a few weeks at most, giving you speedy relief. If the defendant does not appear, you win by default. The judge proclaims a judgment, and the losing party is required to pay damages.

It is important in a small claims court hearing that you be organized, calm, and specific about your complaint. If you are asking for $500 in damages, you must be prepared to show why you deserve that sum. The judge will ask questions of you and the defendant. Usually the judge will make an immediate decision or will take a short break and return with the decision.

CLASS-ACTION LAWSUITS

A **class-action lawsuit** is one in which a large number of people with similar complaints against the same defendant join together to sue. Such lawsuits often involve products that injured many people, and the defendant is the product's manufacturer and others in the supply chain (retailers, parts producers, distributors, and so on). Sometimes employees join together to sue their employer for discrimination affecting all of them. In a class-action suit, a person sues another person or a company on behalf of himself or herself and all others in the same situation. If the plaintiffs win, they split the judgment.

© Corbis

Why might you want to resort to small claims court rather than a jury trial?

In some cases, you can convince a consumer protection group to file a lawsuit on your behalf. For example, the American Civil Liberties Union (ACLU) files lawsuits to protect the rights of groups of citizens. The ACLU collects money from donations to pay the costs involved in filing lawsuits. Many individuals cannot afford to pursue legal remedies without the help of such groups because of the expense involved.

▮ GOVERNMENTAL ASSISTANCE

You may wish to seek help from a government agency to stop some objectionable practice and help you get your money back. Many sources of consumer assistance were discussed in Chapter 29. These types of cases often benefit all consumers by protecting them from fraudulent business practices.

Most states have attorney general offices with consumer protection services available to consumers in the state. You may be able to file a complaint online. The state office will investigate the complaint and take appropriate action. There are also federal government agencies that can assist you with a consumer complaint, many of which are listed in Figure 30.1.

FIGURE 30.1	*Government Assistance*
Automobiles	National Highway Traffic Safety Administration
Collection, Credit	State Consumer Protection Division (at your state capital)
Drugs/Foods	Food and Drug Administration
Household	Consumer Product Safety Commission
Investment Fraud	Federal Trade Commission Securities and Exchange Commission
Medical/Dental	State Board of Medical Examiners State Department of Commerce State Board of Dental Examiners State Health Division State Board of Pharmacy
Medicare	Social Security Administration
Misrepresentation/Fraud	State Consumer Protection Division Local District Attorney Local or State Better Business Bureau
Transportation	Interstate Commerce Commission
Warranties	Federal Trade Commission

ALTERNATIVE DISPUTE RESOLUTION

Alternative dispute resolution (ADR) is a general term covering several other formal methods of settling disputes without using the court system. The services provided in ADR are not free, but they are much less expensive than taking a case to trial. State-certified professionals can help you with negotiation, mediation, or arbitration.

NEGOTIATION

Negotiation is the process of finding a solution that is acceptable to both sides. A neutral third party, called a *negotiator*, assists the parties. Often a negotiator is needed because the parties cannot meet together due to strong emotions that would prohibit them from talking out the problem without yelling or other disruption. For example, when getting a divorce, the two parties may be unable to reach an agreement about division of property, visitation for children, and other economic issues. The negotiator guides the discussion and helps the parties recognize what is most important and reach an agreement.

Negotiation requires tactful give-and-take. You must know the specifics of the problem, what you want done about it, and what you are willing to do to make a settlement. Both sides must be calm and reasonable. Emotional outbursts and confrontational statements create hostility and reduce the chances of finding a remedy that is agreeable to both sides.

MEDIATION

When the parties cannot negotiate a settlement, the next level of ADR is called mediation. **Mediation** is a dispute resolution method in which an independent third person, a *mediator*, helps the parties to reach a solution in a controlled environment. The mediator controls the conversation, allowing both sides to speak separately and state their case. If the parties seem able to do so, the mediator may allow them to speak to each other. The mediator listens carefully and helps both sides sort out what is important and what they would be willing to give up to get it. The mediator proposes a solution and, if the parties agree, prepares a settlement document for the parties to sign. A skilled mediator is able to work with people who otherwise would not be able to come to an agreement.

© Brand X Pictures/Jupiter Images

Why would a person choose ADR rather than taking a case to court?

ARBITRATION

The highest level of ADR is arbitration. **Arbitration** involves an independent third person, called an *arbitrator*, who helps resolve the dispute. But unlike negotiation and mediation, arbitration uses strict rules of procedure. In addition, the arbitrator has subject matter expertise, which means the arbitrator has a legal or professional background related to the issue involved. Arbitrators are often retired judges or attorneys who specialize in the type of issue that is being resolved.

There are two common types of arbitration: voluntary and binding. In *voluntary arbitration*, the arbitrator listens to both sides and makes a recommendation but cannot impose it. Both parties are free to accept or reject it. With **binding arbitration**, the arbitrator makes a decision that is binding on the parties. The parties must agree before arbitration begins that they will accept the decision as final.

Labor disputes are often settled with arbitration decisions. Many labor contracts specify that in the event the employee feels that the employer has done something illegal (or against the terms of the labor contract), they will submit to binding arbitration. If the employee works for the state or other contracted employer, the employee would begin the process by filing a complaint called an **unfair labor practice (ULP)**, which is formal notification to the employer.

An arbitrator (or panel of arbitrators) is appointed to hear the case, and the decision of the arbitrator is final and binding. Often arbitration clauses in contracts specify who pays for the arbitration. Both parties could share the cost, or the losing party could be required to pay it all.

The *Yellow Pages* has listings for ADR professionals in the fields of negotiation, mediation, and arbitration services. You can also find many such resources online. Figure 30.2 lists some dispute resolution resources that you can contact.

FIGURE 30.2 *ADR Resources*

- **American Arbitration Association**
  Dispute Resolution Services Worldwide
  Information about ADR, articles, procedures, online services
  www.adr.org

- **American Bar Association**
  Information about ADR choices
  From home page, enter "alternative dispute resolution" in search box
  www.abanet.org

- **CPR International Institute for Conflict Prevention & Resolution**
  Center for Public Resources
  ADR procedures, information, training
  www.cpradr.org

- **Divorce Mediation**
  Getting a divorce mediator; mediating online
  www.divorceinfo.com/mediation.htm

- **Lawyer Referral and Information Service**
  How to find the right attorney, referrals, classification areas
  www.martindale.com

ISSUES IN YOUR WORLD

RESOLVING DISPUTES FOR E-CONSUMERS

When you buy products online, you are taking a risk. If something goes wrong, you often can't return the product to a physical store and talk to the manager. Online dispute resolution services include the ability to file a complaint and have an independent online service help you get it resolved. If the seller has an ongoing business, the site operator will be willing to discuss and work out an agreement. You can also help to protect yourself with insurance provided through seal owners (companies that guarantee web sites). If you feel you have been misled by a web site, you can file a claim to obtain recourse.

If you buy from a business that displays a seal of approval from a certification or warranty company, such as Square Trade (www.squaretrade.com), Webtrust (www.webtrust.org), or TRUSTe (www.truste.org), you can also find assistance in resolving disputes at these web sites. These companies will keep track of complaints, alert members of problems, and monitor to see that disputes are resolved satisfactorily and within a reasonable period of time.

At the Better Business Bureau "BBBOnline" program (www.bbb.org/online), consumers can file complaints and view complaints filed by others, as well as see which companies have complaints filed against them. For complete alternative dispute resolution services similar to those in the traditional brick-and-mortar world, you can go to official ADR sites, such as Cybersettle. These web sites offer arbitration for those who wish to use the service.

To file a complaint, go to the appropriate web site and complete forms that explain the issue. The online merchant responds, and both of you can continue a dialog until all issues are "on the table." This service is often called hosted message board negotiation, *and it is a free process for consumers.*

You do have avenues for redress when shopping on the Internet. Still, it is wise to shop carefully online and buy only from merchants you know.

THINK *CRITICALLY*

1. *Have you or has someone you know purchased something online that was of poor quality or wasn't what you ordered? How did you resolve the problem?*

2. *In what ways is online shopping riskier than shopping in a physical store?*

3. *Why is it important to look for a seal of approval from a certification or warranty company when shopping online?*

Assessment

KEY TERMS REVIEW

Match the terms with the definitions. Some terms may not be used.

_____ 1. Formal methods of settling disputes without using the court system

_____ 2. Asking the credit issuer to reverse the charge on your account

_____ 3. A court of limited jurisdiction that decides small matters quickly with minimum cost

_____ 4. A complaint filed by an employee claiming violation of a labor contract

_____ 5. A lawsuit in which a large number of people with similar complaints against the same defendant join together to sue

_____ 6. The process of finding a solution to a dispute that is acceptable to both sides through informal discussion

_____ 7. A process in which an independent third person helps resolve a dispute using strict rules of procedure

a. alternative dispute resolution (ADR)

b. arbitration

c. binding arbitration

d. class-action lawsuit

e. disputing a charge

f. mediation

g. negotiation

h. small claims court

i. unfair labor practice (ULP)

CHECK YOUR UNDERSTANDING

8. Why might you choose small claims court over filing a lawsuit in regular court?

9. How is arbitration different from mediation?

APPLY YOUR KNOWLEDGE

10. If you were involved in a dispute, what steps would you take before involving third persons or the court? Why?

THINK _CRITICALLY_

11. Why do people join class-action lawsuits? Is this a good idea? Why or why not?

12. Under what circumstances would you consider filing a complaint with a government agency as a means of obtaining redress?

13. Under what circumstances would you seek the assistance of a negotiator? Explain the types of situations where people are unable to resolve an issue without help.

Chapter Assessment

SUMMARY

30.1

- *The U.S. legal system is built on several sources of law, including constitutional, statutory, and common law. Common law is based on decisions made in court cases that serve as models for future cases.*

- *Trial courts have original jurisdiction, or the authority to hear cases first. Appellate courts review decisions of lower courts.*

- *Civil courts hear noncriminal cases. Criminal courts hear cases involving punishable offenses against society.*

- *The judge, clerk, reporter, and bailiff are court employees.*

- *Both federal and state court systems consist of district trial courts, courts of appeal, and a supreme court. Issues that fall under both state and federal laws are said to be under concurrent jurisdiction.*

- *All states have a statute of limitations that defines a time limit in which a lawsuit may be filed for various complaints.*

- *Court proceedings begin with pleadings, where a plaintiff files a complaint. The defendant may respond with a counterclaim. After the defendant responds, a period of discovery follows, which may include taking depositions. Then the case goes to trial. The losing party may appeal.*

- *With jury trials, the attorneys select jurors from the pool of citizens called by the court. The judge instructs the jury on relevant laws. The jury reaches a verdict and the court enters a judgment.*

30.2

- *Consumers can resolve most disputes themselves through informal discussions. If discussions fail, the consumer may withhold payment, return or refuse merchandise, or dispute charges with the credit card company.*

- *Small claims court requires no attorney and small filing fees, but the decision of the judge is final.*

- *A large number of people with similar complaints against the same defendant may join together in a class-action lawsuit.*

- *Alternative dispute resolution means settling disputes without using the court system. ADR includes negotiation, mediation, and arbitration.*

- *Negotiators help parties reach a solution. Mediators control a conversation where parties are unable to work things out. The mediator also proposes a solution and draws up an agreement if issues are settled.*

- *In voluntary arbitration, the arbitrator makes a recommendation that the parties are free to accept or reject. In binding arbitration, the parties must accept the arbitrator's decision.*

APPLY WHAT YOU KNOW

1. *A case that involves a dispute in a city is filed with the circuit court of a county in the same state. After a trial court hears the case, where can it be appealed?*

2. *A plaintiff files a lawsuit. Explain what happens until a court renders a judgment. What happens if the losing party thinks the court made a "legal" error in the case?*

3. *As a store customer, you are dissatisfied with a product you purchased. Explain the self-help remedies and actions to consider in resolving the dispute.*

4. *Why are small claims courts easy to use and, in some cases, more advantageous than a formal court proceeding?*

5. *Use the Internet to investigate government agencies that can assist you with consumer complaints. For what types of complaints is each agency responsible? Describe a past consumer complaint you or a member of your family has had. Which agency would you choose for help with this consumer problem?*

6. *Search the Internet for information about mediators or arbitrators. Write a one-page report on what they do, how they do it, and how consumers can employ their services.*

MAKE ACADEMIC CONNECTIONS

7. **Math** *Suppose you file a lawsuit and enter into an agreement with your lawyer to pay costs and attorney's fees of 30 percent of the award. If court costs are $300, investigation fees are $500, and you are awarded a judgment of $30,000, how much will your attorney receive in fees? How much will you receive?*

8. **Communication** *Write a paper about the legal system and tort law (personal injury claims filed by attorneys). Explain what is meant by "tort reform" and how it could affect large lawsuit damages awarded to victims of torts. Explain how this affects everyone. Cite your sources, including at least one online source.*

9. **Research** *Conduct online legal research. Enter the keywords "Martindale-Hubbell" and report your findings. Key in other terms that you'd like to know more about, such as "real estate law" or "Miranda v. Arizona." You will be able to find many sources of legal information about cases, decisions, and legal matters. Explain how the Internet has changed the way people do research on legal topics.*

10. **International Studies** *Select one European country and another country in the Middle East or other region where the legal system is very different from the system in the United States. Find information about the structure of their legal system and the basis of their laws. Prepare a report on your findings.*

Solve Problems and

Explore Issues

11. Visit your local law library located at the county courthouse, a public university, or at a law school if there is one in your area. List five types of references available. Look up the statute of limitations for filing lawsuits in your state and tell how long you have to file actions in the following situations: (a) wrongful death or injury, (b) real property infringement, (c) civil action where you are the injured party in a contract. Also in your law library, you will find books that summarize cases tried and decided in your state. Find a case that interests you and summarize the issues involved, the court's decision, and your reactions.

12. With your instructor's permission, spend a half-day at a local county courthouse. Make arrangements to observe a case being tried. Generally, you will not be allowed to leave the room until the court adjourns, nor will you be allowed to enter while court is in session. You may observe a civil or criminal case. Write a report on what you observe.

13. Examine a lawsuit that has been filed. You can look at records of cases that have been filed in your county, although you will not be given copies free of charge. Read through each case and make notes about the plaintiff, the defendant, the issue at hand, what the plaintiff was asking, and how the matter was resolved.

14. Work in groups to determine the appropriate legal remedy for each of the following situations: (a) The plaintiff was driving his vehicle in a northerly direction when the defendant ran a stop sign going in an easterly direction and caused severe damage to the plaintiff's vehicle, including personal injuries to the plaintiff. (b) A person has paid money to a telemarketer for a product that was promised but never received. (c) A local restaurant served food that caused people who ate there on a particular night to get sick. No one died, but several people were very sick for several days, causing medical bills amounting to several thousand dollars.

EXTEND YOUR LEARNING

15. **Legal Issues** Punitive damages are often awarded by juries to send a message that deters others from committing the same violation. Many people feel that punitive damages in cases such as medical malpractice can have a staggering effect on insurance rates for doctors, thus raising costs for everyone. Do you agree that juries should award punitive damages? Should an established limit be placed on the amount of punitive damages that can be awarded? How would limiting punitive damages by statute affect the judicial system?

For related activities and links, go to **www.cengage.com/school/pfinance/mypf**

Ralph Nader

Ralph Nader has been a U.S. presidential candidate in four elections. He is most famous, however, for his long career in consumer rights, humanitarianism, and environmentalism.

© AP Photo/Charles Dharapak

Nader was born in Winsted, Connecticut on February 27, 1934. He graduated from Princeton University in 1955 and Harvard Law School in 1958. He was a professor at the University of Hartford, and in 1964, he moved to Washington, D.C., where he worked for Assistant Secretary of Labor Daniel Patrick Moynihan. He also advised a U.S. Senate subcommittee on car safety. He went on to serve as a faculty member at the American University Washington College of Law, but his exposure to politics would lead him back to it again and again.

Nader's first consumer safety articles appeared in *The Harvard Law Record*. He first criticized the auto industry in an article he wrote for *The Nation* in 1959. In 1965, Nader wrote *Unsafe at Any Speed*, a study that asserted that many American cars were unsafe, especially the Chevrolet Corvair. Many young activitists, inspired by Nader's work, joined him on other projects. They became known as "Nader's Raiders." They investigated government corruption and published dozens of books.

In the 1970s and 1980s, Nader was a key leader in the antinuclear movement. By 1976, Nader also became allied with the environmental movement. In 1980, Nader began campaigning against what he believed were the dangers of large multinational corporations. He started a variety of nonprofit organizations such as the Citizen Advocacy Center, the Disability Rights Center, the Equal Justice Foundation, and Democracy Rising, a group focused on empowering citizens. In both 1990 and 1999, Ralph Nader was named by *Time* magazine to be among the 100 most influential Americans in the 20th century.

THINK *CRITICALLY*

1. *How has Ralph Nader made a difference in the lives of consumers today?*

2. *How did Ralph Nader get into the political arena? How has he used his law background to further his interests?*

3. *What can you learn from someone like Ralph Nader who has dedicated his life to consumer issues?*

4. *Why is it important to get involved in political movements?*

Philanthropy and Ethical Issues

Overview

Philanthropy is the act of donating money, goods, time, or effort to support a societal cause, often over an extended period of time. Although many philanthropists are wealthy, many people not possessing great wealth perform philanthropic acts. Philanthropists want to leave the world a better place than they found it. Everyone has the opportunity to give something back.

  Ethics is the study of right versus wrong, good versus bad, just versus unjust. Legal and ethical responsibilities are not the same thing. We can decide to do the moral minimum (do no harm), or we can resolve to do better. In the very least, we as human beings should realize that learning leads to knowledge, knowledge leads to wisdom, and wisdom leads to understanding. Only when we realize the need for ethics can we begin the process of learning what will lead us to the desire to do the right thing.

© Photodisc/Getty Images

WHY PHILANTHROPY IS IMPORTANT

The major reason why philanthropy is important is because it is the primary source of funding for the fine arts, the performing arts, and religious and humanitarian causes, as well as private (and some public) schools and universities. Many valuable institutions of culture would not continue to exist without the generosity of private philanthropists.

In addition to wealthy individuals, companies, and foundations that have donated vast sums of cash and assets, many nonwealthy people donate substantial portions of their time, effort, and wealth to charitable causes. When you give your time, you are in fact giving the most valuable thing you have. Time is something that cannot be stored, cannot be regained once it is gone, and is in very limited supply for each of us. When you give your time, you are sharing more than monetary wealth; you are giving of yourself and sharing that which is most precious of all.

Philanthropy is important because it feeds the soul of the nation. That is to say, when those whose needs are greatest are given a hand, the entire nation feels the benefit. We are all able to enjoy the richness of culture that results when events are sponsored by those who can afford to pay so that those who cannot afford to pay can experience them as well.

FORMS OF PHILANTHROPY

Every year, wealthy people give massive amounts of money to various causes. The largest individual bequest was a $37 billion gift from Warren Buffett to the Bill and Melinda Gates Foundation (which funds projects from education to the arts) in 2006. *Reader's Digest* gave $424 million to the Metropolitan Museum of Art. Joan Kroc gave $200 million to the National Public Radio. Henry Rowan gave $100 million to Glassboro State College. While these massive dollar donations grab media attention, there are many other forms of philanthropy that go almost unnoticed in comparison, such as those described below.

- A recent and growing trend in philanthropy is the concept of giving circles. With *giving circles*, a group of individuals who are or who become friends pool their charitable donations and decide together how to use the money to benefit the causes that they care about.
- *Volunteerism* is a very important form of philanthropy. Young people who provide service during their youth reap considerable benefits, not only for those they serve but also in their own character development. When people learn to give as they go along, rather than at the end of their lives, it changes their perspective.
- Many *charitable organizations* exist to support worthy causes. These organizations seek donations from individuals. Some of their supporters are wealthy individuals, but most charitable organizations receive the bulk of their funding from many private individuals who give less than $100 each.

Thus, we realize that anyone can be a philanthropist, and anyone can participate in funding causes, programs, and needs that exist within society.

SO MANY WORTHWHILE CAUSES

How do you know which charity is the right one to which you should donate your money, time, assets, or talents? You are right to suspect that in the world of charity, there are those persons, groups, and organizations that would take advantage of your generosity and provide nothing of value to society.

The American Institute of Philanthropy (AIP) is a watchdog group that keeps track of, rates, and publishes reports on more than 500 charitable organizations. You can learn about any charity—what it does (and does not do), how it is run, and what percentage of your donation will actually be used for the purposes you specify. The AIP also provides tips for giving wisely, instructions for how to give online, and answers to your questions. You can then give money with the assurance that the charity of your choice is what it says it is and is doing what it says it is doing. You can visit the AIP web site and ask questions online at http://www.charitywatch.org. To assess your strengths and weaknesses and make a decision about the type of philanthropist you can be, complete Worksheet 1 (My Philanthropy Plan) provided for you in the *Student Activity Guide* and also presented on the next page for reference.

ETHICS AND VALUES

Ethical duties are not the same as legal responsibilities. The law does not require us to "do good," but merely to "do no harm." But just because we can do something (and get away with it), doesn't mean we should. Ethics involves making choices that are based on values. It is a measure of the depth of our character and reveals who we really are. Before making a decision that fringes upon doing something unethical, ask yourself these questions: Is this something I will feel good about later? Is this how I would like to be treated by someone else? Would I be proud if my family and friends were to know about it?

To further explore the issue of ethics, analyze the case studies on the following pages involving ethics in the marketplace, in the workplace, and on the Internet. Record your answers in the space provided on Worksheets 2, 3, 4, 5, and 6 provided for you in the *Student Activity Guide* and also presented on pages 709–713 for reference. In analyzing each case, you must (1) identify the problem, (2) apply relevant knowledge to the solution of the problem, and (3) draw a conclusion or reach a decision based on careful analysis of the problem.

People base ethical decisions on their personal values and principles, which they develop through individual life experiences. Therefore, since everyone has different experiences, decisions about each case will probably vary.

You can probably discuss an ethical issue that you yourself have experienced in the last few weeks or months. How did you resolve the issue? Do you feel good about your decision? If you could do it over again, would you do something different?

We all make mistakes. The important thing is to learn from them. Remember, you can't always be perfect, but you can always strive to do better. Thus, in the end, you will be able to say, "I did the best I could. And when I knew better, I did better."

Let's all resolve to do the best we can!

WORKSHEET 1
My Philanthropy Plan

Answer the following questions about yourself and what you can do to help others who are less fortunate than you are. Then make a commitment to give during your lifetime, so that you can help make the world a better place.

1. If you had money to spare, far beyond your wants and needs, how would you choose to spend it? Be specific.

2. What is your favorite charitable organization or cause? Why?

3. What do you consider to be your greatest gift (talent)? How could you use that gift to help others?

4. If you had enough time to spare and didn't need to work for a living, what would you do?

5. Looking back at your life, 100 years after your death, for what would you like to be remembered?

6. List organizations you would like to help and the ways you can help.

WORKSHEET 2
Cutting It Close

Valerie wanted to earn extra money over the summer, so she decided to start a lawn-mowing business in her neighborhood. To advertise her business, she composed a flyer to put in her neighbors' mailboxes. On the flyer, she listed her services: mowing, trimming, and blowing grass clippings off the driveway and sidewalk when she finished. She offered all of these services for one low price.

Several neighbors wanted her service. In fact, more people asked than she had time to serve. Not wanting to pass up the opportunity to earn so much money, Valerie agreed to do the lawns of all who asked. She figured she would find some way to mow them all. Since she was dealing with neighbors, she did not offer any written contracts. They just agreed verbally.

For three weeks, Valerie worked very hard but still could not finish all the lawns she had agreed to mow. She realized, though, that if she didn't trim the lawns, she could mow one additional lawn each weekend, so that's what she decided to do. Valerie reasoned that her mower could cut grass very close to trees and walls, so the trimming didn't really seem necessary. She was giving her customers a very low price, so it was a good deal even without the trimming. Besides, she could now satisfy more customers who otherwise would have to mow their own lawns or take the time to find someone else to do them.

1. Since Valerie and her neighbors did not sign a written contract, is Valerie obligated to perform the services she listed on her flyer? Why or why not?

2. Valerie is 16, so she is a minor. How does this fact affect her legal and ethical obligations to her neighbors?

3. Do you agree with Valerie's reasons for not trimming? Why or why not?

4. Are the benefits she is offering her neighbors worth giving up the trimming service?

5. If you were in Valerie's situation, what would you do? Why?

WORKSHEET 3
I'm Anonymous

Rajesh works full time and lives in an apartment with two roommates. He has met many people online, and he uses several screen names. He visits chat rooms and reads personal ads frequently and sometimes responds to them. He never provides correct information because he doesn't want anyone finding out who he really is. On several occasions, Rajesh made arrangements to meet someone, but often he did not show up as agreed.

As a joke, Rajesh sometimes sends insulting or vaguely threatening messages to coworkers he doesn't like. He enjoys hearing them talk about the messages at work. Because Rajesh doesn't mean them any real harm, he believes the messages don't hurt anybody. And because he's anonymous, he doesn't think he's taking any risks.

1. Do you think Rajesh is acting appropriately on the Internet? Why or why not?

2. Have you ever acted in similar ways toward people on the Internet? Explain.

3. How would you feel if you received an insulting or threatening e-mail from an anonymous sender?

4. What suggestions would you make to Rajesh about behaving appropriately and staying safe on the Internet?

WORKSHEET 4
Something for Nothing

Jared and Kayla work together for a fast-food restaurant. They are both good workers and have been employed for over a year. Each Christmas the company they work for has a big party for all employees. Gifts are given away to employees who provide outstanding service during the year.

Jared and Kayla's manager has worked for the company for over ten years. She discovered a way to falsify information in the computer to her advantage. She gets more than her fair share of gifts while others in the company do not get as much. Jared and Kayla accidentally discovered this scam. The manager encouraged Jared and Kayla to participate in the scheme.

"You two can get more gifts if you participate. If you try to turn me in, I'll have both of you fired," she said.

1. What is the ethical problem involved in this situation?

2. What are Jared and Kayla's options?

3. What would you do if you were in this situation? Why?

4. How is this case an example of employee theft in the workplace?

WORKSHEET 5
It's a Good Deal

When Reynaldo flew to see his relatives last year, he was able to earn enough air miles for a free ticket. The frequent flyer club rules are clear: The ticket is nontransferable.

Reynaldo bought a ticket for a flight across the country but later discovered he couldn't go. A friend of his was planning a similar trip, so Reynaldo offered him the ticket for $100—much cheaper than the cost of a full fare.

When Reynaldo's friend tried to use the ticket on his return flight, the agent discovered that the ticket belonged to someone else. The airline refused to allow him on the plane without paying the full price for a new ticket. When he told Reynaldo about the problem, Reynaldo said it wasn't his concern.

1. Discuss the issues involved in Reynaldo's dilemma.

2. What's wrong with the owner of a ticket giving or selling it to someone else?

3. Would you participate in this type of a deal? Why or why not?

4. If offered a similar deal, what should you do before accepting it?

WORKSHEET 6
Nobody Got Hurt

Loriann bought a new dress to wear for a special occasion. During the course of the evening, she spilled some juice on the dress and was unable to remove all of the stain. The stain was small and not really visible at first glance.

The next day, Loriann decided that she would probably never wear the dress again. The dress didn't fit as well as she would have liked, so she decided to get her money back. That afternoon she returned the dress to the store. She claimed the dress was a gift that she didn't like. The store gave her credit for the dress, and Loriann bought something else.

When asked how she could do something like that, Loriann replied, "Why not? Nobody got hurt."

1. Was there anything wrong with what Loriann did? Did anybody get hurt? Who?

2. Why do some stores have lenient return policies? Why do some stores have "no return" policies?

3. What would you do if you worked in the store and knew what Loriann had done?

4. Discuss the ethical principles involved in this case.

Glossary

20/10 Rule   A plan to limit the use of credit to no more than 20 percent of yearly take-home pay, with payments of no more than 10 percent of monthly take-home pay.

401(k) Plan   A defined-contribution plan for employees of companies that operate for a profit.

403(b) Plan   A defined-contribution plan for employees of schools, non-profit organizations, and government units.

A

A-Rating   An excellent credit rating.

Absenteeism   The record and pattern of absence rates of workers.

Adjustable-Rate Mortgage (ARM)   A mortgage for which the interest rate changes in response to the movement of interest rates in the economy as a whole.

Adjusted Gross Income   Gross income less adjustments.

Adult Foster Care Facility   A shelter for adults who need care beyond what can be provided at home.

Advanced Degrees   Specialized, intensive programs (taken after obtaining the first college degree) that prepare students for higher-level work responsibilities with more challenges and higher pay.

Agency Bond   A bond issued by a federal agency.

Allowances   Reduction in the amount of tax withheld from your paycheck.

Alternative Dispute Resolution (ADR)   Formal methods of settling disputes without suing the court system.

Annual Percentage Rate (APR)   The cost of credit expressed as a yearly percentage.

Annual Percentage Yield (APY)   The actual interest rate an account earns stated on a yearly basis.

Annual Report   A summary of a corporation's financial results for the year and its prospects for the future.

Annuity   Income from an investment paid in a series of regular payments made for a set number of years.

Appeal   A request to a higher court to review the decision of a lower court.

Application Letter   Also called a cover letter, it serves to introduce you to a potential employer.

Appraised Value   Home value determined by examining the structure, size, features, and quality as compared to similar homes.

Aptitude   A natural, physical or mental ability that allows you to do certain tasks well.

Arbitration   A dispute resolution method in which an independent third person, called an arbitrator, helps resolve the dispute.

Arbitrator   An independent third person who resolves a dispute.

Assessed value   Value set by the city or county that is used to compute property taxes.

Assets   Items of value that a person owns.

Assigned-Risk Pool   A group of people who are unable to obtain automobile insurance due to high risk.

Attractive Nuisance   A dangerous place, condition, or object that is particularly attractive to children.

Audit   An examination of your tax return and records by the IRS.

Automatic Deductions   Represent money you have authorized your bank or other organization to move from one account to another at regular intervals.

B

B-Rating   A good credit rating.

Bait and Switch   An illegal sales technique in which a seller advertises a product with the intention of persuading consumers to buy a more expensive product.

Balanced Fund   A mutual fund that seeks both growth and income but attempts to minimize risk by investing in a mixture of stocks and bonds rather than stocks alone.

Bank Reconciliation   The process of matching your checkbook register with the bank statement.

Bankruptcy   A legal process that relieves debtors of the responsibility of paying their debts or protects them while they try to repay.

Basic Health Coverage   Coverage which includes medical, hospital, and surgical costs.

Basic Needs   Items necessary for maintaining physical life.

BBB   A clearinghouse of information about local businesses, called the Better Business Bureau.

Bear Market   A prolonged period of falling stock prices and a general feeling of investor pessimism.

Benefits   1. Forms of employee compensation in addition to pay. 2. The amount received by the beneficiary from a life insurance policy, also called proceeds.

Binding Arbitration   When the arbitrator makes a decision that is binding on the parties.

Blank Endorsement   The signature of the payee written exactly as his or her name appears on the front of the check.

Blue Chip Stocks   Stocks of large, well-established corporations with a solid record of profitability.

Body   The message section of the letter.

Bond Default   When a bond issuer cannot meet the interest or principal payment on a bond.

Bond Fund   A group of bonds that have been bundled together for investment purposes.

Bond Rating   Tells the investor the risk category that has been assigned to a bond.

Bond Redemption   Occurs when a bond is paid off at maturity.

Bonds   Debt obligations of corporations or state or local governments.

Budget   A spending and saving plan based on your expected income and expenses.

Bull Market   A prolonged period of rising stock prices and a general feeling of investor optimism.

Bundling   Combining services into one package.

C

Callable Bond A bond that the issuer has the right to pay off before its maturity date.

Canceled Check A check that has cleared your account.

Capacity The financial ability to repay a loan with present income.

Capital The value of property you possess after deducting your debts.

Capitalism An economic system in which producers and consumers are free to operate and compete in business transactions with minimal, if any, government interference or regulation.

Car Detail A service provided by specialists who clean and polish the outside as well as clean and treat the interior of a car.

Car Registration A license tag fee that must be renewed annually.

Car Title A legal document that establishes ownership of the vehicle.

Car-Buying Service A service that allows you to choose the vehicle features you want, and a professional car buyer takes over the price negotiation for you.

Care Labels Labels that give instructions for cleaning.

Cash Value The savings accumulated in a permanent life insurance policy that you would receive if you canceled your policy.

Cashier's Check A check written by a bank on its own funds.

Certificate of Deposit (CD) A time deposit where a fixed rate of interest is earned for a specified length of time.

Certified Check A personal check that the bank guarantees or certifies to be good.

Chapter 7 Bankruptcy A liquidation form of bankruptcy for individuals which wipes out most debts in exchange for giving up most assets.

Chapter 13 Bankruptcy A reorganization form of bankruptcy for individuals that allows debtors to keep most of their property and use their income to pay a portion of their debts over three to five years.

Character A responsible attitude toward honoring obligations, often judged on evidence in the person's credit history.

Check A written order to a bank to pay the amount stated to the person or business named on it.

Checkbook Register A booklet used to record checking account transactions.

Child Support Monthly payments to the custodial parent to help provide food, clothing, and shelter for the children.

Civil Case A case which involves one person who has a dispute with another person or entity.

Civil Ceremony A wedding performed by a public official, such as a judge or justice of the peace, rather than a member of the clergy.

Class-Action Lawsuit A lawsuit in which a large number of people with similar complaints against the same defendant join together to sue.

Classic Cars Older vehicles in excellent condition that appreciate if valued as collectors' items.

Clearance When a merchant wants to clear out all the advertised merchandise, but not necessarily at a reduced price.

Closed-End Credit A loan for a specific amount that must be repaid in full, including all finance charges, by a stated due date.

Closing Costs The expenses incurred in transferring ownership from buyer to seller in a real estate transaction.

Co-Insurance Clause A provision requiring policyholders to insure their building for a stated percentage of its replacement value in order to receive full reimbursement for a loss.

Co-Op A room similar to one in a dormitory at lower cost but with added responsibilities.

COBRA A law that allows people who leave employment to continue their health insurance under the company plan for a limited period of time.

Codicil A legal document that modifies parts of a will and reaffirms the rest.

Collateral Property pledged to assure repayment of a loan.

Collective Bargaining The process of negotiating a work contract for union members.

Collective Values Things that are important to society as a whole.

Collision Coverage Automobile insurance that protects your own car against damage from accidents.

Common Law A system of laws based on decisions made in court cases.

Common Stock Represents a type of stock that pays a variable dividend and gives the holder voting rights.

Communist Economic System A system in which the government owns and controls most, if not all, of the productive resources of a nation.

Company Advertising Advertising intended to promote the image of a store, company, or retail chain.

Comparison Shopping Checking several places to be sure you are getting the best price for equal quality.

Competition The rivalry among sellers in the same market to win customers.

Complaint A document outlining the issues of the case and the relief (damages) that the plaintiff requests.

Complimentary Close A courteous phrase used to end a letter.

Comprehensive Coverage Automobile insurance that protects you from damage to your car from causes other than collision or vehicle overturning.

Compressed Workweek A work schedule that fits the normal 40-hour workweek into less than five days.

Condominium Also called a condo, it is an individually owned unit in an apartment-style complex with shared ownership of common areas.

Consideration Something of value exchanged for something else of value.

Consumer Advocate A person who actively promotes consumer causes.

Consumer Credit Protection Act Also known as Truth in Lending, this law requires lenders to fully inform consumers about the costs of credit.

Contact A member of your network, such as a relative, friend, member of a group to which you belong, or a former work associate.

Contract A legally enforceable agreement between two or more people.

Conventional Loan Mortgage agreement that does not have government backing and that is offered through a commercial bank or mortgage broker.

Convertible Bond A corporate bond that can be exchanged for common stock.

Cooperative Education Students attend classes part of the day and then go to a job that provides supervised field experience.

Coordination of Benefits A group health insurance provision that specifies how the insurers will share the cost when more than one policy covers a claim.

Cosigner Someone who promises to pay if the borrower fails to pay.

Counterclaim An accusation that the plaintiff is at fault and should pay damages to the defendant.

Counteroffer A rejection of an offer with a listing of what terms would be acceptable.

CPSC An agency that protects consumers from unreasonable risk of injury or death from potentially hazardous consumer products.

Creative Listening Listening with an open mind to new ideas.

Credit The use of someone else's money, borrowed now with the agreement to pay it back later.

Credit Bureau A business that gathers, stores, and sells credit information to other businesses.

Credit Counseling A service to help consumers manage their debt load and credit more wisely.

Credit Guard A service that monitors your credit records.

Credit History The complete record of your borrowing and repayment performance.

Credit Management Following an individual plan for using credit wisely.

Credit Payment Plan A record of your debts and a strategy for paying them off.

Credit Rating A measure of creditworthiness based on an analysis of your credit and financial history.

Credit Repair The process of reestablishing a good credit rating.

Credit Report A written statement of a consumer's credit history, issued by a credit bureau to businesses.

Credit Score The total of assigned points used to determine the likelihood that you will repay debt as agreed.

Creditor A person or business that loans money to others.

Creditworthy A determination that you are a good credit risk.

Cremation A process of reducing a body to ashes in a high-temperature oven.

Criminal Case A case which involves a government unit who is accusing an individual of committing a crime.

Critical Listening The ability to differentiate facts from opinion.

Custom A long-established practice that takes on the force of an unwritten law.

D

Database A computer program that sorts data for easy search and retrieval.

Dealer Add-Ons High-priced, high-profit dealer services that add little or no value to an automobile.

Debenture A corporate bond that is based on the general creditworthiness of the company.

Debit Card A plastic card that deducts money from a checking account almost immediately to pay for purchases.

Debt Adjustment The formal process of taking over your debt situation for a period of time, after which you will be free of debt.

Debt Collector A person or company hired by a creditor to collect the overdue balance on an account.

Debt Management Plan (DMP) A plan which involves giving money each month to a credit counseling organization.

Debt Negotiation Program Hiring a company to call your creditors to negotiate reductions in the amounts owed.

Debtor A person who borrows money from others.

Deception Occurs when false or misleading claims are made about the quality, the price, or the purpose of a particular product.

Deductible The specified amount of a loss that you (the insured) will have to pay.

Deductions Amounts subtracted from your gross pay.

Deed The legal document that transfers title of real property from one party to another.

Defendant The person against whom the lawsuit is filed.

Deferred Billing A service available to charge customers whereby purchases are not billed to the customer until much later than the standard billing time.

Defined-Benefit Plan A company-sponsored retirement plan in which retired employees receive a set monthly amount based on wages earned and number of years of service.

Defined-Contribution Plan A company-sponsored retirement plan in which employees can receive a periodic or lump-sum payment based on their account balance and the performance of the investments in their account.

Demand Deposit A type of bank account from which funds may be withdrawn at any time.

Dependability A character trait that means you can be counted on to do what you say you will do.

Dependent A person who lives with you and for whom you pay more than half of his or her living expenses.

Deposition A sworn statement of a witness that is recorded and often videotaped to preserve the memory of the issues at hand.

Depreciation The decline in the value of property due to normal wear and tear.

Direct Deposit Your net pay is deposited electronically into your bank account.

Direct Investment Buying stock directly from a corporation.

Disability Insurance An insurance plan that makes regular payments to replace income lost when illness or injury prevents the insured from working.

Discharged Debts Debts erased by the court during bankruptcy proceedings.

Discount Bond A savings bond that is purchased for less than its maturity value.

Discount Points Used to lower the mortgage interest rate.

Discrimination Treating people differently based on prejudice rather than individual merit.

Disposable Income The money you have left to spend or save after taxes and other required deductions are taken.

Disputing a Charge Asking the credit issuer to reverse the charge on your account.

Dissolution of Marriage The breakdown of a marriage due to irreconcilable differences (no-fault).

Diversification The spreading of risk among many types of investments.

Dividend Reinvestment Using dividends previously earned on the stock to buy more shares.

Dividends Money paid to stockholders from the corporation's earnings.

Divorce Decree A final statement of the dissolution decisions.

Dormitory An on-campus building that contains many small rooms that are rented out to students.

Double Indemnity A rider that allows the beneficiary to be paid double the face amount of the insurance policy in the event of accidental death.

Down Payment The amount paid at purchase to bring down the amount owed.

Driving Record Includes the number and type of traffic tickets you've received for driving infractions and misdemeanors along with the number of accidents in which you've been involved.

Duplex A building with two separate living quarters.

Earnest-Money Offer An offer to buy property accompanied by a deposit.

Economic Risk A risk that may result in gain or loss because of changing economic conditions.

Economy Refers to all activities related to production and distribution of goods and services in a geographic area.

Electronic Funds Transfer (EFT) A computer-based system that moves money from one account to another without writing a check or using cash.

Employee Assistance Plan (EAP) A group benefit that allows employees and their families to seek counseling and other mental-health services.

Employee Expenses Any costs of working paid by the employee that are not reimbursed by the employer.

Employment Agencies Help job seekers find a job for which they are qualified.

Employment Application Also called a job application, it is a form that asks questions of people who apply for a job.

Encryption A code that protects your account number and other information online.

Endorsement A written amendment to an insurance policy.

Engaged Being formally pledged or in a committed relationship.

Entrepreneur Someone who organizes, manages, and assumes the ownership risks of a new business.

Equity Difference between the market value of property and the amount owed on it.

Escrow Account A fund where money is held to pay amounts that will come due during the year.

Estate All that a person owns, less debts owed, at the time of the person's death.

Estate Tax A tax on property transferred from an estate to its heirs.

Evaluation A report that discusses the employee's strengths and weaknesses in performing the job and how well the employee helped to meet the company goals.

Eviction The legal process of removing a tenant from rental property.

Exclusions Specific losses that the insurance policy does not cover.

Exempt Status Available only to people who will not earn enough in the year to owe any federal income tax.

Exempted Property Assets considered necessary for survival that a bankrupt debtor is allowed to keep.

Exemption An amount you may subtract from your income for each person who depends on your income to live.

Experience The knowledge and skills acquired from working in a career field.

F

FAA An agency of the U.S. Department of Transportation that controls air traffic and certifies aircraft, airports, pilots, and other personnel.

Face Value The amount the bondholder will be repaid at maturity.

Fake Sale A consumer fraud where a merchant advertises a big sale but keeps the items at regular price or makes the price tags look like a price reduction when there actually is none.

FCC An agency that regulates interstate and international communications by radio, television, wire, satellite, and cable.

FDA An agency that enforces laws and regulations preventing distribution of mislabeled foods, drugs, cosmetics, and medical devices.

FHA Loan A government-sponsored loan that carries mortgage insurance.

Fiat Money Money which is not backed by gold, but by faith in the general economy and government of the country.

Filing Status Your tax-filing group based on your marital status.

Finance Charge The total dollar amount of all interest and fees you pay for the use of credit.

Finance Company An organization that makes high-risk consumer loans.

Financial Plan A set of goals for spending, saving, and investing the money you receive.

Fixed Expenses Costs that do not change from month to month.

Fixed-Rate Loans Loans for which the interest rate does not change over the life of the loan.

Fixed-Rate Mortgage A mortgage on which the interest rate does not change.

Flammability The capacity for catching on fire.

Flex 125 Plan An employee benefit program that allows employees to set aside money, pretax, to help pay deductibles, copayments, and other health expenses during the year that are not covered by insurance.

Flextime A type of work schedule that allows employees to choose their working hours within defined limits.

Floating a Check Writing a check and hoping to cover it with a deposit before it clears.

Follow-Up Contact with the employer after the interview but before hiring occurs to remind the employer of who you are and possibly improve your chance of getting the job.

Form W-2 A summary of the income you earned during the year and all amounts the employer withheld for taxes.

Form W-4 A form that asks for your name, address, Social Security number, marital status and the number of exemptions you are claiming for income tax purposes.

Formal Wedding A wedding with long gowns and tuxedos worn by the wedding party and guests.

Front-end load A mutual fund that charges its fee up front.

FTC An agency that regulates unfair methods of competition, false or deceptive advertising, deceptive product labeling, inaccurate or obsolete information on credit reports, and concealment of the true cost of credit.

FTC Rule Requires that dealers fully disclose to buyers what is and is not covered under warranty for a used vehicle.

Furnished Rental A rental unit in which basic furnishings—bed, dresser, sofa, chairs, lamps, and so on—are provided.

Futures Contracts to buy and sell commodities or stocks for a specified price on a specified date in the future.

G

Garnishment A legal process that allows part of your paycheck to be withheld to pay a debt.

Gems Natural, precious stones, such as diamonds, rubies, sapphires, and emeralds.

General Obligation Bond A municipal bond backed by the power of the issuing state or local government to levy taxes to pay back the debt.

Generic Drugs Less-expensive medications with the same composition as the equivalent brand-name drugs.

Gift Tax A tax applied to a gift of money or property.

Global Fund A mutual fund that purchases international stocks and bonds as well as U.S. securities.

Goal A desired end toward which efforts are directed.

Grace period A timeframe within which you may pay your current balance in full and incur no interest charges.

Grants Forms of educational funding that do not have to be repaid.

Gross Income All taxable income you receive, including wages, salaries, and tips.

Gross Pay The total amount you earn before any deductions are subtracted.

Group Insurance A type of health insurance in which all those insured have the same coverage and pay a set premium.

Growth and Income Fund A mutual fund whose investment goal is to earn returns from both dividends and capital gains.

Growth Fund A mutual fund whose investment goal is to buy stocks that will increase in value over time.

Growth Stocks Stocks in corporations that reinvest their profits into the business so that it can grow.

H

Headhunter Type of employment agency that seeks out highly qualified people to fill important positions for an employer.

Health Insurance A plan for sharing the risk of high medical costs resulting from injury or illness.

Hearing Process of perceiving sound.

Hedge Any investment or action that helps offset against loss from another investment or action.

Heir A person who will inherit property from someone who dies.

HMO A group plan offering prepaid medical care to its members.

Homeowner's Policy Insurance that protects property owners from property and liability risks.

Hospice A nonprofit agency that has trained, compassionate people who assist those who are dying and their families.

HSA A health savings account used in association with a medical plan that carries a high deductible.

Human Relations The art of getting along with others.

Hybrid A type of vehicle that uses alternate energy sources, such as natural gas or battery power, in addition to gasoline.

Hygiene Factors Job elements that dissatisfy when absent but do not add to satisfaction when present.

Identity Who a person is and how they fit in.

Identity Theft Stealing personal information, such as credit card numbers and Social Security numbers, to gain access to a person's finances, often to make purchases with credit.

Impulse Buying Buying something without thinking about it.

Incentive Pay Money offered to encourage employees to strive for higher levels of performance.

Income Fund A mutual fund whose investment goal is to produce current income in the form of interest or dividends.

Income Stocks Stocks that have a consistent history of paying high dividends.

Incontestable Clause A provision in an insurance policy that prevents denial of coverage after a period of time.

Indemnification Putting the policyholder back in the same financial condition he or she was in before a loss occurred.

Index Fund A mutual fund that tries to match the performance of a particular index by investing in the companies included in that index.

Individual Retirement Account (IRA) A retirement savings plan that allows individuals to set aside up to a specified amount each year and delay paying tax on the earnings until they begin withdrawing it at age 59½ or later.

Industry Advertising Advertising intended to promote a general product group without regard to where these products are purchased.

Inflation An economic period where prices are rising and purchasing power is decreasing.

Infomercial A lengthy paid TV advertisement that includes testimonials, product demonstrations, and presentation of product features.

Informal Wedding A wedding which may be held outside with no special attire needed.

Inheritance Tax A tax imposed on an heir who inherits property from an estate.

Initiative Taking the lead, recognizing what needs to be done, and doing it without having to be told.

Innovations New ideas, products, or services that bring about changes in the way we live.

Insurable Interest Any financial interest in life or property such that, if the life or property were lost or harmed, the insured would suffer financially.

Insurable Risk A pure risk that is faced by a large number of people and for which the amount of the loss can be predicted.

Insurance A method for spreading individual risk among a large group of people to make losses more affordable for all.

Interest Earnings on principal.

Interests The things you like to do.

Investing The use of long-term savings to earn a financial return.

Investing Risk The chance that an investment's value will decrease.

Investment-Grade Bonds A bond that is considered of the highest quality.

Invoice Price The price the dealer paid for a car.

Involuntary Bankruptcy Bankruptcy that occurs when creditors file a petition with the court against a debtor.

Itemized Deductions Expenses listed on Schedule A that you can subtract from adjusted gross income to determine taxable income.

Itinerary A detailed schedule of events, times, and places.

Job Analysis An evaluation of the positive and negative attributes of a given type of work.

Job Interview A face-to-face meeting with a potential employer to discuss a job opening.

Job Rotation A job design in which employees are trained to do more than one specialized task.

Job Shadowing Spending time with a worker in the type of job that interests you to see how activities are performed on a daily basis.

Job Sharing A job design in which two people share one full-time position.

Judgment The final court ruling that resolves the key issues and establishes the rights and obligations of each party.

Junk Bond A bond that has a low rating or no rating at all.

Keogh Plan A tax-deferred retirement savings plan available to self-employed individuals and their employees.

L

Labor Union A group of people who work in the same or similar occupations, organized for the benefit of all employees in these occupations.

Landlord The owner or owner's representative of rental property.

Lease A written agreement that allows a tenant to use property for a set period of time at a set rent payment.

Lemon A car with substantial defects that the manufacturer has been unable to fix after repeated attempts.

Lemon Laws Laws that protect consumers from the consequences of buying a defective car.

Lessee The tenant or person who will take possession of the property.

Lessor The landlord or person responsible for the property.

Letter Address Also called the inside address, it contains the name and address of the person or company to whom you are writing.

Leverage The use of borrowed money to buy securities.

Liabilities Money or debts that you owe to others.

Liability Coverage Insurance to protect against claims for bodily injury to another person or damage to another person's property.

Liability Risk The chance of loss that may occur when your errors or actions result in injuries to others or damages to their property.

Lien A financial claim against property.

Life Insurance Insurance that provides funds to the beneficiaries when the insured dies.

Life-Enhancing Wants Items beyond basic needs that add to your quality of life.

Lifelong Learner Actively seeking new knowledge, skills, and experiences that will add to your professional and personal growth throughout your life.

Lifestyle The way people choose to live their lives, based on the values they have chosen.

Line of Credit A preestablished amount that can be borrowed on demand with no collateral.

Liquidation A type of bankruptcy (straight) where assets are sold and debts are paid as much as possible; there is no repayment plan.

Liquidity A measure of how quickly you can get your cash without loss of value.

Listening An active hearing process that requires concentration and effort.

Load The sales fee charged for buying mutual funds.

Loan Consolidation Combining many loans into one large loan with one monthly payment.

Loan Origination Fee The amount charged by a bank or other lender to process the loan papers.

Loan Sharks Unlicensed lenders who charge illegally high interest rates.

Lobbying An attempt to influence public officials to pass laws and make decisions that benefit a profession.

Long-Term Needs Expenses that are costly and require years of planning and saving.

Loss Leader An item of merchandise marked down to an unusually low price, sometimes below the store's cost.

Low-Balling Advertising a service at an unusually low price to lure customers and then attempting to persuade them that they need additional services.

Loyalty A work habit based on respect.

M

Major Medical Coverage Coverage which provides protection against the catastrophic expenses of a serious injury or illness.

Market Economy An economy where both market forces and government decisions determine which goods and services are produced and how they are distributed.

Market Value The price for which stock is bought and sold in the marketplace.

Marketable Of such quality that the employer can sell it or use it to favorably represent the company.

Maturity Date The date on which an investment becomes due for payment.

Mediation A dispute resolution method in which an independent third person, a mediator, helps the parties to reach a solution in a controlled environment.

Micromarketing A marketing strategy designed to target specific people or small groups who are likely to want certain products.

Minimum Wage The lowest wage that an employer may pay an employee as established by law.

Money Anything that can be used to settle debt.

Money Market Account A type of savings account that offers a more competitive interest rate than a regular savings account.

Money Market Fund A mutual fund that invests in safe, liquid securities, such as Treasury Bills and bonds that mature in less than a year.

Monopoly A market with many buyers but only one seller.

Mortgage A loan to purchase real estate.

Motivators Job elements that increase job satisfaction.

Moving costs Expenses of packing, loading, transporting, unloading and unpacking.

Municipal Bond A bond issued by state and local governments.

Mutual Fund A professionally managed group of investments.

N

Negotiable An instrument that is legally collectible.

Negotiation The process of finding a solution to a dispute that is acceptable to both sides through informal discussion.

Net Asset Value The market price for a share of a mutual fund.

Net Pay The amount left after all deductions are taken out of your gross pay.

Net Worth The difference between assets and liabilities.

Networks Informal groups of people with common interests who interact for mutual assistance.

NIST An agency that develops and rewards standards of excellence in business.

No-Fault Insurance Automobile insurance in which drivers receive reimbursement from their own insurer, no matter who caused the accident.

Notarized A process that verifies the signature of a person who signs a document.

O

Odd-Number Pricing The practice of setting prices at uneven amounts rather than whole dollars to make them seem lower.

Open-End Credit A credit arrangement in which a borrower can use credit up to a stated limit.

Open-Ended Questions Require you to respond in paragraphs and talk about yourself.

Opportunity Cost The value of your next best choice—what you are giving up.

Option The right, but not the obligation, to buy or sell a commodity or stock for a specified price within a specified time period.

Overbook To sell more reservations than an airline can fulfill.

Overdraft A check written for more money than your account contains.

Overdraft Protection A bank service that covers checks even if you have insufficient funds in your checking account.

Overtime Time worked beyond regular hours.

Oxidize A chemical reaction with air that causes paint to lose its color and shine.

P

Par Value An assigned dollar value given to each share of stock.

Pawnbroker (or Pawnshop) A legal business that makes high-interest loans based on the value of personal possessions pledged as collateral.

Payroll Savings Plan A plan in which you authorize your employer to make automatic deductions from your paycheck each pay period.

Penny Stocks Low-priced stocks of small companies that have no track record.

Permanent Investments Investment choices held for the long run.

Permanent Life Insurance A life insurance policy that remains in effect for the insured's lifetime and builds a cash value.

Personal Injury Protection (PIP) Automobile insurance that pays for medical, hospital, and funeral costs of the insured's family and passengers, regardless of fault.

Personal Preferences Your tastes, or likes and dislikes.

Personal Property Floater Insurance coverage for the insured's movable property wherever it may be located.

Personal Risk The chance of loss involving your income and standard of living.

Personality Made up of the many individual qualities that make you unique.

Phishing A scam that uses online pop-up messages or e-mail to deceive you into disclosing personal information.

Pigeon Drop Any method used by experienced con artists to convince vulnerable people to invest in phony investments, swampland real estate, or other swindles.

Placement Centers A service offered at schools to help students and former students with careers and employment.

Plaintiff The person who brings a lawsuit by filing the complaint.

Point System 1. A method of evaluation in which points are assigned by a credit bureau based on several factors. 2. A rating system to determine insurance rates.

Polishing Compound A substance that can smooth out surface scratches, scuffs, and stains.

Portability The feature that allows a group policy to be converted into an individual policy.

Portfolio A collection of investments.

Power of Attorney A legal document authorizing someone to act on your behalf.

PPO A group of health care providers who band together to provide health services for set fees.

Preapproval The process of getting a new- or used-car loan prearranged through your bank or credit union.

Precious Metals Tangible metals that have known and universal value worldwide.

Preferred Stock Represents a type of stock that pays a fixed dividend but has no voting rights.

Premium The cost (usually monthly) of an insurance policy.

Prime Rate The interest rate that banks offer to their best business customers.

Principal 1. The total amount borrowed. 2. Amount deposited on which interest will be paid.

Product Advertising Advertising intended to convince consumers to buy a specific good or service.

Productivity The relationship between the cost of paying for workers and the output that is received from their work.

Progressive Taxes Taxes that take a larger share of income as the amount of income grows.

Promotion The ability to advance to positions of greater responsibility and higher pay.

Property Risk The chance of loss or harm to personal or real property.

Property Settlement Agreement A document specifying division of assets agreed to by a divorcing couple outside of court and submitted for the judge's approval.

Proportional Taxes Taxes for which the rate stays the same, or is flat, regardless of income.

Prospectus The legal document that offers securities or mutual fund shares for sale.

Proxy A stockholder's written authorization to transfer his or her voting rights to someone else, usually a company manager.

Prudent Layperson A reasonable untrained person in a similar position.

Public Goods The goods and services provided by government to its citizens.

Punctuality Being ready to start work at the appointed time.

Pure Risk A chance of loss with no chance for gain.

Pyramid Schemes Multilevel marketing plans that promise distributors commissions from their own sales and those of other distributors they recruit.

R

Rate The percentage of interest you will pay on a loan.

Reaffirmation The agreement to pay debts that have been legally discharged.

Real Estate Land and the buildings on it.

Rebate Plan A plan in which you get back a portion of what you spent in credit purchases over the year.

Recall A request for consumers to return a defective product to the manufacturer for a refund or repair.

Redress A remedy to a problem.

Reference Letter Statement attesting to your character, abilities, and experience, written by someone who can be relied upon to give a sincere report.

References People who have known you for at least a year and can provide information about your skills, character and achievements.

Regressive Taxes Taxes that take a smaller share of income as the amount of income grows.

Rent-To-Own Option Renting furniture with an option to buy at a reduced price at the end of the rental period.

Rental Agreement A written agreement that allows you to leave anytime as long as you give the required notice.

Rental Inventory A detailed list of current property conditions.

Renter's Policy Insurance that protects renters from property and liability risks.

Renting The process of using another person's property for a fee.

Reservation An advance commitment to receive a service at a specified later date.

Restrictive Endorsement An endorsement that limits the use of a check.

Resume Often called a personal data sheet, biographical summary, professional file or vita that describes your work experience, education, abilities, interests, and other information that may be of interest to an employer.

Retraining Learning new and different skills so that an employee can retain the same level of employability.

Return Address The first thing to appear at the top of the application letter.

Revenue Incoming funds to the government collected from citizens and businesses in the form of taxes.

Revenue Bond A municipal bond issued to raise money for a public-works project.

Reverse Mortgage A loan against the equity in the borrower's home.

Rewards Program A payback in the form of points that can be redeemed for merchandise.

Risk Assessment Understanding the types of risk you will face and their potential consequences.

Risk Assumption Accepting the consequences of risk by self-insuring to absorb the loss.

Risk Avoidance Lowering your chance of loss by not doing high-risk activities.

Risk Management An organized strategy for controlling financial loss from pure risks and insurable risks.

Risk Reduction Taking measures to lessen the frequency or severity of losses that might occur.

Risk Shifting Transferring risk by buying insurance to cover potential losses.

Roth IRA A type of IRA where contributions are taxed, but earnings are not.

Rule of 72 A technique for estimating the number of years required to double your money at a given rate of return.

S

Safe Deposit Box A place at your bank available to store valuable items or documents.

Safety of Principal A guarantee that you will not lose your savings deposit.

Salary The amount of monthly or annual pay that you will earn for your labor.

Salutation The greeting that begins your letter.

Scarcity A situation in which consumers' wants are unlimited, while the resources for producing the products to satisfy those wants are limited.

Scholarships Cash allowances awarded to students to pay education costs.

SEC An agency that protects investors and maintains the integrity of the securities markets. (Securities and Exchange Commission)

Secured Bond A bond that is backed by specific assets as collateral.

Securities Exchange A marketplace where brokers who are representing investors meet to buy and sell securities.

Security Deposit A refundable amount a renter pays in advance to protect the owner against damage or nonpayment.

Self-Actualization The need to reach one's full potential to grow and to be creative.

Self-Assessment Inventory Lists your strong and weak points along with plans for improvement as you prepare for a career.

Self-Employment Tax The total Social Security and Medicare tax, including employer-matching contributions, paid by people who work for themselves.

Self-Esteem Self-respect and recognition from others.

Semiformal Wedding A wedding which is usually held during the afternoon or early evening, with less formal wear required of guests.

Seniority Refers to the length of time on the job and is used to determine transfers,

promotions, and vacation time according to most union contracts.

Service Credit The providing of a service for which you will pay later.

Short Selling Selling stock borrowed from a broker that must be replaced at a later time.

Short-Term Needs Expenses beyond your regular monthly items.

Simple Interest Interest computed only on the amount borrowed, without compounding.

Simplified Employee Pension (SEP) A tax-deferred retirement plan available to small businesses.

Small Claims Court A court of limited jurisdiction that decides small matters quickly with minimum cost.

Socialist Economic System A system characterized by a large degree of government control of many of the decisions within the nation.

Space-Shifting Copying the contents of CDs and other media to portable devices.

Special Endorsement An endorsement that transfers the right to cash the check to someone else.

Speculative Risk A risk that may result in either gain or loss.

Spousal Support Money paid by one former spouse to support the other.

Spreadsheet A computer program that organizes data in columns and rows.

Standard Deduction A stated amount you can subtract from adjusted gross income if you do not itemize deductions.

Statute of Limitations A legally defined time limit in which a lawsuit may be filed for various complaints.

Sticker Price The manufacturer's suggested retail price (MSRP) shown on the tag in the car's window.

Stock Unit of ownership in a corporation.

Stock Split An increase in the number of outstanding shares of a company's stock.

Stockholders People who own shares of stock.

Stop-Loss Provision An insurance clause that caps or sets a maximum that the insured has to pay during any calendar year.

Stop-Payment Order A request that the bank not honor a specific check.

Student Loans Money borrowed to pay for education.

Studio Apartment An apartment with one large room that serves as the kitchen, living room, and bedroom.

Subscribers Businesses that supply information to credit bureaus about their customers.

Sunk Cost An expense that occurred in the past for which the money cannot be recovered.

Supervision Providing new and current employees with the information and training they need to do their job well.

Sympathetic Listening Often called empathic listening, which is the ability to perceive another person's point of view and to sense what the person is feeling.

T

Target Market A specific consumer group to which advertisements are designed to appeal.

Tax Brackets Income tax ranges from 10 to 35 percent based on income.

Tax Credit An amount subtracted directly from the tax owed.

Tax Evasion Willful failure to pay taxes.

Taxable Income The amount on which you will pay income tax.

Teamwork Working cooperatively in order to achieve a group goal.

Temporary Agency Commonly referred to as a "temp agency," provides part- or full-time temporary job placement.

Temporary Investments Investment choices that will be reevaluated in the short term.

Temporary Life Insurance A life insurance policy that remains in effect for a specified period of time.

Tenant A person who rents property.

Term Life Insurance The most common form of temporary life insurance—a life insurance policy that remains in effect for a specified period of time.

Thank-You Letter Shows appreciation to the employer for taking time to speak with you.

Time-Shifting Recording a video or audio for later viewing or listening.

Time The period during which the borrower will repay a loan.

Title Legally established ownership to property.

Title Insurance A policy that protects you from any claims arising from a defective title.

Townhouse A living space that has two or more levels.

Tradeoff Giving up one option in exchange for another.

Traditional Economic System A system in which the people decide what decisions will be made and how they will be made.

Traditional IRA An IRA for which you can deduct your contribution each year from your taxable income.

Transcripts School records that include a listing of courses you have taken along with the credits and grades you received for them.

Travel Agency A business that arranges transportation, accommodations, and itineraries for customers.

Traveler's Checks Check forms in specific denominations that are used instead of cash while traveling.

Trust Deed A debt security instrument that shows as a lien against property.

Trust A legal document in which an individual gives someone else control of property, for ultimate distribution to another person.

U

Umbrella Liability Insurance A supplement to your basic auto and property liability coverage that expands limits and includes additional risks.

Unemployment Insurance Provides benefits to workers who lose their jobs through no fault of their own.

Unfair Labor Practice (ULP) A complaint filed by an employee claiming violation of a labor contract.

Unfurnished Rental A rental unit in which furnishings generally are not included; however, basic kitchen appliances such as a stove and refrigerator may or may not be included.

Uninsured/Underinsured Coverage Automobile insurance that pays for your injuries when the other driver is legally liable but unable to pay.

Uninvited Guest A person presumed to have permission to be on your property.

Unused Credit The remaining credit available to you on current accounts.

Upgrading Advancing to a higher level of skill to increase your usefulness to an employer.

Upholstery The seat-covering material in a car.

USDA An agency that protects the food supply in the United States.

USPIS A federal law enforcement agency that investigates consumer problems pertaining to illegal use of the mail.

Usury Law A state law that sets a maximum interest rate that may be charged for consumer loans.

V

Values The ideals in life that are important to you.

Variable Expenses Costs that vary in amount and type, depending on the choices you make.

Variable-Rate Loans Loans for which the interest rate goes up and down with inflation and other economic indicators.

Vehicle Emission Test A test to verify that a vehicle meets the minimum clean-air standards.

Vehicle Identification Number (VIN) An alphanumeric number that identifies each vehicle manufactured or sold in the United States.

Verdict The decision reached by a jury.

Vested The point at which employees have full rights to their retirement accounts.

Voluntary Bankruptcy Bankruptcy that occurs when you file a petition with a federal court asking to be declared bankrupt.

Voluntary Compliance A system in which all citizens are expected to prepare and file income tax returns of their own accord without force.

Warning Labels Product labels that advise consumers of risks and safety issues.

Warranty A written statement about a product's quality or performance. Warranties can also be implied (assumed to exist).

Wedding Party Active participants in a wedding ceremony.

Will A legal document that tells how an estate is to be distributed when a person dies.

Work Characteristics The daily activities of the job and the environment in which they must be performed.

Work History A record of the jobs you have held and how long you stayed with each.

Work Rules The do's and don'ts of fitting in successfully and having a positive work experience.

Work-Study A program where students work on campus to earn money.

Workers' Compensation An insurance program that pays benefits to workers and/or their families for injury.

Z

Zero-Coupon Bond A bond that is sold at a deep discount, makes no interest payments, and is redeemable for its face value at maturity.

Index